Multidisciplinary Perspectives on Human Capital and Information Technology Professionals

Vandana Ahuja
Jaypee Institute of Information Technology, India

Shubhangini Rathore
IBS Gurgaon, India

A volume in the Advances in Information Security, Privacy, and Ethics (AISPE) Book Series

Published in the United States of America by
    IGI Global
    Information Science Reference (an imprint of IGI Global)
    701 E. Chocolate Avenue
    Hershey PA, USA 17033
    Tel: 717-533-8845
    Fax: 717-533-8661
    E-mail: cust@igi-global.com
    Web site: http://www.igi-global.com

Library of Congress Cataloging-in-Publication Data

Names: Ahuja, Vandana, editor. | Rathore, Shubhangini, 1986- editor.
Title: Multidisciplinary perspectives on human capital and information
  technology professionals / Vandana Ahuja and Shubhangini Rathore, editors.
Description: Hershey : Information Science Reference, [2018]
Identifiers: LCCN 2017038370| ISBN 9781522552970 (hardcover) | ISBN
  9781522552987 (ebook)
Subjects: LCSH: Personnel management. | Information technology--Management.
Classification: LCC HF5549 .M837 2018 | DDC 004.068--dc23 LC record available at https://lccn.loc.gov/2017038370

This book is published in the IGI Global book series Advances in Information Security, Privacy, and Ethics (AISPE) (ISSN: 1948-9730; eISSN: 1948-9749)

British Cataloguing in Publication Data
A Cataloguing in Publication record for this book is available from the British Library.

For electronic access to this publication, please contact: eresources@igi-global.com.

Advances in Information Security, Privacy, and Ethics (AISPE) Book Series

Manish Gupta
State University of New York, USA

ISSN:1948-9730
EISSN:1948-9749

MISSION

As digital technologies become more pervasive in everyday life and the Internet is utilized in ever increasing ways by both private and public entities, concern over digital threats becomes more prevalent.

The **Advances in Information Security, Privacy, & Ethics (AISPE) Book Series** provides cutting-edge research on the protection and misuse of information and technology across various industries and settings. Comprised of scholarly research on topics such as identity management, cryptography, system security, authentication, and data protection, this book series is ideal for reference by IT professionals, academicians, and upper-level students.

COVERAGE

- Cookies
- Data Storage of Minors
- Network Security Services
- IT Risk
- Access Control
- Cyberethics
- Privacy-Enhancing Technologies
- Risk Management
- Electronic Mail Security
- Security Classifications

IGI Global is currently accepting manuscripts for publication within this series. To submit a proposal for a volume in this series, please contact our Acquisition Editors at Acquisitions@igi-global.com or visit: http://www.igi-global.com/publish/.

Titles in this Series

For a list of additional titles in this series, please visit: www.igi-global.com/book-series

Algorithmic Strategies for Solving Complex Problems in Cryptography
Kannan Balasubramanian (Mepco Schlenk Engineering College, India) and M. Rajakani (Mepco Schlenk Engineering College, India)
Information Science Reference • ©2018 • 302pp • H/C (ISBN: 9781522529156) • US $245.00 (our price)

Information Technology Risk Management and Compliance in Modern Organizations
Manish Gupta (State University of New York, Buffalo, USA) Raj Sharman (State University of New York, Buffalo, USA) John Walp (M&T Bank Corporation, USA) and Pavankumar Mulgund (State University of New York, Buffalo, USA)
Business Science Reference • ©2018 • 360pp • H/C (ISBN: 9781522526049) • US $225.00 (our price)

Detecting and Mitigating Robotic Cyber Security Risks
Raghavendra Kumar (LNCT Group of College, India) Prasant Kumar Pattnaik (KIIT University, India) and Priyanka Pandey (LNCT Group of College, India)
Information Science Reference • ©2017 • 384pp • H/C (ISBN: 9781522521549) • US $210.00 (our price)

Advanced Image-Based Spam Detection and Filtering Techniques
Sunita Vikrant Dhavale (Defense Institute of Advanced Technology (DIAT), Pune, India)
Information Science Reference • ©2017 • 213pp • H/C (ISBN: 9781683180135) • US $175.00 (our price)

Privacy and Security Policies in Big Data
Sharvari Tamane (MGM's Jawaharlal Nehru Engineering College, India) Vijender Kumar Solanki (Institute of Technology and Science Ghaziabad, India) and Nilanjan Dey (Techno India College of Technology, India)
Information Science Reference • ©2017 • 305pp • H/C (ISBN: 9781522524861) • US $210.00 (our price)

Securing Government Information and Data in Developing Countries
Saleem Zoughbi (UN APCICT, UN ESCAP, South Korea)
Information Science Reference • ©2017 • 307pp • H/C (ISBN: 9781522517030) • US $160.00 (our price)

Security Breaches and Threat Prevention in the Internet of Things
N. Jeyanthi (VIT University, India) and R. Thandeeswaran (VIT University, India)
Information Science Reference • ©2017 • 276pp • H/C (ISBN: 9781522522966) • US $180.00 (our price)

701 East Chocolate Avenue, Hershey, PA 17033, USA
Tel: 717-533-8845 x100 • Fax: 717-533-8661
E-Mail: cust@igi-global.com • www.igi-global.com

Table of Contents

Detailed Table of Contents

Contemporary industries face new competition requiring employees to work for longer hours under competitive time-bound deadlines. Prolonged exposure to such stressful situations leads to a depletion and exhaustion of resources in the mind and body with dysfunctional effects on job performance and overall organizational effectiveness. The Indian IT industry is a fast-paced service industry that is characterized by such stressful work situations and related outcomes. This chapter analyses the various factors that contribute to organizational stress and the role of demographic factors on role stress among the professionals of the Indian IT industry. A sample of 250 employees has been collected from the Delhi NCR region. Role stress has been measured by using the ORS scale which comprises of 10 dimensions of the role of stress that are measured by 50 items. The results show that there is a considerable amount of work related stress along with a significant impact of demographic factors on the role of stress amongst the IT professionals.

Chapter 2

Recruitment is the process of identifying and hiring the right talent for a job in an organization, within a timeframe and by incurring the least expenses. The life cycle of the recruitment process starts from identification of an open position which needs to be filled to the candidate joining the organisation formally. On hearing the word recruitment, what flashes in an individual's mind is the process the HR group would follow to choose a candidate, get him interviewed, cross levels, offer, joining formalities completion, and to integrate the new joinee with the organization's philosophy. But, over a period, this process has evolved and it has transformed its existence from a simple process to a much more organized and digitally equipped one. The importance of a recruitment service though has remained the same, that is, the candidate should have the right skills, right knowledge, aptitude, and most importantly, attitude. But what has been the focus of improvement of the Human resources is the time duration and the cost effectiveness.

Chapter 3

Shubhangini Rathore, IBS Gurgaon, India

The acknowledgement to develop emotional competencies of the workforce is a focal point of concern for human resource practitioners today. This chapter attempts to explore the relationship between organizational role stress and emotional intelligence in the Indian IT industry. Data was collected from a total of 250 employees, both managers and non-managers working in the Delhi NCR region. Emotional intelligence was measured by developing a scale consisting of 27 items. Stress was measured using the organizational role stress questionnaire comprising of 50 items. The results show a strong correlation between role stress and emotional intelligence. It was seen that by altering and increasing the levels of EI among the employees; workplace stress could be effectively reduced. There was also seen to be a and significant impact of emotional intelligence on organizational stress. Regression was applied to see the result of the EI variables on different factors of stress. It was seen that there is a significant impact of variables on organizational stress.

Chapter 4

Shirin Alavi, Jaypee Institute of Information Technology, India

This chapter seeks to impart understanding of the role of employee online communities for enhanced employee engagement and retention in an organization. The highly engaged and motivated employees would contribute more towards accomplishing the organizations goals. The various research studies conducted in the past across the world identify job satisfaction as a major determinant of employee engagement and retention. The role of internal communication through employee online communities of organizations or intranets is theoretically suggested to be a major influencer for the enhancement of employee engagement efforts. This can help to enhance and support culture, corporate values, mission statement, and annual company goals. The purpose of this chapter is to investigate the role that the employee online communities of organizations play in order to support the twin objectives of employee retention and engagement. Engaging employees can be the catalyst for inducing positive change among employees and, as a result, boosting an organization's success.

Chapter 5

Eleni Berki, University of Tampere, Finland
Juri Valtanen, University of Tampere, Finland
Sunil Chaudhary, Deerwalk Institute of Technology, Nepal
Linfeng Li, Beijing Institute of Petrochemical Technology, China

Cybersecurity professionals face increased demand to acquire the knowledge and develop the skills required to keep citizens safe from cyberattacks, predict the latter with scientific methods, and advance citizens' social awareness. A proactive multidisciplinary approach against cyberattacks is effective via the combination of multidisciplinary and multi-professional knowledge. Increased public awareness with total quality multi-domain knowledge and social computing skills is likely to decrease cyberattacks' victims and improve cyber systems quality in general. This chapter 1) outlines the basic multidisciplinary research needs and multilevel strategic steps to be taken for timely citizens' protection, and 2) proposes multidisciplinary strategic research approaches and multilevel adult education directions for improving cybersystems' total quality management through collaborative research and by focusing on: a) increasing public awareness, b) predicting cyberattacks, and c) utilising multidisciplinary and multi-professional knowledge in social computing approaches.

Chapter 6

Manuel Palomo-Duarte, University of Cadiz, Spain
Anke Berns, University of Cadiz, Spain
Alberto Cejas, University of Cadiz, Spain
Juan Manuel Dodero, University of Cadiz, Spain
Juan Antonio Caballero-Hernández, University of Cadiz, Spain
Iván Ruiz-Rube, University of Cadiz, Spain

The acquisition of foreign language competencies has become one of the main concerns of current ICT educational policies. Mobile smart devices allow teachers to provide students with personalized learning environments in line with their needs. However, most of the available apps, especially in the area of foreign language learning, still focus on form-based learning supporting mainly one-way interaction. In this chapter, the authors designed a learning system based on a dynamic, asynchronous and constructive learning approach. The chapter illustrates how the system helped students to get involved in their learning process by creating, sharing, and assessing their own learning resources and how teachers could benefit from students' logs to retrieve indicators for assessment processes. Finally, two algorithms that guide students' learning processes are compared: the first algorithm is based on community-driven behaviour, the second one on students' individual behaviour. Results show that both algorithms provide similar outcomes.

Chapter 7

Francisco Antunes, Beira Interior University, Portugal
Manuela Freire, University of Coimbra, Portugal
João Paulo Costa, University of Coimbra, Portugal

Data collected from online social networks offers new possibilities for supporting organizations' daily activities. It is also common knowledge that the opinion exchange in online social networks provides a decisive contribution in decision making. It is, thus, necessary to review and bare present the motivations by which people engage in online social network and the ways in which firms can make use of such motivations in order to take advantage of online social networks as information sources for decision-making support. To do so, the authors of this chapter developed the decision-support social networks to extract such information, which encompasses the intertwined use of human interaction and network structure by combining human capabilities, social network analysis (SNA), and automatic data mining. In this chapter, a brief summary of the performed case studies over the proposed information model is also presented.

Chapter 8

This chapter stresses the importance of the dataflow in business process models and illustrates a notation called DMA that is meant to fulfill two major goals: promoting the integration between business processes and information systems and leveraging the dataflow to provide flexibility in terms of human decisions. The first goal is fulfilled by considering both tasks and business entities as first-class citizens in process models. Business entities form the dataflow that interconnects the tasks: tasks take the input entities from the input dataflow and deliver the output entities to the output dataflow. Human decisions encompass the selection of the input entities when a task needs more than one, and the selection of the task with which to handle the input entities when two or more tasks are admissible. DMA provides a number of patterns that indicate how tasks affect the dataflow. In addition, two compound patterns, called macro tasks, can be used to represent task selection issues. An example related to an order handling process illustrates the notation.

Chapter 9

Globalization in the contemporary information society outlines new important challenges in privacy and personal data protection that apply to user security in cyberspace. This is also the case e-learning environments, which use new network technologies, such as remote access, distributed processing, information sharing, cloud services, social computing, etc. Strong security procedures based on authentication, authorization, and data protection should be proposed to protect system resources, user profiles, personal information, educational materials, and other specific information. The chapter presents the opportunities and challenges of some digital technologies that could increase the effectiveness of e-learning processes by developing a combined e-learning environment. A functional architecture with two sub-systems (front office and back office) and different information resources (public, internal, external) is discussed. Investigation by using formalization and modelling is made and assessments are presented.

Chapter 10

The aim of the chapter is to explore university students' perceptions about the effectiveness of interactive and collaborative tools to improve written skills in a blended-learning environment. Based on this goal, a mixed methods research approach was adopted to enhance the mutual invigoration of the two types of methods, and the validity and reliability of data. Three-hundred fifty-eight learners participated in the quantitative study and 91 in the qualitative one. All of them were enrolled in the subject English I. The instruments used to collect data were two tests and semi-structured interviews. The findings suggested students' positive perspective towards the possibilities offered by online glossaries, online quizzes, wikis, and forums to improve written skills and foster effective written communication in different contexts. It highlights their potentiality to create a learning community in which students could participate actively in the construction of knowledge, abandoning their passive role as simple observers.

Chapter 11

Shivani Pandey, Mediterranean Shipping Company, India

Workaholism, in recent years, has become a regular behaviour pattern among professionals. While self-negligence is assumed as a hallmark of workaholism, empirical data in this case stands to be both narrow and paradoxical. Modern developments like high-speed data connections add more to this belief, as this makes it possible for employees who would like to work at any place and at any given point of time to work. Workaholism is found to affect several important domains of life. With regards to work domain, workaholics commonly seem to have poor associations with their peer/colleagues, most likely on the grounds that they often feel the need to control them and experience issues with delegating work. Given that the amount of time they invested in their work leaves little energy for them for other activities, also the social life outside work gets hampered. This chapter explores the relationship between workaholism, perceived work-related stress, different job conditions, and intensifying anxiety among IT professionals in Delhi/NCR.

Chapter 12

Luis Fernández Sanz, Universidad de Alcalá, Spain
Josefa Gómez-Pérez, Universidad de Alcalá, Spain
Ana Castillo-Martinez, Universidad de Alcalá, Spain

The rapid evolution and expansion of ICT labor markets requires a common language to manage offer and demand of talent, which is especially critical and complex in a transnational integration scenario like the European Union. Models and frameworks represent useful tools for this purpose. This chapter analyzes the most relevant e-competences frameworks in the European Union (e-CF or EN16234, ESCO, and Body of Knowledge or BoK) as well as their integration and similarities. The present impact of these European frameworks in the ICT labor market and their connection to training and education is presented through data and several examples taken from two EU-funded projects: e-Skills Match and e-CF Council.

Chapter 13

Mounira Ilahi-Amri, PRINCE Research Laboratory, Tunisia
Lilila Cheniti-Belcadhi, PRINCE Research Laboratory, Tunisia
Rafik Braham, PRINCE Research Laboratory, Tunisia

In light of trends toward increased requirements for skilled workers, e-assessment presents many challenges. It should address learners' real performance in life. Recognizing the inadequacy of current traditional knowledge-based assessment systems in higher education to achieve performance visibility, we need to rethink how we design new assessment systems that can respond to the corporate requirements of the twenty-first century and mirror the learners' competences. This concern has not been sufficiently investigated. This chapter considers the competence-based assessment. The authors explore the importance of competency and competence modeling conceptual understanding. The research reviews the benchmark literature on the concepts, models, and approaches of competence and competency and explores the confusion surrounding the pair of concepts. They propose a service-oriented framework for competence-based e-assessment to validate the above proposals. The experimentation results support the research goals and learners received a competence-based assessment, which they appreciated.

Chapter 14

Anita Singh, Institute of Management Studies Ghaziabad, India
Lata Bajpai Singh, Institute of Management Studies Ghaziabad, India

This chapter aims to identify different factors of job satisfaction responsible for different types of commitment (i.e. affective, continuance, and normative commitment among the employees of IT organizations). The primary data was collected from 401 respondents of IT organizations using validated scales on organizational commitment and job satisfaction. The exploratory factor analysis was conducted to identify different factors of job satisfaction and scale reliability of organizational commitment scale. The reliability and validity of all the constructs were further done through confirmatory factor analysis. Then related hypotheses were tested using structural equation modeling through AMOS 21.0. Three factors of job satisfaction were extracted, namely growth opportunities and management practices, working condition, and fair treatment. Growth opportunities and management practices are the prominent reasons for affective commitment, whereas fair treatment ensures continuance and normative commitment among the employees of IT organizations with the given sample.

Chapter 15

Aishwarya Singh, Jaypee Business School, India
Santoshi Sengupta, Jaypee Institute of Information Technology, India
Swati Sharma, Jaypee Institute of Information Technology, India

The upheavals in the current times are driving us toward a purposeful need for more effective and "genuine" leadership skills so as to enhance business sustainability. This chapter empirically investigates the concept of authentic leadership and considers the pathways to develop authentic leadership by exploring and examining empathy and mindfulness as predictors of authentic leadership. An intense literature review reflects that only a few studies have been conducted that focus on the antecedents of authentic leadership. The study attempts to fill this void. A questionnaire was completed by 250 respondents from the IT industry. Regression analysis was applied to study the inter-relationships among the variables. Findings reveal that while empathy of a leader is significantly related to the development of authentic leadership, mindfulness is not. Wider geographical selection and replication of the study in other industry is recommended. The chapter promotes development of OB interventions intended to foster the development of authentic leaders for positive organizational outcomes.

The purpose of this chapter is to examine the effect of high involvement work processes on employee withdrawal behaviors in information technology sector in India. It draws from the structured questionnaire data from 300 software engineers working in Infosys, CTS, and HCL. Data was analyzed to find out details related to the relationship between high involvement work processes and employee withdrawal behaviors. It was found that high involvement work processes have a strong negative impact on withdrawal behaviors. The relationship was found to be stronger in the case of work withdrawal behaviors compared to that of job withdrawal behaviors.

Chapter 17

This chapter aims to highlight three viable fields of research within the domain of time banking (TB), a time-currency-based complementary economy system that has been implemented in various frameworks now for more than three decades. The areas of information management (IM), knowledge management (KM), and open source software (OSS) are almost totally unexplored within time banking. In information management, attention has mainly been devoted to IM frameworks. One link (among others) between knowledge management and open source software has been found in a core concept of the time bank called co-production. Finally, all three of these fields can be related directly to time banking and should have a place in further research, the results of which could also have applications in the field of complementary economic systems in general.

Foreword

As a technologist and academician, it is my pleasure to write the foreword for this book. I have always believed that people, process and technology go hand in hand. Human Capital is, and has always been the most significant resource in any organisation. With each passing day, companies face newer challenges, as contemporary times witness humongous technological innovation and path breaking modernisation. These are challenges with respect to cross functional approaches, challenges with respect to the need to keep individuals and organisations abreast with changing technological offerings, challenges with the need to keep employees in organisations constantly motivated.

The business environment has witnessed significant changes across five major arenas, which has given rise to the need for a multidisciplinary approach to handling the problems of the Human Resources in organisations today. These are:

1. The changing government policies;
2. Social changes;
3. Changes across business trends;
4. Advances in IT;
5. The impact of globalisation.

The world is constantly opening up new markets, new products, innovative processes and new delivery mechanisms. The Changes in governmental regulations, privatisation, new agreements for trade and new rules to protect employees, consumers and the environment are placing a constant pressure on companies. Rising consumer expectations and a more socially aware consumer is making organisations wake up to the need for a greater degree of customer centricity and hence more customer oriented employees. A greater number of strategic alliances, the process of outsourcing, and the ever-increasing emphasis on enhancing the productivity of the employees is making organisations revisit past practices. There is a constant need to evolve in the competitive spaces and create new benchmarks, with each passing day. The growth of the internet, wireless networking and technology, digitisation of text, graphic, and audio, the advent of the smartphone, the era of the cloud and big data are other issues which traditional organisations are grappling with, in the present times. Predictive analytics and artificial intelligence are bringing new products, methods and processes to the fore. Issues like international mergers and the dissolution of geographical boundaries in a virtual era, while enhancing project productivity, are constantly placing organisations and employees under continuous stress.

The book provides an inclusive and multidisciplinary discussion on how the above changes impact the diverse facets of the organisational workplaces, the technological interfaces and the learning mechanisms.

The book traces how the IT sector is witnessing an era of *workaholism*, work-related stress, different job conditions and intensifying anxiety. Specific chapters focus on the growing need for organisations to realise the importance of employee engagement and retention. There are newer methods for learning that can be used both in the organisations as well as in the education sector. The book demonstrates how organisations are constantly focussing on the need to bring in efficient work processes, by leveraging the offerings of technology. New methods for recruitment are creating efficiencies in the context of time and money. Newer methods supporting decision making are springing up. There is tremendous opportunity for combining the information prevalent across social networks and human capabilities through datamining. Collaborative business processes and information systems are creating flexibility in terms of human decisions with data flow. There are significant opportunities for integration of information and creation of smooth dataflows, across functional silos as well as across the different hierarchical levels in organisations.

This book was conceptualised keeping the above thoughts in mind and focuses on a wide range of aspects including competencies, skills, knowledge, job profiles, qualifications or occupations years to come. It delineates the need for organisations to focus on the need to strengthen employee commitment at the workplace and the role of job satisfaction in increasing the same. The chapters trace how leadership styles need to be revisited and how authentic leadership can significantly lead to positive outcomes at workplaces.

Hopefully this book will help you understand the opportunities available at the workplaces in the new age. Hope you enjoy reading the contents.

Ricardo Colomo Palacios
Østfold University College, Norway

Ricardo Colomo-Palacios *is a Full Professor at the Computer Science Department of the Østfold University College, Norway. Formerly he worked at Universidad Carlos III de Madrid, Spain. His research interests include applied research in information systems, software project management, people in software projects, business software, software and services process improvement and web science. He received his PhD in Computer Science from the Universidad Politécnica of Madrid (2005). He also holds a MBA from the Instituto de Empresa (2002). He has been working as Software Engineer, Project Manager and Software Engineering Consultant in several companies including Spanish IT leader INDRA. He is also an Editorial Board Member and Associate Editor for several international journals and conferences and Editor in Chief of International Journal of Human Capital and Information Technology Professionals.*

Preface

The word multidisciplinary typically refers to combining or involving several academic disciplines or professional specializations in a bid to evolve something new. Innovative approaches to diverse fields focus on drawing from dissimilar fields, and merging multiple thoughts to generate fresh perspectives. When we look at a problem from a new angle, sometimes new paradigms can emerge. At times, different academic fields can be complimentary to each other and multidisciplinary approaches redefine problems outside normal boundaries and arrive at solutions based on a new understanding of complex situations. Multidisciplinary approaches are the right way of handling organisational issues, as organisations need to understand not to work in well defined silos, but to draw from different disciplines and proceed across functional boundaries to identify remedies and find solutions.

Human Capital is the most significant resource in an organisation and optimal resource utilisation of this asset is the key to successful Human Capital Management in organisations today. The basic premise of maintaining this capital in the organization is the additional value that the strength of this capital can leverage for performance related organizational outcomes. On the whole it is the strongest organizational asset that can be used and developed for incorporating constant changes in the organization. Research on the investment in human capital focuses mainly on increasing the experience, skills and abilities of the human resources, as each of these is linked to economic value and outcomes. HR's role is essentially critical in this industry due to differentiation the ongoing and upcoming service that can be directly attributed to the talent in the organization.

Today, organisations are increasingly facing two challenges in the context of their Human Capital: (1) The need to keep pace with contemporary times and (2) The need to understand that a multidisciplinary comprehension of the organisational fabric will improve the productivity of the HR function and result in a better Return on Investment. It is seen that on the IT sector, the life expectancy of products and programs decline each year, while the demands on employees continue to increase due to the unique set of environmental pressures in IT functions; such as continuous re-engineering, outsourcing, more demanding customers and general information overload.

Thus, several organisational challenges can be resolved if organisations are able to acknowledge the following:

1. Top skills required by recruiters.
2. Recognise the emerging practices with regard to the Human Resource Management Function in organisations.
3. Leverage technology for Human Resource Management.
4. Recognise the need for Training.
5. Accept the importance of Analytics for Decision Making.
6. Appreciate the role of Emotional Intelligence contribute towards positive workplace outcomes.

Each of the above perspectives can be instrumental in helping an organization to leverage its Human Resources for overall success. It is crucial that the IT function would have to understand the essential pillars of management in this sector. The Understanding of the top skills that are most sought after by contemporary recruiters, can help talent gaps while hiring Talent. The recognition of emerging practices that are time, cost and resource efficient can lead to competitive advantage. Leveraging of technology can be effective with respect to continuous development of skills in the workforce and updated methods to keep pace with the requirements of changing roles.

Rigorous Training Need analysis& skill assessment can be useful in conducting an ongoing training and development. A focus on behavioural and technical competencies should go hand in hand for the overall development of talent. The acceptance of the importance of Analytics is absolutely crucial to the changing role of HR professionals in the current times. Moving on to Big Data from Data and using analytics as a decision-making tool would help the HR department in a big way. Appreciation of Emotional Intelligence is absolutely necessary for performance related aspects of an individual, considering the EI is a mediator towards various positive job outcomes.

This book on *Multidisciplinary Perspectives on Human Capital and Information Technology Professionals* focuses on the above related issues. It is a compilation of the thoughts of a host of academicians and corporate practitioners on the myriad dimensions of Human Capital and the need for organisations to recognise specific issues plaguing IT professionals. Various researches incorporated in the book through light on the importance of multitude aspects & challenges of HRM in the IT industry.

In context of the afore mentioned issues; thematic justice to the contributing contents of the book can be done by elaborating each of these issues with respect to the role of Management Research:

1. Top Skills Required by Recruiters

The process of evolution witnesses a constant change in careers from generation to generation. Each fresh batch of graduates from educational institutes enters the workforce with special skills and competencies-some of which are immensely valued by employers. Constantly updated curriculum and learning experiences create the need to revisit recruitment approaches completely. Top skills required by recruiters vary across professions. Key skills required for Management professionals include Communication skills, Analytical Skills, Ability to work in collaborative environments and Strategic Thinking. Engineering graduates need a good mix of Cognitive, Analytical and communication skills. As technology cruises into every facet of a typical workspace, basic technical and internet usage skills are the prerequisites to stepping into the workforce today. Needless to say, Ability to work in teams is the most significant skill requires across all professions.

2. Recognise the Emerging Practices With Regard to the Human Resource Management Function in Organisations

It is vital for organisations to change with the times.HRM practices are fast changing, with the advent of new practices. Recruiters in the past had been using the KSA model for recruitment. The KSA Model-Knowledge (of frameworks, models and concepts), Skills (ability to accomplish a specific task) and Attitudes (emotions, mindset, beliefs etc.). This model has found stiff competition from the new model proposed by the World Economic Forum-the WEF 21ˢᵗ Century skills model which is based on the three broad sets of Foundation literacy, competence and character qualities. With the emergence of an all pervasive growth of the Human Resource function, organisations are getting sensitive to several issues pertaining to employees-these include stress on the job, degree of employee involvement, and handling the dataflow across the varied business processes. The objective remains to achieve cost, time and resource effectiveness.

3.   Leverage Technology for Human Resource Management

According to the World Economic Forum's Future of jobs report, technological megatrends like Mobile Internet, Cloud Technology, Big Data, New Energy Technology, IoT, Sharing economy, and demographic trends like change in nature of work, rise of middle class, etc. are the key drivers of change at the workplace. Increased competition in the market, progress in field of information and communication technologies and globalization of work has changed the entire outlook of the organizations. The arrival of the internet has changed the way employees exchange information and work across geographical boundaries. Virtual teams and virtual communities are proliferating and this helps organizations to stay connected 24*7 across different time zones. Equally important is the role of social media, whereby employees are interacting with each other in an online environment and communities of trust, information sharing as well as knowledge exchange are fast emerging. Strengthened by participation and reciprocity, culturally diverse and geographically dispersed communities, the online domains give individuals a chance to plug and play, cooperate and strive, share knowledge, information and work. Maintenance of HR related data using relevant software modules has improved the efficiency and productivity of the HR function. At the same time, this streamlines an optimal resource utilisation in organisations. Data Analytics has changed the face of the HR function. Companies are also waking up to the need to secure their online databases, ensure privacy and streamline access to selected employees.

4.   Organisations Need to Recognise the Need for Training

The development of its human resources is one of the biggest responsibilities of an organization today. It is crucial for organisations to prepare a resource that can be skilled to utilize the large base of technological advancement, through a quick up gradation of skills.

If an organization wants to achieve excellence, it is important for the same to assess the competencies of its human resources and identify the areas where they can be improved, by subjecting them to appropriate training programs. Training and Development is one of the major activities in organization today. As expectations from employees increase exponentially, there is tremendous pressure for industry to be more innovative, productive and quality driven. Growth and productivity are directly proportional to the employee's skills, their commitment and job performance on the job. To become a competitive organization, it's important that employees gain proper knowledge and skills needed to meet the environmental changes. This can be best facilitated by the training programs tailored according to the needs of the employee and their current job and should focus on three basic things: a) Benefiting employees in their current job-profile, b) Benefiting employees during their job transition, in case of any prospective offer and c) Benefiting employees in their career development. Also the aim is to keep a balance between behavioural and technical training, as none can be fruitful without the other.

5. Organisations Need to Accept the Importance of Analytics

Business Analytics is rapidly entering every field. The era of big data is prompting organisations to invest in data mining and analytics to extract actionable information from available data sources. Large volumes of employee data, when subjected to analytical tools, can be transformed into actionable information which can aid decision making. Employee profiling is an emerging practise which helps the strategic decision-making process and better action planning. The advantages of managing and analysing data can be seen in strategic decision making in all HR related functions. The larger aim is to use the applications of big data for recruitment, performance management, succession planning, benefits and compensation and other HR functions. The role of subjectivity and intuition is to be minimised, moving to a more objective analysis.

6. Organizations Need to Appreciate How Emotional Intelligence Contribute Towards Positive Workplace Outcomes

In all service industries, individual differences and emotions form an important part of the day to day business operations. Emotional Intelligence helps in devising self awareness into ones' strengths, weaknesses, and limitations. Development of qualities that are associate with EI such as adaptability, conscientiousness, persuasion, collaboration and high performance can be instrumental in leading to positive job outcomes such as job satisfaction and better performance. Employees' Emotional Intelligence can also be used for Leadership development in organizations.

This book was conceptualised in the context of the above discussion. The book editors went through the large number of papers published with the International Journal of Human Capital and Information Technology professionals and felt that the journal hosted a significant volume of research which could be further expanded by the authors. There was scope for further researching specific topics across industry verticals, or empirically validating certain hypothesis or even discussing the managerial implications of certain findings by some researchers. After a careful evaluation of the work of several authors, a selected set of authors was invited to share the enhanced versions of their previous contributions. Authors with contributions in the following domains were given preference.

- Competence management within the IT profession
- Ethics, as well as professional and social responsibilities of IT professionals
- Human capital within the IT industry
- Human resource management in the IT sector
- IT careers
- IT personnel in new production environments IT profession
- IT professional associations
- IT professionalism
- IT professionals assessment methods
- IT professionals roles
- IT professionals under the scope of IT governance
- Licensing and certifying of IT professionals
- Mentoring, coaching, and counselling of IT professionals

- Personnel issues in IT standards, models, and frameworks
- Recruiting, staffing, retaining, and rewarding IT professionals

The following section throws light on the diverse chapters presented in the book.

Chapter 1, "Analysis of Role Stress in the Indian IT Industry" by Shubhangini Rathore, focuses on how contemporary industries face new competition requiring employees to work for longer hours under competitive time bound deadlines. Prolonged exposure to such stressful situations leads to a depletion and exhaustion of resources in the mind and body; with dysfunctional effects on job performance and overall organizational effectiveness. Particularly in the IT organizations; organizational culture is seen to be lacking in terms of assisting the employees on the knowledge about stress and coping for psychological problems. The work process are highly dynamic and time bound, as employees have definite targets to meet, that are incubated in different time zones. The life expectancy of products and programs declines each year, while the demands on employees to provide better solutions increases. Internal IT departments that cannot keep pace with the changes and are not sufficiently adaptable are in a danger of being outsourced. The Indian IT industry is a fast paced service industry that is characterized by such stressful work situations and related outcomes. The present study analyses the various factors that contribute to organizational stress and the role of Demographic Factors on Role Stress; among the professionals of the Indian IT industry. A sample of 250 employees has been collected from the Delhi NCR region. Role stress has been measured by using the ORS scale which comprises of ten dimensions of role stress that are measured by 50 items. The results show that there is significant impact of demographic factors on the Role Stress amongst the IT professionals.

Chapter 2, "Recruitment Trends in the Contemporary Era" by Anu Chhabra and Vandana Ahuja, focuses on how the Recruitment landscape has evolved across organisations. It traces how the landscape of recruitment has changed from a simple process to a much more organized and digitally equipped practice. The current economic and political scenario have majorly influenced the Recruitment Industry and hence the HR processes in organizations. The outcomes of the business relationship with other countries, GST (Goods & Service Tax) and more flexible FDI (Foreign Direct Investment) policies have made organisational managements put on their thinking caps to streamline the Human Resource processes Human resources group in any domain can feel the air of transformation all around. These changes are predominantly brought in by technology, years of experience, values, skill, talent and knowledge, organizational structure and to top them all, the evolution of an industry which is very distinct from the past organizations. The chapter explains how the importance of a recruitment service has remained the same, that is, the candidate should have the right skills, right knowledge, aptitude and most importantly the right attitude. But what has been the focus of improvement of the Human Resources, is the time duration and the cost effectiveness. Both these aspects have resulted in a major transition in the whole process. This chapter focuses on the new recruitment trends in contemporary times viz. Increase in Temp Staffing, Analysis of HR Data, Referral Schemes, Video Interview Interactions, Artificial Intelligence, Digitally equipped-App Based era, Mobile recruitment- the Game changing recruitment trend and Employer Branding. The chapter further elaborates how the same can benefit from efficiencies in the context of time and money.

Chapter 3, "What Emotional Intelligence Does to Organizational Stress: Exploring the Indian Information Technology sector" by Shubhangini Rathore, attempted to explore the relationship between organizational Role Stress and Emotional Intelligence in the Indian IT industry. Workplace stress has been studied from various historic and contemporary perspectives. In the history of managing employees, the tradition of keeping emotions at distance from the professional space was always found more appropriate. Logical thinking and rational analysis were always considered effective for handling and solving people and business issues. With an eventual rising importance of the human resources, the contemporary organizational milieu sees a drift in this accepted thought process. The role of emotions and feelings as determinants of one's ability to work in groups is recognized as a considerable factor in managing human resources. Data was collected from a total of 250 employees, both Managers and Non- Managers working in the Delhi NCR Region. Emotional Intelligence was measured by developing a scale consisting of 27 items. Stress was measured using the Organizational Role Stress questionnaire comprising of 50 items. The results show a strong correlation between Role Stress and Emotional Intelligence. It was seen that by altering and increasing the levels of EI among the employees; workplace stress could be effectively reduced. There was also seen to be a significant impact of Emotional Intelligence on Organizational Stress. Regression was applied to see the result of the EI variables on different factors of Stress. It was seen that there is a significant impact of variables on Organizational stress.

Chapter 4, "Employee Online Communities: A Tool for Employee Engagement and Retention" by Shirin Alavi, seeks to impart an understanding of the role of employee online communities for enhanced employee engagement and retention in an organization. A more engaged employee means higher company morale, increased productivity, better collaboration and lower employee turnover. The business intranets of today harness the existing power and momentum of social networks and route them into business advantages. Improving employee management, collaboration and engagement is a goal of every organization. Employees who feel they are a part of something larger than themselves and that their work is valued tend to be more productive, innovative and loyal. A community used to contribute to these results in a higher ROI, improved bottom line and more sustainable company success. The highly engaged and motivated employees would contribute more towards accomplishing the organizations goals. The various research studies conducted in the past across the world identify job satisfaction as a major determinant of employee engagement and retention. The role of internal communication through employee online communities of organizations or intranets is theoretically suggested to be a major influencer for the enhancement of employee engagement efforts. This can help to enhance and support culture, corporate values, mission statement and annual company goals. The purpose of this chapter is to investigate the role that the employee online communities of organizations play in order to support the twin objectives of employee retention and engagement. Engaging employees can be the catalyst for inducing positive change among employees and, as a result, boosting an organization's success.

Chapter 5, "The Need for Multi-Disciplinary Approaches and Multi-Level Knowledge for Cyber-Security Professionals" by Eleni Berki, Juri Valtanen, Sunil Chaudhary and Linfeng Li, talked about how Cybersecurity professionals face the increased demand to acquire the knowledge and develop the skills required to keep citizens safe from cyber attacks, predict the latter with scientific methods, and advance citizens' social awareness. Every day multiple deceitful and convincing attempts with trustworthy content, known as *social engineering* techniques, occur through various communication and dissemination means and, most notably, through the Internet. Hence, thousands of people are convinced to reveal personal, vulnerable information such as social security ids, bank account details, home and email addresses, and the list can go on. A proactive multidisciplinary approach against cyber attacks is effective via the combination of multidisciplinary and multi-professional knowledge. Increased public awareness with total quality multi-domain knowledge and social computing skills is likely to decrease cyber attacks' victims and improve cyber systems quality in general. This chapter 1) outlines the basic multidisciplinary research needs and multilevel strategic steps to be taken for timely citizens' protection, and 2) proposes multidisciplinary strategic research approaches and multilevel adult education directions for improving cyber systems' total quality management through collaborative research and by focusing on: a) increasing public awareness, b) predicting cyber attacks, and c) utilising multidisciplinary and multi-professional knowledge in social computing approaches.

Chapter 6, "A Community-Driven Mobile System to Support Foreign Language Learning" by Manuel Palomo-Duarte, Anke Berns, Alberto Cejas, Juan Manuel Dodero, Juan Antonio Caballero-Hernández and Iván Ruiz-Rube, focuses on the acquisition of foreign language competencies that has become one of the main concerns of current ICT educational policies. Due to the increasing trend towards globalisation foreign language competencies together with generic competencies have become two of the main job requirements in all professional areas especially in leading Information and Communication Technologies (ICT) companies. Even though most ICT professionals are required to understand technical documentation in English or, sometimes, even German, they often lack the language competencies they would need in order to effectively communicate and collaborate with other speakers of the target language. Mobile smart devices allow teachers to provide students with personalized learning environments in line with their needs. However, most of the available apps, especially in the area of foreign language learning, still focus on form-based learning, supporting mainly one-way interaction. In this study, the authors designed a learning system based on a dynamic, asynchronous and constructive learning approach. Finally, two algorithms that guide students' learning process are compared: the first algorithm is based on community-driven behaviour, the second one on students' individual behaviour. Results show that both algorithms provide similar outcomes.

Chapter 7, "From Motivation and Self-Structure to a Decision-Support Framework for Online Social Networks" by Francisco Antunes, Manuela Freire and João Paulo Costa, focussed on the use of data collected from online social networks offers new possibilities for supporting organizations' daily-based activities. The participation in online social networks has become extremely popular, corresponding to more than two-thirds of the global online population. In fact, social networking and blogging account for nearly thirty percent of all time spent on the Internet suggesting that online social networks have become a fundamental part of the global online experience and has introduced a new organizational framework for online communities and, with it, a vibrant new research context It is also common knowledge that the opinion exchange in online social networks provides, nor rarely, a decisive contribution in decision-making. It is, thus, necessary to review and bare present the motivations by which people engage in online social network and the ways in which firms can make use of such motivations, in order to take advantage of online social networks as information sources for decision-making support. To do so, the authors of this paper developed the decision support social networks to extract such information, which encompasses the intertwined use of human interaction and network structure, by combining human capabilities, Social Network Analysis (SNA) and automatic data mining. In this paper, a brief summary of the performed case studies over the proposed information model is also presented.

Chapter 8, "Handling the Dataflow in Business Process Models" by Giorgio Bruno, stresses on the importance of the dataflow in business process models and illustrates a notation called DMA which is meant to fulfil two major goals: promoting the integration between business processes and information systems and leveraging the dataflow to provide flexibility in terms of human decisions. Over the years, various approaches and notations have been proposed to define business process models. They are based on different perspectives and the most important ones are the activity-centric, the artefact-centric and the case-centric perspective. The activity-centric approach has inspired the industry standard BPMN (Business Process Model and Notation) whose focus is on the tasks (work units) and the control flow. The first goal is fulfilled by considering both tasks and business entities as first-class citizens in process models. Business entities form the dataflow that interconnects the tasks: tasks take the input entities from the input dataflow and deliver the output entities to the output dataflow. Human decisions encompass the selection of the input entities when a task needs more than one, and the selection of the task with which to handle the input entities when two or more tasks are admissible. DMA provides a number of patterns that indicate how tasks affect the dataflow: in addition, two compound patterns, called macro tasks, can be used to represent task selection issues. An example related to an order handling process illustrates the notation.

Chapter 9, "Principles of Secure Access and Privacy in Combined E-Learning Environments: Architecture, Formalization, and Modelling" by Radi Petrov Romansky and Irina Stancheva Noninska, outlines new important challenges in privacy and personal data protection which reflect on the applied principles of user's security in the cyberspace. This is also the case with e-learning environments which use new network technologies as remote access, distributed processing, information sharing, cloud services, social computing, etc. It is well known that e-learning is learning based on Information and Communication Technologies (ICT) for remote access to educational curriculum and materials outside of a traditional classroom. Many terms are used for describing e-learning as online learning, internet learning, distance education, etc. The contemporary ICT permits to extend these definitions with distributed learning, mobile learning, and social learning and cloud learning, etc. Yes, e-learning has many benefits, but developed e-learning systems and environments must propose services with a high level of user's security and personal data protection. The chapter highlights the need for Strong security procedures based on authentication, authorization and data protection which should be proposed to protect system resources, user's profiles, personal information, educational materials and other specific information. The chapter presents a point of view about opportunities and challenges of some digital technologies which could increase the effectiveness of e-learning processes by developing a combined e-learning environment. A functional architecture with two sub-systems (front office and back-office) and different information resources (public, internal, external) is discussed. Investigation by using formalization and modelling is made and assessments are presented.

Chapter 10, "A Research on Students' Perceptions on a B-Learning English Environment to Improve Written Skills" by Ana María Pinto-Llorente, Mª Cruz Sánchez-Gómez and Francisco José García-Peñalvo, explored university students' perceptions about the effectiveness of interactive and collaborative tools to improve written skills in a blended learning environment. Web tools have changed the way in which users take part in the communicative and learning process. They state that Web 2.0 philosophy facilitates the access to knowledge, the communication between individuals and the possibility of being a content author. Students learn, practice, and communicate with all the protagonists of the teaching-learning process. This enhances a collective construction of knowledge in which students have an active role, against individualism of traditional methods. Based on this goal, a mixed methods research approach was adopted to enhance the mutual invigoration of the two types of methods, and the validity and reliability of data. 358 learners participated in the quantitative study and 91 in the qualitative one. All of them were enrolled in the subject English I. The instruments used to collect data were two tests and semi-structured interviews. The findings suggested students' positive perspective towards the possibilities offered by online glossaries, online quizzes, wikis and forums to improve written skills and foster effective written communication in different contexts. It was highlighted their potentiality to create a learning community in which students could participate actively in the construction of knowledge, abandoning their passive role as simple observers.

Chapter 11, "An Empirical Study of the Indian IT Sector on Typologies of Workaholism as Predictors of HR Crisis" by Shivani Pandey and Vinky Sharma, focuses on the issue of Workaholism. Workaholism, in recent years has taken a regular behaviour pattern among professionals. Researchers have shown that working conditions have changed expeditiously. Ambiguity of clear role expectations at work is high and the balance between work and personal being has become vaguer. Stress rates at work have upsurge in the past decade resulting in psychiatric health problems and turning down of work productivity. It is also evident from numerous reports that a high level of perceived stress at work is related to low level of satisfaction with job and poor mental condition. While self-negligence is assumed as a hallmark of Workaholism, empirical data in this case stands to be both narrow and paradoxical. The modern developments like high speed data connections add more to this belief, as this makes possible for the employees who would like to work at any place and at any given point of time. Workaholism is found to affect several important domain of life. With regards to work domain, workaholics commonly seem to have poor associations with their peer/colleagues, most likely, on the grounds that they often feel the need to control them and experience issues with delegating work Given that the amount of time they invested in their work leaves little energy for them for other activities, also the social life outside work gets hampered. This study has made a modest effort in exploring the relationship between workaholism, perceived work-related stress, different job conditions and intensifying anxiety among IT professionals in Delhi/NCR.

Chapter 12, "Analysis of the European ICT Competence Frameworks" by Luis Fernández Sanz, Josefa Gómez-Pérez and Ana Castillo-Martinez, focuses on the rapid evolution and expansion of ICT labor markets requires a common language to manage offer and demand of talent which is especially critical and complex in a transnational integration scenario like the European Union. Competences, skills, knowledge, job profiles, qualifications or occupations are some of the concepts most commonly used in the present within the IT profession. They can be easily found in all types of information written in e.g. job ads, training courses and CV of jobseekers. Ensuring that these terms are used consistently with a common language is essential for a correct match of needs between employers, job candidates and training providers. Models and frameworks represent useful tools for this purpose. This chapter analyzes the most relevant e-competences frameworks in the European Union (e-CF or EN16234, ESCO and Body of Knowledge or Book) as well as their integration and similarities. The present impact of these European frameworks in the ICT labor market and their connection to training and education is presented through data and several examples taken from two EU-funded projects: e-Skills Match and e-CF Council.

Chapter 13, "Competence E-Assessment Based on Semantic Web: From Modelling to Validation," has been contributed by Mounira Ilahi-Amri, Lilila Cheniti-Belcadhi and Rafik Braham speaks in light of trends toward increased requirements for skilled workers, e-assessment presents today many challenges; and its trace on learners' real performance in life. In recognition of changes to the typical patterns of working life, Higher Education in overall the world is currently laying great stress on Competence-based learning. This is receiving attention particularly on competence-based development to improve the learner's potential value within lifelong learning and universities are currently looking for the best way to competently manage learning. Thus, and recognizing the inadequacy of current traditional knowledge-based assessment systems in higher education to achieve performance visibility, we need to rethink how we design new assessment systems that can respond to the corporate requirements of the

21st century and mirror the learners' competences. This concern has not been sufficiently investigated. This paper considers the Competence-Based Assessment. We explore the importance of competency and competence modelling conceptual understanding. The research reviews the benchmark literature on the concepts, models and approaches of competence and competency and explores the confusions surrounding the pair of concepts.

Chapter 14, "Determinants of Job Satisfaction and Its Impact on Affective, Continuance, and Normative Commitment of Employees: An Empirical Study" by Anita Singh and Lata Bajpai Singh, aims to identify different factors of job satisfaction responsible for different types of commitment i.e. affective, continuance and normative commitment among the employees of IT organizations. Of late with the rapid change in the environment and technology, the role of HR has become more dynamic and complex for IT companies. It has been observed that role of HR is shifting from traditional personnel, administration, and transactional to strategic utilization of employees. Most of the companies now refer HR activities as 'Human Capital Management' to reflect the strategic and leadership development role of HR. The primary data for the study was collected from 401 respondents of IT organizations using validated scales on organizational commitment and job satisfaction. The exploratory factor analysis was conducted to identify different factors of job satisfaction and scale reliability of organizational commitment scale. The reliability and validity of all the constructs were further done through confirmatory factor analysis. Then related hypotheses were tested using structural equation modelling through AMOS 21.0. Three factors of job satisfaction were extracted namely Growth opportunities and Management practices, Working condition and Fair treatment. Growth opportunities and Management practices is prominent reason for affective commitment and whereas Fair treatment ensures continuance and normative commitment among the employees of IT organizations with the given sample

Chapter 15, "Empathy and Mindfulness: Exploring the Possible Predictors of Authentic Leadership" by Aishwarya Singh, Santoshi Sengupta and Swati, focuses on how the upheavals in the current times are driving us toward a purposeful need for more effective and 'genuine' leadership skills so as to enhance business sustainability. The recent economic crisis in Greece as well as scams such as Vyapam in India calls for leaders who do not deny responsibility, defy their stakeholders or hide information but instead lead with authenticity and integrity. Authentic leadership (AL) that emerges from the earlier theories of social intelligence and multiple intelligence has attracted the attention of researchers and practitioners worldwide. This chapter empirically investigates the concept of Authentic Leadership and considers the pathways to develop authentic leadership by exploring and examining empathy and mindfulness as predictors of authentic leadership. Intense literature review reflect that only few studies have been conducted that focus on the antecedents of authentic leadership. The study attempts to fill this void. A questionnaire was completed by 250 respondents from the IT industry. Regression analysis was applied to study the inter-relationships among the variables. Findings reveal that while empathy of a leader is significantly related to the development of authentic leadership, mindfulness is not. Wider geographical selection and replication of the study in other industry is recommended. The chapter promotes development of OB interventions intended to foster the development of authentic leaders for positive organizational outcomes.

Chapter 16, "High Involvement Work Processes: Implications for Employee Withdrawal Behaviours" by Manu Melwin Joy, focuses on examining the effect of high involvement work processes on employee withdrawal behaviours in information technology sector in India. The study draws from the structured questionnaire data from 300 software engineers working in Infosys, CTS and HCL. Data was analyzed to find out details related to the relationship between high involvement work processes and employee withdrawal behaviours. It was found that high involvement work processes have a strong negative impact on withdrawal behaviours. The relationship was found to be stronger in the case of work withdrawal behaviours compared to that of job withdrawal behaviours. In contrast to previous studies, the perspective of employees on the implementation of High Involvement Work Processes and its effectiveness was captured. The proposed model of the study, serves as an excellent tool for manager to see things from employee's point of view and bring down attrition rates.

Chapter 17, "Open Ways for Time Banking Research: Information and Knowledge Management and Open Source" by Lukas Valek, underlined three possible fields of research in field of time banking which is complementary economy system based on a time currency. These fields of Information and Knowledge management and Open Source software are almost totally unexplored areas of time bank phenomenon, which is known already for more than three decades. The TB concept has faced many challenges, and in terms of cultural environment it is often adapted to reflect a particular regional reality, this adaptation including the management of information and knowledge contained within a time bank, but also various information technology solutions. Nowadays many Time Banking movements have emerged around the world, with the number ever-increasing, thus it is quite difficult to determine precise count. Nevertheless, their focus on social economy gives users a tool to help themselves rather than expect support from authorities. In field of Information Management the attention is mostly on Information Management Frameworks. For Knowledge Management and Open Source, among others, link is found in core concept of time bank called co-production. In conclusion, all these three fields are related to time banking and have place in further research, which can be beneficial for the field of complementary economic systems in general.

The value and contribution of an academic reserve can be evaluated based on the empirical evidences and reviews that it resonates. This book hopes to throw light on some fascinating issues associated with Human Capital in an era marked with Technology and hopes to be of value to aspiring practitioners and researchers in this domain. All the contributions made towards the chapters in the book are based on authentic and rigorous researches in the field of Information Technology that can be summated from HR point of view. The essence of multidisciplinary perspectives adds to the various shades of management thought and development. The book makes for a supporting of various aspects of effective management of professionals working in the IT industry worldwide. The challenges faced by this work section are mostly common to all, at difference stages of incitement.

The Human Resource Management function, in organisations, is constantly evolving as new technologies, concepts and ideologies proceed to shape individual mindsets. These individuals include organisational employees as well as decision makers. As organisations emphasise the need for greater collaboration across cross-functional boundaries, several new means of communication have emerged. These include Skype, live meetings, video conferencing, drop boxes, group chats, workload and document management. Clearly, Internet and communication technologies have made it possible for people sitting at different locations to share information through a common platform, as effectively managing people who do not meet physically is best done through trust. The focus towards better management of human resources is also moved into a perspective of data and the use of analytics for decision making and effective management. The source of online resources and virtual media make virtual sharing an idea that can take leaps and bounds in the area of multidisciplinary management of human resources. This book aims at providing this diverse set of people, with food for thought which can help them in their individual spheres of work and influence. Several chapters showcase the research of scholars in specific fields. Future research directions stated by some of the authors can serve as an ideation platform for other aspiring researchers in those specific fields. Hence, this book serves as a multidisciplinary forum for authors to present and discuss the most recent innovations, trends and practical challenges encountered, and solutions adopted.

This book has drawn immensely from the research contributions published in the International Journal of Human Capital and Information Technology professionals, published by IGI Global. Several authors of journal papers have extended their contributions, to provide a more comprehensive article, for the book. We would like to thank each of the authors. Without their support, this endeavour would not have been possible. The book also hosts some interesting original contributions. We would like to extend our gratitude to the new authors as well as all those individuals who have served as reviewers for those chapters.

Vandana Ahuja
Jaypee Institute of Information Technology, India

Shubhangini Rathore
IBS Gurgaon, India

Chapter 1
Analysis of Role Stress in the Indian IT Industry

Shubhangini Rathore
IBS Gurgaon, India

ABSTRACT

Contemporary industries face new competition requiring employees to work for longer hours under competitive time-bound deadlines. Prolonged exposure to such stressful situations leads to a depletion and exhaustion of resources in the mind and body with dysfunctional effects on job performance and overall organizational effectiveness. The Indian IT industry is a fast-paced service industry that is characterized by such stressful work situations and related outcomes. This chapter analyses the various factors that contribute to organizational stress and the role of demographic factors on role stress among the professionals of the Indian IT industry. A sample of 250 employees has been collected from the Delhi NCR region. Role stress has been measured by using the ORS scale which comprises of 10 dimensions of the role of stress that are measured by 50 items. The results show that there is a considerable amount of work related stress along with a significant impact of demographic factors on the role of stress amongst the IT professionals.

INTRODUCTION

The India Information Technology (IT) Sector is seen in conjunction with the Information Technology enabled Services (ITeS). The sector has a substantial contribution to the national economy as it caters to domestic and foreign markets. The rise of exports makes it account for almost 75% of its total earned revenue. Broadly, the sector is divided into four large segments that comprise of IT services, ITES-BPO and Software; which includes both Research and Development and Engineering.

Apart from various other accolades this sector has also been instrumental in energizing economic growth through its interaction with the higher education sector pertaining to computers and all the Engineering fields.

As economic times get harder; there arises diminishing security of jobs, because of which people remain in jobs that are consistent; but not fulfilling. The IT sector is seen to be characterized with high

DOI: 10.4018/978-1-5225-5297-0.ch001

Role Stress (Colomo-Palacios et al., 2014b; Karad, 2010). The nature of work pressures in contemporary organizations requires employees to work longer hours, under stressful conditions of workload, performance pressure and competition. The IT industry is seen to be characterized by challenging conditions of organizational Stress 4 6. Stress has highlighted itself in the visibility of a rising trend of employee sickness, premature labour turnover, and premature retirement due to ill health, lost production. In 1936, Prof. Hans Selye, "The father of modern stress", researched on dysfunctional effects of stress on the human body due to overarching demands on it. The empirical research in the field began only after Hans Seyle's first article on stress in 1956 20. Stress can be categorized into positive and negative aspects. Positive stress is also called *eustress* and can be defined as a pleasant or curative stress that helps a person to perform better, given the situational demands. The General Adaptation syndrome considers *eustress* as a part of the initial indication of the alarm in the body, but problem seems to arise when the alarm is ignored and ones resources are completed depleted and result in a burnout 21. Negative stress is reached by the body when the body alarms are ignored and the body heads towards a burnout. Increasing workplace demands along with increasing professional aspirations create a point of dissonance for the employee by making him work against all odds of time and resources. A big challenge for organizations now is to create an environment that equips employees with well suited coping mechanisms and programs in fruitful stress management.

Particularly in the IT organizations; organizational culture is seen to be lacking in terms of assisting the employees on the knowledge about stress and coping for psychological problems. The work process are highly dynamic and time bound, as employees have definite targets to meet, that are incubated in different time zones. The life expectancy of products and programs declines each year, while the demands on employees to provide better solutions increases. Internal IT departments that cannot keep pace with the changes and are not sufficiently adaptable are in a danger of being outsourced. Because of the unique set of environmental pressures in IT functions - continuous re-engineering, outsourcing, more demanding customers, general information overload (Karad, 2010) and hard decisions (Colomo-Palacios et al., 2013).

In the Indian IT industry, the trend towards aspiring youngsters who would work extra hours to acquire material comforts; seems to increase. Researchers have shown that broadly the major causes of workforce attrition in the IT sector are work-related, psychological and emotional. The specific variables are effort- reward imbalance, perceived workload and emotional exhaustion. Research shows that there is a very common practice of software engineers who have less than five years of work experience; to leave work. This is a resultant of issues like a shrinking student base, low attractiveness of the profession in terms of image and status (García-Crespo et al., 2008; Day, 2007). A direct outcome of stress is seen in the high levels of attrition that the industry faces. A big challenge for contemporary organizations is to create an environment that equips employees with well suited coping mechanisms and programs in stress management. Research shows that, high levels of stress can lead to emotional exhaustion, lower organizational commitment, and increased turnover intentions (Cropanzano et al. 2003). More recently, research by Colomo-Palacios et al. (2014) shows that stress also leads to IT career abandonment.

A big challenge that the organizations face is that, stress interventions cannot be used as a blanket strategy for all the employees. Apart from individual differences that exist in the workforce; there are always generic differences that are brought forward by demographic factors. The present study explores in detail, the role of various demographic factors in studying workplace stress among the professionals of the IT industry. There are extremely few researches that explore this aspect in the Indian IT industry. The IT sector is also seen to be characterized with high role stress (Karad, 2010). The employees have definite targets that they have to meet, as most of the projects are time bound and incubated in different time zones. Employees need to work through night shifts and deliver the services. Apart from this, the nature of the IT industry makes it subject to phenomenal and increasingly rapid changes. Internal IT departments that cannot keep pace with the changes and are not sufficiently adaptable are in danger of being outsourced. Thus, given the scenario, the employees of the sector need to develop the 1) the ability to learn, 2) the ability to work in teams, 3) oral and written communication, 4) problem solving and reasoning, and 5) a point of reference to health and wellness (Colomo-Palacios, R. et al,2014). More recently, research by Colomo-Palacios et al. (2014) shows that stress also leads to IT career abandonment (Korczynski,2001)

The outcomes of the study will be beneficial for the management professionals in dealing with different strata of employees, when it comes to the issue of workplace stress.

ORGANIZATIONAL STRESS: A REVIEW OF LITERATURE

Lazarus (1993) explained Stress, as a condition or feeling experienced when a person perceives that the, "environmental demands exceed the personal and social resources that the individual is able to mobilize". Hans Selye referred to stress as the, "non-specific response of the body to any demand for change" (Selye, 1997). Research shows that Stress has been studied from various contemporary and historic perspectives. Its impact on work outcomes has been heavily research upon. Researchers have also tried to identify the role of different cultural, demographic and social factors on stress. While on the one hand it has been reported that there are no differences between women and men in relation to workplace stress, it has also been noted that there are differences in both stressors and the severity of stress between the genders.

Spielberger & Reheiser (1994) conducted a study with 1781 working adults, measuring gender differences in occupational stress using the Job Stress Survey (JSS) in American university and corporate settings. It was found that there were no significant differences in the overall stress levels for the two genders, although occupational stress level was highly significant with managerial/professional participants (Spielberger & Reheise, 1994).

Nelson, and Quick (1998) explored the various reasons of work stress in organizations. The researchers have identified four basic factors which are; *Role Factors, Job Stressors, Physical Stressors and Interpersonal* Stressors (Michailids & Elwaki,2001). They explained *Role* based factors causing stress by virtue of an expectation set that is placed on an individual within an organization; especially if these are confusing, ambiguous or conflicting. *Job stressors* are explained as factors related to the basic quality and quantity of work performed as well as the feedback and appraisals that individuals receive regarding their job performance. *Physical Stressors* are explained as stressors that affect the senses, such as light, noise, vibration, smell, temperature, etc. *Interpersonal Stressors* are the factors that deal with one's inability to manage and cope with co workers, friends, family and all associates in general.

Russell & Zinta (2000) investigated the relationship of Organizational Stress and exhaustion to work outcomes such as commitment, turnover intentions, and organizational citizenship behaviors. Based on the Conservation of Resources (COR) model, it was found that stress & emotional exhaustion were negatively related to organizational commitment and supervisory commitment. Emotional exhaustion effected turnover intentions positively. Organizational citizenship behaviors were studied and were found to be negatively related to organizational stress & emotional exhaustion. Therefore a stressed employee was more likable to quit his job.

Neelamegam & Asrafi (2001) identified & measured the level of stress of bank employees that was resultant of the changes in the banking sector due to policy changes, globalization and liberalization and increased competition from the entrance of more private (corporate) sector banks. The study established that stress levels were negatively correlated to years of service and qualification. Incongruent roles, insults, long work hours were identified as major factors of work related stress.

Oi-ling Siu (2002) examined the levels of stress in Managerial and Non Managerial employees in organizations in China and Hong Kong. Standard instruments were used to carry out this research. The study showed that occupational stressors play a significant role in determining job satisfaction, mental and physical well-being. It was also seen that organizational commitment and well-being are positively related to each other, emphasizing that committed employees would have less levels of stress and vice versa.

Michailids & Elwkai (2003) studied factors contributing to workplace stress in the fast-food industry. The Occupational Stress Indicator was used for examining these factors with a sample size of 100 respondents working in different fast food restaurants. It was found that factors such as, ones feeling about their job, behaviour, interpretation of events around them and coping differences contributed to stress. There was significant difference in the perception of stress between women and men as well as individuals in managerial and non-managerial positions with regards to their personality, the degree of ambition and work dedication they possess.

Bacchino et al. (2003) Studied the congruence between personal and organizational values (P-OC), perceived psychological contract violations (PCV), and work stress in the context of age, gender, and job tenure. The results of the study showed that employees reporting higher levels of psychological contract violations are more likely to experience organizational stress. Male Employees were reported higher amounts of stress. Beehr et al. (2003) studied the congruence between sources of the stressor and social support. A sample of 117 respondents was chosen. Two social support measures were used; mainly social support from the supervisor and from the co-workers. A social support scale was used for analysis. The results showed that the Congruence between the sources of stressors and of social support appeared to make little difference in determining the moderating effect of social support on the relationship between stressors and strain. It was seen that role ambiguity and workload originating from the supervisor were positively related to stress.

It has been reported that although women and men are exposed to the same stressors, women are also facing unique stressors. This is particularly important according to Hofboll et al. (2003) as several studies have found that the provision of workplace support was more effective in reducing occupational stress in men than in women. It was reported that women in particular are exposed to the following stressors: multiple roles; lack of career progress; and discrimination and stereotyping.

Aziz (2004) examined the levels of organizational *Role Stress* among women in the IT private sector organizations. The ORS Scale was used on a sample of 256 women professionals. Amongst the major stressors, it was seen that, Resource *inadequacy (RIN)* was ranked as the most potential stressor and was followed by Role *Overload (RO)* and *Personal Inadequacy (PI)*. It was seen that there was significant difference in the stress levels of professionals who were not married and married (Rydstedt, L. W.,et al,2004).

Loosemore & Waters (2004) studied the influence of gender on stress levels in the construction industry. The studies significantly found that overall; men experience slightly higher levels of stress than women. They added that men get more stressed by risk taking, disciplinary matters, and implications of mistakes, redundancy, and career progression. Women on the other side were more influenced with factors such as, opportunities for personal development, rates of pay, keeping up with new ideas, business travel, and the accumulative effect of minor tasks.

Sharma (2004) examined the role and causes of stress in the lives of doctors working in private and public hospitals. Role overload and conflict were seen to be the major reasons of stress. Torkelson & Muhnonb (2004) studied the relationship between coping and health problems in the context of gender and level in the organization. Data was collected from a sample of 279 women and men (100 managers and 179 non-managers) at a sales department in a Swedish telecom company. The nature of work for both men and women were kept similar. The analysis showed that with the level and gender kept controlled, there was no relation between problem-focused strategies and health. On the other hand, emotion-focused strategy of seeking emotional support was associated with fewer health problems. It was observed that the coping mechanisms of individuals were related to the levels that they held. At senior levels, similar coping strategies were used where as at non managerial levels, conventional coping patterns were used.

Michailidis & Georgiou (2005) examined occupational stress of employees in the banking sector by taking a sample of 60 bank employees working at different levels. The Occupational Stress Indicator (OSI) was used for analysis. The results showed that employees' educational levels affect the degree of stress they experience in various ways. Factors such as educational background, the strength of the employees' family support, and the amount of time available for them to relax was also instrumental in contributing towards workplace stress experienced by individuals.

Härenstam and MOA Research Group (2005) studied the management strategies and working conditions in 72 establishments by classifying these elements by type of operations and company position, in order to learn about the increase in occupational stress and sick leaves. The results showed that management technologies distribute risks between segments of the labour market and different groups of the labour force. The developments were most favorable in high tech and knowledge-based operations and least favourable.

Rydstedt et al. (2004) studied the lay theories of stress .The researchers aimed at studying the lay beliefs concerning work stress and perceived strain. A sample of 2270 was used to build on an earlier study of lay beliefs that were assessed by a scale consisting of 36 items. Factor analysis gave a solution with five factors on perceived causes and four factors of perceived alleviation of work stress. Significant relations was found between lay beliefs of work stress and perceived mental strain as well as job stress. It was also found that individual's subjective beliefs about work stress were a potentially mediating factor between objective working conditions and stress outcomes.

Dasgupta & Kumar (2009) analyzed the sources of *Role Stress* among a sample of female doctors working in Shimla. The study revealed that *Self-Role Distance (SRD), inter-role distance (IRD), Role Stagnation (RS), Role Ambiguity (RA), Role Overload (RO), Role Isolation (RI), Role Expectation Conflict (REC)* and *Role Inadequacy* (RI) are the major sources of role stress. The study also showed that there was no significant difference among the male and female doctors, except on the parameters of inter-*role distance* (IRD) and *role inadequacy (RI).The male* doctors were found to have greater mean scores on these two parameters 110.

Nikolaou & Tsaousis (2009) studied the relationship between emotional intelligence and stress in a sample of professionals in mental health institutions. A total of 212 participants were administered the Emotional Intelligence Questionnaire as well as the Organizational Stress Screening Tool (ASSET), a new organizational screening tool, which measures workplace stress. The results of the study showed that Emotional Intelligence was negatively co related to stress and positively related to affective commitment.

Smith (2011) researched on the effect of demographic and diversity statistics on stress and highlighted that here is a need to establish a unified definition of perceived stress as it means different things to different people. A universal understanding and role of individual differences is still unclear through research.

Wirtz et al. (2013) Investigated whether occupational role stress is associated with differential levels of the stress hormone. Findings suggested that occupational role stress in terms of role uncertainty acts as a background stressor that is associated with increased HPA-axis reactivity to acute stress.

Yongkang (2014) explored the relationship among role conflict, role ambiguity, role overload and job stress among the middle-level cadres in the Chinese local government. A sample of 220 employees was selected. The results showed that time pressure was significantly correlated with role conflict and role overload. Along with this, the study also established that job anxiety and job stress were significantly and positively correlated with role ambiguity, role conflict and role overload; role ambiguity had a significant and positive effect on job anxiety and job stress; role conflict and role overload had a significant and positive effect on time stress, job anxiety and job stress.

ORGANIZATIONAL STRESS

As shown in chapter 2, a detailed review of literature was done in order to analyze the various key words in definitions and constructs that have been used to explain Stress.

Steps and Procedures in Factor Identification

Step 1

Table 1 shows the different groups in which key words of similar meaning and application are grouped together

Table 1. Identification of key words from literature review

Key Words (Research Definitions)	Group
Physical damage as a result of the bodies general over adaptation to the stressor (Selye, 1997)	Physical damage felt by the body
Discrepancies between the way in which individuals view themselves, the ways in which they perceive others as responding to them, and the actually do evaluate them. (Lundgren, 1978)	One's sense of self concept
• Non-specific response of the body to, demand for change, perception (Selye, 1997) • Perceiving stressor as a stressor (Briner et al. 2004) • Responding to an event that could be imaginary or real (Brieir & Elliott, 1988) • Individual's own judgment (Holroyd & Lazarus 1982)	Stress as one's individual perception
• Discrepancy in environment its demands of us • A reaction of a particular individual to a environmental stimulus. (Hinkle 1973). • Individual and environment coexisting in a dynamic relationship.(Folkman, Lazarus, Gruen & De Longis, 1986)	Strain of Environmental demands
• An over or under load of information or matter (Steinberg & Ritzmann 1990) • Demands exceed the personal and social resources (Lazarus 1993)	Work Overload& under load
• Incompatible behaviour, multiple expectations or obligations associated with a single social role (Levi, 1996) • A misbalance between what we actually need versus what we are capable to provide (Levi, 1996)	Non clarity of one's roles
• Individual difference in stress inception such as; personality, self esteem, locus of control, coping style, hardiness, type A, attribution style, demographics, expectations, preferences, commitment, health related factors and abilities (Payne, 1988; Parkes, 1994) • Individual Differences such as locus of control, hardiness, and coping resources (Cox & Ferguson, 1991)	Individual differences and Personality

Step 2

After identifying the key variables that explain the various dimensions of *Organizational Stress*, an analysis of the variables is done with the four ***Historical Approaches*** of Workplace Stress

Four Major approaches of stress that highlight the eminent works of researchers such as Canon, Lazarus, Kahn and Levinson have been studied

Historic Approaches of Stress

- **The Homeostatic/Medical Approach:** This approach highlights the work of Walter Cannon who discovered the stress response, initially called the "the emergency response," or "the militaristic response." In this case an external demand spoils the homeostasis of the body, which is more or less a neutral and natural bodily state; ultimately causing stress.
- **The Cognitive Appraisal Approach:** Richard Lazarus contributed to the field of success and highlighted that individual differences play a key role in the inception of stress. Thus individuals may not see a stressor in the same capacity as another person. As, individuals differ widely in their appraisal of situations of people, Perception and cognitive appraisal formed major parts of the stress process in an individual.
- **The Person–Environment Fit Approach:** Robert Kahn explained this as a fit between ones expected demands from his role and the skills that he is capable of providing. Thus confusion between the two leads to stress. A good person – environment fit arises when there is a good balance between expectations and demands.
- **The Psychoanalytic Approach:** Harry Levinson took from the Freudian approaches to explain stress in terms of the ideal self and the real self. Where an ideal self is desirable by a person; a real self is a person's direct witness of self personality. Thus a difference between the two leads to stress between individuals.

As identified in the literature; Table 2 shows the groups of the key words that have been highlighted by various researchers. The factor, "Physical distress", finds its congruence with the Homeostatic approach as both talk about the nature of stress that is imbibes in physical distress or strain in the body. Stress tends to grow in the individual as the physical strain grows. The Cognitive Appraisal Approach finds congruence with the factor, "Individual Perception", or the way in which one perceives his role in the organization. The way in which individuals appraise their stressor is also a matter of perception. Role under load is one such factor in which a sense of insecurity and a feeling of under competence start to develop.

The Person–Environment Fit Approach finds congruence with factor named "Role Overload & Under load, Personality & Work Environment"; which explains concepts of, role conflict, ambiguity and individual differences in perceiving the environment, as the individual is incapable of understanding the exact and reasonable demand from his resources in the organization. The Psychoanalytic Approach finds congruence with the factor, "Self Image"; which explains a person's self image as a major reason as perception of stressor in one's mind as an off shoot of his self concept.

Table 2. Congruence of historic approaches with identified key words of stress

Keyword Identified/Concepts Evolving From the Review of Literature	Congruence With Approaches	Identified Factor
Physical damage as a result of the bodies general over adaptation to the stressors (Selye, 1936)	Homeostatic Approach	Physical Distress
• Discrepancies between the way in which individuals view themselves, the ways in which they perceive others as responding to them, and the actually do evaluate them. (Lundgren, 1978) • Belief in ones capacities (Payne, 1988; Parkes, 1994)	The Psychoanalytic Approach	Self Image
• Non-specific response of the body to, demand for change, perception (Selye, 1936) • Perceiving stressor as a stressor (Briner et al., 2004) • Responding to an event that could be imaginary or real (Brieir & Elliott, 1988) • Individual's own judgment (Holyroyd and Lazarus 1982)	The Cognitive Appraisal Approach	Individual Perception
• A reaction of a particular individual to an environmental stimulus. (Hinkle 1973). • Individual and environment coexisting in a dynamic relationship.(Folkman, Lazarus, Gruen & DeLongis)	Person–Environment Fit Approach	Work Environment
• Under load or overload of matter, energy or information • Demands exceed the personal and social resources (Lazarus 1993)	Individual - Environmental Fit	Work Overload & Work under load
• Incompatible behaviour, multiple expectations or obligations associated with a single social role (Davis, 1995) • A misbalance between what we actually need versus what we are capable to provide (Levi, 1996)	Person–Environment Fit Approach	Role clarity
• Incompatible behaviour, multiple expectations or obligations associated with a single social role(Davis, 1995) • Individual difference in stress inception such as ; personality, self esteem, locus of control, coping style, hardiness, type A, attribution style, demographics, expectations, preferences, commitment, health related factors and abilities (Payne, 1988; Parkes, 1994) • Individual Differences such as locus of control, hardiness, and coping resources.(Cox & Ferguson, 1991)	Person–Environment Fit Approach	Personality

List of Variables Identified for the Study

1. Physical Distress
2. Individual's Perception
3. Role overload
4. Personality
5. role clarity
6. Self Image
7. Workplace Environment
8. Role Under load

Rationale for Adapting Organizational Resource Stress Scale (ORS): Dr.Udai Pareek

After reviewing the various approaches and concepts of workplace stress, a comprehensive list of variables has been identified.

Step III

Organizational Role Stress Scale

The scale comprises of ten factors, namely; Inter-role distance (IRD), Role expectation conflicts (REC) Role isolation(RI), Self-role distance (SRD), Role erosion (RE), Role ambiguity (RA), Resource inadequacy (RIN), Role stagnation (RS),), Personal inadequacy (PI), Role overload (RO),

Table 3. Congruence between identified factors and ORS scale factors

Identified Factors (Literature Review)
1. Physical Distress 2. Individual's Perception 3. Role overload 4. Personality 5. Role clarity 6. Self Image 7. Workplace Environment 8. 8) Role Under load
ORS Scale (Dr.Pareek)
• Role stagnation (RS) • Role expectation conflicts (REC) • Role erosion (RE) • Role overload (RO) • Role isolation(RI) • Self-role distance (SRD) • Role ambiguity (RA) • Role Inadequacy(RIN) • Inter Role Distance (IRD) • Personal Inadequacy(PI)

Physical Distress, Resource Inadequacy (RIN)

Resource Inadequacy (RIN): is seen to arise in a situation where one perceives that his personal and material resources are not enough to accomplish his role requirements and demands. An outcome of this is physical pressures on the body. Physical distress as previously explained is explained as Hardship, pain, torture, exertion starvation and physical damage are a result of the bodies general over adaptation to the stressors. It has also been studied as Physical damage as a result of the bodies general over adaptation to the stressors (Selye, 1936).

Self Image, Self-Role Distance (SRD), Inter-Role Distance (IRD)

Self-Role Distance (SRD) arises from a discrepancy that arises between ones concept of the, "self", and the demands made on him by the role that he performs. Thus the individual perceives himself as incompetent for the job. Discrepancies between the way in which individuals view themselves, the ways in which they perceive others as responding to them, and they actually do evaluate them (Lundgren, 1978). It is also reflected in one's Belief in ones capacities (Payne, 1988; Parkes, 1994). Inter-Role Distance (IRD) is experienced when there is a stress due to in congruence between the roles that one performs in his professional life versus his personal roles.

Role Clarity, Role Expectation Conflict (REC), Role Ambiguity (RA)

In a broad perspective, role clarity can be related to Inter-Role Distance, Role Expectation Conflict and Role Ambiguity.

1. **Role Expectation Conflict (REC):** Arises out of conflicting demands originating from an individual's superiors, subordinates or peers.
2. **Role Ambiguity (RA):** Arises due to a non clarity that arises due to the multitudinous the expectations of one's professional.

Role Clarity arises as a result of Incompatible behaviour, multiple expectations or obligations associated with a single social role (Davis, 1995).A misfit between our capability and role demands (Levi, 1996).

Role Overload, Role Overload (RO), and Personal Inadequacy

Role Overload (RO): This arises from a feeling that one is burdened with a lot of work and responsibilities. Researchers have this as an an over or under load of information or matter (Steinberg & Ritzmann 1990). Personal Inadequacy arises when the individual feels that his resources are not enough to take up the demands of the environment.

Role Under Load, Role Stagnation (RS)

Role Stagnation (RS): arises when one perceives that he has been stagnant and stuck in one role for a considerably long time, also due to a scarcity of developmental opportunities. As previously explained; factors such as underuse of skills, work under load, poor leadership and poor career progress can be attributed to role under load.

Unique Factors Literature From Literature Review, Not Covered by the ORS

The study of organizational stress covers many aspects of stress. Yet, the review of literature shows limitations, in terms of the two factors; Personality and Perception; that are not heavily researched on. The role of personality and individual perception cannot be undermined, as one tries to understand the causes of workplace stress.

1. **Personality:** Incompatible behavior, multiple expectations or obligations associated with a single social role. Individual difference in stress inception such as; personality, self esteem, locus of control, coping style, hardiness, type A, attribution style, demographics, expectations, preferences, commitment, health related factors and abilities (Payne, 1988; Parkes, 1994)Individual Differences such as locus of control, hardiness, and coping resources (Cox & Ferguson, 1991)
2. **Perception:** A Non-specific response of the body to, demand for change, perception (Selye, 1936). It can be explained as perceiving stressor as a stressor (Briner et al., 2004). Responding to an event that could be imaginary or real (Eliot, 1988). It is also a matter of an Individual's own judgment (Holyroyd and Lazarus 1982)
3. **Work Environment:** This can be explained in the discrepancy in environment its demands of us. A reaction of a particular individual to an environmental stimulus. (Hinkle 1973). Individual and environment coexisting in a dynamic relationship (Folkman, Lazarus, Gruen & DeLongis).

Unique Factors From ORS, Not Covered by Literature Review

1. **Role Erosion (RE):** This arises as one perceives that tasks that are a part of his role are being performed by others.
2. **Role Isolation (RI):** This arises as a person feels that his role is secluded form all the mainstream organizational activities.

Unique Factors Literature From Literature Review, Not Covered by the ORS

Research Instrument

The ORS scale (Pareek, 1993), was used to measure the levels of stress among the employees on ten dimensions of workplace stress. One of the pioneers of research on organizational role stress, Pareek (1993) has reiterated that the performance of any role in an organization has built in potential for conflict due to which stress may arise. The scale has been widely used through researches on Role stress. Pestonjee (1992) observed that ORS is certainly one of the best instruments available presently for measuring role stress, as it has a very high reliability and validity.

The Ten dimensions that measure Role Stress are:

Organizational Role stress was measured using the Organizational Role Stress scale by Dr. Udai Pareek; comprising of 50 items that measure stress on the following 10 dimensions

3. **Inter-Role Distance (IRD):** Is experienced when there is a conflict between organizational and non-organizational roles.
4. **Role Stagnation (RS):** Is the feeling of being stuck in the same role for long due to lack of opportunities or development.
5. **Role Expectation Conflict (REC):** Arises out of conflicting demands originating from Superiors, subordinates or peers.
6. **Role Erosion (RE):** Arises when a role occupant feels that others are performing certain Functions, which should have been a part of his role.
7. **Role Overload (RO):** Is the feeling that one is required to do too much.
8. **Role Isolation (RI):** Arises when a person feels that his role is isolated from the mainstream of organizational life.
9. **Personal Inadequacy (PI):** Is created by the lack of adequate skills and the resulting inability to meet the demands of one's role.
10. **Self-Role Distance (SRD):** Arises from a gap between one's concept of self and the demands of his role.
11. **Role Ambiguity (RA):** Is experienced when there is a lack of clarity about the demands of the role.
12. **Resource Inadequacy (RIN):** Arises when human and material resources allocated are Inadequate to meet the demands of the role.

For *Role Stress*, the score on each role stress thus ranges from 0 - 20 as the dimension includes 5 items each, having minimum 0 and maximum 4. The overall organizational role stress score is obtained by adding the score of all dimensions. The total organizational role stress score thus ranges from 0 - 200. *Inter-role distance (IRD)* is measured by adding items 1,11,21,31,41 *Role stagnation (RS)* 2,12,22,32,42, *Role expectation conflicts (REC)* 3,13,23,33,43, *Role erosion (RE)* 4,14,24,34,44, *Role overload (RO)* 5,15,25,35,45, *Role isolation(RI)* 6,16,26,36,46, *Personal inadequacy(PI)* 7,17,27,37,47, *Self-role distance (SRD)* 8,18,28,38,48, *Role ambiguity (RA)* 9,19,29,39,49, *Resource inadequacy (RIN)* 10,20,30,40,50.

Inter-role distance (IRD) is measured by adding items 1,11,21,31,41 *Role stagnation (RS)* 2,12,22,32,42, *Role expectation conflicts (REC)* 3,13,23,33,43, *Role erosion (RE)* 4,14,24,34,44, *Role overload (RO)* 5,15,25,35,45, *Role isolation(RI)* 6,16,26,36,46, *Personal inadequacy (PI)* 7,17,27,37,47, *Self-role distance (SRD)* 8,18,28,38,48, *Role ambiguity (RA)* 9,19,29,39,49, *Resource inadequacy (RIN)* 10,20,30,40,50.

Pretesting of ORS Questionnaire

In order to test the reliability and validity ORS, the same was administered to 150 respondents of the hospitality & it industry. The collected responses were tabulated. Reliability and validity tests were conducted on the data to check the validity and usability of the instrument. Cronbach's alpha, KMO measure of adequacy and Bartlett's test of sphericity were checked and found suitable.

The analysis of Table 4 shows that all the items of the ORS scale load appropriately on the factors and have acceptable levels of alpha value >0.5.The ORS scale was thus used as a tool to measure Organizational Stress in the study.

Table 4. Summary of factor analysis

Factor	KMO	Item No.	Loading	Reliability-Alpha Value
Inter Role Distance	.735	01	.788	.784
		41	.766	
		21	.716	
		11	.697	
		31	.693	
Role Stagnation	.712	12	.762	.761
		32	.747	
		42	.715	
		02	.705	
		22	.651	
Role Expectation Conflict	.635	03	.817	.655
		13	.856	
		33	.888	
		43	.841	
		23	.871	
Role Erosion	.680	34	.742	.693
		24	.831	
		04	.817	
		14	.653	
		44	.874	
Role Overload	.761	25	.836	.760
		15	.729	
		35	.678	
		45	.676	
		05	.642	

continued on following page

Table 4. Continued

Factor	KMO	Item No.	Loading	Reliability-Alpha Value
Role Isolation	.774	26	.851	.805
		36	.841	
		46	.770	
		16	.685	
		06	.624	
Personal Inadequacy	.709	17	.822	.690
		47	.694	
		27	.632	
		37	.602	
		07	.586	
Self Role Distance	.629	08	.819	.624
		48	.803	
		38	.524	
		18	.897	
		28	.759	
Role Ambiguity	.811	39	.860	.821
		09	.813	
		29	.763	
		19	.724	
		49	.645	
Role Inadequacy	.738	20	.817	.698
		30	.766	
		40	.765	
		10	.616	
		50	.506	

Sample Profile

The study consisted of a sample of 250 professionals. The details of the sample are shown in Table 5.

Table.5 shows the descriptive representation of the sample group. Among the participants, 163 (65 percent) were men and 87 (35 percent), women. There were 120 (48 percent) managers and 130 (52 percent) Executives. In the qualification demographics, there were 115 (46 percent) Post Graduates and 135 (54 percent) Graduates. After collecting the data, the demographics were analyzed for age. The sample was divided into four brackets of age, 20-26 years 99 (40 percent) respondents, 27-35 years 59(24 percent) respondents, 36-45 years, 78 (31 percent) respondents and 46-58 years, 14 (5 percent). In the work experience category, the brackets were from 1-5 years, 35 (14 percent) respondenrs,6-10 years,118 (47 percent) respondents 11-20 years,85 (34 percent) respondents and Above 20 years, 12 (5 percent) respondents.

Table 5. Descriptive representation of the Respondents (N=250)

Variable		Frequency	Percentage
Gender	Male	163	65
	Female	87	35
Designation	Manager	120	48
	Executives	130	52
Qualification	Post Graduate	115	46
	Graduate	135	54
Age	20-26years	99	40
	27-35years	59	24
	36-45years	78	31
	46-58years	14	05
Work Experience	1-5years	35	14
	6-10years	118	47
	11-20years	85	34
	Above 20 years	12	05

Result and Analysis

The following section explains the results of the present study. The Table 6, shows the mean values and SD of the employees on the parameters of role stress.

The highest levels of stress as seen in Table 6. are seen on the parameter of Role Ambiguity, (M=16.12,SD=4.48), followed by Role Overload (RO) (M=16.00,SD=4.48), Inter Role Distance (M=15.87,SD=4.71), (IRD)Personal Inadequacy (PI) (M=15.83,SD=4.62), Role Stagnation (RS) (M=15.80,SD=4.52), Role Erosion (RE) (M=15.66,SD=4.25), Role expectation Conflict (REC) (M=15.48, SD=4.43), Inter Role Distance (SRD) (M=15.20, SD=4.90), Role Isolation (RI) (M=15.14,SD=4.62)

Table 6. Showing mean and standard deviation of role stress of employee in the IT

Variables	No. of Items	Score Range	Mean Score	Std. Deviation	Cronbach Alpha
Inter Role Distance (IRD)	5	5-25	15.87	4.71	.818
Role Stagnation (RS)	5	5-25	15.80	4.52	.839
Role expectation Conflict (REC)	5	5-25	15.48	4.43	.802
Role Erosion (RE)	5	5-25	15.66	4.25	.802
Role Overload (RO)	5	5-25	16.00	4.48	.819
Role Isolation (RI)	5	5-25	15.14	4.62	.837
Personal Inadequacy (PI)	5	5-25	15.83	4.62	.836
Self Role Distance (SRD)	5	5-25	15.20	4.90	.867
Role Ambiguity(RA)	5	5-25	16.12	4.48	.820
Resource Inadequacy (RIN)	5	5-25	14.78	5.04	.889

and Resource Inadequacy (RIN)(M=14.78,SD=5.04). It is seen that the overall levels of stress in the employees of the IT industry are moderate. It is important to keep in mind that measures to control stress are essential in order to control any aggravation in the levels of stress among the employees.

Examining the Impact of Demographic Variables on Organizational Stress

An in-depth review is done by analyzing the impact of the demographic variables on the organizational stress experienced by the employees. The demographic variables include Gender, Age, Qualification, number of years of work experience and designation of the employee.

The results of Table 7 indicate that there is no significant difference between the Male and Female respondents of the IT sector in terms of Organizational Stress, except for significant difference, p<0.05 on the parameter of Inter Role Distance (IRD), and Resource Inadequacy (RIN). The result shows that Female employees experience greater levels of role stress than their male counterparts.

The results of Table 8 indicate that There exists significant difference p<0.05, among the Managers and Executives of the IT industry in the parameter of Inter Role Distance (IRD), Role Overload (RO), Personal Inadequacy and Self Role Distance (SRD), As indicated by the mean scores, the results show that the Managers show higher levels of stress than the executives of the IT Industry.

Table 7. t- value of male and female respondents of IT industry in relation to organizational stress

	Gender	N	Mean	Std. Deviation	t-Value	df	Sig. (2-Tailed)
Inter-Role Distance (IRD	Male	163	13.1043	4.03628	2.043	248	.041*
	Female	87	14.2414	4.40920			
Role Stagnation (RS)	Male	163	13.7914	4.07106	1.999	248	.141
	Female	87	14.6207	4.52189			
Role Expectation Conflict (REC)	Male	163	12.7178	4.36952	1.429	248	.055
	Female	87	13.8506	4.52006			
Role Erosion (RE)	Male	163	14.7607	3.99820	1.909	248	.360
	Female	87	15.2299	3.56240			
Role Overload (RO)	Male	163	13.2147	4.43574	.950	248	.256
	Female	87	13.9080	4.86954			
Role Isolation (RI)	Male	163	13.4540	4.21374	1.106	248	.380
	Female	87	13.9655	4.67166			
Personal Inadequacy (PI)	Male	163	13.7423	4.14787	.853	248	.367
	Female	87	14.2644	4.70146			
Self-Role Distance (SRD)	Male	163	13.6810	4.24221	871	248	.369
	Female	87	14.1839	4.14148			
Role Ambiguity (RA)	Male	163	12.0184	4.49893	.907	248	.067
	Female	87	13.1609	4.98573			
Resource Inadequacy (RIN)	Male	163	13.1656	4.36493	1.785	248	.018*
	Female	87	14.5402	4.35571			

**Significant at 0.01 level, *Significant level 0.05 level

Table 8. t- value of managers and non managers of IT industry in relation to organizational stress

	Designation	N	Mean	Std. Deviation	t-Value	Df	Sig. (2-Tailed)
Inter-Role Distance (IRD	Manager	120	14.1667	4.31790	2.437	248	.016*
	Executive	130	12.8846	3.99929			
Role Stagnation (RS)	Manager	120	14.3083	4.52963	.817	248	.415
	Executive	130	13.8692	3.96572			
Role Expectation Conflict (REC)	Manager	120	13.6167	4.90957	1.731	248	.085
	Executive	130	12.6462	3.93328			
Role Erosion (RE)	Manager	120	15.3333	3.99439	1.620	248	.107
	Executive	130	14.5462	3.68973			
Role Overload (RO)	Manager	120	14.0917	4.89211	2.117	248	.035*
	Executive	130	12.8692	4.23421			
Role Isolation (RI)	Manager	120	14.2083	4.63798	2.013	248	.045
	Executive	130	13.1000	4.06507			
Personal Inadequacy (PI)	Manager	120	14.6000	4.69829	2.385	248	.018*
	Executive	130	13.3000	3.90914			
Self-Role Distance (SRD)	Manager	120	14.5000	4.75271	2.347	248	.020*
	Executive	130	13.2615	3.54496			
Role Ambiguity (RA)	Manager	120	12.8500	5.17695	1.407	248	.161
	Executive	130	12.0154	4.18373			
Resource Inadequacy (RIN)	Manager	120	14.1167	4.79703	1.637	248	.103
	Executive	130	13.2077	3.97218			

**Significant at 0.01 level, *Significant level 0.05 level

The results of Table 9 indicate that there is no significant difference in the levels Organizational Stress based on qualification levels of the employees of the IT industry .We cannot make a clear distinction that based on qualification levels, that either group would be experiencing more or less stress.

Table 10 shows the F-value, significance levels and an interpretation of means through sub script, 'a' and 'b'; with the help of post hoc *Duncan analysis*. As noted above, there is significant difference p<0.01 for above given parameters of Organizational Stress. Results indicated that for all the parameters; except Role Overload (RO), Role Isolation (RI) and Personal Inadequacy (PI), there is a significant difference in the mean scores of the Age Group (46-58 years).The overall results indicate that this age group experiences the least levels of Stress among the other age groups of employees, as indicated by the mean scores. For all role stress parameters, there is significant difference p<0.05, with the age group (46-58years), showing the least amount of role stress as indicated by the mean scores. As shown by the transcripts, the other employees in the age groups (20-26 years) (27-35 years) and (36-45) have similar levels of stress within which, the age group (27-35 years) shows higher levels of role stress. Similar results were confirmed by previous literature that showed the existence of maximum stress among the young professionals of the IT industry, which makes them leave their jobs. Various other studies have also confirmed that stress tends to decrease with ones age and tenure in the organization. There can be various reasons for the same, which could include; increased comfort level, emotional intelligence and

Table 9. t- value based on qualification levels of IT industry employees in relation to organizational stress

	Qualification	N	Mean	Std. Deviation	t-Value	df	Sig. (2-Tailed)
Inter-Role Distance (IRD	Post_Graduation	115	13.2870	4.19433	.740	248	.460
	Graduation	135	13.6815	4.20492			
Role Stagnation (RS)	Post_Graduation	115	13.5652	4.45076	1.778	248	.077
	Graduation	135	14.5185	4.02205			
Role Expectation Conflict (REC)	Post_Graduation	115	12.8174	4.68027	.967	248	.335
	Graduation	135	13.3630	4.23843			
Role Erosion (RE)	Post_Graduation	115	14.5652	4.11700	1.362	248	.175
	Graduation	135	15.2296	3.59714			
Role Overload (RO)	Post_Graduation	115	13.5130	4.44926	.181	248	.857
	Graduation	135	13.4074	4.72891			
Role Isolation (RI)	Post_Graduation	115	13.5217	4.36764	.367	248	.714
	Graduation	135	13.7259	4.39713			
Personal Inadequacy (PI)	Post_Graduation	115	14.2957	4.41484	1.249	248	.213
	Graduation	135	13.6074	4.27784			
Self-Role Distance (SRD)	Post_Graduation	115	14.0870	4.27675	.801	248	.424
	Graduation	135	13.6593	4.15046			
Role Ambiguity (RA)	Post_Graduation	115	12.0348	4.97702	1.186	248	.237
	Graduation	135	12.7407	4.43521			
Resource Inadequacy (RIN)	Post_Graduation	115	13.3478	4.64917	.982	248	.327
	Graduation	135	13.8963	4.18111			

**Significant at 0.01 level, *Significant level 0.05 level

Table 10. Post hoc comparisons using the Duncan Analysis, to assess the difference in the levels of organizational stress based on the age group of employees

	Age Groups	20-26 Years	27-35 Years	36-45 Years	46-58 Years	Sig-Value
	N=250	99	59	78	14	
Inter Role Distance (IRD)	Means	12.33a	14.13a	13.65a	9.13b	$F(3,246)=6.01, P=0.001$
Role Stagnation (RS)		14.03a	14.76a	13.62a	8.60b	$F(3,246)=7.35, P=0.000$
Role expectation Conflict(REC)		12.17a	13.95a	13.01a	9.10b	$F(3,246)=5.38, P=0.001$
Role Erosion (RE)		15.70a	15.25a	14.14a	10.40b	$F(3,246)=10.09, P=0.000$
Self Role Distance (SRD)		13.23a	14.25a	13.23a	10.70b	$F(3,246)=2.80, P=0.040$
Role Ambiguity(RA)		11.69a	13.32a	12.08a	7.60b	$F(3,246)=5.95, P=0.001$
Resource Inadequacy (RIN)		13.25a	14.39a	13.05a	10.20b	$,F(3,246)=3.84, P=0.010$

Note: Means with similar subscripts do not differ significantly and means with different subscript differ significantly.

one's life tenure. The younger generations are mostly stressed due to aspirations of over achievement and starting family responsibilities. There seems to be no difference for the parameters Role Overload (RO), Role Isolation (RI) and Personal Inadequacy (PI).(Role Overload) and (Role Isolation) and (Personal Inadequacy), arises as one feels burdened due to job responsibilities and a lack of being adept to handle the same with existing resources. It is seen that the young and older employees may feel overburdened. Previous studies confirm that managers and senior positions in the IT industry, shoulder greater responsibilities based on accountabilities; that may lead to greater stress (Spielberger & Reheise, 1994).

Table 11 shows the F-value, significant levels and an interpretation of means through sub script, 'a' and 'b'; with the help of post hoc Duncan analysis. As noted above, there is significant difference $p<0.01$ & $P<0.05$ for all the parameters of Role Stress.

There is no significant differences in the mean scores except on the parameter of Self Role Distance (SRD).For the parameter of Role expectation Conflict (REC), Role Overload (RO) and Role Isolation (RI); there is a significant difference in the mean scores. As indicated, the highest mean scores are for the group (6-10years) and (11-20years) and the lowest for the (Above 20 years) group. For the parameter of Inter Role Distance (IRD), there is significant difference in the groups (1-5 years) and (above 20 years), the group (6-10years) and (11-20years) forms one group with the highest mean scores. For the parameter of Role Stagnation (RS), there is significant difference in the mean scores of the group (above 20 years), with the lowest mean score. For the parameter of Role Erosion (RE), there is significant difference brought about by the group (11-20 years), also having the least mean scores. For the parameter of Personal Inadequacy (PI), there is significant difference $p<0.05$ between the groups, with the (above 20 years) group) having the lowest men score. For Role Ambiguity (RA), there is significant difference between the three groups, with the group (6-10years) having the highest mean scores and the group (above 20) with the lowest means scores. For Resource Inadequacy (RIN), there is significant difference between the three groups (1-5years), (above 20 years) and the mid group (6-20 years), with this group having the highest mean scores on the parameter.

Table 11. Post hoc comparisons using the Duncan to assess the difference in the levels of organizational stress based on the number of years of work experience of employees

	Work Ex Groups	1-5 Years	6-10 Years	11-20 Years	Above 20 Years	Sig- Value
	N	35	118	85	12	
Inter Role Distance (IRD)		12.15a	14.55b	14.96b	10.42a	F(3,246)=11.63,P=0.000
Role Stagnation (RS)		13.01a	15.98b	14.79 a,b	9.64c	F(3,246)= 13.72,P=0.000
Role expectation Conflict (REC)		11.80a	14.42b	14.21b	10.64a	F(3,246)=8.26,P=0.000
Role Erosion (RE)		14.72a	15.57a	15.39a	10.92b	F(3,246)=6.46, P=0.000
Role Overload (RO)	Means	11.91a	15.27b	14.33b	11.78a	F(3,246)=9.14, P=0.000
Role Isolation (RI)		12.27a	14.69b	15.06b	10.78a	F(3,246)=10.1, P=0.000
Personal Inadequacy (PI)		13.22a,b	14.44b	14.73b	12.21a	F(3,246)=2.81, P=0.04
Role Ambiguity(RA)		11.19a	13.94b	13.56b	8.21c	F(3,246)=10.76, P=0.000
Resource Inadequacy (RIN)		12.71a	15.11b	14.39b	9.78c	F(3,246)=8.76, P=0.000

Note: Means with similar subscripts do not differ significantly and means with different subscript differ significantly

The results show that the least stress is experience by the employee's whit the maximum tenure in the organization. As cited earlier, age is inversely proportional to the inception of stress in an individual. Hence older employees with greater work experience seem to experience the least amount of stress. As one spends more time in an organization, he becomes familiar with the ways to handle workplace demands. The age and life situation also make the person complacent, as his understanding of work is well developed. Thus organizations need to deal more effectively with the work experience group (6-10 years) and (11-20 years); as that is the most stressed group due to career inhibitions and rising competition.

CONCLUSION

There are many reasons for the inception of role stress amongst the professionals of the IT industry. Overall, results indicate that the professionals experience moderate levels of stress. These moderate levels need attention of the human resource professionals, as they could further lead to mild and alarming rates of stress. Wells et al. (2009) conducted a study that showed a positive relationship between job stress and organizational commitment and a negative relationship between job stress and career commitment. However, this commitment can be improved by means of tools like mentoring (Casado-Lumbreras et al., 2009; Casado-Lumbreras et al., 2011). In any case, the nature of work in this industry is characterized by large workgroups comprising of hundreds of members allocated working together in teams. There may be limited scope towards ownership of a complete process, which could be a reason for dissatisfaction among the employees.

Role Ambiguity (RA) seems to be evolving as the most significant stressor in this industry. Role Ambiguity is a result of non clarity of the expectations of work. A clarity in roles and is experienced by the professionals. Thus, the organizations can make their employees more competent by imparting adequate time bound trainings which will help the employees to see more personal and professional growth prospects. This is followed by Role Overload (RO) and Inter Role Distance (IRD). Role overload is resultant of a feeling of having too much work to do, without apt resources. Inter Role distance occurs of the incumbent feels that the various professional roles and personal roles that he plays, are at a clash with each other. This indicates that the employees of the IT industry experience a sense of limitation in resources and time. The hard pressed time lines force them to work under pressures of quick delivery which could lead to role stress. Similar results were confirmed by a study conducted by (Sharma, 2004). Other stressors like Personal Inadequacy (PI) and Resource Inadequacy (RI) are created by the lack of adequate skills and the resulting inability to meet the demands of one's role. This is sometimes results of sufficient training programs that are designed for these professionals.

Comparing with other business sectors the time pressures make it difficult for team members to relieve other members to attain three training programs. Role Isolation is bound to occur when a person feels that his role is isolated from the mainstream of organizational life. This is mostly a result of the nature of tasks that are handled by different teams and their contributions in the overall process. A software developer would have the product or service passed on to the software tester, such that all important appropriations can be made. A lack of ownership in the end product is likely to arise, creating a sense of role isolation. Research and current training practices in the IT industry also show that the training is mostly related to technical skills. The industry needs to focus on behavioral training also that will help the employees in dealing with attitudinal issues related to work and this would help in developing coping mechanisms and well-being.

19

The role of demographic factors on the conception of organizational stress is also important. We notice that in terms of gender; on the parameters of Inter role distance (IRD) and Resource Inadequacy; women feel more stressed than their male counter parts. Inter Role Distance (IRD) can be explained as a gap between one's concept of self and the demands of his role For example, the role of an executive vs. the role of a husband/wife that one plays in his day to day life. Mostly women have to multitask and play their professional and personal roles parallel, that paves way for a feeling of distance amongst the two extreme roles and the inability to suffice any successfully. Resource Inadequacy (RIN) arises when human and material resources allocated are inadequate to meet the demands of the role. This is also a cause of stress for women. Role Erosion (RE) and Role stagnation (RS) occur as one sees a lack of advancement opportunities in one's career. Previous researches also show that women experience more subjective stress than men (Aziz, 2004). Within the IT industry, it is seen that the skill requirements vary through different projects and the skills of a professional; need to be updated with the fast paced evolution in technology. Thus the cycle time for training needs to be taken care of.

The results also show that education does not contribute to any significant difference among the employees. Both graduate and post graduate employees face equal amounts of stress. In terms of age and work experience, we see that there is significant difference $p<0.05$, with the age group (46-58years), showing the least amount of role stress as indicated by the mean scores. The age group (27-35 years) shows higher levels of role stress. In terms of work experience, we see that the least amount of stress is the group with work ex (above 20) years and the maximum in the age group (11-20 years). The results of the study can be further used to analyze the reasons and initiatives that can be undertaken to reduce role stress amongst the employees of the IT sector. Though the sector shows moderate levels of stress, yet a step in the right direction would be helpful in ensuring that the same does not lead to future burnout and exhaustion.

REFERENCES

Beehr, T. A., Jex, S. M., Stacy, B. A., & Murray, M. A. (2001). Work stressors and coworker support as predictors of individual strain and job performance. *Journal of Organizational Behavior, 21*(4), 391–403. doi:10.1002/(SICI)1099-1379(200006)21:4<391::AID-JOB15>3.0.CO;2-9

Bocchino, C. C., Hartman, B. W., & Foley, P. F. (2003). The relationship between person-organization congruence, perceived violations of the psychological contract, and occupational stress symptoms. *Consulting Psychology Journal: Practice and Research, 55*(4), 203–214. doi:10.1037/1061-4087.55.4.203

Briere, J., & Elliott, D. M. (1998). Clinical utility of the Impact of Event Scale: Psychometrics in the general population. *Assessment, 5*(2), 171–180. doi:10.1177/107319119800500207 PMID:9626392

Briner, R., Harris, C., & Daniels, K. (2004). How do work stress and coping work? Toward a fundamental theoretical reappraisal. *British Journal of Guidance & Counselling, 32*(2), 223–234. doi:10.1080/03069880410001692256

Casado-Lumbreras, C., Colomo-Palacios, R., Gomez-Berbis, J. M., & Garcia-Crespo, A. (2009). Mentoring programmes: A study of the Spanish software industry. International. *Journal of Learning and Intellectual Capital, 6*(3), 293–302. doi:10.1504/IJLIC.2009.025046

Casado-Lumbreras, C., Colomo-Palacios, R., Soto-Acosta, P., & Misra, S. (2011). Culture dimensions in software development industry: *The effects of mentoring. Scientific Research and Essays*, *6*(11), 2403–2412.

Colomo-Palacios, R., Casado-Lumbreras, C., Misra, S., & Soto-Acosta, P. (2014b). Career abandonment intentions among software workers. *Human Factors and Ergonomics in Manufacturing & Service Industries*, *24*(6), 641–655. doi:10.1002/hfm.20509

Colomo-Palacios, R., Casado-Lumbreras, C., Soto-Acosta, P., & García-Crespo, Á. (2013). Decisions in software development projects management. *An exploratory study. Behaviour & Information Technology*, *32*(11), 1077–1085. doi:10.1080/0144929X.2011.630414

Colomo-Palacios, R., Casado-Lumbreras, C., Soto-Acosta, P., García-Peñalvo, F. J., & Tovar, E. (2014a). Project managers in global software development teams: A study of the effects on productivity and performance. *Software Quality Journal*, *22*(1), 3–19. doi:10.1007/s11219-012-9191-x

Cox, T., & Ferguson, E. (1991). Individual Differences, Stress and Coping. In C. L. Cooper & R. Payne (Eds.), *Personality and Stress: Individual Differences in the Stress Process*. Wiley.

Cropanzano, R., Rupp, E. D., & Byrne, S. Z. (2003). The Relationship of Emotional Exhaustion to Work Attitudes, Job Performance, and Organizational Citizenship Behaviors. *The Journal of Applied Psychology*, *88*(4), 160–169. doi:10.1037/0021-9010.88.1.160 PMID:12675403

Dasgupta, H., & Kumar, S. (2009). Role Stress among Doctors Working in a Government Hospital in Shimla (India). *European Journal of Soil Science*, *9*(3), 356–370.

Day, A. L., & Carroll, S. A. (2004). Using ability based measure of emotional intelligence to predict individual performance, group performance, and group Citizenship Behaviors. *Personality and Individual Differences*, *36*(6), 1443–1458. doi:10.1016/S0191-8869(03)00240-X

García-Crespo, Á., Colomo-Palacios, R., Gómez-Berbís, J. M., & Tovar-Caro, E. (2008). The IT Crowd: Are We Stereotypes? *IT Professional*, *10*(6), 24–27. doi:10.1109/MITP.2008.134

Härenstam, A., & Group, T. M. R. (2005). Different development trends in working life and increasing occupational stress require new work environment strategies. *Work (Reading, Mass.)*, *24*(3), 261–277. PMID:15912016

Hinkle, L. E. (1973). The Concept of Stress in the Biological and Social Sciences. *Science, Medicine and Man*, *1*(1), 31–48. PMID:4610743

Hofboll, S. E., Geller, P., & Dunahoo, C. (2003). Women's coping: Communal versus individual orientation. In M. J. Schabracq, J. A. M. Winburst, & C. L. Cooper (Eds.), *The Handbook of Work and Health Psychology*. Wiltshire, UK: John Wiley & Sons.

Karad, A. (2010). Job Stress in the Information Technology Sector- The cause and effect analysis. *Journal Of Commerce and Management Thought*, *1*(3), 247–271.

Korczynski, M. (2002). *Human resource management in service work*. Hampshire, UK: Palgrave. doi:10.1007/978-1-137-10774-9

Lazarus. (1993). Coping Theory and Research: Past, Present, and Future. *Psychosomatic Medicine, 55*, 234-247.

Levi, L. (1996). *Managing Physical Stress*. Australia Thomson Delmar Learning.

Loosemore, M., & Waters, T. (2004). Gender Differences in Occupational Stress among Professionals in the Construction Industry. *Journal of Management Engineering, 20*(3), 126–132. doi:10.1061/(ASCE)0742-597X(2004)20:3(126)

Lundgren, B., Jonsson, B., Pangborn, R. M., Sontag, A. M., Barylko-Pikielna, N., Pietrzak, E., & Yoshida, M. et al. (1978). Taste discrimination vs. hedonic response to sucrose. *An interlaboratory study*. *Chemical Senses, 3*(3), 249–265. doi:10.1093/chemse/3.3.249

Michailidis, M., & Georgiou, Y. (2005). Employee occupational stress in banking. *Work (Reading, Mass.), 24*(2), 123–137. PMID:15860902

Michailids, M. P., & Elwkai, M. E. A. (2002). Factors contributing to occupational stress experienced by individuals employed in the fast food industry. *Work (Reading, Mass.), 21*(2), 125–140. PMID:14501091

Mohsin, A. (2004). Role stress among women in the Indian information technology sector. *Women in Management Review, 19*(7), 356–363. doi:10.1108/09649420410563412

Neelamegam, R., & Asrafi, S. (2010). Work Stress Among Employees of Dindigul District Central Cooperative Bank, Tamil Nadu: A Study. The IUP Journal of Management Research, 5(2), 57-69.

Nikolaou, I., & Tsaousis, I. (2009). Emotional Intelligence in the workplace: Exploring its effects on occupational stress and organizational commitment. *The International Journal of Organizational Analysis, 10*(4), 37–42.

Pareek, U. (1982). *Organizational role stress scales (manual, scale, answer sheet)*. Ahmedabad: Navin Publications.

Pareek, U. (1983). Organizational roles stress. In L. D. Goodstein & J. W. Pfeiffer (Eds.), The 1983 annual (pp. 115-123). San Diego, CA: University Associates.

Pareek, U. (1993). *Making Organizational Roles Effective*. McGraw-Hill.

Pareek, U. (1993). *Making organizational roles effective*. New Delhi: Tata McGraw-Hill Publishing.

Pareek, U. (1998).The Pfeiffer Library (2nd ed.). Jossey/Bass.

Payne, R. (1988). *Individual Differences in the Study of Occupational Stress*. New York: Wiley.

Pestonjee, D. M. (1992). *Stress and Coping. The India experience*. New Delhi: Sage Publication.

Russell, C., & Zinta, S. (2000). The Relationship of Organizational Stress to organizational commitment, and Organizational Citizenship Behaviors. *Journal of Industrial and Organizational Psychology*.

Rydstedt, L. W., Devereux, J., & Furnham, A. F. (2004). Are lay theories of work stress related to distress? A longitudinal study in the British workforce. *Work and Stress, 18*(3), 245–254. doi:10.1080/02628370412331323906

Selye, H. (1997). The general adaptation syndrome and the diseases of adaptation. *The Journal of Clinical Endocrinology, 6*(2), 117–123. doi:10.1210/jcem-6-2-117 PMID:21025115

Sharma, E. (2004). Doctors in Jaipur: Working under higher levels of Stress. *Journal of Health Management, 7,* 151-156.

Siu, O.-L. (2002). Occupational Stressors and Well-being among Chinese Employees: The Role of Organisational Commitment. *Applied Psychology, 51*(4), 527–544. doi:10.1111/1464-0597.t01-1-00106

Smith, A. (2011). Perceptions of stress at work Human Research. *Human Resource Management Journal, 11*(4), 74–78. doi:10.1111/j.1748-8583.2001.tb00052.x

Spielberger, C. D., & Reheiser, E. C. (1994). The job stress survey: Measuring gender differences in occupational stress. *Journal of Social Behavior and Personality, 9,* 199–218.

Steinberg, A., & Ritzmann, R. F. (1990). A Living Systems Approach to Understanding the *Concept of Stress. Behavioral Science, 35*(2), 138–146. doi:10.1002/bs.3830350206 PMID:2327936

Torkelson, E., & Muhonen, T. (2004). The role of gender and job level in coping with occupational stress. *Work and Stress, 18*(3), 267–274. doi:10.1080/02678370412331323915

Wells, J. B., Minor, E., Anger, A., & Amato, N. (2009). Predictors of job stress among staff in juvenile correctional facilities. *Criminal Justice and Behavior, 36*(3), 245–258. doi:10.1177/0093854808329334

Wirtz, P. H., Ehlert, U., Kottwitz, M. U., & Semmer, N. K. (2013). Occupational role stress is associated with higher cortisol reactivity to acute stress. *Journal of Occupational Health Psychology, 18*(2), 121–131. doi:10.1037/a0031802 PMID:23566275

Chapter 2
Recruitment Trends in the Contemporary Era

Anu Chhabra
Winning Edge, India

Vandana Ahuja
Jaypee Institute of Information Technology, India

ABSTRACT

Recruitment is the process of identifying and hiring the right talent for a job in an organization, within a timeframe and by incurring the least expenses. The life cycle of the recruitment process starts from identification of an open position which needs to be filled to the candidate joining the organisation formally. On hearing the word recruitment, what flashes in an individual's mind is the process the HR group would follow to choose a candidate, get him interviewed, cross levels, offer, joining formalities completion, and to integrate the new joinee with the organization's philosophy. But, over a period, this process has evolved and it has transformed its existence from a simple process to a much more organized and digitally equipped one. The importance of a recruitment service though has remained the same, that is, the candidate should have the right skills, right knowledge, aptitude, and most importantly, attitude. But what has been the focus of improvement of the Human resources is the time duration and the cost effectiveness.

INTRODUCTION

The current economic and political scenarios have majorly influenced the Recruitment Industry and hence the HR processes in organizations. The outcomes of the business relationship with other countries, GST(Goods & Service Tax) and more flexible FDI(Foreign Direct Investment) policies have made organisational managements put on their thinking caps to streamline the Human Resource processes. LinkedIn in its *India Recruiting Trends for 2017*, survey mentioned that 63% talent leaders expect an increase in hiring budgets, higher than the global average of 37%. Although, 2016 was a gamechanger for the recruitment industry, 2017-18 would also experience a high-voltage change for organizations, to create a competitive workforce.

DOI: 10.4018/978-1-5225-5297-0.ch002

Human resources groups in organisations are witnessing the air of transformation all around. These changes (Girard, Fallery, 2009) are predominantly brought in by technology, years of experience, values, skill, talent and knowledge, organizational structure and to top them all, the evolution of an industry which is very distinct from the past organizations.

Many technology companies have come up with beautiful and well equipped campuses for their employees, which have in house facilities for their talent to grow. But the focus of HR departments has been to implement and innovate processes which are cost-effective to match the work-incentive-performance needs of their employees. It is identified by the HR visionaries, that whatever be the size of an organization, domain, geography; the major focus of an employee(Breaugh and Mann, 1984) has always been the take home salary.

The HR landscape is now changing and the transition can be attributed to the eight factors of

1. Increase in Temp Staffing
2. Analysis of HR Data
3. Referral Schemes
4. Video Interview Interactions
5. Artificial Intelligence
6. Digitally equipped-App Based era
7. Mobile recruitment- the Game changing recruitment trend
8. Employer Branding

The following section discusses each of these eight factors in detail.

Increase in Temp Staffing

The concept per se is not new. The manufacturing and service sector industries have been following this pattern since ages now. However, in the last decade, there has been a significant increase in the contract/ temporary hiring in the IT & ITES sector. Many temp staffing organizations have seen a rapid growth. Organizations like TeamLease, Randstad (earlier known as Mafoi), Adecco, Kelly, Manpower, Collaberra, IKYA, etc. have established themselves well in India. Most them are growing at the rate of 18-21% despite economic slowdown. TeamLease within a decade has emerged as of India's largest temp staffing company with 1400+ clients and outsourced employee count is over 70000 associates.

Earlier it was thought that the temporary positions were usually a path where the person gets absorbed in the organization (Houseman, Susan, and Carolyn Heinrich, 2016). The organizations had the opportunity to see how a temporary worker performed on the job and if the performance was good, the permanent position was offered. Such employees were labelled as Temp-to-hire resource which did give confidence on either side to perform well. But by the industry analysis 7% of all temporary help assignments ended in a hire by the organization. The hire rate when looked industry specific came as 8.8% for professional and technical workers, office job employees was around 8% and Industrial workers 6.6%. An individual also works on a couple of assignments before he decided to formally take up a position.

But now this trend has been changing. Companies hire temporary employee for a stipulated time. This makes the employee and the organization commitment free after the mentioned time is completed. Organizations hire temp staffing depending on a project it takesup-the size, the tenure and the skills.

Figure 1. IT temp staffing cost in billion in the US market

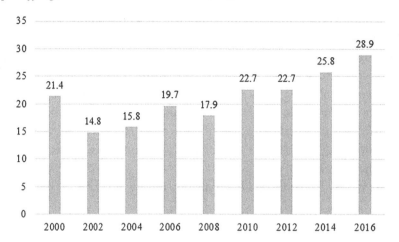

A recent study conducted on the recruitment industry by Ernst & Young and Executive research Association (ERA) estimated the temporary staffing market in India is close to Rs. 17,200 cr. The report states while temporary staffing is not as big in India as it is in the western countries, it is likely to account for 2.5 to 3% of the country's total workforce soon, which will be a substantial number considering the size of Indian workforce.

The IT Sector now prefers contract hires or temporary staff to fulfil its talent crunch as and when it arises. Companies such as NIIT, HCL, Wipro and Capgemini are looking at hiring niche talent for special contracts rather than keeping permanent staff. The rapidly growing trend of contract staffing has given some companies a chance to reduce their budgets and still get the project completed within the given time frame. As competition forces businesses to continually become leaner and more flexible, the importance of focusing on core business has driven the industry to consider and deploy temporary staffing. As organizations are trying to recruit and retain temporary talent, they are offering them all possible ways. These employees are hired on flexible terms and salary structures. This doesn't imply that the demand of the permanent employees has gone down. Temporary Staffing has significantly gained its space in the corporates worldwide, and the employee staffing firms support organizations for the temporary staffing. It has indeed become a well-accepted norm. As cited earlier, this is to strike a balance in the hiring styles of an organization to focus more on the core business and outsource the profiles which vary with the time and demand. The contracts range from 3 months to 1 year depending upon the skillsets and the level.

Analysis of HR Data

HR data plays a significant role in any organization and time and again needs to be analyzed with precision. Talent Mapping and usage of in-house resources rather than keeping them on bench is a must step for all organizations. This allows HR to adapt their tactics based on work history (Garimella, Uma, and Praveen Paruchuri 2015) and behavioral outlines. It would considerably build a competent HR system, organization dependent and improves employee retention. Human resources are stepping into the spotlight with HR analytics. Earlier, one of the HR's primary goals was to collect and keep track of employees' personal and professional information, such as payroll, health benefits and performance reviews. Now, the tide of technology has reached HR's shores and is carrying it into deeper waters where it can analyze data to play a more active role in the organization. It's important to note that HR metrics are not the same as HR analytics. HR managers typically used metrics to measure such data as turnover rates and sick days. With HR analytics, they can gauge employee engagement and whether workers have the skills to reach company goals. HR representatives can now talk with business leaders, find out what they need and hire accordingly. HR analytics allows human resources to interpret data, recognize trends or issues, and take proactive steps with different departments to keep the organization running smoothly and profitably.HR analytics, data scientists and its combination with technology is growing rapidly. This is clear from the number of Vendors who have shown interest in the Data Analytics portfolio, talent management suites are now available with embedded HR analytics. Organizations are also moving their focus to employee engagement parallelly with HR analytics. Live analysis on an employee job satisfaction, employee engagement and fidelity towards the organization is been measured. This analysis is turn helping the HR teams and business units to can help companies get a handle on their workforce and add fact-based reasoning to hire or to give pink slips.

Referral Schemes

Referral Schemes are basically an internal recruitment process used by the HR group to get references for a position from the existing set of employees. With the changing industry scenario, more profitable referral programs are being initiated in the organizations. Statistics shows that the employee referral continues to score higher percentage in terms of the quality of the person joining an organization. The talent is just not on the aptitude but also the attitude of the person who joins the group. Amongst the various divisions, the support groups- business development, sales, marketing emerge as organization centric role which require effective recruitment strategies to get the right candidate boarding the team. This in turn customizing the employer branding content to attract the right talent from references. Top players such as Coca-Cola, Infosys, Genpact, Capgemini, Deloitte, Jubilant and more are reporting that over 40% of their hires come through referrals.

If we go further to discuss on the various types of strategies organizations have started over the past year, we would like to highlight few of them under the broad industry domain vertical-

FMCD Organization

Few months back, Lenovo India started the initiative to strengthen its diversity numbers across the organization. For this, they originated the process by tapping into the Referral Scheme. The organization seek for references from the current set of employees, and decided to reward and acknowledge the employee who shared the reference of a woman for that role. As employee referral became an established method to onboard the right talent, the organization have started to use the application driven platform to make a steady pipeline of referrals. This also ensures that no referral is missed and no employee feels left out. A fair chance is given to all.

Apart from the referral amount, if a woman is hired, an added incentive is given to the employee who had referred her. This has contributed to more woman referrals coming in and hence string a balance in the diversity numbers in the organization.

ITeS and Software Industry

The major challenge these ITeS organization face till date is the rate of attrition, techies declining near the joining dates, having several offers while identifying a movement in the job. So, the positions open with them are always on an upward curve. To churn out candidates from the traditional old ways becomes very difficult not only for the HR team but even from the hiring supporting source that they have. To facilitate them in their hiring process, they come out with Employee Referral schemes. This will ensure that the person whom they are offering through a reference will surly join them and not decline at the last moment.

Also, will like to highlight the step taken by the leading IT giant Infosys, for instance, has enhanced the use of technology for the employee referral process. They have created employee referral application system where employees can view requirement, submit profiles of candidates directly and check the status of their referral real-time in terms of the interviewing process. Due to this total transparency in the system, they are motivated to share more references.

Richard Lobo, Sr. VP and head HR, Infosys, feels that the employee referral has been a success story for them as people referring has been in line with the aspirations of the candidate and maps well with the requirements and culture of the company.

Consulting Organization

Seeing the trend even the Consulting firms Deloitte are also focusing on the internal reference schemes and hence 45% of their recruitments are been taken care. Next, they are building an application on the similar lines as the Industry to make their referral process completely streamlined and digital, so that someone who wants to refer a candidate can take less than a minute to do so.

Commodity Based Groups

Jubilant Food Works depends majorly on referrals as the major chunk of the group works in the store. For the store, the referral candidate is better suited as he understands the working style as well as criticality of the role. The total employee strength of the group is above 30,000, of which 27,000 work in the

Figure 2. Sources of quality hire

outlets. Last year's figure touched around 9,000 employees for their outlet coming as references from the existing team and this number is picking up further.

Their referral application is called 'Skilled Tree'. This works on mobiles, the references are used through one's social media networks and sends out job openings, invite messages on the company's behalf.

Video Interview Interactions

LinkedIn is already a popular social platform for most candidates, consultants and recruiters for recruiting. The other social networking platforms are also encouraging video interactions. Recruitment Specialists are geared up conduct video interviews, collate data and analyze profiles to streamline the interview process. Many organizations are getting into the mode of video interview in their hiring process to identify the body language, personality and evaluate the executive presence of the candidate. In many organizations, the first round itself, the HR prefers to have a skype round to evaluate the soft skills- dressing, looks, and body language of the person. Specially Philips-the HR of a Business Unit, would do such rounds before the hiring manager gets into an evaluation process. This is because, they feel that interacting virtually face-to-face with candidates, leads to better evaluation of the candidate by an interviewer. By doing a video interview as a first round interview, helps the hiring team to decide which candidate will go to the second round and who will not make it in the system, more so than a phone interview. This helps organizations to *speed up* the interview process. Either a face to face interaction or video interaction, generates the speed to evaluate the person under consideration. This way the candidate also gains momentum and shows interest to complete the interview process to understand his fitment in an organization. The timelines have even come down to merely two weeks to complete the whole process. Also, it saves on the time, as in, the availability of the candidate to fly to meet the interviewer. A video interview can typically be scheduled quicker and that can speed up the process.

Video Interviews are cost effective, as they do away with all the travel expenses incurred. Organizations till now where spending huge amount of funds in the interview process. They were making the candidates travel to meet the interviewer. So, video interactions are saving on the cost as well the time. This helps to review the interaction again and again. To analyze and infer from the video interaction, many companies record video interviews to get feedback, suggestion from other team members, who may not be a part of the actual interview process. The different types of applications used for video interviews are Skype, Google Talk, WhatsApp, Facetime. These technologies are the ones that most candidates and employers have an easy access to and they are free to use for one-on-one video calling. But the challenge is they cannot be recorded. Skype currently does not have a built-in recording feature. Facetime has but then not everyone uses Apple products. There are also scenarios wherein in an interaction we have 2 or more people logging in from different geographies at the same time to interact with the candidate. Some of these applications allow multiple people to join in for a group video interaction. PC World gives a good overview of the some of the better interviewing platforms out there. The list includes, Interview4, Montage, InterviewStream, Jobvite and Zoom. Hirevue is another very popular service.

Challenges of Video Interactions

As discussed, we do understand that the Video interviews are quicker, efficient and cost-effective, but are people really happy with it? Not everyone has the best experience with them. Video interactions have led to many barriers between the candidate and the employer. The candidate feels that these are avoidable if they meet in person. The candidates at times get camera conscience that they are unable to give their 100%. The thought of some kind of technology glitch might disrupt the interaction, also breaks the flow of the interview.The positive and negatives to conduct video interviews in place of phone or in-person interviews go hand in hand. So, this becomes a recruiters prerogative to decide when to use face to face interactions and when video connect.

Artificial Intelligence

Technology is constantly evolving itself to act like a bridge between the right candidate, recruiter and the organization. With artificial intelligence rapidly entering the HR domain, the point that needs to be thought about is an extreme experimental and emotionless environment. Though it will be easier to perform many HR processes but amongst the drawbacks, the major one is the absence of an human interface. This will miss the *Human* in every process. Organizations will recruit on-demand and fill positions; utilization of data analytics and artificial intelligence tools will increase, focus being now towards skillsets over professional education degrees. Also, ways to increase diversity hiring. Along with this the emphasis is also moving towards on passive candidates that is candidates who are not actively looking out but exist in the system; through hyper-personalization(The use of data to provide more personalized and targeted products, services, and content).Three important tools are:

Algorithm Driven Applications for Personality Evaluation

Algorithms are prepared which can analyze the voice of a candidate and infer what type of personality the individual has. It not only tracks the years of experience, but also tries to match with the years of experience required in an opening. Today, not just what one says would matter, but how it is said, the tone modulation, emphasis on specific words, which part of sentence would be the most important parameter to draw the analysis etc. are most significant. When an HR personnel has a detailed conversation with a candidate to gauge whether the person is engaged in the role, dull or passionate about the opening and identify his personality traits, he does invest quality time with him. To save their times, the recruiters are shifting the process on the computer based application. A pre-recorded number gives a call to the candidate, he answers a set of pre-defined questions and the analysis is generated by the computer algorithm.

One such example is the speech analysis tool by Precrie Technologies. This helps in decoding the SOFT SKILLS-personality, attitude, behavior, communication of an individual. Another example is of a tool from Jobalign that is used to analyze the interest level of a candidate with respect to that job opening viz. how truthful, calm and serious one is to explore the opportunity and not disappear after taking the offer. This evaluation is majorly adopted by companies where the primary job involves a vocal interaction of the employee- ales or call center jobs. The tool is not used to identify 1 such candidate for the role, but helps to filter out top 10 candidates from whom the Business group and the HR personnel then further identifies. It is just used as a filter.

Usage of Chatbots to Filter Candidates

A chatbot (also known as a talkbot, chatterbot, Bot, chatterbox, IM bot, interactive agent, or Artificial Conversational Entity) is a computer program which conducts a conversation via auditory or textual methods. Automation has reduced a lot of interface. But at times the usage of thesedo help us being productive and correct in our research. Since the last few years, with Chatbots coming in, we see a remarkable shift in the recruitment curve. The transition has been from SmarterChild, AOL Instant Messenger in 2000 to today's Chatbots. Today, many organizations have shifted to AI-enabled chatbots like Mya and Job Pal for the initial steps of recruitment process performed by a recruiter- sourcing, screening, and scheduling interviews. Chatbots are never hibernate, they are always active to respond immediately to an application query and the first level filtration takes place to screen out candidates who do not match the basic skillsets of the job. They are so user friendly that they adapt to any interface that is from an online browser, text messaging, Facebook Messenger to mobile apps etc. Relax, chatbots cannot replace recruiters, the human interface. They will be used as a filter process– to filter out the resumes which would match a Job Description. But we need to understand that clicking a panic button will not work. What is important is to understand how our role will be defined and re-defined over a period. If we have got a basic filtration, we need to refine our screening skills in a more powerful manner.

Reference Check-Automated

Reference check is a very tedious and time consuming job. But this level is the most important level that the recruiters cannot skip it. So, it needs to be handled with umpteen care. To call a reference, to get into a deep discussion, to figure out each aspect of employee's life span, takes good amount of time. But now, this is automated. There are several solutions available in the market like SkillSurvey's Pre-Hire 360, Checkster, VidRecruiter, RefLynk and more. Emails are send across to the candidates for references. These references are then send emails through this software which have certain set of questions that they need to answer. These are then collated by a centralized division who does an analysis of the data and the update is then provides to the concerned Recruiter.

Digitally Equipped-App Based Era

Recruiting the best candidates is vital to the success of any company. Social recruiting has been on the increase, with job boards no longer having enough range to find quality candidates. Traditional ads are becoming ineffective, with most jobseekers finding them mundane and unattractive. So, with that said, it's time to for organizations to spice up their online advertising. For a potential candidate, a job advertised on social media looks far more appealing than the one that he has to search down. Such openings when advertised on the digital media, do enhance the image of the business group. When hiring through these social media channels, it does allow the recruiter to target people based on their area, interests and behavior. There is also one important observation through the post analytics that the people engaging with this job posting increase every minute. It enables the social community to ask questions about the job and further share it with someone they think it might be suitable for.

When posting a job advert through social media it's important that the candidate gets a CTA (Call-to-action) button. Facebook advertising has grown exponentially in recent years, with giving way to a massive audience. Facebook has over 1.8 billion active monthly users and people still prefer this platform to connect and communicate. It promotes an organizations brand, and it also helps as the Facebook interface is super easy to use.

We do see a decline in the hiring standards because of the transition of the recruitment systems, moving towards an application driven system. It has become the matter of concern for the recruiters to filter out 'the one' candidate amongst the large volumes of applicants. Mobile recruitment has simplified the recruiters' challenges by streamlining the hiring process and creating quick skill assessment. Mobile apps are being developed with a job preview process. This in turn help the candidates to assess whether the position they are applying for is of their interest or not. If they wish to pursue, they will explore it further; else they will remove themselves from the application and end the process. These recruitment applications also help in the screening process as they have the talent screening tool. This will also shorten the screening time and filter out the suitable candidates for the recruiter. The biggest advantage that the recruiters feel is accessibility to talent in small towns. In this way, they can access candidates from metro, satellite towns and small cities. This will also help them to broaden their talent pool in turn helping them screen a wider pool to find the right talent.

Mobile Recruitment: The Game Changing Recruitment Trend

These days, one does everything through his mobile phone- pay bills, research, shop, invest, videos etc. Take a step further now, think of applying for a job through your mobile phone. A friend send you a link through WhatsApp, you go to the organizations mobile site and login and submit your resume. Mobile recruiting has finally gained momentum as recruiters and HRs have initiated the process of mobile functionality from their ATS and other recruiting technology. In 2017, we'll see less friction on the candidate's side with "one-click" job applications becoming more common and the ability to send your resume from your phone. Today, the scenario is shifting to mobile recruitments and keeping in mind the benefits attached to it, the organizations are inclining in incorporating this system in the core recruiting system of an organization. The benefit of mobile recruitment is that the recruiters can now actively reach out to the passive candidates. Globally, the trends to target and hire the passive candidates are as - India ranks 3rd-69%; US-83% and China -72% continue to be the top hires. It has been observed that the emphasis is given to the candidate's experience while been hired by an organization. A successful hire becomes an excellent marketing pitch for an organization, while a depressing hiring experience leads to the right candidate declining the job opportunity. Organization do have a process of minimum 7 to 8 rounds for a position which gets scattered over a period of 6weeks in a win-win scenario. But when this process gets delayed, the candidate loses interest in the opportunity; also, potential candidates in the market can get an offer from some other organization. Consultants and HR teams are trying their bit to engage with the candidate, keep him warm during this interim period so that he is well connected for the entire period. Many cloud based software organizations and third part recruitment application software organizations are gaining pace and will be in demand in the coming years. Though the recruitment of any organization has become 100% digital the mobile recruitment is still at an early stage. It will take some time for it to establish itself. The trends show that 75% of active candidates visit an organizations mobile site to explore their career opportunities out of which 45% go ahead and apply for a job through the mobile itself. Still, only 12% organizations are wisely investing in the mobile recruitment space. It is also believed and shared by experts that the next step of innovation in Mobile Technology will be in voice recognition and artificial intelligence tools that will further enhance the whole experience.

Employer Branding

Employer branding is considered the core of any great recruiting strategy an organization can have. So, the HR teams have been quite conscious of this while they build it. A strong employer brand is an influential business tool to connect an organization's value system, strategy, people in the system and

HR policies to the corporate brand. Two decades back, employer brand development was interdependent on recruitment advertising. But, today over 59% of employers say that employer branding represents an organization's overall HR strategy.

The change in the style of advertising has come in with the onset of the digitalization era. An employer must broadcast the organizations branding information are varied. Never did an organization face such a situation Rise in the usage of social media, across Business Units, across levels has become fundamental responsibility for any organization to evaluate its branding and positioning day in day out. Many candidates follow the organizations that they wish to join, they do tend to follow them on various sites for the reviews, updates and the action happening in the organization. Apart from these followers, others as well read all feedbacks, updates and solutions on digital media; that it has become a conscience effort of the HR to monitor its branding.

Brand visibility on social media and digitally is important, and at the same time is vital to manage the online brand presence an organization has created. Whatever one posts, updates or even comments on the social media, does lead to an influence on the masses. The key fundamental point that an organization should remember is to be transparent. This doesn't mean that the factsabout the organization are revealed but enough information is gained to build the trust and respect from the followers. So, the crucial point here becomes is to maintain a balance between the key role and the organization.

In today's world, what candidates look out in an organization is an Employee friendly environment. A place which has a strong work life balance, amiable atmosphere so that it becomes a great place to work. This aspect can be featured well through advertisements and branding done on different digital media sites. Organizations have uploaded situations showcasing many such aspects-compassion, empathy, employee centric, etc. The organizations also seek for followers on their Facebook and LinkedIn pages with voluntary ideas and updates. When people update such facts about an organization on social media, like-minded candidates get attracted to comment and thus brings out an open forum discussions about ideas and other aspects.

But, to keep a check and monitor all pages at the same pace is a big challenge. Digital media sites like Twitter, Facebook, LinkedIn,and Glassdoor along with more common place advertising tools like job portals (Monster, Indeed, Naukri), empowers the recruiter to post the opening and other requirements to focus and attract a suitable audience. There are also so many sites like Sheroes, womenforhire, jobsforher which help to target the diversity hiring concern an organization has.

Figure 3. Trends to choose your employer

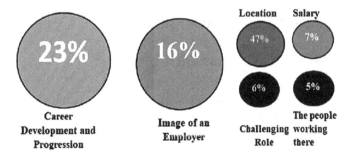

STRATEGIES FOR EMPLOYEE BRANDING

Amongst the various processes organizations follow to work on their employee branding, few are listed below-

- **Internal Brand Ambassadors:** Couple of employees from each Business Group are identified to form a team to use social media to write and tweet about the organizations. There are also Blog pages created which are managed by these Internal Brand Ambassadors. They update information about their team, the workplace, fun post and videos and do cater to some internal team issues. What becomes crucial here is the choice of brand ambassador. He is chosen in such a way that this person would be consistent, controlled and adheres to the company's image and brand messaging.
- **LinkedIn:** Organizations create their LinkedIn pages to enhance the employer's brand creating content rich employer page. This page would also showcase the top management, the current business impact, the mission and the vision statement are highlighted to give emphasis on the organizations existence, employee size and the financial trends. Apart from this they also direct you to their career page so that someone who was reviewing about the organization doesn't miss on the career opportunities open. Also, within LinkedIn, the organizations do post the current open positions so that people can directly apply through LinkedIn.

There are many definitions for employer branding but they all essentially seek to explain a company's ability to differentiate itself from competitors through a unique Employee Value Proposition (EVP). A strong EVP will communicate the company values in a way that highlights what makes that workplace unique and attractive to individuals sharing the same values. As employer brands are based on intangible factors such as image, identity, and perception, being able to discover what it is about a brand that creates an emotional inclination and a sense of identification with the company, can prove invaluable to employers.

The best place to start exploring what motivates people to join an organization, why they stay and why they leave is internal feedback. Existing data from employee feedback, employee engagement and culture surveys, focus groups, employee forums, new hire surveys or exit interviews can often paint a good picture of the prospective and existing employees' experiences. As per industry reports, the number of companies measuring, analyzing and developing strategies based on 'brand attractiveness' is on the rise; as many as 39% of businesses are expected to increase investment in employment branding strategy this year.

CURRENT TRENDS AND BEST PRACTICES

Candidates Are the Same as Customers

With the changing trends, organizations are also focusing in such a way that they create a positive impact and an experience for candidates throughout the recruitment process. The way candidates are treated in the due course of the interview, leads them to form an opinion about the organization. The hR is said to be the face of an organization as they are the very first one to interact and describe the role, the opportunity in detail to the candidate. Organizations are also aware that the candidates do share their experience, the opinion they form about the organization and the culture, with other candidates and friends. This also helps people form a mindset whether they should be a part of an organization or not.

Creation of Talent Groups

The candidates who had applied for a particular position, but did not make to the final round are potential candidates for future openings. This leads to creation of a Talent Group for future references. When an urgent opening, or a number of positions generate randomly in the organization, the first place the recruitment team would go to is the Talent Bench. So, with this talent bench available, the business can quickly start evaluating profiles for the positions and close them.

Social and Visual Revolution

Social media has left an impactful impression of employer branding, improving the way a job opening evolves. From the inception of the position in the system to the application, from the evaluation of the candidates to the offer stage; the interaction between the HR and the prospects plays a significant role. Earlier, the organizations did not get a chance to showcase their qualities digitally. But today, the prospective candidates can voice and write more about their views and form an opinion even before they become a part of the organization. Platforms like Facebook, Glassdoor, and Payscale in particular, have become very useful channels for candidates to research and assess an employer's offering, and HRs must therefore ensure that recruitment messages align with an employee perceptions on these platforms. If in past, companies rarely got publicly contested. But, today, social media offers a platform for current and prospective employees to voice their own views and paint a more realistic picture of their workplace. Channels such as Facebook, Glassdoor, and Payscale in particular are now useful tools for candidates to research and assess an employer's offering, and organizations must therefore ensure that recruitment messages align with employee perceptions. For HR employees of organizations, social media has made a remarkable step towards creation and maintaining large talent pool, which is an updated one. LinkedIn tops amongst recruiters' as the preferred social channel for identifying, evaluating and creating a database of candidates (93%), while Facebook (62%) and Twitter (50%) are used by businesses to project the employers brand. Further, platforms such as YouTube, Pinterest and Instagram are also gaining speed and popularity amongst employers. From global giants, such as Apple, Google and Intel, to smaller companies such as Innocent and Hubspot, videos also make place as powerful tools for communicating companies' organizational culture and attracting potential talent towards the organization.

Planning for Change

In today's competitive, dynamic corporate environment, the organizations focus has shifted. It needs to stay agile and be more aware of the social environment than ever before. As the number of temporary workers have increased drastically over the last few years, HR teams do face a big challenge to create an amiable corporate environment across the organization, and to create a sense of fidelity amongst employees for the organization.

Some organizations which are making use of contemporary HR practices are-

- **L'Oréal:** It has been one of the favorite places where talent would want to work for. But since the last few years the top talent has not joined the brand. Somehow, they have faced the challenge to attract talent which is because their branding. This has resulted in a question on their branding parameters and hence they need to be evaluated. Though L'Oréal has a very well defined branding taglines and focus. But, to carry on the trend has become a challenge. Each tagline used by the organization emphasizes that it is a thrilling place to work for, an organization that motivates its employees and also a School of Excellence. For years, these strategies have been able to attract and retain talent across levels, across the globe.

- **Google:** Google has always been ranked amongst the top 5 places to work for. But has anyone ever thought how do they do that and what are the challenges they face to reach the top position? Their entire business is driven on 1 major strategy -INNOVATION. Time and again Google does invest in employee feedbacks and surveys to draw analysis to work on their problems and resolve them. For example, they did a survey to analyze how their employees were coping with the Work Life Balance, which has been a major concern across the Industry. While doing this, they did infer that the employees were facing issues related to work segmentation. They did showcase the analysis across employees, putting in front the concern for employees' well-being and satisfaction on the front foot. This branding leads to low attrition and brand satisfaction for the employees.

- **Starbucks:** Starbucks, everyone loves to go and have a coffee at this coffee joint. But what's the scene on the other side of the table? The organization really works very hard to attract the number of customers that they have on a daily basis at their outlet. They do heavy social media branding to attain the level of branding. The employees in the organization use the digital language "hashtag" and the candidates who are potential employees can interact with the Instagram and Twitter accounts targeting to work only at Starbucks. By expressing this level of interest and sincerity- in being a part of an organization, the fresh talent gets empowered by the employee feedbacks and updates which highlights how they score towards employee satisfaction.

- **Salesforce:** Salesforce has been ranked top 10 for Best Companies to work for in Fortune this year. The branding an organization follows plays a major role for it to reach that level. Salesforce employer branding is majorly monitored by their employees only. They have a very strong employee referral program which is supported by strong perks and has been really motivating for employees to refer. This has also led them to create an environment with high values, connections and community.

- **Acuity Insurance:** Acuity Insurance has been listed in the Fortune List of top work places and it took entry in 2015. They entered the list by grabbing position 3 itself. They reached that level primarily because of the employer branding that they had created for themselves and the loyalty attached by the employees towards the brand. The perks associated with each hire, and the reimbursements starting from travel, education and leisure are remarkable. The organization does 10% of company contribution to employee's funds followed by intensive family medical insurance plans. They devote a lot of time towards its employees and hence their town halls and quarterly meets play a significant part in building the employee culture for the organization. The charity donations are also present, directed by employee values.

CONCLUSION

To match pace with the changing times, an individual should the following strategies:

- **Lateral Shift:** Rather than moving up in one direction, ambitious employees can move sideways, tapping into new networks, as the corporate lattice allows free-flowing ideas and career paths.
- **Skill Enhancement:** This would imply the effective use of all acquired skills. In some cases, adapting to change includes the use of other skills as well—skills which an individual might not have mastered, or even begun to acquire. In the fast-changing work environment, skills also become redundant. One needs to be prepared to deal with these change successfully. It is therefore important to enhance and acquire your skills. There is no limit, but as many skills as one can, before their use becomes essential for organizational survival. So, constant value addition is the mantra.
- **Digital Presence:** An Individual should be digitally updated on all social media platforms-LinkedIn, Facebook, Twitter. His profiles should be updated with the right key skills, current projects handled, his forte areas so that the researcher can reach his profile while searching.

REFERENCES

Breaugh, J. A., & Mann, R. B. (1984). Recruiting source effects: A test of two alternative explanations. *Journal of Occupational Psychology*, *57*(4), 261–267. doi:10.1111/j.2044-8325.1984.tb00167.x

Garimella, U., & Paruchuri, P. (2015). An Agent for Helping HR with Recruitment. *International Journal of Agent Technologies and Systems*, *7*(3), 67–85. doi:10.4018/IJATS.2015070104

Girard, A., & Fallery, B. (2009). *E-recruitment: new practices, new issues. An exploratory study. In Human Resource Information System* (pp. 39–48). INSTICC Press.

Houseman, S., & Heinrich, C. (2016). The Nature and Role of Temporary Help Work in the U.S. Economy. *Employment Research*, *23*(1), 1–4. doi:10.17848/1075-8445.23(1)-1

Chapter 3
What Emotional Intelligence Does to Organizational Stress:
Exploring the Indian Information Technology Sector

Shubhangini Rathore
IBS Gurgaon, India

ABSTRACT

The acknowledgement to develop emotional competencies of the workforce is a focal point of concern for human resource practitioners today. This chapter attempts to explore the relationship between organizational role stress and emotional intelligence in the Indian IT industry. Data was collected from a total of 250 employees, both managers and non-managers working in the Delhi NCR region. Emotional intelligence was measured by developing a scale consisting of 27 items. Stress was measured using the organizational role stress questionnaire comprising of 50 items. The results show a strong correlation between role stress and emotional intelligence. It was seen that by altering and increasing the levels of EI among the employees; workplace stress could be effectively reduced. There was also seen to be a and significant impact of emotional intelligence on organizational stress. Regression was applied to see the result of the EI variables on different factors of stress. It was seen that there is a significant impact of variables on organizational stress.

INTRODUCTION

Workplace stress has been studied from various historic and contemporary perspectives. In the history of managing employees, the tradition of keeping emotions at distance from the professional space was always found more appropriate. Logical thinking and rational analysis were always considered effective for handling and solving people and business issues. With an eventual rising importance of the human resources, the contemporary organizational milieu sees a drift in this accepted thought process. The role of emotions and feelings as determinants of one's ability to work in groups is recognized as a considerable factor in managing human resources. The Service Industry of India is one of the most rapidly growing

DOI: 10.4018/978-1-5225-5297-0.ch003

sectors in national and international markets. The industry is of prime importance due to its enormous support to the national economy with special regard to employment opportunities that it provides along with its role on the GDP of the country. This sector is credited with a contribution of approximately 60 percent to the country's Gross Domestic Product (GDP) and an estimated 35 percent of employment. The India Information Technology (IT) Sector is seen in conjunction with the Information Technology enabled Services (ITeS).The sector has a substantial contribution to the national economy as it caters to domestic and foreign markets. The rise of exports makes it account for almost 75% of its total earned revenue. Broadly, the sector is divided into four large segments that comprise of IT services, ITES-BPO and Software; which includes both Research and Development and Engineering. The IT industry being a service industry is characterized by an intense use of emotional intelligence.

Hochschild (1983) contended that such jobs require the employee to interact face to face or voice to voice with other stakeholders such as clients, customers and guests. They are also required to produce emotional states in another person under expressions that are guided by the organizations display rules requirement; making the employee the actor, the client the audience and the shop floor the stage (Goleman, 1998). Researchers have highlighted the concept of 'emotional labor'; which is a requirement for employees to act in an empathetic, positive and friendly manner at all times when dealing with customers, in order to make them feel wanted and welcomed (Grandey, 2003) .Emotional Intelligence has an important role to play on the emotional labor outcomes because individuals with high Emotional Intelligence have better emotional management strategies such as deep acting; whereas people with lower Emotional Intelligence adopt only surface acting to regulate their emotional expression (Cheung & Tang, 2009). This leads to stressful encounters for the employee, as he is forced to display feelings and emotions that he may or may not genuinely feel.

The IT industry is seen to be characterized by challenging conditions of Organizational Stress (O'Neill, 2011) In the IT industry, the life expectancy of products and programs declines each year, while the demands on employees increase; due to the unique set of environmental pressures such as continuous re-engineering, outsourcing, more demanding customers and general information overload (Karad 2010). Organizations are now recognizing the importance of effective management of Information Technology professionals for effective performance and functioning (Yeh, Lee & Pai, 2011), yet empirical evidence proves that problems associated with employees and their issues, are the major impediments in this context (Hazzan & Hadar, 2008). Amongst the major issues, there are problems like a shrinking student base, low attractiveness of the profession in terms of image and status (Day, 2007) and career commitment and turnover (Korunka, Hoonakker & Carayon, 2008); (Quan & Cha, 2010). The reason for this turnover has historically been attributed to stress (Engler, 1998). Research has emphasized an inverse role between Emotional Intelligence and Organizational Stress. It is believed that aspects of Emotional Intelligence pertaining to Self and the other; will help an employee to understand himself and deal with challenges such as Organizational Stress (Gani, 2012). The acknowledgement to develop Emotional Intelligence of the workforce therefore becomes a focal point for human resource practitioners and trainers in the service industry.

In the Indian IT industry, the trend towards aspiring youngsters to would work extra hours to acquire material comforts; seems to increase (Ghapanchi & Aurum, 2011); yet there is also a very common practice of software engineers who have less than five years of work experience; to leave work (Colomo-Palacios, 2012). Researchers have shown that the major causes of workforce turnover in the IT sector are; work-related, psychological and emotional in nature. The specific variables are effort- reward imbalance, perceived workload and emotional exhaustion. Given the current scenario, it is important to explore if Emotional Intelligence can be leveraged to make the employees handle the environmental pressures and stress in a better way; that may also lead to reduction in turnover. Work stress is also seen in direct antithesis with the advantages of having a highly committed workforce. Nikolaou & Tsaousis (2002) found a positive correlation between Emotional Intelligence and organizational commitment and a negative correlation between Emotional Intelligence and stress at work. Though considerable studies have attempted to understand the relationship between Emotional Intelligence and Organizational Stress in other sectors; no research has been undertaken in the Indian IT sector.

The present study is also unique from previous studies, as it uses an Emotional Intelligence scale that has been developed by the researchers in a previous study by integrating Indian and Western perspectives on Emotional Intelligence (Rathore et al. 2012).

From Intelligence to Emotional Intelligence

There is empirical evidence which suggests that only intelligence cannot explain our achievements in life; emotions also play a key role (George, 2000).Thus, individuals having the same IQ levels may not necessarily achieve the same levels of academic and professional success, because they all possess different levels of Emotional Intelligence (Brown and Brooks, 2002). The evolution of a dynamic work environment demands equal importance for both technology and human needs to sustain business growth. It is evident that as businesses progress toward rapid globalization, there is a breakdown of trade barriers and an opportunity for people to work with diverse people and enter diverse sets of markets. To manage this diverse workforce, managers need to exhibit Emotional Intelligence. Emotional Intelligence can be explained in the context of being aware of one's own emotions and the emotions of others and managing each of them effectively. Competencies and skills that are a part of Emotional Intelligence (EI) have been identified as important in satisfying both internal and external customers (George, 2000; Higgs & Aitken, 2003).

In 1920, it was suggested by Thorndike that humans have several types of intelligence, one form of this is, "social intelligence" or the ability to, "understand and manage men and women, boys and girls, and to act wisely in human relations" (Thorndike, 1920).A new concept of intelligence was defined by David Wechsler in 1940 as he defined intelligence as, "the aggregate or global capacity of the individual to act purposefully, to think rationally, and to deal effectively with his environment"(Wechsler, 1958).

Howard Gardner proposed that the foundation for most of the models created on Emotional Intelligence were based on interpersonal and intrapersonal intelligence .Gardener believed that these intelligences were as significant as the type of intelligence typically measured by IQ tests (Gardner, 1983). Peter Salovey and John Mayer were the theorist who initially and primarily focused on the studies about social intelligence and concluded that the research on emotional intelligence was based on the notion of social intelligence (Salovey and Mayer 1990) and also that both concepts are linked and interconnected. Going forward, Emotional Intelligence was defined by Boyatzis and Sala (2004) as an, "ability to recognize, understand and use emotional information about oneself or others that leads to or causes effective or superior performance".

Daniel Goleman took inspiration from Salovey and Mayer's manuscripts on the evolving notion of emotional intelligence. The concept of emotional intelligence was made a household word by his best-selling books on emotional intelligence .To comprehend and improve their research models; different researcher's profoundly borrowed from Goleman's model of intelligence.

EVOLUTION OF EMOTIONAL INTELLIGENCE MODELS

Ability Model of Emotional Intelligence by Mayer and Salovey

John Mayer and Peter Salovey (1990) viewed emotional intelligence as a pure form of mental ability. Mayer et al., (2000) explained that an individual's ability to process emotional information and emotional processing varies from person to person. They suggested a four branch model of emotional intelligence, each representing processes of integrating emotions and cognitions. Emotional perception is the first branch which is the ability to recognize and review one's emotions and expressing our emotional requirements to others. Emotional assimilation is the second one which shows the ability to discriminate among emotions and prioritizing emotions which affects their thought process. Emotional understanding is the third one which shows the ability of reasoning the composite emotions and also to identify transitions from one to another. Fourth is the emotional management, which is the ability to regulate the emotional instability depending upon its usefulness in a situation and ability to observe them frequently (Chaudhary & Rathore, 2013).

Mixed Model of Emotional Intelligence by Bar On

Reuven Bar On (1997) proposed a model based on personality theory which highlights the co-dependence of ability with personality traits and their application on personal well-being. His model relates to the use of emotions for performance and success. His model reviews five major constituents of emotional intelligence which are; intrapersonal, interpersonal, adaptability, stress management and general mood with sub constituents under each category. He also states that emotional intelligence can be developed and improved in the workplace. Bar on stated that emotional and cognitive intelligence contributes to a person's general intelligence which shows one's potential to achieve success in life (Chaudhary & Rathore, 2013).

Mixed Model of Emotional Intelligence by Goleman

This model of emotional intelligence was proposed by Goleman. Four main emotional intelligence constructs were outlined by Goleman's model. The First is Self-Awareness, which is the ability to read one's emotions and identify their effect to make decisions. Second is Self-Management, which means regulating one's emotional instincts and adjusting to shifting conditions. Third is Social Awareness, which is the ability to sense, comprehend and respond to emotions of others while understanding social networks. Fourth is Relationship Management; which means, the ability to motivate guidance and develop others while handling conflict (Goleman1998). Within each constructs of emotional intelligence, there are other related competencies; which are the learned capabilities that must be worked and developed to achieve success. Goleman suggests that every individual is born with a general emotional intelligence which determines his potential for learning emotional competencies. The association of competencies is not random; they appear in collaborative groups that support and enable each other (Boyatzis et al. 1999).

Mixed Model of Emotional Intelligence by Dalip Singh

Emotional intelligence in the Indian context has been researched upon by Dr. Dalip Singh (2007). Singh bases his model of Emotional Intelligence upon differences of cultural perspective. According to Singh, the Indian culture is dissimilar from the Western culture and the various models of Emotional Intelligence by western researchers fall short of capturing Emotional competencies that are adequate in the Indian scenario. His model defines Emotional Intelligence in terms of three competencies, which are; Emotional Maturity, Sensitivity and Competency.

Our previous research shows that Dalip Singh's work has a lot of similarities with Goleman's model of Emotional Intelligence. In fact, Singh had taken extensively form Goleman's model. The facets of self-awareness, developing others, delaying gratification, adaptability and flexibility in Goleman's model are broadly explained in terms of Emotional Maturity in Singh's model. The concept covers facets of identifying our and others sentiments, inspiring and developing other members of team, regulating instant instincts and being flexible and adaptable.

The facets of handling emotional upsets, egoism, inferiority complex and developing high self-esteem in Goleman's model are broadly explained in terms of emotional competency in Singh's model. It emphasizes on handling negative feelings, emotional enervation, taking challenges, decreasing self-interest and high optimistic self-worth. The facets of understanding verge of empathy, emotional arousal and developing inter- personal relations in Goleman's Model are broadly explained in terms of emotional sensitivity in Singh's model which roughly manages areas of self-awareness of relation between feelings and actions, replying to low intensity stimuli, understanding and sharing others sentiments, improving positive interpersonal relationships and sharing positive emotions from verbal and non-verbal communication (Rathore et al.2012).

Organizational Role Stress

The nature of work pressures in contemporary organizations requires employees to work longer hours, under stressful conditions of workload, performance pressure and competition. The IT industry is seen to be characterized by challenging conditions of organizational Stress (John.O Neill, 2011; Quan & Cha, 2010). Stress has highlighted itself in the visibility of a rising trend of employee sickness, premature labor turnover, and premature retirement due to ill health, lost production. In 1936, Prof. Hans Selye, "The father of modern stress", researched on dysfunctional effects of stress on the human body due to overarching demands on it. The empirical research in the field began only after Hans Seyle's first article on stress in 1956 (Neelamegam & Asrafi, 2010). Stress can be categorized as positive stress and negative stress. Positive stress is called, "eustress "and is explained as a pleasant or curative stress that helps a person to perform better, in the situational demands. The General Adaptation syndrome considers eustress as a part of the initial indication of the alarm and reaction in the body, but problem seems to arise; when bodily resources are further depleted and result in a burnout. Negative stress is reached by the body when the body alarms are ignored and the body heads towards a burnout. A big challenge for organizations now is to create an environment that equips employees with well suited coping mechanisms and programs in fruitful stress management.

A major problem in devising causal models for stress is the limitations faced by experts in categorizing it. Hinkle explains that it is difficult to explain the term stress, as it carries a different meaning in different disciplines. "In the Biological Literature, it is used in relation to single organisms, populations of organisms, and ecosystems, whereas Social scientists are more concerned about people's interaction with their environment and the resulting emotional disturbance that can sometimes accompany it" (Hinkle 1973). Cox and Griffiths (2000) make a distinction between two types of psychological model of work stress: interactional or structural approaches, and transactional or process models.

Interactional and Transactional Models of Stress

Interactional models focus on the structural characteristics of the stress process, i.e. which stressors are likely to lead to which outcomes in the workplace. They explain the associations of work characteristics with the psychology of the individual. In popular literature, many studies differentiate between the causes and symptoms of work related stress and personal stress. Most importantly, that what is stressful for one person may be of little effect on others. Therefore, the concept of stressor and coping is individualistic in nature. Transactional models are more cognitive, and focus on the dynamic relationship between individuals and their environment in terms of mental and emotional processes (Cox et al. 2000). Transactional models analyse the subjective perceptions of the environment and relate coping to cognitive and appraisal factors based on individual capacity. The models with these features in the occupational stress literature are described below.

Role Stress Model by Udai Pareekh

The current research adapts the model of role stress by Udai Pareekh. Pareek's (1993) scale of role stress is based on ten Role Stress factors that measure organizational stress. These are:

1. **Inter-Role Distance (IRD):** Is experienced when there is a conflict between organizational and non-organizational roles.
2. **Role Stagnation (RS):** Is the feeling of being stuck in the same role for long due to lack of opportunities or development.
3. **Role Expectation Conflict (REC):** Arises out of conflicting demands originating from Superiors, subordinates or peers.
4. **Role Erosion (RE):** Arises when a role occupant feels that others are performing certain Functions, which should have been a part of his role.
5. **Role Overload (RO):** Is the feeling that one is required to do too much.
6. **Role Isolation (RI):** Arises when a person feels that his role is isolated from the mainstream of organizational life.
7. **Personal Inadequacy (PI):** Is created by the lack of adequate skills and the resulting inability to meet the demands of one's role.
8. **Self-Role Distance (SRD):** Arises from a gap between one's concept of self and the demands of his role.
9. **Role Ambiguity (RA):** Is experienced when there is a lack of clarity about the demands of the role.
10. **Resource Inadequacy (RIN):** Arises when human and material resources allocated are Inadequate to meet the demands of the role.

Relationship Between Emotional Intelligence and Organizational Role Stress

A review of literature suggests that there is a significant relationship between emotional intelligence and role stress.

Abraham (2000) studied the relationship between Stress and Emotional Intelligence. She concluded that Emotional Intelligence was inversely proportional to lower levels of perceived stress, positive conflict styles and other measures of positive adaptations in difficult work environment.

Thingujam and Ram (2000) tried to make an Indian adaptation of the emotional intelligence scale (Schulte et al, 1998) but no item modification was made. The results showed that Emotional Intelligence was correlated strongly and positively with coping, moderately and negatively with trait-anxiety, and slightly and positively with belief with social relation.

Slaski and Cartwright (2002) explored the relation between measures of emotional quotient, subjective stress, distress, general health, morale, quality of working life and management performance. A sample of 224 managers of a retail organization in Ireland was selected. Significant co relations were seen to emerge in one direction. The results showed that managers who scored high on emotional quotient were less prone to subjective stress, experienced better health and well-being and better management performance.

Nikolaou and Tsaousis (2002) found that those who could control their emotional states were healthier because they could assess their emotional states, convey their feelings and control their moods. They also mentioned that people with high level of emotional intelligence are able to cope with their emotions more effectively than those with low level of emotional intelligence.

Chabungban (2005) concluded that stress can be costly both to the organization and individuals, if left unnoticed. By developing emotional intelligence, stress can be reduced and productivity increased. Emotional intelligence can also help employees to control negative emotions, frustration.

Gohm, Corser and Dalsky (2005) studied the relationship between emotional intelligence and stress in a group of 158 freshmen. The study concluded that emotional intelligence was a predictor of stress and would help in stress reduction to a great extend. The results suggest that in some cases the highly stressed participants have average levels of emotional intelligence, but do not make optimal use of it because they lack confidence in their emotional ability.

Day, Therrien and Carroll (2005) researched on the ability of emotional intelligence's to predict health outcomes pertaining to stress and strain. The study explored the relationships among EI (as assessed by a trait-based measure, the EQ-i) daily hassles, psychological health and strain factors.

Kulshshrestha et al. (2006) researched on the relation between the subjective well being and locus of control to emotional intelligence among Indian executives. The results of the study revealed that emotional intelligence and locus of control have significant correlation with subjective well being.

Shulman and Hemenover (2006) studied the effect of EI on psychological health. The participants completed measures of perception, understanding and regulation of emotions, psychological well being and emotional distress. The results showed that dispositional EI is related to health outcomes cross-section ally and are strong predictors of health.

S. K., and, S. (2008) investigated the relationship as well as the impact of emotional intelligence on to the perception of role stress of medical professionals in their organizational lives. The findings of the study indicated no significant difference in the level of emotional intelligence and perceived role stress between the genders, but significantly negative relationships of emotional intelligence with organizational role stress for both the genders.

Klohnen (1996) suggested that there are many benefits of applying EI in the workplace for increasing the tolerance for stress, better people management skills and more effective performance as part of a team. On the same lines, Morrison (2008) also tried to successfully determine the relationship between EI and preferred conflict handling styles of registered nurses working in three south Mississippi health Care facilities. 92 valid sets of data instruments were collected for this study. Results showed that higher levels of EI, positively correlated with collaborating and negatively with accommodating.

Akerjordet and Severinsson (2009) conducted a study that focused on the perceptions of emotion intelligence reactions and thoughts. A sample of 250 women was taken and statistical inferences were used. The Results confirmed emotional intelligence to be an important component in relation to stress management and mental health. It was seen that emotionally perspective women seemed to be affected by stress and depression to a greater extent. The relative strength of the association between the score also provides valid and useful overall measures of new mother's perceptions. Li-chuan Chu (2010) studied the advantages of mediation in regard to EI, perceived stress and negative mental health among 351 participants. It was seen that employees with higher EI experienced lesser negative health conditions.

Research Methodology

The sample for the present study comprises of 250 professionals, both managers and non managers; employed at different Software organizations in the National Capital Region, India. A list of software organizations from National Association of Software and Services Companies (NASSCOM) was used for inviting the software organizations for participating in the research. Equal distribution of respondents between small/individual and large/chain organizations was ensured. The sample was collected by the way of stratified random sampling. Senior executives of these organizations were briefed about the research objectives and participation requirements.

Tools for Data Collection

The study uses two distinct scales for the analysis. Emotional Intelligence was used by a self constructed scale, the details of which are mentioned below. Organizational Stress was measured using Pareekh's Organizational Role Stress scale that has been used extensively by researchers in various studies; to measure Role Stress.

Emotional Intelligence Scale

A scale has been constructed for Emotional Intelligence, by adapting to Goleman (ref) and Dalip Singh's (ref) research on Emotional Intelligence in the American and Indian construct respectively. The scale was developed with the help of Content analysis, Factor analysis and Confirmatory factor analysis. The scale consists of 27 items that measured the emotional intelligence of the participants on the parameters of Self Awareness, Self Management, Social Awareness and Relationship Management. The parameters are covered by the 8 factors in the scale ; namely - Self Esteem (Self awareness), Threshold of Emotional Arousal, Flexibility & Adaptability, Handling Egoism (Self Management), Empathy (Social Awareness) and Building Bonds, Communication and Developing Others (Relationship Management). That scale had been developed in our previous research emotional intelligence. The reliability of the scale is >0.07 (Rathore et al. 2012)

Organizational Stress was measured using Pareekh's Organizational Role Stress scale that comprises of ten Role Dimensions:*Inter-Role Distance (IRD), Role Stagnation (RS), Role Expectation Conflict (REC),Role Erosion (RE), Role Overload (RO),Role Isolation (RI)Personal Inadequacy (PI),Self-Role Distance (SRD),Role Ambiguity (RA) and Resource Inadequacy (RIN).*The data was analyzed using t – tests, ANOVA, Correlations and Regression.

Results and Interpretations

The analysis starts by examining the levels of Organizational Stress and Emotional Intelligence in the IT industry. Table 1 shows the percentage means scores of Emotional Intelligence among the employees of the IT industry.

Discussion Table 1

The Table 1 shows that for the IT industry; for *Self Awareness* the parameters are *Self Esteem* (M=3.32, SD=0.86) and *Threshold Of Emotional Arousal* (M=3.32, SD=0.96). For *Self Management* the parameters are Adaptability *& Flexibility* are (M=3.11,SD=0.84) and for *Handling Egoism* (M=3.35,SD=0.99) .For *Social Awareness* the parameters is *Empathy* (M=3.39,SD=0.83) and for Relationship Management, the parameters are *Building Bonds* (M=3.20,SD=0.84), *Communication* (M=3.25,SD=.91) and *Developing Others* (M=3.52,SD=0.83). Overall, the employees of the IT industry have the highest mean scores for *Social Awareness (60%);* which includes *Empathy.* It is seen that the employees have the minimum scores for *Self Management (55%),* which includes *Flexibility & Adaptability* and *Handling Egoism.* It is seen that the employees have the minimum scores for *Self Management,* which includes *Flexibility & Adaptability* and *Handling Egoism.* Adaptability is the ability to be flexible when faced with change. Handling Egoism is the ability to discourage overconfidence or superiority complex. In the present busi-

Table 1. Means, SD, and percentage of emotional intelligence in IT industry

	No. of Items	Score Range	N	Cronbach Alpha	Mean	Stnd. Dev.	Mean Score as %
Self_esteem	6	6-30	250	.843	3.32	0.86	58
Threshold_emo_arousal	2	2-10	250	.720	3.32	0.96	58
Self Awareness: Total Mean:6.64; Mean as %: 58%							
Flexibility_adaptability	4	4-20	250	.711	3.11	0.84	53
Handling_egoism	3	3-15	250	.679	3.35	0.99	59
Self Management Total Mean: 6.46; Mean as %: 55%							
Empathy	3	3-15	250	.979	3.39	0.83	60
Social Awareness Total Mean: 3.39; Mean as %:60%							
Building_bonds	5	5-25	250	.805	3.20	0.84	55
Communication	2	2-10	250	.711	3.25	0.91	56
Developing_others	2	2-10	250	.705	3.52	0.83	63
Relationship Management Total: 9.97; Mean as %:58%							

ness times, it is important to be adaptable to changing customer expectations. This ability needs to be strengthened in the employees such that they can improvise and adapt to environmental changes. Being in the service sector, one is expected to be able to handle egoism so that it does not lead to undesirable behaviors with clients or co workers. It would be useful for the IT industry professionals to develop these competencies in their employees.

Each score range was converted into percent score by the formula:

$$\frac{Mean\ Score - Lowest\ Point\ Of\ Score\ Range}{Highest\ Score - Lowest\ Point\ Of\ Score\ Range}$$

Discussion Table 2

Table 2 shows mean values of *Organizational Stress* among the respondents of the IT industry. The mean scores are *Inter Role Distance (IRD)*(M=2.70,SD=0.84), *Role Stagnation (RS)*(M=2.81,SD=0.85), *Role Expectation Conflict (REC)*(M=2.62,SD=0.89), *Role Erosion (RE)* (M=2.98,SD=0.77), *Role Overload (RO)*(M=2.68,SD=0.92), *Role Isolation (RI)*(M=2.72,SD=0.87), *Personal Inadequacy (PI)* (M=2.78,SD=0.87), Self *Role Distance (SRD)*(M=2.77,SD=0.84), *Role Ambiguity (RA)* (M=2.48,SD=0.93) and *Resource Inadequacy (RIN)*(M=2.70,SD=0.88)

Discussion Table 3

As seen in Table 3. In the IT industry the top five stressors that emerge are; *Role Erosion (RE), Role Stagnation (RS), Personal Inadequacy (PI), Self Role Distance (SRD) and Role Isolation (RI).* In the IT industry

As a stressor, Role Erosion is ranked 1st in the IT industry. In this the occupant feels that others are performing certain functions, which should have been a part of his role. The employees feel stressed

Table 2. Percentage mean scores of organizational stress among the employees of the IT employees

Variables	No. of Items	Score Range	Cronbach Alpha	Mean Score	Std. Deviation	Mean Score as %
Inter Role Distance (IRD)	5	5-25	.789	2.70	0.84	54.0
Role Stagnation (RS)	5	5-25	.743	2.81	0.85	56.2
Role expectation Conflict (REC)	5	5-25	.786	2.62	0.89	52.4
Role Erosion (RE)	5	5-25	.716	2.98	0.77	59.6
Role Overload (RO)	5	5-25	.805	2.68	0.92	53.6
Role Isolation (RI)	5	5-25	.821	2.72	0.87	54.4
Personal Inadequacy (PI)	5	5-25	.788	2.78	0.87	55.6
Self Role Distance (SRD)	5	5-25	.756	2.77	0.84	55.4
Role Ambiguity (RA)	5	5-25	.820	2.48	0.93	49.6
Resource Inadequacy (RIN)	5	5-25	.803	2.70	0.88	54.0

Table 3. A comparative of the Top 5 role stressors in the IT industry

Hospitality Industry	
Variables	**Ranking**
Self Role Distance (SRD)	1
Role Overload (RO)	2
Personal Inadequacy (PI)	3
Role Stagnation (RS)	4
Inter Role Distance (IRD)	5

due to the lack of ownership. Role erosion can be also linked to a feeling of a lack of opportunity that is felt by the software professionals, in terms of lack of advancement in career. Role Stagnation (RS) is ranked as the top 2nd stressor. (RS) is the feeling of being stuck in the same role for long due to lack of opportunities or development. The results indicate that employees face stress and challenges and feel threatened by a feeling of lack of advancement and growth opportunities. In most cases it is seen that these professionals may run out of assignments, if their skill sets are no longer in demand by the clients. Many times the skills possessed by them, only find a scope abroad. Personal inadequacy (PI) is ranked as the top 3rd stressor. In the IT industry there may arises a lack of new training that is required to cope with the dynamic technological changes and requirement. SRD is ranked as the top 4th stressor. Even in this industry; the employees feel similar compulsions to of behaving differently from their real selves. This may create a difference in the way in which the employee actually sees himself, and in the way he is forced to behave. Role Isolation is ranked as the top 5th stressor. It occurs when a person feels that his role is isolated from the mainstream of organizational life.

Discussion Table 4

A Pearson's correlation was administers on the sample, to assess the relationship between organizational stress and Emotional Intelligence on the sample of 250 IT professionals. The study shows that emotional intelligence is negatively and significantly related to workplace stress. All dimensions of emotional

Table 4. Correlation between emotional intelligence and organizational role stress

	IRD	**RS**	**REC**	**RE**	**RO**	**RI**	**PI**	**SRD**	**RA**	**RINA**
Self_Esteem	-.401**	-.458**	-.544**	-.271**	-.476**	-.455**	-.409**	-.494**	-.510**	-.509**
Threshold_emo_awareness	-.343**	-.324**	-.439**	-.184*	-.370**	-.376**	-.242**	-.253**	-.346**	-.341**
Flexibility_Adaptability	-.384**	-.399**	-.434**	-.251**	-.348**	-.358**	-.350**	-.364**	-.431**	-.452**
Handling_Egoism	-.341**	-.347**	-.371**	-.156*	-.291**	-.282**	-.227**	-.280**	-.375**	-.366**
Empathy	-.292**	-.369**	-.366**	-.214**	-.395**	-.335**	-.274**	-.296**	-.459**	-.395**
Building_Bonds	-.355**	-.330**	-.433**	-.249**	-.443**	-.421**	-.373**	-.361**	-.394**	-.411**
Communication	-.256**	-.153	-.396**	-.123	-.360**	-.228**	-.276**	-.386**	-.241**	-.312**
Developing_others	-.369**	-.341**	-.488**	-.334**	-.440**	-.431**	-.441**	-.431**	-.467**	-.443**

** Significant at .01 level

intelligence are moderately and highly related to workplace Stress. This implies that individuals with high emotional intelligence would be less prone to stress and would have better mechanisms of coping.

Regression Analysis

A stepwise linear regression was run on the sample, in order to assess the impact of emotional intelligence competencies on organizational stress. The results of this table would also help in predicting the most important factors of emotional intelligence that contribute to organizational stress. Organizational Stress was the dependent variable in the study and all the emotional intelligence variables were kept as independent variables in the study.

- **Dependent Variable:** Organizational Stress
- **Independent Variable:** Emotional Intelligence
- **Predictors:** Self-esteem, Developing Others

Discussion Table 5

The second model is selected from the results of Table 5. Total Stress here has been computed by taking the mean scores of all the ten role dimensions of Role Stress. It is seen that the R Square value = .301, which means that Approx. 30.1% of role stress can be predicted by two predictors of emotional intelligence, which are; Self Esteem and Developing others. Self esteem is ones belief in one's own capabilities and developing others is the ability to feel a sense of responsibility towards others by helping them develop. An individual's belief in his self worth and capability to develop subordinates would help him in dealing with stress. The nature of work in the IT industry can often lead to a sense of Role Erosion and diminishing significance; which may lead to a lack of self esteem. The professionals thus need responsibilities that involve development of self esteem in the professionals, such that they can deal with stress. In behavioral studies, it is seen that an R square value of .301, is important as a predictor. The value is also seen to be significant p<0.000. Thus emotional intelligence can be used to deal with individual stress.

Table 5. Regression model summary

Model	R	R Square	Adjusted R Square
1	.516[a]	.267	.262
2	.549[b]	.301	.292

Model		Unstandardized Coefficients		Standardized Coefficients	Individual Contribution (Standardized Beta* Zero Order Correlation)
		B	Std. Error	Beta	
2	(Constant)	237.558	13.820		
	Self-esteem	-3.108	.761	-.358	16.4%
	Developing others	-5.698	2.050	-.244	13.6%

In Table 6, the percentage of contrition of EI for each OF THE top 5 variable of Stress can be seen clearly.

In the IT industry, FOR IRD; predictors that have evolved are *Empathy (Beta= -.510, p<0.01), Threshold of Emotional Arousal (Beta = -.547,p<0.01),Communication (Beta= -.391,p<0.01), and Handling Egoism(Beta = -.187,p<0.05).* The R^2 value = .594, which explained that 59.4 percent of the variance in the dependent variable is explained by four dependent variables .The overall ANOVA table is found to be significant. All the t- values of the predictors are found to be significant $p<0.01$. The individual contributions show *of Empathy is 25.9%, Threshold Of Emotional Arousal 16.9%, Communication 10.3% and Handling Egoism 6.2%.*

For RS, In the IT industry, the predictors that have evolved are *Empathy* (Beta=-.881, p<0.01) & *Handling Egoism* (Beta=-.207, p<0.05. The R2 value = .489, which explained that 48.9 percent of the variance in the dependent variable is explained by four dependent variables .The overall ANOVA table is found to be significant. All the t- values of both predictors are found to be significant p<0.01. The individual contributions show of *Empathy* is 42.6%, and *Handling Egoism* is 6.3%

Table 6. Predictors of organizational stress in the IT industry

Predictors	β	Standardized β	t-Value	Sig	Zero-Order Correlations	Individual Contribution	Dimension of Role Stress
Empathy	-0.51	-0.36	-5.24	0.000	-0.72	25.92%	
Threshold_emo_arousl	-0.547	-0.25	-3.93	0.000	-0.676	16.90%	Inter Role Distance (IRD)
Communication	-0.391	-0.17	-3.02	0.003	-0.608	10.33%	
Handling egoism	-0.187	-0.113	-2.09	0.038	-0.55	6.20%	
**F= 89.48 df=(4,245)	R=.770	R square=.594 Adjusted R square:.587					Variance Explained=59.4%
Empathy	-0.881	-0.615	-10.5	0	-0.692	42.60%	Role Stagnation(RS)
Handling_egoism	-0.207	-0.123	-2.11	0.036	-0.509	6.30%	
**F= 118.04 df=(2,247)	R=.669	R square=.489 Adjusted R square:.485					Variance Explained=48.9%
Empathy	-0.564	-0.363	-4.38	0	-0.67	24.30%	
Building_bonds	-0.291	-0.262	-3.08	0.002	-0.656	17.20%	Role Overload(RO)
Communication	-0.368	-0.146	-2.43	0.016	-0.536	7.80%	
**F =79.97 df=(3,246)	R=.703	R square=.494 Adjusted R square:.488					Variance Explained=49.4%
Building_bonds	-0.376	-0.358	-5	0.000	-0.596	21.30%	
Threshold_emo_arousl	-0.42	-0.185	-2.63	0.009	-0.536	9.90%	Personal Inadequacy (PI)
Communication	-0.425	-0.178	-2.63	0.009	-0.522	9.30%	
**F =55.95 df=(3,246)	R=.637	R square=.406 Adjusted R square:.398					Variance Explained=40.6%
Empathy	-0.643	-0.453	-8.23	0.000	-0.674	30.50%	Self Role Distance (SRD)
Communication	-0.831	-0.36	-6.55	0.000	-0.638	23.00%	
**F =142.0 df=(2,247)	R=.731	R square=.535 Adjusted R square:.531					Variance Explained=53.5%

FOR RO In the IT industry, the predictors that have evolved are *Empathy (Beta =-.564, p<0.01), Building Bonds (Beta=-.291, p<0.05) and Communication (Beta =-.368, p<0.01).* The R^2 value = .494, which explained that 49.4 percent of the variance in the dependent variable is explained by three independent variables. The overall ANOVA table is found to be significant. All the t- values of both predictors are found to be significant $p<0.01$. The individual contributions show of *Empathy 24.3%, Building Bonds 17.2% and Communication 7.8%.*

For PI In the IT industry the predictors that have evolved are *Building Bonds, Threshold of Emotional Arousal and Communication.* The R2 value = .406, which explained that 40.6 percent of the variance in the dependent variable is explained by three independent variables .The overall ANOVA table is found to be significant. All the t- values of both predictors are found to be significant p<0.01. The individual contributions of *Building Bonds is 21.3%, Threshold of Emotional Arousal 9.9% and Communication 9.3%.*

For SRD In the IT industry the predictors that have evolved are *Empathy* and *Communication.* The R2 value = .535, which explained that .535 percent of the variance in the dependent variable is explained by two independent variables. The overall ANOVA table is found to be significant. All the t- values of both predictors are found to be significant p<0.01.The individual contribution of the predictors are; *Empathy is 30.5% and Communication is 23%*

CONCLUSION

Within the service industry; the nature of the relationship between Emotional Intelligence and Organizational Stress was found to be negative; which indicates that higher emotional levels will lead to lower levels of stress and vice versa. The result of these findings is similar to results of previous studies that reported Emotional intelligence is negatively correlated with stress. [Slaski and Cartwright (2002), Nikolaou and Tsaousis (2002), Abraham (2005), Chabungban (2005), Day, Therrien and Carroll (2005), Gohm, Corser & Dalsky (2006), S. K. & S. (2008) Morrison (2008) and Akerjordet and Severinsson (2009)].

There is a pressing need nowadays to improve and develop an emotionally intelligent workforce, if we consider the benefits of understanding and regulating emotions to deal with stress. In today's scenario many organizations can have the same type of technologies, machinery, land and capital but what makes an organization different and better from other is its human resource or the kind of people it possess. Emotionally intelligent employees not only perform better but also create an environment for others to do their best and hence form a positive atmosphere to work.

Over the past decade, strong demands have placed India amongst the fastest growing IT markets in the Asia – Pacific region. Low cost services that are demanded by the employers in strict time lines, that becomes a cause of stress for the employees. It has been reported that customer service employees reporting chronic stress exhibit particularly poor job performance (Beehr, Jex, Stacy, & Murray, 2000). Software solutions in contemporary times are no longer offered in wrapped boxes; a new range of operations, systems and computing has lead to intense competition in delivering solutions, products and services. Software engineers are now expected to deliver technical expertise and leadership; over and above the technical roles.

The strengths of software engineers mostly lie in logic, algorithms and problem solving; but it is important to reach out and work with clients and customers who have no technical backgrounds. In the IT industry, the employees are expected to deliver to the expectations of the consumer; based on virtual mediums of exchange. It is extremely important for the employees to work in teams, in order to make a delivery possible. Since the major roles are undertaken by the professionals on the shop floor, amidst strict display rules of emotions; it leads to stress; the outcome of which is seen in the form of high attrition in both industries. The results of the present study are in line with previous researches, which have explored and confirmed similar factors of Role Stress (Love et al. 2007); (Casado-Lumbreras et al., 2011) (Sethi, King and Quick, 2004).

The findings of the present study establish emotional intelligence as a predictor of stress and thus can be linked with significant potential to stress management techniques. Many organizations are benefitting from the advantages of leveraging emotional intelligence trainings for employee and consumer satisfaction .The trainings are widely used in connection with various executive development programs. Nevertheless, its use as part of an organized stress management program may have additive effects in maintaining and increasing work-life balance for all employees. The results show a significant impact of emotional intelligence in Organizational stress, which means that developing emotionally competent employees can be of advantage to the employers; in dealing with issues of employee stress The result of these findings is in line with earlier studies that reported Emotional intelligence is negatively correlated with stress. (Slaski & Cartwright, 2002), (Klohnen, 1996), (Nikolaou & Tsaousis 2002), (Therrien & Carroll, 2006), (Akerjordet & Severinsson 2009).

The study reiterates that emotional intelligence training and competencies can be instrumental in reducing the stress levels of employees. As the results show, by increasing the self esteem and the ability to develop others; stress management coping can be exercised. Moreover, the relationship between EI and occupational stress may also be examined under the frame of various human resources practices. For example, a battery of tests should be used and selection procedures to ensure credible and emotionally competent people to join the organization. Although there is lack of a well-established and widely researched instrument of EI recruiting and selecting employees with high levels of EI, mostly in very stress full positions, as shown in the current study, may have a positive influence on their performance at work, since they will be able to deal with stress at work more effectively (Dulewicz &Higgs, 2000).

Implications for Organizations

1. Huang et.al. (2010) said that employees in service possessing higher levels of emotional intelligence perform better as they do not react instantly or get stressed easily. Also displayed emotions of employees can act as control moves for customers.

2. In a service industry, situations that require surface acting may intervene with the real feelings of the employee and make him work under stress. Literature explains how Emotional Intelligence, can be used to cope up with this stress.

3. A few organizations today provide stress management and counselling sessions to the employees. The study reiterates that developing emotional intelligence competencies can be instrumental in reducing the stress levels of employees.

4. Moreover, the relationship between Emotional Intelligence and Role stress may also be examined under the frame of various human resources practices. For example, a battery of tests should be used in selection procedures to ensure that credible and emotionally competent people join the organization.

REFERENCES

Abraham, R. (2000). The role of job control as a moderator of emotional dissonance and emotional intelligence - outcome relationships. *The Journal of Psychology, 134*(2), 169–184. doi:10.1080/00223980009600860 PMID:10766109

Akerjordet, K., & Severinsson, E. (2008). Emotionally intelligent nurse leadership: A literature review study. *Journal of Nursing Management, 16*(5), 265–577. doi:10.1111/j.1365-2834.2008.00893.x PMID:18558927

Akerjordet, K., & Severinsson, E. (2009). Emotional intelligence, reaction and thought: A Pilot study. *Nursing & Health Sciences, 11*(3), 213–220. doi:10.1111/j.1442-2018.2009.00435.x PMID:19689628

Bar-On, R. (1997). *Bar-On Emotional Quotient Inventory (EQ-I): Technical Manual*. Toronto, Canada: Multi-Health Systems.

Blau, G. J. (1985). The measurement and prediction of career commitment. *Journal of Occupational Psychology, 58*(4), 277–288. doi:10.1111/j.2044-8325.1985.tb00201.x

Boyatzis, R. (1982). *The competent manager: a model for effective performance*. New York: John Wiley and Sons.

Bradley, G. (2007). Job tenure as a moderator of stressor-strain relations: A comparison of experienced and new-start teachers. *Work and Stress, 21*(1), 48–64. doi:10.1080/02678370701264685

Brown, R., & Brooks, I. (2002). Emotion at work: Identifying the emotional climate of night nursing. *Journal of Management in Medicine, 16*(5), 327–344. doi:10.1108/02689230210446517 PMID:12463648

Casado-Lumbreras, et al.. (2011). Culture dimensions in software development industry: The effects of mentoring. *Scientific Research and Essays, 6*(11), 2403–2412.

Chabungham, P. (2005). *The Soft Art of Being a Tough Leader*. Indian Management Journal.

Chaudhary, S., & Rathore, S. (2013). *Developing Emotional Intelligence for Workplace Success. Innovation, Social Networking and Technologies, an Approach*. Bloomsbury Publishing India Pvt. Limited.

Cheung, F. Y., & Tang, C. S. (2009). The influence of emotional intelligence and affectivity on emotional labor strategies at work. *Journal of Individual Differences, 30*(2), 75–86. doi:10.1027/1614-0001.30.2.75

Chu. (2010). The benefits of meditation vis-à-vis emotional intelligence, perceived stress and negative mental health. *Stress and Health, 26*(2), 169-180.

Colomo-Palacios, R., Casado-Lumbreras, C., Misra, S., & Soto-Acosta, P. (2012). Career abandonment intentions among software workers. *Human Factors and Ergonomics in Manufacturing & Service Industries*.

Cox, T., Griffiths, A., & Rial-Gonzalez, E. (2000). *Research on Work-Related Stress*. Luxembourg: Office for Official Publications of the European Communities.

Day, A. L., & Carroll, S. A. (2004). Using ability based measure of emotional intelligence to predict individual performance, group performance, and group Citizenship behaviours. *Personality and Individual Differences, 36*(6), 1443–1458. doi:10.1016/S0191-8869(03)00240-X

Day, A. L., Therrien, D. L., & Carroll, S. A. (2005). Predicting psychological health: Assessing the incremental validity of emotional intelligence beyond personality, Type A behaviour, and daily hassles. *European Journal of Personality, 19*(6), 519–536. doi:10.1002/per.552

Day, J. (2007). Strangers on the train the relationship of the IT department with the rest of the business. *Information Technology & People, 20*(1), 6–31. doi:10.1108/09593840710730536

Dulewicz, V., & Higgs, M. (1998). Emotional intelligence: Can it be measured reliably and validly using competency data? *Competency, 6*(1), 1–15.

Engler, N. (1998). IS managers under stress. *Computing, 12,* 44–48.

Gani, S. H. (2012). Job Stress among bank employees: A case study of selected banks. *Internatioanl Journal of Business and Managment Tomorrow, 2*(3), 1–9.

Gardner, H. (1983). *Frames of mind: The theory of multiple intelligences.* New York: Basic Books.

George, J. M. (2000). Emotions and leadership: The role of emotional intelligence. *Human Relations, 53*(8), 1027–1055. doi:10.1177/0018726700538001

Gohm, C. L., Corser, G. C., & Dalsky, D. J. (2005). Useful, unnecessary, or irrelevant? *Personality and Individual Differences, 39*(1), 1017–1028. doi:10.1016/j.paid.2005.03.018

Gohm, C. L., Corser, G. C., & Dalsky, D. J. (2005). Emotional Intelligence under stress: Useful, unnecessary, or irrelevant. *Personality and Individual Differences, 39*(6), 1017–1028. doi:10.1016/j.paid.2005.03.018

Goleman, D. (1998). *Working with emotional intelligence.* New York: Bantam.

Hapanchi, A. H., & Aurum, A. (2011). Antecedents to IT personnel's intentions to leave: A systematic literature review. *Journal of Systems and Software, 84*(2), 238–249. doi:10.1016/j.jss.2010.09.022

Higgs, M., & Aitken, P. (2003). An exploration of the relationship between emotional intelligence and leadership potential. *Journal of Managerial Psychology, 18*(8), 814–823. doi:10.1108/02683940310511890

Hirschheim, R., & Newman, M. (2010). Houston, we've had a problem...... offshoring, IS employment and the IS discipline: Perception is not reality. *Journal of Information Technology, 25*(4), 358–372. doi:10.1057/jit.2010.23

Hochschild, A. (1983). *The managed heart: Commercialization of human feeling.* Berkley, CA: University of California Press.

O'Neill, & Davis, K. (2011 *International Journal of Hospitality Management 30* 2385390 doi:10.1016/j.ijhm.2010.07.007 PMID:23794780

Karad, A. (2010). Job Stress in the Information Technology Sector-The cause and effect analysis. *Journal Of Commerce and Management Thought.*, *I*(3), 247–271.

Kaur, N. (1992). *Team Cohesion, Adjustment and Achievement motivation as related to performance and gender in team sports* (Unpublished Doctoral thesis). Dept of Physical Education, Publish University, Chandigarh, India.

Klohnen, E. C. (1996). Conceptual analysis and measurement of the construct of ego-resiliency. *Journal of Personality and Social Psychology*, *70*(2), 1067–1079. doi:10.1037/0022-3514.70.5.1067 PMID:8656335

Korunka, H. (2006). Evaluating causes and consequences of turnover intention among IT workers: The development of a questionnaire survey. *Behaviour & Information Technology*, *25*(5), 381–397. doi:10.1080/01449290500102144

Kulshrestha, . (2006). Subjective Well Being in Relation to Emotional Intelligence and Locus of Control among Executives. *Journal of the Indian Academy of Applied Psychology*, *32*(2), 93–98.

Love, P. E. D., & Irani, Z. (2007). Coping and psychological adjustment among information technology personnel. *Industrial Management & Data Systems*, *107*(6), 824–844. doi:10.1108/02635570710758743

Mayer, J. D., & Salovey, P. (1997). What is emotional intelligence? In P. Salovey & D.J. Sluyter (Eds.), Emotional Development and Emotional Intelligence: Educational Implications (pp. 3-31). New York: Basic Books.

Morrison, J. (2008). The relationship between emotional intelligence competencies and preferred conflict-handling styles. *Journal of Nursing Management*, *16*(8), 974–983. doi:10.1111/j.1365-2834.2008.00876.x PMID:19094110

Neelamegam, R., & Asrafi, S. (2010). Work Stress Among Employees of Dindigul District Central Cooperative Bank, Tamil Nadu: A Study. The IUP Journal of Management Research, 5(2), 57-69.

Nikolaou, I., & Tsaousis, I. (2002). Emotional Intelligence in the workplace: Exploring its effects on occupational stress and organizational commitment. *The International Journal of Organizational Analysis*, *10*(4), 45–65. doi:10.1108/eb028956

Pareek, U. (1993). *Making Organizational Roles Effective*. New Delhi: Tata McGraw-Hill.

Quan, J., & Cha, H. (2010). IT certifications, outsourcing and information systems personnel turnover. *Information Technology & People*, *24*(4), 330–351. doi:10.1108/09593841011087798

Rathore, S., Ningthoujam, S., & Medury, Y. (2012). Understanding Emotional Intelligence: Integrating Indo Western Perspectives. *Metamorphosis. Journal of Management Research*, *12*(2), 44–54.

Salovey, P., & Mayer, J. D. (1990). Emotional intelligence. *Imagination, Cognition and Personality*, *9*(3), 185–211. doi:10.2190/DUGG-P24E-52WK-6CDG

Sethi, V., King, R. C., & Quick, J. C. (2004). What causes stress in information system professionals? *Communications of the ACM*, *47*(3), 99–102. doi:10.1145/971617.971623

Shulman, T. E., & Hemenover, S. H. (2006). Is dispositional emotional Intelligence synonymous with personality? *Self and Identity*, *5*(2), 147–171. doi:10.1080/15298860600586206

Singh, D. (2007). Emotional Intelligence at Work; A Professional Guide (3rd ed.). Sage Publications.

Singh, S. K., & Singh, S. (2008). Managing Role Stress through Emotional Intelligence: A Study of Indian Medico Professionals. *International Journal of Indian Culture and Business Management*, *1*(4), 377–396. doi:10.1504/IJICBM.2008.018620

Slaski, M., & Cartwright, S. (2002). Health performance and Emotional Intelligence: An exploratory study of retail managers. *Stress and Health*, *18*(2), 63–68. doi:10.1002/smi.926

Soto-Acosta, P., Martínez-Conesa, I., & Colomo-Palacios, R. (2010). An empirical analysis of the relationship between IT training sources and IT value. *Information Systems Management*, *27*(3), 274–283. doi:10.1080/10580530.2010.493847

Thingujam, N. K. S., & Ram, U. (2000). Emotional Intelligence scale: Indian Norms. *Journal of Education & Psychology*, *58*, 40–44.

Thorndike, E. L. (1920). Intelligence and its use. *Harper's Magazine*, *140*, 227-235.

Wallgren, L. G. (2013). Department of Psychology, University of Gothenburg, Gothenburg, Sweden. *International Journal of Human Capital and Information Technology Professionals*, *4*(4), 1–17. doi:10.4018/ijhcitp.2013100101

Wechsler, D. (1958). *The measurement and appraisal of adult intelligence* (4th ed.). Baltimore, MD: The Williams and Wilkins Company. Kerry S. Webb, Texas Woman's University. doi:10.1037/11167-000

Yeh, C. H., Lee, G. G., & Pai, J. C. (2011). Influence of CIO'S knowledge-sharing behavior on the quality of the IS/IT strategic planning (ISSP) process in Taiwan. *African Journal of Business Management*, *5*(6), 2465–2.

Chapter 4
Employee Online Communities:
A Tool for Employee Engagement and Retention

Shirin Alavi
Jaypee Institute of Information Technology, India

ABSTRACT

This chapter seeks to impart understanding of the role of employee online communities for enhanced employee engagement and retention in an organization. The highly engaged and motivated employees would contribute more towards accomplishing the organizations goals. The various research studies conducted in the past across the world identify job satisfaction as a major determinant of employee engagement and retention. The role of internal communication through employee online communities of organizations or intranets is theoretically suggested to be a major influencer for the enhancement of employee engagement efforts. This can help to enhance and support culture, corporate values, mission statement, and annual company goals. The purpose of this chapter is to investigate the role that the employee online communities of organizations play in order to support the twin objectives of employee retention and engagement. Engaging employees can be the catalyst for inducing positive change among employees and, as a result, boosting an organization's success.

INTRODUCTION

Employee online communities are a powerful tool for managing any enterprise, but more and more organizations are realizing that these communities can be a powerful employee engagement tool as well. A more engaged employee means higher company morale, increased productivity, better collaboration and lower employee turnover. The business intranets of today harness the existing power and momentum of social networks and route them into business advantages. Improving employee management, collaboration and engagement is a goal of every organization. Employees who feel they are a part of something larger than themselves and that their work is valued tend to be more productive, innovative and loyal. A community used to contribute to this results in a higher ROI, improved bottom line and more sustainable company success.

DOI: 10.4018/978-1-5225-5297-0.ch004

The rules of building an employee community are identical to the external communities. Flexible hours and the globalization of the work force are only a few trends in the changing work environment (Asif, S., & Sargeant, A.2000) Companies are also recognizing the importance of providing creative and comfortable spaces for their employees and are building a sense of community among them by sponsoring team-building activities during business hours. The new generation of employees think not only about what they want to do, but how, when, and where they want to do it, it becomes increasingly important to think about how these businesses will communicate internally. With employees located in such diverse locations, it is important to offer a centralized way of communicating knowledge and building a strong corporate culture

An employee online community is a group of employees of an organization with some shared interest who connect and interact with each other over time. Relationship of some sort is implied. The dawn of the information age found groups communicating electronically rather than face to face. A computer mediated community uses social software to regulate the activities of the employees. These are places where employees gather to share knowledge, build recognition and tap opportunities. Initially sensed to be resource pools for value addition, where employees ventured to fulfill their need for self-actualization, participation in employee online communities and forums started as a medium for exchange of ideas and information, and now organizations have started using these communities for employee evangelism and support. To be effective in this new environment, managers must consider the strategic implications of the existence of different types of both virtual community and community participation (Kozinets, R., 1999). Employees join these forums because of the multifaceted opportunities they provide to them.. As likeminded employees converge together, these are new cliques where organizations can use internal opinion leaders for evangelism.

BACKGROUND

Employee Engagement

Almost all mangers realize that there is a direct relationship between employee engagement and financial success of an organization. Harvard.Gallup's meta-analysis of studies shows that corporations with highly engaged employees have 10 percent higher customer rates, 21 percent higher productivity and 22 percent higher profitability than those with low engagement levels. A UK taskforce found that companies with high levels of engagement had employee turnover rates 40% lower than their low-engagement-level competitors. This data supports that employee engagement matters, and yet worldwide only 13% of employees report being "engaged" at work. And fewer than half would recommend their current employer to their personal networks. Employee engagement is a vast construct that touches almost all parts of human resource management facets (Kompaso, S. M., & Sridevi, M. S. 2010). Gallup organization defines employee engagement as the involvement with and enthusiasm for work. Gallup as cited by Dernovsek (2008) likens employee engagement to a positive employees' emotional attachment and employees' commitment. Robinson et al. (2004) define employee engagement as a positive attitude held by the employee towards the organization and its value. An engaged employee is aware of business context, and works with colleagues to improve performance within the job for the benefit of the organization. The organization must work to develop and nurture engagement, which requires a two way relationship between employer and employee. The employees fail to give their best to the organization if every part of human resource is not addressed properly by an organization. The cognitive aspect of employee engagement concerns employees' beliefs about the organization, its leaders and operational conditions. The emotional aspect concerns how employees feel about each of those three factors and whether they have positive or negative attitude towards the organization and its leaders. The physical aspect of employee engagement concerns the physical energies exerted by individuals to accomplish their roles. Thus, according to Kahn (1990), engagement means to be psychologically as well as physically present when occupying and performing an organizational role. Most often employee engagement has been defined as emotional and intellectual commitment to the organisation (Baumruk, R., Gorman, B., & Gorman, R.E. 2006) or the amount of discretionary effort exhibited by employees in their job (Frank et al 2004).

The construct employee engagement is built on the foundation of earlier concepts like job satisfaction, employee commitment and organizational citizenship behaviour. Though it is related to and encompasses these concepts, employee engagement is broader in scope. Employee engagement is stronger predictor of positive organizational performance clearly showing the two-way relationship between employer and employee compared to the three earlier constructs: job satisfaction, employee commitment and organizational citizenship behaviour. Engaged employees are emotionally attached to their organization and highly involved in their job with a great enthusiasm for the success of their employer, going extra mile beyond the employment contractual agreement. The construct, employee engagement emanates from two concepts that have won academic recognition and have been the subjects of empirical research-Commitment and Organizational Citizen Behaviour (OCB) (Robinson, Perryman and Hayday, 2004). Employee engagement has similarities to and overlaps with the above two concepts. Robinson et al. (2004) state that neither commitment nor OCB reflect sufficiently two aspects of engagement-its two-way nature, and the extent to which engaged employees are expected to have an element of business awareness, even though it appears that engagement overlaps with the two concepts. Rafferty et al (2005) also distinguish employee engagement and the two prior concepts- Commitment and OCB, on the ground that engagement clearly demonstrates that it is a two-way mutual process between the employee and the organization. Fernandez (2007) shows the distinction between job satisfaction, the well-known construct in management, and engagement contending that employee satisfaction is not the same as employee engagement and since managers cannot rely on employee satisfaction to help retain the best and the brightest, employee engagement becomes a critical concept. Other researchers take job satisfaction as a part of engagement, but it can merely reflect a superficial, transactional relationship that is only as good as the organization's last round of perks and bonuses; Engagement is about passion and commitment-the willingness to invest oneself and expand one's discretionary effort to help the employer succeed, which is beyond simple satisfaction with the employment arrangement or basic loyalty to the employer (Blessing White, 2008; Erickson, 2005; Macey and Schnieder, 2008). Therefore, the full engagement equation is obtained by aligning maximum job satisfaction and maximum job contribution. Stephen Young, the executive director of Towers Perrin, also distinguishes between job satisfaction and engagement contending that only engagement (not satisfaction) is the strongest predictor of organizational performance (Human Resources, 2007). According to Penna research report (2007) meaning at work has the potential to be valuable way of bringing employers and employees closer together to the benefit of both where employees experience a sense of community, the space to be themselves and the opportunity to make a contribution, they find meaning. Employees want to work in the organizations in which they find meaning at work.. Once an employee satisfied these needs, then the employee looks to development opportunities, the possibility for promotion and then leadership style will be introduced to the mix in the model. The Blessing White (2006) study has found that almost two third's (60%) of the surveyed employees want more opportunities to grow forward to remain satisfied in their jobs. Strong manager-employee relationship is a crucial ingredient in the employee engagement and retention formula.

Employee Retention

The employment relationship is undergoing fundamental changes that have implications for the attraction, motivation and retention of talented employees (Horwitz *et al.*, 2003; Roehling *et al.*, 2000; Turnley and Feldman, 2000). Growing international competition, deregularization and globalization of markets require organizations to become more flexible in order to increase their productivity. This has reduced the job security of employees at all levels in the organization (King, 2000). At the same time HR managers are pressed to attract and retain talented employees who have competencies that are critical for organizational survival (Horwitz *et al.*, 2003; Mitchell *et al.*, 2001; Roehling *et al.*, 2000; Steel *et al.*, 2002). Often, however, those employees are difficult to retain because they attach more importance to marking out their own career path than to organizational loyalty; a tendency which results in increased rates of voluntary turnover (Cappelli, 2001).Not surprisingly, then, retention management has become a popular concept within the HRM literature. It refers to the portfolio of HR practices that organizations develop to reduce voluntary turnover rates (Cappelli, 2001; Mitchell *et al.*, 2001; Steel *et al.*, 2002). Another concept that has gained interest as a construct relevant for understanding and managing contemporary employment relationships is the psychological contract, which refers to employees subjective interpretations and evaluations of their employment deal (Rousseau, 1996, 2001; Turnley and Feldman, 1998). Researchers in this field argue that for retention management to be effective, it is not only important to create an optimal portfolio of HR practices, but also to manage employees perceptions regarding what their organization has promised them in return for their loyalty and commitment. So, while retention management addresses the type of organizational inducements and HR strategies that are effective in reducing voluntary employee turnover, the psychological contract focuses on employees' subjective interpretations of those promised inducements and the relationship with employee outcomes including intentions to stay.In order to create a successful company, employers should consider as many options as possible when it comes to retaining employees, while at the same time securing their trust and loyalty so that they have less of desire to leave in future.. The costs associated with turnover may include lost customers, business and damaged morale. In addition there are the hard costs of time spent in screening, verifying credentials, references, interviewing, hiring, and training the new employee just to get back to where you started. In today's environment it becomes very important for organizations to retain their employees. When an employee leaves, he takes with him valuable knowledge about the company, customers, current projects and past history (sometimes to competitors). Often much time and money has been spent on the employee in expectation of a future return. When the employee leaves, the investment on him is not realized. Customers and clients do business with a company in part because of the people. Relationships are developed that encourage continued sponsorship of the business. When an employee leaves, the relationships that he built for the company are severed leading to potential customer loss.

Employees as Customers of a Business

In the recent past (Cardy & Lengnick Hall 2011) have presented an interesting study which relates employee turnover and employee satisfaction. The outcome of the study depicts that employee satisfaction is higher in those organizations where employees are treated as parallel to a customer. This has helped organizations to understand the factors that contribute in making employees stick to their organizations in the same manner as a satisfied customer is loyal to an organization. The customer equity is concerned with the long term and future value of a customer rather than the immediate profitability of products or services in the similar manner employee life time value depends not only on the immediate value or quality of contribution of the employee to an organization but also on the length of relationship between the employee and the organization. Thus an employee who has contributed highly to the business but stays with the business for a short time may have lower life time value as compared to an employee whose contribution is of substantially lower quality for the same period but who stays with the business for a longer period of time. Employee equity in turn depends on the total discounted life time value of an employee.

Demographics and Significance of Employee Online Communities

The demographic composition of the employee population has also changed to include people of all ages, different cultures, educational backgrounds, and experience and technical skills. Hence employee online communities appear to have significant potential for organizations trying to interact and build relationships with their employees. Here employee orientation is given a new meaning and the contents and processes of exchange between companies and employees are reconsidered if firms want to retain their employees and cooperate with them (Smidts, A., Pruyn, A., & Riel, C. 2001). What deserves a significant mention is that employee online communities represent a set of core values like company culture, building employee perceived value, conviviality, and strong democracy, thereby building employee equity and employee retention.

There is a concept of empathy and trust prevalent in employee online communities as it is said that greater similarities amongst employees forge better understanding. Furthermore, when employees discover they have similar problems, requirements, opinions or experience, they may feel closer, more trusting and be prepared to reveal even more. This has a "snowball effect" in that the more people discover that they are similar to each other, the more they tend to like each other and the more they will disclose about themselves. This is known as "self disclosure reciprocity" and it is powerful online. The reciprocity can be in the form of exchanges of the same kind of aid or helping a mutual friend in the network. Even if reciprocity does not happen immediately, it can happen months or years later, possibly with another person in the community. In healthy communities, reciprocity is a general and accepted norm amongst members.

Employee online communities have *policies*, in the form of tacit assumptions, rituals, protocols, rules, and laws that guide people's interactions. One of the other important constituents of the community dynamics, i.e. the purpose for the existence and creation of the community from the perspective of the company, aims at obtaining increased efficiency, serving as a breeding ground for innovative ideas, and building stronger relationships. To provide them with a better management and technical support, a systematic analysis of the community dynamics is required. The community's internal structural dynamics also influence members' ongoing participation. 'People', the possible customers, which are one of the important constituents of the community dynamics can be divided into four groups, namely by the geography, demography, topic or profession. Use of cyberspace, usage of computer based information technology to support the activities in an online community, communication and interactivity, content typology as driven by community participants and value of volume and frequency of participation (Lee, F.S., Vogel D., Limayem M., 2003) are significant parameters of online communities. There are five stages in community evolution: A potential stage, in which initial connections are developed, a building stage for context and community memory creation, an engaged stage which focuses on access to one another and community learning, an active stage in which serious collaboration starts, an adaptive stage for innovation and generation (McDermott, 2000) (Wenger, 2002), (Gongla and Rizutto, 2001). A successful online community should be able to achieve its purpose. (e.g. targets can be hard like creating a new methodology as well as soft like leveraging collective intellect.) But some goals are highly measurable and some were highly resistant to quantification. The amount and quality of participation is considered as the primary indicator of success (Cothrel, J. and Williams, R., 1999). Employees in these communities may not only be able to develop innovations that can be integrated into the firm, but also may come up with new perspectives on and ways of framing problems.

In an employee online community, the members share the same physical space i.e. co-presence and have access to shared resources. Co-presence breeds kinship amongst employees. These members have a shared goal, interest, need or activity that provides the primary reason for belonging to the community. If organizations seed these communities with their internal evangelists and they are able to become opinion leaders, they can influence the opinion and decision of entire employee communities. Employees are engaged in repeated, active participation and there are often immense interactions, strong emotional ties and shared activities occurring between participants. Reciprocity of information, support and services between members is thus obvious. These communities can be used for Employee Engagement which ultimately leads to Employee Empowerment. These communities act as catalysts for strengthening the bond between company and employees, building long lasting relationships with the employees, creating, maintaining and tightening the feedback loop, identification and resolution of employee issues, creating employee loyalty through personal investment in order to maintain competitive business edge. These communities allow for greater interactivity among members giving boost to self-disclosure reciprocity. These communities are also a useful complement to employee relationship management solutions. Last but not the least, these employee communities help companies to design a path for growth and change.

For organizations, attracting online community users is not an end in itself, as the goal is to have people share information or contribute ideas and the community is a means of achieving this goal. As a result, organizational efforts tend to focus more on the results and less on the dynamics of the community which may not be correct. The online community managers should devote significant time in understanding who members are, what is the nature of their work, what tools and skills they have, who they work with and share knowledge with, and most importantly what kinds of knowledge tools and relationships they want and need. In some organizations where community members have a high level of subject matter knowledge, comfort with technology and access to a superior quality infrastructure, the online community is almost entirely self sustaining. But in most cases the online communities require a significant investment of time and effort to maintain and sometimes this effort is even greater than the effort required to launch the community.

Formal Roles in Maintaining Employee Online Community

In some organizations where community members have a high level of subject matter knowledge, comfort with technology and access to a superior quality infrastructure, the employee online community is almost entirely self sustaining. But in most cases these communities require a significant investment of time and effort to maintain and sometimes this effort is even greater than the effort required to launch the community.

The most commonly cited formal roles in maintaining the communities are:

1. Subject Matter expert,
2. Knowledge Manager,
3. Moderator
4. Help Desk

A Knowledge Manager is a person who does some kind of manipulation of online content, ranging from editing to categorizing and archiving. They also have other responsibilities relating to supporting the employee online community. Often online community managers personally solicit participation from individuals who they thought could offer value to the community. Further, the type of industry in which the organization operates is very important. In industries characterized by a rapid change the employee online communities tend to be more active. Employees struggling with complex new problems are compelled to seek out others with more experience. Here the usage of online tools in an organization is linked to the leadership style. As observed, the introverts and extroverts adapted very differently to online tools. The introverts sometimes take a more active role in online discussions depending on their comfort with the technology and confidence in conveying their thoughts by writing. In contrast extroverts often failed to adapt to the online environment since their strongest temptation is to pick up a phone and call someone. As observed, majority of employee online communities use some kind of event to build the traffic or increase participation in the community. 3/5th of these events are online events either on line training or web events in which members are able to hear from experts, ask questions or air views. Physical events like "promotional tours" can be introduced to the prospective members and a celebratory event that recognized participation of leading members can be conducted. Informal roles are a good indicator for the health of a community. *When members are willing to serve in informal roles, it means that the community is an entity that people value and want to be part of. Some common informal roles include:*

1. **Community Advocate:** Employees who are major supporters of the online community often take an active role in encouraging others to participate. These people also get involved in setting guidelines or organizing community activities.
2. **Leader:** They possess superior knowledge and expertise and are respected and acknowledged by other members. They play an important role in the evolution of the community. Experts serve as informal leaders and are essential in creating the boundaries of discussion. They are permitted to stretch the boundaries thus allowing the discussion to grow and change over time. The presence of these experts is also one of the many draws that bring other employees online as knowledge seekers go where the answers are.
3. **Instigator:** These members distinguish themselves by raising important but controversial issues. This role is more common in Internet communities, but can occur in any online group.

Employee Online Communities Life Cycle

The first stage in the employee online community life-cycle is inception. At *inception*, the idea for an employee online community emerges because of members needs for information, support, recreation, or relationships. Depending on the type of need, interested individuals, begin forming a vision for a community where people can disseminate information, communicate, and interact (Wegner et al. 2002). In addition to the vision, incipient communities begin with a focus and some rules of behaviour and communication, which helps the communities, maintain focus. Once the vision is clear, the required technological components, including Internet applications such as email, listserv, bulletin board, discussion forums, or chats, may be selected and gradually incorporated, responding to the needs and preferences of creators and initial and potential members. The *creation* of the employee online community begins when these technological components are in place and when the initial group of members can begin to interact and spread the word for other members to join (Malhotra et al. 1997).

In time and when enough members have joined, a culture and identity for the community begins to develop. Members start using a common vocabulary and, as the community grows, members select the roles they will play in the community. Additionally, communication and participation etiquette rules surface. Some members lead discussions, some provide support, while many look for support and information. Some members become leaders while others become followers or lurkers, who read messages posted by other members but do not actively, contribute to the community. Some volunteer information while others use this information (Maloney Krichmar D., and Preece J., 2005; Butler et al. 2005; Nonnecke and Preece 2000; Ridings et al. 2006). These characteristics, common to both online and physical communities, initiate the *growth* stage of the employee online community. As the employee online community matures the need for a more explicit and formal organization with regulations, rewards for contributions, subgroups, and discussion of more or less specific topics is evident. In this stage, the community is strengthened and trust and lasting relationships begin to emerge. Throughout the life of the community, new members join in and old members whose needs are satisfied or whose initial excitement for joining the community wears down leave the community. As new members join, the community evolves and a cycle of interaction repeats. New members bring new ideas for discussion and their roles change (Nonnecke and Preece 2001; Burkett 2006). Many communities thrive in this stage for long periods. Other communities change course, or add new features to maintain user interest, iterating in a mature state. Still others lose momentum and member interest completely and begin to *die* down when they face poor participation, lack of quality content, unorganized contributions, and transient membership (Jarvenpaa S. L. and Knoll K., 1998). Activities and needs of members change in each stage of the employee online community evolution. Each stage requires different tools, features, mechanisms, technologies, and management activities. Developers in an organization have to identify the needs in each stage and add the right technology components that will better support the community, in the way the information systems life cycle prescribe. Thus matching features with each community life-cycle stage may more efficiently lead to success.

MAIN FOCUS OF THE CHAPTER

An employee online community is a potential source of loyalty, commitment, and increased retention of employees. These create value for all the employees of an organization. They can be used for value exploration in the employee cognitive space and enhancement of the employee equity of the firm. When enough employees actively participate, and as relationships, trust, and reciprocity build up in the community, the community fulfills its goals and can even achieve collective goals and actions for the benefit of all. Thus the features of employee online communities which make them part of the value delivering and enhancing mechanisms in organizations range from co-presence, reciprocity, building trust and conviviality. These features have well defined roles to play in building relationships with employees and furthering the employee relationship management goals of the organization. The following features of employee online communities have been identified through extensive literature review.

SOLUTIONS AND RECOMMENDATIONS

Employee engagement improves the personal attitudes of employees as well as their performance and behavior on the job. Engaged employees report higher job satisfaction, are more likely to be proactive, are more committed to the organization and are less likely to seek other opportunities. The employee online communities provide a platform for collaboration on ideas and chatting about work with employees irrespective of time zones and geographical boundaries that is impossible in a real life setting. The following steps are recommended to maximize employee engagement using an online community.

- **Enhanced Interface and Communication:** Employees at all levels desire to feel that they are as valuable as top management. Many organizations fail to apprehend that employee engagement can be improved through employee online communities. These communities are a built in channel for communication, collaboration and organization wide interaction that can make employees at all levels feel that they are important for the success of the organization.
- **Existing Employee Engagement Programs Should Be Linked to Online Community:** The employee online community can be used to support the objectives of the existing employee engagement programs by implementing things like transparent leadership communications, online Q&A, information sharing and public acknowledgement of goals and rewards. Some of the employee engagement programs that could be linked to an employee online community could be innovation award programs, Idea jam sessions, employee recognition programs, employee volunteer programs and group health challenges.
- **Low Power Distance Between Leaders and Employees:** In order to increase engagement the leaders of any organization can participate in an ask me anything session in an online community .A list of questions can be prepared in advance and employees are asked to post questions in a community group dedicated to the event .
- **User Friendliness and Ease of Navigation:** The community should be as user friendly as possible to minimize confusion and maximize benefits. Complexity will be necessary for some applications, but simplicity for the user should be a priority. Benefits of collaboration and increased employee engagement will be enhanced by a more user-friendly system.
- **Provides Platform for Expression:** The community must allow the employees to share their opinions and ideas in a manner that they are heard and responded. This will elevate their respect and loyalty towards the organization
- **Positive Vibes:** The environment of the community should be based upon a foundation of mutual respect. Any other type of communication should not be tolerated, as the community should always remain a safe and supportive place for employees to feel secure in expressing themselves

Table 1.

Participation	A new type of communities is gaining momentum on the web and is reshaping online communication and collaboration patterns and the way information is consumed and produced (Kolbitsch., J.and Maurer, H., 2006). A community can further serve as a value delivery mechanism to enhance the perceived value to the employees and stimulating greater content contribution and participation. Individual desires for self actualization, belonging to a group and gaining prestige facilitate participation and mutually maximize the collective intelligence of the participants. The value attributed to these applications is not based on the classic employee value approach, but rather on some feeling of achievement through personal gratification. The incentives offered by employee online communities can lead to higher levels of participation. A community participant is both a member and a user who is also a virtual value initiator for other members (Sangwan., S. 2005).
Degree of Participation	The degree of participation of employees in an online community primarily depends on the member's ability to navigate the internet and around the community. High interactivity with other employees, reciprocity, volume of content contributed by a member and ability to provide correct responses to other members leads to higher degree of participation. Thus higher levels of degree of participation are related to purposive values and self interest. Communication is multi-directional with members responsible for both providing material and consuming information. As more content is available, members find the community even more valuable and degree of participation increases. The content generation can break down if members feel unappreciated or apathetic. The most valuable members and their actions should be rewarded or at least acknowledged. Even a link to their contribution or a status indicator under their name is sufficient. Sometimes having a list of top contributors displayed on the main page of the community will boost at least their ego. If an individual participates more heavily than others in the same online community at a given time, it indicates that he or she expects higher benefits from participating than others at that time, either because of high value of participation, high expected benefits, low perceived participation costs or lack of other alternatives. Thus the higher an individual's level of participation at a given time as compared to other participants, the more likely the individual will continue in the community in the immediate future.
Emotional Attachment	It refers to the members' relationships and attachments within online communities. (Blanchard, A.L., 2004) and (Blanchard, A.L., and Markus, M.L., 2004) studied sense of community including feelings of belonging, safety, and attachment to the group. When these feelings are present, employees develop lasting relationships with other employees, feel attachment to the community, and perceive the online community as a source of emotional support. In one specific employee online community, it was found that active participants develop personal friendships that in some cases move into private and face-to-face interactions.
Online Trust	In simple terms trust can be defined as the belief by one party about another party that the other party will behave in a predictable manner. Trust refers to employee willingness to rely on an exchange partner, in whom one has confidence, and it can be a multifaceted construct and it can be transformed to value and employee loyalty. Trust in the e-vendor is one of the critical factors of success in e-commerce (Torkzadeh, G., Dhillon, G., 2002).Online trust continues to be important as customers and other stakeholders such as employees, suppliers, distributors and regulators now have access to more information and options on the Web, making it critical for firms to earn and retain the trust of their current or potential employees and other stakeholders thus an understanding of how online trust is created and maintained can lead to improved web sites, sales revenues, profitability and ultimately shareholder value. Credibility and benevolence are the underlying dimensions of trust (Shanker, Sultan, 2002). Online Trust is positively associated with returns on employee relationship management initiatives because employee relationship management is focused on targeted employee segments and effective communication and interaction with these segments and employees is directly related to Online Trust. Trust can be defined as "the willingness of a party to be vulnerable to the actions of another party based on the expectation that the other will perform a particular action important to the trustor" (Mooradian T., Renzl B., and Matzler K., 2006).Online trust is important in both business-to-business and business-to-consumer e-business. Consumers and businesses, feeling the pressure of economic downturn and terrorism, increasingly look to buy from and do business with organizations with the most trusted Web sites and electronic networks. Companies' perception of online trust has steadily evolved from being a construct involving security and privacy issues on the Internet to a multidimensional, complex construct that includes reliability/ credibility, emotional comfort and quality for multiple stakeholders such as employees, suppliers, distributors and regulators, in addition to customers. Further, trust online spans the end-to-end aspects of e-business rather than being just based on the electronic storefront.
Commitment	A commitment to the community leads to volunteering, willingness to help coordinate and manage the community and an audience for online postings and messages. Both employees and businesses need to be committed to the community. (Anderson and Weitz., 1989), (Wilson and Mummalaneni., 1990) and (Mummalaneni and Wilson., 1991) present models of relationship development where factors such as trust, satisfaction, social bonds and relational investments are said to impact the development of commitment. Employee loyalty is usually taken to be an indication of the existence of a relationship and some commitment to the organization on the part of the employee. Commitment and loyalty are generally linked to value creation. A commitment perspective focuses on the psychological attachment to a community that makes employees in a community think positively about it, leading them to stay with the organization for a long period of time and continuously contribute to it (Meyer, J.P., and Allen, N.J., 1991; Meyer, J.P., and Allen, N.J., 1997).
Employee Loyalty	Employee loyalty promotes value to members through increased usage and user satisfaction. Peer-to-peer interaction relies on both the number of users and their intensity of use. The development of employee loyalty involves building and sustaining a relationship with an employee, which leads to the repeated purchase of products or services over a given period of time. A loyal employee base allows employee online communities to devote their energies to business matters (Gefen, D., 2002; Rowley, J., & Dawes, J., 2000). Employees can demonstrate their loyalty in several ways. They can choose to stay with the community, draw other members to join the community, participate in case of new product development and respond if the company asks for a feedback. Employees engaged through these online communities can become an important source of competitive advantage where loyal employees become competitive assets.The organizations through these communities should give special treatment to loyal employees by giving recognition in identity, expertise and other extrinsic rewards in the form of gift, social recognition and feedback (Ireberri, A. and Leroy,G.,2009).
Reciprocity	It represents a pattern of behaviour where employees respond to friendly or hostile actions with similar actions even if no material gains are expected. Furthermore when employees discover they have similar problems, requirements, opinions or experiences they may feel closer, more trusting and be prepared to reveal even more.
Attitude Towards Switching	The employee online communities help in enhancing employee loyalty, employee satisfaction and involvement which are the three main factors that will not let the employees switch over from the organization. The employee online communities further help the firms in formulating relevant appraisal strategies based on the switching behaviour of the employees.

and being treated well. Effective communication, positive interaction and respectful responses are vital in creating a community that increases employee engagement.

- **Content Organization:** The content that should be shared in the community should be beneficial for employees. From industry articles and trends to employee tips and tools, sharing useful content helps workers to feel supported. Content can be articles, blog posts, videos, audios or photos. Employees should also be encouraged to share content via the community if it fits with company specifications and guidelines for relevance and appropriateness.

- **Platform for fun and Humour:** A community is a business tool that is intended to improve workflow and engagement; it shouldn't be just about being serious and business like all of the time. A sense of humour can go a long way in promoting employee engagement and morale, as long as it is handled in a professional manner. Programs like "Fun Fridays" can be introduced where employees can share some thought provoking or entertaining item via the community. In line with making room for entertainment, there should also be a thread or area where employees are allowed to discuss non-work topics with co-workers on breaks or after hours. This could take the form of a chat room or forum that's just for socialisation. Fostering personal connections among employees makes them more likely to value their job and keep working there.

- **Timely Feedback:** As the community is created, launched and used, time should be taken to elicit direct employee feedback. A short survey asking employees to rate different aspects of the community as well as their overall opinion will offer feedback about its utility and effectiveness. A mixture of questions with 0 to 10 ratings as well as open-ended questions allowing employees to give details can be very useful in measuring engagement and finding out how the community could be strengthened further.

- **Flexible Procedures:** A community can allow for flexibility in changing processes, procedures, workflow and other aspects of the work on demand. A flexible atmosphere and ease of change enhances engagement. With easier, more efficient communication, changes can be rolled out and enacted in hours or days instead of weeks or months. Businesses should take advantage of the speed and efficiency of a community to keep business procedures as streamlined and up to date as possible. Central document storage, video tutorials, online meetings and instant messaging can all help to spread the word about internal changes

CONCLUSION

Employee online communities are a powerful tool for attaining the twin objectives of employee engagement and retention. The drivers of employee engagement are complex, and studies suggest that everything matters be it the office environment or the meaningfulness of the corporate mission, but virtually all of these studies agree that employee engagement increases when three things happen: 1. Employees clearly understand how their job contributes to the corporate mission – how they can personally make a difference. 2. High performers are publicly recognized for their efforts. 3. Leadership closes the loop, providing frequent, transparent updates on the success of corporate initiatives and changes in corporate strategy. Each of these actions requires information sharing. Thus the employee online communities have become essential for employee engagement in all organizations irrespective of size. If an employee poses a question in the community some other employee will have that same question tomorrow, next week, or next year. Rather than asking the question again, employee can search discussions, resource libraries, and other text-based content to find the answer quickly. This creates an easy way for employees to tap into the knowledge of all current and past employees in one site. The access to knowledge can quickly increase productivity, efficiency, and quality of work irrespective of the industry vertical. In order to utilize the full potential of these communities the organizations should focus on the features of online communities namely participation, degree of participation, emotional attachment, online trust, commitment, employee loyalty, reciprocity and attitude towards switching. Online communities sustain if employees participate. Companies will benefit if they are able to solicit long term employee participation which results in developing employee relationship capital. The ability of an employee online community to increase the credibility of the organization and improve communication across varied organizational functions can be achieved by resolving the problems of employees aptly, increasing inter employee reliability and creating an environment which mitigates employee uncertainty.

REFERENCES

Anderson, E., & Weitz, B. (1989). Determinants of continuity in conventional industrial channel dyad. *Marketing Science*, 8(4), 310–323. doi:10.1287/mksc.8.4.310

Asif, S., & Sargeant, A. (2000). Modelling internal communication in the financial services sector. *European Journal of Marketing*, 34(3/4), 299–317. doi:10.1108/03090560010311867

Baumruk, R., Gorman, B., & Gorman, R. E. (2006). Why managers are crucial to increasing engagement. *Strategic HR Review*, 5(2), 24–27. doi:10.1108/14754390680000863

Blanchard, A. L. (2004). The effects of dispersed virtual communities on face-to-face social capital. In Social Capital and Information Technology. MIT Press.

Blanchard, A. L., & Markus, M. L. (2004). The experienced sense of a virtual community: Characteristics and processes. Data Base Advance Information System, 35(1), 65–79.

Blessing White. (2006). *Employee Engagement Report 2006*. BlessingWhite, Inc. Available: www.blessingwhite.com

Blessing White. (2008). *The Employee Engagement Equation in India*. Presented by BlessingWhite and HR Anexi. Available: www.blessingwhite.com

Burkett, S. (2006). Scott Burkett's pothole of the infobahm: The life cycle of online community members [Weblog post]. Retrieved from http://www.scottburkett.com/intek/php/online-communities/2006-01-09/the-lifecycleof- online-community-members.html

Butler, . (2005). Community effort in online groups: Who does the work and why. In S. Weisband & L. Atwater (Eds.), *Leadership at a Distance*. Mahwah, NJ: Lawrence Erlbaum Associates Inc.

Cappelli, P. (2001). A market-driven approach to retaining talent. Harvard Business Review, 27-50.

Cardy, R. L., & Lengnick-Hall, M. L. (2011). Will they stay or will they go? Exploring a customer-oriented approach to employee retention. *Journal of Business and Psychology*, 26(2), 213–217. doi:10.1007/s10869-011-9223-8

Cothrel, J., & Williams, R. (1999). Online Communities helping them form and grow. *Journal of Knowledge Management, 3*(1), 54–60. doi:10.1108/13673279910259394

Dernovsek, D. (2008). *Creating highly engaged and committed employee starts at the top andends at the bottom line Credit Union Magazine, May 2008.* Credit Union National Association, Inc.

Erickson, T.J. (2005). *Testimony submitted before the US Senate Committee on Health, Education, Labour and Pensions, May 26.* Academic Press.

Fernandez, C. P. (2007). Employee engagement. *Journal of Public Health Management and Practice.* Available: http://find.galegroup.com

Frank, F. D., Finnegan, R. P., & Taylor, C. R. (2004). The race for talent: Retaining and engaging workers in the 21st century. *Human Resource Planning, 27*(3), 12–25.

Gefen, D. (2002). Customer loyalty in e-commerce. *Journal of the Association for Information Systems, 3*, 27-51.

Gongla, P., & Rizzuto, C. R. (2001). Evolving Communities of Practice: IBM Global Services Experience. *IBM Systems Journal, 40*(4), 842–862. doi:10.1147/sj.404.0842

Horwitz, F. M., Heng, C. T., & Quazi, H. A. (2003). Finders, keepers? Attracting, motivating and retaining knowledge workers. *Human Resource Management Journal, 13*(4), 23–44. doi:10.1111/j.1748-8583.2003.tb00103.x

Human Resources. (2007). *Research: Employee engagement ROI-rules of engagement.* Available: http://global.factiva.com/ha/default.aspx

Iriberri, A., & Leroy, G. (2009). A life cycle perspective on online community Success. *ACM Computing Surveys, 41*(2), 11. doi:10.1145/1459352.1459356

Jarvenpaa, S.L., & Knoll, K. (1998). Is anybody out there Antecedents of trust in global virtual teams. *Journal of Management Information System, 14*, 29–65.

Kahn, W. A. (1990). Psychological conditions of personal engagement and disengagement at work. *Academy of Management Journal, 33*(4), 692–724. doi:10.2307/256287

King, J. E. (2000). White-collar reactions to job insecurity and the role of the psychological contract: Implications for human resource management. *Human Resource Management, 39*(1), 79–92. doi:10.1002/(SICI)1099-050X(200021)39:1<79::AID-HRM7>3.0.CO;2-A

Kolbitsch, J., & Maurer, H. (2006). The Transformation of the Web: How Emerging Communities Shape the Information We Consume. *Journal of Universal Computer Science, 12*(2), 187–213.

Kompaso, S. M., & Sridevi, M. S. (2010). Employee engagement: The key to improving performance. *International Journal of Business and Management, 5*(12), 89. doi:10.5539/ijbm.v5n12p89

Kozinets, R. (1999). E tribalized marketing: The strategic implications of virtual communities of consumption. European Management Journal, 17(3), 252-264.

Lee, F.S., Vogel, D., & Limayem, M. (2003). Virtual Community Informatics: A review and research agenda. *The Journal of Information Technology Theory and Application, 5*(1), 47-61.

Macey, W. H., & Schneider, B. (2008). The Meaning of Employee Engagement. *Industrial and Organizational Psychology: Perspectives on Science and Practice, 1*(01), 3–30. doi:10.1111/j.1754-9434.2007.0002.x

Malhotra. (1997). Evolution of a virtual community: Understanding design issues through a longitudinal study. *Proceedings of the Eighteenth International Conference on Information Systems.*

Maloney Krichmar, D., & Preece, J. (2005). A multilevel analysis of sociability, usability, and community dynamics in an online health community. ACM Trans. Comput-Hum. Interaction, 12(2), 1–232.

McDermott, R. (2000). Community Development as a Natural Step: Five Stages of Community Development. *Knowledge Management Review, 3*(5).

Meyer, J. P., & Allen, N. J. (1991). A three-component conceptualization of organizational commitment. *Human Resource Management Review, 1*(1), 61–89. doi:10.1016/1053-4822(91)90011-Z

Meyer, J. P., & Allen, N. J. (1997). *Commitment in the workplace: Theory, research, and application.* Newbury Park, CA: Sage.

Mitchell, T. R., Holtom, B. C., & Lee, T. W. (2001). How to keep your best employees: Developing an effective retention policy. *The Academy of Management Executive, 15*(4), 96–109. doi:10.5465/AME.2001.5897929

Mooradian, T., Renzl, B., & Matzler, K. (2006). Who trusts? Personality, trust and knowledge sharing. *Journal of Management Learning, 37*(4), 523–540. doi:10.1177/1350507606073424

Mummalaneni, V., & Wilson, D. (1991). *The influence of close personal relationships between a buyer and a seller on the continued stability of the role relationships* (Working Paper 4). Institute for the Study of Business Markets, Pennsylvania State University.

Nonnecke, B., & Preece, J. (2000). Lurker demographics: Counting the silent. In *Proceedings of the SigchiI Conference on Human Factors in Computing Systems.* ACM Press. doi:10.1145/332040.332409

Nonnecke, B., & Preece, J. (2001). Why lurkers lurk. *Proceedings of the Seventh Americas Conference on Information Systems.*

Penna. (2007). *Meaning at Work Research Report.* Available: http:// www. e-penna.com/ newsopinion/ research.aspx

Rafferty, A. M., Maben, J., West, E., & Robinson, D. (2005). *What makes a good employer?* Issue Paper 3 International Council of Nurses Geneva.

Ridings. (2006). Psychological barriers: Lurker and poster motivations and behaviour in online communities. Commun. AIS, 18, 329–354.

Robinson, D., Perryman, S., & Hayday, S. (2004). *The Drivers of Employee Engagement Report 408.* Institute for Employment Studies.

Robinson, D., Perryman, S., & Hayday, S. (2004). *The Drivers of Employee Engagement.* Brighton, UK: Institute for Employment Studies.

Roehling, M. V., Cavanaugh, M. A., Moynihan, L. M., & Boswell, W. (2000). The nature of the new employment relationship: A content analysis of the practitioner and academic literatures. *Human Resource Management, 39*(4), 305–320. doi:10.1002/1099-050X(200024)39:4<305::AID-HRM3>3.0.CO;2-V

Rousseau, D. M. (1996). Changing the deal while keeping the people. *The Academy of Management Executive, 10,* 50–58.

Rousseau, D. M. (2001). The idiosyncratic deal: Flexibility versus fairness? *Organizational Dynamics, 29*(4), 260–273. doi:10.1016/S0090-2616(01)00032-8

Rowley, J., & Dawes, J. (2000). Disloyalty: A closer look at non-loyals. *Journal of Consumer Marketing, 17*(6), 538-549.

Sangwan, S. (2005). Virtual Community Success: A Uses and Gratifications Perspective. *Proceedings of the 38th Annual Hawaii International Conference.* doi:10.1109/HICSS.2005.673

Shankar, V., Urban, G.L., & Sultan, F. (2002). Online Trust: a stakeholder perspective, concepts, implications and future directions. *Journal of Strategic Information Systems, 11,* 325–344.

Smidts, A., Pruyn, A., & Riel, C. (2001). The impact of employee communication and perceived external prestige on organizational identification. *Academy of Management Journal, 49*(5), 1051–1062. doi:10.2307/3069448

Steel, R. P. (2002). Turnover theory at the empirical interface: Problems of fit and function. *Academy of Management Review, 27,* 346–360.

Torkzadeh, G., & Dhillon, G. (2002). Measuring factors that influence the success of internet commerce. *Information Systems Research, 13*(2), 187–204. doi:10.1287/isre.13.2.187.87

Turnley, W. H., & Feldman, D. C. (1998). Psychological contract violation during corporate restructuring. *Human Resource Management, 37*(1), 71–83. doi:10.1002/(SICI)1099-050X(199821)37:1<71::AID-HRM7>3.0.CO;2-S

Turnley, W. H., & Feldman, D. C. (2000). Re-examining the effects of psychological contract violations: Unmet expectations and job dissatisfaction as mediators. *Journal of Organizational Behavior, 21*(1), 25–42. doi:10.1002/(SICI)1099-1379(200002)21:1<25::AID-JOB2>3.0.CO;2-Z

Wegner, . (2002). *Cultivating Communities of Practice: A Guide to Managing Knowledge.* Cambridge, MA: Harvard Business School Press.

Wegner, . (2002). *Cultivating Communities of Practice: A Guide to ManagingKnowledge.* Cambridge, MA: Harvard Business School Press.

Wilson, D. T., & Mummalaneni, V. (1990). Bonding and commitment in buyer-seller relationships: a preliminary conceptualisation. In D. Ford (Ed.), *Understanding Business Markets* (pp. 408–420). London: Academic Press, Harcourt Brace Jovanovich.

Chapter 5

The Need for Multi-Disciplinary Approaches and Multi-Level Knowledge for Cybersecurity Professionals

Eleni Berki
University of Tampere, Finland

Juri Valtanen
University of Tampere, Finland

Sunil Chaudhary
Deerwalk Institute of Technology, Nepal

Linfeng Li
Beijing Institute of Petrochemical Technology, China

ABSTRACT

Cybersecurity professionals face increased demand to acquire the knowledge and develop the skills required to keep citizens safe from cyberattacks, predict the latter with scientific methods, and advance citizens' social awareness. A proactive multidisciplinary approach against cyberattacks is effective via the combination of multidisciplinary and multi-professional knowledge. Increased public awareness with total quality multi-domain knowledge and social computing skills is likely to decrease cyberattacks' victims and improve cyber systems quality in general. This chapter 1) outlines the basic multidisciplinary research needs and multilevel strategic steps to be taken for timely citizens' protection, and 2) proposes multidisciplinary strategic research approaches and multilevel adult education directions for improving cybersystems' total quality management through collaborative research and by focusing on: a) increasing public awareness, b) predicting cyberattacks, and c) utilising multidisciplinary and multi-professional knowledge in social computing approaches.

DOI: 10.4018/978-1-5225-5297-0.ch005

INTRODUCTION

Every day multiple deceitful and convincing attempts with trustworthy content, known as *social engineering* techniques, occur through various communication and dissemination means and, most notably, through the Internet. Hence, thousands of people are convinced to reveal personal, vulnerable information such as social security ids, bank account details, home and email addresses, and the list can go on. For instance, online identity theft and (online) *phishing* are examples of social engineering that is often associated to cyberattacks, by obtaining and using personal information. Social engineering is the psychological manipulation of people in order to make them divulge their confidential information or perform activities which can be harmful for security and privacy (see Harley, 1998; Hadnagy, 2011; Berki et al., 2014; Heartfield & Loukas, 2015). In common terms social engineering can also be understood as *hacking the human factor in cybersecurity*. In fact, social engineers have socio-psychological knowledge, technical skills and they have been associated with dark creativity and deceitful information acquisition and processing. The social engineers become more and more sophisticated and they are familiar with knowledge from many scientific domains. Notably, social engineers and social engineering resembled, once, terms of positive connotations and application of interdisciplinary knowledge from socio-technical domains for societal problem solving.

Notwithstanding, deceiving citizens to reveal theirs and others' credentials is considered unethical and raises questions related to law and order. Undoubtedly, it would be beneficial for the State, science and society to i) know and ii) be able to timely predict the frequency of social engineering activities that compromise the citizens' confidentiality, privacy and safety. Hence, a relevant research question here could be the following:

- **Research Question:** What types of multidisciplinary knowledge and skills do cybersecurity professionals need in order to i) proactively advice citizens and ii) predict the time and frequency of cyberattacks and other social engineering attempts that compromise privacy and safety?

Combining and advancing *multiprofessional* knowledge and social awareness can result in better and *timely* protection of citizens' vulnerability and privacy. *Multidisciplinary* education is sometimes used interchangeably with multiprofessional education meaning *occasions when professions learn side by side for whatever reason* while interprofessional education *occurs when students or members of two or more professions learn with, from and about each other to improve collaboration and the quality of care* (Barr & Low, 2013). Such a trustworthy multilevel and multidisciplinary approach to cybersecurity can encourage citizens' active participation in society and could eventually have a long term social impact, leading to social transformation (Berki et al., 2014). It can further prove to be the most cost-effective option for the State, the citizens and the IT professionals, including all information systems stakeholders.

Cyberattacks Through the Lenses of Cybersecurity Professionals

According to Techopedia (2017) *cyberattacks* are deliberate exploitations of computer-based systems, ICT-dependent enterprises and networks. A cyberattack normally uses malicious code to change computer code, logic or data, resulting in disruptive consequences that can compromise data and lead to various types of cybercrime, such as information and identity theft. In cyberattacks (e.g. phishing attacks), technical subterfuge techniques (e.g., *pharming*) are employed to modify host files in the victims' computers, proceed to *DNS cache poisoning*, utilize *domain name typos*, exploit *cross-site scripting* vulnerabilities, and organize *man-in-the-middle* attacks in order to redirect a website's traffic to another, fake site (Milletary, 2013). Further, techniques such as *cross-site request forgery*, specialized malware, rogue Wi-Fi (i.e. *evil twin*), rogue Quick Response (QR) code, and hacking techniques are also utilized to conduct cyberattacks and, in particular, phishing attacks.

Techopedia (2017) mentions that cyberattacks may include the following consequences: i) identity theft, fraud, extortion, ii) malware, pharming, phishing, spamming, spoofing, spyware, Trojans and viruses, iii) stolen hardware, such as laptops or mobile devices, iv) Denial-of-Service and distributed Denial-of-Service attacks, v) breach of access, vi) password sniffing, vii) system infiltration, viii) website defacement, ix) private and public web browser exploits, x) instant messaging abuse, and xi) intellectual property (IP) theft or unauthorized access.

Cyberattacks can be categorized into *physical attacks* (e.g., physical outage of power, data, or otherwise), *syntactic attacks* (e.g., attacks against the operating logic of computer systems, vulnerabilities in software products, problems with cryptographic algorithms and protocols) and *semantic attacks* (i.e., target the way human users perceive and interpret Internet contents). These days, semantic attacks are more serious threats than other types of attack, since they target the human/computer interface, often referred as the most insecure interface on the Internet (Schneier, 2000).

A Worthy to Mention Frequent Cyberattack: (Social) Phishing

Nowadays, social engineering is more prevalent in phishing, which is a frequent cyberattack, utilized for identity theft, fraud and other types of cybercrime. The four phases of a cycle in social engineering-related cyberattacks are: information gathering, developing relationship, exploitation, and execution (see Allan et al., 2005). *Phishers*, *spammers*, and other (e.g. *pharmers*) employ more specialized targeted attacks such as *spear phishing*, *clone phishing*, and *whaling* and invest considerable time preparing for such cyberattacks. Such attacks use *hunting technique*, in which the attackers make their victims to divulge information after a minimal interaction, generally in one interaction, after which the communication is ended or *farming technique*, in which the attackers establish a relationship with their victims and continue to extract confidential information over a longer period of time (Samani and McFarland, 2014). They employ social engineering techniques such as *masquerading, dumpster diving, leftover, hoax virus alerts* and other such as chain letters, spam, direct psychological manipulation (Harley, 1998), *chat-in-the-middle* attack, *vishing, smishing* (RSA, 2009), to name just a few attempts of cyberattacks that target to sensitive information elicitation. Notably, there is no limit to social engineering techniques, as long as there is creativity and societal events and situations to exploit, which exit in abundance. Whether it was a global/local event or a festival or a holiday season or a natural calamity, all of them have been targeted by cyberattackers.

The Potential Victims of Cyberattacks: The State, the Society, and the Citizens

The dynamics of social surroundings can affect citizens' trust and compromise the security of the State and the society in general. Phishing is one of the most typical offline (e.g. by post) and online cyberattacks that happen daily. Phishers, who design and conduct mainly online attacks, efficiently combine i) advanced technological knowledge and ii) current social and situation-specific information. Various intelligent combinations of i) and ii) are used in order to exploit evoked feelings from turbulent and unstable world circumstances such as war situations, financial crises, ethical conflicts and other (Chaudhary et al, 2015a). In their attempts to gain citizens' trust for successful phishing, phishers are inventive and act with dark creativity.

The (online) citizens of e-society utilize virtual communities and social media for social networking. They also use online services such as e-shopping, e-banking, online games, music and films from cloud services, e-mail, e-governance, e-health, online tickets sales and the list can go on. The list of the compromised online services and social networks is so long that seems endless. For gathering information on trustworthy relationships and common interests phishers can simply observe online services and/ or look at any social network sites (Ramzan, 2006), and redesign their strategy of attacks, for example, context-aware phishing, socially-aware phishing, and reverse social engineering.

Recent happenings due to socio-economical reasons, such as wars, earthquakes, immigration, refugee-situations and other, show that when the real communities are in danger, people consider e-groups and cybercommunities as safety shelters, where through *anonymity, eponymity, nonymity* or *polynymity* (Berki & Jäkälä, 2009), citizens can interact and share their interests, feelings, worries and concerns. In most of these cases (Jäkälä & Berki, 2013), information that is produced by individuals, groups and communities of people is openly available for use but also for misuse and abuse.

In the long run the amelioration target should be the enhanced and safe functioning of social interaction systems e.g. social/mass media. In order to safeguard the security, communication, privacy, and openness of the interactive processes of the society, one must be aware and active and be encouraged by socio-technical factors to do so. Additionally, the authors posit that social awareness is dependent on social computing, which in turn, is concerned with information and communication systems of social media and networks and the mechanisms and principles that underlie their usability, maintainability, and use. Some examples of the latter and proposed ways to be used to improve total quality, and usable security (Li & Helenius, 2007; Kainda et al., 2010; Akhawe & Felt, 2013; Yuan et al., 2014) are presented next.

TOTAL QUALITY MANAGEMENT AND CITIZENS READINESS

Quality management has been a significant part of anti-phishing software and tools design. Quality criteria and metrics for *functionality, security and accuracy, usability, maintainability,* and *efficiency* have been essential measures in the fight against phishing (Chaudhary et al., 2015a). Developing phishing-resistant systems (Li et al., 2007) is one way by which software quality can participate in counteracting phishing attacks. Another way is strengthening the general quality of anti-phishing tools in many levels. Yet, both ways, no matter how informative and practical may be, are not sufficient in assuring citizens' security and privacy protection. Unless it is combined with social computing, user-psychology and social behavior knowledge, anti-phishing technology design can merely offer software quality measures and criteria for corrective and reactive maintenance, only. On the contrary, it is the proactive and preventive maintenance that multilevel quality and social computing should prompt for. Thus considering total quality management principles and integrated multidisciplinary knowledge could comprise an effective cybersecurity research and IT professional's education strategy.

Multi-Domain Knowledge for Designing Cyberattacks-Resistant Information Technology

An absolutely correct and complete cyberattack-resistant system is not possible. One main reason for this is that cyberattacks apply not just more and more sophisticating technology but also consider recent social events and cultural norms, exploited by social engineers and cybercriminals worldwide. It is the humans who are the weakest link in cybercrime activities. Humans are often exploited by cybercriminals e.g. pharmers and phishers when the latter employ intelligent semantic attacks. An exact (and possibly correct and complete up to some point) solution could somehow be achieved for technical problems. Human factors, however, do not fit to a 'precise' solution! Adverse effects due to the human nature and emotions (e.g. gullibility, greed, fear, diffidence, anxiety, thoughtlessness, apathy, sympathy, and curiosity) could be identified, controlled and minimized, but still can be unpredictable. Apparently, there still exist possibilities to control certain factors that can limit cyberattacks or, for instance, increase the efforts and time that cybercriminals need to act.

First, it is necessary to identify and fix these vulnerabilities which can be cybersecurity risks in a network system. To prevent system users from cyberattacks and social phishing Li et al. (2007) emphasize i) improving the quality of systems design and ii) the need for well-defined security requirements. From the systems design perspective they suggest misuse-oriented prevention, i.e., protection from phishing attacks with the help of the misuse case method. The *misuse-case* method is an effective approach to capture security requirements (Sindre & Opdahl, 2005) and analyze secure software architecture to identify security threats and vulnerabilities (Pauli & Xu, 2005). In a different way from them, Flechais et al. (2007) recommended an integrated methodology called *Appropriate and Effective Guidance for Information Security (AEGIS)*, used for developing secure and usable systems. This interdisciplinary approach integrates security and usability into the design process of the system development.

Another approach is focusing on *phishing resistant authentication method*. A question that arises is the following: *Is it feasible to create such an authentication method?* Despite the availability of diversified authentication schemes, a username-password pair is the most widely used authentication method. To improve its phishing resistance, mechanisms such as *one-time passcode*, multifactor authentication, *multistep authentication*, *gesture-based password*, and *graphical password* are a constant practice.

Another cognitive features multilevel authentication protocol, the *'Delayed Password Disclosure (DPD)'*, was proposed by Jakobsson & Myers (2008) .Their main idea was to provide users with visual character-by character feedback as they type their password. In so doing, they can stop entering the password as soon as it is realized that the website is unauthentic. However, the problem with this approach is that it allows partial disclosure of a password, which can be very helpful in cracking the password; for instance, using *password guessing attack*.

Some authentication schemes are based on the process of previewing or trial. Such are *picture password* (see Sinofsky, 2011) by which a user can authenticate by freeform gestures on picture. Likewise, Google research is focused on *'USB key'* which will be alternative to password (See Simonite, 2013). The 'USB key' will hold a cryptographic key and authenticate by correctly responding to mathematical (computational) challenges posed by the online service. The progress in biometrics is also heading in the right direction and has evolved to acquire the position of an underlying authentication technique in diverse applications (Mabry, 2015). Such research may result in new authentication methods and technologies from *what you know*, *what you have* and *what you are* categories. However, it is crucial to understand that the resulting technologies and methods must scale up security, be economical to implement, and are easy and convenient to use, in order to get accepted by the users (Bonneau et al., 2012; Li et al., 2012). At the same time, their developers must keep in mind the dynamically changing scenario of technology, for example, the emerging Internet of Things (IoT), and strive towards developing *sustainable* methods and technologies.

Example of Cybersecurity Multilevel Quality: Usable Security and Energy-Efficient Technology Solutions

Planning appropriately tailored to human needs tools, thus improving the multilevel quality of cybersecurity technology can be an effective multidisciplinary research and development strategy in the fight against cyberattacks and phishing in particular. Multidisciplinary knowledge is needed because anti-phishing tools are available in different forms, for example embedded in most of the anti-virus software, inbuilt in popular web browsers, as independent add-ons (SpoofGuard, Netcraft, and EarthLink). In these anti-phishing tools *accuracy and precision* in result is one major stakeholders concern. There is no anti-phishing tool, which can detect each and every single phishing attack. The reason for this may be that techniques adopted for phishing purposes are continuously changing, embracing all different information and communication technologies, e.g. snail mail, phone call, email, SMS, advertisement banner in website, and fraudulent websites. Moreover, social engineers quickly adapt to newly appeared information and knowledge and accordingly increase the sophistication in the technology and social engineering knowledge that they combine to carry out their illegal activities.

To keep pace with the changing, growing needs scenarios and often with the business reality, cybersecurity tools have to upgrade accordingly, which is possible only through the consideration of *maintainability factors and built-in design properties*. There has also been a necessity to design *proactive measures* to counteract cyberattacks and not just limit the efforts to corrective and reactive measures. Regarding anti-phishing tools' design and use, another serious concern is found to be the tools' poor *usability* (Dhamija et al., 2006; Wu et al., 2006; Li & Helenius, 2007). Due to poor usability of anti-phishing tools, plenty of Internet users remain exposed to online threats. They either do not pay attention to or fail to understand the warnings displayed by anti-phishing tools. Ultimately, they fail to act as directed by the anti-phishing tools; or disobey the directions because they are not appropriately advised. As a multilevel quality property, usability itself involves, by and large, the consideration of human factors. Therefore, the design of usable security must take into account what humans can and cannot do well (Dhamija et al., 2006) and what type of knowledge/information do they need to counteract well. Security and usability should be considered in a complementary manner when designing anti-phishing tools. Both security and usability requirements should be integrated throughout the system/tool design process, by iterative analysis and design, and evaluation cycles for usability and security while incorporating them (Yee, 2004; Kainda et al., 2010).

Naturally, plenty of Internet users widely use Smartphone and tablets to browse the Internet, performing security-sensitive activities like e-banking and online shopping. Surprisingly, these particular online activities have attracted cyberattacks targeting users of such specific devices (Ruggiero & Foote, 2011; RSA, 2009). A natural problem with these devices is that they are battery-powered and pose limited computing power. Therefore, it is crucial to design a *lightweight* cybersecurity tool; thus targeting towards increasing the overall *efficiency* (performance) of anti-phishing tools. Energy wise, such lightweight cybersecurity tools have to be i) energy-friendly with conformance to green computing principles; ii) effective through usable security rules against cyberattacks; iii) should not involve exhaustive computing tasks (defined in complex ways) that can quickly drain the available battery and other resources, but rather utilize natural, computational design logic and iv) consider ethical design rules.

The significance of human and social awareness is discussed next along with the necessity of *resilience* in the fight against cyberattacks. Subsequently, in the upcoming sections we expose our research concern on the multidisciplinary knowledge needed by cybersecurity professionals so that social awareness can increase, influence and assist cyberattacks' prediction and prevention through social computing approaches.

Caring for Citizens' Multilevel Knowledge and Readiness

As mentioned in the aforementioned sections, cyberattackers, e.g., phishers use semantic attacks to exploit human vulnerabilities. It does not matter how many firewalls, encryption software, certificates, or two-factor authentication mechanisms an organization has; the human behind the keyboard can still fall for a phish (Hong, 2012). In cyberattacks such as phishing attacks there are many cues, which can help Internet users to identify them. Surveys and research studies alarmingly revealed that Internet users lack proper knowledge on phishing recognition (Bravo-Lillo et al., 2011; Kirlappos & Sasse, 2012; Chaudhary et al., 2015b) and other cyberattacks. Therefore, educating Internet users and raising their awareness regarding phishing and other types of cyberattacks can be a potential effective measure for protection.

At present, in order to make their clients more aware, banks, financial companies, online shops and other organizations, whose online clients are vulnerable to phishing and other cyberattacks, include static information about cyberattacks in their websites. Regarding online security and privacy, there is publicly available online training material, published by various governmental and non-governmental organizations, business, security companies, universities and other. This material has been proved useful for the readers, who admit that there is multilevel information about many issues that they did not know before reading. Web-based training materials, contextual training, embedded training, and interactive games have also been found effective in educating Internet users about cybersecurity and helping them to avoid cyberattacks such as phishing (Kumaraguru et al., 2007; Sheng et al., 2007). Examples here include the interactive game "Anti-Phish Phil", and the interactive training system "PhishGuru". These were designed by CyLab Usable Privacy and Security (CUPS) Laboratory at Carnegie Mellon University. CUPS targets to educate Internet users about phishing emails and websites. Similarly, the online quiz "Phish or Not Phish", developed by VeriSign, is available for free. Kuo et al. (2007) suggested to include tutorials with detailed information about the potential problems, focusing on problem-focused adult education (Valtanen, 2016) in anti-phishing tools. In so doing the potential online users can read them and increasingly advance their multilevel knowledge on phishing. Hence humans can, gradually, become aware of the dangers.

Wu et al. (2006) found out significant improvement in the ability of Internet users to detect phishing attacks, before and after reading a tutorial by email on phishing attacks. Sheng et al. (2007) experimented on the role of games (see also Mystakidis et al., 2017) to educate Internet users on cybersecurity and phishing attacks' recognition. The experiment indicated that gaming results in more effective user awareness than other means such as reading text or following online tutorials.

Multidisciplinary knowledge notably increases awareness about cyberattacks and can be very helpful in reducing the numbers of people falling for social engineering online attacks. However, it is essential to realize how effective are the instructions included in multilevel training materials and how they are perceived by the users/learners. Herley (2009) argues that the current training materials teach users to look for visible cues. This approach offers only limited protection against social engineering online. Cyberattackers can modify visible cues in emails and websites. Moreover, these training materials assume that users are keen to avoid risks; on the contrary, another study showed that people judge for relevance before authenticity (Jakobsson, 2007).

Admittedly, too sensitive interfaces about security can backfire, and make users to doubt every email and website. The citizens/users can have misconceptions about security from beforehand. Therefore, multidisciplinary and multilevel training materials should not just limit their contents to inform on visible cues. They should also challenge misconceptions of the users (Kirlappos & Sasse, 2012; Chaudhary et al., 2015b) on the resilience of technologies, and cognitively prepare them so that they can intelligently assess potential risks.

"How to design methods and materials for cyberattacks awareness?" is another crucial question that seeks to be answered. Factors such as IT literacy, age, gender, prior exposure, personal traits and national culture of the learners are found to be directly linked to their vulnerabilities to cyberattacks, primarily to phishing (Jagatic et al., 2007; Sheng et al., 2010; Halevi et. al., 2013; Chaudhary et al. 2015b; Berki et al., 2017). For example, 18-25 age group is more vulnerable to phishing attacks than other ages may be due to their inherent tendency towards risks. Hence, such factors must be comprehended and incorporated in the design of learning materials and methods for cyberattacks awareness and education.

Cyber-Resilience and Tools: Multidisciplinary Anti-Phishing Knowledge and Long Term Social Impact

Cyber-resilience is a significant quality property, dealing with the degree of flexibility, rigidity, resistance, and toughness of a cyber-physical system and associated tools. It is rather imperative and implicit that resilience is interconnected with all other quality properties discussed earlier. According to the United States Department of Homeland Security (2013), resilience includes the ability to withstand and recover from deliberate attacks, accidents, or naturally occurring threats and incidents. Cyber-resilient anti-phishing technologies can help to reduce the immediate short-term negative impact on users/citizens and could moderate the long-term social impact.

A generally used method to reduce the impact of phishing and other cyberattacks is to *take the websites down*. There is, though, a limitation in this type of counteraction. Not all countries have essential laws or legal provision principles to remove such websites.

Another approach is to flood the phishers' databases with false information. This is also called *poisoning*, but is not *Denial of Service (DoS)* attack. Although this is related to pharming techniques, the concept behind this method is to make it difficult for phishers to differentiate between valid and false data. This can, sometimes, make the database completely useless. This technique also has a serious limitation. It requires tracking the spoofed websites without any *false negative* result.

McRae & Vaughan (2007) proposed a technique, which employs web-bugs and *honeytokens*. The concept behind their technique was not simply to minimize the damage but also to track down the phishers. Although this approach is not fully proved, it raises a noble issue which is to track down the phishers and punish them for their illegitimate activities. It is debatable whether punishment can deter phishers or not; however, it might be legally and morally required.

Further than user awareness about phishing attacks and consciousness of the cyberattack situation, social awareness and social consciousness are needed for adopting a proactive, and where possible predictive, total quality engineering approach; thus, not simply following a reactive problem-solving method as the ones described above. The rest of the paper is dedicated in exposing societal needs and proposing strategic ways of multilevel research for increasing social awareness (and, thus, social consciousness) through instilling multidisciplinary knowledge and competencies to cybersecurity professionals.

STRATEGIC MULTIDISCIPLINARY RESEARCH AND KNOWLEDGE SCHEMES FOR CYBERSECURITY MULTIPROFESSIONALS

The structure and social order of the information society and the local/global events influence cyber attacks and social engineering techniques. It is a social need to research how certain and uncertain situations of real and virtual communities affect citizens' trust and influence personal safety, privacy and social security. There is also a strategic social need to predict when these activities might occur, with accuracy and clarity. Effective remedies for cyberattacks could be achieved by relating cyberattacks activities to the current or/and recent phenomena of the society and their frequency. Multidisciplinary knowledge and related skills could lead to timely identification and prediction. Ultimately, this combined knowledge and information scheme could form a proactive cybersystems research and development strategy that could, practically, enhance preventive maintenance (Berki et al., 2014) through informed choices.

Questions Leading to Multidisciplinary Knowledge

The social context/environment with its timely internal/external events and particular phenomena/ situations in information society increase i) cyberattacks such as social engineering activities and, thus, ii) cyberattackers. Subsequently, iii) the victims of cyberattacks are increased, while more and more citizens are in danger in daily life and work. Considering this hypothesis and attempting to formulate an effective cybersecurity research strategy, someone could further consider the next questions:

1. *Which* phenomena /events in societies increased the amount of cyberattacks recently?
2. *How* the content of the cyberattacks-oriented activities is related to the social context?
3. *Why* cyberattackers chose these particular happenings as the content of their cyberattacks?
4. *Could* a prediction model of future cyberattacks be constructed and realized?

The answers to questions 1-3 can reveal new, significant, multilevel knowledge considering the social dimensions of trust and the consequences of cyberattacks to the citizens' life in the absence of privacy and social security. Hence, answers to questions 1-3 will result in increased *social awareness*. The answer to question 4 could also increase social awareness and, most importantly, *public readiness*. A prediction model could be part of protection guidelines for citizens' education and training to recognize and rather predict anticipated cyberattacks.

Multidisciplinary Knowledge-Based Research Aims to Increase Public Readiness

At this point, the research steps towards understanding and capturing cyberattacks should target to address the following issues that correspond to the research questions 1-4 (exposed in the earlier section), in a more explanatory manner:

1. *Which* societal situations generate cyberattacks and cyberattackers?
2. *What* do cyberattckers search for?
3. *Which* data and kinds of information are likely to become strong potential cyberattacks 'baits' for the citizens?
4. *How* cyberattacks could be predicted?
5. *How* individual/public readiness could be raised?

Hence the research design should primarily aim at developing individual and public awareness regarding cyberattacks, for the sake of citizens' privacy and social security. In so doing, and utilizing suitable data, the research stages and steps followed must have the next inputs and deliverables:

Stage 1: Research and social learning on the dynamics of social relationships between citizens, online groups and services and special events/situations in virtual/real communities; classification of the cyberattacks.

Stage 2: The research should result in i) protection guidelines for the citizens and ii) a prediction model for cyberattacks. These two outcomes will assist in the development of social awareness.

Such kind of strategic research on cyberattacks must be qualitative and quantitative in nature and have international collaboration. Thus, we propose the collection, analysis and comparison of international data and information on cyberattacks. An excellent data source, for instance, for correlation and meta-analysis is the international data reported in the APWG reports (2008-2014) of every 6 months/year, during the last years. These are collections of online phishing attacks and, perhaps, the most reliable and relevant data source internationally regarding social engineering online. It is, however, a relatively limited source of available, real data, and also incomplete because not each and every phishing attempt is reported.

Researchers already utilized many resources with collected data available for anti-phishing research (Li, 2013; Chaudhary, 2016). Other sources of data available are the incidents mentioned in the news by mass media and social media. These can be researched and scrutinized through many viewpoints in order to reveal:

1. Common conditions for cyberattack activities that include common actions
2. Cyberattacks patterns (and anti-patterns) and human roles, and
3. Social consequences they create

The emergence of elements i) – iii) can constitute an abstraction of the social reality that it can be decisively useful when prescribing cyberattacks remedies and setting software quality criteria such as resilience and usable security for cybersecurity software.

Information that targets social awareness is of strategic significance and has to be monitored and released with great care for the citizens. As an example of how publicly available information can be used or abused by different groups, we next analyze a recent social engineering online case that abused information from a real event in China.

Social Awareness and Reporting of Online Social Engineering Attack in China

Recently, with the development of the Internet, new media channels have been introduced into daily life in China. Chinese people may go to some popular websites, such as sohu.com, sina.com.cn, ifeng.com, to read public news. These new (social) media bring the information faster, and also provide their audience with a public virtual space to share comments on what they read. While though people have enjoyed the convenience of these media, they also have to be very careful with sensitive personal or non-personal information sharing unwillingly and, sometimes, unconsciously, as described next.

An Example of Abused Information With Unintended Consequences

The emerging media channels also host situations where people can be victims of phishing and other potential cyberattacks, like in the following event, which generated unnecessary suffering from financial loss caused by phishing messages. The information used in the phishing messages was revealed during the facts reporting on a police incident.

On the 9th of February 2014, soon after the 2014 Chinese New Year, the police in Guangdong province launched a raid on saunas, karaokes and other venues of ill repute in Dongguan, a city in Guangdong province famous for manufacturing and a highly developed sex industry (Rauhala, 2014). The police detained 67 people and shut down 12 venues. The news should have confirmed that the sex industry is not protected by the law in China, however. Some people got phished because of (the reporting of) these social events happening. According to the text from a newspaper published in Guangdong (News.163. com, 2014), some victims reported that they received phishing SMS messages saying: "Dad, I have been caught by the police when I played in Dongguan last night, please transfer ***yuan as bail to the bank account ******."

Question Asking for Increasing Public Awareness and Advancing Social Consciousness

We thought of the following a) – e) question-based analysis and *subsequent quick remedy-based answer*, in an attempt to reflect and analyze on this event's consequences:

1. *What could these media tell people about the particular social event?*

In the Dongguan raid, the media could only tell the audience the time, the organizer, the general process and the results of the event. No individual information was exposed, nor should it be exposed.

2. *What will likely be the social awareness impact on the individuals?*

In the Dongguan raid, individuals may see the determination and attitude of Chinese central/local government towards the sex industry. Some individuals may also be informed on the whereabouts of the famous sex industry centre in the province of Guangdong. Some individuals may also start looking for other places for entertainment. Some people may start worrying about their friends, i.e. whether they were involved in this event or not; and the list can go on.

3. *Which is/are the role(s) of the authorities?*

The authorities actually play the role of the leader in this event. They planned the event, they recorded the whole process, and assisted in publishing the details they (were) allowed.

4. *Which is/are the role(s) of the individual citizens?*

Many roles can be attributed to the individual citizens. They can be part of the audience watching and listening to the event. They can also be the reporters disclosing more or less critical details on the event. They can also be these individuals (actors) catching others or being caught by the police.

5. *What are the benefits/costs for the individuals?*

People may receive rewards from taking part in the raid operation, e.g. as a policeman, an undercover, a reporter, a leader, an informant and other. They could also be punished if they are a detained person in the raid operation.

In addition to the question-based analysis, many other right questions can be asked in order to enhance understanding of the socio-cultural and geo-political factors and make citizens aware of the seriousness and the dangers of the incident. Except specific questions, other cross-disciplinary analysis means of communicating facts, news and events can be utilized, through different actors/roles in different socio-cultural contexts. Some examples of cross-disciplinary and multidisciplinary analysis models are mentioned next.

Situation Understanding and Awareness via Multilevel Information Communication and Modeling

Situation understanding and situation awareness can derive from the use of appropriate analysis and communication means that appeal to different *socio-cognitive domains*. For instance, in case of cyberattacks (see phishing example in previous section), except mere news reporting and analysis, international statistical correlations and annual tabular data, as well as other analysis and presentation means can advance situational knowledge. Modeling techniques, for instance, can be borrowed from SSM - Soft Systems Methodology (Checkland & Scholes, 1990). These techniques include the CATWOE (Customer, Actor, Transformation, Worldview, Owner, Environment) analysis, various alternative system's Root Definitions, and Rich Pictures (Checkland & Scholes, 1990). These techniques depict and describe the structured and unstructured social systems situations in a realistic and analytical manner. The authors borrowed methodological knowledge from the SSM techniques in order to form questions a) –e) in the previous section and reflected on the analysis of the particular example in China. The main reason for this choice is that SSM techniques can provide holistic (systemic) views of the society and the effects of cyberattacks on citizens and other social partners and stakeholders. In an effort to construct a hybrid, multiview and multidisciplinary methodology that can increase multilevel knowledge regarding cyberattacks, the authors of this chapter also suggest: 1) Contextual PEST (Political, Environmental, Social and Technical) analysis that can initially be used for a more systemic understanding of the cyberattack situation. 2) Further SWOT (Strengths, Weaknesses, Opportunities and Threats) analysis could be used in categorizing cyberattacks, as pointed for phishing attempts regarding the email content (see Li et al., 2011; Berki et al., 2014).

Social networking, virtual community engagement and cultural interaction through social and mass media make online worlds complex and chaotic to understand. Cyber threats could be seen as social phenomena, initiating from people gathered around screens to play games to the emergence of email and social media. As technologies have evolved, so too have the socio-cognitive and socio-cultural issues with which they are entwined. The technical knowledge of advanced ICT challenges humans. (Chaudhary et al., 2015b) Understanding the social contexts and cultural practices constitutes considerable challenges, too (see e.g. Eggers, 2014). Cyberattackers, however, are aware of such vulnerabilities and needs and in their attacks interact with certain socio-cognitive and cyber psychological knowledge that can allure other humans on the Internet.

Further research on cybersecurity technology and social/mass media should be handled through predominant and multidisciplinary research frameworks that contain concepts and conceptual modeling through which humans can typically conceptualize the dynamic and evolutionary nature of societal structure and regular or irregular events. For example, cognitive science and social computing comprise one potential integrated knowledge area that can be utilized in the study of cybersecurity technologies and digital media as socio-cognitive and cultural phenomena. The next section elaborates further to this target.

Social Computing and Integrated Multidisciplinary Knowledge for Modeling and Predicting Cyberattacks

Social computing is an area of computer science that is concerned with the intersection of social behavior and computational systems. Social computing involves supporting any sort of social behavior in or through computational systems (Surowiecki, 2005; Berki, 2001). It is based on creating or recreating social conventions and social contexts through the use of software and technology. Thus, blogs, email, instant messaging, social network services, wikis, social bookmarking and other instances of what is often called social software illustrate ideas from social computing, but also other kinds of software applications where people interact socially.

Social computing is believed to adequately handle computations that are carried out by groups of people; hence, it has recently become popular because of its relationship to free/open source, social software, and social network analysis (see e.g. Berki, 2001; Surowiecki, 2005). These are believed to influence ways of thinking and practice and social order. Apparently, computational social choice and prediction modeling can be used in the fight of cyberattacks and social phishing (Li et al. 2015; Chaudhary et al., 2017) because social behavior, except social awareness, provides a social knowledge basis on human interaction to plan and coordinate in advance and, above all, draw inferences.

Humans develop abilities and skills for interacting, expressing themselves in multiple ways (Jäkälä & Berki, 2013). Humans are considerably sensitive to i) the behavior of others around them and ii) their social context. They possess emotions generated from situations i) and ii) and make a number of decisions that are influenced by these and other feelings. Except human-computer interaction, human to human interaction, social behavior and socio-cognitive factors (Berki, 2001; Berki et al., 2004; Surowiecki, 2005) form a potential research domain where critical and reflective scientific research can be carried out. For this reason, there are many socio-technical factors in many types of cyberattacks for potential conceptual computational modeling (see e.g. Berki, 2001; Berki et al., 2004; Li et al., 2015; Chaudhary et al., 2017). For example, social computing could assist in designing cyberattacks-resistant systems and cybersecurity technology that support useful functionality by making socially-triggered and -filtered information available to the information systems' users (Li et al., 2015; Chaudhary et al., 2017).

An Example of Multidisciplinary Knowledge: Socio-Cognitive Conceptual Computational Modeling of Trust Assumptions in User Behavior

A frequent case of social phishing can happen through a personal message, like in the earlier discussed case of the 9th of February 2014, in Dongguan, city in Guangdong, China. Another case of social phishing can happen through the following message: *Your flight is cancelled; please transfer 100 euro to bank account xxxx-xxxx-xxxx-xxxx as collaterals to reserve the seat for your next flight. We will refund the money back to you after your trip.*

Both behavioral patterns of the receiver in the above two messages are depicted in Figure 1, adapted here from Chaudhary et al. (2017), where there is a full description of a socio-cognitive and computational model for decision making and user modeling in social phishing.

From the figure, one can easily compare and find out the most vulnerable behavioral pattern, i.e. the path in the diagram with the biggest weighted value of trust attitude.

In Figure 1, let us assume that the sum value of trust weight is $\sum W$, now:

- If the trustor (i.e., the SMS receiver) chooses the first path, then $\sum W = wk_1 + Wk_2$ (where $k_1 = 1...6$; $k_2 = 1...n$)
- If the trustor chooses the second path, then $\sum W = Wk_1' + wk_2'$ (where $k_1' = 1...n$; $k_2' = 1...6$).

In order to trust the message, the sum value of trust has to be positive, i.e., $\sum W > 0$. The higher will be the sum value of trust, so will be the possibility that the trustor will respond to the phishing attack. For the zero and negative values, i.e., $\sum W \leq 0$, the chance that the trustor will respond to the SMS will be minimal.

Humans have always been the main target of deceitful cyberattacks. If the question is why humans are easily deceived one can find many personal factors and reasons. Among the first, are, the socio-cultural factors. Such issues can influence as follows: a person might wonder how s/he will be remembered (was s/he helpful or not) or a person might not want to insult the other person (follows a high moral code),

Figure 1.

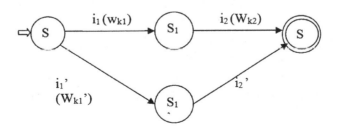

or a person thinks this is a good relationship investment (since social relationships are valued high), or a person is in a much lower social/power status (and thus does not dare to reject requests from others) (Chaudhary et al., 2017).

It constitutes a great challenge to essentially argue why people lie and deceit, and why people trust and how they make trust decisions. Chaudhary et al. (2017) studied and conceptualized social arguments and assumptions on trust and constructed a computational model of social values as they appear in interpersonal collaboration. Their study supports the need for adopting theories of vulnerable behaviour detection in assisting victims from social phishing and other cyberattacks.

Towards Cybersecurity Multi-Professionals: Multidisciplinary Research and Education Strategies

A socio-economical strategy for the fight of cyberattacks and social engineering is important because it will involve high level planning and design to achieve readiness and pre-recognition of cyberattacks targets among citizens in society, under certain or uncertain conditions. A resource-based strategy can be effective because the resources available to manage the fight against cyberattacks (e.g. phishing and other criminal actions of social engineering) are, normally, limited and the future online threats unknown. The necessity of a nation-wide strategy is about shaping the future, while constitutes a human attempt to get to desirable ends with all available and possible means.

A cybersecurity research strategy based (not only) on principles of social computing and software quality management could be defined as i) a social abstract pattern in a stream of phenomena and decisions, or as ii) a systematic approach of finding, formulating, and developing a contingency research framework. Both i) and ii) could strive for readiness to recognize attempts of cyberattacks and, in the long run, future prediction mechanisms of cyberattacks-related activities. Further, the citizens would be encouraged for participation and be empowered with suitable knowledge for situational analysis and situational awareness.

The authors, considering their and others' research outcomes (see e.g. Dhamija et al., 2006; Li et al., 2011; Li, 2013; Chaudhary & Berki, 2013; Li et al., 2014), have concluded the following: In order to determine the future research directions and challenges of cybersecurity artifacts design (Berki et al., 2014) it is essential to: firstly, achieve an improved understanding of the current cybersecurity research and education internationally; and secondly, define a strategic resource-based critical knowledge framework through which international multidisciplinary researchers and cybersecurity multi-professionals can pursue particular courses of multidisciplinary and cross-disciplinary research and development action.

Figure 2, next, depicts the knowledge domains from which the most useful cross-disciplinary knowledge, models and information needed for cybersecurity professionals can derive. Most of the knowledge abstracted in figure 2 has already been discussed and demonstrated for its applicability and usefulness in the previous sections. Other knowledge has been theoreticize and utilized in international multidisciplinary research (see e.g. Wilson and Pirrie, 2000), essentially in cybersecurity, with applications and theoretical extensions spanning the domains of cryptography and steganography, user psychology, human and social sciences, design sciences, aspects of policy, law and ethics, identity management, risk management, and other (Gagliardi et al, 2016; McCanny & Hooper, 2016).

Following the conceptualization of cybersecurity multi-professionals knowledge (figure 2) and considering the fundamental principle of strategic planning *hope for the best, plan for the worst*, a strategic

Figure 2.

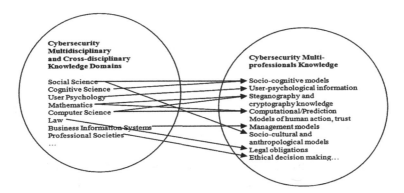

research contingency approach (Li, 2013; Chaudhary, 2016) for effective cybersecurity technologies and policies in society must, at least, address the next generic questions, as exposed in (Berki et al 2014) and (Chaudhary et al, 2015a):

1. *What* should and could be done, and *why*?
2. *For whom* should this be done, and *why*?
3. *How* could this be done best, and *why*?
4. *Who* should do this best, and *why*?
5. *With whom* else could and should this be done best, and *why*?

These polymorphic considerations are relevant as analysis guidelines at many levels and originate from different knowledge domains. They can be used, for instance, in cyberattacks activity analysis, in cybersecurity policy design and realization, and other situations like citizens' education and training schemes and in problems that their nature is of law and social order origin. However, often the legal and ethical security design requirements can be contradictory for IT/cybersecurity professionals and their personal values. Apparently, the (private) information provided for social awareness cannot be anonymous; but it is, however, significantly precise and accurate because it is linked to the shared personal experiences of (eponymous or anonymous) people, who are, in turn, connected to other people. The reliability and validity of it derives from the social consciousness and both citizens' and IT/cybersecurity professionals' empowerment and responsibility for social transformation.

SUMMARY AND CRITICAL THOUGHTS

Cyberattacks empowered by *dark creativity* techniques (e.g., semantic attacks or social engineering) seem to currently constitute the most severe problem for information security professionals and cybersecurity professionals in particular. They target the weakest link in the cybersecurity chain, which is its human factor. The demand for multidisciplinary scientific knowledge that covers a wide range of business, socio-technical, legal and other matters and derives from multiple domains such as social science, software, hardware, design sciences, user psychology, aspects of law, ethics and education, and other is of paramount importance for future cyberprofessionals. Specific knowledge and relevant information through total quality criteria on corrective, reactive, proactive or preventive maintenance are rather limited and exercised in a limited fashion.

Except socio-technical management approaches towards situational readiness and public awareness, other strategic multi-domain knowledge and multilevel strategies and design considerations with legal and ethical awareness for IT/cybersecurity professionals can also contribute towards the previous. One of these professional challenges is the secure, ethical and legal design of social behavior-based computational systems. These systems could support the collection and dissemination of information through collective social interaction, for example from and to online groups, work teams, web-based communities, online organizations, and local/global capital markets.

This chapter investigated and further reported on the significance of i) a multidisciplinary strategic research and education approach and ii) multilevel international scientific collaboration between IT professionals and other concerned social partners to fight cyberattacks. Citizen's social awareness can act as a protection mechanism in the social context of cybersociety. Cybersecurity protection guidelines, multidisciplinary adult education and multilevel training programs, as well as simple trust management strategies can make citizens re-think their online interaction.

It is unfortunate that currently, cybersecurity knowledge and techniques against cyberattacks constitute an esoteric situation of specialized information shared by a few research teams, governmental (e.g. military, national law and other) and a small number of cybersecurity technology companies worldwide. Nonetheless it has become an obstacle for widening the useful knowledge for the society that can lead to timely public awareness for the citizens. This situation is often considered as a competitive advantage for commercial exploitation. However, the same international situation has been an obstacle in widening the epistemological and practical knowledge that can lead to IT skills and digital culture development, increased social awareness and individuals' safety in cybersociety. The cybersecurity/IT professionals carry a huge responsibility for this. On the other hand, cyberattackers (e.g. phishers) are very knowledgeable and intelligent, (perhaps well-respected IT professionals!), aware of the socio-technical facts and security gaps that can be utilized to interact with potential victims and convince them to reveal information on themselves and others. Such deceitful efforts with trustworthy content through online services and face to face conversations frequently appear and go on increasing in (cyber)society. Thus, everyone working on cybersecurity must understand the fast evolving threat of cyberattacks, and require to collaborate across all sectorial disciplines and national boundaries (McCanny & Hopper, 2016).

Recent research also showed (Li et al., 2011; Hong, 2012; Li, 2013; Chaudhary and Berki, 2013) that cyber activities like phishing become increasingly difficult to recognize, while phishers and other cyberattackers become more sophisticated with multilevel knowledge. It seems inevitable that future cyberattacks will utilize more (trustworthy) elements of social and personal contexts, becoming thus more dangerous for citizens' welfare and society. Protecting citizen's vulnerability and privacy in the era of e-society through increased social awareness is a huge challenge for cybersecurity experts. The latter are called upon to care for and realize, among other, two challenging targets in e-society: i) improving trust relationships and, thus, security and safety ii) securing freedom of speech and expression, which belong to the basic human rights.

An essential cross-disciplinary conceptualization of knowledge for cybersecurity multiprofessionals is not a remedy-for-all solution. Scientific or ideological orientations of isolated cybersecurity research and development approaches have suffered as a result of reductionist abstractions (Berki et al., 2014). Accordingly, *the problem of personal security (the problem of law and order) cannot be adequately explained by reducing it either to criminality (i.e. the problem between individuality and universality) or to politics (i.e. the conflict between particulars).... (Berki, 1986).*

In addition, cybersecurity professionals are IT professionals and multidisciplinary knowledge workers, who are under constant pressure to learn something new that regularly appears in cybersecurity/IT subject fields. This adds to the stress of IT professionals (Rathore & Ahuja, 2015), which can derive from many work-related sources. A constant demand for continuous training can be a positive feature in knowledge work as far as it is related to interesting work tasks and autonomy. The downside of the current emphasis on multidisciplinarity, flexibility and lifelong learning is that work may also involve multilevel stress due to tight schedules, quick decision-making rhythms and unrealistic expectations to keep work-related skills up-to-date. (Pyöriä, Melin & Blom, 2005; Rathore & Ahuja, 2015).

Regarding cyberattacks, complementary actions are also the following: i) citizens could and should, eventually, acquire useful social skills and digital competencies, and ii) the Law and Justice could be able to utilize predictive practical information. Socially aware citizens appreciate freedom of expression, privacy, confidentiality and other human rights. Empowered and knowledgeable citizens, in turn, can collaborate better with cybersecurity professionals in supporting safe social interaction and stability. Social awareness and multilevel knowledge lead to secure active participation. This is the first step towards social consciousness and caring, reflective and critical thinking, that are necessary items for social activism and societal transformation.

REFERENCES

Akhawe, D., & Felt, A. P. (2013). Alice in wonderland: A large-scale field study of browser security warning effectiveness. *Proceedings of the 22nd USENIX Security Symposium*, 257-272.

Allan, A., Noakes-Fry, K., & Mogull, R. (2005). *Management update: How businesses can defend against social engineering attacks*. Gartner Inc.

APWG. (2008-2014). *Phishing attacks trends reports*. Anti-Phishing Working Group.

Barr, H., & Low, H. (2013). *Introducing interprofessional education*. Centre for the Advancement of Interprofessional Education. doi:10.1007/978-94-6209-353-9_16

Berki, E. (2001). *Establishing a scientific discipline for capturing the entropy of systems process models: CDM-FILTERS - A computational and dynamic metamodel as a flexible and integrated language for the testing, expression and re-engineering of systems* (PhD Thesis). University of N. London, UK.

Berki, E., Chaudhary, S., Li, L., & Valtanen, J. (2014). Increasing social awareness through software quality and social computing – Towards effective anti-phishing research strategies. *Proceedings of the 22nd SQM Conference*, 149-164.

Berki, E., Georgiadou, E., & Holcombe, M. (2004). Requirements engineering and process modelling in software quality management – Towards a generic process metamodel. *Software Quality Journal*, *12*(3), 265–283. doi:10.1023/B:SQJO.0000034711.87241.t0

Berki, E., & Jäkälä, M. (2009). Cyber-identities and social life in cyberspace. In Hatzipanagos, S. & Warburton, S. (Eds.), Handbook of Research on Social Software and Developing Community Ontologies (pp. 27-39). IGI Global. doi:10.4018/978-1-60566-208-4.ch003

Berki, E., Sharma-Kandel, C., Zhao, Y., & Chaudhary, S. (2017). A comparative study of cloud services use by prospective IT professionals in five countries. *Proceedings of the 9th EDULEARN.*

Berki, R. N. (1986). *Security and society: Reflections on Law, order and politics.* London: J. M. Dent & Sons Ltd.

Bonneau, J., Herley, C., van Oorschot, P. C., & Stajano, F. (2012). The quest to replace passwords: a framework for comparative evaluation of web authentication schemes. *Proceedings of the IEEE Symposium on Security and Privacy*, 553-567. doi:10.1109/SP.2012.44

Bravo-Lillo, C., Cranor, L. F., Downs, J., Komanduri, S., Reeder, R. W., Schechter, S., & Sleeper, M. (2013). Your attention please: designing security-decision UIs to make genuine risk harder to ignore. *Proceedings of the Symposium on Usable Privacy and Security.* doi:10.1145/2501604.2501610

Chaudhary, S. (2016). *The use of usable security and security education to fight phishing attacks* (PhD Thesis). University of Tampere, Finland.

Chaudhary, S., & Berki, E. (2013). Challenges in designing usable anti-phishing solutions. *Proceedings of the 21st SQM Conference*, 189-200.

Chaudhary, S., Berki, E., Li, L., & Valtanen, J. (2015a). Time Up for phishing with effective anti-phishing research strategies. *International Journal of Human Capital and IT Professionals*, 6(2), 49–64. doi:10.4018/IJHCITP.2015040104

Chaudhary, S., Berki, E., Li, L., Valtanen, J., & Helenius, M. (2017). A socio-cognitive and computational model for decision making and user modelling in social phishing. *Proceedings of the 25th SQM Conference.*

Chaudhary, S., Zhao, Y., Berki, E., Valtanen, J., Li,L., Helenius, M., & Mystakidis, S. (2015b). A cross-cultural and gender-based perspective for online security: Exploring knowledge, skills and attitudes of higher education students. *IADIS International Journal on WWW/Internet, 13*(1), 57-71.

Chaudhary, S., Zolotavkin, Y., Berki, E., Helenius, M., Nykänen, P., & Kela, J. (2016). Towards a conceptual framework for privacy protection in the use of interactive 3600 video surveillance. *Proceedings of the IEEE 22nd International Conference on Virtual Systems & Multimedia,.*

Checkland, P., & Scholes, J. (1990). *Soft systems methodology in action.* Wiley & Sons.

Dhamija, R., Tygar, J. D., & Hearst, M. (2006). Why phishing works. *Proceedings of the Conference on Human Factors in Computing Systems*, 581-590.

Eggers, D. (2014). *The circle.* Vintage Books.

Flechais, I., Mascolo, C., & Sasse, M. A. (2007). Integrating security and usability into the requirements and design process. *International Journal of Electronic Security and Digital Forensics*, *1*(1), 12–26. doi:10.1504/IJESDF.2007.013589

Gagliardi, F., Hankin, C., Gal-Ezer, J., McGettrick, A., & Meitern, M. (2016). *Advancing cybersecurity research and education in Europe major drivers of growth in the digital landscape*. ACM.

Hadnagy, C. (2011). *Social engineering: The art of human hacking*. Wiley Publishing.

Halevi, T., Lewis, J., & Memon, N. (2013). A pilot study of cyber security and privacy related behavior and personality traits. *Proceedings of the 22nd International Conference on World Wide Web*, 737-744. doi:10.1145/2487788.2488034

Harley, D. (1998). Re-floating the Titanic: Dealing with social engineering attacks. *Proceedings of the European Expert Group for IT Security*.

Heartfield, R., & Loukas, G. (2016). A taxonomy of attacks and a survey defense mechanisms for semantic social engineering attacks. *ACM Computing Surveys*, *48*(3).

Herley, C. (2009). So long, and no thanks for the externalities: The rational rejection of security advice by users. *Proceedings of the New Security Paradigms Workshop*, 133-144. doi:10.1145/1719030.1719050

Hong, J. (2012). The state of phishing attacks. *Communications of the ACM*, *55*(1), 74. doi:10.1145/2063176.2063197

Jagatic, T. N., Johnson, N., Jakobsson, M., Menczer, F. (2007). Social phishing. *Communications of the ACM, 50*(10), 94-100.

Jäkälä, M., & Berki, E. (2013). Communities, communication and online identities. In Digital Identity and Social Media (pp. 1-13). IGI Global.

Jakobsson, M. (2007). The human factor in phishing. *Proceedings of the Privacy and Security of Consumer Information*.

Jakobsson, M., & Myers, S. (2008). Delayed password disclosure. *International Journal of Applied Cryptography*, *1*(1), 47–59. doi:10.1504/IJACT.2008.017051

Kainda, R., Flechais, I., & Roscoe, A. W. (2010). Security and Usability: Analysis and Evaluation. *Proceedings of the 5th International Conference on Availability, Reliability and Security*. doi:10.1109/ARES.2010.77

Kirlappos, I., & Sasse, M. A. (2012). Security education against phishing: A modest proposal for a major rethink. *IEEE Security and Privacy*, *10*(2), 24–32. doi:10.1109/MSP.2011.179

Kumaraguru, P., Sheng, S., Acquisti, A., Cranor, L. F., & Hong, J. (2007). Teaching Johnny not to fall for phish. *ACM Transactions on Internet Technology*, *10*(2).

Kuo, C., Parno, B., & Perrig, A. (2007). Browser enhancements for preventing phishing attacks. In M. Jakobsson & S. Myers (Eds.), *Phishing and countermeasures: Understanding the increasing problem of electronic identity theft* (pp. 351–367). John Wiley & Sons, Inc.

Li, L. (2013). *A contingency framework to assure the user-centred quality and to support the design of anti-phishing software* (PhD Thesis). University of Tampere, Finland.

Li, L., Berki, E., Helenius, M., & Ovaska, S. (2014). Towards a contingency approach with whitelist- and blacklist-based anti-phishing applications: What do usability tests indicate? *Behaviour & Information Technology, 33*(11), 1136–1147. doi:10.1080/0144929X.2013.875221

Li, L., Berki, E., Helenius, M., & Reijo, S. (2012). New usability metrices for authentication mechanisms. *Proceedings of the SQM and INSPIRE International Conference.*

Li, L., & Helenius, M. (2007). Usability evaluation of anti-phishing toolbars. *Journal of Computer Virology, 3*(2), 163–184. doi:10.1007/s11416-007-0050-4

Li, L., Helenius, M., & Berki, E. (2007). Phishing resistant information systems: security handling with misuse cases design. *Proceedings of the SQM Conference.*

Li, L., Helenius, M., & Berki, E. (2011). How and why phishing and spam messages disturb us? *Proceedings of the IADIS International Conference ICT, Society and Human Beings.*

Li, L., Nummenmaa, T., Berki, E., & Helenius, M. (2015). Phishing Knowledge based User Modelling in Software Design. *Proceedings of the SPLST Conference.*

Mabry, J. (2015). *Recent progress in biometrics.* Clanrye International.

McCanny, J., & Hopper, A. (2016). *Progress and research in cybersecurity: Supporting resilience, trust and digital identities.* The Royal Society.

McRae, C. M., & Vaughn, R. B. (2007). Phighting the phisher: Using web bugs and honeytokens to investigate the source of phishing attacks. *Proceedings of the 40th Hawaii International Conference on System Sciences.* doi:10.1109/HICSS.2007.435

Milletary, J. (2013). *Technical trends in phishing attacks.* Retrieved on 16 August 2017 from: https://www.us-cert.gov/sites/default/files/publications/phishing_trends0511.pdf

Mystakidis, S., Berki, E., & Valtanen, J. (2017). Toward successfully integrating mini learning games into social virtual reality environments: Recommendations for improving open and distance learning. *Proceedings of the 9th EDULEARN.* doi:10.21125/edulearn.2017.1203

News.163.com. (2014). *The police raid in Dongguan becomes a spoofing resource.* Retrieved on 12 August 2014 from: http://news.163.com/14/0213/03/9KUCEQKI00014Q4P.html

Pauli, J. J., & Xu, D. (2005). Misuse case-based design and analysis of secure software architecture. *Proceedings of the International Conference on Information Technology: Coding and Computing, 2,* 398-403. doi:10.1109/ITCC.2005.199

Pyöriä, P., Melin, H., & Blom, R. (2005). *Knowledge workers in the information society.* Tampere: Tampere University Press.

Ramzan, Z. (2006). *Context-Aware phishing realized*. Retrieved on 15 August 2017 from: https://www.symantec.com/connect/blogs/context-aware-phishing-realized

Rathore, S., & Ahuja, V. (2015). A study of role stress among the IT professionals in India: Examining the impact of demographic factors. *International Journal of Human Capital and IT Professionals*, 6(2).

Rauhala, E. (2014). *In China, police raid on notorious 'Sin City' greeted with ridicule*. Retrieved on 12 September 2014 from: http://time.com/6064/in-china-police-raid-on-notorious-sin-city-greeted-with-ridicule/

RSA. (2009). *Phishing, vishing and smishing: Old threats present new risks*. RSA.

Ruggiero, P., & Foote, J. (2011). *Cyber threats to mobile phone*. US-CERT.

Samani, R., & McFarland, C. (2014). *Hacking the human operating system:Tthe role of social engineering within cybersecurity*. Intel Security McAfee.

Schneier, B. (2000). *Cryoto-gram*. Retrieved on 24 August 2017 from: https://www.schneier.com/crypto-gram/archives/2000/1015.html

Sheng, S., Holbrook, M., Kumaraguru, P., Cranor, L., & Downs, J. (2010). Who Falls for Phish? A demographic analysis of phishing susceptibility and effectiveness of interventions. *Proceedings of the Conference on Human Factors in Computing System*.

Sheng, S., Magnien, B., Kumaraguru, P., Acquisti, A., Cranor, L. F., Hong, J., & Nunge, E. (2007). Anti-phishing Phil: The design and evaluation of a game that teaches people not to fall for phish. *Proceedings of the SOUPS*, 88-99. doi:10.1145/1280680.1280692

Simonite, T. (2013). *Google wants to replace your password with a ring*. Retrieved on 16 August 2014 from: http://www.technologyreview.com/news/512051/google-wants-to-replace-all-your-passwords-with-a-ring/

Sindre, G., & Opdahl, A. (2005). Eliciting security requirements with misuse cases. *Requirements Engineering*, 10(1), 34–44. doi:10.1007/s00766-004-0194-4

Sinofsky, S. (2011). *Signing in with a picture password*. Retrieved on 16 August 2014 from: http://blogs.msdn.com/b/b8/archive/2011/12/16/signing-in-with-a-picture-password.aspx

Surowiecki, J. (2005). *The wisdom of crowds*. Anchor Books.

Technopedia. (2017). *Definition of cyberattack*. Retrieved on 14 August 2017 from: https://www.techopedia.com/definition/24748/cyberattack

U.S. Department of Homeland Security. (2013). *What is security and resilience?* Retrieved on 16 August 2014 from: http://www.dhs.gov/what-security-and-resilience

Valtanen, J. (2016). *What is the Problem? The meaning of problem in problem-based learning context – Towards problem-aware students* (PhD Thesis). University of Tampere, Finland.

Wilson, V., & Pirrie, A. (2000). *Multidisciplinary teamworking beyond the barriers? A review of the issues*. Scottish Council of Research in Education SCRE.

Wu, M., Miller, R. C., & Garfinkel, S. L. (2006). Do security toolbars actually prevent phishing attacks? *Proceedings of the Conference on Human Factors in Computing System*, 601-610. doi:10.1145/1124772.1124863

Yee, K. (2004). Aligning security and usability. *IEEE Security and Privacy*, 2(5), 48–55. doi:10.1109/MSP.2004.64

Yuan, X., Guo, M., Ren, F., & Peng, F. (2014). Usability analysis of online bank login interface based on eye tracking experiment. *Sensors & Transducers*, *165*(2), 203–212.

Chapter 6
A Community–Driven Mobile System to Support Foreign Language Learning

Manuel Palomo-Duarte
University of Cadiz, Spain

Anke Berns
University of Cadiz, Spain

Alberto Cejas
University of Cadiz, Spain

Juan Manuel Dodero
University of Cadiz, Spain

Juan Antonio Caballero-Hernández
University of Cadiz, Spain

Iván Ruiz-Rube
University of Cadiz, Spain

ABSTRACT

The acquisition of foreign language competencies has become one of the main concerns of current ICT educational policies. Mobile smart devices allow teachers to provide students with personalized learning environments in line with their needs. However, most of the available apps, especially in the area of foreign language learning, still focus on form-based learning supporting mainly one-way interaction. In this chapter, the authors designed a learning system based on a dynamic, asynchronous and constructive learning approach. The chapter illustrates how the system helped students to get involved in their learning process by creating, sharing, and assessing their own learning resources and how teachers could benefit from students' logs to retrieve indicators for assessment processes. Finally, two algorithms that guide students' learning processes are compared: the first algorithm is based on community-driven behaviour, the second one on students' individual behaviour. Results show that both algorithms provide similar outcomes.

DOI: 10.4018/978-1-5225-5297-0.ch006

INTRODUCTION

Due to the increasing trend towards globalisation foreign language competencies together with generic competencies have become two of the main job requirements in all professional areas especially in leading Information and Communication Technologies (ICT) companies (EGFSN, 2013). Even though most ICT professionals are required to understand technical documentation in English or, sometimes, even German, they often lack the language competencies they would need in order to effectively communicate and collaborate with other speakers of the target language (ICT Ireland, & ISA, 2011). Due to the growing rise and availability of the ICTs coupled with the need to support students' in their learning process, especially out of class, many educational institutions have started integrating in their teaching process different kinds of online learning tools. Among the most widespread ones are Learning Management Systems (LMSs) such as Moodle, Blackboard, WebCT, etc. (Del Blanco et al., 2011; Berns et al., 2013a & b) since they provide both, teachers and students with new opportunities to facilitate and enhance teaching and learning processes. Apart from LMSs there are other types of learning platforms such as Personal Learning Environments (PLEs) or mobile Personal Learning Environments (mPLEs) (Humanante-Ramos et al., 2017; Kukulska-Hulme, 2016) that are becoming increasingly popular, since they allow teachers as well as students to manage and control their teaching/ learning contents according to their needs. Furthermore, PLEs allow for a more ubiquitous teaching/learning process enabling teachers to more easily manage and administer their course contents and teaching resources, students to access learning resources at any time and place (Berns et al., 2017a) and finally, to allow its users to create highly versatile and learner-centered learning environments (Viberg & Grönlund, 2012).

In line with the growing trend and interest in taking advantage of mobile devices for educational purposes (Iglesias Rodríguez, García Riaza, 2017, & Nielson, 2017), especially in the area of Mobile Assisted Language Learning (MALL), the authors of the current study have designed a dynamic mobile learning system, called *Anon_app* (Berns et al., 2015 & 2017b) that aims at enhancing students' language learning process by means of a collaborative learning environment. Since gamification has been identified as a potential tool to increase students' motivation as well as learning outcomes (Bytheway, 2011; Connolly et al., 2001; Hamari et al., 2014; Berns et al., 2016), the use of games has attracted the interest of many practitioners in the area of education (Burston, 2013; Minovic et al., 2012; Vassilev, 2015; Síthigh, 2011). This together with the fact that nowadays devices such as smartphones and tablets are amongst students' most frequently used gadgets (Agudo et al., 2011; Chinnery, 2006; Berns & Palomo-Duarte, 2015) encouraged the authors of the current chapter to integrate a gamified app in the course syllabus of a German foreign language course. By using game elements the authors intended to increase students' motivation towards language learning, especially outside class. In a context in which students often lack the language input and practice they would need to acquire the level, they are expected to have at the end of the term, the current study aims to take advantage of the possibilities of a community-driven mobile learning system to support students in their language learning process, while at the same time helping teachers to more easily monitor and assess students' learning process (Garrison & Kanuka, 2004; Berns et al., 2013a; Berns et al., 2013b).

The current chapter illustrates first, how the mobile learning system helped students to become actively involved in their own learning process by creating, sharing and assessing their own learning resources and second, how teachers can benefit from students' logs to retrieve objective indicators to enhance assessment processes. Finally, the software system implements two different algorithms in order to support students' in their learning processes. While the first algorithm is based on students' interaction with the app as part of a learner community, the second algorithm, that was implemented in the second version of the app, was based solely on students' individual behaviour. In this study, the authors analyse and compare the impact of both algorithms on students' learning outcomes. Results show that both algorithm provide similar learning outcomes.

This chapter is organized as follows: Section 2 sets out the context of the current study within related works, followed by Section 3, which outlines the teaching background for the learning experience. Section 4 describes the learning design that has been implemented, followed by Section 5 which presents the experimental settings and discusses the results of the study. Finally, in Section 6 the authors draw some conclusions and future lines of work.

RELATED WORKS

The potential of smartphones and tablets to provide students with dynamic and personalized learning environments in line with their needs is well-known. However, a review of the literature shows that most of the available apps, especially in the area of MALL, still focus on form-based learning supporting mainly one-way interaction (teacher to learner or computer-learner interaction) rather than exploring the wide range of interactive tools, current smartphones (tablets) provide, to support collaborative and constructive learning approaches (Sa'don & Iahad, 2017; Calderón-Márquez et al., 2017; Olmo-Gil, 2017; Berns et al., 2017a).

Mobile learning (m-learning) has created a new learning paradigm in educational settings as an extension of distance and blended learning approaches, offering new possibilities for developing learning tools that can easily be adapted to students' particular learning needs -hence nurturing more conventional teaching/learning approaches. The Information Gathering and Lesson Tool (IGLOO) is one example of the many tools and applications that have been developed in this context. IGLOO is a mobile learning system that supports teachers and students during their learning process by means of different formal as well as informal learning scenarios (Samuel et al., 2009; García-Peñalvo et al., 2012; Colomo-Palacios et al., 2014). Another example for a mobile learning system is the one created by the e-Learning Laboratory of the Shanghai Jiao Tong University. The system delivers live broadcast of real-time classroom teaching to online students with mobile devices, allowing students to customize their ways of receiving, based on when and where they are tuning into the broadcast. To increase interactivity between the teacher and online students in large classes, the system also supports short text-messaging and instant polls. This way, students can pose questions and make suggestions in real time, while teachers can address them immediately, hence providing students with instant feedback (Qi et al., 2006).

Additionally, mobile learning frameworks such as the one designed by (Girão et al., 2010) have been proposed to cover the main topics of an analog electronics course (semiconductors theory, diodes, transistors, etc.). Besides these generic applications and learning tools, other applications such as mobile learning games have been developed for a huge variety of learning contexts (Berns et.al., 2016 & 2017b). Game-Based Learning (GBL) uses the motivational potential of computer games to engage students in learning processes (Prensky, 2005) by providing them with fun, interactive and often experiential virtual learning experiences. Another interesting aspect of using computer games for educational purposes is the huge variety of game plays: from casual, direct subject up to cooperative games (Cornillie et al., 2012). Due to their variety of content, design and player modes teachers are able to implement different types of games in line with their students' interests and specific learning needs. However, several researchers, especially from the area of MALL, have underlined the need for designing games based on open-source software to allow teachers and other stakeholders to easily adapt game contents to students' specific learner profiles, learning needs and language level (Berns et al., 2013a & b).

Another interesting study on GBL is the one carried out by (Lilly & Warnes, 2009). The study provides three game templates for mobile Game-Based Learning (mGBL) that were developed for educational purposes in the fields of e-commerce, e-health and e-career. While Game Template 1 is based on a quiz module and a simulation module, Game Template 2 employs an adventure game that aims at improving the player's avatar characteristics in an e-career context. Finally, Game Template 3 allows for modeling games which require the user to focus on real world problems and to solve these. Game templates include tools such as text chats in order to communicate with other players, quizzes and simulations as well as different kinds of media collection and sharing.

Apart from the above mentioned studies, other studies have analysed the use of mobile games to foster the development of more specific skills. In (Sánchez & Olivares, 2011) three mobile games were developed and played by teams of four students in order to collaboratively solve a series of problems. The first mobile game, called *Evolution*, used sophisticated 3D graphics, where the design of some elements such as time, actions, logic and resources were aligned with real-time strategy games. The added value of real-time strategy games especially lies in their potential to help players developing problem solving skills. The second and third game (*BuinZoo* and *Museum*) were trivia-based games, that aimed at guiding young learners during their virtual visits through a zoo or museum. Both games were designed to help students fostering their knowledge on subjects related to the science curriculum (Sánchez & Olivares, 2011).

Other interesting works on using game-based apps to increase students' motivation and interaction in the target language can be found in the area of MALL (Berns & Palomo-Duarte, 2015; Berns et al., 2016). One example is the *VocabTRAINER A1* app, which is based on 9 mini-games that are played individually and offline, providing students with different exercises to foster their vocabulary and grammar skills. Once a student has successfully completed the different mini-games, the app allows him to participate in a collaborative online game, called *Catch me, if you can!*. During the game students must identify together with their game partners (2 policemen and 1 detective) a virtual murderer to prevent him from committing another crime. To do so players must coordinate their actions by communicating amongst each other vía an in-app text chat.

Another popular learning approach has been the use of serious games, which aim to provide learners adaptive learning scenarios and personalized itineraries (Del Blanco., 2012) to better meet their learning needs. An example for such an approach can be found in (Burgos et al., 2007) where the authors present an authoring tool for creating and playing point-and-click adventure games called <e-Adventure>. <E-Adventure> allows to integrate within the developed games adaptive Units of Learning (UoL) by using flags as game states. In case that the state of flags is modified, the game can adopt a completely different behaviour and deliver new UoLs (Moreno-Ger et al., 2008).

Learning through games has traditionally been assessed through summative assessment, focusing on learning outcomes rather than on learning processes. However, in recent years there has been an increasing trend to focus more on students' learning process by integrating formative assessment, also known as real-time assessment. Real-time assessment aims at giving students instant feedback on their performance -hence helping them to succeed in their learning process (Caballero-Hernández et al., 2017). Learning through digital games is often evaluated by using pre- and post-tests in order to measure content knowledge. However, research has shown that such traditional assessment methods often do not allow for analysing the complex learning process by providing for instance information on the competencies a learner might have acquired due to the game (Shute & Ke, 2012). One way to improve assessment procedures and measures, in terms of quality and utility, consists in using Evidence-Centered Design (ECD) (Mislevy et al., 2003). ECD supports the design of valid assessments, yielding real-time estimation of students' competence levels, based on a wide range of knowledge and skills. One popular way of assessing students' competencies is using Stealth assessment, which refers to ECD-based assessment procedures that are interwoven with the game-environment itself and thus invisible for the player (Shute & Venture, 2013). During the game-play, players produce different sets of actions, whereas the interest of Stealth assessment focuses on analysing and assessing the different skills students use to complete the game task. As a result, stealth assessment procedures focus on the analysis of students' interaction while playing a game in order to obtain data on students' skills and game performance. Another popular assessment procedure for educational settings refers to authentic assessment which plays an important role for assessing students' competencies. However, researchers differ in their opinions on this topic. While some researchers consider authentic assessment as an evaluation of students' performance (Torrance, 1995), others (Herrington & Herrington, 1998) argue that authentic assessment emphasises the meaningful content of the task and its context. After reviewing different definitions Gulikers et al. (2004) describe authentic assessment as one that requires students using the same competencies and attitudes they would need to apply to common situations in their professional life. So, this approach could be integrated in games through an analysis of the player's behaviour, whereas the required competencies are used to solve very specific situations.

Another emerging field in the area of GBL is Learning Analytics (LA), which aims at making an efficient and effective use of educational data. LA includes capturing, tracking, aggregating, analysing and utilising/visualising information on both, students' interactions with the learning content itself as well as on their learning progress. A key issue when using LA is to determine which information is going to be extracted (Shoukry et al., 2014). The classification of the data collected depends on whether a general (extensive data) or more detailed observation (intensive data) is desired. Collecting data from a single-player game differs from collecting data from a multi-player game mode, since in this last one students interact with other players, hence generating a greater amount of data. Mobile devices are very promising platforms for LA. Due to their wide availability, accessibility and ease of use, they make data collection much more natural and non-invasive than sometimes traditional platforms do. Furthermore, ubiquitous LA are becoming increasingly popular as it allows considering additional information concerning the context learning takes place. This way factors such as time, location, activity, noise, light and social environment can be analysed (Aljohani & Davis, 2012).

Educational Data Mining (EDM) is a concept related to LA. The International Educational Data Mining Society defines EDM as "an emerging discipline, concerned with developing methods to explore the unique types of data that come from educational settings and to use these methods to better understand students' learning processes." So both disciplines aim to use collected data to improve learning processes as well as their assessment. However they also differ from each other in some of the following ways: the type of discovery that is prioritised (while EDM focus on automated discovery, LA focus on leveraging human judgement), the type of adaptation and personalisation typically supported (EDM models are more often used as the basis of automated adaptation and LA models are more often designed to empower instructors and learners), the distinction between holistic (LA) and reductionists (EDM) frameworks, the most common origins (semantic web or intelligent curriculum for LA and educational software and student modelling for EDM) and methods and techniques used (social network analysis or sentiment analysis for LA and classification or clustering for EDM) (Siemens & Baker, 2012).

Apart from the previously mentioned approaches another popular learning approach is the use of educational games based on competition. In this kind of approach learning is achieved throughout the competition between two or more players, using the element of competition to increase students' motivation (Palomo-Duarte et al., 2012). Literature review has shown that there are numerous examples of game-based learning through competition. One example is the Free Libresoft Educational Quizzbowl game (FLEQ), which is a tournament management software, that allows its participants to synchronously play against other players on an Internet Relay Chat (IRC) channel. The game mechanism consists in competing amongst each other, answering Trivia-like questions (Robles et al., 2012). As such, it is a competitive out of class GBL learning initiative.

Another relevant aspect of mobile GBL refers to Location-based learning which offers different possibilities to enrich students' learning experiences. Learning processes can be extended from traditional classroom settings to those beyond classroom and thus more closely related to students' everyday life. This allows, for instance, to create learning environments in which their users can interact with physical or virtual objects, developing productive learning experiences involving exploration and cooperation (Hwang et al., 2008; Mota, Ruiz-Rube, Dodero, & Figueiredo, 2016) or even accessing contextualised information, communication, analysis and interrelation of real places (Roschelle, 2003).

In location-based learning games usually several students have to share a single mobile device to jointly perform a game task. An analysis of this situation is done in (Melero et al., 2015). The analysis is done through the design and evaluation of a location-based learning game in which students had to play in groups sharing a mobile device whilst visiting a contemporary museum. During the game, students are asked to visit specific places in the museum solving a number of questions, which are placed all over the museum. Players are provided with positive and negative feedback on their game performance, indicating the correct and incorrect answers. To successfully complete the game all questions need to be answered correctly. After evaluating different characteristics of location-based learning games the authors conclude that this type of game is more suitable for smaller learner groups, especially if it aims to keep all learners actively involved in the game task.

Additionally there are some ethical considerations that should be taken into account when using games, simulations and virtual worlds for educational purposes. Generally, considerations about ethics start with social concepts on what is right or wrong concluding with several moral principles on what people are expected to do in terms of rights, fairness and responsibilities to local and global benefits. In a research work on this topic (Warren & Lin, 2013) some guidelines and key issues are provided along with an illustrative example. Furthermore, to minimise risks, the authors recommend designers to critically reflect on questions such as: if a game, simulation or virtual world is appropriate for the target audience, if there are means to measure whether the product influences learning or not and if the design variables can be controlled to minimise social, psychological and learning risks for its users.

THEORETICAL BACKGROUND

The mobile learning system designed for the current project is based on the pedagogical framework of mobile learning. As outlined by Sharples and other researchers (Sharples et al., 2005) mobile learning theories recognises not only "(...) the essential role of mobility and communication in the process of learning (...)" but also the importance of the context for meaning construction. Mobile learning has also been described as a process in which knowledge is gained throughout multiple contexts amongst people and personal interactive technologies". In line with the aforementioned aspects Sharples et al. propose a framework that is based on Engeström's expansive activity model (Engeström, 1987) and which aims to analyse the interdependencies between learning and technology. The framework he proposes is mainly based on five factors (subject, object, context, tools and communication), which are themselves analysed under two different layers: a technological and a semiotic layer. The technological layer describes learning as "an engagement with technology, in which devices such as mobile phones (...) function as interactive agents (...)" that help its users to acquire knowledge, to communicate amongst each other, to share and negotiate contents and meanings and, finally, to reflect on them. In contrast, the semiotic layer describes learning as "a cognitive system in which learners' objective-oriented actions are mediated by cultural tools and signs".

Anon_app has been designed on the aforementioned framework combined with a social constructivist approach which conceives learning as "an active process of building knowledge and skills through game-based learning activities within a supportive community" (Sharples et al., 2005). Hence some of the key-issues, when starting with the design, were that in order to guarantee an effective learning environment, the mobile learning system should be *learner-*, *knowledge-*, *assessment-* as well as *community centered* (Moreno-Ger et al., 2008; Belloti et al., 2013). This means firstly, that content builds on students' competences, background knowledge and interests (Krashen, 1985; Sharples et al., 2005), secondly, that the curriculum is built from "sound foundation of validated knowledge" (*knowledge centered*) (Sharples et al., 2005), thirdly, that assessment is matched to our students' ability offering them individualised feedback and formative guidance (assessment centered). And fourth, that the system should engage learners in sharing knowledge and in supporting weaker students (*community centered*) (Sharples et al., 2005; Moreno-Ger et al., 2008).

Anon_app provides students with a dynamic learning environment allowing them to asynchronously get and produce new language in- and out-put. This is done through a variety of tasks which focus on students' reading and writing competencies. All tasks are based on the idea of guessing and explaining words previously selected by the teacher from the A1 level of the Common European Framework of Reference for Languages (CEFR). The corpus is gradually created, assessed and reported by the players themselves (Taras, 2002; Van Zundert et al., 2010; Gikandi et al., 2011). This way, students are encouraged to become actively involved in their own learning process by reviewing and reflecting on the target language and hence gradually co-constructing the system knowledge (Marty & Carron, 2011; Berns et al., 2013b). Additionally, in order to make the learning experience more engaging a score system was incorporated (Dondlinger, 2007; Berns et al., 2013a).

DESIGN AND ARCHITECTURE

The software (Figure 1) the authors have developed specifically for the current project is available as GPL free software in its forge[1]. While the system in its first version, launched in 2014, was only available for Android devices, the authors decided in 2015 to launch a second version of the app, by rewriting its source code and using the multi-platform library libGDx (Saltares Márquez & Cejas Sánchez, 2014). Since then the app is both available for Android devices as well as the iPhone/iPad or PC. Once

Figure 1. Architecture diagram of the system

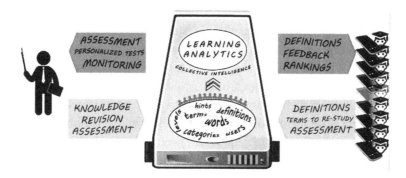

students have installed the client software in their Android smartphones or tablets, this identifies them and interacts with the server through the Internet to implement the learning process.

The typical application work-flow starts by asking the users to select the language they want to focus on. At the moment the system supports English, German and Russian, but it can easily be implemented by including other languages simply translating a couple of text files. The target language is used both, for the design of the interface as well as the learning tasks to perform. Once the user has selected the language he wants to focus on, he is asked to identify himself by introducing his email address and password. This allows him to play on different devices (smartphone, tablet or laptop) in line with his personal needs, circumstances, etc.

Apart from this, before each game-session players must choose the level and categories they want to play. This allows for a customisable learning process in line with the students' learning needs. This way students with a higher language level compared to the rest of the language course can play more advanced levels, whereas those with a lower language proficiency can repeat already played terms, as many times as they need. Once within the app screen (Figure 2), the system provides players first with a selected definition of a term, which they must guess. Moreover, the app provides students with the option to ask for an additional clue (e.g. Definition of cold: In Alaska it is always _____. The first letter is "c". Clue: In the summer it is usually hot, but in the winter it is often _____).

For each term players have to guess they are given the opportunity to guess the required answer three times. Once they have failed the third attempt the system automatically provides them with instant and explicit feedback by indicating the player the correct answer. Feedback here aims to be constructive, supporting and guiding students during their learning process (Sun et al., 2008).

To enhance students' incidental vocabulary learning players are allowed to copy definitions (or part of them) to their notebook and thus to store them in their app for later review (Brown et al., 2008). Finally, before getting access to the next definition, users are always asked to grade the previously played definition. In 2016 the grading system was finally refined in order to enhance learning students' outcomes: while in the first version of the app (2015) students were asked to provide a general rating for each definition they had played (based on the question whether the definition they had played was a good or bad definition, that helped them in their learning process), this time students were asked to assess each definition, they had played, by answering a number of questions related with grammatical and linguistic aspects. Questions were randomly chosen from a pool of questions and aimed at focusing students' attention on linguistic aspects such as the position or conjugation of a verb within a sentence (definition), the use of capital letters when using nouns, etc. Additionally, in case students considered

Figure 2. Screenshot of the app displaying a definition to guess

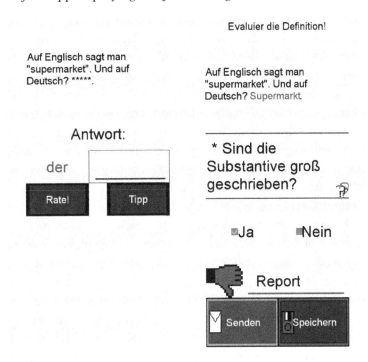

a definition wrong or inappropriate (in terms of linguistics or content), they were allowed to report the respective definition by always indicating the reason for their report: improper or offensive content, linguistic mistakes or inaccurate definition.

At the end of each game-session, an overall summary is shown along with some stats to gamify the app. Furthermore, the *Statistics* option from the main menu will always preserve the last game-session data along with a bulk of additional useful information regarding the definitions played and results obtained. The Statistics provide players with data on their success ratio, the number of definitions, which have been played, the categories in which the player guessed the most or the least definitions as well as the frequency with which each level has been played and selected. Furthermore some additional information on players actions are provided. This is for instance, on the definitions introduced by the users themselves, including the average rating, the average success ratio and number of reports.

In addition to the previously commented usual game flow, students are allowed to contribute to the system by creating and deciding on his own learning resources (Berns et al., 2017b). As a result, once a student has played a certain number of definitions, he is invited to create a new definition for a word the system automatically provides him with. Once a student has created a definition this will be automatically included in the database together with those previously introduced by other peers or the teacher. Allowing students to get actively involved in the learning process, by tailoring learning contents to their personal needs, makes the app a dynamic learning tool. As new definitions will be played and peer-assessed, students are encouraged to do their best when adding a new definition to the system. This way, the platform's knowledge base is being increased and continuously reviewed by the users themselves. As a result of this process, the server will contain different graded definitions for each term.

The knowledge base, which is being stored by the server program includes the following data: the definitions available for each term, the definitions each student guessed or failed during each game-session, the assessment of each player and the terms that each player considered interesting to be restudied. Thanks to this information the system provides its users with constant feedback on their individual learning progress. In addition, since this knowledge base is increased and continuously assessed by the users themselves, the server will contain not only different definitions for each term, but also different grades.

With regard to teachers' assessment of students' learning process the mobile learning system provides teachers with a web portal that allows them to easily monitor and assess students' interaction with the app by accessing different learning analytics, that provide valuable data on: the usage, each student has made of the app (Figure 3), the grades students obtained (according to the terms that have been guessed and the grades students' definitions received) (Figure 4) along with the grades each student gave when assessing the played definitions (Figure 5).

Finally, a report of the low-graded definitions provides teachers with an insight into the difficulties a specific student (or a group of them) might have encountered when playing the app. In addition, those definitions that unfairly received high grades can help identifying students who are unable to detect mistakes related to linguistic or in the target language. Furthermore the system will provide the teacher with different recommendations. For example, if the ratio of students guessing a concrete definition is below a certain threshold, it may indicate that its linguistic level is too complex.

Additionally, the server allows teachers to automatically create personalised tests for each player, in line with teachers' interests and needs with regard to students' assessment. In particular, the tests can include a certain number of random definitions as well as definitions a concrete student successfully guessed when playing the app. This way, the teacher is able to check whether a student introduced the correct answer with the help of additional resources such as en extra dictionary or whether he/she guessed them due to his language proficiency/knowledge of the target language. Additionally, the personalised tests might also include a certain number of definitions that a student either did not guess or did not focus on during the different game sessions.

Finally, the software system implements two algorithms, based on two different criteria, to select from the knowledge base the definitions that each student must guess during the different game ses-

Figure 3. Interface of the teacher's web portal in order to generate statistics on student's learning process

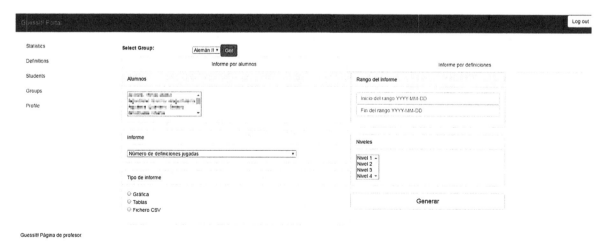

Figure 4. Statistics on students' interaction with the app and the definitions played by each student

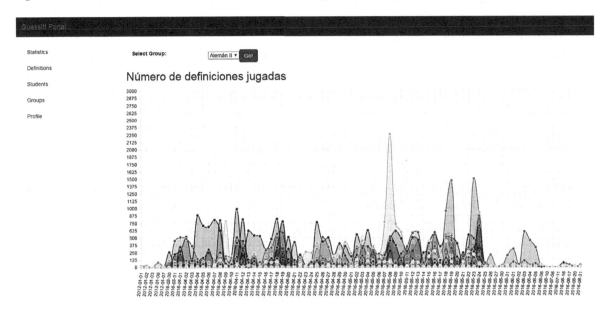

Figure 5. Statistics on the number of definitions each student created and added to the knowledge base

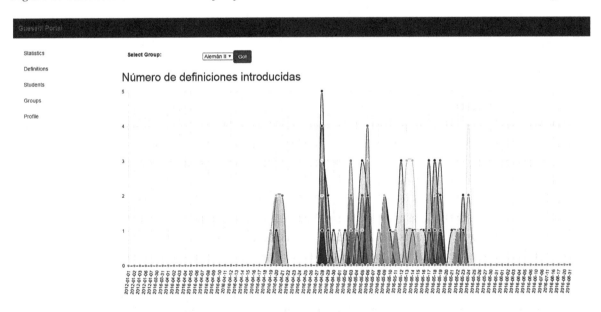

sions. Since the knowledge base is constantly increasing, due to students' interaction with the system, the authors were particularly concerned about providing students with the most suitable definitions from the knowledge base in order to guarantee that the language input provided by the system, would help them strengthening their language level. To this end the authors implemented in their first version of the software an algorithm, that allowed the system to select and deliver, for each game round, definitions to be played by the students according to the grades these had previously been given to by the community of players. While those definitions with higher grades were delivered more often by the system, those with lower grades were delivered less frequently. To take into account students' learning progress, the grades a definition received more than two weeks ago had lower weight on the algorithm (as students are supposed to have a higher proficiency).

With the purpose to harness the potential of the app and to support students' in their learning process the authors developed in 2016 a second version of the mobile learning system, by implementing two types of algorithm: one, based on the behaviour of the entire learner community and one, based on students' individual game behaviour and interaction with the app. The added value of the second algorithm was that it allowed to combine the definitions to be played by the students, from two different sources: while the first kind was made of those definitions a student had not played, making up to 50% of each game round, the second one was made of those definitions a student had already played, but was not able to guess. This way the authors wanted to make sure, on the one hand, that students would play all available definitions and, on the other, that students would be able to focus especially on those definitions they struggled with and thus apparently still present some linguistic barrier for them, which they need to overcome by replaying the respective definitions. In case there are enough new definitions for the player, at least half of each game round will be based on those new definitions. However, the ratio on which those definitions will be offered depends on student's performance: the lower the guessing ratio of a student is, the more new definitions will be offered to him in order to help him focusing especially on his weaknesses in the target language and to gradually overcome them.

EXPERIMENT

Settings

The experiment was carried out with more than 52 students from a CEFR A1.1 level German foreign language course (6 ECTS) at a Spanish University. The course lasted one semester and was based on 48 contact hours combined with 104 independent learning hours. From the very first moment of their German language course students were exposed to the target language and used to employ this as the only vehicle to interact and communicate with the language teacher as well as other peers.

The experience lasted about 4 weeks, during which students were asked to use the *Anon_app* for their independent learning beyond class, by focusing each week on a different level. Before giving students access to the *Anon_app* the authors asked students to take part in a pre-test in order to test their vocabulary and grammar knowledge at the outset of the experiment. The test was made of 60 questions that were randomly selected from the knowledge base comprising vocabulary and grammar items from all four levels. As our target students were from the A1.1 level of the CEFR the vocabulary and grammar items of the mobile learning system as well as the different pre- and post-tests were based on this level.

Once students had taken part in the pre-test (which focused on the vocabulary and grammar items from all four levels of the app), they were invited to use the app for their independent and out of class learning. To become familiar with the app students were asked to focus first on levels 1 and 2 (which were based mainly on already known vocabulary from previous language classes) and second, on levels 3 and 4. Unlike the first two levels, levels 3 and 4 were only in part known to the students -hence providing student with new language input and the opportunity to foster and widen their knowledge on the target language.

Additionally, and in order to analyse the apps' impact on students' learning process, they were asked to take each week a test that focused on the levels and language items they had previously played. After one week using the app, students were asked to fill in a first post-test, followed by a second and third one, each of which took place in an interval of one week. All tests were completed off-line and focused as the pre-test did, on 60 questions, that were randomly selected from the knowledge base. Nonetheless, unlike the pre-test, that focused on language items from all four levels, the three post-tests were based on vocabulary from different levels in line with the levels students were asked to play during each week of the experiment. While post-test 1 focused on levels 1 and 2, post-test 2 focused on levels 1 to 3 followed by post-test 3, which were based on levels 1 to 4. Moreover, in the case of post-test 3 content had been selected on the basis of a much larger corpus (376 definitions) compared to when learners took part in the pre-test (224 definitions). Since students started introducing (from the second week of the experiment onwards), new definitions, the knowledge base increased significantly each week and differed significantly from the initial knowledge base, that is at the outset of the experiment.

Previous works on *Anon_app* had already highlighted the app's potential for supporting students' language learning processes (Palomo-Duarte et al.). In 2016 year, an A/B test was implemented in the experience in order to compare the results of a traditional learning process (based on individual behaviour and a community-driven approach. This way, in 2016, half of the students used the original community-driven algorithm, and the other half used the second algorithm that was based on students' individual performance. Students were randomly assigned to each algorithm and played a total number of 138,149 definitions while the knowledge base contained 376 definitions of which 152 were created and added to by the students themselves.

ANALYSIS AND DISCUSSION

An analysis of the different tests and their results allows for the following insights: Firstly, all of the students, who took part in the 4 tests (one pre-test plus three post-tests), significantly improved their test scores, comparing their results from the pre-test with those obtained in post-test 3. The latter was completed by all students at the end of the game experience, allowing teachers to evaluate students' learning progress. The positive results are especially remarkable taking into account that the knowledge base increased on a daily basis. When preparing the different tests, the authors were always concerned about including at least 50% of the definitions created and introduced by the learners themselves mixed up with another 50% of definitions, which were created and introduced by the language teacher. All definitions were selected due to linguistic as well as content-based criteria. This means that the authors selected those definitions, which were very good definitions in terms of linguistic criteria combined with those which were very clever and outstanding in terms of content.

Additionally, in the last post-test the authors included an exercise in which students were asked to propose their own definitions for a number of terms they were provided. This way, the authors aimed to reward especially those students, with additional scores, who enriched the knowledge base by introducing new definitions, rather than only playing those already provided by their peers or the language teacher.

A comparison between pre-test and post-test 3 underlines the apps impact on students' vocabulary learning. And thus there is an average of 44.26 points of difference in a range of 0 to 100 (18.18 std.

dev.). The difference in the post-test 1 and post-test 2 are negative: students got an average of 4.55 points less from pre-test to post-test 1 (12.85 std. dev.) and 2.40 less from the pre-test to post-test 2 (12.73 std. dev.). While these figures are low in a range from 0 to 100, it seems that students did not play a lot during the first two weeks. According to their comments, it seems that students dedicated the first two weeks to study using traditional methods (they had received the list of words is a PDF document in the first week), and only after realising the added value of the app for studying those words in context they used it massively.

It is noteworthy, that students' learning outcomes are similar, regardless the type of algorithm that has been used. This means, there was no significant difference in terms of learning outcomes. While students using the "A" algorithm (based on the community-driven behaviour) gained an average of 45.23 points (15.99 std. dev.) from pre-test to post-test3, losing 3.23 from pre-test to pos-test 2 (10.35 std. dev.) and losing 2.85 (12.34 std. dev.) on average, those students who used instead the "B" algorithm (based on individual behaviour) gained an average of 42.69 points (21.17 std. dev.) from pre-test to post-test3, losing 6.69 from pre-test to post-test 2 (15.87 std. dev.) and losing 1.68 (13.32 std. dev.) on average.

An analysis of the server logs provides interesting automated indicators for different skills. For instance, if we look at the time dedicated to play, we could easily check constant study skills. This could be done either by seeing if each student played a certain minimum number of definitions during a period of time (day, week) or by checking the total work effort (if we check the whole experiment length). In fact, the students registered in the system, played a total amount of 138,149 definitions. This means that each student played an average of 2,657 definitions. If we estimate that every definition needs a minimum of 20 seconds to be read and answered, and another 10 seconds on average to be assessed and if considered relevant, to be copied down by the users in their app notebook. According to this estimation, each student had dedicated at least more than 22 hours to study using the app. The authors consider this to be a significant amount considering that our pilot study lasted only 4 weeks.

Values are not so similar for students using both algorithms in this aspect. Students using the "A" community-drive algorithm played an average of 2,431 definitions, guessit 80% of them. Those using the "B" algorithm based on individual behaviour 2,617 definitions (similar amount), guessit 87% of them (7% more). Interestingly, students using "A" algorithm added 2.55 definitions, while those using "B" added 3.04 (significantly more). It seems that they felt more comfortable using the app.

To measure participation skills the teacher can check the number of contributions from each student. In our case, the app started with 224 definitions, that were previously introduced by the teacher and ended up with 376 definitions. This means that students' active participation in the development of learning contents helped increasing the number of definitions by almost tripling the definitions, which were initially available. By introducing in total 152 definitions, this is a mean of almost 3 definitions per student. At first sight, it looks as if the figure was not very high, but taking into account that writing in a foreign language in general and definitions in particular is quite difficult, especially at the A1.1 level (CEFR), the results obtained are quite positive.

CONCLUSION

In this chapter, the authors have described the workflow of the gamified multilingual *Anon_app* and the learning objectives the app can be used for. *Anon_app* is a client-server computer software which has been developed specifically for the current research project. While most of the currently available apps

(Heil et al., 2016; Burston 2013, 2014 & 2015; Calderón-Márquez et al., 2017) only offer static and teacher or designer created content, *Anon_app* is dynamically enriched with new content from each of its users. This way, students are actively involved in their own learning process making significant decisions on the learning content and resources they want to use and focus on. In line with this, each player is constantly invited to enter new definitions for the terms the system has previously provided him with. Once a student has introduced a definition, the definition is entered into the system and becomes part of its knowledge base. Since all definitions are peer-assessed by other classmates, while playing the app, the author of each definition gets the opportunity to receive constant feedback on his performance. This feedback aims at providing players with the opportunity to critically review and to develop their language skills. In addition, this process facilitates monitoring and automated assessment by the language teachers.

In the experiment using *Anon_app* the authors used the mobile learning system in a German foreign language course (A1.1 level of the CEFR) at a Spanish University. Students played the app for a period of one month, focusing on four different levels. Results from the pre- and post-tests have shown a significant improvement in terms of vocabulary and grammar acquisition. Probably this is related to the time students spent on playing the app, which was probably a much longer time they usually dedicate for their learning out of class. These results are complemented with objective indicators on the acquisition of other skills that are automatically extracted from system logs. Those results refer, for instance, to students' ability to explain words in a foreign language or the competence to assess definitions, that were created and added by other players. In particular, results show that both algorithm provide similar learning outcomes, hence being the two approaches suitable for guiding the learning process. However, further research is needed to draw some stronger conclusions on the validity of the specific usage students' made of the app and the impact of both algorithms on students' learning.

Future work will focus on making a more detailed analysis of the results obtained in order to identify possible correlations between the different indicators the authors obtained, due to the analysis of students' logs, and students' final course grades. This way, the authors will be able to early identify students' learning profiles and individual learning needs and thus to provide them with almost instant feedback on their learning process. Additionally, the authors intend to develop a Domain Specific Language as the one described by (Balderas, A. et al., 2017) to help language teachers retrieving customized reports of the experience.

ACKNOWLEDGMENT

This work has been funded by the Andalusian Government under the University of Cadiz programme for Researching and Innovation in Education (SOL-201500054668-TRA). The authors would also like to thank the OSLUCA, Aula Universitaria Hispano-Rusa (AUHR), as well as Elihú Salcedo, Juan Miguel Ruiz Ladrón, Manuel Rodríguez-Sánchez Guerra, Sammy Kleinberg, Salvador Sánchez Reyes, Alicia Garrido Guerrero, Mercedes Paez Piña for their much-valued support.

REFERENCES

Agudo, J. E., Rico, M., Sánchez, H., & Valor, M. (2011). Accessing mobile learning records in Moodle through web services. *The IEEE Journal of Latin-American Learning Technologies*, *6*(3), 95–102.

Aljohani, N. R., & Davis, H. C. (2012). Learning analytics in mobile and ubiquitous learning environments. 11th World Conference on Mobile and Contextual Learning: mLearn 2012.

Balderas, A., Berns, A., Palomo-Duarte, M., Dodero, J. M., & Ruiz-Rube, I. (2017). Retrieving Objective Indicators from Student Logs in Virtual Worlds. *Journal of Information Technology Research*, *10*(3), 69–83.

Bellotti, F., Kapralos, B., Lee, K., Moreno-Ger, P., & Berta, R. (2013). Assessment in and of serious games: An overview. *Advances in Human-Computer Interaction*, *2013*, 1. doi:10.1155/2013/120791

Berns, A., Gonzalez-Pardo, A., & Camacho, D. (2013a). Game-like language learning in 3-D virtual environments. *Computers & Education*, *60*(1), 210–220. doi:10.1016/j.compedu.2012.07.001

Berns, A., Palomo-Duarte, M., Dodero, J. M., & Valero-Franco, C. (2013b). Using a 3D online game to assess students' foreign language acquisition and communicative competence. In D. Hernández-Leo, T. Ley, R. Klamma, & A. Harrer (Eds.), Lecture Notes in Computer Science*: Vol. 8095. *Scaling up learning for sustained impact*: Proceedings of the 8th European Conference, on Technology Enhanced Learning (EC-TEL)* (pp. 19-31). Berlin, Germany: Springer-Verlag. doi:10.1007/978-3-642-40814-4_3

Berns, A., & Palomo-Duarte, M. (2015). Supporting Foreign Language Learning through a gamified app. In R. Hernández & P. Rankin (Eds.), *Higher Education and Second Language Learning: Promoting Self-Directed Learning in New Technological and Educational Contexts* (pp. 181–204). Oxford, UK: Peter Lang.

Berns, A., Palomo-Duarte, M., Dodero, J. M., Ruiz-Ladrón, J. M., & Calderón-Márquez, A. (2015). Mobile apps to support and assess foreign language learning. In F. Helm, L. Bradley, M. Guarda, & S. Thouësny (Eds.), *Critical CALL – Proceedings of the 2015 EUROCALL Conference* (pp. 51-56). Academic Press. doi:10.14705/rpnet.2015.000309

Berns, A., Isla-Montes, J. L., Palomo-Duarte, M., & Dodero, J. M. (2016). Motivation, students' needs and learning outcomes: A hybrid game-based app for enhanced language learning. *SpringerPlus*, *5*(1), 1305. doi:10.1186/s40064-016-2971-1 PMID:27547679

Berns, A., Palomo-Duarte, M., Isla-Montes, J. L., Dodero, J. M., & Delatorre, P. (2017a). Agenda colaborativa para el aprendizaje de idiomas: Del papel al dispositivo móvil. *Revista Iberoamericana de Educación a Distancia RIED*, *20*(2), 119–139. doi:10.5944/ried.20.2.17713

Berns, A., Palomo-Duarte, M., & Dodero, J. M. (2017b). A mobile learning system to allow students developing their own learning resources. In. J. Colpaert, A. Aerts, R. Kern, & M. Kaiser (Eds.), *CALL in context- Proceedings of the 2017 CALL conference* (pp. 83-90). Academic Press.

Brown, R., Waring, R., & Donkaewbua, S. (2008). Incidental Vocabulary Acquisition from Reading, Reading-While-Listening, and Listening to Stories. *Reading in a Foreign Language*, *20*(2), 136–163.

Burgos, D., Moreno-Ger, P., Sierra, J. L., & Fernandez-Manjon, B. (2007). Authoring game-based adaptive units of learning with IMS Learning Design and e-Adventure. *International Journal of Learning Technology*, *3*(3), 252–268. doi:10.1504/IJLT.2007.015444

Burston, J. (2013). Mobile-assisted language learning: A selected annotated bibliography of implementation studies 1994-2012. *Language Learning & Technology*, *17*(3), 157–224.

Bytheway, J. A. (2011). *Vocabulary learning strategies in massively multiplayer online role-playing games* (Master's thesis). University of Wellington.

Caballero-Hernández, J. A., Palomo-Duarte, M., & Dodero, J. M. (2017). Skill assessment in learning experiences based on serious games: A Systematic Mapping Study. *Computers & Education*, *113*, 42–60. doi:10.1016/j.compedu.2017.05.008

Calderón-Márquez, A., Palomo-Duarte, M., Berns, A., & Dodero, J. M. (2017). Tendencias y tipos de aprendizaje en MALL: una revisión sistemática de la literatura (2012-2016). *V Congreso Internacional sobre Aprendizaje, Innovación y Competitividad. (CINAIC 2017)*. doi:10.26754/CINAIC.2017.000001_061

Chao, P. Y., & Chen, G. D. (2009). Augmenting paper-based learning with mobile phones. *Interacting with Computers*, *21*(3), 173–185. doi:10.1016/j.intcom.2009.01.001

Chinnery, G. (2006). Emerging technologies. Going to the mall: Mobile assisted language learning. *Language Learning & Technology*, *10*(1), 9–16.

Colomo-Palacios, R., Casado-Lumbreras, C., Soto-Acosta, P., & Misra, S. (2014). Providing knowledge recommendations: An approach for informal electronic mentoring. *Interactive Learning Environments*, *22*(2), 221–240. doi:10.1080/10494820.2012.745430

Connolly, T. M., Stansfield, M., & Hainey, T. (2001). An alternate reality game for language learning: ARGuing for multilingual motivation. *Computers & Education*, *57*(1), 1389–1415. doi:10.1016/j.compedu.2011.01.009

Cornillie, F., Thorne, S. L., & Desmet, P. (2012). ReCALL special issue: Digital games for language learning: challenges and opportunities: Editorial Digital games for language learning: From hype to insight? *ReCALL*, *24*(03), 243–256. doi:10.1017/S0958344012000134

Del Blanco, Á., Torrente, J., Moreno-Ger, P., & Fernández-Manjón, B. (2011). Enhancing adaptive learning and assessment in virtual learning environments with educational games. In Q. Jin (Ed.), *Intelligent Learning Systems and Advancements in Computer-Aided Instruction: Emerging Studies* (pp. 144–163). Hershey, PA: Information Science Reference.

Dondlinger, M. J. (2007). Educational video game design: A review of the literature. *Journal of Applied Educational Technology*, *4*(1), 21–31.

Expert Group on Future Skills Needs (EGFSN). (2013). *Addressing Future Demand for High-Level ICT Skills (November 2013)*. Forfás / EGFSN.

Engeström, Y. (1987). *Learning by expanding: an activity-theoretical approach to developmental research*. Helsinki, Finland: Orienta-Konsultit Oy.

García-Peñalvo, F. J., Colomo-Palacios, R., & Lytras, M. D. (2012). Informal learning in work environments: Training with the Social Web in the workplace. *Behaviour & Information Technology, 31*(8), 753–755. doi:10.1080/0144929X.2012.661548

García-Peñalvo, F. J., Conde, M. A., Alier, M., & Colomo-Palacios, R. (2014). A Case Study for Measuring Informal Learning in PLEs. *International Journal of Emerging Technologies in Learning, 9*(7), 47–55. doi:10.3991/ijet.v9i7.3734

Garrison, D. R., & Kanuka, H. (2004). Blended learning: Uncovering its transformative potential in higher education. *The Internet and Higher Education, 7*(2), 95–115. doi:10.1016/j.iheduc.2004.02.001

Gikandi, J., Morrow, D., & Davis, N. (2011). Online formative assessment in higher education: A review of the literature. *Computers & Education, 57*(4), 2333–2351. doi:10.1016/j.compedu.2011.06.004

Girão, P. S., Pires, V. F., Dias, O. P., & Martins, J. F. (2010). Development of a mobile learning framework for an analog electronics course. In *Sixth International Conference on Education Engineering (EDUCON) 2010* (pp. 561-567). Madrid: IEEE.

Gulikers, J. T., Bastiaens, T. J., & Kirschner, P. A. (2004). A five-dimensional framework for authentic assessment. *Educational Technology Research and Development, 52*(3), 67–86. doi:10.1007/BF02504676

Hamari, J., Koivisto, J., & Sarsa, H. (2014). Does gamification work? – a literature review of empirical studies on gamification. In *2014 47th Hawaii International Conference on System Sciences (HICSS)* (pp. 3025-3034). Waikoloa, HI: IEEE.

Herrington, J., & Herrington, A. (1998). Authentic assessment and multimedia: How university students respond to a model of authentic assessment. *Higher Education Research & Development, 17*(3), 305–322. doi:10.1080/0729436980170304

Humanante-Ramos, P., García-Peñalvo, F., & Conde-González, M. (2017). Mobile Personal Learning Environments: A systematic literature review. *Revista Iberoamericana de Educación a Distancia, 20*(2), 73–92. doi:10.5944/ried.20.2.17692

Hwang, G., Tsai, C., & Yang, S. J. H. (2008). Criteria, strategies and research issues of context-aware ubiquitous learning. *Journal of Educational Technology & Society, 11*(2), 81–91.

Ireland, I. C. T. (Leadership in Information and Communications Technology) & ISA (Irish Software Association). (2011). The need for language skills in the high-tech sector. ICT & ISA.

Krashen, S. D. (1985). *The input hypothesis: Issues and implications*. New York: Addison-Wesley Longman Ltd.

Kukulska-Hulme, A. (2016). *Personalization of language learning through mobile technologies: Part of the Cambridge Papers in ELT series*. Cambridge, UK: Cambridge University Press.

Lilly, J., & Warnes, M. (2009). Designing mobile games for learning: The mGBL approach. In O. Petrovic & A. Brand (Eds.), Serious Games on the Move (pp. 3-27). Springer-Verlag/Wien.

Marty, J. C., & Carron, T. (2011). Observation of collaborative activities in a game-based learning platform. *IEEE Transactions on Learning Technologies, 4*(1), 98–110. doi:10.1109/TLT.2011.1

Melero, J., Hernández-Leo, D., & Manatunga, K. (2015). Group-based mobile learning: Do group size and sharing mobile devices matter? *Computers in Human Behavior*, *44*, 377–385. doi:10.1016/j. chb.2014.11.078

Minovic, M., Štavljanin, V., & Milovanovic, M. (2012). Educational Games and IT Professionals: Perspectives from the Field. *International Journal of Human Capital and Information Technology Professionals*, *3*(4), 25–38. doi:10.4018/jhcitp.2012100103

Mislevy, R. J., Steinberg, L. S., & Almond, R. G. (2003). Focus article: On the structure of educational assessments. *Measurement: Interdisciplinary Research and Perspectives*, *1*(1), 3–62. doi:10.1207/ S15366359MEA0101_02

Moreno-Ger, P., Burgos, D., Martínez-Ortiz, I., Sierra, J. L., & Fernández-Manjón, B. (2008). Educational game design for online education. *Computers in Human Behavior*, *24*(6), 2530–2540. doi:10.1016/j. chb.2008.03.012

Mota, J. M., Ruiz-Rube, I., Dodero, J. M., & Figueiredo, M. 2016. Visual environment for designing interactive learning scenarios with augmented reality. In *Proceedings of 12th International Conference on Mobile Learning* (pp. 67–74). Algarve, Portugal: mlearning.

Nielson, K. B. (2017). Mobile-Assisted Language Learning: Research-Based Best Practices for Maximizing Learner Success. In Blended Learning: Concepts, Methodologies, Tools, and Applications (pp. 818-842). Hershey, PA: IGI Global.

Olmo-Gil, M., Berns, A., & Palomo-Duarte, M. (2017). *Exploring the Potential of Commercial Language Apps to Meet Students' Learning Needs when Studying English at High School and University* (Academic dissertation). Retrieved from Universidad de Cádiz institutional repository. (handler 10498/19542)

Palomo-Duarte, M., Dodero, J. M., Tocino, J. T., García-Domínguez, A., & Balderas, A. (2012). Competitive evaluation in a video game development course. In *17th ACM Annual Conference on Innovation and Technology in Computer Science Education (ITiCSE '12)*, (pp. 321-326): ACM. doi:10.1145/2325296.2325371

Palomo-Duarte, M., Berns, A., Cejas, A., Dodero, J. M., Caballero, J. A., & Ruiz-Rube, I. (2016). Assessing Foreign Language Learning Through Mobile Game-Based Learning Environments. *International Journal of Human Capital and Information Technology Professionals*, *7*(2), 53–67. doi:10.4018/ IJHCITP.2016040104

Prensky, M. (2005). Computer games and learning: Digital game-based learning. In J. Raessens & J. Goldstein (Eds.), *Handbook of computer game studies* (pp. 97–122). Cambridge, MA: MIT Press.

Qi, H., Wang, M., Tong, R., Shen, R., Wang, J., & Gao, Y. (2006). The design and implementation of an interactive mobile learning system. In *The 6th IEEE International Conference on Advanced Learning Technologies 2006* (pp. 947-951). Kerkrade: IEEE.

Robles, G., González-Barahona, J. M., & Moral, A. (2012). A synchronous on-line competition software to improve and motivate learning. In *Global Engineering Education Conference (EDUCON)*, 2012 (pp. 1-8). Marrakech: IEEE. doi:10.1109/EDUCON.2012.6201118

Roschelle, J. (2003). Unlocking the learning value of wireless mobile devices. *Journal of Computer Assisted Learning*, *19*(3), 260–272. doi:10.1046/j.0266-4909.2003.00028.x

Rodríguez, A. I., & Riaza, B. G. (2016). Learning Goes Mobile: Devices and APPS for the Practice of Contents at Tertiary Level. In D. Fonseca & E. Redondo (Eds.), *Handbook of Research on Applied E-Learning in Engineering and Architecture Education* (pp. 472–496). Hershey, PA: IGI Global. doi:10.4018/978-1-4666-8803-2.ch021

Saltares Márquez, D., & Cejas Sánchez, A. (2014). *Libgdx Cross-platform Game Development Cookbook*. Packt Publishing.

Samuel, O. O., Botha, A., Ford, M., Tolmay, J. P., & Krause, C. (2009). Igloo: Mobile learning system to facilitate and support learners and educators. In A. Gyasi-Agyei, & A. Ogunfunmi (Eds.), *2nd International Conference on Adaptive Science & Technology (ICAST) 2009* (pp. 355-360). Accra: IEEE. doi:10.1109/ICASTECH.2009.5409702

Sánchez, J., & Olivares, R. (2011). Problem solving and collaboration using mobile serious games. *Computers & Education*, *57*(3), 1943–1952. doi:10.1016/j.compedu.2011.04.012

Sa'don, N. F., & Iahad, N. A. (2017). Collaborative Mobile Learning: A Systematic Literature Review. In Blended Learning: Concepts, Methodologies, Tools, and Applications (pp. 676-690). Hershey, PA: IGI Global. doi:10.4018/978-1-5225-0783-3.ch033

Sharples, M., Taylor, J., & Vavoula, G. (2005). Towards a theory of mobile learning. In H. van der Merwe & T. Brown (Eds.), *Proceedings of 4th World Conference on mLearning (mLearn)* (pp. 1-9). Cape Town: mLearn.

Shoukry, L., Göbel, S., & Steinmetz, R. (2014). Learning Analytics and Serious Games: Trends and Considerations. In *Proceedings of the 2014 ACM International Workshop on Serious Games* (pp. 21-26). Orlando, FL: ACM. doi:10.1145/2656719.2656729

Shute, V. J., & Ke, F. (2012). Games, learning, and assessment. In D. Ifenthaler, D., Eseryel & X. Ge (Eds.), Assessment in Game Based Learning (pp. 43-58). New York, NY: Springer. doi:10.1007/978-1-4614-3546-4_4

Shute, V. J., & Ventura, M. (2013). *Stealth assessment: Measuring and supporting learning in video games*. Cambridge, MA: MIT Press.

Siemens, G., & Baker, R. (2012). Learning analytics and educational data mining: towards communication and collaboration. In S. Buckingham, D. Gasevic, & R. Ferguson (Eds.), *Proceedings of the 2nd international conference on learning analytics and knowledge* (pp. 252-254). Vancouver: ACM. doi:10.1145/2330601.2330661

Síthigh, D. M. (2011). Legal games: The regulation of content and the challenge of casual gaming. *Journal of Gaming & Virtual Worlds*, *3*(1), 3–19. doi:10.1386/jgvw.3.1.3_1

Sun, P. C., Tsai, R. J., Finger, G., Chen, Y. Y., & Yeh, D. (2008). What drives a successful e-learning? An empirical investigation of the critical factors influencing learner satisfaction. *Computers & Education*, *50*(4), 1183–1202. doi:10.1016/j.compedu.2006.11.007

Taras, M. (2002). Using Assessment for Learning and Learning from Assessment. *Assessment & Evaluation in Higher Education*, 27(6), 501–510. doi:10.1080/0260293022000020273

Torrance, H. (1995). *Evaluating authentic assessment: Problems and possibilities in new approaches to assessment*. Open University.

Trinder, J. (2005). Mobile technologies and systems. In A. Kukulska-Hulme & J. Traxler (Eds.), *Mobile learning. A handbook for educators and trainers* (pp. 7–24). London: Routledge, Taylor & Francis Inc.

Van Zundert, M., Sluijsmans, D., & Van Merriënboer, J. (2010). Effective peer assessment processes: Research findings and future directions. *Learning and Instruction*, 20(4), 270–279. doi:10.1016/j.learninstruc.2009.08.004

Vassilev, T. I. (2015). An Approach to Teaching Introductory Programming for IT Professionals Using Games. *International Journal of Human Capital and Information Technology Professionals*, 6(1), 26–38. doi:10.4018/ijhcitp.2015010103

Viberg, O., & Grönlund, Å. (2012). Mobile assisted language learning: A literature review. In *11th World Conference on Mobile and Contextual Learning* (pp. 9-16). Helsinki, Finland: mLearn.

Warren, S. J., & Lin, L. (2013). Ethical considerations for learning game, simulation, and virtual world design and development. In K-12 Education: Concepts, Methodologies, Tools, and Applications (pp. 292-309). Hershey, PA: Information Science Publishing.

KEY TERMS AND DEFINITIONS

A/B Test: A method for conducting experiments where two different versions of a same app are presented to the users randomly.

CEFR: The Common European Framework of Reference for Languages, which provides a set of guidelines for the design of learning materials and the assessment of proficiency in a diversity of languages.

Competencies: The set of abilities or skills of a person to properly perform a given task.

Gamification: A technique for improving user engagement and learning by including common game elements (rewards, competition, etc.) into the learning activities.

GPL: This is the GNU general public license, which means that all the pieces of software derivate from an original one must be distributed under the same license term.

Learning Analytics: The process of collecting and analyzing data of individual student interactions in learning activities supported by online tools.

Mobile Learning: The application of the mobile technologies (mobile phones, tablets, etc.) to enable students to learn out of the classroom.

ENDNOTE

[1]   https://github.com/JuanMNGA/GuessIt2016

Chapter 7

From Motivation and Self-Structure to a Decision-Support Framework for Online Social Networks

Francisco Antunes
Beira Interior University, Portugal

Manuela Freire
University of Coimbra, Portugal

João Paulo Costa
University of Coimbra, Portugal

ABSTRACT

Data collected from online social networks offers new possibilities for supporting organizations' daily activities. It is also common knowledge that the opinion exchange in online social networks provides a decisive contribution in decision making. It is, thus, necessary to review and bare present the motivations by which people engage in online social network and the ways in which firms can make use of such motivations in order to take advantage of online social networks as information sources for decision-making support. To do so, the authors of this chapter developed the decision-support social networks to extract such information, which encompasses the intertwined use of human interaction and network structure by combining human capabilities, social network analysis (SNA), and automatic data mining. In this chapter, a brief summary of the performed case studies over the proposed information model is also presented.

INTRODUCTION

The participation in online social networks have become extremely popular, corresponding to more than two-thirds of the global online population. In fact, social networking and blogging account for nearly thirty percent of all time spent on the Internet (Mander & McGrath, 2017), suggesting that online social

DOI: 10.4018/978-1-5225-5297-0.ch007

networks have become a fundamental part of the global online experience (Benevenuto, Rodrigues, Meeyoung, & Almeida, 2009) and has introduced a new organizational framework for online communities and, with it, a vibrant new research context (Boyd & Ellison, 2008).

The use of social web data offers new possibilities for supporting organizations' daily-based activities. According to Pang and Lee (2008), "what others think" has always been an important piece of information in decision-making for almost everyone. It is also common knowledge that family and friends assume, and not in rare occasions, a decisive role in individual decision-making (choosing the color for a new car, the next holiday destination, a gift for the spouse/husband, etc.). The weight of such opinions may well match or overcome other criteria thought to be more rational or rigorous. This situation is not awkward or inexistent in firm management, as polls and market studies on costumer habits or opinion-based preferences are often incorporated into corporate decisions. The social web has made possible, as never before, to directly collect the opinions and experiences (personal and professional) of a wide range of people without any "formal inquiries", thus allowing to change the way we look at the whole decision process. Tollinen, Jarvinen, and Karjaluoto (2012), argue that social web monitoring, rather than using explicit surveys, provides more objective results on people's intentions. However, according to Murugesan (2010), several issues are still open and unsolved, like the management of the social web content (that grows day by day), its heterogeneity and the effectiveness of its extraction, just to mention a few. In addition, as reported by Batagelj, Doreian, Ferligoj, and Kejzar (2014), the majority of specific social networks (such as enterprise-based) are context limited and ignoring such contexts can impose large constraints on understanding the underlying phenomena or situation.

It is, thus, necessary to review and bare present the motivations by which people engage in online social network and the ways in which firms can make use of such motivations, in order to take advantage of online social networks as information sources for decision-making support. To do so, we developed an information model – the decision support social networks – to extract decision-making information from the interaction of people involved in online social networks (Antunes & Costa, 2011, 2012b), which allows different working modes, ranging from very small to very large groups, without any constraint neither on how the group will organize itself nor on how it will be constituted. The idea behind such information model is that it remains an *ad hoc* self-organized structure, formed by people who do not have to belong to a specific firm, motivated to contribute to problem-solving (whether by firm mechanisms or by an independent self-motivation).

In this paper we take a step forward in a research field that is recognized to be in its early stages (Davenport, 2014), by providing actual implementations of the proposed information model, to extract, process, structure and analyze the collected data from context-specific online social networks. Such framework incorporates the intertwined use of human interaction and network structure, by combining human capabilities, Social Network Analysis (SNA) and automatic data mining. In the next section, a definition of online social networks is elaborated, as well as a deeper understanding of social networking phenomena, a classification and building blocks. The section ends up with the concept of group or community. Motivation to participate, language and the importance of context is also reviewed when using online social networks for decision-making purposes. After that, the decision support in social networks is deepened and the developed framework and the way to implement it is presented. Three examples of usage of the framework are then mentioned. The conclusions of these examples are also presented. Naturally, the paper ends with reference to future research and final remarks.

ONLINE SOCIAL NETWORKS

There is not a unique definition for online social networks. While the term "social software" became a name to denote contemporary technology that supports social interaction (Boyd, 2006), there are many concurrent names for what it stands, namely groupware, computer-mediated communication software, social computing, just to mention a few.

Social software can be loosely defined as software which supports, extends, or derives added value from, human social behavior – message-boards, musical taste sharing, photo-sharing, instant messaging, mailing lists, social networking (Coates, 2005). Due to the panoply of terms, is fair to say that online social networks are web-based services, whose nature and nomenclature may vary from site to site. They allow individuals to construct a public or semi-public profile within a bounded system, articulate a list of other users with whom they share a connection, view and traverse their list of connections and those made by others within the system (Boyd & Ellison, 2008) and interact with people in their networks (Subrahmanyama, Reich, Waechter, & Espinoza, 2008).

While boundaries are blurred, most online social networks share a core feature: individuals offer a representation of themselves (a "profile") to others to peruse, with the intention of contacting or being contacted by others, to share opinions and facts, to meet new friends or dates, find new jobs, receive or provide recommendations, and much more (Gross & Acquisti, 2005). They are also being used to support the creation of brand communities or for marketing research (Maclaran & Catterall, 2002).

According to Kaplan & Haenlein (2010), online social networks can be classified by the cross-over of social presence/media richness and self-presentation/self-disclosure (see Table 1).

Kietzmann, Hermkens, McCarthy, & Silvestre (2011) stand that online social networks are built on seven functional blocks (see Figure 1), namely: identity, conversations, sharing, presence, relationships, reputation and groups. The authors, however, do not stand that the building blocks are mutually exclusive, nor do they all have to be present in a social media activity.

- **The Identity:** Represents the extent to which users reveal their identities in a social media setting (name, age, gender, profession, location, and information that portray users in certain ways), bearing privacy concerns as well;
- **Conversations:** Represent the extent to which users communicate with other users in a social media setting. These postings can be rich and useful, but not necessarily connected to a greater social media exchange on the same subject. Firms often need tools and capabilities that allow them to combine the information in order to produce an overall image or message;
- **Sharing:** Represents the extent to which users exchange, distribute, and receive content as well as the implied reasons why they meet online and associate with each other and the mapping of users' connectivity, across their entire social network;

Table 1. Social presence/media richness and self-presentation/self-disclosure

		Social Presence/Media Richness		
		Low	**Medium**	**High**
Self-presentation / Self-disclosure	High	Blogs	Social networking sites	Virtual social worlds
	Low	Collaborative projects	Content communities	Virtual game worlds

Source: Adapted from Kaplan & Haenlein (2010).

Figure 1. The honeycomb of social media
Source: *Kietzmann et al. (2011).*

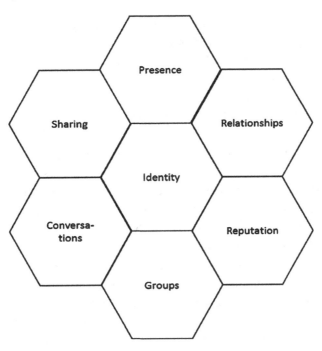

- **Presence:** Represents the extent to which users can know if other users are accessible. The implication of presence is that firms need to pay attention to the relative importance of user availability and user location. A firm might also want to investigate if users have a desire for selective presences, where one can be visible to some people while staying hidden to others. Another direct implication of presence is that it is linked to the traits of other functional blocks, including conversations and relationships;

- **Relationships:** Represent the extent to which users can be related to other users, by some form of association that leads them to converse, share objects of sociality, meet up, or simply just list each other as a friend or fan. Research shows that the denser and larger a user's portfolio of relationships is, and the more central his or her position in the portfolio, the more likely that user is to be an influential member in their network. Firms seeking to engage with their users must understand how they can maintain or build relationships, or both;

- **Reputation:** Is the extent to which users can identify the standing of others, including themselves, in a social media setting. In most cases, reputation is a matter of trust and has significant implications for how firms should effectively engage social media. If firms and users value their reputations and those of other users, then a metric must be chosen to provide this information. For a firm, this means that the engagement needs of its community should inform the choice of the reputation system. Once a firm has identified appropriate metrics for the reputation of its community's social media engagement, the appropriate evaluation tool must be chosen. This could be based on either objective data (e.g., the number of views or followers) or collective intelligence of the crowd (e.g., a rating system).;

- **Groups:** Represent the extent to which users can form communities and sub communities. Two major types of groups exist. Firstly, individuals can sort through their contacts and place their "buddies", friends, followers, or fans into different self-created groups. Secondly, groups online can be analogous to clubs in the offline world: open to anyone, closed (approval required), or secret (by invitation only). A firm would benefit from studying the groups within the community and their engagement with the other building blocks.

Motivation to Participate and Timely Decisions

Knowing that people add value, online social networks depend of their users to create a dynamic database that change and adapts continuously in time, as a result of the interactions among users and between the users and the system. Therefore, a fundamental issue is to create a critical mass of users that regularly and create, update and share knowledge (Gehrke & Wolf, 2010; Jones, Failla, & Miller, 2007). In order to be useful to organizations, thus taking advantage of the "wisdom of the crowds", online social networks needs to encompass enough people (please see Burke, Marlow, and Lento (2009) for a discussion on this issue, concerning generic social networks). Nonetheless, when using or analyzing an online social network for decision-making purposes, within specific contexts, the concept of "enough" people becomes blurred.

Most organizations do not possess all required knowledge within their formal boundaries and might benefit from external network connections by gaining access to new information, expertise, and ideas not available locally, while interacting informally, free from the constraints of hierarchy and local rules. Even though the employing organizations can be a direct competitors, informal and reciprocal knowledge exchanges between individuals are valued and sustained over time, because knowledge sharing is an important aspect of being a member of a technological community (Bouty, 2000; Teigland & Wasko, 2003). The problem here is that the availability of electronic communication technologies is no guarantee that knowledge sharing will actually take place (Alavi & Leidner, 2001; Orlikowski & Iacono, 2001) and, therefore, the decision support social network could be dependent of the mere willingness or "kindness" of users to participate.

Creating and maintaining a core of centralized individuals is of adamant importance to overcome the problem. These individuals, should possess experience in the practice by using extrinsic motivators such as enhanced reputation to actively promote contributions and sustaining the network (Wasko & Faraj, 2005). This core of individuals primarily built upon internal human resources, can be engaged in different types of incentives to participation, besides social rewards (personal satisfaction, reputation, feeling of belonging, tenure within the network, etc.), namely through economic incentives or career enhancements (Munson, 2008). To help generating a critical mass, managers should target individuals with longer tenure and more experience in the practice.

Another method to promote individual participation in the critical mass is the development of techniques that help to build an individual's reputation in the profession. For example, it could be helpful to assign status to individuals and make it visible. Individual reputations could become more salient when managers build bridges between physical and virtual networks, finding ways to spread the online-developed reputations, to the profession as a whole and motivating individuals, by gaining status and recognition in this way, to participate more in electronic networks of practice (Hippel & Krogh, 2003; Wasko & Faraj, 2005).

As in any problem-solving process, within a decision support social network, management should set a foreseeable time for solving a problem, *i.e.*, disseminating the problem in hand throughout the network, gathering enough people around it and performing the decision process until a solution is attained. Within a decision support social network, management opportunities for decision are, therefore, closely tied to the speed of the process, meaning that problems (or types of problems), people and decision processes need an adequate time framework to unveil.

To address this problem, it is necessary: an information cascade, where messages spread throughout the network; that the information spreads quickly, aided by the affordances of social network platforms; and that the process enables a broad reach by bridging multiple networks. The sum of these characteristics provides us nonetheless than the definition of viral information. A viral information event creates a temporally bound, self-organized, interest network in which membership is based on an interest in the information content or in belonging to the interest network of others (Hemsley & Mason, 2013). In the case of decision support social networks, management should focus on spreading the information, regarding a decision problem, quickly and widely, making it a viral event. This should be done especially by targeting individuals with longer tenure and more experience in the practice to generate a critical mass of people, responsible for pushing the information, at least in the early stage of its propagation. It is known that if individuals are scattered throughout the network, then the information is unlikely to diffuse. If, on the other hand, they are close together, as in more context-based online social networks, then information has an increased chance for propagation (Leskovec, Adamic, & Huberman, 2007). Therefore, the critical mass, once again, plays an important role in gathering and bringing closer external individuals.

According to Hemsley & Mason (2013), to go viral, events are subject to two decisions by individuals in a social media network. The first is whether to watch/read the message and the second is whether to forward a viewed message. Each person who participates in a viral event has effectively voted on the content twice through his or her duel decisions, so that the resulting event has been deemed relevant and worth spreading in some way. Repeated viral events filtered in this way may result in the formation of interest networks that will grow or decay based on the accumulated social capital within the interest network. Over time, the interest networks initiated (or reinforced) by the viral event may evolve into more stable communities of practice and such evolution over time can be analyzed by Social Network Analysis as it can provide a visual (qualitative), as well as a mathematical (quantitative) analysis of human the established relations.

Communication, Language, and Context

As idea is to promote participation and information propagation within online social networks, confidentiality and language selection should not be trivial issues. On one hand, when a decision support social network only relies on internal human resources, the confidentiality expectation around problem solving is naturally bounded by corporate confidentiality agreements (implicit or explicit). On the other hand, if external human resources are implied in the process of problem solving or idea discussion, the ability for controlling the level of confidentiality is likely to be diluted. As internal and external human resources do not share the same set of motivation factors, it is not likely that they abide to confidentiality concerns in same way. Therefore, firms should be aware that open forums, are able to gather a larger amount of knowledge on a specific problem, but this is done at the expense of confidentiality loss. As a result, management should weight, beforehand, the importance of expanding the network outside the boundaries of the firm with the loss of control over confidentiality, thus expanding or restricting the network (using adequate profiles, for instance) accordingly to its needs.

When discussing a problem within a large or expanding online network of people, there is the need to ensure that a common language is used or, otherwise, linguistic barriers may occur. Participation will be likely hindered if people are not comfortable in expressing themselves using a certain language. In the extreme case, participation will not even take place if people do not know the used language. The use of a specific language can also inhibit or promote participation and, consequently, the network expansion might be tied to this matter. To broaden the network, the use of English language (even if it is bad English…) seems proper for fully developing the network, as English remains a dominant force within certain Internet realms. A study conducted by the Organization for Economic Co-operation and Development found that while some seventy eight percent of Web sites in OECD countries were in English, ninety one percent of Web sites on "secure-servers" were in English, and a fully ninety six percent of Web sites on secure servers in the ".com" domain were in English (Warschauer, Said, & Zohry, 2002).

The solution for this problem is twofold. Firstly, it relies outside management boundaries, namely on the use of automated translation mechanisms (some browsers already integrate such features) or imposing the use of a common language, such as English (especially when not in control of the involved people). Secondly, because decision support situations are context-dependent, it is necessary to adjust data processing features accordingly (preferably combining human-based and automatic features), and to take into account the language where the web discourse is being produced. Only then, data become relevant and expressive in terms of substance and social context.

Particularly within online social networks, people tend to mix linguistic and non-linguistic resources in order to expedite communication. Literature review shows a perceived difficulty in structuring social networks data (Shum, Cannavacciuolo, De Liddo, Iandoli, & Quinto, 2011), as people, in order to accelerate communication, tend to reduce the number of characters that are typed to express an idea (Freire, Antunes, & Costa, 2015a), which poses greater strain in semantic extraction (in fact, some intervention do not even contain text, but only links and/or tags).

Altogether, this means that this data is possibly tangled, incomplete and sometimes error-prone (Antunes, Freire, & Costa, 2016). In this case, semantics lie hidden in speech content created by the interveners and in order to reveal them, literature has focused on the study of computer mediated communications (S. Herring, 2010, 2013), natural language processing, web content analysis (S. C. Herring, 2010; Kok & Rogers, 2016) or discourse analysis (Moser, Groenewegen, & Huysman, 2013), just to mention a few. Most of existing studies turn out to focus on describing network properties, rather than focusing on a deep semantic analysis of the *posts* and later use of the findings. Although there are studies of greater complexity, that deepen the semantic analysis of web discourse contents, they do not integrate it with the analysis of network properties nor with users' interaction. The studies that incorporate SNA, as well as the semantic analysis of the *posts* are scarce and they remain mainly theoretical (S. C. Herring, 2013; Power & Phillips-Wren, 2012).

Even harder to grasp, are the artifices of language such as rhetoric and wordplay (that turn out to be discursive strategies), origin, destination, intentions and reception of speech, which help to define how these interactions and respective arguments do come out.

DECISION SUPPORT IN ONLINE SOCIAL NETWORKS

It is known that one of the most common means to collect data (regarding, for instance, marketing purposes like testing new products acceptance, determining the level of client satisfaction, accessing after-sales quality, etc.) is the use of direct surveys (whether personal or online). Nonetheless, it is also largely recognized that this type of approach possesses intrinsic problems, as people do not always reveal their true opinions or intentions, especially in face-to-face situations, which may lead to significant errors in predicting activities such as future sales or poll. The idea of collecting people's true opinions seems far more feasible within the context of social webs, than in face-to-face environments, as people can use made-up profiles to express their true ideas, instead of using their "official" profiles (please see Tollinen et al. (2012)). In term of the earlier stages of decision-making process, especially at the intelligence and design stages (as defined by Simon (1977)), this means getting better information quality, thus enhancing the possibility of better or more reality-tuned decisions, even though direct surveys have its own advantages, such as simplicity, cost and simpler data processing, that social web content analysis does not. However, the task of collecting and analyzing the content of online social networks (or web discourse) remains quite challenging as is encompasses social and technical problems that need an integrated approach.

Antunes and Costa (2012a) enlightened the interconnections of online social networking and decision support systems (DSS) concepts. They underwent a large study, using four major bibliographic resources (ISI WOK, SCOPUS, SCIRIUS and EBSCO) and, at the end of the research process, 89 papers were selected as actual interconnections of both fields. In order to reveal the concepts encompassed in the literature, network text analysis was used, as it assumes that language and knowledge can be modeled as networks of words and relations, encoding links among words to construct a network of linkages, analyzing the existence, frequencies, and covariance of terms or concepts. Social network analysis was then used to analyze and represent the obtained network of concepts (Carley, 1997). The process returned four concept clusters, which represent that the central pillars that need to be addressed when implementing a decision support social network, regardless of it size (general or context-based):

- **Technical Infrastructure:** Encompassing research that elaborates, develops, proposes and analyzes social networking infrastructures, for distinct purposes like data-gathering purposes, information extraction, taxonomy building, web computing, consumer support, decision automation, etc.
- **Online Communities:** Focusing on people, users, teams, and providing a view on the effects of online social networking among established online communities; research is directed towards group dynamics (formation, cohesion, behavior, etc.) and its effects (actual or perceived) among specific online communities.
- **Network Analysis:** Encompassing the analysis of organizations, companies and distributed structures, providing interpretation and decision support by means of social network analysis measures (centrality, betweenness, closeness, degree, etc.).
- **Knowledge Management:** Addressing the so-called "wisdom of the crowds", using the lens of knowledge management, namely its use (actual and perceived), usefulness and setbacks towards the objectives of knowledge creation, sharing, encoding, retrieval and representation.

Integrating Discursive and Technical Issues

Understanding why people participate in online social networks seems, therefore, crucial for developing and engaging users within a decision support social network (Antunes & Costa, 2014) and to integrate the all above mentioned issues we developed a framework to extract, process, structure and analyze the collected data from context-specific social networks. Such framework incorporates human interaction and network structure, by combining human capabilities, Social Network Analysis (SNA) and automatic data mining. According to Marmo (2011), the combination of SNA and web mining gives an innovative degree of detail in the analysis of social networks that can be useful for decision-making, by providing a better structuring and understanding of the logical sequence of the produced contents of an online social network (Antunes & Costa, 2011).

Although online social networks seem to be well fitted for searching information (Suki, Ramayah, Ming, & Suki, 2011) and for developing divergence processes (typical activities within the intelligent phase of the decision process), how to use online social networks for structuring and/or convergence procedures or activities remains elusive. Nonetheless, produced contents, need to be tagged by users or automatically supplied by the system, creating a *folksonomy* that can be used afterwards for convergence purposes. Classifications according to argumentation models can be available, or created by the users, for which semantic techniques (Web 3.0/semantic) seem to be quite promising (Schneider, Groza, & Passant, 2013; Turoff, Hiltz, Bieber, Fjermstad, & Rana, 1999). The combination of information filtering, classification, sorting and displaying techniques, becomes essential to support the different cognitive styles of decision-makers engaged in contingent decision processes (Colombo, Antonietti, Sala, & Caravita, 2013).

However, as in the previous section, there are several limitations, which cannot be disregarded, making the treatment, organization and retrieval and analyzing the content of social web content (or web discourse), commonly known as *posts*, quite challenging:

- **Processing the Text of Posts:** Processing the textual data contained in the *posts* requires tools to clean and standardize them (as the ideas contained in *posts* can be diffused along sentences full of characters and punctuation, to emphasize situations), in order to capture the semantic aspects that allow to go beyond the mere identification of keywords, ranking of concepts, etc. (Robinson, Webber, & Eifrem, 2013). The writing style commonly used in these platforms has a pattern out of the ordinary that sometimes makes it incomprehensible to those who are not part of the conversation and/or that culture or context, thus making it very hard to make it "machine- understandable" (Antunes et al., 2016). This is because social actors often make mistakes, spelling and/or grammar, use abbreviations (ASAP = as soon as possible), symbols (:(= sad) "stretch" the words ("nooooo"), include links, images, audio and video (Bodomo, 2010).

- **Semantics:** Usually, *posts* do not share common ontologies, as they are created and changed constantly. The non-existence of standards to express web data semantics hinders the possibilities for integrating applications to analyze them. In addition, the interaction within social networks, and its consequent discursive exchanges, often produces information in an informal and unstructured language, that social tagging, used in folksonomies, fails to address;

- **Post Dimension (Number of Characters):** In order to accelerate communication people tend to reduce the number of characters that are typed to express an idea (Antunes & Costa, 2015), which poses greater strain in semantic extraction;
- **Data Characteristics:** Social networks are much more than a simple set of links and texts. They are interactive and dynamic complex networks with several links that correspond not only to users and "friends" (followers), but also a set of links between *posts*, videos, photos, etc. (S. C. Herring, 2010; Robinson et al., 2013). In addition, a user can comment *posts* in a successively way (*post* → comment; comment → comment) and share them. This raises the issues of visualization and graphical analysis. The collected data falls into three categories: structured (users), semi-structured (*posts*) and unstructured (*concepts* found within *posts*);

Processing the data contained in the textual interchanges, within an online social network, usually known as posts, requires tools to clean and standardize them (as the ideas contained in posts can be diffused along sentences full of characters and punctuation, to emphasize situations). This is done to capture the semantic aspects that allow to go beyond the mere identification of keywords, ranking of concepts, etc. (Robinson et al., 2013). To do so, the developed framework, depicted in Figure 2, starts by extracting data from a context-specific online social network. Throughout the process, an iterative three-stage process will generate several networks, which are recurrent and iterative.

Figure 2. Workflow of the developed approach
Source: (Freire, Antunes, & Costa, 2017).

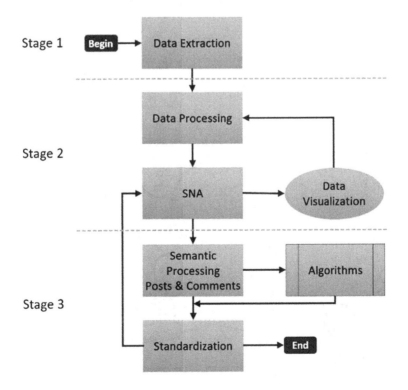

Data Extraction

The first step is to gather data with all interacting social actors (user → user) and respective *posts* (user → *post*) and data regarding the *posts* and comments.

Such data makes it possible to study the social interaction (user → user), as well as to study the semantics of the content of a *post*. To that purpose, a two-mode network is used, as it allows to represent three sets of nodes in the same graph (Ikematsu & Murata, 2013), allowing to analyze the three levels of interactions between social actors, i.e. the interaction between: users; user and *posts*; *posts* and concepts. The main issue here is to be able to affect a *post* to a user and, in turn, a concept to a *post*, in order to know who said what, as shown in Figure 3.

Data Processing and Interpretation

In order to simultaneously analyze the three levels of the network (the interaction between: users; user and *posts*; *posts* and concepts) a transformation of the two-mode network into a one-mode network (Borgatti, 2009) is required. This method binds the two datasets using common nodes. By doing so, data can be represented by a square matrix, where rows and columns represent the nodes of the two unified datasets. In this matrix, a "1" in a given position means that there is a connection between the line node and the column node of that position.

Figure 3. Levels of analysis
Source: (Freire et al., 2017).

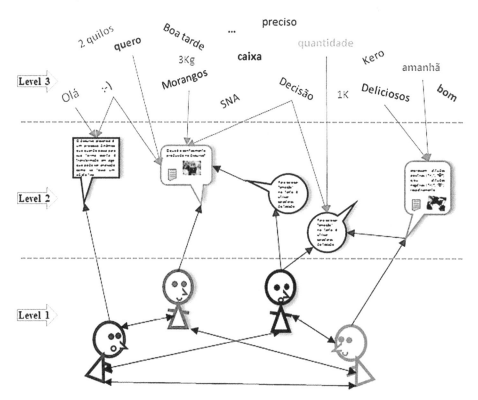

It is then necessary to interpret the data using SNA, namely by using in-degree and out-degree metrics, to eliminate irrelevant data of unconnected nodes, i.e., nodes with in-degree and out-degree equaling zero. These *posts* usually are derived from automatic messages. After this cleaning, it is necessary to perform the junction of the data with all interacting social actors (user → user) and respective *posts* (user → *post* interactions) and data regarding the *posts* and comments, in order to create a single network.

Semantics Processing

The first step in this stage is to transform *posts* and comments, into networks of words, as a basis to perform the semantic analysis of *posts* using text mining and SNA. The process of data analysis is an iterative recurrent process, where human involvement is essential for a systematic analysis of the obtained results and to verify if any adjustments are deemed necessary. The visualization of the data by means of SNA tools and metrics helps to accelerate this process.

A simple way to transform text into SNA interpretable data is to "split" every discursive exchange (*posts* and comments) into individual words. The result of this action is a network where each concept is a node, regardless of its existence in another *post* or comment. In doing so, the content of each *post* is summarized through a semantic sub-network, which is constructed by establishing a relationship between the pairs of words contained in each *post*.

In order to identify standardized network concepts, our proposal establishes the creation of a *Cleaning Database* (Provost & Fawcett, 2013) to process the unstructured data from the *posts*. After identifying irrelevant data, the *Cleaning Database* is then configured to discard them in a second processing.

The next step is to detect keywords, since the extraction of keywords is an important technique for identifying the most used and relevant concepts in *posts* (Aggarwal, 2011). For that purpose, a new network, consisting of the users, received *posts* and concepts contained in them, is then created. In this network, each concept constitutes an entity with its own ID. Concepts with the same semantic meaning are then sought (knowing that each concept has a different ID), and the same ID is assigned to all concepts bearing the same meaning, by replicating the links from the keyword to the *post*. We find that the graphical visualization of the network can be very helpful in this step. A network of keywords is then created, constituted by users, *posts* and concepts contained therein. This network is built with concept's unicity (keywords), allowing to count (using the out-degree metric) the number of times each relevant concept was posted or linked.

As described, the devised iterative process needs a combination of human and computerized procedure that allow to build semantic networks that summarize the discursive exchanges between users, where text mining allows to convert users' *posts* into multiple pieces (as many, as the concepts that exist in a post). In addition, the use of SNA software over the obtained networks, which incorporates a variety of visualization techniques and algorithms, translates concepts, extracted from posts and comments, into something more compact and, therefore, more understandable. Through SNA metrics (please see Arif (2015) for a detailed review), it is not only possible to identify the structure of the users' network, but also to "translate" the network into a graphical representation. Such representation makes it possible to identify users acting as leaders (who will make most of the orders) and/or who influence others (product recommendation), as well as to determine the relative strength of the leader through a key concept. Such information can help to devise more adjusted (we could almost say "chirurgical") marketing strategies that target the users that will better propagate its effects on a lesser cost.

APPLICATION CASE STUDIES

To test and illustrate how the described framework can be used to decision support, we present in this section a brief summary of three distinct situations, which allowed the refinement over its sequential application, over different case settings and participation motivations (the references for the detailed case studies are provided ahead).

Although the framework does not specify any online social network for its application, we used Facebook in all presented cases, in order to use the app Netvizz (https://apps.facebook.com/netvizz/), a free tool that provides a simple and quick way to import data by using the module "group data", to collect the data. The module allowed extracting tabular files of users' activities around the posts of the created Facebook groups.

To perform data extraction we used *NodeXL* (https://nodexl.codeplex.com/) and *Gephi* (https://Gephi.org/), an open-source software that allows a simple visualization and manipulation of networks, as well as the calculation of the most important metrics of SNA, was used for data processing along the stages of the framework.

Regarding semantic analysis, in order to interconnect concepts to posts and comments, two approaches were followed. The first one obtained a summary of each discursive exchange, while the second identified the network of keywords. We explored the data with text mining, building semantic networks that summarized the discursive exchanges between users. Text mining allowed to convert posts into multiple pieces (as many, as the concepts that exist in a post). In addition, the SNA software that incorporated a variety of visualization techniques and algorithms, helped to translate the concepts, extracted from posts and comments, into something more compact and, therefore, more understandable. The calculation of different SNA metrics and the analysis of multiple networks allowed a richer, more structured view of those involved in discourse, as well as the most used concepts.

The identification and standardization of network concepts was performed using Microsoft Excel VBA (Visual Basic for Applications) algorithms. Data were then processed, using MS-Excel, producing Cleaning Databases that were created and imported into *Gephi*, making it possible to generate and graphically visualize the produced networks.

The Collaborators' Annual Lunch

We created a closed group for a small group of collaborators of a large company, geographically spread all over the country, to debate the location of their traditional annual lunch (Freire et al., 2015a). They voluntarily participated with different levels of engagement. Some gathered information (mainly web-based) on the topic and reasoned about it. The organization of a simple lunch had an associated logistics process, because when gathering a group, the number of people conditions the choice of the location. Consequently, the organizer needed to know who would attend, as well as their menu and location preferences, in order to satisfy the attendees. Accordingly, the decision-making required a thorough search of the suggested alternatives, reliable information on the consequences and preferences, to get the intended results.

This was the first attempt to use the framework as a decision-support tool, encompassing a situation where all involved users were internal to the company, self-motivated and bearing a strong group feeling.

The data were collected between 22-Nov-2014 and 11-Jan-2015 and, afterwards, we applied SNA techniques in order to study the network, which was analyzed from the ego-centric perspective (Ma, Gustafson, Moitra, & Bracewell, 2010). The group were aware of the language in use, as well as the associated semantics and therefore, there was no need for ontologies to decipher what is implied within the speech. The use of this relatively small network allowed limiting the number of elements under review. In this way, it was possible to study, more thoroughly, the network in terms of its composition, characteristics (through metrics on the type of interaction established between the different social actors) and structure.

The group interaction had low activity, with short and simple posts, providing a low number of keywords found in the analyzed speech. This situation was expected as it is known that the language used in web discourse is usually characterized by a tendency to reduce the amount character to express an idea and, consequently, to speed up the communication process. It was possible to state that, within the analyzed posts, only one had a larger number of concepts.

The analysis of the multiple networks, as well as the calculations of different SNA metrics, allowed a rich and structured view of the discourse, as well as most used concepts. This allowed to effectively produce a decision reconstruction (especially when gathering information on the problem and when seeking alternatives for its resolution – that could be translated into the design and intelligence phases of the decision process), thus producing a clear understanding on how many people would attend the lunch, the intended place and menu.

A General Strike of an Airline Company

The objectives of this study (Freire, Antunes, & Costa, 2015b) were to analyze costumer-generated data, during a period of a ten days strike (in May of 2015), encompassing a situation where the involved users were external to the company, self-motivated and without a group feeling. The main goal was to understand if it was possible to structure the produced posts within the airline's Facebook social network, in order to check service and responsiveness of the airline company to customers, as well as to develop indicators to review and/or fortify strategies in customer service on a strike situation, using SNA methodology.

The data, collected not only during the ten days strike, but also during the following five days, allowed constructing several networks and subnetworks. By analyzing the content of the posts we perceived that they could be categorized, which meant that posts provided the means to better focus/create task groups to address cases of complaints, requests for help/support in changing a reservation, requests for information (about hotel, luggage collection, refund procedures, etc.).

In the analyzed posts, many customers complained that the call center did not answer calls, they had no response to e-mails, airports with service counters (personal assistance) were closed and the airline company website did not have any information on the strike. Visualization allowed to identify relevant conversations and to provide direct and immediate insights about the customers' feelings, allowing faster reactions to whether or not client dissatisfaction sentiment is being developed or aggravated.

Posts' analysis and network visualization could have helped the airline company to identify the problems in traditional channels (call centers, e-mail, etc.) and to address them more quickly in order to prevent future service breakdowns due to strike situations. In addition, visualization and identification of keywords could have been used to reinforce the need for delivering permanent information (for instance through online channels or service counters) on: whether a flight needed to be canceled or not; the list of canceled or available flights; how to reschedule/change the date of a flight.

The Strawberries Sale

The "strawberries sale" was implemented within a group of potential customers (Freire et al., 2017). A small promotional box of strawberries was delivered at the potential customers' workplaces, with the following attached message: "Directly from the producer to the customer. To place order intentions, please join the Strawberries group created on Facebook and leave yours". Then, a strawberry grower was contacted to deliver those orders at customers' workplaces.

The decision support problem was to estimate the required strawberries quantity to meet the customers' requests (as no pre-established order form was available), solely based on their *posts* on Facebook. We intended to verify if the semantic analysis of the *posts* could be used to effectively recommend the necessary quantities to transport and deliver, solely based on expressed intentions (there were no actual purchase orders involved). We concluded that it was possible to extract insights for decision support, namely to predict the behavior of customers, thus allowing to create new visions based on real data, resulting from the interaction and discursive exchanges between users. By using SNA metrics it was not only possible to identify the structure of the users' network, but also to "translate" the network into a graphical representation. Such representation made possible to identify users acting as leaders (who would make most of the orders) and/or who influenced others (product recommendation), as well as to determine the relative strength of the leader through a key concept. Such information could help to devise more adjusted (we could almost say "chirurgical") marketing strategies to target the users that could better propagate its effects on a lesser cost.

We concluded that not only it was possible to recommend the needed quantities to be transported and delivered to customers, but also we have identified the customers who ordered the most and the leaders of the customers' group.

FUTURE RESEARCH DIRECTIONS

The analysis and visualization of concepts extracted from the web discourse can be used as insights for follow-up decisions, as they allow efficient access to key information. The obtained results provided information on the key terms that were used during the discursive exchanges, in order to be used to analyze different alternatives to support decision-making.

We intend to determine if the combination of context-specific and context-generic semantics extraction procedures would benefit from an integrated approach, as well as the development of a deeper combination of text and data mining and graphical visualization of the text and data mining results improve the effectiveness of semantic extraction frameworks, especially for prediction purposes. To do so, we plan to broaden the scope of our studies, in order to determine to what extent it can be used for prediction. Some of the planned case studies regard: the number of club fans that will go to a stadium; the number of people attending a demonstration and/or event; the number of people interested in a particular promotional campaign; the number of people who oppose a measure or policy; the acceptance of a new product and/or service.

In addition, we aim to explore and develop new feature/algorithms that could identify interest and dishonest behavior in social web networks (or at least to flag the suspicion to the users), as the actual implementation is unable to do so.

CONCLUSION

Starting from the existing connections between online social network and decision support, the motivations for people to engage in online social networks were reviewed. There are extrinsic and intrinsic factors. People contribute to social networks when they understand that it enhances their reputation and recognition and to some extend because they feel it is enjoyable to help others. The participation or contribution of people engaged in social networking is not without problems.

Considering that a solution to a certain problem is expected within a decision support social network, some potential problems may arise: the network can be dependent of the mere willingness or "kindness" of users to participate; decisions can emerge out of time; a common language may not be easy to find; and confidentiality can be out of control. These potential problems were framed and several tactics or policies were put forward so that firms could overcome them.

The analysis and visualization of concepts used in web discourse can be used as insights for follow-up decisions, as it allows efficient access to key information. The obtained results provide information on the key terms used during the discursive exchanges and can be used to analyze various alternatives of a problem and to support decision-making. By identifying the number of times that the concepts appear in all posts, it is possible to determine any possible preferences and opinions of users. By putting all the group members and their respective interests in the same level, we get an outline of the views and group positions (in favor or against). Therefore, when a choice has to be made, argumentation gets into the "game" and network analysis can help to capture it. Therefore, network analysis is particularly suitable for the study of social network decision-making because it allows to recognize the dynamic nature of networks, providing tools and techniques for measuring and evaluating its changes.

To do so, we used the proposed framework to extract, process, structure and analyze the collected data from a social network. We explored social networks, combining two different perspectives: the social interactions between users and the semantic analysis of their discourse.

It should be noted that the construction of datasets obtained from Facebook are inexpensive and easy to extract, so it is easier and faster to obtain reports on the opinions of customers, as compared to conducting market researches or surveys. Increasingly, customers have the ability to express their needs, feelings, desires, and frustrations about a product, service and/or company in real time. Therefore, we stand that the proposed framework can be useful to extract a set of orientations for decision-making. We could conclude that it is possible to extract insights for decision support, namely to predict the behavior of customers.

ACKNOWLEDGMENT

This research was supported by the by the Portuguese Foundation for Science and Technology (FCT). [Grant number UID/MULTI/00308/2013].

REFERENCES

Aggarwal, C. C. (2011). *Social Network Data Analytics*. New York: Springer. doi:10.1007/978-1-4419-8462-3

Alavi, M., & Leidner, D. E. (2001). Review: Knowledge management and knowledge management systems: Conceptual foundations and research issues. *Management Information Systems Quarterly*, *25*(1), 107–136. doi:10.2307/3250961

Antunes, F., & Costa, J. P. (2011). *Decision Support Social Network*. Paper presented at the 6th Iberian Conference on Information Systems and Technologies (CISTI), Chaves, Portugal.

Antunes, F., & Costa, J. P. (2012a). *Disentangling Online Social Networking and Decision Support Systems Research Using Social Network Analysis*. Paper presented at the EWG-DSS Liverpool-2012 Workshop on Decision Support Systems & Operations Management Trends and Solutions in Industries, Liverpool, UK.

Antunes, F., & Costa, J. P. (2012b). Integrating decision support and social networks. *Advances in Human-Computer Interaction*, *2012*, 1–10. doi:10.1155/2012/574276

Antunes, F., & Costa, J. P. (2014). Reviewing Motivations for Engaging in Decision Support Social Networks. *International Journal of Human Capital and Information Technology Professionals*, *5*(1), 1–14. doi:10.4018/ijhcitp.2014010101

Antunes, F., & Costa, J. P. (2015). The Impact of Online Social Networks on Decision Support Systems. In L. Mola, F. Pennarola, & S. Za (Eds.), From Information to Smart Society (Vol. 5, pp. 75-85). Springer International Publishing. doi:10.1007/978-3-319-09450-2_7

Antunes, F., Freire, M., & Costa, J. P. (2016). Semantic web and decision support systems. *Journal of Decision Systems*, *25*(1), 79–93. doi:10.1080/12460125.2015.1087293

Arif, T. (2015). The Mathematics of Social Network Analysis: Metrics for Academic Social Networks. *International Journal of Computer Applications Technology and Research*, *4*(12), 889–893. doi:10.7753/IJCATR0412.1003

Batagelj, V., Doreian, P., Ferligoj, A., & Kejzar, A. (2014). Understanding Large Temporal Networks and Spatial Networks: Exploration, Pattern Searching, Visualization and Network Evolution. Chichester, UK: John Wiley & Sons Ltd. doi:10.1002/9781118915370

Benevenuto, F., Rodrigues, T., Meeyoung, C., & Almeida, V. (2009, November 4–6,). *Characterizing User Behavior in Online Social Networks*. Paper presented at the Internet Measurement Conference (IMC'09), Chicago, IL. doi:10.1145/1644893.1644900

Bodomo, A. B. (2010). *Computer-Mediated Communication for Linguistics and Literacy: Technology and Natural Language Education*. Hershey, PA: Information Science Reference. doi:10.4018/978-1-60566-868-0

Borgatti, S. P. (2009). 2-Mode Concepts in Social Network Analysis. In R. A. Meyers (Ed.), *Encyclopedia of Complexity and System Science* (pp. 8279–8291). Larkspur, CA: Springer. doi:10.1007/978-0-387-30440-3_491

Bouty, I. (2000). Interpersonal and interaction influences on Informal resource exchanges between R&D researchers across organizational boundaries. *Academy of Management Journal, 43*(1), 50–65. doi:10.2307/1556385

Boyd, D. M. (2006). The significance of social software. In T. N. Burg & J. Schmidt (Eds.), *BlogTalks Reloaded. Social Software - Research & Cases* (pp. 15–30). Norderstedt, Germany: Books on Demand GmbH.

Boyd, D. M., & Ellison, N. B. (2008). Social network sites: Definition, history, and scholarship. *Journal of Computer-Mediated Communication, 13*(1), 210–230. doi:10.1111/j.1083-6101.2007.00393.x

Burke, M., Marlow, C., & Lento, T. (2009). *Feed Me: Motivating Newcomer Contribution in Social Network Sites.* Paper presented at the CHI 2009, Boston, MA. doi:10.1145/1518701.1518847

Carley, K. M. (1997). Network Text Analysis: The Network Position of Concepts. In C. W. Roberts (Ed.), *Analysis for the Social Sciences: Methods for Drawing Statistical Inferences from Texts and Transcripts* (pp. 79–100). Mahwah, NJ: Laurence Erlbaum Associates, Inc.

Coates, T. (2005). An addendum to a definition of Social Software. *PLASTICBAG. ORG, 5.* Retrieved from http://www.plasticbag.org/archives/2005/01/an_addendum_to_a_definition_of_social_software/

Colombo, B., Antonietti, A., Sala, R., & Caravita, S. C. S. (2013). Blog Content and Structure, Cognitive Style and Metacognition. *International Journal of Technology and Human Interaction, 9*(3), 1–17. doi:10.4018/jthi.2013070101

Davenport, T. H. (2014). *Big data at work: dispelling the myths, uncovering the opportunities.* Harvard Business School Press. doi:10.15358/9783800648153

Freire, M., Antunes, F., & Costa, J. P. (2015a). *Exploring social network analysis techniques on decision support.* Paper presented at the 2nd European Conference on Social Media ECSM 2015, Porto, Portugal.

Freire, M., Antunes, F., & Costa, J. P. (2015b). *Social network analysis to support decision-making.* Paper presented at the Workshop on Assessment Methodologies – energy, mobility and other real world applications (WAM 2015), Coimbra, Portugal.

Freire, M., Antunes, F., & Costa, J. P. (2017). A Semantics Extraction Framework for Decision Support in Context-Specific Social Web Networks. In L. S. Linden I., Colot C (Ed.), Decision Support Systems VII. Data, Information and Knowledge Visualization in Decision Support Systems (pp. 133-147). Springer. doi:10.1007/978-3-319-57487-5_10

Gehrke, N., & Wolf, P. (2010). *Towards Audit 2.0 – A Web 2.0 Community Platform for Auditors.* Paper presented at the 43rd Hawaii International Conference on System Sciences (CD-ROM), Kauai, HI. doi:10.1109/HICSS.2010.407

Gross, R., & Acquisti, A. (2005). *Information Revelation and Privacy in Online Social Networks.* Paper presented at the 2005 ACM Workshop on Privacy in the Electronic Society (WPES'05), Alexandria, VA. doi:10.1145/1102199.1102214

Hemsley, J., & Mason, R. M. (2013). Knowledge and Knowledge Management in the Social Media Age. *Journal of Organizational Computing and Electronic Commerce, 23*(1-2), 138–167. doi:10.1080/109 19392.2013.748614

Herring, S. (2010). Web Content Analysis: Expanding the Paradigm. In J. Hunsinger, L. Klastrup, & M. Allen (Eds.), *The International Handbook of Internet Research* (pp. 233–249). New York: Springer.

Herring, S. (2013). Discourse in Web 2.0: Familiar, Reconfigured, and Emergent. In D. Tannen & A.-M. Trester (Eds.), *Discourse 2.0: language and new media* (pp. 1–25). Washington, DC: Georgetown University Press.

Herring, S. C. (2010). Web Content Analysis: Expanding the Paradigm. In J. Hunsinger, L. Klastrup, & M. Allen (Eds.), *The International Handbook of Internet Research* (pp. 233–249). New York: Springer.

Herring, S. C. (2013). Discourse in Web 2.0: Familiar, Reconfigured, and Emergent. In D. Tannen & A. M. Trester (Eds.), *Discourse 2.0: language and new media* (pp. 1–25). Washington, DC: Georgetown University Press.

Hippel, E., & Krogh, G. (2003). Open Source Software and the "Private-Collective" Innovation Model: Issues for Organization Science. *Organization Science, 14*(2), 208–223. doi:10.1287/orsc.14.2.209.14992

Ikematsu, K., & Murata, T. (2013). A Fast Method for Detecting Communities from Tripartite Networks. In A. Jatowt, E.-P. Lim, Y. Ding, A. Miura, T. Tezuka, G. Dias, & B. T. Dai et al. (Eds.), *Social Informatics* (pp. 192–205). Springer. doi:10.1007/978-3-319-03260-3_17

Jones, B., Failla, A., & Miller, B. (2007). Tacit Knowledge in Rapidly Evolving Organisational Environments. *International Journal of Technology and Human Interaction, 3*(1), 49–71. doi:10.4018/jthi.2007010104

Kaplan, A. M., & Haenlein, M. (2010). Users of the world, unite! The challenges and opportunities of Social Media. *Business Horizons, 53*(1), 59–68. doi:10.1016/j.bushor.2009.09.003

Kietzmann, J. H., Hermkens, K., McCarthy, I. P., & Silvestre, B. S. (2011). Social media? Get serious! Understanding the functional building blocks of social media. *Business Horizons, 54*(3), 241–251. doi:10.1016/j.bushor.2011.01.005

Kok, S., & Rogers, R. (2016). Rethinking migration in the digital age-transglocalization and the Somali diaspora. *Global Networks*, 1–24.

Leskovec, J., Adamic, L. A., & Huberman, B. A. (2007). The Dynamics of Viral Marketing. *ACM Transactions on the Web, 1*(1).

Ma, H., Gustafson, S., Moitra, A., & Bracewell, D. (2010). Ego-Centric Network Sampling in Viral Marketing Applications. In I.-H. Ting, H.-J. Wu, & T.-H. Ho (Eds.), *Mining and Analyzing Social Networks* (pp. 35–50). Springer. doi:10.1007/978-3-642-13422-7_3

Maclaran, P., & Catterall, M. (2002). Researching the social Web: Marketing information from virtual communities. *Marketing Intelligence & Planning, 20*(6), 319–326. doi:10.1108/02634500210445374

Mander, J., & McGrath, F. (2017). *Flagship Report Q1 2017 - Time Spent on Social Networks or Services*. Global Web Index Media.

Marmo, R. (2011). Web Mining and Social Network Analysis. In H. Zhang, R. S. Segall, & M. Cao (Eds.), *Visual Analytics and Interactive Technologies: Data, Text and Web Mining Applications* (pp. 202–211). Hershey, PA: Information Science Reference. doi:10.4018/978-1-60960-102-7.ch012

Moser, C., Groenewegen, P., & Huysman, M. (2013). Extending Social Network Analysis with Discourse Analysis: Combining Relational with Interpretive Data. In T. Özyer, J. Rokne, G. Wagner, & A. Reuser (Eds.), *The Influence of Technology on Social Network Analysis and Mining* (pp. 547–561). New York: Springer. doi:10.1007/978-3-7091-1346-2_24

Munson, S. A. (2008). *Motivating and enabling organizational memory with a wrokgroup Wiki*. Paper presented at the WikiSym08 2008 International Symposium on Wikis, Porto, Portugal.

Murugesan, S. (2010). *Handbook of Research on Web 2.0, 3.0, and X.0- Technologies, Business, and Social Applications*. Hershey, PA: IGI-Global. doi:10.4018/978-1-60566-384-5

Orlikowski, W. J., & Iacono, C. S. (2001). Desperately Seeking the "IT" in IT Research - A Call to Theorizing the IT Artifact. *Information Systems Research, 12*(2), 121–134. doi:10.1287/isre.12.2.121.9700

Pang, B., & Lee, L. (2008). *Opinion Mining and Sentiment Analysis* (Vol. 2). Now Publishers Inc.

Power, D. J., & Phillips-Wren, G. (2012). Impact of Social Media and Web 2.0 on Decision-Making. *Journal of Decision Systems, 20*(3), 249–261. doi:10.3166/jds.20.249-261

Provost, F., & Fawcett, T. (2013). *Data Science for Business: What You Need to Know about Data Mining and Data-Analytic Thinking*. O'Reilly Media.

Robinson, I., Webber, J., & Eifrem, E. (2013). *Graph Databases. Gravenstein Highway North*. Sebastopol, CA: O'Reilly Media, Inc.

Schneider, J., Groza, T., & Passant, A. (2013). A review of argumentation for the Social Semantic Web. *Semantic Web, 4*(2), 159–218. doi:10.3233/SW-2012-0073

Shum, S. B., Cannavacciuolo, L., De Liddo, A., Iandoli, L., & Quinto, I. (2011). Using Social Network Analysis to Support Collective Decision-Making Process. *International Journal of Decision Support System Technology, 3*(2), 15–31. doi:10.4018/jdsst.2011040102

Simon, H. A. (1977). *The New Science of Management Decision*. Upper Saddle River, NJ: Prentice Hall.

Subrahmanyama, K., Reich, S. M., Waechter, N., & Espinoza, G. (2008). Online and offline social networks: Use of social networking sites by emerging adults. *Journal of Applied Developmental Psychology, 29*(6), 420–433. doi:10.1016/j.appdev.2008.07.003

Suki, N. M., Ramayah, T., Ming, M. K. P., & Suki, N. M. (2011). Factors Enhancing Employed Job Seekers Intentions to Use Social Networking Sites as a Job Search Tool. *International Journal of Technology and Human Interaction, 7*(2), 38–54. doi:10.4018/jthi.2011040105

Teigland, R., & Wasko, M. M. (2003). Integrating Knowledge through Information Trading: Examining the Relationship between Boundary Spanning Communication and Individual Performance. *Decision Sciences, 34*(2), 261–286. doi:10.1111/1540-5915.02341

Tollinen, A., Jarvinen, J., & Karjaluoto, H. (2012). *Opportunities and Challenges of Social Media Monitoring in the Business to Business Sector.* Paper presented at the The 4th International Business and Social Science Research Conference, Dubai, UAE.

Turoff, M., Hiltz, S. R., Bieber, M., Fjermstad, J., & Rana, A. (1999). Collaborative Discourse Structures in Computer Mediated Group Communications. *Journal of Computer-Mediated Communication, 4*(4), 1050–1079.

Warschauer, M., Said, G. R. E., & Zohry, A. (2002). Language Choice Online: Globalization and Identity in Egypt. *Journal of Computer-Mediated Communication, 7*(4).

Wasko, M. M., & Faraj, S. (2005). Why should I share? Examining social capital and knowledge contribution In electronic networks of practice. *Management Information Systems Quarterly, 29*(1), 35–57.

KEY TERMS AND DEFINITIONS

Case Study: A process or record of research into the development of a particular person, group, or situation over a period of time in order to analyze a particular instance of something used or analyzed in order to illustrate a thesis or principle.

Data Extraction: The act or process of retrieving data out of (usually unstructured or poorly structured) data sources for further data processing or data storage (data migration).

Decision-Making: The thought process of selecting a logical choice from the available options by weighting the positives and negatives of each option and considering all the alternatives. For effective decision making, a person must be able to forecast the outcome of each option as well, and based on all these items, determine which option is the best for that particular situation.

Group: A set of people who act together in a certain context and work environment.

Online Social Network: A web-based service, whose nature and nomenclature may vary, that permits individuals to construct public or semi-public profiles and allows their interaction.

Semantics: Regards the branch of linguistics and logic concerned with meaning. The two main areas are logical semantics, concerned with matters such as sense and reference and presupposition and implication, and lexical semantics, concerned with the analysis of word, phrase and text meanings and relations between them.

Social Network Analysis: The mapping and measuring of relationships and flows between people, groups, organizations, computers, URLs, and other connected information/knowledge entities. The nodes in the network represent the entities, while the links show relationships or flows between the nodes. SNA provides both a visual and a mathematical analysis of the created networks.

Chapter 8
Handling the Dataflow in Business Process Models

Giorgio Bruno
Politecnico di Torino, Italy

ABSTRACT

This chapter stresses the importance of the dataflow in business process models and illustrates a nota-tion called DMA that is meant to fulfill two major goals: promoting the integration between business processes and information systems and leveraging the dataflow to provide flexibility in terms of human decisions. The first goal is fulfilled by considering both tasks and business entities as first-class citizens in process models. Business entities form the dataflow that interconnects the tasks: tasks take the input entities from the input dataflow and deliver the output entities to the output dataflow. Human decisions encompass the selection of the input entities when a task needs more than one, and the selection of the task with which to handle the input entities when two or more tasks are admissible. DMA provides a number of patterns that indicate how tasks affect the dataflow. In addition, two compound patterns, called macro tasks, can be used to represent task selection issues. An example related to an order handling process illustrates the notation.

INTRODUCTION

Over the years, various approaches and notations have been proposed to define business process mod-els. They are based on different perspectives and the most important ones are the activity-centric, the artifact-centric and the case-centric perspective.

The activity-centric approach has inspired the industry standard BPMN (Business Process Model and Notation) (OMG-BPMN, 2013), whose focus is on the tasks (work units) and the control flow. The control flow is mainly based on the completion events of the tasks through the intermediation of control-flow elements called gateways: the choice of the paths in the process is carried out automatically on the basis of conditions related to the process variables. This approach provides an efficient way to handle repetitive situations (i.e., routines): the process orchestrates work by distributing tasks to automatic services or to human participants through their worklists. However, participants are mainly considered

DOI: 10.4018/978-1-5225-5297-0.ch008

as resources needed to carry out tasks that are not automatable; human choices are limited and they are not explicitly represented in process models.

The artifact-oriented approach has shifted the focus to the business entities involved in the process; its roots can be found in past research on entity-based dynamic modeling (Sanz, 2011). The term artifact has been introduced to designate a concrete and self-describing chunk of information used to run a business (Nigam & Caswell, 2003). It encompasses both the informational aspects of an entity type and its life cycle consisting of states and transitions. The major benefit is the right level of granularity, which facilitates communication among the stakeholders and helps them focus on the primary purposes of the business (Chao et al, 2009).

However, the artifact-oriented approach does not pay more attention than the activity-oriented one to human tasks: the participants in the process continue to be considered as mere resources needed for tasks that are not automatable.

Flexibility (Schonenberg, Mans, Russell, Mulyar & van der Aalst, 2008) is at the heart of knowledge-intensive processes (Di Ciccio, Marrella & Russo, 2015), i.e., processes calling for some degree of creativity and adaptation to specific circumstances (Alvesson, 2004). What distinguishes knowledge-intensive processes from routines is that participants are not considered as mere resources needed to carry out tasks which are not automatable; on the contrary, their involvement is required at a higher level where they can make choices which affect the control flow.

Flexibility is needed in situations calling for customized treatment: they are called cases and are well known in the medical and legal realms. In the treatment of a case, the participants can decide the tasks to be carried out on the basis of the circumstances. The recent standard CMMN (Case Management Model and Notation) provides a notation to define the process governing the evolution of the case under consideration (OMG-CMMN, 2016). The process is based on an information structure called case file: it is a hierarchical structure (made up of case file items) similar to the one used in document management systems. However, the notation does not show the dataflow in the process model in that there is no visual representation of the inputs and outputs of tasks in terms of the case file items affected.

This chapter stresses the importance of the dataflow and illustrates a notation called DMA (Dataflow-oriented Modeling Approach) for the representation of business processes. The major purposes are as follows.

First, DMA promotes the integration between business processes and information systems: for this reason, the dataflow in process models is based on the entities of the underlying information systems, and process models are complemented by information models that show the types of the entities along with their relationships and attributes. The business entities form the dataflow that interconnects the tasks: tasks take the input entities from the input dataflow and deliver the output entities to the output dataflow. The dataflow in DMA shows the types of the entities involved in the process as well as their states; the states indicate the progress in their life cycles. Therefore, DMA pays tribute to the artifact orientation in that the process models can be thought of as combinations of artifact life cycles.

The second purpose is to leverage the dataflow to provide flexibility in terms of human decisions.

They encompass the selection of the input entities when a task needs more than one, and the selection of the task with which to handle the input entities when two or more tasks are admissible. The ability of selecting the input entities is needed, for example, by an account manager who is in charge of producing a procurement order out of a number of requisition orders. An example of task selection can be found in the operation of a broker who combines requests and offers in transactions and can reject requests and offers. A request and an offer may then be involved in two mutually exclusive actions: one rejects the request or the offer and the other produces a transaction.

The notation provided by DMA considers both tasks and business entities as first-class citizens in business process models. Tasks are classified in a number of patterns that indicate how they affect the dataflow: particular attention is given to aggregation and disaggregation issues. In addition, two compound patterns, called macro tasks, can be used to represent task selection issues.

This chapter is structured as follows. In the first part, it presents background information, gives an overview of DMA with the help of a simple order-handling process, and illustrates the major features of tasks as well as the major task patterns. The second part addresses human task selection and shows the related macro tasks in an extended version of the order-handling process. Finally, the conclusion is presented.

BACKGROUND

The research reported in this chapter has been stimulated by work on the artifact-oriented perspective (Hull, 2008), flexible processes (Schonenberg, Mans, Russell, Mulyar & van der Aalst, 2008) and case management (Marin, Hull & Vaculín, 2013).

A well-known approach in the artifact-oriented domain is the GSM (Guard-Stage-Milestone) one (Hull et al., 2011): its major components are the artifacts, which contain informational aspects (attributes and associations), life cycles and coordination items (events and rules). While the approach is very flexible, its major drawback is the difficulty to figure out what the actual flow of activities is. Moreover, tasks are not first-class citizens in that they are intermediated by calls to external services. Other approaches in the domain are PHILharmonicFlows (Künzle & Reichert, 2011) and COREPRO (Müller, Reichert & Herbst, 2007).

BPMN (OMG-BPMN, 2013) and UML Activity Diagrams (OMG-UML, 2015) provide dataflow-oriented features, in terms of data objects with states (BPMN) and input and output pins with states (UML Activity Diagrams). As a consequence, the control flow and the dataflow coexist: this coexistence in BPMN makes it difficult to handle situations requiring a many-to-many mapping between entities, such as the one between requisition orders and procurement orders (Meyer, Pufahl, Fahland & Weske, 2013). On the contrary, DMA can easily handle aggregation and disaggregation issues as is shown in the enhanced version of the order handling process.

The mapping between activity-oriented models and artifact-oriented ones has been addressed in several papers. Extraction approaches have been presented for UML Activity Diagrams (Eshuis & van Gorp 2012; Kumaran, Liu & Wu, 2008; Ryndina, Küster & Gall, 2007) as well as for BPMN models (Cabanillas, Resinas, Ruiz-Cortés & Awad, 2011) so as to obtain the life cycles of the entity types appearing in activity models. The opposite direction, i.e., the generation of process models from life cycles, has also been investigated (Küster, Ryndina & Gall, 2007). Roundtrip transformations between lifecycle-oriented models and extended activity-oriented ones have been presented by Meyer and Weske (2014). A technique for extracting the life cycles of the entity types from a dataflow model has been presented by Bruno (2017).

Human choices have been addressed by research on flexible processes based on declarative approaches. For example, in Declare (Pesic, Schonenberg & van der Aalst, 2007) any task of an ad-hoc sub-process may be performed as long as the mandatory constraints are not violated. However, the dataflow is not represented explicitly and then the choice of the tasks cannot be put in relation to the input entities. This limitation has been overcome in DMA because the input and output flows of the tasks are shown in process models.

The notion of case management has evolved over years and a number of approaches have been proposed (Van der Aalst, Weske & Grünbauer, 2005; De Man, 2009; Marin, Hull & Vaculín, 2013; Motahari-Nezhad & Swenson, 2013; Hauder, Pigat & Matthes, 2014). The recent standard CMMN has been inspired by GSM; however the dataflow is not included in the process model. Bruno (2016) has proposed an extension to CMMN for the representation of the dataflow between tasks.

OVERVIEW OF DMA

DMA integrates the notions of artifact and task: it is a dataflow language in that the activation of tasks depends on the availability of suitable input entities. On the contrary, in the activity-oriented approach, tasks are mainly activated on the basis of the completion events of the tasks previously performed.

DMA models are connected bipartite graphs made up of tasks and dataflow nodes. The symbols of tasks and nodes are the rectangle with rounded borders and the circle, respectively. Tasks and nodes are connected by means of oriented arcs: they establish input relationships from nodes to tasks and output relationships from tasks to nodes.

The structure of DMA models has been inspired by Petri nets (Murata, 1989): nodes correspond to places and tasks correspond to transitions.

Nodes denote flows of business entities of the same type and state; their labels show the types and the states, separated by commas. The states indicate the progress of the entities in their life cycles.

If a node has two or more input tasks, it is a merge node; if it has two or more output tasks, it is a branch node. If a node has only one input task and only one output task, it may be absorbed in the arc connecting the source task to the destination one. This arc has the label of the included dataflow node and is called dataflow arc.

Tasks are divided into automatic tasks and human ones. The former are performed by services, and the latter are carried by the participants in the process. A human task is accompanied by a role denoting the participants entitled to perform it. The role is shown next to the task symbol.

An example of process model is shown in Figure 1. It is a simple order handling process that enables the account managers of a given organization to interact with customers and suppliers. An account manager handles the relationships with a number of customers. The process enables customers to place requisition orders, and account managers to place procurement orders with suppliers. Each requisition order refers to a product type; in the information system of the organization, each product type is associated with a number of suppliers.

The mapping between requisition orders and procurement orders is many to one; therefore one or more requisition orders can be associated with one procurement order, provided that the supplier the procurement order is directed to handles all the product types related to the requisition orders. Suppliers fulfill procurement orders, and when a procurement order has been fulfilled, the corresponding requisition orders are considered fulfilled and the respective customers will be notified automatically.

DMA promotes a tight integration with information systems and, for this reason, an information model including the types of the business entities along with their relationships and attributes complements the process model.

The information model draws on the UML (Unified Modeling Language) class model (OMG-UML, 2015) and extends it on the basis of a number of conventions, such as the categories of the entity types and the required relationships. The information model related to the order handling process is shown in Figure 1.

Entity types are divided into three major categories: role types, managed types and complementary ones. Role types, such as Customer, Supplier and AccountMgr, match the role labels of human tasks. Managed types represent the entities forming the dataflow of the process; they match the entity types appearing in the labels of the dataflow nodes and arcs. The complementary types, such as ProductType, denote entities that provide background information: the process does not generate complementary entities but may introduce associations between managed entities and complementary ones.

Relationships show the constraints on the number of associations by means of multiplicity indicators. The symbols "n" and "*" mean one or more associations, and zero or more associations, respectively.

Required relationships represent associations that must be set when new entities are generated; they are shown as oriented links, i.e., connections ending with an arrow on one side. For example, the relationship between POrder and ROrder expresses the constraint that a new procurement order is based on a number of requisition orders. The multiplicity on the side of required entities is an integer number or "n"; if it is omitted, it is assumed to be 1. If the multiplicity on the side of non-required entities is omitted, it is assumed to be "*".

In a process model, there are tasks with no input entities and tasks with no output entities. The former (e.g., placeROrder) enter entities in the process and the latter (e.g., notifyCustomer) remove entities from the process; they are called entry tasks and exit tasks, respectively.

Tasks have a number of properties, i.e., post-conditions, output directives and assignment rules, which are illustrated in the next section. Post-conditions express the effects of tasks in a declarative way, output directives specify the output entities of tasks, and assignment rules determine the performers of tasks

Figure 1. The model of process HandleCustomerOrders1

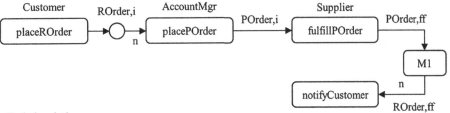

Task descriptions
placeROrder: Post: isNew ROrder as order. Out: order.
placePOrder: Post: (with Supplier s, where s.productTypes includes rOrders.productType) isNew POrder order.
Out: order. Assignee: rOrder.customer.accountMgr.
fulfillPOrder: Assignee: pOrder.supplier.

Information model

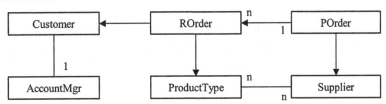

on the basis of the input entities. The definitions of the properties are introduced by the keywords Post, Out and Assignee, respectively.

The effect of task placeROrder is to enter a requisition order into the information system. The output of the task is the newly generated order; the process sets the state of the order to the initial one (named i by convention) on the basis of the label of the output node.

Any customer can perform task placeROrder. On the contrary, the next task, placePOrder, is performed by a specific account manager who is the one that takes care of the relationships with the customer who placed the requisition orders. The assignment rule in task placePOrder is a navigational expression that maps a requisition order to the intended account manager. Navigational expressions are explained in the next section.

The effect of task placePOrder is to produce a procurement order directed to a supplier who supplies the product types required by the requisition orders that have been selected by the performer of the task from among those available in the input node. This kind of selection is called input selection; the weight "n" indicates that the number of requisition orders to be selected is not predetermined.

The procurement order is then fulfilled by the specific supplier; the details are not provided and therefore the post-condition is missing. The task emits the input entity and the process changes its state according to the label of the output dataflow arc: the procurement order gets the state fulfilled (ff).

A mapping task (M1) follows task fulfillPOrder: it is an automatic task whose operation is explained in the next section. In this case, its function is to output the requisition orders associated with the procurement order; these orders get the state fulfilled (ff). The reason is that the procurement order needs no further treatment while the fulfillment of the requisition orders has to be notified to the customers. The notification is performed by automatic task notifyCustomer.

The order handling process combines the life cycles of two artifacts, ROrder and POrder, as shown by the labels of the dataflow arcs.

FEATURES OF TASKS

This section illustrates the major features of tasks, namely the post-conditions, the output directives and the assignment rules for human tasks. These features take advantage of the information model that accompanies the process model.

Post-Conditions

Although the implementation of tasks is outside the scope of process models (and usually consists of web applications), it is important to express the intended effects and the constraints of tasks. A common way is to use a declarative approach based on conditions. The syntax of conditions in DMA is inspired by OCL (OMG-OCL, 2014). In addition, DMA leverages the implications of the required relationships in the information model.

For example, the post-condition "isNew ROrder as order" of task placeROrder in Figure 1 specifies that the effect of the task is the generation of a new requisition order. This new entity, referred to as order, will be outputted when the execution of the task is completed, as established by the output directive "Out: order".

The generation of a new entity involves additional implicit effects, if its type is subject to required relationships. Type ROrder has two required relationships with types Customer and ProductType: therefore a new ROrder needs to be connected to a Customer entity and to a ProductType entity. The entities fulfilling the required relationships are called partner entities: they may be determined automatically or through a selection made by the task performer.

A partner entity is automatically determined if its type is included in the contextual types of the task under consideration: the contextual types encompass the type of the role associated with the task and the types of the input entities of the task. Therefore the customer entity to be associated with a newly generated ROrder entity is the performer entity (i.e., the entity representing the person who is in charge of performing the task), because Customer is the role of the performers of task placeROrder. On the other hand, the productType entity will be selected by the performer during the execution of the task in that its type is not a contextual type of the task.

If the selection of a partner entity is subject to constraints a selection rule is introduced in the post-condition as it takes place with task placePOrder: "(with Supplier s, where s.productTypes includes rOrders.productType) isNew POrder order". The selection rule, written between parentheses and introduced by the keyword with, is about choosing a supplier who handles the product types associated with the input entities. The input entities are referred to as rOrders. The plural form of the type name with the initial in lower case is used, if the number of entities may be more than one; otherwise, the singular form is used. The supplier entity selected by the task performer is referred to as "s"; it will be connected implicitly to the newly generated POrder entity as a consequence of the required relationship from POrder to Supplier. The other required relationship, i.e., the one from POrder to ROrder, brings about the connection between the POrder entity and the input entities of the task.

The expressions "s.productTypes" and "rOrders.productType" in the selection rule are navigational expressions. The former returns the product types related to the chosen supplier: the plural (with the initial in lower case) of the name ProductType is used because the relationship from Supplier to ProductType has multiplicity $>= 1$. The latter provides the ProductType entities associated with the task input entities.

Output Directives

Output directives specify the contributions of the tasks to the dataflow, in terms of output entities. The process sets the state of the output entities on the basis of the labels of the output nodes and arcs. If an output entity is a newly generated one it gets the initial state (named i by convention). If a task emits the input entities no directive is needed.

Assignment Rules

A human task may be performed by any member of the role associated with the task or by a specific member. In the second case, an assignment rule is needed.

In particular, this chapter addresses the situation in which the assignee depends on the input entities. For example, task placePOrder is carried out by several account managers but each of them operates on the requisition orders placed by the customers they take care of.

The assignment rule is introduced by the keyword "Assignee" and consists of a navigational expression that maps input entities to performers. The mapping is carried out by means of a navigational expression: for example, "rOrder.customer.accountMgr" in task placePOrder means that each input requisition order, referred to as rOrder, will be handled by the account manager related to the customer that is associated with it. The expression corresponds to the path "ROrder - Customer - AccountMgr" in the information model: the path starts with the type of the input entities and ends with the role type associated with the task. The path is valid, if it returns one and only one performer.

For the sake of simplicity, the assignment rule can be provided automatically, if there is one and only one valid minimal path starting with the type of the input entities and ending with the role type associated with the task. A valid minimal path is a path that has the minimum number of elements and denotes exactly one performer. Therefore, on the basis of this assumption, there is no need to explicitly write the assignment rule for task placePOrder.

Task placeROrder has no input entities and then it is an entry task, as is explained in the next section. It may be performed by any customer, i.e., by any member of the role associated with the task.

Weights of the Arcs

If a single execution of a task may take more than one entity from an input node or may deliver more than one entity to an output one, a weight is put on the corresponding arc. The weight is an integer number greater than 1, if the number of entities involved is fixed; it is "n", if the number is not predetermined. If the weight is missing its value is assumed to be 1.

A weight greater than one means that the input entities are chosen by the performer of the task: this kind of human decision is referred to as entity selection.

TASK PATTERNS

This section presents the most common task patterns that can be found in DMA models; they are shown in Figure 2. Only the basic version is presented for each pattern. The weights of the arcs are not shown: in general, the patterns can handle more than one input (and output) entity. Moreover, the patterns that may have two or more input (or output) arcs are shown with two input (or output) arcs.

Figure 2. Task patterns

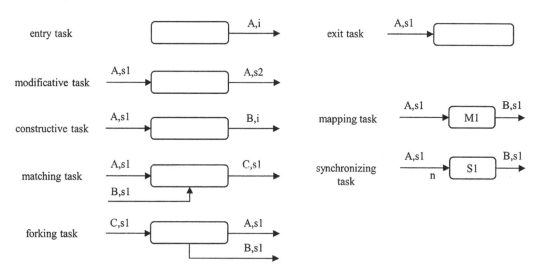

Entity types are represented by capital letters such as A and B. States are indicated as s1, s2, etc. The initial state is named "i".

A short description of the purposes of the patterns is as follows.

Entry tasks enter new entities into the process; they have no input entities as they act as data sources. On the contrary, exit tasks remove entities from the process because they emit no output entities. Task placeROrder in Figure 1 is an entry task while task notifyCustomer is an exit one.

Modificative tasks emit the input entities; the input arc and the output one have the same type but different states. Constructive tasks emit newly generated entities that are associated with the input entities: the state of the new entities is the initial one. Task placePOrder in Figure 1 is a constructive task while task fulfillPOrder is a modificative one.

Matching tasks select input entities of different types, and forking tasks emit entities of different types. A task may be a matching task and a forking one at the same time, if it has two or more input arcs and two or more output arcs.

A synchronizing task assumes that the input type, say, A, and the output one, say, B, are related with a many-to-one multiplicity. When all the entities A that are related to the same entity B are available in the input node, the task removes the entities A from the input node and outputs the entity B. Synchronizing tasks are depicted with smaller icons and their names are S1, S2, etc.

A mapping task assumes that the input type, say, A, and the output one, say, B, are related; it emits all the entities B related to the input entity A. Mapping tasks are depicted with smaller icons and their names are M1, M2, etc.

MACRO TASKS FOR TASK SELECTION

In addition to entity selection, which is exemplified by task placePOrder in Figure 1, there is another kind of selection, referred to as task selection. It takes place when a performer may handle the input entities with two or more mutually exclusive tasks (called competing tasks); then, he or she is in charge of selecting the task taking into account the content of the input entities.

Two patterns for human selection are provided by DMA: they are called macro tasks and are shown in Figure 3. Macro tasks include all the tasks that have some common input entities; these tasks may be the starting points of different courses of action. A macro task is depicted as a box including the competing tasks; the name of the macro task is shown in the upper part of the box.

Figure 3. Macro tasks for human selection

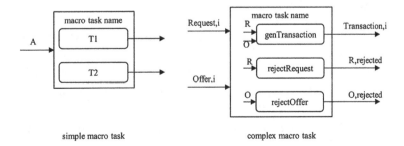

145

Macro tasks may be simple or complex. In a simple macro task, all the tasks share the same input flows. In the example, the input A may be handled with task T1 or task T2 and it is up to the performer of the macro task to decide.

In a complex macro task, the input flows of the tasks may be different; the box then contains the transitive closure of all the tasks having some common input flows.

In the example, the complex macro task has two input flows: one contains requests and the other contains offers. Task genTransaction is a matching task: it enables the performer to combine one request and one offer so as to produce a new transaction. The other tasks are modificative ones and can be carried out to reject a request or an offer. The input flows of the tasks are shown explicitly using the initial of the types (R and O) of the input flows of the macro task. The use of macro tasks is exemplified in the next section.

THE ENHANCED MODEL OF PROCESS HANDLECUSTOMERORDERS

Task selection is illustrated with an extended version of the order handling process presented in section "Overview of DMA". The extensions are as follows.

Requisition orders are made up of lines each one referring to a product type. Account managers may reject or accept requisition orders, and may bundle the lines of accepted ones into procurement orders directed to suitable suppliers, i.e., suppliers that are able to provide the product types required by the lines. A newly generated procurement order remains in the initial state until the account manager closes it; then it will be made available to the intended supplier. In the meanwhile, the account manager can associate additional lines with the procurement order.

The process model and the companion information model are shown in Figure 4 and in Figure 5, respectively.

The process model includes two macro tasks: a simple one (checkROrder) and a complex one (issuePOrder). The performer of macro task checkROrder has to decide whether to accept or reject an incoming requisition order. Both competing tasks are modificative ones. Task acceptROrder is followed by mapping task M1, which emits the lines associated with the input requisition order.

Macro task issuePOrder has two input nodes: "Line, i" and "POrder, i". The latter is also an output node and then a bidirectional arc appears between the node and the box of the macro task.

The weight "n" on the input arc from node "Line, i" means that the performer has to select the input lines for tasks genPOrder and addLines from among those available in the input node.

The performer may generate a new procurement order on the basis of the input lines selected or may add them to an open procurement order (i.e., a procurement order in the initial state); in addition, he or she may decide to close an open procurement order.

The selection rule "(with lines, Supplier s, where s.productTypes includes lines.productType)" in the post-condition of task genPOrder means that the intended supplier must be able to provide the product types required by the lines selected. The selection rule "(with lines, pOrder, where pOrder.supplier.productTypes includes lines.productType)" in the post-condition of task addLines signifies that the lines and the procurement order must be compatible, i.e., the supplier of the procurement order must be able to provide the product types required by the lines.

The bidirectional arc (PO) of task addLines means that "POrder, i" is both an input node and an output one of the task.

Figure 4. The model of process HandleCustomerOrders2

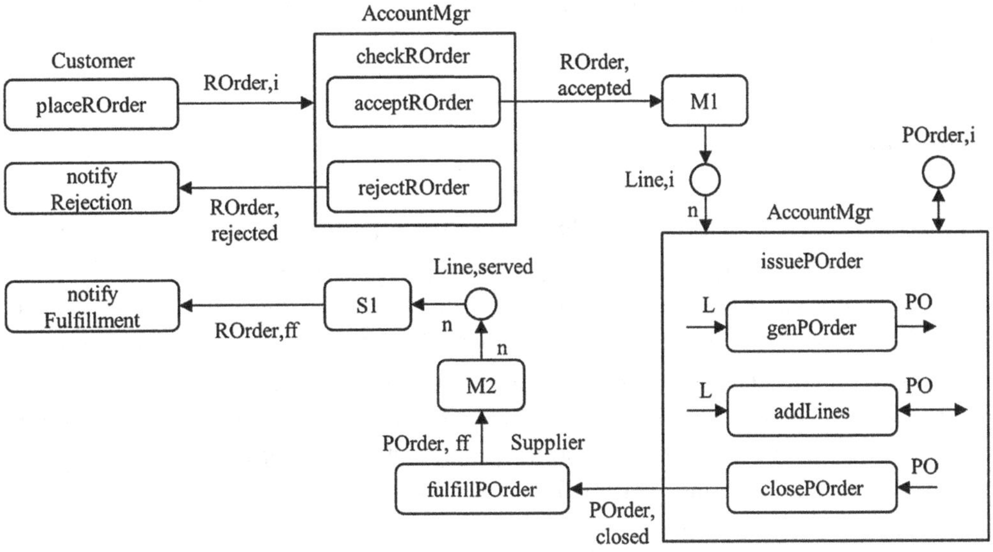

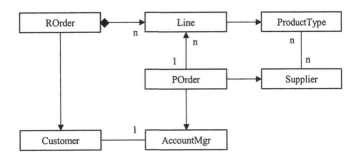

Task descriptions
placeROrder: Post: isNew ROrder as order. Out: order.
genPOrder: Post: (with lines, Supplier s, where s.productTypes includes lines.productType)
 isNew POrder order. Out: order.
addLines: (with lines, pOrder, where pOrder.supplier.productTypes includes lines.productType)
 lines.pOrder == pOrder. Out: pOrder.

Figure 5. The information model of process HandleCustomerOrders2

The assignment rules for the tasks are omitted as they can be inferred automatically from the information model. As an example, the lines are handled by the account manager that results from the path "Line - ROrder - Customer - AccountMgr"; it corresponds to the navigational expression "line.rOrder. customer.accountMgr".

When a procurement order is closed, the specific supplier can fulfill it; the output of task fulfillPOrder enters mapping task M2, which emits the lines associated with the procurement order. When node "Line, served" includes all the lines related to the same requisition order, the synchronizer S1 outputs the order, and then a notification of fulfillment is sent to the customer.

The process handles an indirect many-to-many mapping between requisition orders and procurement ones: the mapping is based on the lines of requisition orders. A procurement order may include lines from different requisition orders. Mapping task M2 decomposes the flow of procurement orders into a flow of served lines; synchronizer S1 recomposes the flow of fulfilled requisition orders from the flow of served lines.

CONCLUSION

This chapter has illustrated a notation, called DMA (Dataflow-oriented Modeling Approach), that leverages the dataflow to promote the integration between business processes and information systems. The dataflow in process models is based on the entities of the underlying information systems, and process models are complemented by information models that show the types of the entities along with their relationships and attributes. The presence of the information model is essential for the definition of the properties of tasks, namely the intended effects, the contribution to the output dataflow and, in case of human tasks, the assignment rules for the appointment of suitable performers.

The explicit representation of the dataflow in DMA allows human decisions to be easily represented. Two kinds of them have been illustrated: entity selection and task selection.

This chapter has also presented a number of patterns that show how tasks affect the dataflow.

The patterns enable the construction of a process model as a composition of building blocks consisting of single tasks or macro tasks; the latter represent situations in which the input entities may be handled with different tasks and the selection of the one to be carried out implies a human decision.

Current work is devoted to improving the flexibility of the approach in order to tackle case management issues such as those addressed by the recent standard CMMN (Case Management Model and Notation) (OMG-CMMN, 2016). Moreover, an improvement to the structure of work lists, which include the tasks assigned to the participants in the process, will be investigated.

REFERENCES

Alvesson, M. (2004). *Knowledge work and knowledge-intensive firms*. Oxford, UK: Oxford University Press.

Bruno, G. (2016). Tasks and assignments in case management models. *Procedia Computer Science*, *100*, 156–163. doi:10.1016/j.procs.2016.09.135

Bruno, G. (2017). A dataflow-oriented modeling approach to business processes. *International Journal of Human Capital and Information Technology Professionals*, *8*(1), 51–65. doi:10.4018/IJHCITP.2017010104

Cabanillas, C., Resinas, M., Ruiz-Cortés, A., & Awad, A. (2011). Automatic generation of a data-centered view of business processes. In *Lecture Notes in Computer Science, 6741* (pp. 352–366). Heidelberg, Germany: Springer. doi:10.1007/978-3-642-21640-4_27

Chao, T. (2009). Artifact-based transformation of IBM Global Financing. In *Lecture Notes in Computer Science, 5701* (pp. 261–277). Heidelberg, Germany: Springer.

De Man, H. (2009, January). Case management: A review of modeling approaches. *BPTrends*.

Di Ciccio, C., Marrella, A., & Russo, A. (2015). Knowledge-intensive processes: Characteristics, requirements and analysis of contemporary approaches. *Journal on Data Semantics, 4*(1), 29–57. doi:10.1007/s13740-014-0038-4

Eshuis, R., & van Gorp, P. (2012). Synthesizing object life cycles from business process models. In *Lecture Notes in Computer Science, 7532* (pp. 307–320). Heidelberg, Germany: Springer. doi:10.1007/978-3-642-34002-4_24

Hauder, M., Pigat, S., & Matthes, F. (2014). Research challenges in adaptive case management: a literature review. In *Proceedings of the 18th IEEE International Enterprise Distributed Object Computing Conference Workshops and Demonstrations* (pp. 98–107). New York: IEEE Press. doi:10.1109/EDOCW.2014.24

Hull, R. (2008). Artifact-oriented business process models: brief survey of research results and challenges. In *Lecture Notes in Computer Science, 5332* (pp. 1152–1163). Heidelberg, Germany: Springer.

Hull, R. (2011). Introducing the Guard–Stage-Milestone approach for specifying business entity lifecycles. In *Lecture Notes in Computer Science, 6551* (pp. 1–24). Heidelberg, Germany: Springer. doi:10.1007/978-3-642-19589-1_1

Kumaran, S., Liu, R., & Wu, F. Y. (2008). On the duality of information-oriented and activity-oriented models of business processes. In *Lecture Notes in Computer Science, 5074* (pp. 32–47). Heidelberg: Springer.

Künzle, V., & Reichert, M. (2011). PHILharmonicFlows: Towards a framework for object-aware process management. *Journal of Software Maintenance and Evolution: Research and Practice, 23*(4), 205–244. doi:10.1002/smr.524

Küster, J. M., Ryndina, K., & Gall, H. (2007). Generation of business process models for object life cycle compliance. In *Lecture Notes in Computer Science, 4714* (pp. 165–181). Heidelberg, Germany: Springer. doi:10.1007/978-3-540-75183-0_13

Marin, M., Hull, R., & Vaculín, R. (2013). Data centric BPM and the emerging case management standard: A short survey. *Lecture Notes in Business Information Processing, 132*, 24–30. doi:10.1007/978-3-642-36285-9_4

Meyer, A., Pufahl, L., Fahland, D., & Weske, M. (2013). Modeling and enacting complex data dependencies in business processes. In *Lecture Notes in Computer Science, 8094* (pp. 171–186). Heidelberg, Germany: Springer. doi:10.1007/978-3-642-40176-3_14

Meyer, A., & Weske, M. (2014). Activity-oriented and artifact-oriented process model roundtrip. *Lecture Notes in Business Information Processing, 171*, 167–181. doi:10.1007/978-3-319-06257-0_14

Motahari-Nezhad, H. R., & Swenson, K. D. (2013). Adaptive case management: overview and research challenges. In *Proceedings of the 15th IEEE Conference on Business Informatics* (pp. 264–269). New York: IEEE Press. doi:10.1109/CBI.2013.44

Müller, D., Reichert, M., & Herbst, J. (2007). Data-driven modeling and coordination of large process structures. In *Lecture Notes in Computer Science, 4803* (pp. 131–149). Heidelberg, Germany: Springer. doi:10.1007/978-3-540-76848-7_10

Murata, T. (1989). Petri nets: Properties, analysis and applications. *Proceedings of the IEEE, 77*(4), 541–580. doi:10.1109/5.24143

Nigam, A., & Caswell, N. S. (2003). Business artifacts: An approach to operational specification. *IBM Systems Journal, 42*(3), 428–445. doi:10.1147/sj.423.0428

OMG-BPMN. (2013). *Business Process Model and Notation, V.2.0.2*. Retrieved July 17, 2017, from http://www.omg.org/spec/BPMN/2.0.2/

OMG-CMMN. (2016). *Case Management Model and Notation, V.1.0*. Retrieved July 17, 2017, from http://www.omg.org/spec/CMMN/1.1/

OMG-OCL. (2014). *Object Constraint Language, V.2.4*. Retrieved July 17, 2017, from http://www.omg.org/spec/OCL/2.4/

OMG-UML. (2015). *Unified Modeling Language, V.2.5*. Retrieved July 17, 2017, from http://www.omg.org/spec/UML/2.5/

Pesic, M., Schonenberg, H., & van der Aalst, W. M. P. (2007). Declare: Full support for loosely-structured processes. In *Proceedings of the 11th IEEE International Conference on Enterprise Distributed Object Computing* (pp. 287-298). New York: IEEE Press. doi:10.1109/EDOC.2007.14

Ryndina, K., Küster, J. M., & Gall, H. (2007). Consistency of business process models and object life cycles. In *Lecture Notes in Computer Science, 4364* (pp. 80–90). Heidelberg, Germany: Springer. doi:10.1007/978-3-540-69489-2_11

Sadiq, S., Orlowska, M., Sadiq, W., & Schulz, K. (2005). When workflows will not deliver: the case of contradicting work practice. *Proceedings of the 8th International Conference on Business Information Systems*.

Sanz, J. L. C. (2011). Entity-oriented operations modeling for business process management - A multi-disciplinary review of the state-of-the-art. In *Proceedings of the 6th IEEE International Symposium on Service Oriented System Engineering* (pp. 152-163). New York: IEEE Press.

Schonenberg, H., Mans, R., Russell, N., Mulyar, N., & van der Aalst, W. (2008). Process flexibility: A survey of contemporary approaches. *Lecture Notes in Business Information Processing, 10*, 16–30. doi:10.1007/978-3-540-68644-6_2

Van der Aalst, W. M. P., Weske, M., & Grünbauer, D. (2005). Case handling: A new paradigm for business process support. *Data & Knowledge Engineering, 53*(2), 129–162. doi:10.1016/j.datak.2004.07.003

KEY TERMS AND DEFINITIONS

Business Process: A standard way of organizing work in a business context. It consists of a number of tasks to be carried out by human participants or automated services.

Case Management: The handling of a situation that requires a customized treatment. The case workers can decide the tasks to perform as well as their ordering.

Dataflow: The information entities used and produced by tasks.

Entity Selection: A situation in which a performer has to select the input entities of the task to be carried out.

Performer: For a given task, the person in charge of performing it.

Task: A unit of work in the system.

Task Selection: A situation in which a performer may operate on the same input entities with a number of alternative tasks.

To-Do List: A list of pending tasks for a certain performer. By clicking on an entry, he/she can perform the specific work related to the task.

Chapter 9

Principles of Secure Access and Privacy in Combined E-Learning Environment:
Architecture, Formalization, and Modelling

Radi Petrov Romansky
Technical University of Sofia, Bulgaria

Irina Stancheva Noninska
Technical University of Sofia, Bulgaria

ABSTRACT

Globalization in the contemporary information society outlines new important challenges in privacy and personal data protection that apply to user security in cyberspace. This is also the case e-learning environments, which use new network technologies, such as remote access, distributed processing, information sharing, cloud services, social computing, etc. Strong security procedures based on authentication, authorization, and data protection should be proposed to protect system resources, user profiles, personal information, educational materials, and other specific information. The chapter presents the opportunities and challenges of some digital technologies that could increase the effectiveness of e-learning processes by developing a combined e-learning environment. A functional architecture with two sub-systems (front office and back office) and different information resources (public, internal, external) is discussed. Investigation by using formalization and modelling is made and assessments are presented.

INTRODUCTION

It is well known that e-learning is learning based on Information and Communication Technologies (ICT) for remote access to educational curriculum and materials outside of a traditional classroom. Many terms are used for describing e-learning as online learning, internet learning, distance education, etc. The contemporary ICT permit to extend these definitions with distributed learning, mobile learning, social

DOI: 10.4018/978-1-5225-5297-0.ch009

learning, cloud learning, etc. Yes, e-learning has many benefits, but developed e-learning systems and environments must propose services with a high level of user's security and personal data protection.

The digital world based on Internet proposes many opportunities for collaboration and remote access, making communications easy and fast. Implementation of cloud and social computing technologies contributes to the success of the understanding and accepting e-learning policy as a whole (Peytcheva-Forsyth, 2015). There are different proposals for e-learning architectures based on cloud services and social media (Joshi, 2014; Neville, 2013; Riahi, 2015; Khedr, 2017; Yang, 2017). These new technologies have many advantages which sometimes could cause difficulties with protection of information and user's privacy (Chen, 2013).

All information resources should be regarded as an integration of information (structured data) that are supported by technological and technical units (computer equipment; program tools; meta-data for description of information objects; means for designing, developing and managing; etc.). Globalization and opportunities for distributed access to different information resources impose adoption of information security policy and strong control over user's personal data processing (Romansky, 2015a). This is very important as the use of Internet is permanently increasing. o be done bearing in mind permanent increasing of Internet using. All new opportunities of globalization could have a negative effect on digital privacy and this is valid for all components of Information Society as virtual environments (Guazzini, 2017), distributed and online learning (Bandara, 2014; Chen, 2013), cloud computing (Viti, 2014; Lavanya, 2017), mobile communications (Hasan, 2015; Jung, 2015; Olawumi, 2017), social computing (Kinast, 2014; Misra, 2015), Internet of Things in education (Burd, 2017), etc. The Web applications which usually share personal information, determine a necessity for secure Internet connections, hence network providers must guarantee user's privacy (Fisher, 2014; Kinast, 2014). It is well known that the privacy is a fundamental human right and very often it depends on secure processing of personal data. Different components of the digital word require creation of personal profiles that consist of personal data and they should be protected by improving the legislation and implemented clear privacy strategy (Werner, 2017) and strong security conception (Gabor, 2017).

Different models and schemes for digital education are used as basic components of contemporary digital world and all aspects of digital privacy and secure access to the profiles with personal data must find adequate solution. Nowadays e-Learning environments are extended by opportunities that give social computing (Neville, 2013; Rotkrantz, 2015) and cloud services (Joshi, 2014; Riahi, 2015; Lavanya, 2017) which outline new challenges for digital privacy (Romansky, 2015a; Romansky, 2015b).

The purpose of this chapter is to summarize the main opportunities of the contemporary technologies used for supporting e-learning processes and to determine their challenges for user's security and privacy. The goal is to propose a functional architecture of combined e-learning environment (CeLE) with two system levels – front office (input point for preliminary registration and identification) and back office responsible for access control and security management by using means and tools for authentication, authorization, digital right management and personal data protection. Formalization of the proposed procedures in CeLE by using directed graph is made. The effectiveness of processes in CeLE is investigated based on designed models in discrete and stochastic aspects and some statistical assessments obtained by the software Develve are presented.

OPPORTUNITIES AND CHALLENGES OF THE DIGITAL WORLD

The contemporary digital world proposes many opportunities which could be used and implemented in different distributed environments during the phase of design and/or as an additional functionality. However, each of these technologies could create situations that will disturb one or more principles of user's security and privacy.

For example, the grid technology increases the performance of task realization in case of very large size of data (big data), but at the same time it increases the risk for attacks to the information resources (Ashok, 2014). The new aspect of grid technology is so called "smart girds" determined by Yu & Xue as

... electric networks that employ advanced monitoring, control, and communication technologies to deliver reliable and secure energy supply, enhance operation efficiency for generators and distributors, and provide flexible choices for prosumers. Smart grids are a combination of complex physical network systems and cyber systems that face many technological challenges. In this paper, we will first present an overview of these challenges in the context of cyber-physical systems (Yu, 2016).

The authors present in the paper several challenges that smart grids could be made for cyber-physical systems.

Another contribution of the digital world is cloud computing and cloud environments. It is well known that this technology has many opportunities for institutions and business. This theme is often discussed in the scientific literature, for example (Allen, 2017) determines the cloud service "Software as a Service" (SaaS) as "*a form of remote software access that has primarily targeted research supercomputer systems for computation*". The authors note that the SaaS-based services are based on the multitenancy and "*such multitenancy insures the most fundamental benefit of the SaaS model which is the ease and expediency with which new users can begin using the software*". Yes, cloud services are good means to increase the performance and effectiveness of work in the network, but they have different challenges for the user's privacy.

Organization of e-Learning Environments

The Information Society is an organization of distributed information resources in the global network with remote access and information sharing. Different distributed environments exist as components of the contemporary digital world, including e-governance/e-government, e-health, e-business/e-commerce, e-learning, etc. An extension of e-learning is so called Distributed Learning (DL) that unites the principles of e-learning and networking. DL is an instructional model based on location of main participants and resources (instructors, teachers, students, system administrators, moderators, content, user's profiles, etc.) in different places in the global network and information servicing realization (Romansky, 2017).

The model of DL is an organization of distributed and common-used informational resources in a heterogeneous environment with local management. In this reason, the design of such Distributed Learning Environment (DLE) requires to build an adequate conceptual model and previously investigation based on formalization and modelling of the processes of information servicing. This will increase the effectiveness of the architectural and software design.

The traditional e-learning system consists of sub-systems as a virtual learning environment for collaboration and assessment, library management and sub-systems for grading and content management.

At the same time, contemporary e-learning processes usually are realized via the Internet using different web technologies. In this reason, an e-learning environment could be defined as an integration of educational, information, network and knowledge based technologies and platforms. A version of traditional e-learning model for e-learning is presented in (Kim, 2013). This model includes two basic groups of participants that have created their own personal profiles, as shown in Figure 1. These profiles usually consist of personal data that should be protected. Main processes supported in this e-learning system are communication between participants; learner's access to learning resources; moderator's activities for learning resources preparation and evaluation procedures. All these processes use databases that should be protected as well.

This structure could be extended by combining different techniques including audio over the Internet, video via the Internet, opportunities of social computing (social media & social networks, social web-sites like YouTube and messaging programs such as Skype, Adobe Connect could be used too), blogs/micro-blogs for sharing comments and additional information, mobile devices for access to web sites (so called m-learning), virtual classrooms based of virtual reality, interactive white-boards or smart-boards, virtual learning environments (known as learning platforms), etc.

Social computing is a possible element that could be implemented in DLE because "*social media are now a cornerstone of everyday life*" (Selwin, 2016). The authors determine the aim of the article "*to look back at the impact of social media on education, and revisit some of the central questions and challenges*". In addition, in (Greenhow, 2016) is proposed a model for social media using as a space for learning with varying attributes. The authors conclude, that "*model could reveal new understandings of social media in education, and outline future research directions*". The benefits for e-learning procedures are determined in (Manca, 2016) by the text "*Social Media refer to a wide range of applications enabling users to create, share, comment and discuss digital content. They are also depicted as 'dynamic', 'interactive', 'democratic', 'people centric', 'volatile', 'social' and 'adaptive'*". Another opportunity of social media is that it "*enable the development of new didactical models underlying MOOCs*" (Rothkrantz, 2015) and it "*can provide a virtual meeting place*". The author formulates the question "*how to select your friends to cooperate successfully in study activities*" and a tool for recommendation best matching students are described in the article.

Cloud computing is another important opportunity for organization of DLE based on using suitable cloud services and data centres for information and education resources storing. Riahi determines that

Figure 1. Ordinary model for e-learning system
Kim, 2013.

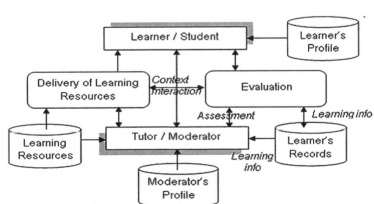

"As with rapid growth of the cloud computing architecture usage, more and more industries move their focus from investing into processing power to renting processing power from a specialized vendor but education field is no different" (Riahi, 2015). The author write that e-learning systems require many hardware and software resources and cloud computing is a suitable decision for infrastructure of DLE because it can to use cloud services for running application, storing different information and profiles, using infrastructural components, etc. Using cloud infrastructure will permit DLE to be *"feasible and it can greatly improve the efficiency of investment and the power of management, which can make E-learning system development into a virtuous circle and achieve a win-win situation for suppliers and customers"*. An architecture of e-learning cloud is presented in this article and five main layers are described: Hardware resource layer; Software resource layer; Resource management layer; Service layer; Business application layer. The idea for using cloud's opportunities for realization of e-learning processes is supported in (Yang, 2017). Several advantages are determined in this article: (1) e-learning developers (teachers & trainers) will have lower engagements with balancing between hardware and resources; (2) users of DLE (students & workers) *"would only require having some light weight, low cost devices, such as tablet, ultra book, or smart phone, to interact with e-learning systems through internet connection"*; (3) the information resources, educational materials and personal data will be saved in cloud with needed data management and the personal storage space could be greatly reduced and improved. In this direction, an enhancement process framework is proposed in (Khedr, 2017). This framework uses the cloud layers SaaS which permits to provide a single instance on the cloud for multiple users. According the article *"students can sign in these layers through the profile and can use the preferred style which is built in profile"*. The paper focuses in the enhancement of e-learning process through two points of views: (1) by offering different learning styles; (2) enhanced model of the e-course and e-learning process and better system performance. Finally, a proposal for implementation of cloud-based e-learning solutions in performance-centric architecture is made in (Joshi, 2014). The author marks that the basic problems of DLE are limited availability of infrastructural resources, increasing demands for resources, time, space and cost constraints and all these problems increase the degradation of the system performance.

Internet of Things (IoT) and Machin to Machin (M2M) communication are two new paradigms which propose new point of view about units' control and processes management. The key part of IoT is the cloud and this concept is generally used to describe the network of objects – objects with embedded small sensors are turn linked through wireless connection to the Internet. In the IoT, everyday objects share data over networks, with or without human intervention. What is the connection with the education and partially with e-learning systems? An answer of the question "How will the IoT impact education?" is given in (eLeaP, 2016): *"Today, more and more researchers are attempting to use wireless technologies to create smarter classrooms and more specifically, classrooms that can give real-time feedback to instructors on what is and is not working"*. The on-line material cites Nenad Gligorić (leader of researchers' team) who notes: *"Combining the IoT technology with social and behavioural analysis, an ordinary classroom can be transformed into a smart classroom that actively listens and analyses voices, conversations, movements, behaviour, etc., in order to reach a conclusion about the lecturers' presentation and listeners' satisfaction"*. The article concludes that *"theoretically, in the classroom of the future, every desk will be equipped with a sensor"*.

Every of the presented above technologies could cause different threats to information resources and personal profiles supported in DLE. Cloud technology and social computing, extending their activities in e-learning processes, must take into account user's privacy, keeping information availability, integrity and confidentiality. Viti et al. (Viti, 2014) specify that increasing cloud threats and vulnerabilities *"creates the need for monitoring tools and services, which provide a way for administrators to define and evaluate security metrics for their systems"*, and a monitoring tool for cloud computing security is proposed in this article.

At the same time, mobile communications and remote access to information resources by mobile units could cause other specific security embarrassments. Jung et al. (Jung, 2015) introduce the metric "security rating" that *"... denotes the trustworthiness of the context information..."* and define it as follows: *"The Security Rating is a global indicator expressing difficulty and challenge for an adversary to counterfeit a context information source"*. The authors determine 5 levels for this rating – from very low (1) to very high (5).

Information Security and User's Security in DLE

According to (Gabor, 2017) *"An e-learning platform is a web-based software application, depending on the utilized technology and Internet environment. Due to the close connection between e-learning platforms and the web, platforms are threatened and vulnerable to various cyber-attacks"* and the paper discusses security issues in e-learning platforms (DLE). The goal of information security in DLE is to protect information from all possible threats via the Internet communications. An overview made in (Alwi, 2010) which is cited in (Bandara, 2014) defines the main vulnerabilities as follows:

- Deliberate software attacks (viruses, worms, macros, denial of service);
- Technical software failures and errors (bugs, coding problems, unknown loopholes);
- Acts of human error or failure (accidents, employee mistakes);
- Deliberate acts of espionage or trespass (unauthorized access and/or data collection);
- Deliberate acts of sabotage or vandalism (destruction of information or system);
- Technical hardware failures or errors (equipment failure);
- Deliberate acts of theft (illegal confiscation of equipment or information);
- Compromises to intellectual property (piracy, copyright, infringement);
- Quality of Service deviations from service providers (power and WAN service issues);
- Technological obsolescence (antiquated or out-dated technologies);
- Deliberate acts of information extortion (blackmail for information disclosure).

An e-learning environment usually implements different procedures for control over users' activities, preventing unallowed access and data modification. (Gabor, 2017) determines the choose of a strong password as a first measure for blocking unauthorized access and proposes an algorithm *"that generates strong passwords to secure personal data, while offering the possibility to check the strength of the generated password"*.

In the frame of information and communication security reliable authentication schemes could be applied on the base of specialized hardware, software or biometric tools and cryptographic algorithms. They must be put at the root of a Digital Rights Management System (DRMS) which is able to guarantee successful data protection during input, processing, archiving and transfer via the Internet. In addition, each e-learning environment should enforce strong policy for personal data protection having in mind that data exchanged via the global network are frequently subject of non-authorised using, modification, corruption or loss. Information vulnerability in clouds and social networks is as high as in enterprise applications for computing systems communicated via the Internet. Frequently applied attempts in practice which could successfully overcome proposed security measures and violate privacy are summarized into the following four groups:

- Embarrassment with identification of data controller, data processor and data subject in the frame of data processing obligations;
- All rights of a user concerning data subject could not be guaranteed, bearing in mind that every user must know the goal of data collection and policy for their protection, he/she should be able to revise and block some data, require data deletion, etc.;
- Possibility for multiple data transfers between different locations including to the countries with low level of personal data protection policy;
- Low level of organizational and technical measures used for personal data protection, which is main obligation of data controllers.

An Information Security Management (ISM) system consists of tools and measures, applied to oppose all these threats. Main dimensions of this structure are: information security policy; organizational and technical components for data protection; rules for hardware, software and biometric identification; authorization by determining levels of digital rights for resources' using; rules for access restriction to information and systems' resources, rooms and servers for external (unauthorized) persons, etc. Most popular and efficient mechanisms for information security in e-learning recommended by different authors (Kim, 2013; Alwi, 2010; Bandara, 2014) are summarized here as follows:

- Development of ICT policy in accordance with security requirements and implementation of a relevant ISM system;
- Installing and periodical renewing software for information and system resources protection from the Internet threats (firewalls, antivirus programs, etc.);
- Improving applied authentication scheme by using suitable techniques for users' identification – passwords (standard means for user identification); biometric identification (based on one or more individual biological characteristics as fingerprints, flat of the hand, voice, face, retina, sign, etc.) and smart card (it usually uses cryptographic algorithms based on public key encryption and provides efficient identification and authentication;
- Authorization on the base of a relevant Digital Rights Management System (DRMS) which can to ensure access to learning and systems' resources from authorized users only. This mechanism could guarantee high level of information confidentiality including personal profiles. E-learning resources must be kept secret implementing strong schemes, able to revoke unallowed access by any unauthorized person. In order to control access and security in e-learning system different approaches are proposed, as single sign for authentication and authorization; protection of intellectual property by permanent control of copyright; implementation of devices for digital identity, etc.;
- Using cryptography in communications and data archiving;
- Managing security training programs for professionals and staff.
- In this context, the rules of ISM should be adapted to opportunity for using mobile communications and it should apply adequate security countermeasures to protect the resources in the information environment (Hasan, 2015). The author of article cited above discusses authentication and authorization as important measures for protection organised by different means to guarantee secure mobile physical security.

The main goal of information security in e-learning is to provide availability, integrity and accountability of information. Availability in e-learning could be defined as assurance that a DLE could be accessed by authorized users only and published information resources' relevance is kept successfully. Integrity in e-learning is the protection of information (including personal data) from unauthorized changes and it depends on access control. Integrity could be compromised by hacker attacks, unprotected downloaded files, viruses, and other threats. Accountability reveals the ability to clarify security events.

One side of the DLE is to ensure effective distribution, sharing and accessing information and teaching materials. A possible solution for this could be using cloud storage which leads to efficient scale mechanism (Lavanya, 2017). The paper determines that *"e-learning materials are critical in providing essential security measures to protect valuable data of users from vulnerable securities in materials"* and proposes a cloud based e-learning system which realizes two important aspects of information security – confidentiality and integrity. The goal of the proposed system is *"e-learning materials in the cloud to be kept and secret"* and the elliptic curve cryptography algorithm is used for this goal. The presented in (Lavanya, 2017) architecture of cloud based e-learning system consists of

… local server, centralized server and a web browser in which multiple client will access their local server to upload or receive their material through internet. The learning material repository will consist of all learning material for the E-learners. The client will send a request to the cloud storage for the materials.

The basic modules of the proposed system are "accessing the document", "identifying possibility of attacks", "preventing attack" and "false positive attack verification".

Data Protection and User's Privacy in DLE

The right of privacy is the ability of individuals to determine what part of their personal information has been collected (Maher, 2014). A user of DLE has no obligation to provide personal data, but in most cases, he/she will not be able to use some application without fulfilling name, address or other personal data. The required information collected during the registration could be determined as a *personal identifiable information* (first/last name, user name, password, e-mail address, geographic location, mobile phone number, birthday, birthplace, age, gender, race, health, social media account, community/forum discussions, chats, facial photo) or as a *sensitive information* that could be automatically collected by the system (learner preferences, grades, assignments, learning history, and learning outcomes IP address, user's URL, browser type, length and number of visited pages, credit/payment card number and expiration date). All sensitive data must be protected by using adequate measures – *"for effectively managing applications and resources, the use of models and tools is essential for the secure management of identities and to avoid compromising data privacy"* is written in (Werner, 2017). The authors present that *"there are models and tools that address federated identity management, and it is important that they use privacy mechanisms to assist in compliance with current legislation"* and make a survey of privacy in cloud identify management.

All participants who are intended to use services via the global network space, including online learning services, must be informed about the main privacy protection procedures. Every user must know what personal information is required for the creation of personal profile during registration and the purpose, i.e. the reason for personal data collection and processing. Policy and measures for personal data protection (PDP), if personal data will be transferred to third party (data controller or other country) should be clearly determined. Each participant in e-learning processes has rights to revise his/her own personal data and to require data actualization, correction, blocking or erasing when it is necessary. Data controller is obliged to erase personal data for every user who have already finished activities with e-learning system or archiving data if this is required by the national law. In this reason, each e-learning environment should enforce strong policy for personal data protection to oppose corruption, loss or illegal using.

Privacy protection in DLE must be clearly explained to users who should know the purposes of data collection through the web browser and other activities concerning personal data protection. Privacy policy and disclosure practices give additional possibility for public review of data security. All e-learning institutions should protect the information resources as educational, research data, personal information by measures that are compliant with the Data Protection Act and the last European regulation from 2014 when the European Commission has proposed the new paradigm "right to be forgotten / to be erased" about privacy regulation in the cyber space.

Many of the data controller's obligations could be realized by developing united system for information security and PDP. An organizational structure of System for Information Security & Privacy (SISP) is shown in Figure 2.

The problems of data protection and privacy are very important for personal information stored in the cloud. A study of privacy control with audit of e-learning processes based on cloud services is made in (Al-Khafaji, 2017). The goal of the authors is to present a concept *"of ensuring privacy to protect information shared between e-learning system and cloud platform by proposing a mechanism to preserve the privacy of quite distinctive that supports public scrutiny on the information shared between these important technologies"*. The uploaded by users own personal information could be protected by encryption mechanism based on AES encryption algorithm for protection of shared information.

The uniting e-learning processes and cloud services generates concept for DLE based on cloud. Many papers discuss this idea. For example, (Camillo, 2017) proposes *"an architecture that allows an individual to obtain services without the need of releasing all personal attributes. The architecture achieves that outcome evaluating the targeted policy in the domain of the identity provider, that is, policies are sent from service providers to identity providers to be evaluated, without the need of releasing some PIIs to the service provider side"*. The project is realized to oppose to the disclosure of personal data in e-learning system. Several papers discussed cloud based DLE have been presented in the beginning of this section (Khedr, 2017; Riahi, 2015; Yang, 2017).

Figure 2. Organizational scheme of SISP
Romansky, 2016a.

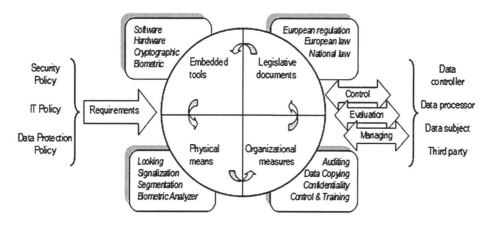

ORGANIZATION OF A COMBINED E-LEARNING ENVIRONMENT

The general organization of CeLE is shown in Figure 2. The main components are Front office, Back office, Space of information & education resources (public, internal, external).

- Front office is a sub-system for supporting user's access to e-learning services by input point (web portal). The functions of this system are the user's identification, checking the legitimate access, starting the procedure for registration (for a new user) and preliminary identification. The registration procedure creates a personal profile and every user must be informed for this and for his/her rights. Additional procedures of these systems are registration of each login (time, IP address and additional attributes), supporting audit journal (file) for the parameters of each access and collection of statistical information for accessed components.
- Back office performs basic administrative procedures and guidance of requests to a suitable component for processing. This system should analyse each access for defining type and rights for realization requested work with system, information and education resources. In this reason, the important part is SISP which collect system and personal profiles, administrative software, DRMS and technical measures for security and user's data protection. The main procedures are *authentication* (procedure able to guarantee secure and reliable access to environment for registered users); *request (access) analysis* (preliminary analyses of user's request based on checking user's profile with Personal Data – PD and level of rights for accessing internal or external learning resources based on Digital Right Management System – DRMS principles); *authorization* (determining user's status and defined rights to use requested information – learning resource, evaluation information, administrative information, personal data processing, etc.); *request processing* (realization of a permitted request after successful authorization).
- Space of distributed resources – it unites different educational and information resources used in e-learning process and supported administrative procedures. The space is constructed by three types of resources – public (without restricted access); internal (stored in the own memories and managed based on internal administrative software and operation systems); external (stored in cloud data centres and accessed via the Internet on the base of rent service or by providers). Each external system (cloud, social media, IoT system, etc.) must have its own personal security system and is obliged to support an adequate policy for PDP.

Discrete Formalization

The goal of the formalization is to determine a conceptual model of CeLE and to support next phases of architecture development and model investigation. Each process could be presented as a set of discrete states and transitions between which permits to describe this process by directed graph (Romansky, 2016b). In this reason, a preliminary graph formalization is shown in Figure 4. This formal description determines the basic sub-systems and formulates the main procedures for each of them.

The choice of the graph apparatus is made based on following conditions:

- Number of investigated events at the structure is finite and this permits defining a finite set of states presented by nodes in a directed graph.

Figure 3. Organizational scheme of CeLE

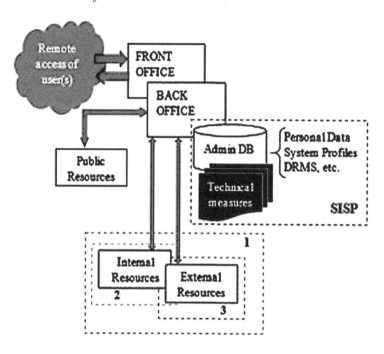

Figure 4. Preliminary graph formalization

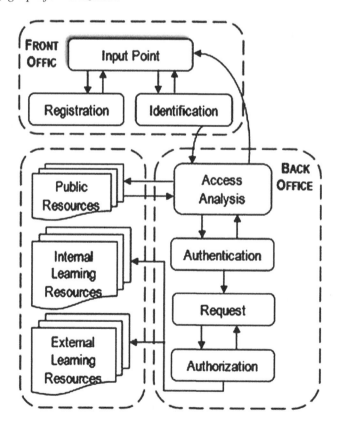

- Each observed event in the architecture has constant behaviour presented by fixed procedure (algorithm), but realization is made under a stochastic flow.
- Graph nodes present all observed events (sub-processes) and transitions between nodes describe possible realization of an e-learning process.

An extended formal description is proposed in Figure 5 (Romansky, 2016a). Following basic states determine the functionality of the basic procedures in CeLE: *input point* (access to official portal of e-learning environment); *registration* (every new user should make a registration before accessing and using different resources and services); *identification* (preliminary checking the user's identify); *access analysis* (procedure for determining if the requested resource is public or protected); *authentication* (realization of the second phase after preliminary identification to validate the user's request based on the stored user's profile; *request analysis* (determining the type of requested resource for selection suitable procedure for the next step); *authorization* (activation of mechanism for user's right checking based on the result from the previous procedure – for internal or for external resource); *request processing* (realization of a permitted request after successful authorization).

Different resources are included in the state "request processing" – administrative, personal data, educational materials, learning resources. Some of these resources could be stored or implemented in external environments associated to CeLE. The collaborated external resources unite spaces in the field of cloud computing (services IaaS, SaaS, PaaS, data centres), social computing (social media, social networks, social aggregators, blog/microblogs, forums, etc.), personal specialized web sites, and elements

Figure 5. Graph formalization of the access to the system resources

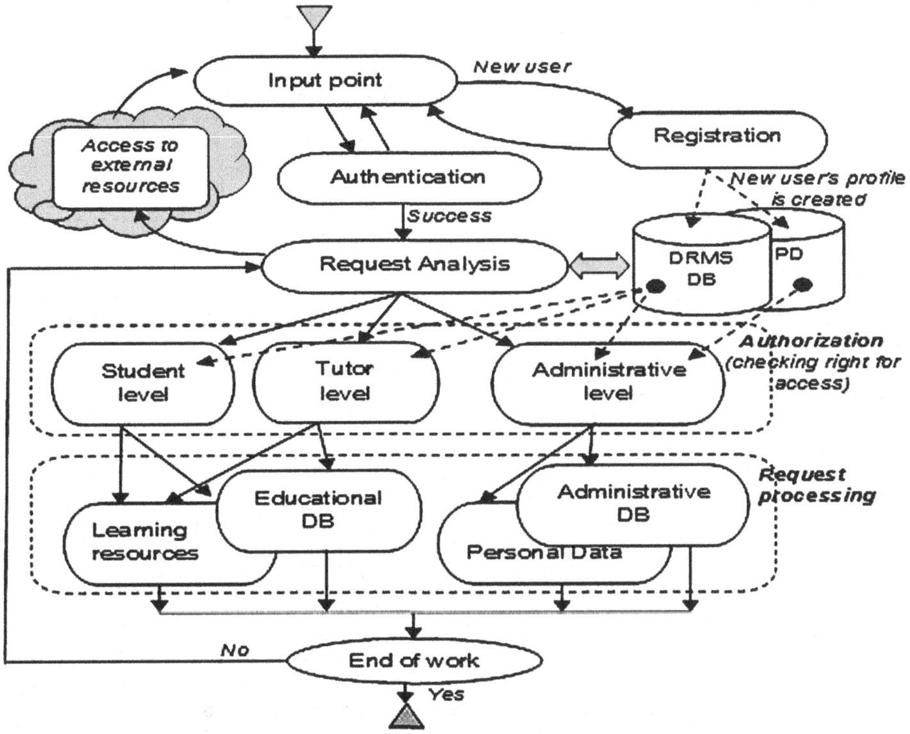

of IoT and M2M communications (units, sensors, applications, etc.). All these spaces and technological opportunities could be used by rent, so it is accepted that they are reliable protected, applying recommendable information security and privacy protection standards as an obligation of service owner and/ or service provider.

Architecture Development

Functional architecture of CeLE is presented in figure 6. Practically the users could be two types – internal and external. Internal users are these which work directly with the CeLE hardware and software infrastructure (administrators, teachers, trainers, tutors). The external users could use the system's functionality by accessing the input point of the CeLE web portal and after identification and registration (for new users). The procedure "authentication" could be realized in two steps. The first step is "identification" and could be realized in the Front Office. The second step is "verification" and must be realized in the Back Office.

The gate of the Back Office is the module "Request Analysis" which has very important role as a main requests' analyser and distributor. If a current request is intended to access any collaborated external resource (cloud services, data centres, social media networks, specialized web sites, etc.) it is directed to the security shell of these resources (it is assumed that each attached external environment

Figure 6. Functional architecture of CeLE

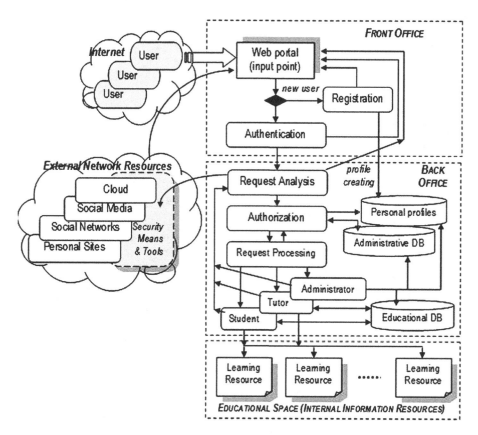

accessed via the Internet has individual system for security and data protection – in reason of the rules of the EU legislation). If a request needs any internal resource, then the internal security sub-system will start with preliminary authorization on the rules of the realized internal DRMS. An authorization procedure ensures access to two databases – with personal profiles and with administrative information to determine access rights for concrete resources by user's profile (student, tutor or administrator). The first database should be reliable protected by organizational and technical measures according to the rules of the data protection law. The next steps are processing of valid and authorized requests by access and using resources in the educational space.

The "obligations" of this architecture could be extended with procedures for managing secure access to the external resources as a first phase before activation of "Security Means & Tools" system of the external network resource. In this reason the procedure "Authorization" will be activated after preliminary "Request Analysis" and will be realized based on the accessed resource (internal or external).

An algorithm that describes this extended version of CeLE's functionality is shown in Figure 7. The authentication procedure is divided into to two phases and the first one "Identification" is included as a procedure in the Front Office sub-system. Another characteristics is that this architecture allows an additional type resources" Public resources" with free access. The access to the other two types of resources (internal and external) should be regulated. The rights for concrete access to these resources are determined by authorization procedure which must be realized in two versions too.

MODELLING AND INVESTIGATION OF THE PROCESSES

The modelling is very useful approach for systems' investigation and determination of structural discrepancy revealing special features of processes realization. The model investigation could be realized by using discrete or stochastic means. Petri Net (PN) is an asynchronous apparatus for discrete analytical modelling and investigation which permits to determine the sequence of possible states by activation several transactions t_j between places p_i. The execution of PN-model is based on an evaluation tree constructed by activation all permitted transactions starting from an initial state.

Another approach for model investigation of the proposed architecture is stochastic modelling. The functionality of CeLE can be generalized as a family of discrete-time stochastic processes each of them described by a random process $X(t, \Phi, \Theta)$, were t is an ordered increased set of discrete time points $t_0 < t_1 < \ldots < t_n \in T$ (T is a parametric space), Φ represents all random factors of the system and Θ is a set with all possible design parameters. The realization of discrete-time stochastic process is a sequence of states $X(t_i)$ for discrete moments $t_i \in T$, for $i=0,1,2,\ldots,n$. In this reason, an apparatus of Markov chain (MC) is used for a model definition and investigation of processes in CeLE by analytical solution. This approach is used in other research works for modelling of e-learning processes, especially those, oriented to investigation of different approaches for security and privacy protection and their efficiency. For example, articles (Taraghi, 2014a; Taraghi, 2014b) present Markov chain and classification algorithms as a tool, applied to investigate database collecting learner's answers to asked questions. Another research based on MC modelling of distributed e-learning resources is presented in (Malini, 2016). This article proposes new Markov model to know the learner's requirements in advance and the research is carried out in the cloud platform and the overall architecture of e-learning system on cloud is presented.

Figure 7. Algorithmic scheme of processes in CeLE with separated function for secure access to different resources
Romansky, 2017b.

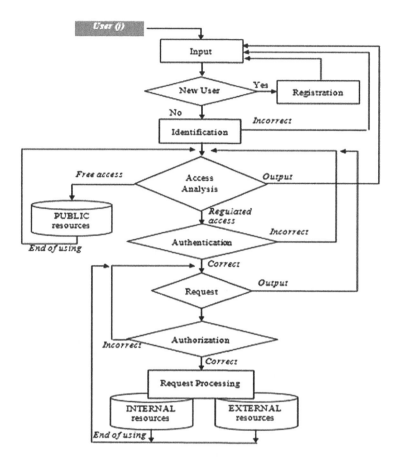

Deterministic Modelling by Using Petri Net

The proposed description is based on the classic Petri Net (PN) apparatus where the main procedures are presented as transitions, and the condition are presented as positions. The theoretical-set definition is presented below (Romansky, 2016b).

Formal definition of Petri Net: $PN = \{T, P, I, O\}$, $T \cap P = \varnothing$

Set of transactions $T = \{t_i \mid i=1 \div 9\}$:

t_1 – remote user's access to the input point;
t_2 – registration of a new user;
t_3 – activate the identification procedure;
t_4 – access to public resources;
•

t_5 – authentication procedure for access to corporative (private) resources (T - correct; F – incorrect);

t_6 – finishing the work;

t_7 – authorization procedure (rights checking) by using DRMS tools (T – correct; F – incorrect);

t_8 – access to external corporative resources;

t_9 – access to internal corporative resources.

Set of positions $P = \{p_j / j=1\div5\}$:

p_1 – user's access is activated;

p_2 – access of a registered user;

p_3 – legitimated user's access;

p_4 – successful authentication;

p_5 – successful authorization.

Input Functions

$$I(t_1) = \varnothing$$

$$I(t_2) = \{p_1, p_1\}$$

$$I(t_3) = \{p_1, p_2\}$$

$$I(t_4) = I(t_5) = I(t_6) = \{p_3\}$$

$$I(t_7) = \{p_4\}$$

$$I(t_8) = I(t_9) = \{p_5\}$$

Output Functions

$$O(t_1) = \{p_1, p_1\}$$

$$O(t_2) = \{p_1, p_2\}$$

$$O(t_3) = O(t_4) = O(F.t_5) = O(F.t_7) = \{p_3\}$$

$$O(T.t_5) = \{p_4\}$$

$$O(t_6) = O(t_8) = \varnothing$$

$$O(T.t_7) = \{p_5\}$$

$$O(t_9) = \{p_4\}$$

The graph scheme of the model based on the presented theoretical-set definition is shown in the Figure 8.

The evolution of the defined PN-model of CeLE is presented by the tree of possible transactions given in the Figure 9. Marking μ_j (j=0, 1, 2, 3, 4, 5) for each new state is presented in the figure. The investigation of the PN-model could be made based on the analysis of the evolution tree and the characteristics are determined below.

- **Reachability:** The model permits cyclic recurrence with reiteration of some phases based on activation of the selected transition.
- **Liveness:** This characteristic deals with initial marking μ_0, bearing in mind that minimum one permitted transaction for each step of the evolution exists.
- **Blocking:** The PN-model has not any blocked marking and the model is active, so there are not conflict situations.
- **Boundless:** The model is 2-limited because the number of marks at each position during the evaluation $<\mu_0 \rightarrow \mu_1 \rightarrow \mu_2 \rightarrow \ldots \rightarrow \mu_0>$ is no more than 2, i.e. $\Sigma\mu(p_i) \leq 2$.

Proposed discrete modelling could be extended based on stochastic approach by using Stochastic Petri Net (SPN) and an example is presented in (Romansky, 2016c).

Figure 8. Graph presentation of the defined PN-model of CeLE

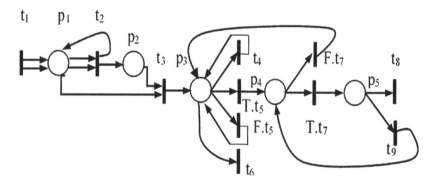

Figure 9. Evaluation tree construction of the defined PN-model

$\mu_0 = (0,0,0,0,0) \xrightarrow{t1} \mu_1 = (2,0,0,0,0)$

$\mu_1 \xrightarrow{t2} \mu_2 = (1,1,0,0,0) \xrightarrow{t3} \mu_3 = (0,0,1,0,0)$

$\mu_3 \xrightarrow{t4} \mu_3$

$\mu_3 \xrightarrow{t5F} \mu_3$

$\mu_3 \xrightarrow{t6} \mu_0$

$\mu_3 \xrightarrow{t5T} \mu_4 = (0,0,0,1,0) \xrightarrow{t7F} \mu_3$

$\mu_4 \xrightarrow{t7T} \mu_5 = (0,0,0,0,1) \xrightarrow{t9} \mu_4$

$\mu_5 \xrightarrow{t8} \mu_0$

$$\mu_0 \rightarrow \mu_1 \rightarrow \mu_2 \rightarrow \mu_3 \begin{cases} \rightarrow \mu_3 \\ \rightarrow \mu_3 \\ \rightarrow \mu_4 \begin{cases} \rightarrow \mu_5 \begin{cases} \rightarrow \mu_0 \\ \rightarrow \mu_4 \end{cases} \\ \rightarrow \mu_3 \end{cases} \\ \rightarrow \mu_0 \end{cases}$$

Stochastic Modelling by Using Markov Chain

This section presents an approach for investigation of the proposed architecture using Markov chain (MC) model. Some parts of the investigation are discussed in (Romansky, 2016a; Romansky, 2017b). The analytical model definition (Figure 10) is based on determined discrete set of states S with power 8 and interaction between main four components (transactions between states) presented by defined matrix of transitive probabilities P. Determined transactions are: a – probability for unregistered (new) user; b – probability for correct authorization of registered user; c – probability for a request to access and using external educational resources; d – probability for an input in the back office and authorization (determining the right) for using an internal resource; e – probability for an internal educational resource using (after correct authorization); f – probability for using system resources and personal data processing. It is assumed that all e-learning processes start with activation of state s_1 – vector of initial probabilities is $\mathbf{P}_0 = \{1, 0, 0, 0, 0, 0, 0\}$.

A preliminary analysis of procedures is made and some assumptions are accepted to simplify the analytical investigation. For example, it is assumed that the probability of access to the system by new unregistered user is no more than 0,3 ($a \leq 0,3$) and the unauthorized access to the resources (including attacks from external nodes) is in the frame [10%, 30%], i.e. $0,1 \leq b \leq 0,3$. The next assumption is that

Figure 10. Definition of analytical MC-model

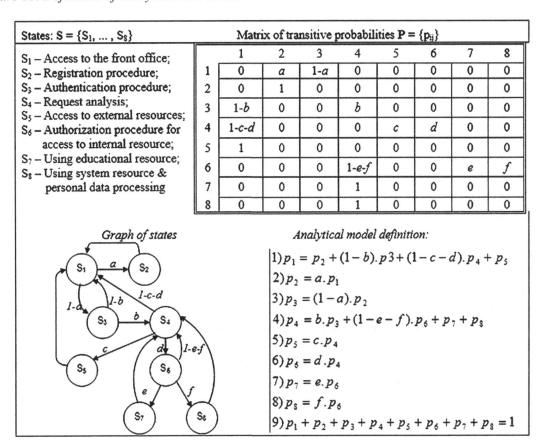

States: S = {S₁, ... , S₈}									

States:
- S₁ – Access to the front office;
- S₂ – Registration procedure;
- S₃ – Authentication procedure;
- S₄ – Request analysis;
- S₅ – Access to external resources;
- S₆ – Authorization procedure for access to internal resource;
- S₇ – Using educational resource;
- S₈ – Using system resource & personal data processing

Matrix of transitive probabilities P = {pᵢⱼ}

	1	2	3	4	5	6	7	8
1	0	a	$1-a$	0	0	0	0	0
2	0	1	0	0	0	0	0	0
3	$1-b$	0	0	b	0	0	0	0
4	$1-c-d$	0	0	0	c	d	0	0
5	1	0	0	0	0	0	0	0
6	0	0	0	$1-e-f$	0	0	e	f
7	0	0	0	1	0	0	0	0
8	0	0	0	1	0	0	0	0

Graph of states

Analytical model definition:

$$1) \, p_1 = p_2 + (1-b).p3 + (1-c-d).p_4 + p_5$$
$$2) \, p_2 = a.p_1$$
$$3) \, p_3 = (1-a).p_2$$
$$4) \, p_4 = b.p_3 + (1-e-f).p_6 + p_7 + p_8$$
$$5) \, p_5 = c.p_4$$
$$6) \, p_6 = d.p_4$$
$$7) \, p_7 = e.p_6$$
$$8) \, p_8 = f.p_6$$
$$9) \, p_1 + p_2 + p_3 + p_4 + p_5 + p_6 + p_7 + p_8 = 1$$

the refusal of service (in the states "Request Analysis" and "Authorization") is no more than 10% of all cases and this permits to determine the values: $(1-c-d) \leq 0,1 \Rightarrow (c+d) \leq 0,9$ and $(1-e-f) \leq 0,1 \Rightarrow (e+f) \leq 0,9$.

Analytical Solution of the MC-Model

The analytical solution of the system of equations is made by presentation the probabilities by using only the probability p_1 and replacement in the last equation (9) of the MC-model (Romansky, 2016a):

$$p_2 = ap_1 ; \; p_3 = (1-a)p_1 ; \; p_4 = \frac{b(1-a)}{1-d} p_1 ; \; p_5 = cp_4 = c\frac{b(1-a)}{1-d} p_1 ;$$

$$p_6 = dp_4 = d\frac{b(1-a)}{1-d} p_1 ; \; p_7 = ep_6 = ed\frac{b(1-a)}{1-d} p_1 ; \; p_8 = fp_6 = fd\frac{b(1-a)}{1-d} p_1 .$$

$$p_1 + ap_1 + (1-a)p_1 + \frac{b(1-a)}{(1-d)} p_1 + \frac{bc(1-c)}{(1-d)} p_1$$
$$+ \frac{bd(1-a)}{(1-d)} p_1 + \frac{bde(1-a)}{(1-d)} p_1 + \frac{bdf(1-a)}{(1-d)} p_1 = 1$$

After solution of this equation and replacing $\pi = [2-2d+b(1-a)(1+c+d+de+df)]$ the results for the probabilities are determined as follows:

$$p_1 = \frac{(1-d)}{\pi} ; p_2 = \frac{a(1-d)}{\pi} ; p_3 = \frac{(1-a)(1-d)}{\pi} ; p_4 = \frac{b(1-a)}{\pi} ;$$
$$p_5 = \frac{bc(1-a)}{\pi} ; p_6 = \frac{bd(1-a)}{\pi} ; p_7 = \frac{bde(1-a)}{\pi} ; p_8 = \frac{bdf(1-a)}{\pi}$$

Experiments and Assessments

The assumptions made in the previous section permit to define the working frame for analytical investigation of the proposed Markov model by determining concrete values for the probabilities: $a \in \{0,2; 0,25; 0,3\}$; $b \in \{0,7; 0,75; 0,8; 0,85; 0,9\}$; $c \in \{0,35; 0,4; 0,45\}$; $d \in \{0,45; 0,5; 0,55; 0,6\}$ and $(1-e-f)=0,1 \Rightarrow e = f = 0,45$ (equal access probabilities to educational or system resource after authorization). This factor environment permits to construct partial *multi-factor experimental plan* based on all combinations of accepted values for the probabilities. Statistical processing of this plan is made over Develve software and several experimental results are presented in Figure 11 and Table 1.

The experimental results show that the probabilities have very small assessments for the characteristics variance, standard deviation (St.Dev.) and confidence interval (Conf.Int.). Equal values for Student's T-distribution and normal distribution are obtained. The difference Δ=MAX-MIN is the largest one for the probability p_1 which presents the loading front office portal by access of different remote users.

Figure 11. Histograms and time series for the probabilities based on the obtained data sets

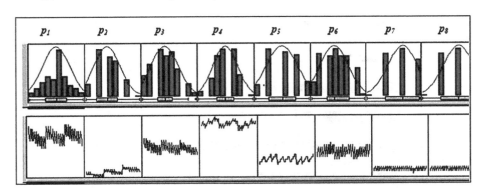

Table 1. Generalization of the statistical assessments for the probabilities

	p1	p2	p3	p4	p5	p6	p7	p8
n	108	108	108	108	108	108	108	108
Mean	0,1995	0,0501	0,1493	0,2505	0,1001	0,1318	0,0593	0,0593
Median	0,1992	0,0492	0,1490	0,2512	0,1003	0,1313	0,0591	0,0591
MIN	0,1501	0,0300	0,1151	0,2198	0,0787	0,0989	0,0445	0,0445
MAX	0,2522	0,0757	0,1885	0,2777	0,1216	0,1666	0,0750	0,0750
Δ=[max-min]	0,1021	0,0457	0,0733	0,0579	0,0429	0,0677	0,0305	0,0305
Variance	0,0006	0,0001	0,0003	0,0002	0,0001	0,0003	0,0001	0,0001
St.Dev.	0,02391	0,01139	0,01757	0,01293	0,01051	0,01778	0,008	0,008
Conf.Int.	0,005	0,002	0,003	0,002	0,002	0,003	0,002	0,002

The average values obtained for the final probabilities (Figure 11) show that the highest value has implementation of the state "Request analysis". On the other hand, the assessments for security procedures, defined in the model – authentication (p_3) and authorization (p_6) have a quite small difference (about 0,017) which is due to external resources' access. The difference between cases of process initialization by access to the Front Office (input point – p_1) and using of the Back-Office procedure "Request Analysis" (p_4) could be explained with the possibility to process many internal requests by other states as authorization, educational resources, system resources or personal data processing. Correlation between some processes presented by probabilities is shown in figure 13. The main states that correspond to the secure procedures are S_3 (authentication), S_5 (access to any external resource) and S_6 (procedure for authorization before access and using internal information and/or educational resource). The boxplots and some statistical assessments for probabilities presenting using of these states are summarized in Table 2.

One factor experimental plan has been made to evaluate dependencies between activities of procedures. The functional dependency of the final probabilities from the level of new unregistered users accessing the input point of front office is investigated by consecutively increasing factor "*a*" from 0,02 to 0,70 by step 0,02 (number of registrations n=36). For each other factor (*b, c, d, e, f*) its average value calculated during the multi-factor experiments is fixed. Figure 14 shows implementation level of

Figure 12. Average values for the final probabilities

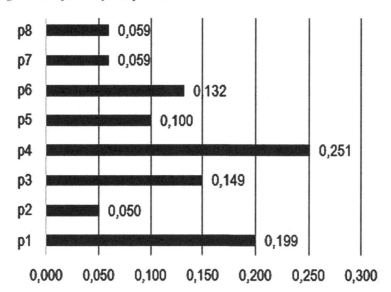

Figure 13. Correlation between selected pairs of probabilities

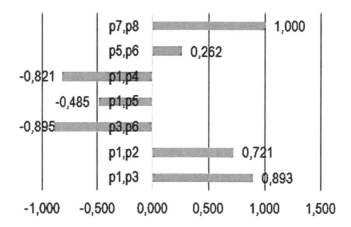

procedures "authentication" and "authorization" and their relation with all access attempts to e-learning environment (input point of the front office).

Diagram in Figure 15 presents a comparison between utilization of "registration" procedure and requesting any external or internal resource. Factor "*a*" accepts the same values and as it is expected registration utilization increases in the large range of the set, but the maximal level is no more than 0,22.

CONCLUSION

Nowadays educational technologies are used by constantly increasing number of learners which is due to easy access to information resources, variety of virtual educational environments, collaboration and

Table 2. Boxplots of secure access probabilities

Authentication Procedure	Access to External Resources	Authorization Procedure
95% Confidence interval mean: 0.146 / 0.153 95% Confidence interval STDEV: 0.015 / 0.020 Right extreme: 0.220 Right tail: 0.180 Q3: 0.140 Median Q2: 0.150 Q1: 0.160 Left tail: 0.120 Left extreme: 0.080	95% Confidence interval mean: 0.098 / 0.102 95% Confidence interval STDEV: 0.010 / 0.013 Right extreme: 0.170 Right tail: 0.120 Q3: 0.090 Median Q2: 0.100 Q1: 0.110 Left tail: 0.080 Left extreme: 0.030	95% Confidence interval mean: 0.128 / 0.135 95% Confidence interval STDEV: 0.016 / 0.021 Right extreme: 0.240 Right tail: 0.170 Q3: 0.120 Median Q2: 0.130 Q1: 0.150 Left tail: 0.100 Left extreme: 0.030

Figure 14. Changing of the security procedures utilization with increasing the new user access

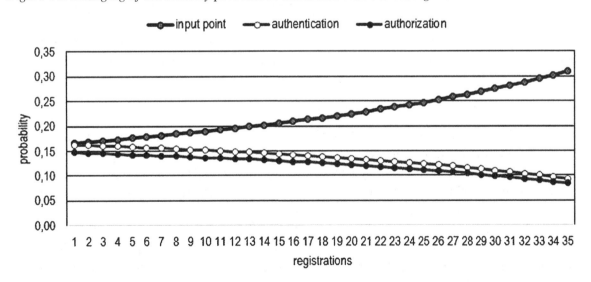

173

Figure 15. Relation between registration and access to the resources

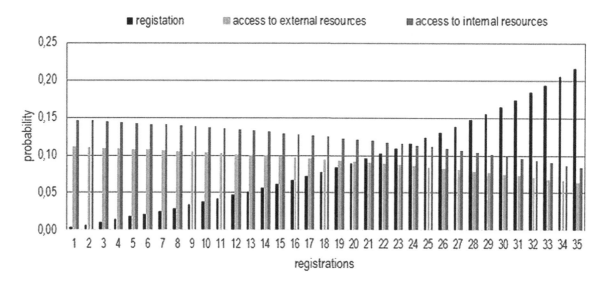

forums, etc. Different forms as e-learning, d-learning, m-learning have been created to help learners and teachers in their educational activities. In addition, development of cloud computing and mobile cloud computing extends concept of Internet importance for e-learning. These cloud technologies with the opportunities of social computing create new functionalities of contemporary e-learning environments. According to published trends cloud computing will be rapidly developed in the future. Many publications emphasis this obstacle and different authors suggest elements of cloud and social computing to be included in all e-learning environments. Since network communication and remote access to different resources will continue to threaten data integrity, strong measures for information security and personal data protection must be implemented. It should be considered that all Internet means and tools ensure easy and convenient access to learning resources but at the same time cyber-attacks and unallowed access to personal data of users quite often succeed in attempts to destroy privacy. Vulnerabilities are more complicated when cloud and social computing are applied, hence before using these technologies specific threats and risks must be analysed.

Authors' point of view for organization of e-learning environment with secure access to all resources (informational, educational and personal data) is presented in this article. The proposal has been made after discussion of main information security management principles and privacy protection requirements, rules for their implementation by authentication and authorization procedures checking user's access rights. A preliminary formalization of processes by using ordered graph structure to determine procedures activity is made and generalized architecture of combined heterogenic e-learning environment is proposed. An approach for investigation of this architecture based on apparatus of Petri Net (PN) and of Markov Chain (MC) is proposed, where a MC-model has been designed and applied for realization of partial multi-factor plan and one-factor plan. The calculated assessments for the final probabilities permit to analyse the frame of components' implementation for security and privacy protection. Relatively high values obtained after analysis outline their importance in this environment. Additional calculation and interpretation using software product "Develve" accomplished investigation and as a result statistical assessments for the processes of secure access and personal data protection were obtained.

The analytical investigation could be extended by realization of a full multi-factor experimental plan which is the goal of a future work in order to make a comparison of probabilities in more large borders. For this purpose, authors are intending to accomplish investigation applying additional apparatus for modelling and simulation.

REFERENCES

Al-Khafaji, K. M. K., & Eryilmaz, M. (2017). Auditor technology and privacy control to secure e-learning information on cloud. *Proceedings of International Conference on Progress in Applied Science.*

Allen, B., Ananthakrishnan, R., Chard, K., Foster, I., Madduri, R., Pruyne, J., . . . Tuecke, S. (2017). Globus: a case study in software as a service for scientists. In *Proceedings of the 8th Workshop Science-Cloud'17* (pp. 26-32). Academic Press. doi:10.1145/3086567.3086570

Alwi, N. H. M., & Fan, I. (2010). E-Learning and Information Security Management. *International Journal of Digital Society*, *1*(2), 148–156. doi:10.20533/ijds.2040.2570.2010.0019

Ashok, A., Hahn, A., & Govindarasu, M. (2014). Cyber-physical security of wide-area monitoring, protection and control in a smart grid environment. *Journal of Advanced Research*, *5*(4), 481–489. doi:10.1016/j.jare.2013.12.005 PMID:25685516

Bandara, I., Ioras, F., & Maher, K. (2014). Cyber security concerns in e-learning education. In *Proceedings of ICERI-2014 Conference* (pp.728-734). Seville, Spain: Academic Press.

Burd, B., Elahi, A., Russell, I., Barker, L., Pérez, A. F., Siever, B., & Guerra, J. G. et al. (2017). The Internet of Things in CS education: current challenges and future potential. *Proceedings of the 22nd ACM Conference on Innovation and Technology in Computer Science Education.* doi:10.1145/3059009.3081331

Camillo, G. L., Westphall, C. M., Werner, J., & Westphall, C. B. (2017). Preserving privacy with fine-grained authorization in an identity management system. In *Proceedings of the 16th International Conference on Networks* (pp. 75-80), Venice, Italy: Academic Press.

Chen, Y., & He, W. (2013). Security risks and protection in online learning: A survey. *International Review of Research in Open and Distance Learning*, *14*(5), 108–127. doi:10.19173/irrodl.v14i5.1632

eLeaP. (2016). *The Internet of Things' impact on elearning.* Available at: https://www.eleapsoftware.com/the-internet-of-things-impact-on-elearning/

Fischer, A. E. (2014). *Improving user protection and security in cyberspace.* Report of Committee on Culture, Science, Education and Media, Council of Europe. Retrieved March 12, 2014, from www.statewatch.org/news/2014/mar/coe-parl-ass-cyberspace-security.pdf

Gabor, A. M., Popescu, M. C., & Naaji, A. (2017). Security issues related to e-learning education. *International Journal of Computer Science and Network Security*, *17*(1), 60–66.

Greenhow, C., & Lewin, C. (2016). Social media and education: Reconceptualizing the boundaries of formal and informal learning. *Learning, Media and Technology*, *41*(1), 6–30. doi:10.1080/17439884.2015.1064954

Guazzini, A., Sarac, A., Donati, C., Nardi, A., Vilone, D., & Meringolo, P. (2017). Participation and privacy perception in virtual environments: The role of sense of community, culture and gender between Italian and Turkish. Future Internet, 9(11).

Hasan, B., Mahmoud, T., Gomez, J. M., Pramode, R., & Kurzhofer, J. (2015). User acceptance identification of restrictions caused by mobile security countermeasures. In *Proceedings of 5th International Conference on Mobile Services, Resources, and Users* (pp.31-37). Brussel, Belgium: Academic Press.

Joshi, N. A. (2014). Performance-centric cloud-based e-learning. *The IUP Journal of Information Technology*, X(2), 7–16.

Jung, C., Eitel, A., Feth, D., & Rudolph, M. (2015). Dealing with uncertainty in context-aware mobile applications. In *Proceedings of 5th International Conference on Mobile Services, Resources, and Users* (pp. 1-7). Brussel, Belgium: Academic Press.

Khedr, A. E., & Indrees, A. M. (2017). Enhanced e-learning system for e-courses base on cloud computing. *Journal of Computers*, 12(1), 10–19.

Kim, H. (2013). E-learning privacy and security requirements [review]. *Journal of Security Engineering*, 10(5), 591–600. doi:10.14257/jse.2013.10.5.07

Kinast & Partner. (2014). *Social media and data protection*. Retrieved from www.kinast-partner.com/data-protection-law/social-media-and-data-protection/

Lavanya, N. A., Buvana, M., & Shanthi, D. (2017). Detection of security threats and vulnerabilities of e-learning systems in cloud computing. *Advances in Natural and Applied Sciences*, 11(7), 550–559.

Maher, A. A., Najwa, H. M. A., & Roesnita, I. (2014). Towards an efficient privacy in cloud based e-learning. In *Proceedings of International Conference on Intelligent Systems, Data Mining and Information Technology* (pp.40-45). Bangkok, Thailand: Academic Press.

Malini, G., Mala, T., & Kannan, A. (2016). Markov model based prediction for effective e-content delivery in the cloud. *Asian Journal of Information Technology*, 15(17), 3280–3286. Available at http://docsdrive.com/pdfs/medwelljournals/ajit/2016/3280-3286.pdf

Manca, S., & Ranieri, M. (2016). Facebook and the other. Potentials and obstacles of Social Media for teaching in higher education. *Computers & Education*, 95(April), 216–230. doi:10.1016/j.compedu.2016.01.012

Misra, G., & Such, J. M. (2015). Social computing privacy and online relationships. In *AISB Social Aspects of Cognition and Computing Symposium* (pp. 1-6). Academic Press. Available at: http://eprints.lancs.ac.uk/74190/1/SACCS_AISB2015_submission_11.pdf

Neville, K., & Heavin, C. (2013). Using social media to support the learning needs of future IS security professionals. *Electronic Journal of e-Learning*, 11(1), 29-38.

Olawumi, O., Väänänen, A., Haataja, U., & Toivanen, P. (2017). Security issues in smart homes and mobile health system: Threat analysis, possible countermeasures and lessons learned. *International Journal on Information Technologies and Security*, 9(1), 31–52.

Peytcheva-Forsyth, R., & Yovkova, B. (2015). How students' experience in e-learning affects their judgements about the quality of an online course. *International Journal of Human Capital and Information Technology Professionals*, *6*(1), 14–25. doi:10.4018/ijhcitp.2015010102

Riahi, G. (2015). E-learning systems based on cloud computing: A review. *Procedia Computer Science*, *62*, 352–359. doi:10.1016/j.procs.2015.08.415

Romansky, R. (2015b). Social computing and digital privacy. *Communication & Cognition*, *48*(3-4), 65–82.

Romansky, R. (2017a). *Information servicing in distributed learning environments*. Saarbrüken, Germany: LAP LAMBERT Academic Publishing.

Romansky, R., & Noninska, I. (2015a). Globalization and digital privacy. *Electrotechnika & Electronica*, *50*(11/12), 36-41. Retrieved from http://ceec.fnts.bg/journal.html

Romansky, R., & Noninska, I. (2016a). Architecture of Combined e-Learning Environment and Investigation of Secure Access and Privacy Protection. *International Journal of Human Capital and Information Technology Professionals*, *9*(3), 89–106. doi:10.4018/IJHCITP.2016070107

Romansky, R., & Noninska, I. (2016b). Discrete Formalization and Investigation of Secure Access to Corporative Resources. *International Journal of Engineering Research and Management*, *3*(5), 97–101.

Romansky, R., & Noninska, I. (2016c). An Approach for Modelling of Security Procedures for Information Resources Protection. *International Advanced Research Journal in Science. Engineering and Technology*, *3*(6), 1–6.

Romansky, R., & Noninska, I. (2017b). Stochastic Investigation of Secure Access to the Resources of a Corporative System. *International Journal of Scientific & Engineering Research*, *8*(1), 578–584.

Rothkrantz, L. (2015). How social media facilitate learning communities and peer groups around MOOCS. *International Journal of Human Capital and Information Technology Professionals*, *6*(1), 1–13. doi:10.4018/ijhcitp.2015010101

Selwyn, N., & Stirling, E. (2016). Social media and education…now the dust has settled. *Learning, Media and Technology*, *41*(1), 1–5. doi:10.1080/17439884.2015.1115769

Shivshankar, S., & Paul, S. (2015). E-Learning Environment – The Security and Privacy Challenges Focusing on the Counter Measures. *Proceedings of the International Conference on Developments of E-Systems Engineering*. doi:10.1109/DeSE.2015.31

Taraghi, B., Ebner, M., Saranti, A., & Schön, M. (2014a). On using Markov chain to evidence the learning structures and difficulty levels of one digit multiplication. In *Proceedings of the 4th International Conference on Learning Analytics and Knowledge* (pp. 68-72). Indianapolis, IN: Academic Press. doi:10.1145/2567574.2567614

Taraghi, B., Saranti, A., Ebner, M., & Schön, M. (2014b). *Markov chain and classification of difficulty levels enhances the learning path in one digit multiplication*. In Lecture Notes in Computer Science: Vol. 8523 (pp. 322–333). Springer. doi:10.1007/978-3-319-07482-5_31

Viti, P. A. F., dos Santos, D. R., Westphall, C. B., Westphall, C. M., & Vieira, K. M. M. (2014). Current issues in cloud computing security and management. In *Proceedings of the 8th International Conference on Emerging Security Information, Systems and Technologies* (pp.36-42). Lisbon, Portugal: Academic Press.

Werner, J., Westphal, C. M., & Westphal, C. B. (2017). Cloud identity management: A survey on privacy strategies. *Computer Networks, 122*, 29–42. doi:10.1016/j.comnet.2017.04.030

Yang, C.-T., Yeh, W.-T., & Shih, W.-C. (2017). Implementation and evaluation of an e-learning architecture on cloud environments. *International Journal of Information and Education Technology (IJIET), 7*(8), 623–630. doi:10.18178/ijiet.2017.7.8.943

Yu, X., & Xue, Y. (2016). Smart grids: A cyber-physical systems perspective. *Proceedings of the IEEE, 104*(5), 1058–1070. doi:10.1109/JPROC.2015.2503119

KEY TERMS AND DEFINITIONS

CeLE: Combined e-learning environment.
DL: Distributed learning.
DLE: Distributed learning environment.
DRMS: Digital rights management system.
EU: European Union.
ICT: Information and communication technologies.
IoT: Internet of things.
ISM: Information security management.
M2M: Machin-to-machine; Markov chain.
PD: Personal data.
PDP: Personal data protection.
PN: Petri net.
SISP: System for information security and privacy.

Chapter 10
A Research on Students' Perceptions on a B-Learning English Environment to Improve Written Skills

Ana María Pinto-Llorente
University of Salamanca, Spain

Mª Cruz Sánchez-Gómez
University of Salamanca, Spain

Francisco José García-Peñalvo
University of Salamanca, Spain

ABSTRACT

The aim of the chapter is to explore university students' perceptions about the effectiveness of interactive and collaborative tools to improve written skills in a blended-learning environment. Based on this goal, a mixed methods research approach was adopted to enhance the mutual invigoration of the two types of methods, and the validity and reliability of data. Three-hundred-fifty-eight learners participated in the quantitative study and 91 in the qualitative one. All of them were enrolled in the subject English I. The instruments used to collect data were two tests and semi-structured interviews. The findings suggested students' positive perspective towards the possibilities offered by online glossaries, online quizzes, wikis, and forums to improve written skills and foster effective written communication in different contexts. It highlights their potentiality to create a learning community in which students could participate actively in the construction of knowledge, abandoning their passive role as simple observers.

INTRODUCTION

The aim of this study is to explore university students' perceptions about the effectiveness of interactive (online glossaries and online questionnaire) and collaborative (forums and wikis) tools to improve English written skills in a blended learning environment. As García-Peñalvo, Colomo-Palacios & Lytras

DOI: 10.4018/978-1-5225-5297-0.ch010

(2012), and García-Peñalvo & Colomo-Palacios (2015) point out all these Social Web tools have changed the way in which users take part in the communicative and learning process. They state that Web 2.0 philosophy facilitates the access to knowledge, the communication between individuals and the possibility of being a content author. Students learn, practice, and communicate with all the protagonists of the teaching-learning process (Pinto-Llorente et al, 2015a). This enhances a collective construction of knowledge in which students have an active role, against individualism of traditional methods (Pinto-Llorente et al, 2014a).

In this study researchers analysed a technological model implemented via the platform Moodle at the Pontifical University of Salamanca to know if its technological tools facilitated the learning experiences and written interactions in English between the participants of the teaching-learning process (Blake, 2000). They focused on the analysis of some of the interactive and collaborative resources provided by Moodle to improve students' written skills in English.

Regarding the interactive resources, they analysed the use of online glossaries and online questionnaires. On one hand, the online glossaries were used to create a dictionary of grammatical terms. Students had to include the definition of two terms, and all their entries and examples. Although that e-activity was designed to do individually, learners shared their definitions with their virtual classmates. Regarding the rules to develop the glossaries, participants had to write everything in English, since the purpose of those e-activities was not only to learn all the new grammatical terms but also to help them to improve their written skills. On the other hand, the online questionnaires were used to design assessment and self-assessment e-activities. They enabled teachers to create a bank of different kinds of questions (multiple choice, true/false questions and short answer) and to design different questionnaires to include them in different sections of the course to practice reading and writing. The assessment and self-assessment questionnaires had different rules. In the case of assessment questionnaires, teachers decided to shuffle the questions and answers randomly, avoiding the same order for questions and answers in the questionnaire. Students only had one attempt to complete the questionnaire, so the grading method was first attempt, time was limited and there were penalties applied for incorrect answers. Moreover the results were available after the questionnaires were closed. In the case of self-assessment questionnaires, questions and answers were not shuffled randomly, time and the number of attempts were not limited and penalties were not applied for incorrect answers. The results were available immediately after each attempt. The purpose of those questionnaires was to help students to learn the contents of the course and to prepare them to do the assessment questionnaires and the final exam. It was a way to help students solve their doubts about contents, and recognize their strengths and weaknesses. All online questionnaires were completed individually. Although they were interactive resources and there was a bidirectional communication, that only took place between learners and computers.

In the model implemented there were also two forums; one was about methodology and another one about English culture. In the first forum, students shared their ideas for teaching English in Primary Education, attaching different documents in which they included good practices. The second forum was used as a complement of the different wikis of English culture, and allowed each group to interact, exchange points of view and make decisions about the content, and format that they wanted to include in their final wikis. Regarding the rules of use of those forums, teachers established that students used English in all their interactions and in all the documents uploaded, since the forums were designed to improve students' written skills.

The second collaborative resource used in the model was the wiki. It was used to carry out a group e-activity about different topics of English culture. Small groups of students developed each wiki and when they finished the e-activities, they shared them with their virtual classmates. As mentioned before, each wiki was complemented with a forum to establish a more fluent interaction and decide the points they wanted to include and their roles in the process. All contents developed through that resource were written in English. Therefore, those e-activities had the purpose of learning different cultural aspects as well as improving students' written skills. Teachers evaluated all the e-activities developed through interactive and collaborative resources as part of students' final grade. They carried out a continuous and summative assessment.

After introducing the hypermedia modular model and the e-activities designed with the tools mentioned before, researchers showed a literature review of studies in which Moodle and those tools were used to create English teaching-learning environments.

LITERATURE REVIEW

Pinto, Sánchez & García (2015b) carried out a quantitative research with an ex-post-facto design to highlight the benefits of some transmissive, interactive and collaborative tools such as podcast, videocast, online questionnaires, online glossary and forum in learning English Phonetics and Phonology. The sample was composed of 87 students enrolled in the subject English Phonetics and Phonology of the Degree in Primary Education: English. A pre-test and a post-test were used to operationalize the variables and collect data. The findings of the research demonstrated that participants were quite satisfied with the model implemented in the blended learning modality as well as with the transmissive, interactive and collaborative resources used to develop the activities to help student to practice and improve their level in English pronunciation level. They considered that the VLE implemented helped them to perceive and produce English more accurately.

The study of Aydin & Yildiz (2014) focused on the use of the collaborative tool wiki in collaborative writing projects in foreign language learning classrooms. The sample of the research was composed of a total of 34 intermediate level university students learning English as a foreign language. During the course learners had to accomplish three wiki-based collaborative writing tasks in groups of four: an argumentative one, an informative one and a decision-making one. Researchers analysed student wiki pages in order to investigate the role of activity type in the number of peer and self-corrections, and the form-related and meaning-related changes. Data were also collected through focus-group interviews and questionnaires that were used to find out students' perceptions about the experience. The results pointed out that the argumentative activity promoted more peer-corrections than the other ones. And the informative task generated more self-corrections than the other activities. Findings also emphasized that 94% of the time, the use of wiki-based collaborative writing activities contributed to the accurate use of grammatical structures. Participants' perceptions were quite and considered that their writing performance improved through the use of wikis.

Ferriman (2013) developed a quasi-experimental study into the impact of a blended e-learning environment on academic writing assignments in English at Thai International College. An experimental group of students used an on-line bulletin board and face-to-face communication in class to share information for essay topics they were preparing. A same size control group used only face-to-face communication for the same task. The experimental and control groups were compared on three variables for each of the 3 essays they write: number of references used; word count; essay score. The results indicated that the experimental group had higher means on six of the nine outcomes, though those were not statistically significant, suggesting that the bulletin board must have more than compensated for the larger class size.

The study of Twu (2010) highlighted the learners' positive attitude toward language learning in Wiki environments, and toward interaction developed in wiki in English as L2 classroom. The results identified some effective strategies to involve students in this activity, and to maximize language in learning environment using wiki as a tool of communication to build a learning community.

Researchers also highlighted the study carried out by Miyazoe & Anderson (2010). They discussed the positive effects of the simultaneous implementation of three written activities through technological tools such as forum, blog, and wiki in a blended learning environment for teaching and learning English at the University of Tokyo. In the final results, the positive perception of these three tools on the part of students was proven, highlighting wiki as the most favourable one, followed by blog and forum. The study established the usefulness of each one of the online writing tools, and observed a general improvement in students' writing abilities. According to the conclusions of that study a significant step forward took place in how teachers must think about online writing and its effectiveness in language teaching, and learning strategies.

The study conducted by Kol & Schcolnik (2008) focused on the use of forum in the teaching-learning process of English. Although the purpose of that research was to establish valid criteria to assess the contributions on the part of students, the research focused on the use of forum for academic purposes. It emphasized students' positive perceptions towards the use of that tool to improve written skills.

Researchers also highlighted the study of Lund (2008) in Norway about the use of wiki as a collaboration tool in teaching English. The results of the study showed that wiki was an appropriate tool to promote collaborative and cooperative abilities in learning foreign languages.

In the research carried out by Franco (2008) the use of wiki was also emphasized. The study was developed in Brazil with students of intermediate level in English. The use of wiki was analysed to promote peer correction in a virtual group environment. The results confirmed once again the positive attitudes of students towards the use of that resource in their progress in learning English.

The study of Mak & Coniam (2008) was conducted in Hong Kong with high school students whose level in English was intermediate. According to the results, the use of wiki helped students develop their writing skills, and it promoted collaborative writing between students with minimal input and support from teachers. Students were able to write authentic texts and to work together.

The study of Kovacic, Bubas & Zlatovic (2008) started in November 2006 at the Faculty of Organization and Informatics, University of Zagreb, Croatia, and was developed during the 2006/2007 and 2007/2008 academic years. They wanted to assess the applicability of wiki technology in teaching English for special purposes to engage students in different individual and collaborative online learning activities; to evaluate these activities, and to allow them to choose the most appropriate activities for learning a L2. The use of this tool allowed students to participate more actively in the course, contributed in the development of activities and demonstrated what they had learned. The students concluded that they had improved both their writing skills and vocabulary. The teachers also had different elements to evaluate the students' participation more precisely and objectively.

The study of Farabaugh (2007) was conducted at Cornell University in different literature courses. The Farabaugh study used two versions of the wiki software: QwikiWiki and MediaWiki. The author concluded that technology was a good tool to carry out reading and writing assignments that encouraged language awareness in the literary domain. The results also emphasized that asynchronous tool was appropriate to improve writing skills, to extend group work outside the class, to promote collaborative writing, and to help students to create their own knowledge rather than just receiving it from teachers.

The study of Fitze (2006) also expressed the positive aspects of using forum to teach a foreign language. In this occasion it combined traditional and online instruction through an e-learning platform. The study concluded that there was a broader range in the vocabulary used, as well as a greater interaction and participation of students in written expression.

Finally, the experience developed by Savignon & Roithmeier (2004) was focused on using forum as a tool to promote cultural exchange and to learn a second language (L2). That exchange took place between students who were learning German in the USA, and students learning English in Germany. Students of both countries participated in different discussion topics during several weeks through forums. The study pointed out that there were evidences of collaborative dialogue, and cooperative construction of texts, as well as the use of asynchronous communication strategies to promote the exchange of knowledge and create a community of learning.

Most researchers developed around learning English as a L2 and the use of technological tools required that more studies must be performed in that field. Building on the results of previous studies, researchers were very motivated to conduct the current study, exploring university students' perceptions about the effectiveness of interactive and collaborative tools to improve student written skills in a blended learning environment. They wanted to contribute to the knowledge base in that area and gather more information for the implementation of educational programmes that allowed teachers to decide better the priorities for educational intervention.

In the following parts of the paper, researchers provided an overview of the research. First of all, they introduced the study by providing the mixed methods research adopted (quantitative and qualitative).

According to Padgett's classification (1998) the research was an example of a study in which it was firstly used a quantitative instrument, a questionnaire, followed by a semi-structured interview, a qualitative instrument, to go deeply into the quantitative results in order to meet the objective of the study. The population of the research was made of 451 students enrolled in the subject English I of the Degree in Primary Education: English, developed under blended learning modality. The quantitative sample was made of 358 people and it was a probability sample while the qualitative sample was made of 91 students and it was non-probabilistic, cumulative and sequential. Secondly, researchers presented the main quantitative and qualitative results of the data analysis. Finally, they showed the main conclusions of the research according to students' perspectives about the effectiveness of interactive and collaborative resources to improve their written skills in English

METHOD

In order to explore university students' perceptions about the effectiveness of interactive and collaborative tools to improve written skills in a blended learning environment a mixed methods research was adopted. This methodology is interesting in the process as well as in the result, so it combines qualitative and quantitative methods which enhances, on the one hand, the mutual invigoration of these two types of methods, and, on the other hand, the validity and reliability of data (Anguera, 2008). As Delgado (2014) points out, this method combines the plasticity of the qualitative approach and the rigour of the quantitative one. Regarding the works done by different experts (Delgado, 2014; Hernández, et al, 2014; Sánchez-Gómez, 2015), the following characteristics can be distinguished in a mixed methods approach:

1. Holistic vision (complete and integral approach)
2. Complementation (clarification of the results of one method on the basis of the other)
3. Development (the results of one method as a support of the processes of the other: sampling, collection, data analysis, new hypotheses, etc.)
4. Initiation (to discover contradictions, new frames of reference, to modify original approaches with the results of the other method)
5. Expansion (one method can expand the knowledge obtained by the other)
6. Compensation (the weaknesses of one method can be made up for the other)
7. Diversity (different views of the problem)
8. Clarity (to display elements which were not detected by a single method)
9. Triangulation (quantitative and qualitative corroboration)
10. Credibility and improvement (reinforcing arguments, results and procedures)

Padgett (1998) identifies three forms of conducting this kind of research. First of all, the research begins in a qualitative way through interviews, discussion group and observation. The variables, ideas or hypotheses are identified and studied later through quantitative methods and hypothesis testing. Secondly, researchers initially use a quantitative method with its specific instruments and the qualitative one later. The results of the quantitative approach are the starting point of the qualitative one that provides information about those questions that cannot be answered through the instruments of the quantitative approach. Finally, the third form is that in which quantitative and qualitative approaches are used simultaneously. According to this classification our research is an example of the second form, since researchers it was firstly used a quantitative instrument, a questionnaire, followed by a semi-structured interview, a qualitative instrument, to go deeply into the quantitative results obtained in order to meet our objectives.

The quantitative study of our research was an ex-post-facto design because researchers could not control and manipulate the variables since the phenomenon occurred naturally, so they only recorded its measures. They studied natural groups already formed and consisted of students enrolled in the subject English I. The research addressed a descriptive study, a survey method, using techniques of descriptive and inferential analysis for the different strata sample of the study (Arnal, Rincón & Latorre, 1994; Kerlinger, 1973), and was developed in three phases (Buendía, Colás & Hernández, 1997). First of all, a theoretical and conceptual phase in which the objectives and research hypotheses were set. Secondly, a methodological phase in which the sample and the variables of the study were selected, and it was carried out the preparation of the pilot questionnaire and its definitive formulation. And finally, statistical and conceptual phase in which it was carried out coding and data analysis to obtain the results from which generalizations could be made, and conclusions could be drawn.

The qualitative approach of our research was based on the Grounded Theory since the process of the Grounded Theory was followed for the categorization of dimensions. The theory emerged and developed inductively from the research data, not deductively from theoretical frameworks. The process of analysis was dynamic and creative, and two fundamental strategies could be distinguished: the theoretical sampling and the method of constant comparison (Glaser & Strauss, 2009). On the one hand, the theoretical sampling referred to the process of data collection, its analysis and categorization on the part of the researcher. Data collection and analysis were carried out until theoretical saturation occurs, that is to say, "when no additional data are found that advance, modify, qualify, extend or add to the theory develop" (Glaser & Strauss, 1967, p.61). On the other hand, the constant comparison method intended to generate theory from a constant comparative analysis of the data collected. Thus, researchers encoded and reflected on the type of data they were collecting from the beginning (Trinidad, Carretero & Soriano, 2006). The method is distinguished by four stages: 1) comparing incidents and data that are applicable to each category; 2) integrating these categories and their properties; 3) bounding the theory; and 4) setting out the theory (Glaser & Strauss, 2009).

Variables and Instrument

The instruments used to collect the quantitative data were a pre-test and a post-test which were divided into three parts: personal data, technology and second language. Researchers designed the initial drafts of the questionnaires. Experts in different areas (research methodology, English and technology) analysed those drafts, the content, clarity and relevance of the items and the adequacy of the terms used in relation to the dimensions studied; and did the reports with several contributions and suggestions. The experts' contributions were analysed and researchers carried out the changes proposed. The participation of those experts in the design of the tests provided the external validity of these instruments. On the other hand, the internal consistency of the questionnaires was assessed using Cronbach's alpha, having high internal consistency $\alpha=0.910$ and $\alpha=0.894$ respectively, so their measures were stable and consistent. The final questionnaires consisted of different kinds of questions: yes/no, open, closed, multiple choice, and a five-point Likert scale to avoid possible negative effects such as the halo effect.

The qualitative instrument was a semi-structured interview to let people express their opinions freely, without being influenced by researchers (Creswell, 2005). The categories were not established a priori but generated by interviewees. Internal validity was achieved because the criteria established by Coleman & Unrau (2005), and Hernández, Fernández & Baptista (2014) were met. Referring to the reliability of the coding, researchers had the collaboration of 16 experts in this matter. They had a copy of the tree of categories and the transcription of the interviews to code them. Researchers compared experts' encodings with theirs to identify the agreements that existed between them, with an agreement of 81%. That level of reliability meant that the encodings were clearly valid and determines which category was part of the final tree.

Participants

The population of the research was made of 451 students enrolled in the subject English I of the Degree in Primary Education: English, developed under blended learning modality. The quantitative sample was cluster sampling, since all members form natural groupings, and a probability sample since any member of the population had the same probability of being selected, and the results of the study could be generalized to a larger population. It was made of 358 learners, 23.2% of them were men and 76.8% women whose ages were between 20 and 58. All of them had finished a previous University Degree and most of them were working. 25.10% had a part-time job and 57% a full-time job. In addition, 86.73% had a job related to education. It was a sufficiently representative sample with a relative error of 2.5%. On the other hand, the qualitative sample was made of 91 students, aged between 20 and 58. In this case, it was a non-probabilistic sample, cumulative and sequential, the sample needed to get enough information, reaching the theoretical saturation to meet the objectives of the study.

Data Collection and Analyses

Participants filled in the questionnaires at the beginning and at the end of the academic year. Both tests were available in the hypermedia modular model implemented in the subject English I. Once the fieldwork was finished, researchers ordered data and prepared the register coding to process the 716 questionnaires collected in an ad hoc file. After creating the data matrix, they introduced and debugged data, and did descriptive and inferential analysis using the SPSS statistical software version 20. They carried out a descriptive analysis of the variables expressed in frequencies and percentages, and an inferential analysis, calculating t-Test for the significance of the difference between the means of two independent samples (student's t-test), a one-way analysis of variance (ANOVA), and chi-square test to see if there was a relationship between two categorical variables. The quantitative obtained results were depicted through graphics and tables using Microsoft Office Word 2013.

On the other hand, the 91 semi-structured interviews were conducted along three months until theoretical saturation occurred. All interviews were videotaped to transcribe them accurately. Researchers followed the scheme proposed by Miles & Huberman (1994) about the processes of qualitative data analysis in which there were three basic tasks: a) data reduction, b) data display, and c) drawing and verifying conclusions. It was a nonlinear design but convergent and recursive, that finished when saturation of information was reached. In the first phase, researchers carried out the separation of units according to thematic criteria, using the line as a textual unit in order not to distort the meaning of the text. They identified and arranged the elements through categorizing and coding of data units to classify them in a certain content category. The categories were defined deductively, with a priori categories, and inductively, introducing modification when data were examined. Researchers used NVIVO11 software to carry out categorizing and coding. Finally, the synthesis and clustering was carried out to lead to a physical grouping of the units belonging to the same category, and synthesizing in a metacategory all the information that was contained in different categories with points in common. In the second phase, researchers arranged data in different charts and crosstabs using Microsoft Office Word 2013 to illustrate the results. In the last phase of the processes of qualitative data analysis, researchers presented the results, their interpretation and the extraction of the conclusions from the study.

RESULTS

In the following subsections, researchers present the qualitative and quantitative results obtained in the study.

Quantitative Results

Regarding the results obtained in the item that referred to the appropriateness of the e-activities available in the hypermedia modular model to improve participants' written skills, the vast majority of students, 96.8% (n=346), considered that they were totally appropriate to help them to improve those aspects of the second language (See Figure 1).

The students were also asked about the frequency of participation in the e-activities designed through forums, wikis, online questionnaires and online glossaries. Regarding the results obtained, participants' assessments were quite positive. In the case of forums, the participants responded with *occasionally*

Figure 1. Appropriateness of the e-activities available in the hypermedia modular model to improve participants' written skills

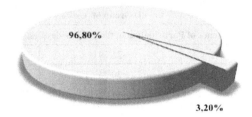

and *almost everytime*. The results in wikis were better, since the learners responded with *occasionally, almost everytime* and *everytime*. Concerning the use of online questionnaires and online glossaries, similar results were obtained, since learners self-assessed their participation in these tasks as *almost everytime* and *everytime* (See Table 1).

The results of analysis of variance according to the different age groups (p=.006, p=.006, p=.000) shows that there were statistically significant differences (CI 95%) in the participation in the e-activities through forums, wikis, online questionnaires and online glossaries. Researchers calculated the Tukey HSD post-hoc test (See Table 2), which showed that there were statistically significant differences between the mean of the youngest (20-24: $\bar{X}$ =3.51) and the groups of students aged between 25 and 29 ($\bar{X}$ =3.02), and between 30 and 34 ($\bar{X}$ =2.94). The youngest ones participated in the e-activities designed through forums with more frequency. In the dependent variable that referred to the frequency of participation in e-activities designed through wikis there were also statistically significant differences between the groups of students aged between 20 and 24 ($\bar{X}$ =3.98), and between 30 and 34 ($\bar{X}$ =3.99), and the group of participants aged between 25 and 29 ($\bar{X}$ =3.54). In that case the students aged between 25 and 29 participated less in these e-activities than the groups whose ages were between 20 and 24, and 30 and 34. The results also showed statistically significant differences between the age groups in the frequency of participation in e-activities designed through online glossaries. There were differences in the groups of students whose ages were between 20 and 24 ($\bar{X}$ =4.00), between 25 and 29 ($\bar{X}$ =3.61) and between 30 and 34 ($\bar{X}$ =3.58), and the oldest participants (35 or more than 35: $\bar{X}$ =2.71). There were also differences between the youngest learners (20-24: $\bar{X}$ =4.00) and those whose ages were between 30 and 34 ($\bar{X}$ =3.58).

Table 1. Statistics of the dependent variables of the frequency of participation in the e-activities designed through forums, wikis, online questionnaires, and online glossaries

Items	Never	Almost Never	Occasionally	ALMOST everytime	Everytime	$\bar{X}$	Sx
Frequency of Participation in Forums	12.3%(n=44)	18.7% (n=67)	24.3% (n=87)	33.8% (n=121)	10.6% (n=38)	3.12	1.198
Frequency of Participation in Wikis	2.2% (n=8)	8.9% (n=32)	24.3% (n=87)	39.1% (n=140)	25.1% (n=90)	3.76	1.001
Frequency of Participation in Online Questionnaires	2.8% (n=10)	6.7% (n=24)	21.8% (n=78)	39.1% (n=140)	29.3% (n=105)	3.86	1.008
Frequency of Participation in Online Glossaries	4.7% (n=17)	18.2% (n=65)	19.3% (n=69)	32.1% (n=115)	25.4% (n=91)	3.55	1.188

Table 2. Multiple comparisons: Dependent variables of the frequency of participation in the e-activities designed through forums, wikis, online questionnaires and online glossaries

	(I) Group of Age	(J) Group of Age	Mean Difference (I-J)	Sig.
Dependent Variable: Frequency of Participation in the E-Activities Designed Through Forums				
Tukey HSD	20-24	25-29	.484*	.033
		30-34	.563*	.004
Dependent Variable: Frequency of Participation in the E-Activities Designed Through Wikis				
Tukey HSD	20-24	25-29	.434*	.020
	30-34	25-29	.448*	.006
Dependent Variable: Frequency of Participation in the E-Activities Designed Through Online Glossaries				
Tukey HSD	20-24	30-34	.423*	.038
		35 or more than 35	1.291*	.000
	25-29	35 or more than 35	.900*	.000
	30-34	35 or more than 35	.868*	.000

* The mean difference is significant at the .05 level. n= 358

Participants were also asked about the effectiveness of e-activities designed through forums, wikis, online questionnaires and online glossaries to help them to improve their written skills in English as second language. Referring to e-activities done through forums and wikis, 69.7% and 66.3% of the students highlighted that the use of these tools helped them *quite a lot*. Just 8.5% and 8.2% of them assessed them as *not very helpful (not much)*, and 1.4% and 1.5% as *not helpful at all (not at all)*. Similar results were obtained when students evaluated the e-activities done through online questionnaires and online glossaries since 65.4% and 61.1% assessed them as *quite helpful*, and only 7.4% and 7.5% of learners assessed them as *not very helpful (not much)*, and 1.8 and 2.5% as *not helpful at all (not at all)* (See Figure 2).

Students were asked to self-assess their level of writing and reading at the beginning and at the end of the academic year (See Figure 3). 32.4% of the learners self-assessed their level of writing as *fair*

Figure 2. Effectiveness of the e-activities designed through forums, wikis, online questionnaires and online glossaries to help participants to improve their written skills

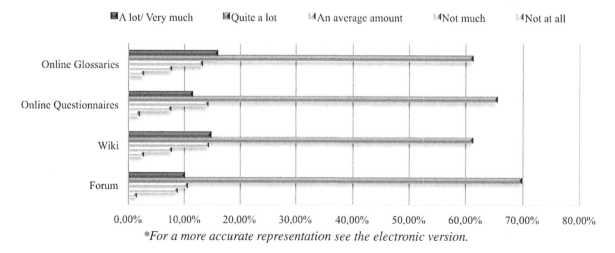

For a more accurate representation see the electronic version.

Figure 3. Participants' self-assessment of written skills (writing and reading)

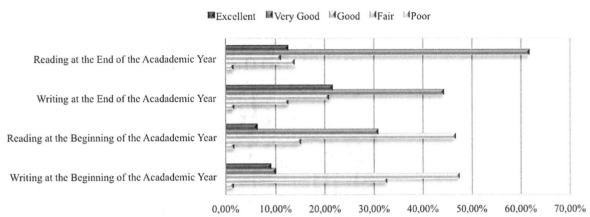

For a more accurate representation see the electronic version.

and 47.2% as *good* at the beginning of the course. These results improved at the end of the course since almost half of the students (44.1%) responded with *very good*. Regarding reading, the results were better. 46.4% self-assessed it as *good* and 30.7% as *very good* at the beginning of the course. These results also improved at the end of the academic year, as 61.5% of the students responded with *very good*.

According to the results obtained, students improved their level in reading and writing. There were differences in the variables that referred to those written skills. To determine whether these differences were statistically significant differences (CI 95%) or not, researchers calculated the student's t-test for related samples. That test showed that there were statistically significant differences between these variables (writing: p=.000, t=14.312; reading: p=.000, t=11.906); therefore the null hypothesis was rejected. In other words, there was a relation between the improvement of reading and writing and the development of the e-activities through the technological tools (forums, wikis, online questionnaires and online glossaries) provided in the hypermedia modular model of the subject English I.

Qualitative Results

In the following subsections, researchers present the results obtained in the qualitative data analyses.

First of all, Figure 4 shows the results of the semantic analyses carried out to know the twenty most frequently occurring words in the semi-structured interviews conducted along three months. The words with the highest frequency were: learning (416), blended (364), technology (362), English (315), Skills (312), written (312), questionnaire (260), forum (258), wiki (258), glossary (257), interaction (256), collaborative (230) and communication (216).

Following the qualitative procedure described before in the data collection analyses section, researchers determined a series of categories and subcategories represented as a conceptual map and organized hierarchically according to students' perspectives (See Figure 5).

Researchers applied thematic networks to organize the thematic analysis of qualitative data. As Attride-Stirling (2001) points out thematic networks arrange the coding text that is presented at the end of the data gathering stage in three classes of themes, three levels and their relationships: Global Theme, Organizing Theme and Basic Theme (See Figure 5). "This core structure has significant parallels with the three basic elements of grounded theory: concepts, categories and propositions" (Attride-Stirling,

Figure 4. Semantic analyses: word cloud

Figure 5. Conceptual map

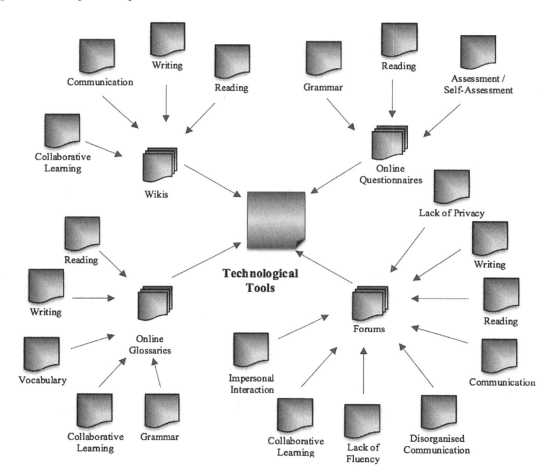

2001, p.387 in Corbin and Strauss, 1990). The *Global Theme* of our research is Technological Tools. It comprises a thematic network consisting of four *Organizing Themes* and twenty *Basic Themes*. This Thematic Network represents students' perspectives on the effectiveness of the e-activities designed through interactive and collaborative resources implemented in the hypermedia modular model of the subject English I to improve written skills. Table 3 shows the qualitative results obtained in the *Global Theme*, the *Organizing Themes* and *Basic Themes*.

In the following subsections, the results obtained in each organizing theme are presented. Two of them refer to interactive tools: online glossaries and online questionnaires in which the interaction takes place between students and computers, and the other two to collaborative tools: forums and wikis which promote a multidirectional communication between the protagonists of the teaching-learning process.

The verbatim quotes from the study participants are labelled in terms of gender and age.

Organizing Theme: Online Glossaries

Based on the overall evaluation of the blended course implemented, the majority of students believed that the e-activities developed through glossaries were effective to improve their written skills. Participants were strongly aware of the necessity of improving these skills, and considered that the e-activities designed through this technological tool allowed them to foster effective written communication in a variety of situations. The data analysis also revealed that those e-activities permitted them to develop their English vocabulary and grammar. They considered that having a good English grammar and vocabulary did not only mean that they could understand longer and more difficult texts, but also they could write in a more appropriate way a wide range of text patterns: reports, articles, reviews, formal and informal letters or essays.

Finally, they highlighted that the use of this technological tool created a favourable environment for collaborative learning, since all of them could share the work that they had done with all the participants of the teaching-learning process. It was a relevant aspect of this kind of education which had a significant impact on the development of this e-activity.

I think that the activity developed through the online glossary has been quite appropriate to achieve the learning objectives, to improve reading and writing (24-year-old man, participant 83).

I would like to say that the activity done through the online glossary has been very effective and we have had the opportunity to improve our writing and English grammar since we have to write everything in this language (35-year-old woman, participant 15).

We also count on our classmates' help and collaboration, so it is promoted the collaborative work or in group (28-year-old man, participant 19).

That fact of using this asynchronous tool gives us the opportunity of sharing our work with the classmates although we don't share the same time and place (37-year-old man, participant 72).

Table 3. From global theme to organizing theme to basic theme

University Students' Perceptions About the Effectiveness of Interactive and Collaborative Tools to Improve Written Skills in a Blended Learning Environment	A Text Units	B Interviews	C % B/ Total Interviews	D Text Units of B	E % A/D	F % A/Total Lines
Global Theme: Technological Tools	7,057	91	100%	19,443	36.3%	36.3%
Organizing Theme: Forums	3,322	91	100%	19,443	17%	17%
1. Basic Theme: Collaborative Learning	716	81	89%	16,023	3.7%	3.7%
2. Basic Theme: Reading	649	74	81%	14,810	3.3%	3.3%
3. Basic Theme: Writing	712	77	85%	16,116	3.7%	3.7%
4. Basic Theme: Communication	621	73	80%	14,685	3.2%	3.2%
5. Basic Theme: Lack of Privacy	123	34	37%	6,915	0.6%	0.6%
6. Basic Theme: Disorganised Communication	264	42	46%	8,865	1.4%	1.4%
7. Basic Theme: Lack of Fluency	176	37	41%	7,132	0.9%	0.9%
8. Basic Theme: Impersonal Interaction	61	32	35%	6,634	0.3%	0.3%
Organizing Theme: Wikis	1,678	83	91%	16,137	10.4%	8.6%
1. Basic Theme: Reading	381	69	76%	13,474	2.4%	2.0%
2. Basic Theme: Writing	442	72	79%	13,998	2.7%	2.3%
3. Basic Theme: Communication	479	76	84%	15,912	3.0%	2.5%
4. Basic Theme: Collaborative Learning	376	69	76%	13,998	2.3%	1.9%
Organizing Theme: Online Questionnaires	989	72	79%	13,998	7.0%	5.1%
1. Basic Theme: Grammar	188	57	63%	12,094	1.3%	1.0%
2. Basic Theme: Reading	532	72	79%	13,998	3.8%	2.7%
3. Basic Theme: Assessment / Self Assessment	269	64	70%	13,121	1.9%	1.4%
Organizing Theme: Online Glossaries	1,068	67	74%	14,387	7.4%	5.5%
1. Basic Theme: Vocabulary	108	45	49%	9,212	0.7%	0.6%
2. Basic Theme: Reading	312	62	68%	12,753	2.2%	1.6%
3. Basic Theme: Writing	268	58	64%	12,156	1.9%	1.4%
4. Basic Theme: Grammar	113	43	47%	9,023	0.8%	0.6%
5. Basic Theme: Collaborative Learning	267	58	64%	12,156	1.9%	1.4%

A = total number of text units retrieved of each theme

B = number of interviews in which participants refer to each theme

C = percentage of the number of interviews in which participants refer to each theme in relation to the total number of interviews

D = number of text units of B

E = percentage of A in relation to the total text units of the interviews in which participants refer to each theme

F = percentage of A in relation to the total text units (19,443) of all interviews (91)

Organizing Theme: Online Questionnaire

The empirical analysis also provided evidences on the positive link between the use of online question-naires, and the development of reading and English grammar.

The vast majority of students believed that online questionnaires allowed teachers to design e-activities to carry out initial, continuous and summative assessment. They considered that this was possible because of the use of that interactive asynchronous tool that eliminated the temporal and spatial barriers of the traditional education. Moreover, the findings also indicated that the students emphasized the positive aspect of the self-assessment e-activities, since they believed that it was essential to know their progress in their level of English. The self-assessment e-activities and the feedback provided immediately after finishing them allowed learners to know their strengths and weaknesses and be prepared for the final exam.

Some of the activities of the model implemented have helped teachers to evaluate our progress and daily work. This is appropriate in this kind of education because we have done a lot of work through the platform and teachers must take it into account (22-year-old woman, participant 5).

I would like to highlight the use of the online questionnaires because they have allowed us to self-assess our progress. It is a very useful tool because we could know our mistakes immediately after finishing them. The teachers have provided the necessary explanations to clarify our doubts (31-year-old woman, participant 24).

We have had access to immediate feedback when we have finished each of the online questionnaires. We have been able to check our answers and know our mistakes and correct answers constantly (23-year-old man, participant 62).

Organizing Theme: Wiki

Wiki was conceptualized as a technological tool that allowed students to communicate in writing in a virtual learning environment. Students also emphasized the potential of that asynchronous tool to develop their written skills and the collaborative learning which was related to a Social Constructivist Learning environment. The findings also indicated that students believed that it was essential to have the capacity to work in groups and collaboratively. They thought that collaborative learning was one of the advantages of that tool and the blended learning education, since it contributed to the creation of a learning community.

I also emphasize how the use of these technologies allows us to work as a team; for example, we have designed together the different wikis and have used different forums to share our ideas. This improves and promotes collaborative learning and teamwork. We have created knowledge, while the teachers have guided us (29-year-old man, participant 77).

It's the first time that I have used the wiki, but my experience has been very positive and I have really improved my written skills. It has been a very collaborative activity (45-year-old woman, participant 38).

Organizing Theme: Forum

Most students pointed out how forums allowed them to interact and decide what they wanted to include in the wikis developed about English culture. Moreover, they emphasized how forums allowed them to exchange their ideas and opinions while respecting different points of view and recognizing their classmates' work. They also thought that the e-activities developed through forums offered the possibility of sharing their works with the rest of the participants of the hypermedia model, enhancing active participation, collaborative learning and the creation of knowledge. However, some students considered that the interactions developed through that collaborative tool were impersonal and disorganised and that caused problems to do the e-activities and communicate suitably. Some of them also pointed out the lack of privacy and fluency in the communications that took place in the e-activities using that technological tool and considered that they were not used to using that technological tool to communicate and had problems to develop the e-activities. Finally, and based on the overall evaluation of participants' opinions about the e-activities developed through forums, students considered that they were appropriate to improve their written skills in English, since it was the only language permitted in all the interactions.

We have had different technological tools, such as forums, to work together. They have helped us develop the wiki of culture, and exchange methodological ideas to teach English in a primary school (32-year-old woman, participant 17).

The forum has been a good tool to develop the wiki of English culture. We have used it to communicate us with all the members of our group in order to divide our tasks and help us to write the text in English. It has been a collaborative work in which we have learned together and we have shared everything (26-year-old woman, participant 65).

The activities were appropriate for this kind of instruction. We need to practice our written skills and to do it like that is perfect (42-year-old woman, participant 37).

It is a good tool, but I also consider that communication is a bit chaotic and I have had problems to communicate with my classmates. I'm not used to using it (46-year-old woman, participant 70).

Clusters by Coding Similarity

In this section, researchers presented the results of the cluster analysis to describe the coding similarities that existed between the age groups and the themes of the research. Researchers decided the column as the criterion to be used for measuring it because the goal of the cluster analysis was to form similar groups. In the following clusters, patterns in the study by grouping nodes that were coded similarly can be visualized. They provided graphical representations to see the similarities of coding (See Figure 6).

As first cluster (See Figure 7) shows the coding similarities happened in the themes that referred to *Online Questionnaires* and *Assessment and Self-assessment* e-activities. There was a clear relation between that interactive tool and the possibilities that it offered not only to design e-activities to assess students, but also to allow them to be aware of their progress in English. It was emphasized the significant changes that there were in the way participants learned and improved *English grammar* and *reading*.

In the second cluster (See Figure 8), the coding similarity happened in the themes that referred to the interactive tool, Online Glossary, and the collaborative learning. They consider that it is essential that students who are enrolled in an English Course in the blended learning modality cooperate and work together in the development of an online glossary, which allows them to develop their vocabulary in English and communicate in a more appropriate and better way.

In the next cluster (See Figure 9) there was closeness in participants' speech in the themes that referred to forum and communication. They strongly agreed with the statement that that collaborative tool was essential in the hypermedia modular model implemented in a blended learning modality, and

Figure 6. Global cluster by coding similarity

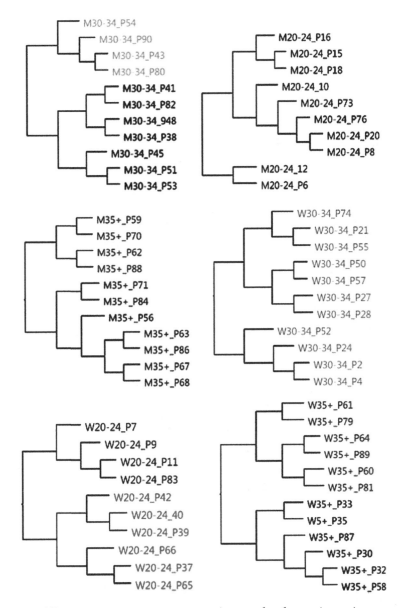

For a more accurate representation see the electronic version.

they emphasized their advantages, specially the collaborative learning and the creation of a learning community in which students worked together and shared opinions.

In the following cluster (See Figure 10) it was emphasized the relation that existed between wiki and collaborative learning. Learners valued the possibilities that that technological tool offered to develop e-activities in groups very positively. Moreover, they considered that it was a good tool that allowed students to communicate at any time and from any place, since being an asynchronous tool broke all the temporal and spatial barriers that could exist.

In the last cluster (See Figure 11), on one hand, there was closeness in students' speech in the themes that referred to the collaborative tool: forum, and the possibilities that it offered to communicate, and

Figure 7. 1ˢᵗ cluster by coding similarity

Figure 8. 2ⁿᵈ cluster by coding similarity

Figure 9. 3ʳᵈ cluster by coding similarity

Figure 10. 4ᵗʰ cluster by coding similarity

Figure 11. 5ᵗʰ cluster by coding similarity

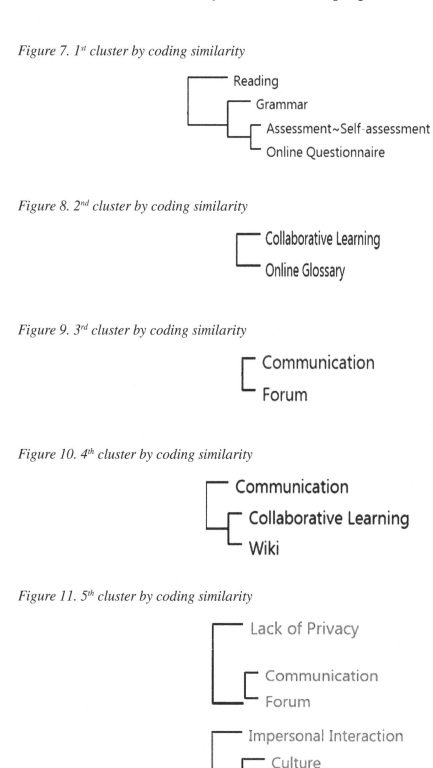

between the development of different English cultural topics and the improvement of their writing. On the other hand, and in view of the results achieved, there were coding similarities between the use of forum and the themes that referred to impersonal interaction and the lack of privacy.

CONCLUSION AND DISCUSSION

To meet the objective of the study researchers analysed university students' perceptions about the effectiveness of interactive and collaborative tools to improve written skills in a blended learning environment. The research proved the benefits and the effectiveness of technological interactive tools (online glossaries and online questionnaires) and collaborative resources (wikis and forums) not only to improve reading and writing, but also to learn grammatical structures, vocabulary, some cultural topics and methodological aspects of teaching English in Primary Education (Aydin & Yildiz, 2014; Pinto, Sánchez & García, 2015b).

The findings of the study emphasized that the use of those asynchronous tools contributed to the creation of a learning community, since they strengthened teamwork, in which all students participated and interacted to do the e-activities provided by teachers (García-Peñalvo, 2008; Lee, 2010; Twu, 2010). There was a change from the traditional individualism to the collective construction of knowledge that was a dynamic, active process in which learners participated actively (Pinto-Llorente, et al 2014a). Therefore, wikis, forums, online questionnaires and online glossaries enabled the development of a collaborative learning process because participants worked together in a participative hypermedia model. As a community of authors, all the members were able to create, modify, or eliminate content. That facilitated the involvement of students in the creation of the contents of the course and promoted multidirectional communication in which students participated actively and abandoned their passive role as simple observers and recipients (Pinto, Sánchez & García, 2015b). This led to the successful creation of a blended learning model, which was tailor-made for the requirements of that kind of instruction and for students' educational needs. With regards to the learning approach in which that model was based on, the empirical study suggested that it supported learner-centred pedagogy, since students were placed at the centre of teaching-learning process and create knowledge that they shared with the rest of classmates (Cortiella & Horowitz, 2014; Evangelidou, 2017).

Special emphasis were placed on the benefits of the asynchronous tools to promote continuous assessment, taking into account the e-activities that students developed through the platform during the whole academic year. They also considered that the model implemented allowed teachers to design different assessment e-activities to carry out a continuous and summative assessment, and to assess all the e-activities developed during the course (Blanco & Ginovart, 2009). They thought that it was possible because the model had different asynchronous tools that eliminated, as mentioned above, the temporal and spatial barriers of the traditional education.

Participants concluded that teachers' work was essential, and, in a way, success depended on them. That was directly related to the involvement of teachers in the process, since they had to master not only the contents, but also technology to plan e-activities, and anticipate learners' difficulties by designing a platform that did not lead to any error that prevented student learning (Jeffrey et al 2014). Moreover, the tools were excellent means to promote peer correction in a virtual environment. Participants of the blended learning model helped each other to solve the tasks and corrected their mistakes in English.

Combined, that also promoted students' self-assessment because they were able to reflect about what they wrote and about their progress in English (Aydin & Yildiz, 2014).

Data showed the potential of forums, wikis, online questionnaires and online glossaries for academic purpose beyond all temporal and spatial barriers of traditional education. Thus, that kind of instruction enabled students to continue studying despite their personal situation and allowed them to reconcile professional and personal obligations with lifelong learning and mobility (Pinto-Llorente et al 2014b).

Nowadays we are witnessing the technological literacy of today's society in which Social web tools afforded us the opportunity of an effective access to knowledge in which students become the protagonists of their learning (Sánchez et al 2011). The use of e-learning platforms and their tools have led to the development of blended learning models which allow and guarantee the education of students, independently of their personal and professional situations. Interactive and collaborative resources have enhanced and facilitated communication between all the protagonist of the teaching-learning process, providing a greater flexibility since they break all the space and time barriers and promoting self and lifelong learning (Pinto-Llorente et al 2014c; Sánchez-Gómez et al 2010).

The results of the research provide more information for future innovative and educational programmes and can be a reference for future researchers and for the implementation of blended learning models in higher education to decide better the preferences in educational intervention and move towards more effective models to improve Students' level of English.

REFERENCES

Anguera, M. T. (2008). Metodologías cualitativas: características, procesos y aplicaciones. In *Metodología en la investigación sobre discapacidad. Introducción al uso de las ecuaciones estructurales* (pp. 141–155). Salamanca: Publicaciones del INICO.

Arnal, J., Rincón, D., & Latorre, A. (1994). *Investigación educativa. Fundamentos y metodología*. Barcelona: Labor.

Attride-Stirling, J. (2001). Thematic networks: An analytic tool for qualitative research. *Qualitative Research*, *1*(3), 385–405. doi:10.1177/146879410100100307

Aydin, Z., & Yildiz, S. (2014). Using wikis to promote collaborative EFL writing. *Language Learning & Technology*, *18*(1), 160–180.

Blake, R. (2000). Computer mediated communication: A window on L2 Spanish interlanguage. *Language Learning & Technology*, *4*(1), 120–136.

Blanco, M., & Ginovart, M. (2009). Creating Moodle Quizzes for the Subjects of Mathematics and Statistics Corresponding to the First Years in Engineering Studies. In *Proceedings of the 1st International Conference on Education and New Learning Technologies* (pp. 1984-1883). Barcelona: AITED.

Buendía, L., Colás, P., & Hernández, F. (1997). *Métodos de investigación en psicopedagogía*. Madrid: McGraw-Hill.

Coleman, H., & Unrau, Y. A. (2010). Qualitative Data Analysis. In R. M. Grinnell & Y. A. Unrau (Eds.), *Social Work: Research and Evaluation. Foundations of Evidence-Based Practice* (pp. 447–464). New York: Oxford University Press.

Corbin, J., & Strauss, A. (1990). Grounded Theory Research: Procedures, Canons and Evaluative Criteria. *Qualitative Sociology, 13*(1), 3–21. doi:10.1007/BF00988593

Cortiella, C., & Horowitz, S. H. (2014). *The State of learning disabilities: facts, trends and emerging issues*. New York: National Center for Learning Disabilities.

Creswell, J. (2005). *Educational Research: Planning, Conducting, and Evaluating Quantitative and Qualitative Research*. Upper Saddle River, NJ: Pearson Education.

Delgado, C. (2014). *Viajando a Ítaca por los mares cuantitativos, manual de ruta para investigar en grado y en postgrado*. Salamanca: Amaru.

Evangelidou, F. (2017). Kavala's 6th Graders towards Mastering Mathematics: A Blended Learning Proposal at Disabled Students' Side. In A. Palalas & P. Pawluk (Eds.), *Blended Learning Theory and Practice Proceedings of the 2nd World Conference on Blended Learning (IABL2017)* (pp. 79-84). Toronto: International Association for Blended Learning and George Brown College.

Farabaugh, R. (2007). "The isle is full of noises": Using Wiki software to establish a discourse community in a Shakespeare classroom. *Language Awareness, 16*(1), 41–56. doi:10.2167/la428.0

Ferriman, N. (2013). The impact of blended e-learning on undergraduate academic essay writing in English (L2). *Computers & Education, 60*(1), 243–253. doi:10.1016/j.compedu.2012.07.008

Fitze, M. (2006). Discourse and Participation in ESL face-to-face and written electronic conferences. *Language Learning & Technology, 10*(1), 67–86.

Franco, C. P. (2008). Using Wiki-based Peer-Correction to Develop Writing Skills of Brazilian EFL Learners. *Novitas-ROYAL, 2*(1), 49–59.

García-Peñalvo, F. J. (2008). *Advances in E-Learning: Experiences and Methodologies*. Hershey, PA: Information Science Reference. doi:10.4018/978-1-59904-756-0

García-Peñalvo, F. J., & Colomo-Palacios, R. (2015). Innovative teaching methods in Engineering. *International Journal of Engineering Education, 31*(3), 689–693.

García-Peñalvo, F. J., Colomo-Palacios, R., & Lytras, M. D. (2012). Informal learning in work environments: Training with the Social Web in the workplace. *Behaviour & Information Technology, 31*(8), 753–755. doi:10.1080/0144929X.2012.661548

Glaser, B. G., & Strauss, A. L. (1967). *The Discovery of Grounded Theory: Strategies for Qualitative Research*. New York: Aldine. Publishing Company.

Glaser, B. G., & Strauss, A. L. (2009). *The Discovery of Grounded Theory: Strategies for Qualitative Research*. New York: Aldine. Publishing Company.

Hernández, R., Fernández, C., & Baptista, P. (2014). *Metodología de la investigación*. McGraw Hill.

Jeffrey, L. M., Milne, J., Suddaby, G., & Higgins, A. (2014). Blended learning: How teachers balance the blend of online and classroom components. *Journal of Information Technology Education: Research*, *13*, 121–140.

Kerlinger, F. N. (1973). *Foundations of Behavioral Research*. New York: Rinehart and Winston.

Kol, S., & Schcolnik, M. (2008). Asynchronous Forums in EAP: Assessment Issues. *Language Learning & Technology*, *12*(2), 49–70.

Kovacic, A., Bubas, G., & Zlatovic, M. (2008). *E-tivities with a wiki: Innovative Teaching of English as a Foreign Language*. In *Proceedings of the 14th Congress of the European University Information Systems Organisation* (pp. 1-13). Aarhus, Denmark: Academic Press.

Lee, L. (2010). Exploring wiki-mediated collaborative writing: A case-study in an elementary Spanish course. *CALICO Journal*, *27*(2), 260–276. doi:10.11139/cj.27.2.260-276

Lund, A. (2008). Wikis: A Collective Approach to Language Learning. *ReCALL*, *20*(1), 35–54. doi:10.1017/S0958344008000414

Mak, B., & Coniam, D. (2008). Using Wikis to enhance and develop writing skills among secondary school students in Hong Kong. System. *An International Journal of Educational Technology and Applied Linguistics*, *36*(3), 437–455.

Miles, M. B., & Huberman, A. (1994). *Qualitative Data Analysis: An Expanded Sourcebook*. Newbury Park, CA: SAGE.

Miyazoe, T., & Anderson, T. (2010). Learning outcomes and students' perceptions of online writing: Simultaneous implementation of a forum, blog, and wiki in an EFL blended learning setting. *System: An International Journal of Educational Technology and Applied Linguistics*, *38*(2), 185–199. doi:10.1016/j.system.2010.03.006

Padgett, D. K. (1998). *Qualitative methods in social work research: Challenges and rewards*. Thousand Oaks, CA: SAGE.

Pinto, A. M., Sánchez, M. C., & García, F. J. (2015b). Developing a VLE to Enable the Innovative Learning of English Pronunciation. In *Proceedings of the 3rd International Conference on Technological Ecosystems for Enhancing Multiculturality* (pp. 83-89). New York: ACM. doi:10.1145/2808580.2808594

Pinto-Llorente, A. M., Sánchez-Gómez, M. C., & García-Peñalvo, F. J. (2014a). Assessing the effectiveness of a technological model to improve written skills in English in higher education. In *Proceedings of the Second International Conference on Technological Ecosystems for Enhancing Multiculturality* (pp. 69-74). New York: ACM.

Pinto-Llorente, A. M., Sánchez-Gómez, M. C., & García-Peñalvo, F. J. (2014c). Students' essential characteristics for learning English in a hypermedia modular model. In *Proceedings of the Second International Conference on Technological Ecosystems for Enhancing Multiculturality* (pp. 107-111). New York: ACM.

Pinto-Llorente, A. M., Sánchez-Gómez, M. C., & García-Peñalvo, F. J. (2015a). To Be or Not to Be Successful? That Does Not Only Depend on Technology, But Also on Human Factors. *Journal of Cases on Information Technology*, *17*(1), 51–69. doi:10.4018/JCIT.2015010104

Pinto-Llorente, A. M., Sánchez-Gómez, M. C., & Palacios-Vicario, B. (2014b). Modelo Blended Learning para la enseñanza-aprendizaje del inglés en educación superior. In *Blended Learning en educación superior. Perspectivas de innovación y cambio* (pp. 121–142). Madrid: Editorial Síntesis.

Sánchez, M. C., Pinto, A. M., & García, F. J. (2011). University students' technological competence. A European higher education area (EHEA). Case study. In *CAL 2011 Learning Futures: Education, Technology & Sustainability*. Manchester Metropolitan University.

Sánchez-Gómez, M. C. (2015). La dicotomía cualitativo-cuantitativo: posibilidades de integración y diseños mixtos. Campo Abierto. Vol. monográfico, 11-30.

Sánchez-Gómez, M. C., Pinto-Llorente, A. M., & García-Peñalvo, F. J. (2010). Blended learning University students' perception of digital competence. In European Applied Business Research (EABR) and European College Teaching & Learning (ETLC), Dublin, Ireland.

Savignon, S. J., & Roithmeier, W. (2004). Computer-Mediated Communication: Texts and Strategies. *CALICO Journal*, *21*(2), 265–290.

Trinidad, A., Carretero, V., & Soriano, R. M. (2006). Teoría fundamentada "Grounded Theory" La construcción de la teoría a través del análisis interpretacional. Madrid: CIS.

Twu, H. (2010). A predictive study of Wiki interaction: Can attitude toward Wiki predict Wiki interaction in High-Context Cultures groups? *Journal of Educational Technology Development and Exchange*, *3*(1), 57–68. doi:10.18785/jetde.0301.05

KEY TERMS AND DEFINITIONS

Blended Learning: A kind of education modality that combines both face-to-face and online lessons.

Collaborative Learning: A situation in which a group of students learn together and have an active role in creating and sharing knowledge.

Higher Education: The third level of education. It is beyond secondary education and is normally provided by universities or colleges.

Learning Community: A group of students who work collaboratively, share knowledge, and have common learning objectives.

Mixed-Methods Research: A research that combines quantitative and qualitative approaches in a single study.

Written Skills: The skills that refer to reading comprehension and written expression. They refer to two of the necessary skills to communicate with native and non-native speakers.

Chapter 11

An Empirical Study of the Indian IT Sector on Typologies of Workaholism as Predictors of HR Crisis

Shivani Pandey
Mediterranean Shipping Company, India

ABSTRACT

Workaholism, in recent years, has become a regular behaviour pattern among professionals. While self-negligence is assumed as a hallmark of workaholism, empirical data in this case stands to be both narrow and paradoxical. Modern developments like high-speed data connections add more to this belief, as this makes it possible for employees who would like to work at any place and at any given point of time to work. Workaholism is found to affect several important domains of life. With regards to work domain, workaholics commonly seem to have poor associations with their peer/colleagues, most likely on the grounds that they often feel the need to control them and experience issues with delegating work. Given that the amount of time they invested in their work leaves little energy for them for other activities, also the social life outside work gets hampered. This chapter explores the relationship between workaholism, perceived work-related stress, different job conditions, and intensifying anxiety among IT professionals in Delhi/NCR.

INTRODUCTION

With the fast leap of technology innovation and competitiveness, the leisure and comfort among today's employees have also improved. A new 24/7 economy has freed the old work environment paradigm, as never before. As an aftermath, an interminable transformation in working pattern is evidently noticeable. With globalization and the pace of technology change in society, the modern economy organizations have become indeed exceptionally demanding. This also has augmented the need for growth, followed with frequent breakdowns among working employees.

Number of studies (Estes & Wang, 2008; Hooks & Hicks, 2002) have shown that working conditions have changed expeditiously. Ambiguity of clear role expectations at work is high and the balance

DOI: 10.4018/978-1-5225-5297-0.ch011

between work and personal being has become vaguer (Srikanth & Jomon, 2013). Stress rates at work have upsurge in the past decade resulting in psychiatric health problems and turning down of work productivity. It is also evident from numerous reports that a high level of perceived stress at work is related to low level of satisfaction with job and poor mental condition (Dhabhar, et al., 2010). Several researches have also reported significant associations between occupational stress, anger, work-family conflict and psychological and physical health. Henceforth, a great deal of attention is being given to the issues of work-related stress and health (Schaufeli, et al., 2008) which is often discussed in daily conversations.

Stress

Stress, over the years, has been defined in diverse ways. Formerly, it was regarded as some kind of pressure from the environment which later on turned into strain within the individual (Shimazu&Schaufeli, 2007). An extreme mode of stress can hinder productivity and impact one's physical and mental health. It can also threaten the individuals as well as organisations from attainment of goals. Mohanty & Jena (2016) has found in their investigation that job turn out to be less fulfilling under extreme stress and that their expected inherent and outward needs are not satisfied. Tomar (2017) found that IT professionals have long work hours with various time zones, add up to cooperation, undertaking to be finished on due date with flawlessness as per customer needs, which requires relational, specialized, and authoritative. These attributes prompt word related stress and work exhaustion.

How Is Stress Caused?

The workplace is an imperative cause for both demands of job and pressures triggering stress. The factors related to workplace stress cited are dearth of managerial support, low inter-personal relations, demanding job, workplace viciousness, lack of flexibility, low self-esteem and being workaholic (Schaufeli & Bakker, 2004), which further results in HR Crisis (Pandey & Sharma, 2014). HR crisis may be defined as an unstable state of affairs occurring in the organisation resulting in drain or loss of personnel, deterioration of morale, inadequate development of human resources, lack of succession plans and managerial inappropriateness leading to a multiple unhealthy consequence in an organisation.

Few researchers have tried establishing relatedness between personality types with stress proneness. One that includes being persistent and highly involved in work was studied by Caplan & Jones (1975). It acted as a catalyst of workload and ambiguity of role resulting further into anxiety, depression and antipathy. Role ambiguity was found to be positively associated with anxiety, depression, and antipathy, whereas workload was found to be positively associated with anxiety only. Research has further more revealed that these individuals who are mostly in a perpetual struggle mode to get things done in the least amount of time will undergo more stress than individuals who rarely have an urge to succeed. Adding to these personality types, there is another vital personality attribute that has come forth to make pace with the demand of the dynamic economy is "workaholism". This popular corporate buzz word has also created hype among scholars across the world. The emphasis of lately, has been on understanding the diverse aspects that constitute workaholism. For the non-professionals, "workaholism" appears to be working exceptionally hard. It's quite apparent that a person who is a typical work addict would be driven by a strong internal motivation rather than being driven by external aspects, such as organizational culture, financial issues, pressure from supervisor or a strong yearning for career encroachment. The diverse notion of "workaholism" put forth a requisite to conceptualize the word "workaholism", as its inimitable outcomes and antecedents has emerged as broadly varied and contradictory. Based on the extant literature it is observed that stress, insecurity related to job and job/occupational burnout are the probable roots of career exodus for IT professionals. In several studies, it's depicted that when stress levels surpass the coping abilities of an individual, the results are unfavourable to the organization as the stress related to the employees has been majorly linked to career change intention. A common link found in different studies related to career exodus is that when employees work under lot of pressure which is common IT industry, they start changing careers in order to lessen stress. Based on such evidences, it is expected that overstressed IT professionals may follow suit and change careers (Rathore & Ahuja, 2015). Managers, thus, looking forward and are keen in retaining these IT talent, should work on implementing changes aimed at improving the work/life balance of the employees. Dealing with information technologies for 99% service uptime is very arduous, both physically and emotionally. In an informal interview conducted, it was indicated that this was a principal cause of burnout and stress. In many IT companies, employees are expected to be available on a 24/7 basis, in case of any technical issues. This requires leaving one's home and return to the office during non- working hours to execute backup service or technical maintenance. The most viable solution managers can provide to elude this job burnout is by expounding the boundary between work and home (Ghapanchi & Aurum, 2011).

REVIEW OF LITERATURE

Using Work Addiction Literature to Theorize About Basics of Workaholism

Oates' unique conceptualization of workaholism mirrored an immaculate enslavement point of view as far as both the impulse to work and the level of contention with one's life:

A workaholic is a man whose requirement for work has turned out to be excessive to the point that it makes observable unsettling influence or impedance with his real wellbeing, individual satisfaction, and relational relations, and with his smooth social working (Oates, 1971; p. 4).

Two exceedingly compelling models in our comprehension of behavioral addictions are the disorder model of habit (Shaffer et al., 2004) and the segment model of enslavement (Griffiths, 2011). Though the previous has been most useful in understanding forerunners and helplessness, the last gives a structure whereupon the key basic components of dependence can be caught on. The parts display draws on Brown's (1993) hedonic administration demonstrate and has been to a great extent enlivened by the symptomatic characterization of phobic behavior. As per this structure, a someone who is addicted presentations indications that speak to each of the accompanying segments: subjective and additionally behavioral remarkable quality (i.e., the action commands one's considerations as well as conduct), state of mind change (i.e., the conduct is utilized as an approach to alter inclination), resistance (i.e., the expanding measure of time required to acquire a similar involvement with the action), withdrawal side effects (i.e., feeling contrary feelings when the action is halted or decreased), backslide and restoration, and loss of control (i.e., the need to come back to a similar level of utilization in the wake of attempting to stop, and losing control over the utilization), and strife (i.e., the conduct clashes with everything in the individual's life, for example, connections, work, as well as training) (Griffiths, 2005).

Workaholism

The word "workaholism" has been interpreted from diverse standpoints viz. nature of work, working hours etc. Definitions (Buelens & Poelmans, 2004; Harpaz & Snir, 2003; Scott, Moore, &Miceli, 1997) say that workaholics spend more time on their work which leaves them psychologically or cognitively fatigued with passage of time. Moreover, they perpetually keep thinking about work when not even at work, ending up in relatively high level of emotional distress and physical complaints.

"Workaholism" and "workaholic" was first interpreted by Oates in 1971. He defined a "workaholic" as "somebody who is so obsessed with work that it creates conspicuous disturbance to health, personal happiness and social functioning". Several other researchers (Cherrington, 1980) have termed different workaholic types with both positive and negative connotations that are in nature both mixed and conflicting. Some researchers (Schaef and Fassel, 1988) with a broader understanding of the subject have quoted that organizational factor play a dominant role in development of Workaholism traits in employees as it is observed that organizations are keen in rewarding workaholics or workaholic behaviour. Employees putting in long hours at work, spending an extra time on job apart from normal office hours, are remunerated with acknowledgments and better career prospects. The fact also stands true for such organisations where extra working hours or workaholic behaviour are considered as a requisite for growth and innovation and are preferred by executives majorly over being or going back early at home (Dasgupta and Gupta, 2009).

Diverse Working Conditions and Work- Related Stress

Nevertheless, of a huge portion of research on individual types of employee's well-being, for example, burnout, work engagement, job satisfaction, furthermore, workaholism is very less thought about on how they may affect each other after some time. How employees feel at work may affect their conduct at work, and furthermore over the long haul (Vogt, et.al 2016).

For both hypothetical and handy reasons, it is imperative to know the potential outcomes of diverse sorts of employee well-being, and furthermore in examination with each other. Environment at workplace is one of the popping elements of external stress factors. In lieu of this, prior researches have revealed that excessive stress and anxiety at job, job dissatisfaction and high work-family conflict experienced by employees are mainly swayed by contextual components. Such toxic work environment can have catastrophic effects on its employees. It is also seen that workaholics put lot of effort in their work, are very stubborn, look for perfection in everything (not restricting it to job) and do not believe in task delegation that in turn creates a lose- lose situation between him and his co-workers. Former definitions have concerted on the frequent non- work consequences that go with workaholism. Robinson (2000) illustrated the individualities of workaholism as being similar to that of alcoholism, i.e. being progressive in nature, an unconscious attempt to resolve unmet psychological desires which can lead to irrepressible life, fragmentation of family, severe health complications and death too". An important facet of the overall concept is that workaholic behaviours are not driven by external needs rather it is internally based. Relatively to the three-segment approach by Maslach et al. (2001), others have contended that job burnout may best be lessened to an unsocial regular torment, to be specific exhaustion (Sinha, et.al, 2014). Conversely, the empathy weakness structure characterizes burnout as a unidimensional build including an absence of prosperity, negative demeanours toward work, or an absence of self-acknowledgment (Reddiyoor & Rajeswari, 2017).

Based on available literature and introspection on severe working conditions in today's organizations, the present study has made an appropriate effort in incorporating work conditions and working attitudes to explore the relationships between perceived or appraised work stress and anxiety among IT professionals in Delhi/NCR.

Demographic Variables and Work-Related Stress

Cox (2010), defined stress as a "perceptual phenomenon arising from a comparison between the levels of demand put on a person versus his ability to cope." The degree to which a stress is experienced by an individual in a particular situation will contrast due to personal factors. When talking on the demographic grounds, researches show that young workers are most likely to be less satisfied with their present jobs than older workers (Srivastava, 2011). Stress is an emotional state of fear and threat that has physical, mental and behavioural consequences. It is practically proved that people usually perform well when they are encouraged, challenged and invigorated rather than being threatened by facets of the work environment that are sometimes over arduous in some way. Gender difference similarly has one of the dynamic roles to play in understanding work-related stress and anxiety due to diverse demands rising from job. Men and women account diverse reactions to work-related stress, both physically and psychologically. Number of researchers put forward that though the probability in women reporting symptoms of clinical depression or anxiety disorder related to work-related stress is high, they are doing a better job in connecting and involving themselves with others which at times are imperative as stress management strategies (Shimazu, Schaufeli &Taris, 2010).When compared to men, 80 percent of them who had high psychological job demands were found to be at greater risk of depression and anxiety disorders than the one with lower demands. It was also observed that nearly half of the depression or anxiety disorder cases were diagnosed at age bracket of 30-35, which was directly related to workplace stress and high job demands condition.

Workaholism Phenomenon, Work Related Stress, Job Conditions: Internal Validity

The expression "workaholism" was begat by Oates (1971), who depicts it as "the impulse or the wild need to work unendingly" (p. 11). This early portrayal involves two center components which return in most later meanings of workaholism: working too much hard and the presence of a solid, compelling internal drive (cf. McMillan, O'Driscoll, and Burke, 2003). The previous focuses to the way that obsessive employees have a tendency to assign an excellent measure of time to work and that they work past what is sensibly anticipated that would meet hierarchical or financial prerequisites. The last perceives that compulsive employees relentlessly and every now and again consider work, notwithstanding when not working, which recommends that compulsive employees are "fixated" with their work. Truth be told, these two components—that speak to the behavioural and subjective part of workaholism, individually—allude to the very inception of the term workaholism which was intended to compare to liquor addiction. We concur with Porter (1996, p. 71), who approaches understudies of workaholism to "... come back to the root of the term as a beginning stage for future research". She places that workaholism ought to be translated as a habit, that is, as intemperate and industrious conduct with unsafe outcomes, along these lines barring sees that think about workaholism as a positive state (e.g. Machlowitz, 1980; Scott, Moore, and Miceli, 1997; Spence and Robbins, 1992). In our view, compulsive employees work harder than their employment medicines require and they put substantially more exertion into their occupations than is normal by the general population with whom or for whom they work, and in doing as such they disregard their life outside their occupation. Ordinarily, they work so hard out of an internal impulse, need, or drive, and not in light of outer factors, for example, budgetary prizes, profession points of view, hierarchical culture, or poor marriage.

Work related stress or burnout is an analogy that is usually used to depict a condition of mental exhaustion. In spite of the fact that there is some discourse about the idea of burnout, the most broadly utilized conceptualization begins from Maslach (1993), who depicts work related stress as a three dimensional develop that comprises of: (1) depletion (i.e. the exhaustion or depleting of mental assets); (2) skepticism (i.e. apathy or a removed state of mind towards one's employment); and (3) absence of expert viability (i.e. the propensity to assess one's work execution adversely, bringing about sentiments of deficiency and poor occupation related confidence). It has been assessed that more than 90 for every penny of the examinations on work related burnout utilize the Maslach Burnout Inventory that depends on this three-dimensional definition (Schaufeli and Enzmann, 1998, p. 71). The way that reviews on burnout and workaholism are for all intents and purposes lacking is all the more surprising on the grounds that as of now 20 years prior it was proposed that workaholism may go about as the underlying driver of burnout since unreasonably and quickly working representatives go through their mental assets, abandoning them exhausted and "wore out" (Maslach, 1986). Plainly, this dispute suggests that workaholism and job burnout are distinctive constructs that can likewise be separated observationally.

The idea of job conditions evolved from researches on job burnout, to be specific as an endeavour to cover the whole range running from employee unwell being to representative prosperity. Not at all like the individuals who experience the ill effects of burnout in job, drew in representatives have a feeling of vivacious and powerful association with their work exercises and they consider themselves to be ready to bargain well with the requests of their employment. All the more particularly, Schaufeli, Salanova, González-Romá, and Bakker (2002a) characterize work engagement as a positive, satisfying, work-related perspective that is portrayed by: (1) energy (i.e. elevated amounts of vitality and mental strength while working, the eagerness to put exertion in one's work, and determination additionally even with challenges); (2) commitment (i.e. a feeling of criticalness, eagerness, motivation, pride, and test); and (3) retention (i.e. being completely moved and fascinated in one's work, whereby time passes rapidly and one experiences issues with withdrawing oneself from work). Job conditions and job burnout are reasonably adversely related. As of late, it was discovered that fatigue and energy and additionally negativity and devotion each traverse a measurement that may be marked activation and distinguishing proof, individually (González-Romá, Schaufeli, Bakker, and Lloret, 2006). Up until this point, the connection between job conditions and workaholism has not been considered. Be that as it may, interviews with drew in representatives who scored high on energy, commitment, and assimilation recommend that they are not dependent on work (Hallberg, U. & Schaufeli, W.B., 2006). Dissimilar to workaholics, they appreciate getting things done outside work, they don't feel regretful when not working, and they don't work hard due to a solid and powerful internal drive but since for them work is entertaining.

CONSEQUENCES

Workaholism can adversely impact private relations, recreation and wellbeing (Grzywacz, J.G. & Marks, N.F., 2000). The side effects are like what we see in different addictions, including impacts on temperament, resistance and withdrawal. Studies demonstrate that when one encounters stress at work, people with a solid interior work drive report an expansion in subjective stress-related physical and mental manifestations contrasted with those with low scores (Linley, P.A., Joseph, S., Harrington, S. & Wood, A. 2006; Taris, Schaufeli &Verhoeven, 2005). In this way, it is conceivable that adapting style controls the connection amongst workaholism and wellbeing (Shimazu, Schaufeli &Taris, 2010).

Two examinations have looked facilitate into how workaholism identifies with rest. In one investigation, people with the most elevated scores on workaholism were more probable than laborers with low scores to report rest issues, tiredness at work, and challenges awakening notwithstanding exhaustion in the mornings (Kożusznik, M.W., Dyląg, A., & Jaworek, M.A., 2014). In the other investigation, Andreassen et al. (2011) found that high fanatical work drive was related with a sleeping disorder.

Moreover, investigate demonstrates that compulsive workers report all the more work–family clashes and poorer working outside work than non-obsessive workers (Ho, V.T., Wong, S.S., & Lee, C.H., 2011; Robinson, B.E., 1999). Since time is a restricted asset, it is regular that workaholism affects the household front. Barely any investigations, be that as it may, have been directed with a nearer examination of how workaholism influences the work–family relationship. In a current report that separates amongst positive and negative overflow it was discovered that fanatical work drive was connected to negative overflow amongst work and family (Andreassen, Hetland et al., 2012). Much more, the observations also state that workaholics are slanted to contribute their assets (e.g., time, vitality, consideration, feelings) in work, and paying little heed to whether they fall flat or succeed, will keep on doing in this way, frequently to the detriment of their private and family lives. (Hakanen & Peeters, 2015).

Taken together, it appears that the centre component of workaholism, inside over the top work drive, is related with a few negative side effects (Grant, J. E., et al., 2010; John, O. P., Naumann, L. P. & Soto, C. J., 2008; McMillan LHW, et al., 2001). Work drive has likewise been connected to bring down life and employment fulfillment. Furthermore, it has been exhibited that workaholism is related with diminished mental prosperity, saw wellbeing, joy and self-detailed work execution ((Taris, T.W., Schaufeli, W.B., Shimazu, A., 2010; Shimazu & Schaufeli, 2009).

Motivation of the Paper

In line with the aforementioned research and on the basis of prevailing literature on the concept of "workhaholism", the present study aims at exploring the relationship between anxiety and work-related stress among IT professionals in Delhi/NCR in context with the rampant working culture and workaholism. The study also emphases on the data with reverence to particular industry i.e. IT industry and demographical variables.

The Pertaining Issues in the Study

Firstly, the innumerable underlying scope of workaholism, working culture and job conditions that may impact the multifarious dimensions of work-related stress and anxiety as observed in IT professionals still provides a window for exploration. Secondly, whether the notion of work-related stress and anxiety differs in IT professionals based on age group and marital status, or for the reason that they are working in different industries needs to be addressed.

To attain the basic objective of the study, it's important to have a comprehensive view of:

1. The level of association among the factors of workaholism, work culture and job conditions with anxiety (of growing age) and a person's physical appeal
2. The level of association among the factors of workaholism, work culture and job conditions with anxiety at work and unreasonable distress
3. The level of association among the factors of workaholism, work culture and job conditions with health issues
4. The difference in values of work-related stress and anxiety pertaining to certain demographic variables

RESEARCH METHODOLOGY

Aforementioned issues were raised and examined using multivariate background. The sampling technique used was purposive in nature, as the focus was on particular characteristics of a population which would best enable us to answer our research questions. For this, IT professionals belonging to middle and upper level of hierarchy across different IT companies in Delhi/NCR were contacted. The age group of respondents varied from 30 years to 50 years. All participants were informed about the objective of the study. Data and responses were collected through a structured questionnaire which was mailed across to the professionals. Though initially 250 respondents were approached the final sample size came about to be 200 only. The questionnaire constructed was subjected to factor analysis with oblique rotation to identify underlying constructs or factors. This would further help in explaining the correlations among a set of items.

Measures

The questionnaire included the following four aspects- workaholism, work culture, job conditions and work-related stress &anxiety. All measures were well validated. Each measure used was rated on a 5-point Likert scale (1= do not agree, 5= absolutely agree).

- **Workaholism:** The scale consists of five subscales (a) Obsession for work, (b) Self-sufficiency with no socialization, (c) Exhaustion from work (d) Timeliness (e) Recognition. The alpha coefficient of the scale results in .880.
- **Work Culture:** The scale consists of two subscales (a) Rewarding long working hours and competitive work culture, (b) Fast Growth and organisational culture of competition. The alpha coefficient of the scale results in .760.
- **Job Conditions:** The scale consists of four subscales (a) Disproportionate Job Responsibilities, (b) Unforeseen work (c) Work pressure with no substitute, (d) Travelling. The alpha coefficients of the scale results in .696.

- **Work-Related Stress and Anxiety:** The scale consists of three subscales (a) Anxiety due to growing age (b) Anxiety due to work evolvement, (c) Health issues. The alpha coefficients of the scale results in .848.

Demographic features of the respondents included age, gender, years of service and marital status as mentioned in Table 1.

RESULTS AND ANALYSIS

To explore the associations between fundamental dimensions of workaholism, Work Culture and job conditions with the multifarious dimensions of work-related stress and anxiety observed in IT professionals, certain research questions were constructed that were further analysed through step-wise multiple regression analyses. The independent variables were (a) Factors of Workaholism, (b) Work Culture and (c) Job Conditions. The dependent variable was (a) Work-related stress and anxiety.

Correlation Results

Correlation Analysis which is applied to quantify the association between two continuous variables was run on the data collected as shown in Table 2. The means, standard deviations, and correlation coefficients resulted in factors of Workaholism showing significant positive correlations with factors of work culture and the factors of dependent variable work-related stress and anxiety (with low values). Work culture is significantly correlated to work-related stress and anxiety (though the value of the coefficients is low). Factors of severe job conditions show both positive and negative correlations with work-related stress and anxiety.

Regression Analysis

In the next step, we conducted an additional analysis, Stepwise regression Analysis to see the pattern of associations among the factors of workaholism, work culture and job conditions with the factor of dependent variable i.e., anxiety (with the growing age) and a person's physical appeal. Stepwise regression adds or removes variables based on the t-statistics of their estimated coefficients. Table 3 depicts the variables that resulted as significant predictors of dependent variable.

With the first regression analysis, the variables that came out as the significant predictors for Work-related stress and anxiety are - Obsession for work, Exhaustion from work, Promoting competitive work culture, Disproportionate job responsibilities and Unforeseen load of work. The variables shared 28% variance with criterion variable 'Work related stress & anxiety.' The result depicts that the factors of Workaholism among the independent variables are the stronger predictors of work-related stress and anxiety than the factors of work culture and job conditions. The beta weights of the two significant predictors of Workaholism are .356 and .351, followed by work culture and job conditions. With negative beta weights (-.178 and -.184) of factors of job conditions it illustrates that there exists an opposite relationship between extreme job conditions and anxiety due to growing age and a person's physical appeal.

The second intent of the research was to analyse the level of association among the factors of workaholism, work culture and job conditions with the dependent variable, anxiety at work and unreasonable distress. Another multiple regression was run to get the result. Table 4 illustrates that only two factors of workaholism emerged as the predictor of anxiety at work and unreasonable distress amongst all the independent variables. Further, obsession for work came out as a stronger predictor with beta as .289than self-sufficiency with no socialization with beta value being.184. R^2 is .191that shows the variance shared by both the variables is 19%.

To have a comprehensive view of the strength of association between the factors of workaholism, work culture and job conditions with the dependent variable, health issues stepwise MRA was run on the data available. Obsession for work having the highest beta value (.511) emerged as strong predictors for dependent variable "health issue" followed by the factors of job conditions. Yet again, the factors of job condition "Travelling and Disproportionate Job Responsibilities" emerged as negative predictors of 'work-related stress and health issues.' Another job condition dimension - Unforeseen work demand has emerged as the positive predictor for DV 'health issues'. All the independent variables showed 45% (R^2=.451) variance with the dependent variable- Table 5.

T-Test Results

To have an understanding of the difference in values of work-related stress and anxiety pertaining to certain demographic variables T-test was applied on the data. Table 6 shows the t-test result in terms of marital status of the employees which reveals a significant difference in terms of perception of work-related stress. Work-related stress and anxiety was seen to be significantly higher among unmarried IT professionals compared to married IT professionals. Further, a dichotomous split of employees in the age group between 24 and 35 and 36 to 55 years was done to find the difference in terms of age group. This split was made on the basis of meta-analyses of age in the applied psychology literature (Thomas & Feldman, 2009). The result showed that work-related stress among employees belonging to 24 years to 35years was significantly high as compared to 36 years to 55 years' age group.

DISCUSSION

It is important to know the sampling technique used in the study as it makes the findings understand better. This study is based upon purposive sampling, wherein a researcher chooses to what is to be known and then selects the sample that can provide the exact information by his experience or knowledge (Tongco, 2007). As the objective of the research was in studying IT professionals who work in extreme job environments in Delhi/NCR, purposive sampling was the ostensive choice.

The study provides a perspective wherein workaholism with a definite work-culture and job conditions takes a toll on IT professionals. It entails the workaholic behaviour pattern that cropped up as (a) Obsession for work, (b) Self-sufficiency with no socialization (c) Exhaustion from work (d) Timeliness (e) Recognition is associated to work-related stress and anxiety among IT professionals. Simultaneously, the work-related stress and anxiety scale emerged with three major elements (a) Anxiety due to growing age (b) Anxiety due to work evolvement, (c) Health issues. The result demonstrates that high obsession towards work if reaches an exhaustion level, has the tendency to influence the perception of anxiety about approaching old age or growing age. Even the factor of work culture of the organization i.e. fast growth and organisational culture of competition has its say on increasing anxiety due to growing age and drooping personal looks. If we put together, the second and third regression addressing the workaholic behaviour representing obsession for work, self-sufficiency and no socialization, included with the type of work that leaves a person with mental and physical exhaustion is yet again linked to work-related stress and anxiety among IT professionals. There is a difference in working hard and being addictive towards work and it becomes all the more unlike when signs comprise of being negligent of personal activities, austere conditions of health and excessive qualms for future prospects. Researchers have found that excess of workaholism has negative impact on a person's health leading to too much work stress and job burnout (Chen, Chang & Ching, 2004).

The preceding academic literature shows that workaholic behaviour pattern along with prevailing work culture in the organization have been influencing the stress perceived by IT professionals. Organizations generally set standards for working hence stimulating a work culture wherein the philosophy revolves round rigorous competition thereby takes its toll on employees. The big run today is to be on the top which has become vicious as the positions vacant are now limited than what used to be a decade and a half formerly (Joseph, Gautam & Bharathi, 2015). To stay ahead and competitive, organizations are promoting a culture of hard work and encouraging employees to go that extra mile. Though academic literature is full of evidences (Vansteenkiste et al., 2007) about the negative impact that competitive work culture has on both physical and mental health, one staggering finding has emerged in this study as well. The study resulted in two factors of job dimensions being negative predictor of a particular type of work-related stress (anxiety due to growing age and changing looks). This explains that extreme working conditions in corporate world, disproportionate job responsibilities and unforeseen work do not affect IT professionals with regard to anxiety due to growing age and changing physical looks. People also take travelling with ease (for work) till they do not find it distressing their overall health. Employees especially from service sectors work for long hours and with the augmented usage of highly developed technology it requires one to be available 24*7 even after duty hours. In lieu of this, other studies too have ascertained that although these jobs have high rewarding structures but employees with such demanding jobs are more susceptible to job burnout.

The Dangerous Allure of Extremes

Some findings that stand contrary to considering extreme job conditions as negative are depicting a change in the social phenomenon of perception of work-related stress. Working for more than 60 hours a week has become a typical norm. Employees take pride and feel exalted in working late in the office and are happy in extended travel for office work. The reasons probably could be being highly achievement oriented; believing in the philosophy of being "extreme" and being under competitive pressure (Shahnaz, Zickar & Michael 2006). Though competitive pressures in corporate world are making "extreme" jobs necessary, there has been an upsurge in regard of activities that increases the adrenaline produced in high-stress situations. Second motivating element found stimulating workaholism was the allure of the job. A culture that promotes "extremes" is not surprising as employees strongly endeavour for such passionate jobs. They do not consider these jobs as exploiting them rather they consider these jobs as honourable, appropriate and much wanted. It's surprising that the drift heading extreme is been considered as an advantage to competitiveness. The organization to some extent by trending towards extreme might gain competitive advantage but then putting excess stress on job would crop a contrary effect too.

The study shows that employees in IT sector have comparatively a higher level of work-related stress and anxiety compared to other sector (Bolhari, Rezaeian et.al 2012).The reason perhaps could be the major push been faced by the service sector in Indian that is high compared to other sectors.

Studies previously have shown that IT professionals often agonize from job burnout due to extremely arduous and hectic job conditions (Sonnentag, S. et al, 1994). Marital status and age level as key factors correspondingly make a difference while perceiving stress and anxiety level. The possibility maybe at the earlier stages of career, expectations and desires being high, individuals do not get easily satisfied. Hence, unmarried and younger age group employees go through more stress and anxiety from work compared to married employees. Research shows that being married conveys support and firmness to personal lives of employees with older adults also being able to regulate their temperaments and exhibit an advanced level of emotional intelligence (Goodman, 2011).

Workaholism: Nature, Sources, and Outcomes in the Global World

Workaholism involves (a) disproportionate spending of time and energy on work (b) difficulty in disengagement from work, eliciting negative emotions (c) obstruction and anxiety (d) restricting oneself from socialization (e) leading to low self-esteem, career dissatisfaction, ill-health and job burnout. This has been further described in form of typologies in Table 7. A workplace that puts forth excess work pressure especially business services is found to be moderately related with higher level of drive for work and low level of work enjoyment. On the contrary, a system with supervisors providing flexibility at work is related with relatively less work-family conflict and more job satisfaction among enthusiastic workaholics. Findings have revealed that regardless of gender, work-related stress and work-life conflict or imbalance is correlated with workaholism (Kumar & Siddique, 2011) which meant that gender did not moderate the associations between workaholism with work-related stress and work-life conflict.

The following conclusion of the researches has persisted to be constant across nations, i.e. respondents with a high level of work-orientation worked comparatively more number of hours per week than respondents with low level of work-orientation. The working hours for men stands out to be more per week than for women. Married women spent comparatively fewer hours per week on work than unmarried women, however married men's working hours were than unmarried men per week. Employees of private sector tend to spend more time on work per week than employees from public-sector. It is also observed that employees in the IT sector, particularly women don't remain with a similar association for a long time because of prolonged working hours/odd planning (Patwardhan, 2014). Subsequently, keeping in mind the end goal to maintain a strategic distance from the strain emerging because of tedium, rebuilding of occupations should be possible to suit the people's attitudes and interests by giving some sort of incitement, by limiting distressing perspectives a presenting development arranged settings, enabling representatives to have control over the occupation and accept choices on the position with confined authority.

CONCLUSION

Even though the word "workaholism" has turned into a piece of our ordinary vocabulary, regardless we know minimal about the logical reason for it. Reasons why a few people move toward becoming obsessive workers are most likely various and complex. For the most part, studies demonstrate that workaholism is likened with negative results. To date, no recorded handling mechanism for workaholism exists. The field is in extraordinary need of longitudinal examinations including target parameters of conduct and wellbeing.

The present study aimed to examine the relationship of workaholism with work related stress, work culture and job conditions amongst IT professionals in Delhi/NCR. The results of the current study indicated that workaholism and its components were significantly and positively related to IT professionals' work-related stress. The results of stepwise multiple regressions demonstrated that workaholism could envisage IT professionals' stress towards work. These findings were in line with the results of Kumari, Joshi, & Pandey (2014), Haq (2015). To substantiate these discoveries, it could be noticed that workaholism forced an incredible pressure on employees, the outcome of which was work related anxiety and as the aftereffect of work related anxiety, the individual's physical and mental vitality masticated. This further led to strain, weariness, and burnout and diminished employment fulfillment. IT professionals had various undertakings and because of high workload and a wide assortment of obligations they had, they bear an abnormal state of working pressure. Obsessive worker IT professionals invest a large portion of their opportunity and vitality at work and oblige little time to their life and different issues. Truth be told, these individuals disregarded their need to rest and overlooked different issues identified with their day by day life which may prompt occurrence of some negative feelings affecting one's conduct and development.

Other findings of the current study indicate that workaholism and it components were significantly and positively correlated with IT professionals' work related stress, work culture and job conditions. To justify these outcomes, it can be noticed that workaholics oppose on attempting to enhance themselves and to wind up plainly fulfilled and they look for satisfaction and delight in their work. These individuals have solid inborn inspiration to work, against which they can't help it. This autonomous inspiration may be because of ecological conditions including monetary situations, environment of the organization, pressure caused by one's manager, work advancement and additionally getting away from the family. These individuals invest a little energy to rest and after some time, they end up noticeably depleted cognitively and inwardly. Since they largely are involved in work, notwithstanding when they are not at work, they encounter thoughtful excitement and turn out to be candidly exasperates and accordingly, they for the most part report different mental issue and physical objections. At the point when a man experiences burnout, he/she is for all time worn out, forceful, skeptical, and irate. He/she has negative musings and is irritable and exhausted. He/she ends up noticeably irate with the smallest uneasiness, and is disappointed and feels misery. IT professionals who are anxious to invest a great deal of energy at work enter their work lives into their own lives unintendedly and more often than not misfortune the harmony between their work lives and individual lives. Because of this extreme weariness which is caused to the idea of educating, IT professionals are confronted with burnout manifestations including lessened viability, exhaustion, and investing a great deal of energy at work. Accordingly, obsessive worker IT professionals end up plainly depleted speedier and this thus, may influence the quality of their administration and may prompt disappointment from work. Workaholism is a sort of enslavement which can be charming and in the meantime monotonous and risky to such an extent that a few scientists considered this state as an illness.

In the interim, since workaholics are not willing to delegate their oomph and obligations, they are in struggle with their colleagues and subsequently, their work turns out to be considerably more confounded. At the point when workaholics invest a considerable measure of time in doing their work, their vitality is debilitated and they experience the ill effects of work related stress. In an investigation, Jansi & Anbazhagan (2017) showed that individuals who are associated with their work are more inclined to mental and physical injuries contrasted with others, since they dedicate a ton of mental vitality and time to their work. This implies they disregard their own issues and invest the greater part of their energy at work. Subsequently, the more the force of the work and the more the occupation's requests, the more the employees' exhaustion.

Overall, results showed that with increasing IT professionals' workaholism, they experience more work-related stress and job burnout. Considering the results of the current study, holding training courses for IT professionals to become familiar with the phenomena of workaholism, stress, job burnout, individual and organizational outcomes, methods of dealing with them and managing time effectively (aiding at devoting time to work, family and oneself) is of great importance. It is recommended that other researchers conduct studies to investigate other sectors and also examine the relationship of workaholism with other occupational consequences based on demographic characteristics (gender, age, marital status, level of education, etc.). These studies can be conducted using a qualitative method or both qualitative and quantitative methods. Moreover, since the questionnaires used in this study were developed in other countries, developing such questionnaires in accordance with the condition of our country is highly recommended. Since this study was carried out on IT sector in Delhi/NCR, hence, generalizing its results has its own limitations. Therefore, when generalizing these results to other group of employees and sectors, great caution should be taken.

Inferences of the Study

The outcome of this exploratory study offers some interesting understandings of the variables that shares employees' perception of work-related stress and thereby suggests prospects for future research. The sampling technique was purposive and was drawn from IT companies located in Delhi/NCR, as Delhi/NCR being a metropolitan city and remarkably attracts people from all part of the world. The sample drawn had their work experience not only in Delhi/NCR but also in various parts of Indian cities as well as world. Thus, the findings of the study are supposed not to be just constrained to IT professionals working in Delhi/NCR but also to other employees working under related conditions. Though the concern towards increasing work-life imbalance has been taken up widely by Indian researchers, there still lies a gap in the empirical research concerning workaholism and its influence on Indian IT industry for a competitive business environment. Also, there is a large gamut of literature related to "workhalism" but it remains varied and conflicting till date. Therefore, there is a dire need to comprehend the phenomena of Workaholism and address the attributes of workaholism in depth. Considering Work-related Stress, Job Conditions and Work culture as main predictors of HR Crisis, with increase in work-related stress HR crisis in the organisation increases which means the predictor is positively related to HR crisis and with increase in job conditions and work culture (i.e. improvement in both the predictors) decreases the probability of occurrence of HR crisis which means the predictor is negatively related to HR crisis. Future research may also try and understand the mindset of the current generation with their choice of job and that what kind of training strategies companies follow to cope up with different types of job stress, if any. Studies, by and large, related to attributes of workaholism holds paucity of data in Indian IT context, which further drove the researchers to deep dive and understand the association between workaholism, job conditions, work culture and work-related stress and anxiety. It is generally observed that employees from IT & ITES sector seem to tussle with work-related stress and anxiety comparatively more; thus, organizations predominantly from this sector need to assess their nature of job and the prevalent work culture. Organisations should give an extra effort in development of skills at individual level, to cope with work-related stress and reducing depression and anxiety levels.

CONTRIBUTION OF THE STUDY AND DIRECTIONS FOR FUTURE RESEARCH

Workaholism, being a derogatory term, much of the literature has covered only the external effects of workaholism which therefore calls for further consideration. This study further summarizes its contribution in (a) categorizing the essential dimensions of workaholism, work culture and job conditions (b) determining the association among predictors and outcome variables. (c) Interpreting the difference in work-related stress and anxiety of IT professionals with respect to their age group and marital status. Present study is valued for its uniqueness in examining an imperative occurrence in the context of contemporary realities catering to Indian IT context specifically. The IT sector is frequently pigeonholed with high role stress (Karad, 2010), as the life expectancy of software products and programs keep waning each year, and the stress on employees keeps intensifying due to distinctive environmental pressures (Colomo-Palacios et al., 2014a). The irony is that it is rarely seen that the organizational culture helps employees in dealing with such stresses and its related problems. Research by Colomo-Palacios et al. (2014b) shows that stress also leads to IT career abandonment as the IT industry is more susceptible to prodigious and increasingly prompt changes. In such a scenario, the employees are thus expected to develop skills to learn fast, stay updated to new things, develop skills to work in team and problem solving and reasoning skill. This research thus, endeavours to recognize the working conditions and Workaholism behaviour along with the varying social milieu. Though there are quite a few limitations of this study but this can open a pathway for other researchers to explore other related factors in continuation to the present research. The results generalization as is restricted due to purposive sampling should therefore be treated with cautiousness. This study lost out on a substantial part of the working professionals as it did not include IT population belonging to the lower hierarchy of the organisational chart. Since this research was purely based upon the authors' own observation, it therefore proposes future scope of substantiating the data across industry or sector and including other population sample to the research (family, friends and associates). Generalization of the present study results to other sectors or industries as well as in other countries awaits further empirical examination.

REFERENCES

Andreassen, C. S., Griffiths, M. D., Hetland, J., & Pallesen, S. (2012). Development of a work addiction scale. *Scandinavian Journal of Psychology*, *53*(3), 265–272. doi:10.1111/j.1467-9450.2012.00947.x PMID:22490005

Bolhari, A., Rezaeian, A., Bolhari, J., & Bairamzadeh, S. (2012). Occupational Stress Level among Information Technology Professionals in Iran. *International Journal of Information and Electronics Engineering*, *2*(5), 682–685.

Brown, R. I. F. (1993). *Some contributions of the study of gambling to the study of other addictions. In Gambling behavior and problem gambling*. Reno, NV: University of Nevada Press.

Buelens, M., & Poelmans, S. A. Y. (2004). Enriching the Spence and Robbins' typology of workaholism: Demographic, motivational, and organizational correlates. *Journal of Organizational Change Management*, *17*(5), 440–458. doi:10.1108/09534810410554470

Caplan, R. D., & Jones, K. W. (1975). Effects of Work Load, Role Ambiguity, and Type A Personality on Anxiety, Depression, and Heart Rate. *The Journal of Applied Psychology*, *4*(2), 713–719. doi:10.1037/0021-9010.60.6.713 PMID:1194173

Chen, T. Y., Chang, P. L., & Ching, W. Y. (2004). A study of career needs, career development programs, job satisfaction and the turnover intentions of R&D personnel. *Career Development International*, *9*(4), 424–437. doi:10.1108/13620430410544364

Cherrington, D. J. (1980). *The Work Ethic*. New York, NY: American Management Association.

Colomo-Palacios, R., Casado-Lumbreras, C., Misra, S., & Soto-Acosta, P. (2014b). Career abandonment intentions among software workers. *Human Factors and Ergonomics in Manufacturing & Service Industries*, *24*(6), 641–655. doi:10.1002/hfm.20509

Colomo-Palacios, R., Casado-Lumbreras, C., Soto-Acosta, P., Garcia-Penalvo, F. J., & Tovar, E. (2014a). Project managers in global software development teams: A study of the effects on productivity and performance. *Software Quality Journal*, *22*(1), 3–19. doi:10.1007/s11219-012-9191-x

Cox, T., & Griffiths, A. (2010). *Work-related stress: a theoretical perspective. In Occupational Health Psychology*. Chichester, UK: Wiley-Blackwell.

Dasgupta, M., & Gupta, R. K. (2009). Innovation in Organizations: A Review of the Role of Organizational Learning and Knowledge Management. *Global Business Review*, *10*(2), 203–224. doi:10.1177/097215090901000205

Dhabhar, F. S., Saul, A. N., Daugherty, C., Holmes, T. H., Bouley, D. M., & Oberyszyn, T. M. (2010). Short-term stress enhances cellular immunity and increases early resistance to squamous cell carcinoma. *Brain, Behavior, and Immunity*, *24*(1), 127–137. doi:10.1016/j.bbi.2009.09.004 PMID:19765644

Estes, B., & Wang, J. (2008). Workplace Incivility: Impacts on Individual and Organizational Performance. *Human Resource Development Review*, *7*(2), 218–240. doi:10.1177/1534484308315565

Ghapanchi, A. H., & Aurum, A. (2011). Antecedents to IT personnel's intentions to leave: A systematic literature review. *Journal of Systems and Software*, *84*(2), 238–249. doi:10.1016/j.jss.2010.09.022

Gonzalez-Roma, V., Schaufeli, W. B., Bakker, A. B., & Lloret, S. (2006). Burnout and work engagement: Independent factors or opposite poles? *Journal of Vocational Behavior*, *68*(1), 165–174. doi:10.1016/j.jvb.2005.01.003

Goodman, C. K. (2011). Work stress can strain marriage. *McClatchy-Tribune Newspapers*. Retrieved from http://articles.chicagotribune.com/2011-06-03/travel/ct-tribu-work-stress-marriage-20110603_1_strain-marriage-job-stress-couples

Grant, J. E., Potenza, M. N., Weinstein, A., & Gorelick, D. A. (2010). Introduction to behavioral addictions. *The American Journal of Drug and Alcohol Abuse*, *36*(5), 233–241. doi:10.3109/00952990.201 0.491884 PMID:20560821

Griffiths, M. D. (2005). A components model of addiction within a biopsychological framework. *Journal of Substance Use*, *10*(4), 191–197. doi:10.1080/14659890500114359

Griffiths, M. D. (2011). Workaholism: A 21st century addiction. *The Psychologist. Bulletin of the British Psychological Society, 24*, 740–744.

Grzywacz, J. G., & Marks, N. F. (2000). Reconceptualizing the work family interface: An ecological perspective on the correlates of positive and negative spillover between work and family. *Journal of Occupational Psychology, 5*(1), 111–126. doi:10.1037/1076-8998.5.1.111 PMID:10658890

Hakanen, J., & Peeters, M. (2015). How do work engagement, workaholism, and the work-to-family interface affect each other? A 7-year follow-up study. *Journal of Occupational and Environmental Medicine, 57*(6), 601–609. doi:10.1097/JOM.0000000000000457 PMID:26053362

Hallberg, U., & Schaufeli, W. B. (2006). "Same same" but different? Can work engagement be discriminated from job involvement and organizational commitment? *European Psychologist, 11*(2), 119–127. doi:10.1027/1016-9040.11.2.119

Haq, G.S.S. (2015). A Study on Job Satisfaction Of It Industry Employees. *Innovative Journal of Business and Management, 4*(1), 1–7.

Harpaz, I., & Snir, R. (2003). Workaholism: Its definition and nature. *Human Relations, 56*(3), 291–319. doi:10.1177/0018726703056003613

Ho, V. T., Wong, S. S., & Lee, C. H. (2011). A tale of passion: Linking job passion and cognitive engagement to employee work performance. *Journal of Management Studies, 48*(1), 26–47. doi:10.1111/j.1467-6486.2009.00878.x

Jansi, A.M., & Anbazhagan, S. (2017). A Study on Personality Traits of Information Technology (IT) Employees and Job Satisfaction. *International Journal of Marketing and Human Resource Management, 8*(2), 1–8.

Joseph, S., Gautam, B., & Bharathi, S. V. (2015). An Empirical Study on the Factors Contributing to Work Family Conflict among Young Employees in the IT Companies. *Indian Journal of Science and Technology, 8*(6), 50–60. doi:10.17485/ijst/2015/v8iS6/62919

Karad, C. A. (2010). Job Stress in the Information Technology Sector-The cause and effect analysis. *Journal of Commerce and Management Thought, 1*(3), 247–271.

Karen, L. H., & Julia, L. H. (2002). Workplace Environment in a Professional Services Firm. *Behavioral Research in Accounting, 14*(1), 105–127. doi:10.2308/bria.2002.14.1.105

Kożusznik, M. W., Dyląg, A., & Jaworek, M. A. (2014). The Polish adaptation of the short form of the Dutch Work Addiction Scale. In T. Marek, W. Karwowski, M. Frankowicz, J. Kantola, & P. Zgaga (Eds.), *Human Factors of Global Society: A System of Systems Perspective* (pp. 311–318). New York: CRC Press Taylor and Francis Group.

Kumar, M. S., & Siddique, Λ. M. (2011). A study on occupational stress among IT professionals Chennai. *International Journal of Enterprise Innovation Management Studies, 2*(2), 119–124.

Kumari, G., Joshi, G., & Pandey, K. M. (2014). Job Stress in Software Companies: A Case Study of HCL Bangalore, India. *Global Journal of Computer Science and Technology, 14*(7).

Linley, P. A., Joseph, S., Harrington, S., & Wood, A. (2006). Positive psychology: Past, present, and(possible) future. *The Journal of Positive Psychology, 1*(1), 3–16. doi:10.1080/17439760500372796

Machlowitz, M. (1980). *Workaholics: Living with them, working with them.* Reading, MA: Addison-Wesley.

Maslach, C., Schaufeli, W. B., & Leiter, M. P. (2001). Job burnout. *Annual Review of Psychology, 52*(1), 397–422. doi:10.1146/annurev.psych.52.1.397 PMID:11148311

McMillan, L. H. W., O'Driscoll, M. P., & Burke, R. J. (2003). Workaholism: A review of theory, research and new directions. In C. L. Cooper & I. T. Robertson (Eds.), *International Review of Industrial and Organizational Psychology* (pp. 167–190). New York: John Wiley.

McMillan, L. H. W., O'Driscoll, M. P., Marsh, N. V., & Brady, E. C. (2001). Understanding workaholism: Data synthesis, theoretical critique, and future design strategies. *International Journal of Stress Management, 8*(2), 69–91. doi:10.1023/A:1009573129142

Mohanty, A., & Lalatendu, K. J. (2016). Work-Life Balance Challenges for Indian Employees: Socio-Cultural Implications and Strategies. *Journal of Human Resource and Sustainability Studies, 4*(01), 15–21. doi:10.4236/jhrss.2016.41002

Oates, W. (1971). *Confessions of a workaholic: The facts about work addiction.* New York: World.

Pandey, S., & Sharma, V. (2014). An Exploratory study on Organisational Crisis in Information Technology industry. *International journal of Research in Computer Application & Management, 4*(9), 22-34.

Patwardhan, N. C. (2014). Work-Life Balance Initiations for Women Employees in the IT Industry. In P. Verma & H. Shah (Eds.), *Work-life Balance: A Global Perspective.* Delhi: Wisdom Publications.

Rathore, S., & Ahuja, V. (2015). Examining the impact of Emotional Intelligence on Organizational Role Stress: An empirical study of the Indian IT sector. *International Journal of Human Capital and Information Technology Professionals, 6*(1), 51–63. doi:10.4018/ijhcitp.2015010105

Reddiyoor, N. A., Rajeswari K. S. (2017). Role of Self-Efficacy and Collective Efficacy as Moderators of Occupational Stress Among Software Development Professionals. *International Journal of Human Capital and Information Technology Professionals, 8*(2), 1-14.

Robinson, B. E. (1999). The work addiction risk test: Development a tentative measure of workaholism. *Perceptual and Motor Skills, 88*(1), 199–210. doi:10.2466/pms.1999.88.1.199 PMID:10214644

Robinson, B. E. (2000). Workaholism: Bridging the Gap between Workplace, Sociocultural, and Family Research. *Journal of Employment Counseling, 37*(1), 31–47. doi:10.1002/j.2161-1920.2000.tb01024.x

Schaef, A. W., & Fassel, D. (1988). *The Addictive Organization.* Francisco, CA: Harper Row.

Schaufeli, W. B., & Bakker, A. B. (2004). Job demands, job resources, and their relationship with burnout and engagement: A multi-sample study. *Journal of Organizational Behavior, 25*(3), 293–315. doi:10.1002/job.248

Schaufeli, W. B., Salanova, M., Gonzalez-Roma, V., & Bakker, A. B. (2002a). The measurement of engagementand burnout and: A confirmative analytic approach. *Journal of Happiness Studies, 3*(1), 71–92. doi:10.1023/A:1015630930326

Schaufeli, W. B., Taris, T. W., & Van, R. W. (2008). Workaholism, burnout and engagement: Three of a kind or three different kinds of employee well-being. *Applied Psychology*, *57*(2), 173–203. doi:10.1111/j.1464-0597.2007.00285.x

Schaufeli, W. S., & Enzmann, D. (1998). *The burnout companion to study and practice: A critical analysis*. London: Taylor & Francis.

Scott, K. S., Moore, K. S., & Miceli, M. P. (1997). An exploration of the meaning and consequences of workaholism. *Human Relations*, *50*(3), 287–314. doi:10.1177/001872679705000304

Shaffer, H. J., LaPlante, D. A., LaBrie, R. A., Kidman, K. C., Donato, A. N., & Stanton, M. V. (2004). Toward a syndrome model of addiction: Multiple expressions, common etiology. *Harvard Review of Psychiatry*, *12*(6), 367–374. doi:10.1080/10673220490905705 PMID:15764471

Shimazu, A., & Schaufeli, W. B. (2007). Does distraction facilitate problem-focused coping with job stress? A one year longitudinal study. *Journal of Behavioral Medicine*, *30*(5), 423–434. doi:10.1007/s10865-007-9109-4 PMID:17522973

Shimazu, A., Schaufeli, W. B., & Taris, T. W. (2010). How does workaholism affect worker health and performance? The mediating role of coping. *International Journal of Behavioral Medicine*, *17*(2), 154–160. doi:10.1007/s12529-010-9077-x PMID:20169433

Sinha, V., Abraham, A., Bhaskarna, B., Xavier, K., & Kariat, K. (2014). Role efficacy: Studying the impact on employee engagement, employee motivation and attrition. *International Journal of Human Capital and Information Technology Professionals*, *5*(4), 35–54. doi:10.4018/ijhcitp.2014100103

Sonnentag, S., Brodbeck, F. C., Heinbokel, T., & Stolte, W. (1994). Stressor-burnout Relationship in Software Development Teams. *Journal of Occupational and Organizational Psychology*, *67*(4), 25–32. doi:10.1111/j.2044-8325.1994.tb00571.x

Spence, J. T., & Robbins, A. S. (1992). Workaholism: Definition, measurement, and preliminary results. *Journal of Personality Assessment*, *58*(1), 160–178. doi:10.1207/s15327752jpa5801_15 PMID:16370875

Srikanth, P. B., & Jomon, M. G. (2013). Role ambiguity and role performance Effectiveness: Moderating the Effect of Feedback seeking Behaviour. *Asian Academy of Management Journal*, *18*(2), 105–127.

Srivastava, S. (2011). Analyzing the impact of mentoring on job burnout –job satisfaction relationship: An empirical study on Indian managers. *Paradigm*, *15*(1/2), 48–57.

Taris, T. W., Schaufeli, W. B., & Shimazu, A. (2010). The push and pull of work: About the difference between workaholism and work engagement. In A. B. Bakker & M. P. Leiter (Eds.), *Work engagement: A handbook of essential theory and research*. New York: Psychology Press.

Taris, T. W., Schaufeli, W. B., & Verhoeven, L. C. (2005). Internal and external validation of the Dutch Work Addiction Risk Test: Implications for jobs and non-work conflict. *Journal of Applied Psychology: An International Review*, *54*, 37–60. doi:10.1111/j.1464-0597.2005.00195.x

Thomas, W. H., & Feldman, D. C. (2009). Age, work experience, and the psychological contract. *Journal of Organizational Behavior*, *30*(8), 1053–1075. doi:10.1002/job.599

Tomar, J. S. (2017). Employee Engagement Practices in IT Sector Vis-à-Vis Other Sectors in India. *International Journal of Human Capital and Information Technology Professionals, Volume, 8*(3), 7–14.

Tongco, M. D. C. (2007). Purposive Sampling as a Tool for Informant Selection. *A Journal for Plant. People and Applied Research, 5,* 147–158.

Vansteenkiste, M., Neyrinck, B., Niemiec, C. P., Soenens, B., Witte, H., & Broeck, A. (2007). On the relations among work value orientations, psychological need satisfaction and job outcomes: A self-determination theory approach. *Journal of Occupational and Organizational Psychology, 80*(2), 251–277. doi:10.1348/096317906X111024

Vogt, K., Hakanen, J. J., Brauchli, R., Gregor, G. J., & Bauer, G. F. (2016). The consequences of job crafting: A three-wave study. *European Journal of Work and Organizational Psychology, 25*(3), 353–362. doi:10.1080/1359432X.2015.1072170

APPENDIX

Table 1. Demographic information

S. No.	Demographic Characteristics	Number
1	Average age of the respondents	36
2	Percentage of respondents (male)	88
3	Percentage of respondents (female)	12
4	Average working hours (per week)	64
5	Hierarchy in the company - Middle Management (%)	60
6	Hierarchy in the company - Senior Management (%)	40
7	Married (%)	80
8	Unmarried (%)	10
9	Divorced (%)	10

Table 2. Means, standard deviations, and correlation analysis

Variables	Obsession for work	Self-sufficiency with no socialization	Exhaustion from work	Timeliness	Recognition	Rewarding long working hours & promoting competitive WC	Organizational culture of competition	Disproportionate job responsibilities	Unforeseen load of work	Work pressure with no substitute	Travelling	Anxiety due to growing age	Anxiety due to work environment	Health issues
Obsession for work	1													
Self-sufficiency with no socialization	.396	1												
Exhaustion from work	.312**	.442**	1											
Timeliness	.218**	.189*	.210**	1										
Recognition	.204*	.251**	.009	.211**	1									
Rewarding long working hours & promoting competitive WC	.315**	.051	.054	.101	.342**	1								
Organizational culture of competition	.082	-.031	.007	.113	.392**	.282**	1							
Disproportionate job responsibilities	.348**	.346**	.381	.146	.171*	.239**	.169*	1						
Unforeseen load of work	.271**	.061	.139	.331**	.252**	.425**	.136	.116	1					
Work pressure with no substitute	.481**	.401**	.291**	.354**	.221**	.336**	.124	.372**	.273**	1				
Travelling	-.041	-.082	.031	-.029	-.124	-.114	-.142	-.084	.006	-.044	1			
Anxiety due to growing age	.361**	.134	.351**	.091	.011	.161*	.174*	.079	-.025	.211**	-.049	1		
Anxiety due to work environment	.365**	.310**	.271**	-.021	.142	.182*	-.072	.147	.087	.159*	-.117	.396*	1	
Health issues	.521**	.151	.191*	.216**	.131	.106	-.027	.032	.139	.359**	-.291**	.481**	.250**	1
Mean	8.74	14.28	6.13	12.58	12.11	11.78	7.68	12.73	5.76	9.16	54.84	7.45	8.67	3.9
SD	2.48	4.45	1.95	2.19	2.06	3.05	1.59	3.42	2.25	2.31	15.25	3.35	3.38	2.1
Sig	**p<.000 *p<.05													

Table 3. Stepwise regression-anxiety at work and unreasonable distress as dependent variable and factors of workaholism, work culture and job condition as independent variables

Variables	Standardized Coefficients		
	Beta	T	Sig
Obsession for work	.356	3.917	.000
Exhaustion from work	.351	4.283	.000
Promoting competitive work culture	.213	2.738	.006
Disproportionate job responsibilities	-.178	-2.398	.014
Unforeseen load of work	-.184	-2.275	.021
R2	.284		
F	9.879		

Table 4. Stepwise regression-anxiety (with the growing age) and person's physical appeal as dependent variable and factors of workaholism, work culture and job condition as independent variables

Variables	Standardized Coefficients		
	Beta	T	Sig
Obsession for work	.289	3.508	.001
Self-sufficiency with no socialization	.184	2.279	.023
R2	.191		
F	14.178		

Table 5. Stepwise regression: Work-related stress and health issues as dependent variable and factors of workaholism, work culture and job condition as independent variables

Variables	Standardized Coefficients		
	Beta	T	Sig
Obsession for work	.511	6.712	.000
Travelling	-.287	-4.451	.000
Disproportionate Job Responsibilities	-.234	-3.419	.001
Unforeseen work demand	.189	2.511	.012
R^2	.451		
F	26.032		

Table 6. Comparison of marital status and age group of employees on work-related stress and anxiety

Variables	Marital Status		Age Group	
	Married (N=170)	Unmarried (N=30)	24-35 yrs. (N=90)	36-55 years (N=110)
Work-related stress & Anxiety	M=23.12 S.D.=8.56	M=25.52 S.D.=9.72	M=25.87 S.D.=8.97	M=23.74 S.D.=7.65
T value	-4.954 P<.000		2.45 P<.023	

Figure 1. Typologies of workaholism

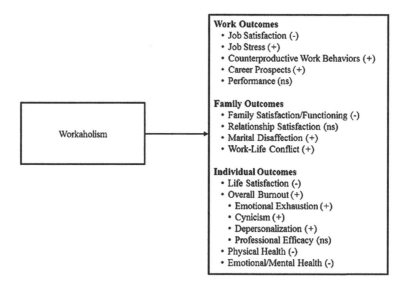

Chapter 12
Analysis of the European ICT Competence Frameworks

Luis Fernández Sanz
Universidad de Alcalá, Spain

Josefa Gómez-Pérez
Universidad de Alcalá, Spain

Ana Castillo-Martinez
Universidad de Alcalá, Spain

ABSTRACT

The rapid evolution and expansion of ICT labor markets requires a common language to manage offer and demand of talent, which is especially critical and complex in a transnational integration scenario like the European Union. Models and frameworks represent useful tools for this purpose. This chapter analyzes the most relevant e-competences frameworks in the European Union (e-CF or EN16234, ESCO, and Body of Knowledge or BoK) as well as their integration and similarities. The present impact of these European frameworks in the ICT labor market and their connection to training and education is presented through data and several examples taken from two EU-funded projects: e-Skills Match and e-CF Council.

INTRODUCTION

Competences, skills, knowledge, job profiles, qualifications or occupations are some of the concepts most commonly used in the present within the IT profession. They can be easily found in all types of information written in e.g. job ads, training courses and CV of jobseekers. Ensuring that these terms are used consistently with a common language is essential for a correct match of needs between employers, job candidates and training providers. When we analyze the case of European Union (EU) where the transnational coordination is a primary objective, this need of a common frame for all actors in ICT employment is urgent and vital for the mobility of ICT people across borders. This is one of the main reasons why EU has promoted different ICT competence frameworks to support a better coordination

DOI: 10.4018/978-1-5225-5297-0.ch012

of the ICT job market where, as it happens in many other developed countries, companies are generally experiencing a shortage of qualified workers to cover their needs of digital transformation of businesses (Hüsing et al., 2015).

The efforts of EU in this area has led to a set of results in the shape of frameworks or competence models. The most relevant ones are the European e-Competence Framework (e-CF) (EN 16234-1, 2016), the European Competence, Skills, Qualification and Occupations (ESCO) classification (European Commission-1) and the European Foundational Body of Knowledge (BoK) (Oliver, 2012). Before continuing it is important to mention that the ICT labor market also considers important the role of certifications. However, there are several reasons why we are not going to devote space to this area in this chapter:

- It is important to point out that certifications are not competence frameworks. We have also analyzed the case of ITIL (Fernández-Balandrón, 2007) which basically is just a model which defines the best practices for IT management. Axelos, the company which manages ITIL, PRINCE and other certifications created under guidance of the UK Government, has launched the Axelos Skills Framework. It has been derived from ITIL and other sources, and embraces a restricted set of skills in Project Management and IT Service Management. Although this framework pretends offering additional value to their certifications, its structure with qualifications, skills/competences and occupations is not exhaustive and is totally inspired in the e-CF Framework mentioned above.
- Certifications are always relevant as sources of information for competences frameworks but they are usually very specific and restricted to the documentation of syllabus and evaluation methods.
- ICT certifications represents a huge number of cases as can be seen in a non-exhaustive non formal catalogue of ICT certifications (http://itcertificationmaster.com/list-of-all-it-certifications/), there are 2313 different IT certifications from 161 vendors/entities.
- Certifications cover a broad range of rigor and quality of design and justification from the worst to the best level something already identified in (García and Fernández-Sanz).

These are the reasons why ICT certifications in general are not considered as sources of information for our analysis of competence frameworks. However, we have also included a short analysis of Axelos Skills Framework to allow readers to also know this case.

As a consequence, we can summarize that the aim of this chapter is to provide a comprehensive view of the above mentioned frameworks and to highlight the need of having a good understanding on such basic and fundamental concepts. But the work does not stop here because an integration of the different views provided by the mentioned frameworks is also needed.

This simple idea of integrating the existing ICT related reference schemes and standards (Fernández-Sanz, et. al., 2017) was the origin of the European Project e-Skills Match (e-Skills Match Project: http://www.eskillsmatch.eu/en/), aimed at providing integrated services for self-assessment of e-Skills and digital competences and further training recommended to reach the target profile as well as market certifications offered by the developed e-Skills platform. It is also directly related to another project, e-CF Council (http://www.ecfalliance.org/) which works with the e-CF Framework to develop training paths for the different competences.

The chapter is organized as follows. The first three sections describe and analyze each of the mentioned frameworks (e-CF, ESCO and BoK) adding a reference to Axelos Skills Framework. Once presented the frameworks, a short section analyzes their similarities and the possible alignment of basic terms coming from the different frameworks. The next section illustrates the impact and utility of these models within the IT profession. We will see how a clear relationship between competence frameworks and the world of education and training can be easily set up as well as an example of the link between competence frameworks and daily practice of recruiters and employers in ICT labor market. The section will also illustrate how the e-CF framework has been linked to qualification profiles and training itineraries as an additional link to ICT labor market needs. The chapter ends with a section on conclusions.

THE E-COMPETENCE FRAMEWORK (E-CF)

The European e-Competence Framework (e-CF) provides a common language to describe and support mutual understanding of the competences required and deployed by ICT professionals, including both practitioners and managers. In 2005, further to the recommendations of the European e-Skills Forum, the CEN ICT Skills Workshop members agreed that national ICT framework stakeholders as well as European ICT industry representatives should consider developing a European e-Competence Framework. ICT framework stakeholders met with representatives from European larger enterprises to carry out this initiative, encouraged and accompanied by the European Commission.

The e-CF version 1.0 was published in 2008 from the outcome of two years e-Skills multi-stakeholder, ICT and human resources experts' work from multiple organization levels. The e-CF version 2.0 was published 2 years later, with dimension 4 fully developed, and accompanied by an updated user guide and a newly developed methodology documentation. The e-CF framework has recently become a standard for the ICT competences in Europe (EN 16234-1, 2016).

This framework is designed to fulfill the requirements of businesses and other organizations and it is based on the following points:

- The e-CF expresses ICT competence.
- The e-CF is an enabler; it is designed to be a tool to empower users, not to restrict them, being them from private or public sector organization, ICT user or ICT supply companies, educational institutions, social partners or individuals.
- A competence can be a component of a job role, but it cannot be used as a substitute for similarly named job titles. Competences can be aggregated to represent the essential content of a job role or profile; moreover, one single competence may be assigned to a number of different job profiles.
- Competence is not to be confused with process or technology concepts. For example, Big Data or Cloud computing represent evolving technologies and they may be included in the e-CF dimension of knowledge and skills.

e-CF is structured from four dimensions that reflect different levels of business and human resource planning requirements in addition to job / work proficiency levels:

- **Dimension 1:** 5 e-Competence areas, derived from the ICT business processes: Plan, Build, Run, Enable and Manage. Plan, Build and Run are core areas whilst Enable and Manage are cross cutting issues referred and related to the former. Each area includes a set of e-Competences.
- **Dimension 2:** A competence is a demonstrated ability to apply knowledge, skills and attitudes for achieving observable results. The e-Competences can then be adapted and customized into differ-

ent business contexts such as e-commerce, e-health, e-banking, etc. According to dimension 2, 40 e-Competences have been identified and described in the e-CF 3.0:

- **Area A:** Plan
  - A.1. IS and Business Strategy Alignment
  - A.2. Service Level Management
  - A.3. Business Plan Development
  - A.4. Product / Service Planning
  - A.5. Architecture Design
  - A.6. Application Design
  - A.7. Technology Trend Monitoring
  - A.8. Sustainable Development
  - A.9. Innovating
- **Area B:** Build
  - B.1. Application Development
  - B.2. Component Integration
  - B.3. Testing
  - B.4. Solution Deployment
  - B.5. Documentation Production
  - B.6. Systems Engineering
- **Area C:** Run
  - C.1. User Support
  - C.2. Change Support
  - C.3. Service Delivery
  - C.4. Problem Management
- **Area D:** Enable
  - D.1. Information Security Strategy Development
  - D.2. ICT Quality Strategy Development
  - D.3. Education and Training Provision
  - D.4. Purchasing
  - D.5. Sales Proposal Development
  - D.6. Channel Management
  - D.7. Sales Management
  - D.8. Contract Management
  - D.9. Personnel Development
  - D.10. Information and Knowledge Management
  - D.11. Needs Identification
  - D.12. Digital Marketing
- **Area E:** Manage
  - E.1. Forecast Development
  - E.2. Project and Portfolio Management
  - E.3. Risk Management
  - E.4. Relationship Management
  - E.5. Process Improvement

- ▪ E.6. ICT Quality Management
- ▪ E.7. Business Change Management
- ▪ E.8. Information Security Management
- ▪ E.9. IS Governance
- **Dimension 3:** Proficiency levels of each e-Competence provide European reference level specifications on competence levels e-1 to e-5, which are related to the European Qualifications Framework (EQF) (European Commission-2), levels 3 to 8 as follows:

The relationship between the proficiency levels of e-CF and EQF is summarized in Table 1.

A proficiency level integrates three facets: context complexity, autonomy and behavior. These three dimensions can be summarized as following:

- Autonomy ranges between "Responding to instructions" and "Making personal choices".
- Context complexity ranges between "Structured – Predictable" situations and "Unpredictable – Unstructured" situations.
- Behavior here represents an observable outcome of attitude and ranges between "the ability to apply" and "the ability to conceive".

Whilst EQF levels represents learning levels, e-CF ones represent the meaningful level of proficiency that a competence can reasonably express. Therefore, a competence can usually be related to no more than 3 e-levels. Some competences make sense at higher levels only; while, some others at the lower ones.

- **Dimension 4:** Exemplificative and not exhaustive samples of knowledge and skills related to each e-Competence. Knowledge and skills are related to competences through some examples. They add value and context, but no list/catalogue is provided.

In summary, e-competences in dimension 1 and 2 are mainly presented from the organizational perspective. Dimension 3 offers a bridge between organizational and individual competences. Dimension 4, with its precise and specific skills and knowledges easily linkable to learning outcomes, can represent a bridge between organization competences and vocational training and qualifications.

The 4-dimension structure of e-CF makes it particularly flexible and valuable for different uses. It provides a pragmatic competence overview of the European ICT labor market from the industry and public sector perspective. It can be used by individuals for self-assess against job roles defined in e-CF

Table 1. Relationship between e-CF proficiency levels and EQF levels

e-CF Level	Related to EQF Level
e-5	8
e-4	7
e-3	6
e-2	4 and 5
e-1	3

competence terminology. It can be used to focus personal development on areas for improvement and, in the same way, understand, find out and match training offers and learning paths.

The ICT profiles cover, at their level of granularity, the full ICT Business process. Structured from six main ICT Profile families, these 23 Profiles reflect the top of a European ICT Profiles family tree, as follows:

- **Family 1:** Business Management
  - Business Information Manager
  - CIO
  - ICT Operations Manager
- **Family 2:** Technical Management
  - Quality Assurance Manager
  - ICT Security Manager
  - Project Manager
  - Service Manager
- **Family 3:** Design
  - Business Analyst
  - Systems Analyst
  - Enterprise Architect
  - Systems Architect
- **Family 4:** Development
  - Developer
  - Digital Media Specialist
  - Test Specialist
- **Family 5:** Service & Operation
  - Database Administrator
  - Systems Administrator
  - Network Specialist
  - Technical Specialist
  - Service Desk Agent
- **Family 6:** Support
  - Account Manager
  - ICT Trainer
  - ICT Security Specialist
  - ICT Consultant

The structure of e-CF is summarized in Table 2.

The e-CF framework is the most popular competence framework in Europe as big effort from European Commission DG Industry supported its design, implementation and testing through several projects. As a consequence of its development, some organizations developed different online tools (e-Competence Quality Self-Assessment Tool; CEPIS; European e-Competence Framework), mainly focused on the self-assessment of ICT user competences and skills. Nevertheless, these online tools do not offer any link to training institutions that recommend training paths for the identified gaps between the candidate's

Table 2. Structure of the e-CF framework

Competences	40
Competence Areas	5
Profiles	23
Proficiency Levels	5
Knowledges	209
Skills	203
Profile Families	6

profile and the target professional profile he/she chose. The connection to competence certifications is also missed as well as the correspondence to other frameworks or references, excepting the EQF.

Finally, the strong points in the framework are the following ones:

- Self-assessment of own ICT user competences
- The identification of ICT user profile is possible starting from competences
- Proficiency levels are linked with EQF
- The framework adopting the "dimension" terminology used by the e-Competence Framework for ICT Professionals
- There are connections with ICT user qualifications.

And the weak points in the framework can be summarized as follows:

- There isn't link with formation institutes, to achieve competence certifications
- There aren't standard ICT user profiles
- The identification of competences isn't possible, starting from ICT profiles.

EUROPEAN CLASSIFICATION OF SKILLS/COMPETENCES, QUALIFICATION, AND OCCUPATION (ESCO)

ESCO is the multilingual classification of European Skills, Competences, Qualifications and Occupations. The European Commission services launched the project in 2010 with an open stakeholder consultation. ESCO is part of the Europe 2020 strategy.

The first version of ESCO was published on 23 October 2013, but it has been gradually developed focusing on sets of sectors to work in occupations, skills and knowledge. This continuous update is needed in order to reflect changes in the European labor market and in education and training. ESCO v1 was launched in 2017, after a complete revision carried out by the sectoral reference groups, groups of experts in each sector selected by the ESCO project secretariat after a public call for applications. The classification is now available free of charge to all stakeholders through the ESCO website.

The ESCO framework was mostly developed to link the gap between the labor market and the world of education and training. Thus, it is possible to minimize the detected mismatch between the skills of jobseekers and the needs of the companies.

The ESCO project is focused on the classification of European Skills, Competences, Qualifications and Occupations, which should be centered in occupational profiles showing the relationships between occupations, skills, competences and qualifications. These pillars are structured hierarchically and interrelated with each other.

ESCO is linked to relevant international classifications, standards and frameworks, such as The Statistical classification of economic activities in the European Community (NACE), the International Standard Classification of Occupations (ISCO) (International Labor Organization) and EQF as some primary inspirational sources or references. However, specificity of some sectors like the one of ICT Services has leaded to decisions which have adjusted the initial common structure and procedures of creation. As an example, NACE classification of economic activity was suggested as guideline for the sectoral breakdown of occupations in all sectors, but in the one of ICT Services was not considered as a good inspiration due to the fact that ICT occupations are transversal by nature and this classification would be not so meaningful.

The ESCO framework can be used to provide different services in several business cases:

- Bridging the communication gap between education and work. Effective communication and dialogue between the labor market and the education and training sector is vital, as the specific occupations, skills, competences and qualifications that people need change over time.
- Online matching of people to jobs. It helps employees to identify new career paths and show what transferable skills they have between occupations. ESCO can enhance recruitment by contributing to better competence-based job matching.
- Enabling mobility. Due to in almost all European countries, employment and career guidance services use different national classifications, mapping them to ESCO increases semantic interoperability. ESCO translates information between different classification systems, functioning as a hub.
- Supporting education and training in the shift to learning outcomes. The standardized terminology proposed by ESCO will facilitate the dialogue between labor market and education and training stakeholders within and across sectors and borders.
- Supporting skills intelligence and statistics. ESCO can serve as a basis for other types of research, such as benchmarking and cross-country comparison.

ESCO identifies and categorizes skills, competences, qualifications and occupations in a standard way, using standard terminology in all EU languages and an open format that can be used by third parties' software.

To facilitate the dialogue between the labor market and the education/training sector, ESCO is structured on the basis of three pillars representing a searchable database in 26 languages. These pillars are:

- **Occupations:** The ESCO occupations pillar contains occupation groups and occupations. An occupation is a grouping of jobs involving similar tasks and which require a similar skills set. An occupation group clusters occupations or occupation groups with common characteristics in a hierarchical way. The initial adopted scheme was the sectoral breakdown that is shown in Figure 1. The first level was structured into four categories: Governance, Management, Development and Operations. A second level was established under each category, except for ICT Governance because it involved a reduced number of occupations (Chief Information Officer, Chief Technology Officer, ICT Market Strategist, etc.). However, the final adopted structure is based on ISCO, the

Figure 1. Sectoral breakdown of ICT services

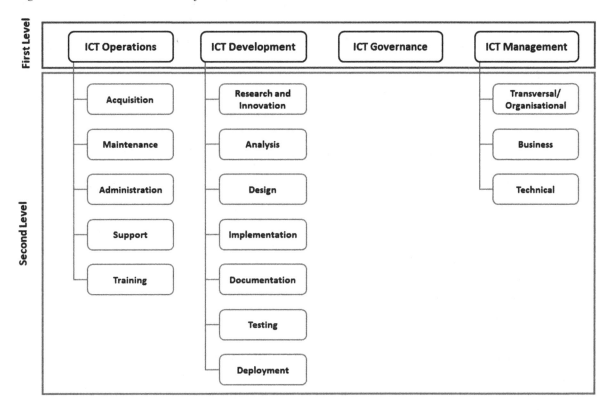

International Standard Classification of Occupations (International Labor Organization NACE) which was implemented by most of European countries in the past.

- **Skills/Competences:** The skills and competences pillar contains skills, competences, knowledge as well as skills and competence group concepts. It also includes other concepts that are frequently used to describe occupational profiles on the labor market, such as tools, materials, hardware, software and work contexts. Work context refers to concepts that can be used to describe the specific context of different jobs that belongs to the same occupation. Work context can, for example, describe a work place, types of company, environmental conditions, products, technologies or business activities. Types of skills and competences:
    - ○ Transversal skills and competences
    - ○ Cross-sector skills and competences
        - ▪ Thinking
        - ▪ Language
        - ▪ Application of knowledge
        - ▪ Social interaction
        - ▪ Attitudes and values
    - ○ Sector-specific skills and competences
    - ○ Occupation-specific skills and competences
    - ○ Job-specific skills and competences

- **Qualifications:** The qualifications pillar contains qualification groups and qualifications. A qualification is the formal outcome of an assessment and validation process which is obtained when a competent body determines that an individual has achieved learning outcomes to given standards. A qualification is defined by:
  - **Category:**
    - National qualifications (indirectly via the EQF portal)
    - Qualifications awarded at national level but regulated at European level (directly in ESCO)
    - (International) qualifications, certificates and licenses linked to tasks, technologies (directly in ESCO)
    - (International) qualifications and certificates linked to occupations and sectors (directly in ESCO)
  - Title.
  - Awarding body
  - Expiring date (optional)
  - EQF level (optional)
  - Definition (optional)
  - Scope note (optional)

The pillars are interlinked to show the relationships between them. Occupational profiles show whether skills and competences are essential or optional and what qualifications are relevant for each ESCO Occupation. Alternatively, the user can identify a specific skill and see which occupation or qualification this skill is relevant to.

The structure of ESCO for ICT Services is summarized in Table 3. As commented, ESCO covers all sectors of economic activities so the global numbers for the whole ESCO structure are much higher: around 3000 occupations and about 13500 skills and knowledge items, including the so-called Cross-Sectoral Skills which are general skills very common to all sectors. Everything is adapted to 26 languages of the European Union.

Finally, the strong points in the framework are the following:

- It is an official labor classification promoted by European Commission and to be adopted in the next future by the employment services of the European countries.
- It is a multilingual classification which will be available in all the official languages of European Union and there is a commitment from European Commission to maintain it in the future.

Table 3. Structure of the ESCO framework for ICT services

Profiles/Occupations	111
Optional Skills/Knowledges	467
Essential Skills/Knowledges	631
Occupation Groups	4
Occupation Subgroups	15
Qualifications	TBD

- It is linked to relevant international classifications and frameworks, such as NACE, ISCO and EQF. In the case of the ICT Services Sector, the e-CF Framework was extensively considered as inspiration and main reference during the work.
- It will be available free of charge to all stakeholders through the ESCO portal.
- ESCO defines the skills, competences, knowledges and other items for a whole list of occupations defined for the ICT Services Sector and just some few examples.
- It provides a specific and extensive catalogue of skills, knowledges and other items for defining an occupation. These items are systematically and specifically created and listed, they are not inferred from a few examples.

The weak points in the framework are the following:

- The qualification pillar in the ICT Services Sector has not been developed in the first stages due to the difficulties of dealing with the huge number of certifications.
- The allocation of skills, knowledges and competences does not allow to specify a qualification level, i.e. there is not an equivalent to the e-CF level or any other similar scale.

THE EUROPEAN FOUNDATIONAL ICT BODY OF KNOWLEDGE (BOK)

The Body of Knowledge (known as BoK) is the complete set of concepts, terms and activities that compose a professional domain, known by the relevant learned society or professional association. The BoK often forms the basis for curricula for most professional programs, setting the essential competencies to get accredited before applying these principles in practice. There are a vast number of Bodies of Knowledge in each area of professional specialization and the ICT field is not an exception. However, despite its high acceptance, there is currently no global or European Body of Knowledge that is all encompassing and which addresses all the ICT knowledge areas required by the industry. This situation is due to, in some cases, several countries have a national ICT BoK adapted to their national context. Besides it is possible to find different BoK on ICT field as outcome from different research projects, as happens with SWEBOK created by the IEEE Computer Society (IEEE Computer Society) and related to the software engineering discipline (Sicilia et al., 2005); with another shape, also the Computing Curricula, created by the ACM IEEE-CS joint committee is a well-known proposal of a set of curricular guidelines on computer sciences (ACM & IEEE, 2013).

These Bodies of Knowledge usually structure the content adopting an industry point of view with the future employability of students in mind or take a purely educational point of view. The European Foundational ICT Body of Knowledge claims to be the base level knowledge required to enter the ICT profession and acts as the first point of reference for anyone interested in working in ICT. BoK is linked to e-CF, since it was created after e-CF was well structured in version 3.0.

The structure of the Foundational ICT Body of Knowledge could be described as an 'inverted T-model'. In this structure the horizontal axis shows the knowledge areas of the ICT domain, while the vertical axis corresponds to specific knowledge and skills to specialize in one domain. Its structure is summarized in Table 4.

Table 4. Structure of the BoK framework

Job Profiles	28
Knowledge	91
Areas	12
Competences	33

The ICT BoK considers 12 areas and each area includes:

1. List of items required as foundational knowledge necessary under this Knowledge Area.
2. List of references to the e-Competence Framework.
3. List of possible job profiles that require having an understanding of the Knowledge Area.
4. List of examples of specific Bodies of Knowledge, certification and training possibilities.

Finally, the strengths in the framework are the following ones:

- It is a European classification sponsored by the European Commission.
- It is directly related to the e-CF framework.
- It is used as a guide to design and develop syllabus.

The weakness of the framework is mainly that:

- It is not as detailed as needed stakeholders: e.g., the description of the foundational knowledge required in each area is too short.

ITIL- AXELOS Skills Framework

ITIL (Information Technology Infrastructure Library) is a trusted and well-established framework based on global best practices for IT Service Management that focuses on aligning the IT services to the needs of the business. Accordingly, ITIL does not include an explicit description of working position, but it provides guidance to organizations and individuals on how to use IT as a tool to facilitate business change, transformation and growth.

ITIL's IT Service Management Best Practice is supported by a qualification scheme that enables individuals and organizations to demonstrate their abilities in adopting and adapting the framework to address their specific needs. The ITIL Qualification Scheme provides a modular approach to the ITIL framework, and is comprised of a series of qualifications focused on different aspects of ITIL best practice.

The scheme structure provides a clear progression from Foundation through to Intermediate, Expert and Master whilst allowing you to focus on the aspects that are most relevant to your role.

The ITIL guidance covers the entire service lifecycle from the identification of business then IT requirements, to designing and embedding a solution to maintaining the new service through continuous review and improvement.

The successful adaptation of ITIL can help to improve services through different ways:

- Managing business risk and service disruption or failure.
- Improving and developing positive relationships with customers by delivering efficient services that meet their needs.
- Establishing cost-effective systems for managing demand for services.
- Supporting business change whilst maintaining a stable service environment.

Actually, the framework in this section is the Axelos Skills Framework. It has been derived from ITIL and other sources, and comprises skills in Project and Programme Management, IT Service Management, leadership and personal management. It provides individuals with a framework for self-assessment and to help them to identify the priorities for personal development. For organizations, it provides a management tool to help align professional development alongside the organization's goals.

The ITIL service design stage of the ITIL service management framework offers global best-practice guidance to IT practitioners and business leaders wanting to move their IT strategy forward. This step-by-step approach to planning focuses on quality and efficiency, leading to robust IT services that will stand the test of time.

ITIL's IT Service Management Best Practice is supported by a qualification scheme that enables individuals and organizations to demonstrate their abilities in adopting and adapting the framework to address their specific needs. In this aspect, the ITIL framework is structured on the following pillars:

- **Qualifications:** The qualifications pillar contains qualification groups and qualifications.
- **Skills/Competences:** The skills and competences pillar contains skills, competences, knowledge as well as skills and competence group concepts.
- **Occupations:** The ITIL occupations pillar contains occupation groups and occupations.

Each skill represents a unique dimension of work, such as risk management or leadership, and provides recognizable descriptions of the main behaviors that an individual demonstrates when operating effectively. Each skill is defined at up to five different levels which represent the full range of responsibility/autonomy:

Level 1: Intern / Entry level. Works primarily under supervision with responsibility for carrying out routine work.

Level 2: Practitioner. Works independently, primarily in non-complex situations, and may take some responsibility for the evaluation and improvement of work activities.

Level 3: Professional / Manager. Works independently where there is unpredictable change; may manage others and be responsible for reviewing and developing performance of themselves and others.

Level 4: Lead Professional / Senior Manager. Manages complex technical or professional activities or projects, taking responsibility for decision-making in complex and unpredictable work; takes responsibility for managing professional development of individuals and groups.

Level 5: Executive. Manages and transforms work contexts that are complex, unpredictable and require new strategic approaches; takes responsibility for contributing to professional knowledge and practice and/or for reviewing the strategic performance of teams. Recognized as an expert by other professionals.

The structure of ITIL-Axelos is summarized in Table 5.

Table 5. Structure of the ITIL-Axelos framework

Occupations	50
Occupation Groups	2
Occupation Subgroups	9
Qualifications	5

It is worthwhile to highlight that certifications like ITIL are not competence frameworks. In the case of ITIL it is just a model which defines the best practices for IT management. In addition, the structure is not equivalent to the rest of the frameworks (it does not include common terms such as competences, occupations, areas, etc.). It is only a proposal for a certification in a very specific area in the universe of occupations in ICT. ITIL is included in this chapter since certifications are always relevant as sources of information for competences frameworks. However, they are usually very specific and restricted to the documentation of syllabus and evaluation methods. On the other hand, as can be seen in a non-exhaustive non-formal catalogue of ICT certifications (IT Certification Master, 2017), there are 2313 different IT certifications from 161 vendors/entities. This represents a vast number of certifications where there is a broad range of rigor and quality of design and validation from the worst to the best level, something already identified in (Fernández-Sanz, García-García, 2006).

As a result. the strong points in the framework are the following ones:

- The classification is related to a well-known certification.
- Unlike ITIL as a certification, the AXELOS model classifies occupations (CIO, Systems Analyst, Service Manager, etc.) instead of classifying roles. The ITIL documentation only considers roles in the IT service management area such as Service Support Manager, Problem Manager, Service Desk Supervisor, etc.

The weak points can be summarized as follows:

- It does not address many other areas of the IT profession like software development, consultancy, technical/business high level management, etc.
- It is not a competence model: it is just a model which defines the best practices for IT management complementary to the ITIL.
- The structure is not so similar to the rest of the models.
- It is only a proposal for a certification within the huge number of them existing in the market (IT Certification Master, 2017).

ALIGNMENT OF CONCEPTS COMING FROM THE DIFFERENT FRAMEWORKS

As mentioned before, having several different frameworks may cause confusion instead of helping to clarify things to stakeholders in the ICT labor market as well as in the training and education side. Once the four main competence frameworks have been described, this section tries to link/align the different concepts that are used in each one. For example, an ESCO occupation and an e-CF profile refer to similar concepts although they are different terms. Table 6 shows the correspondence of terms among the different standards and frameworks.

Another important point for the comparison is that all the analyzed frameworks use "dimensions" to describe and categorize their contents. They are all based on description of skills, knowledge or competences. Some of them can describe profiles or occupation; some others include references to qualifications.

The similarities and some existing cross-references among the most relevant frameworks (E-CF, ESCO and BoK) is a good basis for their integration into a common scheme as demonstrated by the e-Skills Match project and its new integrative framework described in (Fernández-Sanz, et. al., 2017). Obviously this is only the initial integration as the real value of the frameworks comes from their links to labor market, recruitment, career development, and training and education as we can see in the next section.

Table 6. Terms comparison

Concept	ESCO	e-CF	ITIL-Axelos	BoK	Comments
Occupation	Grouping of jobs involving similar tasks and which require a similar skills set.	A job profile provides a comprehensive description written and formal of a job	Defines the roles, responsibilities, skills and knowledge required by a particular person. One job description can include multiple roles.	Same as e-CF	They refer to similar concepts
Competence	Proven ability to use knowledge, skills and personal, social and/or methodological abilities, in work or study situations and in professional and personal development.	Demonstrated ability to apply knowledge, skills and attitudes for achieving observable results.	Is a collection of knowledge, personal attributes, skills and relevant experience needed to be successful in a certain function	Same as e-CF	They refer to similar concepts
Skill	Ability to apply knowledge and use know-how to complete tasks and solve problems	It is related to competences through some examples.	Represents a unique dimension of work, and provides recognizable descriptions of the main behaviors that an individual demonstrates when operating effectively.		They refer to similar concepts. BoK does not consider this concept
Qualification	Formal outcome of an assessment and validation process which is obtained when a competent body determines that an individual has achieved learning outcomes to given standards		(ITIL Service Transition) An activity that ensures that the IT infrastructure is appropriate and correctly configured to support an application or IT service.		ECF and BoK do not consider this concept. ESCO and Axelos refer to similar concept
Knowledge	Outcome of the assimilation of information through learning	It is related to competences through some examples.	Knowledge requires an understanding of relationships, knowing how to apply project management in practical situations as well as interpreting methods	High-level areas of knowledge that represent the base level starting ICT professionals should understand. Each knowledge area includes a list of items required as foundational knowledge necessary under that knowledge area.	They refer to similar concepts.
Area	Occupation Group	Occupation families			ESCO and e-CF refer to similar concepts. Axelos and BoK do not consider this concept.
Proficiency level		Reference level specifications on competences		Responsibility autonomy levels	Axelos and e-CF refer to similar concepts. ESCO and BoK do not consider this concept.

UTILITY AND IMPACT OF EUROPEAN FRAMEWORKS
WITHIN THE ICT PROFESSION

The above mentioned frameworks are currently in use in many fields such as companies recruiting ICT people, companies offering training courses, universities, jobseekers, etc. The situation is more interesting in those countries where the frameworks have been adopted earlier (e.g. those ones such as Italy or Netherlands which were the first in translating e-CF into local language and promoting it as local standard before being approved as EN16234).

For example, a Dutch recruitment company called IT-Staffing has analyzed the number of job vacancies per e-CF competence and the number of candidates that declare to have acquired those competences. As can be seen in Figure 2, the number of candidates is in most cases higher than the number of vacancies, which means that the demand is adequately covered by competent and qualified employees. Nevertheless, there are some cases in which the number of job vacancies is higher than the number of candidates. This means that there are not enough people that have acquired those particular competences. More precisely, the 37% and the 8% of the vacancies for the e-CF competences Component Integration and Digital Marketing are not covered by any qualified candidate. A direct consequence of this analysis is the need of tailored training in order to cover the gap for certain e-CF competences between the offer and the demand in the current labor market. Although this is not a comprehensive study (it is based on 16 e-CF competences instead of 40), it represents a practical application of the e-CF framework in a relevant stakeholder. It is a fact that the interest in this kind of frameworks is growing and the trend is that it will be rising in the coming years.

As part of the e-Skills Match project, good results have also come from an extensive research looking for studies/reports on skills demand, job profiles demand, green-IT demand, demand of innovative profiles/skills, etc. The novelty of this research is that the demand has been linked to the e-CF competences in order to distinguish which are the most/less requested e-CF competences according to

Figure 2. Results of the study with data form IT-staffing

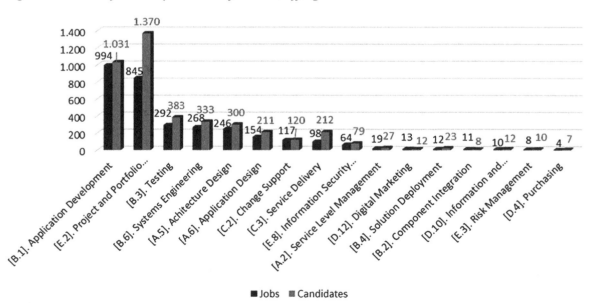

experts and to data coming from job portals and HR companies. This study will also help to find out which type of skills/knowledge gap could exist within the ICT profession. The idea of these studies is to depict the situation of the actual demand for ICT skills (referred to both competences and positions) linked to competences expressed by recruiters and employers as well as the availability of candidates so it is possible to determine which are the most promising profiles and competences to help in career development and employment of citizens.

OF course, it is also possible to use these competence frameworks in order to link competences to training resources such as MOOCs (Massive Open Online Courses) and OERs (Open Educational Resources). This enables the analysis of the existing level of supply of eSkills, both actual and potential future trends, especially based on these online training resources. The results of this analysis are included in the reports of the eSkills Match project although some of them are shown in Table 7.

The analysis addressed a starting list of 2784 courses from an online repository list which were mapped to e-CF. Tt was possible to identify the link of 787 of them to an e-CF competence and level working with the starting list of 4715 tags in the MOOC repository where only 803 of the tags could be connected to the ICT field. Regarding OERs, the final list mapped to e-CF competences has 931 different OERs using a similar procedure.

Another European project involved in exploiting the benefits of the competence frameworks is the e-CF Council Project (e-CF Council Project), a project co-funded by the European Commission through the Erasmus+ Program. Its goal is to develop Competence Qualifications Profiles (CQP), one per e-CF competence, and then design training itineraries oriented to the development of the skills and the acquisition of the knowledge suggested by each particular e-CF competence. The work in the project has already led to relevant results such as the development of specialized training programs for candidates in 15 e-CF competences, the ones most demanded or considered as most important by stakeholders (according to a survey responded by 97 experts). These courses are expected to train 120 people in 4 countries.

This link of the frameworks with the side of training and education is increasingly important. The companies already performing pilot projects of evaluation of the competences of their employees are starting to discover that they need to know the mapping of courses to these competence frameworks when the training providers offer them for covering the detected skill gaps. This represents a challenge for training providers as they need to work with these frameworks and adapt their training design to them. Thus sooner or later companies and training providers will need to adopt these standards ro work with a common language.

We think that this trend will also impact the formal education. Some universities are currently including ESCO/e-CF competence maps in their curricula in order to inform their students about the competences they will acquire if they complete a certain degree: e.g, see the example at (University of Alcalá, 2017). Other very relevant examples are the e-CF-based competence maps provided by the most important certification institutions (e-Competence Quality Label, 2017). They show the e-CF competences acquired when being certified by one of the leading certification providers included in the catalogue published at the website.

Going further the reality on ICT competence frameworks at European level, there is already relevant expressions of international at other international levels. Japanese representatives have been in contact with actors experienced in e-CF to join efforts for better defining models and aligning their classifications/standards to the e-CF framework. Some Chinese companies have already shown interest in using these standards with pilot projects to enhance the professional development of their employees. It is important

Table 7. e-CF competences ordered according to their number of MOOCs

e-CF Competence	MOOCs	OERs
B.1.Application Development	628	86
D.11.Needs Identification	560	16
D.10.Information and Knowledge Management	524	18
D.12.Digital Marketing	393	8
A.9.Innovating	375	36
A.6.Application Design	294	70
D.3.Education and Training Provision	273	56
A.5.Architecture Design	258	21
E.9.IS Governance	233	167
A.8.Sustainable Development	171	37
A.3.Business Plan Development	99	32
E.8.Information Security Management	99	46
A.7.Technology Trend Monitoring	70	26
E.4.Relationship Management	47	100
D.1.Information Security Strategy Development	46	94
E.3.Risk Management	41	42
B.5.Documentation Production	40	8
B.6.Systems Engineering	40	82
E.2.Project and Portfolio Management	40	50
B.2.Component Integration	27	42
C.1.User Support	21	23
E.7.Business Change Management	21	51
C.3.Service Delivery	19	19
D.9.Personnel Development	18	37
E.6.ICT Quality Management	18	47
A.4.Product Service Planning	17	32
B.3.Testing	14	16
D.2.ICT Quality Strategy Development	12	21
D.8.Contract Management	12	18
B.4.Solution Deployment	8	21
A.1.IS and Business Strategy Alignment	7	25
E.5.Process Improvement	5	69
D.4.Purchasing	4	77
C.4.Problem Management	1	74
D.7.Sales Management	1	43
A.2.Service Level Management	0	33
C.2.Change Support	0	12
D.5.Sales Proposal Development	0	33
D.6.Channel Management	0	60
E.1.Forecast Development	0	68

to notice that this convergence would benefit all the stakeholders such as companies, employees, and training providers. A common language based on competences would make easier finding jobs, posting clear job ads, performing general studies by researchers, etc. independently of the country and sector.

CONCLUSIONS

e-Skills or ICT competence frameworks have come to stay because they solve real problems in the daily practice of HR management in ICT. That is the reason why the authorities of the European Commission have committed funds and support to develop these frameworks as a way to overcome clear barriers to European intra-mobility of ICT professionals as well as to ease the matching of profiles to job market needs. The frameworks are providing a common language which is already allowing clearer matching of demand and offer of talent in job portals. They are also helping HR departments to organize career paths and internal training plans with the goal of achieving a better fit of qualifications of employees to the recommended profile for each occupation or position.

Obviously, these frameworks are not simple in terms of elements as they need to map a lot of items on skills, knowledge and occupations (literally hundreds). Even the typical 40 competences of e-CF could be too many elements if no supporting tools and help are available for users. First tools have been too much focused on the automated support to self-assessment of competences through specialized online forms (e.g. the cases of CEPIS e-competence benchmark, Empirica tool, etc.). However, the contribution of new projects, like e-Skills Match (http://www.eskillsmatch.eu/en/), is based on their support to the three pillars needed for a practical solution in the management of ICT competences:

- **Competences:** Assessment and profiling functionality to help job candidates to know themselves in terms of competences, to discover their strengths and weaknesses in relation to a target occupation and to develop their competence-based portrait for recruiters and HR department
- **Training:** Recommendation of training courses and resources (expressed as MOOC or OER) mapped to e-competences, mostly the ones which are below the recommended level for the occupations targeted by a job candidate or an employer: this implies mapping training outcomes to e-competences, a trend which will rise rapidly in the next years reaching both in-company training as well as regular education, including universities.
- **Employment:** Functionality for connecting competences profile and evidences of merits (training, experience, etc.) of candidates with an attractive showing option in the shape of e-portfolio mapped to the competence frameworks. This allows employers to directly match their job profiles (if expressed with e-competences) with the available candidates in the system (those who obviously have granted access to their CVs).

Once the support to these three pillars could be widely implemented and the HR departments started to adopt it (as some big organizations are already doing: e.g. Poste Italiane, Huawei, Indra, etc.), we will see an explosion in the use of the European frameworks in the daily practice of HR in ICT. This is obviously going to happen in Europe (as authorities and standards will push it) but also globally: currently stakeholders in China and Japan are starting to collaborate with Europe in connecting these ideas and frameworks with their own models or practices.

REFERENCES

CEPIS. (n.d.). *e-Competence Benchmark*. Retrieved July 2017, from https://www.cepisecompetence-benchmark.org/survey/survey/index

e-CF Council Project. (n.d.). Retrieved July 2017, from www.ecfalliance.org

e-Competence Quality. (n.d.). *e-Competence Certificates*. Retrieved July 2017, from http://www.e-competence-quality.com/certification-profiles/

e-Skills Match Project. (n.d.). Retrieved July 2017, from http://www.eskillsmatch.eu/en/

EN 16234-1:2016. (2016). *e-Competence Framework (e-CF) – a Common European Framework for ICT Professionals in All Industry Sectors – Part 1: Framework. European e-Competence Framework. e-CF 3.0 Profiling tool on-line*. Retrieved July 2017, from http://www.ecompetences.eu/e-cf-3-0-and-ict-profiles-on-line-tool

European Commission. (n.d.a). *ESCO: European Classification of Skills/Competences, Qualifications and Occupations*. Retrieved July 2017, from https://www.ec.europa.eu/esco/portal/document/en/8e9cf30d-9799-4f95-ae29-e05c725b24c7

European Commission. (n.d.b). *European Qualifications Framework*. Retrieved July 2017, from http://ec.europa.eu/ploteus

Fernández-Balandrón, C. (2007). ITIL: Information Technology Infrastructure Library. *BIT Numerical Mathematics*, *160*, 46–49.

Fernández-Sanz, L., & García-García, M.J. (2006). The human factor in software engineering. *Eur. J. Inform. Prof., 7*(1).

Fernández-Sanz, L., Gómez Pérez, J., & Castillo-Martínez, A. (2017). e-Skills Match: A framework for mapping and integrating the main skills, knowledge and competence standards and models for ICT occupations. *Computer Standards & Interfaces*, *51*, 30–42. doi:10.1016/j.csi.2016.11.004

García, M. J., & Fernández-Sanz, L. (2007). Opinión de los profesionales TIC acerca de la formación y las certificaciones personales. *Novatica*, 32-39

Hüsing, T.,Korte, W. B., & Dashja, E. (2015). *e-Skills in Europe Trends and Forecasts for the European ICT Professional and Digital Leadership Labour Markets (2015-2020)*. Empirica Working Paper, November 2015.

IEEE Computer Society. (n.d.). Retrieved July 2017, from http://www.computer.org

International Labour Organization. (n.d.). *International Standard Classification of Occupations*. Retrieved July 2017, from http://www.ilo.org/public/english/bureau/stat/isco/

IT Certification Master. (n.d.). *The List of Certifications*. Retrieved July 2017, from http://www.itcertificationmaster.com/list-of-all-it-certifications

Joint Task Force on Computing Curricula Association for Computing Machinery IEEE-Computer Society. (2013). *Computer Science Curricula 2013. e-Competence Quality Self-Assessment Tool*. Retrieved July 2017, from http://www.eskills-quality.eu/results-downloads/self-assessment-tool

NACE. (n.d.). *Eurostat Statistics Explained*. Retrieved July 2017, from http://www.ec.europa.eu/eurostat/statistics-explained/index.php/Main_Page

Oliver, G. R. (2012). *Foundations of the Assumed Business Operations and Strategy Body of Knowledge (BOSBOK): An Outline of Shareable Knowledge*. Sydney: Darlington Press.

Sicilia, M. A., Cuadrado, J. J., García, E., Rodríguez, D., & Hilera, J. R. (2005). The evaluation of ontological representation of the SWEBOK as a revision tool. *Proceedings of the 9th Annual International Computer Software and Application Conference (COMPSAC)*, 26-28.

University of Alcalá. (n.d.). *Mapa competencial basado en los marcos europeos e-CF y ESCO*. Retrieved July 2017, from https://www.uah.es/export/sites/uah/es/estudios/.galleries/Archivos-estudios/MU/Unico/AM133_11_1_3_E_MasterDireccionProyectosUAH-mapa-eCF.pdf

Chapter 13
Competence E–Assessment Based on Semantic Web:
From Modeling to Validation

Mounira Ilahi-Amri
PRINCE Research Laboratory, Tunisia

Lilila Cheniti-Belcadhi
PRINCE Research Laboratory, Tunisia

Rafik Braham
PRINCE Research Laboratory, Tunisia

ABSTRACT

In light of trends toward increased requirements for skilled workers, e-assessment presents many challenges. It should address learners' real performance in life. Recognizing the inadequacy of current traditional knowledge-based assessment systems in higher education to achieve performance visibility, we need to rethink how we design new assessment systems that can respond to the corporate requirements of the twenty-first century and mirror the learners' competences. This concern has not been sufficiently investigated. This chapter considers the competence-based assessment. The authors explore the importance of competency and competence modeling conceptual understanding. The research reviews the benchmark literature on the concepts, models, and approaches of competence and competency and explores the confusion surrounding the pair of concepts. They propose a service-oriented framework for competence-based e-assessment to validate the above proposals. The experimentation results support the research goals and learners received a competence-based assessment, which they appreciated.

INTRODUCTION

In recognition of changes to the typical patterns of working life, Higher Education in overall the world is currently laying great stress on Competence-based learning. This is receiving attention particularly on competence-based development to improve the learner's potential value within lifelong learning and

DOI: 10.4018/978-1-5225-5297-0.ch013

universities are currently looking for the best way to competently manage learning. Nevertheless, while lifelong learning is increasingly influencing university and workplace in overall the world, some critical issues still have to be worked out so as to reach its full potential (Ilahi, Cheniti-Belcadhi, & Braham, 2013). Since, it appears to address the assessment expectations of these competences.

The continued growth and importance of this issue is shaping the new learning environments, posing new challenges, fostering the need for new models and approaches both at the learning and assessment levels. Hence, we are now confronted with the challenge to accomplish the initiated shift to a competitive and competence-based educational system in order to guarantee productivity and high quality. To attain such ambitious goal, learning has to fundamentally move from input-based to outcome-based approach. Nowadays, technological, economic, and organizational changes entail new needs for an educational system more responsive and open to the labor market's requirements. To meet the challenges of worldwide increasing competition and to improve the employability of graduate students, education should provide learners with not only knowledge, skills, and competences but also with the proof that these learners could reveal the competences they are supposed to perform in the labor market. Thus, promoting a more dynamic and future-oriented interaction between labor demand and education supply which is evidently the great challenge for the educational system. To establish this interaction, there is a need for mechanisms such as competence models and related assessment tools, which can be used for enhancing the fluency of the key competences of learning and assisting the development of a range of valuable services, e.g. personal and professional development, competence-based learning and employment opportunity exploration.

Although implemented in different ways, current learning management systems share a core common weakness: the assessment process is mainly knowledge-based. This paper presents a comprehensive analysis of competence/y based approaches in the existing literature. The results show that these approaches are far from being able to afford the learner with his valid acquired competence profile. Competence-based assessment is still insufficiently implemented or even not addressed. The findings of the analysis are meant as a starting point for our work aiming at modeling and implementing a new assessment system providing learners with their acquired competences profiles.

Accordingly, we discuss in this paper academic Competence based assessment approach; a formal approach of assessment characterized by the convergence of lifelong, formal, non formal and informal competence-based learning.

Following the introduction, the remainder of the paper is structured as the following: In section 2 we describe the theoretical background on the concepts, models and approaches of competence and competency and explores their relationship to one another. Section 3 reviews relevant related works on and presents the essential findings that could be retained through the comparative study in section 4. We argue that a proper competence modeling solution would increase the efficiency of competence-based learning and competence-based assessment. In section 5, we provide our approach towards competence Web-based assessment modeling using semantic Web. Section 6 presents the related service oriented architecture. The experimental results and the system evaluation are described in sections 7 and 8. Finally, section 9 summarizes the main conclusions of this research and outlines the future research.

THEORETICAL BACKGROUND

Though the rapidly increasing number of related work published in recent years, the theoretical grounding is still weak as a whole, especially in the introduction of concepts. In fact, the concepts of competence and competency are almost used substitutably without distinction. Hence, we introduce in this section the theoretical background of the paper, including the definitions of the concepts competence, competency and the competence-based assessment.

Competence

Competences are treated from different point of views and in an open sort of contexts to enlighten the required abilities for successful actions and efficient management of knowledge and skills (Ivanova & Chatti, 2011). The European Commission (2007) defines competence as a combination of knowledge, skills and attitudes appropriate to a given context. In (Cheetham & Chivers, 2005), competences are defined as 'overall, effective performance within an occupation, which may range from the basic level of proficiency to the highest levels of excellence'. The proposed definition does emphasis that the concept of competence is built on three dimensions:

- A person's competencies - knowledge, skills, attitude, or any psychomotor or mental activity which may require mastery (Cheetham & Chivers, 2005);
- An occupation, which may range from hobbies and sports to professions; we prefer to use the commonly used term context instead;
- The proficiency level of a person with respect to a context;

As persons may have various occupations, they may have various levels of competence for each occupation. For instance, Ahmed might excel in his occupation as a software engineer, but his qualities as a networks engineer are mediocre. Yet, there is an overlap in the knowledge and skills required for both professions, and skills learned in the former profession might increase competence in the latter profession.

Key competences are considered those which all individuals need for personal fulfillment and development, active citizenship, social inclusion and employment (Ivanova & Chatti, 2011).

As (Kou, Jia, & Wang, 2013) states, the model of competence refers to the cluster of competencies for a specific job, the grading behavior standard of each competency and its matching degree to a specific job.

The key dimension of the concept is the specific job. As enlightened by (Ivanova & Chatti, 2011), the behavior standard of the same competency differs according to different occupational contexts. Hence, in order to make the competence model fit for a particular post, (Kou, Jia, & Wang, 2013) argues that the specific jobs should be categorized and picked out, which is often based on analyzing the core value chain of a given firm and clearly identifying occupational categories, occupational families, occupational grades, and occupational positions. The second component of the concept is the cluster of competencies. The third one is the grading behavior standard of each competency and its matching degree to the specific job.

Competency

At present, there are several definitions of the term competency. The HR-XML Consortium states that competencies are "measurable characteristics" (HR-XML Consortium, 2007), and makes out that "some competencies can be objectively measured, whereas others may only be subjectively recognized". The competencies are discerned by their types, the most common are regarded as: basic, generic and specific. The components are broken down into three levels such as: general competency, the unit of competency and elements of competency. The specification is, as the name entails, principally orientated towards business employment and recognition. Nevertheless it is easily adaptable towards educational and training contexts.

Though the competency definition has not reached unanimity over the years, competencies are commonly conceptualized as measurable patterns of knowledge, skills, abilities, behaviors, and other characteristics (KSAOs) that differentiate high from average or poor performance (Rodriguez, Patel, Bright, Gregory, & Gowing, 2002).

The educational model of competency is one of the UNESCO recommendations to support lifelong learning and competency developing. A competency model is a set of competencies, often arranged into some clusters for a specific intention. The competency model is a detailed description of behaviors which employees need in order to have the ability to be effective in a job. Fundamentally, we may regard the competency model as a set of success factors which contribute to achieving high performance and concrete results. The authors in (Schoonover,Schoonover, Nemerov, & Ehly, 2000) argue that the competency model is important because it provides a road map for the range of behaviors that produce excellent performance.

Competence vs. Competency

In light of the differences in the core connotations of competency model and competence model, we argue that the two conceptions should be distinguished and we provide the following figure to highlight this distinction.

This finding is in line with existing research and the literature refers to it as "input competencies" and "output competences" (De Coi, Herder, Koesling, Lofi, Olmedilla, Papatreou, & Siberski, 2007; Ivanova & Chatti, 2011). This builds on the fact that the term competence is seen as an output-based approach focusing on the requirements of a certain job profile and the term competency as an input-based approach correlated to the behavior that should be acquired to carry out the task or job.

Figure 1. Competency vs. competence
Ilahi, Cheniti-Belcadhi, & Braham, 2013.

Further evidence for the distinction between competency and competence models is provided by (Kou, Jia, & Wang, 2013) who points out that "the comparison and identification of competency and competence shows that the two concepts are evidently different in the core connotation and research method."

This research work has led to the choice of the competence model as a basis for the production of our competence Web-based assessment approach.

Competence-Based Assessment

The value of an e-learning management system strongly depends on the proof that learners could reveal the competences they are supposed to perform. Hence, there is currently a growing body of literature about the role that electronic assessment and feedback is playing in the Higher Education sector (Whitelock, Gilbert, & Gale, 2013). In the traditional learning, assessment is usually based on knowledge through objective evidence or essay. In the competence-based learning, assessment could be based on competence rules if any, but mainly in the evidence testing through demonstrations, product design, simulations and portfolios.

Grant (1979) describe the competence based assessment as a "form of assessment that is derived from a specification of a set of outcomes; that so clearly states both the outcomes — general and specific — that assessors, students and interested third parties can all make reasonably objective judgments with respect to student achievement or non-achievement of these outcomes; and that certifies student progress on the basis of demonstrated achievement of these outcomes".

Accordingly, we refer hereinafter to the Competence-Based Assessment as the process of assembling evidence and building judgments on whether competence has been reached. The aim of such an assessment is to verify that an individual can act upon the standard expected in the workplace, as expressed in the related approved competence standards.

RELATED WORK

We discuss in this section proposals having the same goal or theme of this work. Owing to the increasing number of publications on competence/competency-based approaches, this review cannot be exhaustive. In the following we review some representative works.

The authors in (Paquette, Rogozan, & Marino, 2012) address the issue of competency comparison, providing some heuristics to match the competencies of users with those involved in task-based scenario components (actors, tasks, resources). Competencies are defined according to a structured competency model based on domain ontology. The provision of the context for recommendation is done through a learning scenario model.

The work in (Magdaleno-Palencia, García-Valdez, Castañón-Puga, & Gaxiola-Vega, 2011) proposes a model for the study of personalized hypermedia systems with a competency approach. The competency model is used to adapt the course material to the student's needs. The goal is to help students learn and thus reach a suitable competency level.

A review of the main definitions of competence in literature of different application fields is provided in (Sampson & Fytros, 2008). Based on the analysis of the different competence definitions, the authors adopt the following generic definition: "a competence can be defined as a set of personal characteristics (e.g. skills, knowledge, attitudes) that an individual possess or needs to acquire, in order to perform an activity within a specific context, whereas performance may range from the basic level of proficiency to the highest levels of excellence."

The aim of the research in (Nitchot, Gilbert, & Wills, 2012) is to contribute a competence-based system which recommends itself to learners, in order to get appropriate study materials as links from the Web without communication from the teacher's side. The proposed model draws on the (COMBA) model (Sitthisak, Gilbert, & Davis 2008). A 'Competence' within COMBA is composed of an 'Intended learning outcome' and 'Context'. An intended learning outcome is a particular combination of capability and subject matter. 'Capability' indicates what the learner will be able to do with the subject matter of the e-learning objective. 'Context' can refer to a tool and a situation. However, this model gives no consideration to assure the competence-based assessment process.

Another work in (Dolog, Thomsen, Thomsen, & Stage, 2010) describes an experience in building up and teaching Web engineering skills as part of the masters programme in software engineering at Aalborg University. The authors describe how they have incorporated various training on Web engineering related topics into the software engineering masters degree programme. The context in which this training happens is project oriented problem based learning. It's well argued that due to the inherent properties of problem based learning, this teaching style provides more competence based learning and deeper understanding required by industry and also necessary for those students pursuing a research career.

A methodology supported by a technological framework to facilitate communication about informal learning between businesses, employees and learners can be also found in (García-Peñalvo, Johnson, Ribeiro Alves, & Minovic, 2013). This includes a cloud personal learning network, which integrates a portfolio system and institutional tools such as an institutional environment, a repository, and a competence catalogue. It allows the institution to draw formal and non-formal actions in light of the informal learning that is taking place, and to match students to others with similar interests according to their informal learning activities, interests, and development.

Another study conducted in the software industry (Colomo Palacios, Casado-Lumbreras, Soto-Acosta, García Peñalvo, & Tovar Caro, 2013) aims to investigate competence gaps among software practitioners. The authors contrast the 360-degree feedback results and self-evaluations with that of standard competence levels. The authors argue that the results of the research are very valuable to organizations immersed in software development projects.

The Personal Learning Environment (PLE) project in (Ivanova & Chatti, 2011) has showed that students do not possess all needed competences for self-organization, self-learning and self-cognition that would impact the effectiveness of their learning. The aims of the work are to explore the students' competences profiles and their capabilities for behavior activities to organize and plan learning according to a given learning situation and to examine the functionality of a PLE to facilitate the achievement of missing competences. A competences model for personal and professional development is created after a literature review of key competences for engineers and lifelong learners and after gathering the students' opinion through many surveys.

As above enlightened, current specifications focus on the modeling of competencies (not competences) and they miss important information that should be included, such as proficiency level and context. In this perspective, the work in (De Coi, Herder, Koesling, Lofi, Olmedilla, Papatrcou, & Siberski, 2007) addresses the problem of competence representation and exchange. The authors provide a representation of competences, relationships among them and competence profiles. Such a model allows advanced algorithms for competence and profile matching.

However there is no information provided within the latter works to conceptualize the competence-based assessment process.

The authors in (Najjar, Derntl, Klobucar, Simon, Totschnig, Grant, & Pawlowski, 2010) introduced PALO (Personal Achieved Learning Outcome) a data model for capturing information that enables management and exchange of personal data on achieved learning outcomes (knowledge, skills, competences). The Personal Achieved Learning Outcome schema describes the relations between achieved learning outcomes, context where outcomes are achieved, and evidence records of the gained learning outcomes. Information on levels like proficiency level of learner mastering for the learning outcomes are also captured.

In (Alsinet, Barroso, Béjar, & Planes, 2009) authors present a formal knowledge representation model to define a competence-based student-centered education model. The aim of the assessment process is to determine the degree of realization of competences developed by students during the execution of some continuing education activity. The proposed approach uses ontologies as formal knowledge representation model to help teachers in developing an evaluation plan of education activities oriented to determine the degree of competence achievement. The model is composed of five main classes: Student, Assignment, Submission, Grade and Indicator. Nevertheless we think that, similarly to the previous one, this model is rather educational oriented than assessment oriented as it doesn't include some relevant concepts related to the assessment process. As well, this work doesn't consider any distinction between the terms competence, competency and knowledge.

Some other projects in this field are: the TENCompetence Project (Berlanga, Sloep, Brouns, Bitter-Rijpkema, & Koper, 2008), which affords a set of tools to support lifelong learning; and the MyElvin Project (García-Peñalvo, González-González, & Murray, 2012), among others.

These initiatives stand for a step forward to the modeling of competence-based systems. Some of them address very well the issue of competency/competence modeling and achieve the tasks for which they were conceived with respect to the requirements specified by their authors. Nevertheless, we spot some drawbacks in each one of these approaches. As revealed in the following section, while almost all these publications have made efforts to afford competency or competence models, only a minority provided some efforts to grant the distinction between the two concepts, of which and for the best of our knowledge no one provided appropriate assessment Framework based on the proper competence conceptualization.

COMPARATIVE STUDY

Having reviewed different competence Web-based approaches, we propose in this section to compare them based on a set of criteria that we define in the following:

Criterion 1 (C1): Competency/Competence

This criterion is to show if the discussed approach is about competency, competence or doesn't make a difference between the two concepts.

Criterion 2 (C2): Modeling Approach

This criterion c2 is to provide the used model representing the proposed approach. We, particularly, focus on the use of Semantic Web technologies at the design phase as they provide models which are useful for creating a network of data and enable the representation and the dynamic construction of shared and re-usable content.

Criterion 3 (C3): Use of Formal Description

This criterion is about specifying whether the system uses a formal approach to define the different functionalities in a system-independent and re-usable manner, which allows their application in different contexts.

Criterion 4 (C4): Competence Based Assessment

This criterion is to see if the discussed work presents a tool satisfying the competence Based e-assessment functionality based on the proper competence conceptualization (Distinction between the two key concepts of competency and competence, exploit of semantic modeling approach and use of formal description).

Table 1 compares the different competence Based e-assessment approaches according to the already established criteria. An investigation of this table leads to the following deductions:

- The majority of the competence Based e-assessment approaches don't take into account the distinction between the two key concepts of competency and competence.
- The Semantic Web technologies such as ontologies are not employed by most of the discussed approaches.
- All the competence Based e-assessment approaches are domain-specific since they use no formal definition.
- None of the discussed works has provided appropriate assessment Framework based on the proper competence conceptualization.

To sum up, literature did not afford a general system which is able to support Competence Web based Assessment in a convincing way. This was taken into consideration when designing and developing our Competence Web based assessment system. Thus, we try to design and develop a competence Based e-assessment approach that meets the above discussed criteria.

As revealed in this table, it appears also that though the increasing amount of competence-based approaches related papers published nowadays, modeling approaches are rarely tackled. Accordingly we focus on this issue by using ontologies to efficiently enable sharing and reuse through real-world semantics.

Table 1. Competency and competence addressed aspects in the literature

	Competency/ Competence	Modeling Approach	Formal Description	Competence-Based Assessment
Kou, 2013 [65]	+/+	None	-	-
Paquette, 2012 [91]	+/-	Ontology	-	-
Nitchot, 2012 [86]	-/+	XML-schema	-	-
Ivanova, 2011 [71]	+/+	None	-	-
Magdaleno-Palencia, 2011 [69]	+/-	None	-	-
Sampson, 2008 [100]	-/+	None	-	-
De Coi, 2007 [66]	+/+	Object Model	-	-
Alsinet, 2009 [4]/	-/+	Ontology	-	-
PALO, 2010 [84]	-/+	Data Model	-	-
Trailer, 2012 [28]	-/+	None	-	-

COMPETENCE-BASED ASSESSMENT

Scenario Description

For our scenario (Ilahi, Cheniti-Belcadhi, & Braham, 2013) we consider the example of a learner who has just finished his computer science study at university and is looking for a job: he wants to work as a software engineer. He looks for job advertisements and information about companies' requirements and how much he has to learn to be fit for the role. It is not difficult to find job offers in the computer science industry, but quite often specific competences are required.

He needs to have a proof of his real competences within concrete job situations. He searches the Internet to find information and sources about specialization/postgraduate courses, software and applications or Web agencies that offer advice and tips about careers and trainings.

He has a TOEIC certificate from an accredited Language Center. He has also a CISCO IT Certificate. Accordingly, he wishes a formal recognition of these learning opportunities to provide him greater visibility and therefore potential value in the labor market.

Our framework should offer online competence Web based assessment tests to give him his acquired competence profile. Every Competence Item is scored based on his associated evidence. The framework must help him, as a job candidate, to prove his competences by taking assessments, helping better find validated skills. Thus, to enable him sharing his competences profile with third-party applications as social or recruitment systems.

The framework must then present:

- The list of the best job offers that may be of interest, sorting them by relevance and respect to his preferences
- And the gap report between his acquired competence profile and those required

If desired, it might:

- Offer recommendations to access to online or training courses to improve his level of competences
- Give him updates on the status of his applications after any re-assessment of his potential competences. That is, a "Tracking System" for all his job applications.
- And send assessment scores and potential recommendations to prospective employers.

Based on the competence-based assessment results, the university issues the learner a formal and recognized certificate that provides evidence of his gained competences.

Competence-Based Assessment Process

To illustrate the proposed scenario, we provide the following workflow. Such workflow is depicted in Figure 2 and consists on:

- The learner, after signing up, is asked to pick out his potential competences in a predefined competence referential. This information is stored in his portfolio.
- If available, the learner attaches to the Evidence Collector his related Evidence(s).
- The framework proceeds to the review of the provided evidence(s) in the light of the picked competences. It skips over selected competences for which the learner has provided accepted evidence and find out what he should attest further. Decision on which competences need further evidence is made. The mandatory list of corresponding competence-based assessment tests, to confirm whether the picked competences are really acquired, is then presented to the learner.

Upon selection of a competence-based assessment test:

- If the learner is seeking for potential recommendations to prepare himself for the test, these recommendations are provided.
- If not, the assessment test is launched.

After consulting his result, the learner could make the decision to redo the Assessment Test and/or take another mandatory Assessment Test until his satisfaction by the awarded results and/or doing all the mandatory tests. To maximize their potential, all participants are provided with equivalent opportunities to redo the Assessment Tests.

The system provides to the learner an extra option of adding further competence(s) to the referential. In such a case, the learner is redirected to a page containing a form where he has to complete the information of the new suggested competence(s) as well as his potential evidence(s). The add would be pending until potential validation by one of the enabled tutors.

- The certified acquired competence profile is then provided to the learner
- If interested, the system provides insights into the most relevant required competences profiles in the labor market associated with the corresponding gaps, taking into account his acquired competence profile.

Figure 2. Competence-based assessment process

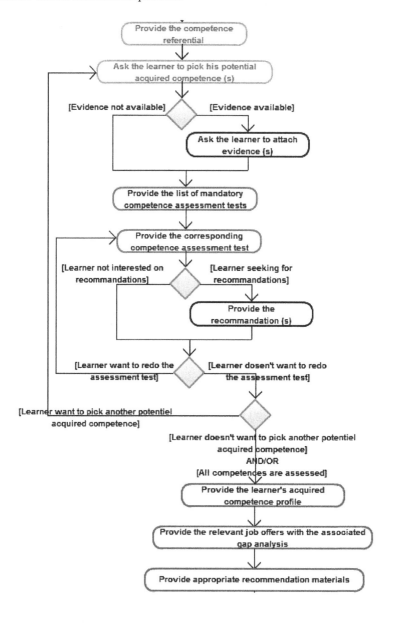

Competence-Based Assessment Model

The Figure 3 provides an overview of the proposed model in an ontological form since ontologies grant a common framework that enables data, information and knowledge to be shared and reused across applications and communities. Ontologies have been subject of recent research in Web-based assessment in (Cheniti-Belcadhi, Henze, & Braham, 2008). However this was typically knowledge oriented. In this work, we use ontologies to model competence Web-based assessment. Our viewpoint is that competence-based assessment environments will be based on contextual check of provided evidence(s) and resources based on a semantic web approach to enable the provision of the acquired competence profile. For a coherence

Figure 3. Competence web-based assessment model
Ilahi, Cheniti-Belcadhi, & Braham, 2013.

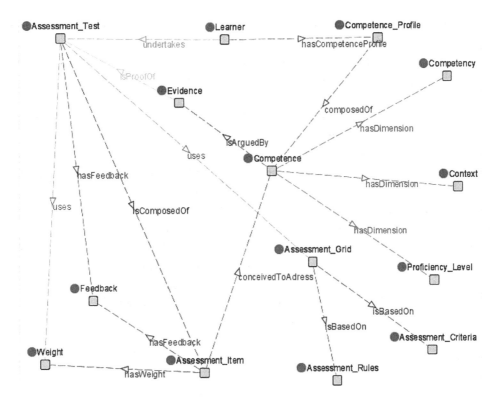

purpose, our assessment model is built on a well-structured conceptual base, which might serve as the foundation both for large scale and classroom assessments. The assessment model could be translated as follows: A Learner has a Competence Profile which is composed of competences. Each Competence consists of a Competency that he/she performs in a given Context with a mastered Proficiency Level. Every Competence is argued by some Evidence(s). These evidences are the proof of an Assessment Test which is comprised of a set of Weighted Assessment Items. Each Assessment Item is conceived to address one or more competences. To deliver the appropriate Feedback, the Assessment Test uses an Assessment Grid which is based on Assessment Criteria and Assessment Rules.

At the heart of our model are four core components. These are: Assessment Item, Evidence, Assessment Grid and Feedback. Assessment Items are the main focus of the system. Assessment Items need to be well arranged for each one of the depicted competences in order to be efficient for the assessment process. They could be categorized according to competences items. Within our proposed model evidence could range from classroom-based assessment to large-scale standardized assessment of competence levels; for example the Amideast or Cisco organizations. This could be: Recognized certifications, practical demonstrations, publications, written tests, projects, and simulations. Competence-based Assessment Grids have two main benefits; they reveal the competence-based expectations for learning. Moreover, they grant a common basis for the competence-based assessment process. The assessment process should provide Feedback to learners on their progress towards the achievement of their competences. Feedback will enable learners to recognize where they have done well and indicate what they could improve on, as well as arguing the assessment awarded score.

Competence-Based Assessment Scenario Model

To assist the development of our approach towards competence-based assessment, we provide the following typical competence-based assessment scenario. To allow reusability and sharing, the model is built upon an ontological structure enabling the formalized representation of the assessment process. Figure 4 shows the proposed scenario model which is composed of the five following phases;

- **Initialization:** During this step the necessary elements for the competence-based assessment process are established. This includes definition of the competence referential, assessment grids, criteria, rules, as well as provision of the assessment tests.
- **Self-Assessment:** This step reflects the learner's personal statement on his potential competences. This provides him the opportunity to give feedback on the success of his lifelong learning activities. It also helps the learner decide when he is ready for the assessment of a competence.
- **Evidence Analytics:** We adopt learner-centered and lifelong learning-oriented approach to the collection of evidence. These evidences are later analyzed to fairly and reliably judge competences.
  - ○ **Evidence Collection:** The learner has to argue his decisions through providing the related evidence. He gathers evidence with regard to the picked competences through the self-assessment stage. This evidence could be from formal, non formal and informal contexts. This information is stored in his portfolio.

Figure 4. Competence-based assessment scenario model

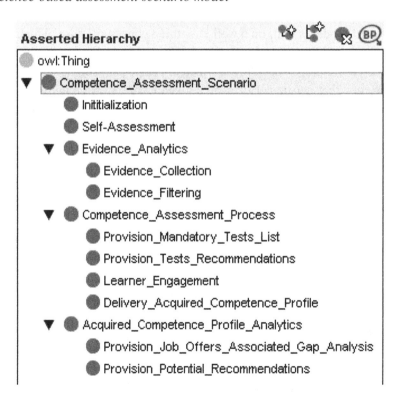

- ◦ **Evidence Filtering:** The objective is to identify which competences are effectively acquired among the picked competences. This relies on the confidence rating of the associated evidence. If the provided evidence is judged unreliable, the associated competence would need further demonstration to be validated. In such a case, the system affords an assessment test to check the related competence. The consideration of the "confidence rating" is currently an item of future work.
- • **Competence-Based Assessment Process:**
  - ◦ **Provision of List of Mandatory Tests:** After making the decision on which competences need further evidence, the mandatory list of corresponding competence-based assessment tests is presented to the learner.
  - ◦ **Provision of Tests and/or Recommendations:** In this stage competences requiring further verification are subject to assessment tests. Upon selection of a test from the proposed mandatory list, the learner could be assisted if he wishes with a recommendation material. Otherwise, the assessment test is launched.
  - ◦ **Learner Engagement:** In the light of his obtained results, the learner decides which of the competences he would further attest. In such a case, another additional test is proposed. To support competence-based assessment decision-making, this process is constantly feasible until his satisfaction by the awarded results and/or doing all the mandatory tests. The assessment decision process is thus iterative, integrative and participative. The goal is to provide a variety of opportunities for learners to demonstrate their competences.
  - ◦ **Delivery of the Acquired Competence Profile:** Finally, the system checks if the obtained results comply with the acquisition of the related competences and provides the validation of the acquired competence profile. The acquired profile includes all learner competences within, formal, non formal and informal contexts.
- • **Acquired Competence Profile Analytics:**
  - ◦ **Provision of Relevant Job Offers Associated With Gap Analysis:** The acquired competence profile allows the system to carry out gap analysis in the light of the available required competence profiles. Related relevant job offers are the provided.
  - ◦ **Provision of Potential Recommendations:** Comparison of the resulting acquired profile with existing required profiles directs to decisions on what training or learning activities could fill the identified gaps.

Though some blueprint do exist, to the best of our knowledge there has been no prior explicit formulation of this model, nor a concrete application or empirical assessment, as presented in this paper. It supports the awareness of employability competence-based requirements by detailing the learner's acquired competence profile so that it becomes clearer and easier to judge the convenience of the graduate learner to the proposed posts. This provides powerful support to both learners and stakeholders.

SERVICE ORIENTED ARCHITECTURE FOR COMPETENCE E-ASSESSMENT

Current trends in Web based assessment systems are towards flexible and scalable approaches that can be applied to a wide range of domains and can be further expanded to incorporate more enhancements.

Recently, Service Oriented Architectures (SOAs) have been used to build modular and flexible systems, and some research works developed new distributed e-learning and assessment approaches, such as SWAP-Learn (Cheniti-Belcadhi, Henze, & Braham, 2008). The service-oriented paradigm has a universal support and is promptly gaining wide recognition within the industry since it relies on a simplified mechanism and uses open standards to connect distributed applications regardless of the technology behind. This empowers flexible orchestration of services through automatic selection, interoperation of existing services, and execution control. Further, it raises application performance, and reduces costs of deployment, testing and maintenance. Hence, we propose this architecture in Figure 5 for Competence based Assessment in a cloud computing environment.

The proposed architecture of this research is inspired from the one in (Cheniti-Belcadhi, Henze, & Braham, 2008). A detailed description of this architecture is available through a workflow in (Ilahi, Cheniti-Belcadhi, & Braham, 2014a). In this section, all functions of the Competence based Assessment scenario, depicted in (Ilahi, Cheniti-Belcadhi, & Braham, 2014b), are modeled as services. We present here the used Web services by providing the description and their interactions;

- **Login Service:** The authentification of learners is accomplished through the login service, which checks the learner's identifications and transfers them to the other services.
- **Competence Referential Provider Service:** This service has to provide the learner with a visualization of the existing competence referential.
- **Evidence Analytics Service:** This composite service adopts a learner-centered and lifelong learning-oriented approach to the collection of evidence. These evidences are later analyzed to fairly and reliably judge competences. It relies on the execution of both:
  - **Evidence Collection Service:** This service helps the learner to argue his/her decisions through providing the related evidence. He/she gathers evidence with regard to the picked competences through the self-assessment stage. This evidence could be from formal, non formal and informal contexts. This information is stored in his/her portfolio.
  - **Evidence Filtering Service:** The objective of this service is to identify which competences are effectively acquired among the picked competences. This relies on the confidence rating of the associated evidence. If the provided evidence is judged unreliable, the associated competence would need further demonstration to be validated. In such a case, the system affords an assessment test to check the related competence. The consideration of the "confidence rating" is currently an item of future work.
- **Connector Service:** This is the mediator service. It enables communication between all other services, except for the login and competence referential provider services.
- **Competence Assessment Service:** This service is composed of two sub-services:
  - **Assessment Delivery Service:** After making decision on which competences need further evidence, the assessment delivery service is invoked to provide the learner with the corresponding assessment test.
  - **Grading Service:** This service receives the response from the learner, evaluates it, assigns a score, changes the state of the related competence and sends the result to the connectivity service. The state of the related competence changes based on a set of logical rules and depending on the awarded score.

- **Acquired Competence Profile Delivery Service:** Finally, after checking if the obtained results comply with the acquisition of the related competences, the acquired competence profile delivery service provides the validation of the acquired competence profile. The acquired profile includes all learner competences within formal, non formal and informal contexts.

Our proposed architecture of Competence based Assessment reflects flexibility and diversity, in which new aspects and services can be connected to afford a suitable level of personalization and therefore enhance the whole system.

EXPERIMENTATION

We proposed in the SWAP-COMP system to test the learners' competences level. This test is only possible in case an efficient and coherent competence modeling have been realized.

In this research we have established a domain ontology for "Computing and Internet Certificate (C2i)" referential (Virtual University of Tunis, 2015) which is organized around five competence areas. This referential allows the acquisition of computer and internet skills. It certifies a first level of competence that can be extended with the C2i level 2. The choice of this referential is motivated by the introduction of qualification of ICT competences in higher education within all universities. This joins in the will that all the students would have this transverse certified competence, both for their successful study and for their future vocational integration.

We first set up the classes of concepts in this referential. We then looked for the subclass relations between these classes, which helped us to define the hierarchy of classes. The ontology that we created is used for the resource description of the "Computing and Internet Certificate (C2i)" referential on which we propose to test SWAP-COMP.

In Figure 6 we present an overview of all the competence instances within the "Computing and Internet Certificate (C2i)" referential.

Figure 5. Service oriented architecture for competence-based assessment

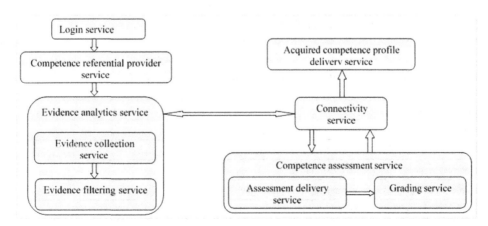

Figure 6. Competences of the "Computing and Internet Certificate (C2i) level 1" referential

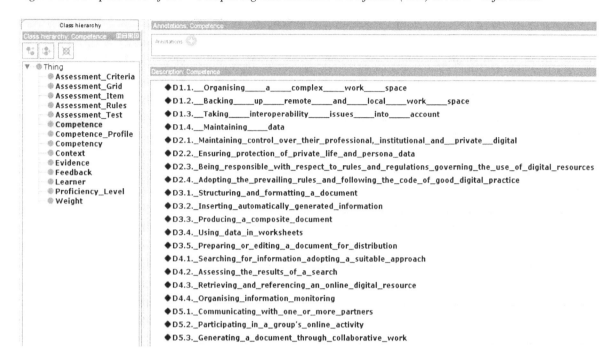

The learner, after signing up, is asked to pick out his potential competences in the competence referential. If available, the learner attaches to the Evidence Collector his related Evidence(s). This information is stored in his portfolio.

To accurately assess competences, we have to define indicators that could be extracted from the activity of each learner in the system. SWAP-COMP records each learner interaction: downloaded files and submitted assignments. For each competence the learner could attach up to three evidences.

For each evidence, a Confidence Rating (CR) is assigned by SWAP-COMP according to Table 2.

This information is used as an indicator of learners' achievements as following: An evidence E is convincing in one of the subsequent cases:

CR>3 (One submitted file for evidence E)

$\sum$CR > 4 (Two submitted files for E={E1, E2}

Table 2. Attributed confidence rating with respect to evidence analytics

0: No evidence
1: Very weak: attests the related competence but with significant weaknesses
2: Weak: attests the related competence but with some weaknesses
3: Acceptable: attests the related competence satisfactorily
4: Good: attests the related competence with some aspects of high quality
5: Very good: attests the related competence with all aspects of high quality

$\sum$ **CR > 5** (Three submitted files for E={E1, E2, E3})

After review of the provided evidence(s) in the light of the picked competences, SWAP-COMP skips over selected competences for which the learner has provided convincing evidence and find out what he should attest further. Decision on which competences need further evidence is made. The mandatory list of corresponding Competence based Assessment tests, to confirm whether the picked competences are really acquired, is then presented to the learner. The final competence level is automatically attributed upon test completion. Therefore, it is:

- **Beginner/ Novice:** if $\sum$ Marks Awarded $\in$[50..65] (Acceptable)
- **Intermediary:** if $\sum$ Marks Awarded $\in$[66..79] (Good)
- **Expert:** if $\sum$ Marks Awarded $\in$[80..100] (Excellent)

EVALUATION

An evaluation of SWAP-COMP was performed, with a particular focus on usability and effectiveness aspects. We experimented it with two categories of learners: undergraduate students and lifelong learners. A panel of thirty learners with different competences profiles was selected; twenty of these were enrolled in the first year of a specialized education curriculum at the Higher Institute of Specialized Education (ISES) at the university of Manouba in Tunisia, and were expected to be part of the "beginners" and/or "intermediaries" category. The remaining learners had already finished their studies and were seeking for a job. They were expected to reach the "Expert level" in our experiment. In this evaluation each learner- without undergoing any prior training on how to operate SWAP-COMP- has used the system; at the end of the course session for the ISES students and in non formal settings (personal meetings) for the others. This gave them the opportunity to navigate through the proposed services and answer some of the assessment tests. To accurately assess competences, we have defined indicators that could be extracted from the activity of each learner in the system. SWAP-COMP recorded each learner interaction: downloaded files and submitted assignments. This information was used as an indicator of learners' achievements.

The real time data were produced during the learners' interaction with the complete system. All the actions that learners performed with the components were recorded and tutors had the possibility to view them as reports. Additionally the scores obtained for the tests were stored within each module and gradebook within real-time. Also the learner's competence profile progress bar was updated on a real-time basis.

A questionnaire was designed to evaluate opinions about SWAP-COMP and was distributed to all learners. The questionnaire was composed of 16 questions. The answer choices for the first fourteen questions ranged from 1 (strongly disagree) to 5 (strongly agree) and the last two questions remained open-ended. The students were observed during this experiment by the lecturer. The questions were designed to check the following hypotheses:

H1: The system is simple and intuitive to use, with a minimum amount of explanation.
H2: The system provides guidance and orientation to the learner, which facilitates navigation through the different services.

H3: Competence based Assessment really affects learner's motivation.

H4: The system can be easily used for other competence ranges.

H5: Tracking of learner progress and instant feedback provided by SWAP-COMP positively affects the learner engagement.

The questionnaire covers all hypotheses. Besides hypothesis testing, another point of the questionnaire was to get information for further development and enhancements of the SWAP-COMP system. It allows evaluating ease of use, motivation, generic feature and engagement aspects. It permits also to determinate student's satisfactions evidencing the SWAP-COMP's performances. This data is also combined with noted observations gathered by the tutor that followed the learners during the experiment.

The system was evaluated as easy to use and learn with a minimum amount of explanation, as reflected through H1. The tutor's observations confirm those findings. The analysis and comparison of results for hypothesis H2 and H3 reveal that the learners were very motivated to undertake the Competence based Assessment tests. They felt well guided through SWAP-COMP and did not need any assistance. This motivation also was perceived through our discussions with the applicants. Indeed, they confirmed that the provided guidance and orientation through SWAP-COMP facilitates navigation through the different services which, therefore, affect their motivation.

From another side, the analysis of the obtained results shows that for most of the hypothesis there are no significant differences between the two kinds of applicants (undergraduate students and lifelong learners). We believe that this may be due to the increasing awareness of the competence concept inside every one.

CONCLUSION AND FUTURE WORK

Despite research in Competence-based approaches has intensified over the last years, there is relatively little research about competence-based assessment in e-Learning environments. In this paper, we first highlighted the importance of competency and competence modeling conceptual understanding and explore their relationship to one another. Then we provide a comparative study illustrating the confusions

Figure 7. SWAP-COM evaluation results diagram

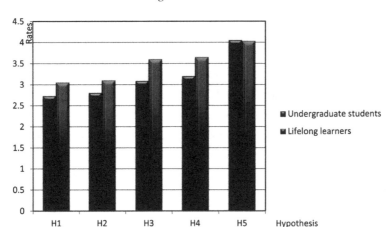

surrounding the pair of concepts; thus enabling to build our competence-based assessment approach within e-learning environments in an effective way. Overviews of our model as well as our scenario model towards Competence Web-based assessment are presented at last. On this basis, the article reports on the whole services oriented architecture of the aforesaid proposal through detailing its corresponding services.

We presented the experimentation of SWAP-COMP with different assessment scenarios thus to evaluate the reliability and flexibility of the proposal as well as to scale the features provided for the assessment process.

This work opens several research themes and we can characterize the future work according to several main directions such as application of SWAP-COMP to other Competence domains and taking into consideration other kinds of assessment items within SWAP-COMP.

REFERENCES

Alsinet, T., Barroso, D., Béjar, R., & Planes, J. (2009): A Formal Model of Competence-Based Assessment. *CCIA*, 428-436.

Berlanga, A. J., Sloep, P. B., Brouns, F., Bitter-Rijpkema, M. E., & Koper, R. (2008). Towards a TEN-Competence ePortfolio. *International Journal of Emerging Technologies in Learning*, *3*, 24–28.

Cheetham, G., & Chivers, G. (2005). *Professions, competence, and informal learning*. Cheltenham, UK: Edward Elgar Publishing.

Cheniti-Belcadhi, L., Henze, N., & Braham, R. (2008). Assessment personalization in the Semantic Web. *Journal of Computational Methods in Science and Engineering*, *8*(3), 163–182.

Colomo Palacios, R., Casado-Lumbreras, C., Soto-Acosta, P., García Peñalvo, F. J., & Caro, E. T. (2013). Competence gaps in software personnel: A multi-organizational study. *Computers in Human Behavior*, *29*(2), 456–461. doi:10.1016/j.chb.2012.04.021

De Coi, J., Herder, E., Koesling, A., Lofi, C., Olmedilla, D., Papatreou, O., & Siberski, W. (2007). A Model for Competence Gap Analysis. *Proceedings of 3rd International Conference on Web Information Systems and Technologies (WEBIST)*, 304-312.

Dolog, P., Thomsen, L. L., Thomsen, B., & Stage, J. (2010). Competence Centered Specialization in Web Engineering Topics in a Software Engineering Masters Degree Programme. *Proceedings of the 1st Educators' Day on Web Engineering Curricula, WECU-2010 in conjunction with International Web Engineering Conference*. http://CEUR-WS.org/Vol-607

European Commission. (2007). *Proposal For A Recommendation Of The European Parliament And Of The Council On Key Competences For Lifelong Learning*. Council Of The European Union.

García-Peñalvo, F. J., González-González, J. C., & Murray, M. (2012). MyElvin: A Web-Based Informal Learning Platform for Languages Practice. *International Journal of Knowledge Society Research*, *3*(1), 26–39. doi:10.4018/jksr.2012010103

García-Peñalvo, F. J., Johnson, M., Ribeiro Alves, G., & Minovic, M. (2014). Informal learning recognition through a cloud ecosystem. *Future Generation Computer Systems*, *32*, 282–294. doi:10.1016/j.future.2013.08.004

Grant, G. (1979). *On Competence: A Critical Analysis of Competence-based Reforms in Higher Education*. San Francisco: Jossey-Bass.

HR-XML. (2007). *HR-XML Consortium Competencies*. Retrieved from http://ns.hr-xml.org/2_5/HR-XML-2_5/CPO/Competencies.html

Ilahi, M., Cheniti-Belcadhi, L., & Braham, R. (2013). Competence Web–Based Assessment for lifelong learning. *First International Conference On Technological Ecosystems for Enhancing Multiculturality*. doi:10.1145/2536536.2536619

Ilahi, M., Cheniti-Belcadhi, L., & Braham, R. (2014a). Semantic Models for Competence-Based Assessment. *International Journal of Human Capital and Information Technology Professionals*, *5*(3), 33–46. doi:10.4018/ijhcitp.2014070103

Ilahi, M., Cheniti-Belcadhi, L., & Braham, R. (2014b). Scenario Model for Competence-Based Assessment. In *2014 IEEE 14th International Conference on Advanced Learning Technologies* (pp. 344-346). IEEE. doi:10.1109/ICALT.2014.103

Ivanova, M., & Chatti, M. A. (2011). Competences Mapping for Personal Learning Environment Management. *Proceedings of the PLE Conference 2011*.

Kou, K., Jia, Z., & Wang, Y. (2013). A Comparative Research on Competency and Competence, Competency Model and Competence Model. *Proceedings of the Sixth International Conference on Management Science and Engineering Management. Lecture Notes in Electrical Engineering*, *185*, 681-693. doi:10.1007/978-1-4471-4600-1_58

Magdaleno-Palencia, J.S., García-Valdez, J.M., Castañón-Puga, M., & Gaxiola-Vega, L.A. (2011). On the Modelling of Adaptive Hypermedia Systems Using Agents for Courses with the Competency Approach. *ICSECS*, (3), 624-630.

Najjar, J., Derntl, M., Klobucar, T., Simon, B., Totschnig, M., Grant, S., & Pawlowski, J. (2010). A data model for describing and exchanging Personal Achieved Learning Outcomes (PALO). *International Journal of IT Standards and Standardization Research*, *8*(2), 87–104. doi:10.4018/jitsr.2010070107

Nitchot, A., Gilbert, L., & Wills, G. B. (2012). *Competence Web-based System for Suggesting Study Materials Links: Approach & Experimental Design*. In EdMedia-World Conference on Educational Media and Technology, Denver, CO.

Paquette, G., Rogozan, D., & Marino, O. (2012). Competency Comparison Relations for Recommendation in Technology Enhanced Learning Scenarios. *Proceedings of the 2nd Workshop on Recommender Systems for Technology Enhanced Learning (RecSysTEL)*.

Rodriguez, D., Patel, R., Bright, A., Gregory, D., & Gowing, M. K. (2002). Developing Competency Models to Promote Integrated Human Resource. *Human Resource Management*, *41*(3), 309–324. doi:10.1002/hrm.10043

Sampson, D., & Fytros, D. (2008). *Competence Models in Technology-enhanced Competence-based Learning. In International Handbook on Information Technologies for Education and Training* (2nd ed.; pp. 155–177). Berlin: Springer. doi:10.1007/978-3-540-74155-8_9

Schoonover, S. C., Schoonover, H., Nemerov, D., & Ehly, C. (2000). *Competency-Based HR Applications: Results of a Comprehensive Survey.* Andersen/Schoonover/SHRM.

Sitthisak, O., Gilbert, L., & Davis, H.C. (2008). Deriving E-Assessment from a Competency Model. *ICALT*, 327-329 .

Virtual University of Tunis. (n.d.). Retrieved from http://c2i.uvt.rnu.tn/Sitec2i/index.php?option=com_content&view=article&id=61&Itemid=48

Whitelock, D., Gilbert, L., & Gale, V. (2013). E-assessment tales: What types of literature are informing day-to-day practice? *International Journal of e-Assessment, 3*(1).

Chapter 14

Determinants of Job Satisfaction and Its Impact on Affective, Continuance, and Normative Commitment of Employees:
An Empirical Study

Anita Singh
Institute of Management Studies Ghaziabad, India

Lata Bajpai Singh
Institute of Management Studies Ghaziabad, India

ABSTRACT

This chapter aims to identify different factors of job satisfaction responsible for different types of commitment (i.e. affective, continuance, and normative commitment among the employees of IT organizations). The primary data was collected from 401 respondents of IT organizations using validated scales on organizational commitment and job satisfaction. The exploratory factor analysis was conducted to identify different factors of job satisfaction and scale reliability of organizational commitment scale. The reliability and validity of all the constructs were further done through confirmatory factor analysis. Then related hypotheses were tested using structural equation modeling through AMOS 21.0. Three factors of job satisfaction were extracted, namely growth opportunities and management practices, working condition, and fair treatment. Growth opportunities and management practices are the prominent reasons for affective commitment, whereas fair treatment ensures continuance and normative commitment among the employees of IT organizations with the given sample.

INTRODUCTION

Of late with the rapid change in the environment and technology, the role of HR has become more dynamic and complex for IT companies. It has been observed that role of HR is shifting from traditional personnel, administration, and transactional to strategic utilization of employees. Most of the companies now refer

DOI: 10.4018/978-1-5225-5297-0.ch014

HR activities as 'Human Capital Management' to reflect the strategic and leadership development role of HR. The focus of the company is not only to recruit new employees but also to encourage and motivate the existing employees for better performance by keeping them satisfied and committed towards their job. Keeping employees happy, satisfied and committed depends on the HR approach towards employee life cycle. The fact that employees are the most important resource of any organization cannot be denied.

Employee Commitment and retention of talented employees are very important for maintaining stability and reducing employee turnover. Various outcomes are influenced by organizational commitment such as decreased turn over, higher motivation and organizational support. Keeping workers happy and satisfied with the job strengthen the organization in reducing employee turnover, increasing productivity, profits and tends to develop high loyalty and commitment level among employees. Job satisfaction among employees develops a sense of mental, physical, financial, technical and human security. It helps in employee retention and develops commitment among them.

The loss of skilled IT professionals is very expensive. Annual rates of turnover in IT departments have been estimated up to 20% or more. In addition to the cost of replacing the experienced staff turnover takes its toll on productivity and morale through disruption of projects, heavier workloads and negative impact on team cohesion. It is evident from few sources that high turnover is an inevitable consequence of huge demand for technology skills .The only remedy for this trend is research and development to increase commitment among IT professionals and it also is widely accepted that one way to reduce voluntary turnover is by strengthening employee commitment to the firm. So it is crucial to identify the level of job satisfaction and its influence on organizational commitment to retain talented work force in the software industry.

The present study is based on the understanding that turnover intentions among software professionals are largely in agreement with theoretical models of job satisfaction, organizational commitment, and turnover. Research does not support much employee turnover and retention in IT does not much support the claim that IT turnover can be independent of job satisfaction, but rather suggest that IT employees seem to be quicker to change jobs than other employees when they are dissatisfied with their current employer (Hacker, 2003).The researchers are of the opinion that HR practices are significantly associated with the Job satisfaction (Ting,1997) and improves the employee's feeling of commitment towards the organization (Anand, 2016, Jiang, Onyema, 2014, Lepak, Hu, & Baer, 2012; Khanna & Sehgal, 2016).

LITERATURE REVIEW

Job Satisfaction

Several studies have been conducted on job satisfaction. Recently the more global organizational commitment has emerged out of the research literature as being important to understanding and predicting organizational behavior. The term 'Satisfaction' refers to a level of achievement of needs, wants and desire (Nancy C. Morse, 1997) and it depends on wants of an individual from the world and that he receives in return. The concept of job satisfaction is widely researched and researchers define it in various manners. According to Knoop(1995), it is the general attitude of an employee towards the job and its dimensions whereas Mc Nsee-Smith views it the feelings of individuals towards their job. Locke (1976) has defined job satisfaction based on Individual's evaluation of one's work or work experiences as a positive state. According to Spector (1997), it is a set of attitude towards different aspects of work, and it is a multidimensional concept indicating cognitive and affective states. In other words it is the degree to which an individual needs can be satisfied (Glimmer, 1966). It is the duty as well as their emotional response to social and physical workplace situations (Trevor, 2001) and reaction towards the job (Gruneberg, 1979; Landy and Conte, 2004). Berry (1997) opined job satisfaction reflects the level of contentment of employees towards the job and reaction to work experiences.

In the similar line Bingol (2010) viewed job satisfaction of employees is linked to meeting their job expectations with their needs and desire and it refers to the attitude of employee's towards working environment and working conditions (Fiorilla & Nappo, 2014, Joung et al., 2015; Randeree & Chaudhry, 2012, Spector, 1997) , and their positive emotional response towards their work performance and jobs (Bigliardi et al., 2012; Chatzoudes et al., 2015; Dierendonck, 2015). Further Bhuiyan and Menguc (2002), elaborates that job satisfaction is positive as well as negative perception of employees towards their job developed in internal or external work situations.

Further research suggests that high level of job satisfaction among the employees helps the organization to retain their experienced, trained and competent employees. It enhances the motivation level of employees (Arif & Ilyas, 2013; Raddaha et al., 2012; Tziner et al., 2014), develops sense of loyalty, and commitment towards the organization (Randeree & Chaudhry, 2012; Zehrer et al, 2007) and enhances employee productivity and reduces absenteeism and turnover (Duxbury & Halinski, 2014 that leads to enhanced organizational effectiveness and efficiency (Bigliardi et al., 2012; Ling & Toh, 2014). The literature supports that measurement of job satisfaction is important as it is indicative of work behaviour like absenteeism, employee turnover, productivity (Cranny, Smith and Stone, 1992), and predictor of organizational citizenship, high attrition rate, motivational level, stress level and turnover of employees (Singh, 2012).

Review of the literature indicates a number of dimensions that are related with overall employee's job satisfaction experience. It reflects that it is related to environmental factors such as physical and psychosocial factors as well as strongly related with emotional, individual and economical factors that influence job turnover, absenteeism and tardiness (Brayfield and Crockett, 1955).It includes fair wages, job security, a balance between job skills and work knowledge pride, social security, management policies, promotion and overall social climate Oral, 2005). According to Luthans (1998) three dimensions of job satisfaction; job satisfaction as an emotional reaction against the job, a concept for meeting employee's acquisitions achievements or expectations and symbol of interconnected different behaviors may be acknowledged.

Recent research reveals that intrinsic satisfaction and extrinsic satisfaction are two major dimensions of job satisfaction (Bigliardi et al., 2012; George & Zakkariya, 2015; Randeree & Chaudhry, 2012; Raddaha et al., 2012) where intrinsic factors are related to internal job factors like growth opportunity, recognition, sense of achievement, responsibility and advancement (Raddaha., 2012).Extrinsic factors are related to external job factors such as company policy, safe healthy and secure career path, supervision, compensation, social integration and status(Mirkamali & Thani, 2011; Randeree & Chaudhry, 2012). Further literature supports both the factors may have a major impact on performance of the employee especially job motivation (Bigliardi et al., 2005; George & Zakkariya, 2015; Seebaluck & Seegum, 2013; Stringer et al., 2011).

The literature review suggests that Job Satisfaction is multidimensional and widely researched area and is an important concept in behavioral science; it refers to general feeling, attitude towards their job, working environment and working conditions of the organizations. Job satisfaction plays an important role to reduce turnover and enhance employee performance and organizational effectiveness and efficiency. It develops a sense of loyalty and commitment among employees.

Organizational Commitment

Organizational commitment gained the major focus of the research during 1990's.Research suggests that commitment is a multidimensional construct and its correlates and consequences vary across the dimensions. The present study is based on Allen & Mayor (1990), three step model of organizational commitment scale that overlaps with other multidimensional concepts (Jaros, Jermier, Koehler, & Sincich, 1993; Mayer & Schoorman, 1992).However, there are variations in multidimensional models but the focus of the study was to just study the Affective (ACS), Continuance (CCS), and Normative (NCS) Commitment (Allen &Meyer, 1990; Meyer, Allen, & Smith, 1993)and also to see the impact of different variables of job satisfaction on Affective (ACS), Continuance (CCS), and Normative (NCS) Commitment.

Organizational commitment can be referred to the relative strength of employee identification with the involvement of specific organization (Armstrong, 2009, Porter et al., 1974). Mowday et al., (1982) identified three characteristics of organizational commitment: a strong desire of an employee to remain a member of the organization, a strong belief and acceptance of the goals and the values of the organization and readiness to put effort on behalf of the organization.

Researchers are of the opinion that committed employees are more engaged in citizenship activities and display enhanced job performance (Jaros, 1997.According to Steers (1977) personal characteristics, job characteristics and work experience are important antecedents and are strongly related to organizational commitment. One of the most important contributions is three component model of organizational commitment proposed by Meyer and Allen (1990).They suggested three kinds of organizational commitment: Affective commitment, Continuance commitment and normative commitment (Allen and Meyer, 1990, 1996; Greenberg, 2005; Karrasch, 2003; Turner and Chelladurai, 2005).Affective Commitment refers to employee desire to continue membership due to emotional bonding, identification with and involvement in the organization, as a result of long work experiences, feeling of comfort and competence. Employees with high level of affective commitment work in the organization voluntarily because they are willing to work and not only because of the job need (Meyer, Allen and Smith, 1993). Continuance Commitment is basically the awareness of the employee related to the cost of leaving the organization (Meyer, Allen and Smith, 1993). Continuance commitment of an employee does not allow them to leave the organization due to the fear of unknown opportunity cost to the organization or they have few alternatives. High degree of continuance commitment allows the employees to continue their membership in that organization due to their need. Normative Commitment refers to the feeling of obligation to remain in the organization due to internalization of the loyalty norms. They wish to remain in the organization as a part of their ethical and moral responsibility (Meyer and Allen, 1991).According to Wiener and Gechman (1977), normative commitment is the result of the experience of an employee during their growing years in the socialization process as a member of the family. It is manifested during their socialization process. Individuals feel indebted to the organization for the investment of resources and time on them, they take the onus to return and repay for the benefits derived from the organization by putting extra effort on the job and staying in the job (Meyer *et al.,* 1993).

Relationship Between Job Satisfaction and Organizational Commitment

Different researchers worked on the two constructs i.e. job satisfaction and organizational commitment and found a significant relationship between both (William and Hazer, 1986; Mathieu & Zajac, 1990; Mannheim & Baruch, 1997; Busch et. al., 1998; Lum et. al. 1998; Yousef, 1998; Al-Aameri, 2000; Lu et. al., 2007; Martin & Roodt, 2008; Ahmad & Oranya, 2010; Azeem, 2010; Maria et. al. 2010; Lumley, et.al. 2011; Kaplan et. al. 2012; Deepa et.al. 2014; Patnaik & Dubey, 2015, Aranya, Kushnir & Valency, 1986; Boshoff & Mels, 1995; Harrison & Hubbard, 1998; Johnston et al., 1990; Knoop, 1995; Kreitner & Kinicki, 1992; Morrison, 1997; Norris & Niebuhr, 1984; Ting, 1997) and it impacts performance and turnover intent (Benkhoff, 1997; Clugston, 2000; Klein & Ritti, 1984; Lum, et al., 1998; Mathieu & Zajac, 1990. On the similar verge a study by Mueller, Boyer, Price, and Iverson (1994) demonstrates that the bond with the organization is strengthened when employees are satisfied as well as committed to the organization, that result in greater cooperation and less likelihood of quitting .However, as far as employees attitude towards the job is concerned it may vary. Mowday, Steers, & Porter, (1979) suggests that the focus of job satisfaction is more on the employees response to the job or to some specific aspects of the job such as supervision, working condition and pay (Sarwar & Abugre, 2013), whereas commitment is more global, attitude of the employees are towards organization and adhering to its goal and values (Porter, Steers, Mowday, & Boulian, 1974; Solinger, van Olffen, & Roe, 2008).

Job satisfaction has been identified as an antecedent of organizational commitment (William & Hazer 1986; Van Scotter, 2000; Leite et. al. 2014) .Job satisfaction is also found as one of the predictors of organizational commitment (Tsai & Huang, 2008; Azeem, 2010; Dirani & Kuchinke, 2011; Field & Buitendach, 2011; Abraham, 2012; Adekola, 2012; Biswas & Bhatnagar, 2013; Cahyono, 2015).

However in a study conducted by Almigo et. al., (2014) no significant relationship was observed between job satisfaction and organizational commitment.

It has been observed that while studying job satisfaction, researchers have studied two aspects of it to have a better understanding, one is overall job satisfaction and the other is facets of job satisfaction (Cherrington 1994). A facet of job satisfaction was described by Spector (1997) as any part of a job that produces feelings of satisfaction or dissatisfaction where as overall job satisfaction focuses on general internal state within an individual about satisfaction or dissatisfaction.

Impact of Factors of Job Satisfaction on Organizational Commitment

McPhee & Townsend (1992) mentioned in their work that it is possible to have high level of job satisfaction without having a sense of attachment or obligation to stay in the organization in an individual, similarly a highly committed individual may dislike the job that they are performing. Eslami & Gharakhani (2012) conducted a study on the factors of job satisfaction and their impact on organizational commitment and found that promotions, personal relationships and favorable condition of work have significant impact o organizational commitment. Suma & Lesha (2013) mentioned in their work that satisfaction from work itself, quality of supervision and pay has a positive impact on organizational commitment. Azeem & Akhtar (2014) found that the facets of job satisfaction significantly related to organizational commitment. Leite et. al. (2014) mentioned in their study that the satisfaction with rewards does not predict organizational commitment whereas satisfaction form interpersonal relationship is an antecedent of commitment at the workplace. Khan & Jan (2015), worked on the determinants of job satisfaction and their impact on organizational commitment and they found that perception about satisfaction from pay, promotion, and work environment are the prominent forecasters of organizational commitment, however some determinants such as work, coworker and supervision play a secondary role in predicting organizational commitment.

Impact of Job Satisfaction on the Factors of Organizational Commitment

Aydogdu et. al. (2011); found in their study that job satisfaction has a significant and positive relationship with three dimensions of organizational commitment. Kaplan et. Al. (2012) identified that the job satisfaction is significantly related to normative and affective commitment however it does not have a positive correlation with continuance commitment. They also concluded that job satisfaction had a positive effect on affective commitment. Whereas Yucel (2012) concluded that job satisfaction positively affects all the three dimensions of organizational commitment i.e. affective, continuance and normative commitment. Further Azeez, et. al. (2016), in their study suggests that there is significant relationship between employee's job satisfactions however, could not find statistically significant relationship between employees 'job satisfaction and the three dimensions of organizational commitment. Askigil (2011) observed significant relationship between internal & external job satisfaction with affective commitment and normative commitment. Apart from it, the positive relationship between external job satisfaction and continuance commitment was found in the same study whereas could not find the positive relationship between internal job satisfaction and continuance commitment.

Rationale of the Study

From the above reviewed literature it can be inferred that different studies confirm the relationship between both the constructs and job satisfaction has also been considered as antecedent or predictor of organizational commitment. Significant studies are conducted to find out the facets, determinants of factors of job satisfaction responsible for organizational commitment. Some researchers also tried to explore the impact of job satisfaction on different dimensions of organizational commitment however the researchers could not witness sufficient evidences of the studies exploring the impact of different determinants of job satisfaction affecting different dimensions of organizational commitment.

Lots of work has been done and there are different measures to ensure job satisfaction, however the practices to be adopted to ensure organizational commitment still require sufficient evidences. Patnaik & Dubey, (2015) also mentioned in their study to extend the research on investigation to distinguish the dimensions of job satisfaction and organizational commitment. Thus in the presented study the researchers aim to examine different factors of job satisfaction and their impact on the organizational commitment i.e. affective, continuance & normative commitment of IT employees and also identify the determinants of job satisfaction primarily responsible for different dimensions of organizational commitment.

METHODOLOGY

The context being investigated is quite specific; the present study was conducted on the technical employees of the Information technology Industry located in Delhi (N.C.R.). Samples were selected from top IT multinational companies drawn from three levels of management including entry level, middle level and top level employees working in Delhi NCR in India.

The information for the study is collected from both primary and secondary sources. For the purpose of primary data collection validated instruments of organizational commitment & job satisfaction scales were used. The data collection was done by giving questionnaires to the respondents and collected it later from them. For the purpose of data collection 685 questionnaires were distributed, however only valid responses from 401 considered for the study.

Data Collection Instrument

For the purpose of the study the scales proposed by different researchers have been used and the details of the same are given below:

Organizational Commitment

To study organizational commitment the revised scale proposed by Allen Mayer (1990) was used. The 24 items scale measures affective, continuance and normative commitment with 8 items each. Some of the items in the scale were 'I would be very happy to spend the rest of my career with this organization', 'I enjoy discussing my organization with people outside it' to measure affective commitment 'It would be hard for me to leave my organization right now, even if I wanted to', 'My life would be disrupted if I decided I wanted to leave my organization now' to measure continuance commitment and 'I think that people these days move from organization to organization too often' to measure normative commitment.

Job Satisfaction

To measure overall job satisfaction structured questionnaire, of 15-item scale developed by Harold Andrew Patrick (2009) was used to measure. Some of the items included in the survey questions were related to 'Opportunity for advancement ', Appreciation (from management) ', 'Company policy and management practices', 'Intrinsic aspects of job (excluding ease)', 'Salary', Supervision ', 'Social aspects of job', 'Working conditions (excluding hours)', Communication ', Hours (from working conditions) ', Ease (from intrinsic aspects of job)', ' Benefits', and 'Fair treatment'.

Data Analysis

After data collection the exploratory factor analysis was done to explore factors of job satisfaction with the help of the responses from selected sample. After EFA a structural model was proposed to be tested using structural equation modeling (SEM) approach. As SEM is a multivariate technique, it can examine the series of dependence relationship in a hypothesized model. SEM approach of the study is a combination of CFA and multiple regression, through CFA i.e. measurement model testing is being done to analyze the reliability and validity of the variables and structural model was further tested to study the path strength and relationship among the variables.

Exploratory Factor Analysis

Exploratory factor analysis was performed on all the 15 items of job satisfaction and 24 items of organizational commitment with Varimax rotation and principal component analysis. During the analysis the factor loading of each item more than 0.50 and the Eigen value of each factor more than 1 was considered to extract the factors. With the help of analysis 3 factors of organizational commitment and 3 factors of job satisfaction emerged. The reliability of all 6 factors i.e. constructs for further study was assessed by the value of Cronbach's alpha. Cronbach's alpha is used to measure the internal reliability of all the items in each construct through the pair wise correlation which ranges between 0 to1. Its value between 0.6 to 0.7 is considered reliable and above 0.7 indicate a good degree of reliability (Sekaran, 2003) and in the present study the values of all 06 constructs appeared between 0.93 to 0.95 and it indicates good internal consistency (Hair et. al. 2010) among the items. Table 1 presents the factor loading and cronbach's alpha values of affective, continuance and normative commitment and also of the 03 factors of job satisfaction.

A separate EFA was done on the responses of job analysis and the KMO (Kaiser-Meyer-Olkin) measure of adequacy was found to be 0.89 which is better than adequate (0.6) and the Bartlett test of sphericity as significant. The total variance explained by the three factor of job satisfaction was found as 80.72%. Further description of the 03 factors of job satisfaction extracted through EFA is explained below:

Factor 1: Growth Opportunities and Management Practices (JSF1)

The study suggests that most prominent factor that leads to job satisfaction among employees is Opportunity for advancement, they would prefer to work in that organizations where they are appreciated for their work and achievement, by the management and would appreciate transparent and employee friendly company policy and management practices that attract them to stay in the organization (Mirkamali & Thani, 2011; Randeree & Chaudhry, 2012). Further other variables like intrinsic aspects of job, salary and benefits also play an important role in overall job satisfaction. Intrinsic factors are related to internal job factors like growth opportunity, recognition, sense of achievement, responsibility and advancement (Raddaha., 2012).

Factor 2: Working Conditions (JSF2)

The next most important factor for IT professionals are working condition, they would prefer to work in the organization that provides best of the working conditions .And this is also confirmed by the study conducted by Sarwar & Abugre, 2013, They would like to work in the organization that maintains work life balance of their employees and maintains transparency and clarity in communication. Thus this study also suggests that job satisfaction may be referred to the employee's attitude towards working environment and working conditions (Fiorilla & Nappo, 2014, Joung et al., 2015; Randeree & Chaudhry, 2012, Spector,, 1997), and also it is connected with the positive emotional response towards their jobs and work performance (Bigliardi et al., 2012; Chatzoudes et al., 2015; Dierendonck, 2015).Working conditions as an important variable of job satisfaction can lead to organizational commitment among IT technical's resulting in better performance.

Factor 3: Fair Treatment (JSF3)

Fair treatment factor in the organization depicts that employees are motivated to perform where there is job security and the task is interesting, it relates with the intrinsic aspects of the job, employees will prefer to work under supervision of seniors provided with proper guidance and autonomy in decision making. Fair and equal treatment in the organization may develop a sense of belongingness among IT professionals and that may reflect positive impact on commitment.

Thus, the study suggests that for employees growth opportunities are preferred need. They want to continuously grow and improve on their skills in order to stay competitive in the market. They prefer job positions which provide them with authority to make decisions pertaining to their job roles and they like to be included in the decisions making process. They want to undertake challenging projects rather than the conventional ones (Singh, A, 2012).

Table 1. Descriptive and rotated component matrix of exploratory factor analysis

Factor	Items	Mean	Variance	Factor Loading	Cronbach's Alpha
Affective Commitment (AC)	I would be very happy to spend the rest of my career with this organization	3.53	1.728	0.766	0.938
	I enjoy discussing my organization with people outside it	4.01	0.970	0.825	
	I really feel as if the organization's problems are my own *	3.64	1.478	0.725	
	I do not think I could become as attached to another organization as I am to this one	3.72	1.059	0.619	
	I feel like part of the family at my organization	3.53	1.246	0.741	
	I feel emotionally attached to this organization	3.690	1.702	0.656	
	This organization has a great deal of personal meaning for me	3.56	1.363	0.627	
	I feel a strong sense of belonging to my organization	3.74	1.711	0.534	
Continuance Commitment (CC)	It would be hard for me to leave my organization right now, even if I wanted to	3.62	1.384	0.809	0.93
	My life would be disrupted if I decided I wanted to leave my organization now	3.7	1.540	0.495	
	I am afraid of what might happen if I quit my job without having another one lined up	3.68	1.234	0.799	
	It would be costly for me to leave my organization now	3.59	1.138	0.49	
	Right now staying with my organization is a matter of necessity as much as desire	3.68	1.173	0.767	
	I feel that I have few options to consider leaving this organization	3.64	1.166	0.625	
	One of the serious consequences of leaving this organization would be scarcity of available alternatives	3.54	1.536	0.654	
	One of the major reasons I continue to work for this organization is that leaving would require personal sacrifice-another organization may not match the overall benefits I have here	3.53	1.195	0.756	
Normative Commitment (NC)	I think that people these days move from organization to organization too often	3.95	1.415	0.829	0.958
	I believe that a person must always be loyal to his/her organization	3.83	1.150	0.623	
	Jumping from organization to organization seems unethical to me	3.93	1.261	0.747	
	I believe that loyalty is important and therefore I feel a strong sense of moral obligation	4.04	1.265	0.623	
	If I got another offer for a better job elsewhere I would not feel it was right to leave my organization	3.76	1.201	0.603	
	I was taught to believe in the value of remaining loyal to one organization	3.84	1.304	0.809	
	Things were better in the days when people stayed with one organization for most of their careers	3.77	1.49	0.579	
	I think that wanting to be a company man or company woman is sensible	3.69	1.61	0.76	
Growth Opportunities& Management Practices (JSF1)	Opportunity for advancement	3.84	1.897	0.63	0.934
	Appreciation (from management)	3.66	1.393	0.845	
	Company policy and management practices	3.86	1.578	0.799	
	Intrinsic aspects of job (excluding ease)	3.4	1.739	0.604	
	Salary	3.76	1.51	0.57	
	Ease (from intrinsic aspects of job)	3.7	1.942	0.715	
	Benefits	3.77	1.638	0.57	
Working Conditions (JSF2)	Social aspects of job	3.7	1.819	0.71	0.9
	Working conditions (excluding hours)	3.98	1.628	0.785	
	Communication	3.77	1.555	0.731	
	Hours (from working conditions)	3.83	1.74	0.829	
Fair Treatment (JSF3)	Job Security	3.5	2.08	0.572	0.94
	Interest (from intrinsic aspects of job)	3.65	1.736	0.546	
	Supervision	3.38	1.895	0.514	
	Fair treatment	3.79	1.647	0.416	

Source: Author's own.

PROPOSED RESEARCH MODEL AND HYPOTHESES

During the exploratory factor analysis, 3 factors were identified and the same were identified as growth opportunities & Management practices; Working conditions and Fair treatment. On the basis of factors extracted the researchers propose a conceptual model and the same is given below as Figure I.

Further, the following hypotheses were tested with the help of Structural Equation Modeling:

1. JSF1 i.e. Growth opportunities & Management practices have an impact on affective commitment.
2. JSF1 i.e. Growth opportunities & Management practices have an impact on continuance commitment.
3. JSF1 i.e. Growth opportunities & Management practices have an impact on normative commitment.
4. JSF2 i.e. working conditions have an impact on affective commitment.
5. JSF2 i.e. working conditions have an impact on continuance commitment.
6. JSF2 i.e. working conditions have an impact on normative commitment.
7. JSF3 i.e. fair treatment has an impact on affective commitment.
8. JSF3 i.e. fair treatment has an impact on continuance commitment.
9. JSF3 i.e. fair treatment has an impact on normative commitment.

Measurement Model

Confirmatory Factor analysis was applied based on the output of EFA using Amos 21. In this few items from all the constructs were dropped to improve the measurement model fit indices. In this one item from affective commitment, 02 items each from continuance commitment and normative commitment, 03 items from JSF1 and 01 items each form both JSF2 & JSF3 were dropped. Thus during CFA total 11 items were dropped including both the scales i.e. job satisfaction & organizational commitment. The final list of items retained with each construct is displayed in Table 2. The fit indices of measurement model using first order constructs appeared with satisfactory scores such as Chi Square = 908.553, Degree of freedom = 354, p value <0.001, CMIN/df = 2.567. The value of other measures were found as GFI = 0.899, CFI = 0.926, TLI=0.915, AND IFI = 0.927, NFI =0.889, PNFI=0.772, PCFI= 0.808, RMSEA = 0.08. The value of normed chi square i.e. 2.56 was below the maximum value of 3 and the values of Goodness of fit index (GFI), comparative fit index (CFI) and normed fit index (NFI) were found close to or more than minimum value of 0.9. The value of root mean square error of approximation (RMSEA) was found as 0.08 which means satisfactory level of unidimensionality and convergent validity. The standardized coefficients for all the items were higher than the twice of their standard errors confirming the convergent validity. The factor loading of all the items was found more than 0.5, the average variance extracted (AVE) values for the all the constructs was also above 0.50 and the composite reliability (CR) of all the scales was found as more than 0.7 (Graver et. al. 1999; Hu & Bantler 1999). Apart from it the composite reliability of all the constructs was also found more than the average variance extracted (AVE).

Discriminant validity can be checked with the comparison of average variance extracted (AVE) with the corresponding inter construct squared correlation estimates and in present analysis the value of square root of each AVE is greater than absolute correlation value between the scales and other scales. The AVE value for each construct was also found to be higher than maximum shared variance (MSV) and average shared squared variance (ASV) values supporting the evidence of discriminant validity. Table 3 presents the value corresponds to discriminant validity matrix.

Structural Model

Structural equation modeling was performed to examine the hypothesized model presented in Figure 1 and the result path diagram of the structural model are presented in Table 4, however the goodness of fit indices for structural model could not be found acceptable with the values of CMIN/df above 4.00, value of root mean square error of approximation (RMSEA) = 0.92 and goodness of fit (GFI) = 0.812.

Then for model fit, rework was done using modification indices and found that the construct JSF2 insignificant with affective and continuance commitment. The value of regression estimate was also not very high for the path analyses between JSF2 and normative commitment as it accounted for 19% of explanation. During model testing through modification indices the construct JSF2 was dropped from the study now the structural model was tested with two independent variables JSF1 and JSF3 and three dependent variables such as affective commitment, continuance commitment and normative commitment. The path analysis of revised structural model is presented in Table 5 and the diagrammatic representation of the same is given in Figure 2.

As the result depicts Growth Opportunities & Management Practices (JSF1) found significant for affective commitment and Fair treatment (JSF3) found to be significant for continuance and normative commitment. The goodness of fit indices for the model was also found marginally adequate with values (CMIN/df = 3.761, GFI= .819, CFI= .909, NFI = .888, TLI= .890 and RMSEA = 0.811, thus the structural model can be depicted as accepted as per fit indices.

As per the result of R square multivariate test of the revised structural model it is estimated that JSF1 predicts 55.5% of variance in affective commitment, similarly JSF3 predicts 59.3% variance in continuance commitment and JSF3 also predicts 58.5% variance in normative commitment.

DISCUSSION

During the literature review, the significance of both organizational commitment and job satisfaction was evident. It was found that job satisfaction is different from organizational commitment as it seems as day to day function at the workplace and both the broad constructs are positively linked to each other

Figure 1. Proposed model

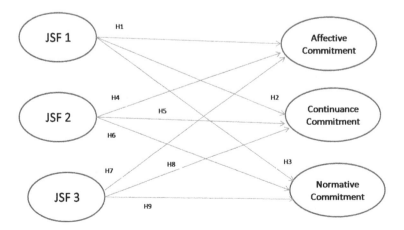

Table 2. Measurement model results

Constructs	Items	Standardized Estimates	p Value	Average Variance Explained (AVE)	Composite Reliability (CR)
AC	AC1	0.918	***	0.677959	2.54
	AC2	0.835	***		
	AC4	0.87	***		
	AC5	0.855	***		
	AC6	0.964	***		
	AC7	0.888	***		
	AC8	0.845	***		
CC	CC1	0.916	***	0.8288	2.03
	CC2	0.882	***		
	CC3	0.91	***		
	CC5	0.926	***		
	CC7	0.911	***		
	CC8	0.917	***		
NC	NC1	0.935	***	0.8338	2
	NC2	0.883	***		
	NC3	0.903	***		
	NC4	0.952	***		
	NC5	0.886	***		
	NC8	0.918	***		
JSF1	JS3	0.967	***	0.7921	1.83
	JS5	0.979	***		
	JS6	0.799	***		
	JS7	0.798	***		
JSF 2	JS9	0.941	***	0.8447	1.79
	JS10	0.875	***		
	JS11	0.748	***		
JSF 3	JS1	0.801	***	0.7534	1.74
	JS2	0.884	***		
	JS15	0.915	***		

Source: Author's own.
* Factor loadings are significant at p< 0.01 level

Table 3. Discriminant validity

	Affective Commitment	Continuance Commitment	Normative Commitment	JSF1	JSF2	JSF3
Affective Commitment	0.8233*					
Continuance Commitment	0.100	0.910*				
Normative Commitment	0.310	0.100	0.9131*			
JSF1	0.610	0.090	0.42	0.89*		
JSF2	0.440	0.110	0.34	0.160	0.919*	
JSF3	0.770	0.190	0.60	0.570	0.49	0.867*

Source: Author's own.
*Square root of average variance extracted (AVE) values

Table 4. Result of hypothesis testing of proposed structural model

Hypotheses	Hypothesized Paths	Standardized Path Coefficients	P Value	Results
1	JSF1 = AC	0.405	***	Accepted
2	JSF1= CC	-0.02	0.824	Not Accepted
3	JSF1 = NC	0.234	***	Accepted
4	JSF2 = AC	0.42	0.488	Not Accepted
5	JSF2= CC	0.095	0.207	Not Accepted
6	JSF2 = NC	0.199	***	Accepted
7	JSF3 = AC	0.383	***	Accepted
8	JSF3= CC	0.551	***	Accepted
9	JSF3 = NC	0.479	***	Accepted

Source: Author's own.

* Implies significant at p <0.01; JSF

Figure 2. Revised structural model
* Significant

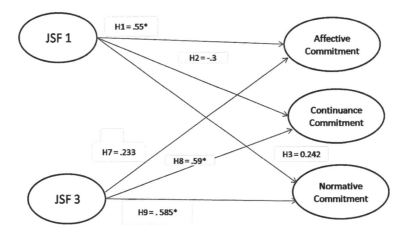

Table 5. Result of hypothesis testing of revised proposed structural model

Hypotheses	Hypothesized Paths	Standardized Path Coefficients	P Value	Results
1	JSF1 = AC	0.555	***	Accepted
2	JSF1= CC	-0.3	0.817	Not Accepted
3	JSF1 = NC	0.242	0.14	Not Accepted
7	JSF3 = AC	0.233	0.26	Not Accepted
8	JSF3= CC	0.593	***	Accepted
9	JSF3 = NC	0.585	***	Accepted

* Implies significant at p <0.01; JSF

(Aranya, Kushnir & Valency, 1986; Boshoff & Mels, 1995; Harrison & Hubbard, 1998; Johnston et al., 1990; Knoop, 1995; Kreitner & Kinicki, 1992; Morrison, 1997; Norris & Niebuhr, 1984; Ting, 1997).

The main purpose of the study was to identify the factors of job satisfaction causing different types of commitment among the sampled respondents. For the said purpose it was important to identify the factors of job satisfaction and then see the causal relationship between the extracted factors of job satisfaction and the types of organizational commitment.

For extraction of factors the exploratory factor analysis was applied on the data set and three factors of job satisfaction emerged from it namely growth opportunities & management practices; working conditions; fair treatment. Among the factors, the first factor i.e. growth opportunities & the management practices have also considered as intrinsic factors of job satisfaction in the study by Raddaha (2012). Apart from it three factors of organizational commitment were also found significant during the reliability and validity testing using measurement model.

On the basis of literature review a conceptual model was proposed, mentioning the impact of factors of job satisfaction on the three types of organizational commitment i.e. affective, continuance and normative. However during multiple hypotheses testing using structural equation modeling only two factors were found with significant impact on the three types of commitment. It was observed that growth opportunities and management practices have an impact on affective commitment that means it affects an employee's desire to continue their association with the organization due to emotional bonding, identification with and involvement in the organization. It can further be understood that once an employee is satisfied with the growth opportunities and management practices they slip in with the feeling of comfort and competence and ultimately their commitment level improves.

Similarly, fair treatment with the employees was found to have significant impact on the continuance and normative commitment. It depicts that transparent and fair treatment of employees create awareness about the cost of leaving the organization among them (Meyer, Allen and Smith, 1993) and they would like to continue with the organization due to the fear of unknown opportunity cost to the organization or they may have few alternatives. Apart from it the employee's satisfaction due to fair treatment further develops the feeling of obligation among them to remain with the organization considering their ethical and moral responsibility (Meyer and Allen, 1991).

Thus the two factors of job satisfaction i.e. growth opportunities & management practice and fair treatment with the employees have a significant role in improving the affective, continuance and normative commitment of employees, however as per the model the other factor i.e. working condition do not have significant impact on employee's organizational commitment. It may be because their working conditions are already taken care of by the employers in terms of infrastructural arrangements at the workplace.

FUTURE RESEARCH DIRECTION

No research work is free from limitation and all have a scope of continuing the research work further. The presented study is based on IT employees of Delhi NCR region only, however, to make the findings generalized the study can be undertaken on a better sample of respondents representing different regional and national culture.

CONCLUSION

A major challenge faced by all IT company is, developing and maintaining Organizational commitment and Job satisfaction. It is in the interest of all organization to secure commitment and reduce employee turnover. From the present study it can be concluded that two factors of job satisfaction have significant impact on the three types of commitment. It suggests that 'growth opportunities and management practices', influences affective commitment and affects an employee's desire to continue their association with the organization Similarly, the other factor 'fair treatment of employees', was identified to have significant impact on the continuance and normative commitment of employees working in IT Companies . In this context it is pertinent for the HR Department or managers to develop human resource policies that are in alignment to the needs and motivation of the employees. The findings of this study have pointed out some salient issues in the IT field specific to job satisfaction, and commitment to minimize employee turnover and enhance their performance and organizational efficiency. To ensure different types of commitment at the workplace the practitioners can focus on the factors of job satisfaction suggested in the study.

REFERENCES

Abraham, S. (2012). Development of Employee Engagement Programme on the Basis of Employee Satisfaction Survey. *Journal of Economic Development, Management, IT, Finance and Marketing*, *4*(1), 27–37.

Adekola, B. (2012). The impact of organizational commitment on job satisfaction: A study of employees at Nigerian Universities. *International Journal of Human Resource Studies*, *2*(2), 1. doi:10.5296/ijhrs.v2i2.1740

Ahmad, N., & Oranye, N. O. (2010). Empowerment, job satisfaction and organizational commitment: A comparative analysis of nurses working in Malaysia and England. *Journal of Nursing Management*, *18*(5), 582–591. doi:10.1111/j.1365-2834.2010.01093.x PMID:20636507

Al-Aameri, A. S. (2000). Job satisfaction and organizational commitment for nurses. *Saudi Medical Journal*, *21*(6), 531–535. PMID:11500699

Allen, N. J., & Meyer, J. P. (1990). The measurement and antecedents of affective, continuance, and normative commitment to the organization. *Journal of Occupational Psychology*, *63*(1), 1–18. doi:10.1111/j.2044-8325.1990.tb00506.x

Allen, N. J., & Meyer, J. P. (1996). Affective, continuance, and normative commitment to the organization: An examination of construct validity. *Journal of Vocational Behavior*, *49*(3), 252–276. doi:10.1006/jvbe.1996.0043 PMID:8980084

Almigo, N., Khan, R. K. A. W., & Hamzah, H. (2014). *Coaches turnover tendency review of job satisfaction and organizational commitment program in the national service*. Academic Press.

Anand, N. (2016). Impact of human resource practices on job satisfaction: Evidence from Indian public sector banks. *International Journal of Engineering Technology Science and Research*, *3*, 122–115.

Aranya, N., Kushnir, P., & Valency, R. (1986). Organisational commitment in a male dominated profession. *Human Relations*, *39*(5), 433–448. doi:10.1177/001872678603900504

Arif, S., & Ilyas, M. (2013). Quality of work-life model for teachers of private universities in Pakistan. *Quality Assurance in Education, 21*(3), 282–298. doi:10.1108/QAE-Feb-2012-0006

Armstrong, M. (2009). Armstrong's handbook of human resource management practice. London: Kogan Page.

Aydogdu, S., & Asikgil, B. (2011). An empirical study of the relationship among job satisfaction, organizational commitment and turnover intention. *International Review of Management and Marketing, 1*(3), 43.

Azeem, S. M. (2010). Job satisfaction and organizational commitment among employees in the Sultanate of Oman. *Psychology (Irvine, Calif.), 1*(4), 295–300. doi:10.4236/psych.2010.14038

Azeem, S. M., & Akhtar, N. (2014). Job satisfaction and organizational commitment among public sector employees in Saudi Arabia. *International Journal of Business and Social Science, 5*(7).

Azeez, R. O., Jayeoba, F., & Adeoye, A. O. (2016). Job satisfaction, turnover intention and organizational commitment, Bvimsr's. *Journal of Management Research, 8*(2), 102.

Benkhoff, B. (1997). Disentangling organisational commitment: the changes of OCQ for research and policy. *Personal Review, 26*(1), 114-20.

Berry, L. M. (1997). *Psychology at work*. San Francisco: McGraw Hill.

Bhuian, S. N., & Mengüç, B. (2002). An Extension And Evoluation Of Job Characteristics, Organizational Commitment And Job Satisfaction In An Expatriate, Quest Worker, Sales Setting. *Journal of Personal Selling & Sales Management, 22*(1), 1–11.

Bigliardi, Dormio, Galati, & Schiuma. (2012). The impact of organizational culture on the job satisfaction of knowledge workers. *VINE, 42*(1), 36 – 51.

Bingöl. (2010). *Dursun*. İstanbul: İnsan Kaynakları Yönetimi, Beta Basım Yayım Dağıtım.

Biswas, S., & Bhatnagar, J. (2013). Mediator Analysis of Employee Engagement: Role of Perceived Organizational Support, P-O Fit, Organizational Commitment and Job Satisfaction. *Vikalpa, 38*(1), 27–40.

Boshoff, C., & Mels, G. (1995). A Causal Model to Evaluate the Relationships Among Supervision, Role Stress, Organizational Commitment and Internal Service Quality. *European Journal of Marketing, 29*(2), 23–42. doi:10.1108/03090569510080932

Busch, T., Fallan, L., & Pettersen, A. (1998). Disciplinary Differences in Job Satisfaction Self- Efficacy, Goal Commitment and Organizational Commitment among Faculty Employees in Norwegian Colleges: An Empirical Assessment of Indicators of Performance. *Quality in Higher Education, 4*(2), 137–157. doi:10.1080/1353832980040204

Cahyono, D. (2015). Modeling Turnover and Their Antecedents Using the Locus of Control as Moderation: Empirical Study of Public Accountant Firms in Java Indonesia. *International Journal of Finance and Accounting, 4*(1), 40–51.

Clugston, M. (2000). The mediating effects of multidimensional commitment on job satisfaction and intent to leave. *Journal of Organizational Behavior, 21*(4), 477–486. doi:10.1002/(SICI)1099-1379(200006)21:4<477::AID-JOB25>3.0.CO;2-7

Cranny, C. J., Smith, P. C., & Stone, E. F. (1992). *Job satisfaction: How people feel about their jobs and how it affects their performance.* New York, NY: Lexington Book.

Deepa, E., Palaniswamy, R., & Kuppusamy, S. (2014). Effect of Performance Appraisal System in Organizational Commitment, Job Satisfaction and Productivity. *The Journal Contemporary Management Research, 8*(1), 72–82.

Dierendonck, D. V. (2015). The influence of planning, support and self-concordance on goal progress and job satisfaction-Evidence-based HRM. *A Global Forum for Empirical Scholarship, 3*(3), 206 – 221.

Dirani, K. M., & Kuchinke, K. P. (2011). Job satisfaction and organizational commitment: Validating the Arabic satisfaction and commitment questionnaire (ASCQ), testing the correlations, and investigating the effects of demographic variables in the Lebanese banking sector. *International Journal of Human Resource Management, 22*(5), 1180–1202. doi:10.1080/09585192.2011.556801

Duxbury, L., & Halinski, M. (2014). Dealing with the Grumpy Boomers, Re-engaging the disengaged and retaining talent. *Journal of Organizational Change Management, 27*(4), 660 – 676. <ALIGNMENT. qj></ALIGNMENT>10.1108/JOCM-05-2014-0106

Elizabeth, G., & Zakkariya, K.A. (2015). Job related stress and job satisfaction: a comparative study among bank employees. *Journal of Management Development, 34*(3), 316 – 329.

Eslami, J., & Gharakhani, D. (2012). Organizational commitment and job satisfaction. *ARPN Journal of Science and Technology, 2*(2), 85–91.

Field, L. K., & Buitendach, J. H. (2011). Happiness, Work Engagement and Organisational Commitment of Support Staff at a Tertiary Education Institution in South Africa. *SA Journal of Industrial Psychology/ SA Tydskrif vir Bedryfsielkunde, 37*(1), 946-955. doi:10.4102/sajip.v37i1.946

Fiorillo, D., & Nappo, N. (2014). Job satisfaction in Italy: Individual characteristics and social relations. *International Journal of Social Economics, 41*(8), 683–704. doi:10.1108/IJSE-10-2012-0195

Florence, Y. Y. L., & Weiyan, T. (2014). Boosting facility managers' personal and work outcomes through job design. *Facilities, 32*(13/14), 825–844. doi:10.1108/F-04-2013-0031

Garver, M. S., & Mentzer, J. T. (1999). Logistics Research Methods: Employing Structural Equation Modelling to Test for Construct Validity. *Journal of Business Logistics, 20*, 33–57.

Glimmer, V. H. B. (1966). *Industrial psychology.* New York: Mc Graw Hill Book Co. G.

Greenberg, J. (2005). *Managing behavior in organizations* (4th ed.). Englewood Cliffs, NJ: Prentice-Hall.

Gruneberg, M. M. (1979). *Understanding job satisfaction.* London: The Macmillan Press Ltd. doi:10.1007/978-1-349-03952-4

Hacker, A. (2003). Turnover: A silent profit killer. *Information Systems Management, 20*(2), 14–18. do i:10.1201/1078/43204.20.2.20030301/41465.3

Hair, J., Black, W., Babin, B., & Anderson, R. (2010). Multivariate Data Analysis. Prentice Hall, Inc.

Harrrison, J. K., & Hubbard, R. (1998). Antecedents to organizational commitment among Mexican employees of a US firms in Mexico. *The Journal of Social Psychology, 138*(5), 609–623. doi:10.1080/00224549809600416

Hu, L., & Bentler, P. M. (1999). Cutoff Criteria for Fit Indexes in Covariance Structure Analysis: Conventional Criteria versus New Alternatives. *Structural Equation Modeling, 6*(1), 1–55. doi:10.1080/10705519909540118

Jaros, S. J. (1997). An assessment of Meyer and Allen's (1991), three component model of organizational commitment and turnover intentions. *Journal of Vocational Behavior, 51*(3), 319–337. doi:10.1006/jvbe.1995.1553

Jiang, K., Lepak, D., Hu, J., & Baer, J. (2012). How does human resource management influence organizational outcomes? A meta-analytic investigation of mediating mechanisms. *Academy of Management Journal, 55*(6), 1264–1294. doi:10.5465/amj.2011.0088

Johns, G. (1996). Theories of Work Motivation. In *Leadership Organizational Behavior*. Harper Collins College Publishers.

Johnston, M. W., Parasuraman, A., Futrell, C. M., & Black, W. C. (1990). A longitudinal assessment of the impact of selected organisational influences on salespeople's organisational commitment during early employment. *JMR, Journal of Marketing Research, 23*(1), 333–344. doi:10.2307/3172590

Joung, H.-W., Goh, B. K., Huffman, L., Jingxue, J. Y., & Surles, J. (2015). Investigating relationships between internal marketing practices and employee organizational commitment in the foodservice industry. *International Journal of Contemporary Hospitality Management, 27*(7), 1618–1640. doi:10.1108/IJCHM-05-2014-0269

Kaplan, M., Ogut, E., Kaplan, A., & Aksay, K. (2012). The relationship between job satisfaction and organizational commitment: The case of hospital employees. *World Journal of Management, 4*(1), 22–29.

Karrasch. (2003). Antecedents and Consequences of Organizational Commitment. *Military Psychology, 15*(3), 225-36.

Kasim, R., & Abdul, G. C. (2012). Leadership – style, satisfaction and commitment. *Engineering, Construction, and Architectural Management, 19*(1), 61–85. doi:10.1108/09699981211192571

Khan, A. S., & Jan, F. (2015). The Study of Organization Commitment and Job Satisfaction among Hospital Nurses, A Survey of District Hospitals of Dera Ismail Khan. *Global Journal of Management and Business Research*.

Khanna, P., & Sehgal, M. (2016). A study of HRM practices and its effect on employees job satisfaction in private sector banks with special reference to ICICI banks in Ludhiana. *International Journal of Management, 4*, 36–43.

Klein, S. M., & Ritti, R. R. (1984). *Understanding organizational behavior* (2nd ed.). Boston: Kent Publishing Company.

Kreitner, R., & Kinicki, A. (1992). *Organizational behavior* (2nd ed.). New York: Irwin.

Landy, F. J., & Conte, J. M. (2004). *Work in 21st century: An introduction to individual and organizational psychology.* New York: McGraw Hill.

Lee, K., Carswell, J. J., & Allen, N. J. (2000). A meta-analytic review of occupational commitment: Relations with person and work-related variables. *The Journal of Applied Psychology, 85*(5), 799–811. doi:10.1037/0021-9010.85.5.799 PMID:11055151

Leite, N. R. P., Rodrigues, A. C. D. A., & Albuquerque, L. G. D. (2014). Organizational commitment and job satisfaction: What are the potential relationships? *BAR - Brazilian Administration Review, 11*(4), 476–495. doi:10.1590/1807-7692bar2014276

Lu, H., Alison, E., While, K., & Barriball, L. (2007). Job satisfaction and its related factors: A questionnaire survey of hospital nurses in Mainland China. *International Journal of Nursing Studies, 44*(4), 574–588. doi:10.1016/j.ijnurstu.2006.07.007 PMID:16962123

Lum, L., Kervin, J., Clark, K., Reid, F., & Sirola, W. (1998). Explaining Nursing Turnover Intention: Job Satisfaction, Pay Satisfaction, or Organizational Commitment? *Journal of Organizational Behavior, 19*(3), 305–320. doi:10.1002/(SICI)1099-1379(199805)19:3<305::AID-JOB843>3.0.CO;2-N

Lumley, E. J., Coetzee, M., Tladinyane, R., & Ferreira, N. (2011). Exploring the job satisfaction and organisational commitment of employees in the information technology environment. *Southern African Business Review, 15*(1), 100–118.

Luthans, F. (1998). *Organizational Behaviour* (8th ed.). Boston: Irwin McGraw-Hill.

Mannheim, B., Baruch, Y., & Tal, J. (1997). Alternative Models for Antecedents and Outcomes of Work Centrality and Job Satisfaction of High-Tech Personnel. *Human Relations, 50*(12), 1537–1562. doi:10.1177/001872679705001204

Maria, M., Pavlos, S., Eleni, M., Thamme, K., & Constantinidis, T. C. (2010). Greek Registered Nurses' Job Satisfaction in Relation to Work-Related Stress: A Study on Army and Civilian Registered nurses. *Global Journal of Health Science, 2*(1), 44–59. Available at www.ccsenet.org/gjhs

Martin, A., & Roodt, G. (2008). Perceptions of organisational commitment, job satisfaction and turnover intentions in a post-merger South African tertiary institution. *SA Journal of Industrial Psychology, 34*(1), 23–31. doi:10.4102/sajip.v34i1.415

Mathieu, J. E., & Zajac, D. M. (1990). A review and meta-analysis of the antecedents, correlates, and consequences of organizational commitment. *Psychological Bulletin, 108*(2), 171–194. doi:10.1037/0033-2909.108.2.171

Mathieu, J. E., & Zajac, D. M. (1990). A review and Meta analysis of the antecedent's correlates and consequences of organizational commitment. *Psychological Bulletin, 108*(2), 171–199. doi:10.1037/0033-2909.108.2.171

McPhee, S. D., & Townsend, L. J. (1992). A study of organisational commitment and job satisfaction among Air force occupational therapy officers. *Military Medicine, 153*(3), 117–121. PMID:1603401

Meyer, J. P., Allen, N. J., & Smith, C. A. (1993). Commitment to organizations and occupations: Extension and test of a three-component model. *The Journal of Applied Psychology, 78*(4), 538–551. doi:10.1037/0021-9010.78.4.538

Mirkamalia, S. M., & Thanib, F. N. (2011). A Study on the Quality of Work Life (QWL) among faculty members of University of Tehran(UT) and Sharif university of Technology (SUT). *Social and Behavioral Sciences, 29*, 179–187.

Mowday, R. T., Porter, L. W., & Steers, R. M. (1982). *Employee organizational linkages: The psychology of commitment, absenteeism and turnover.* New York: Academic Press.

Mowday, R. T., Steers, R. M., & Porter, L. W. (1979). The measurement of organizational commitment. *Journal of Vocational Behavior, 14*(2), 224–247. doi:10.1016/0001-8791(79)90072-1

Mueller, C. W., Boyer, E. M., Price, J. L., & Iverson, R. D. (1994). Employee attachment and non coercive conditions of work. *Work and Occupations, 21*(2), 179–212. doi:10.1177/0730888494021002002

Nancy, C. M. (1977). *Satisfactions in the White-Collar Job.* Ayer publishing.

Nanjundeswaraswamy, T. S. (2013). Quality of Work life of Employees in Private Technical Institutions. *International Journal of Qualitative Research, 7*(3), 3–14.

Norris, D. R., & Niebuhr, R. E. (1984). Professionalism, organizational commitment and job satisfaction in an accounting organization. *Accounting, Organizations and Society, 9*(1), 49–60. doi:10.1016/0361-3682(84)90029-1

Onyema, E. O. (2014). Assessing the relationship between human resource management and employee job satisfaction: A case study of a food and beverage company. *Journal of Business Administration Research, 3*(1), 71–81. doi:10.5430/jbar.v3n1p71

Porter, L. W., Steers, R. M., Mowday, R. T., & Boulian, P. V. (1974). Organizational Commitment, Job Satisfaction and Turnover among Psychiatric Technicians. *The Journal of Applied Psychology, 59*(5), 603–609. doi:10.1037/h0037335

Salleh, R., Nair, M. S., & Harun, H. (2012). Job satisfaction, organizational commitment, and turnover intention: A case study on employees of a retail company in Malaysia. *World Academy of Science, Engineering and Technology, 72*(12), 316–323.

Sarwar, S., & Abugre, J. (2013). The Influence of Rewards And Job Satisfaction on Employees In The Service Industry. *The Business & Management Review*, 23-32.

Seebaluck, A. K., & Seegum, T. D. (2013). Motivation among public primary school teachers in Mauritius. *International Journal of Educational Management, 27*(4), 446–464. doi:10.1108/09513541311316359

Sekaran, U. (2003). *Research methods for business: A skill-building approach* (4th ed.). New York, NY: John Wiley.

Singh, A. (2012). Job Satisfaction in Insurance Sector: An Empirical Investigation. *International Journal of Engineering and Management Sciences, 3*(4).

Solinger, O. N., & Van Oleffen, W. (2008). Beyond the three-component model of organitzacional commitment. *The Journal of Applied Psychology, 93*(1), 70–83. doi:10.1037/0021-9010.93.1.70 PMID:18211136

Spector, P. E. (1997). *Job satisfaction: Application, assessment, cause and consequences.* Thousand Oaks, CA: Sage Publication.

Steer, R. M., Mooday, R. T., & Porter, L. W. (1982). *Employee organisation linkages.* New York: Academic Press.

Stringer, C., Didham, J., & Theivananthampillai, P. (2011). Motivation, pay satisfaction, and job satisfaction of frontline employees. *Qualitative Research in Accounting & Management, 8*(2), 161–179. doi:10.1108/11766091111137564

Suma, S., & Lesha, J. (2013). Job satisfaction and organizational commitment: The case of Shkodra municipality. *European Scientific Journal, ESJ, 9*(17).

Ting, Y. (1997). Determinants of job satisfaction of federal government employees. *Public Personnel Management, 26*(3), 313–335.

Trevor, C. O. (2001). Interactions among actual ease-of-movement determinants and job satisfaction in the prediction of voluntary turnover. *Academy of Management Journal, 44*(4), 621–638. doi:10.2307/3069407

Tsai, M. T., & Huang, C. C. (2008). The relationship among ethical climate types, facets of job satisfaction, and the three components of organizational commitment: A study of nurses in Taiwan. *Journal of Business Ethics, 80*(3), 565–581. doi:10.1007/s10551-007-9455-8

Turner, B. A., & Chelladurai, P. (2005). Organizational and occupational commitment, intention to leave and perceived performance of intercollegiate coaches. *Journal of Sport Management, 19*(2), 193–211. doi:10.1123/jsm.19.2.193

Turner, C., & Chelladurai, P. (2005). Organizational and Occupational Commitment, Intention to Leave, and Perceived Performance of Intercollegiate Coaches. *Journal of Sport Management, Vol, 19*(2), 193–211. doi:10.1123/jsm.19.2.193

Tziner, E., Fein, E. C., & Oren, L. (2012). Fein, L. Orenn Human motivation and performance outcomes in the context of downsizing. *Is Less Still More, 1*, 103–133. doi:10.1017/CBO9780511791574.008

Van Scotter, J. R. (2000). Relationships of task performance and contextual performance with turnover, job satisfaction, and affective commitment. *Human Resource Management Review, 10*(1), 79–95. doi:10.1016/S1053-4822(99)00040-6

Wiener, Y., & Gechman, A. S. (1977). Commitment: A behavioral approach to job involvement. *Journal of Vocational Behavior, 10*(1), 47–52. doi:10.1016/0001-8791(77)90041-0

Williams, L. J., & Hazer, J. T. (1986). Antecedents and consequences of satisfaction and commitment in turnover models: A re-analysis using latent variable structural equation methods. *The Journal of Applied Psychology*, *72*(1), 219–231. doi:10.1037/0021-9010.71.2.219

Yousef, D. A. (1998). Satisfaction with Job Security as a Predictor of Organizational Commitment and Job Performance in a Multicultural Environment. *International Journal of Manpower*, *19*(3), 184–194. doi:10.1108/01437729810216694

Yücel, İ. (2012). Examining the relationships among job satisfaction, organizational commitment, and turnover intention: An empirical study. *International Journal of Business and Management*, *7*(20), 44. doi:10.5539/ijbm.v7n20p44

Zehrer, A., Crotts, J. C., & Magnini, V. P. (2011). The perceived usefulness of blog postings: An extension of the expectancy-disconfirmation paradigm. *Tourism Management*, *32*(1), 106–113. doi:10.1016/j.tourman.2010.06.013

Chapter 15
Empathy and Mindfulness:
Exploring the Possible Predictors of Authentic Leadership

Aishwarya Singh
Jaypee Business School, India

Santoshi Sengupta
Jaypee Institute of Information Technology, India

Swati Sharma
Jaypee Institute of Information Technology, India

ABSTRACT

The upheavals in the current times are driving us toward a purposeful need for more effective and "genuine" leadership skills so as to enhance business sustainability. This chapter empirically investigates the concept of authentic leadership and considers the pathways to develop authentic leadership by exploring and examining empathy and mindfulness as predictors of authentic leadership. An intense literature review reflects that only a few studies have been conducted that focus on the antecedents of authentic leadership. The study attempts to fill this void. A questionnaire was completed by 250 respondents from the IT industry. Regression analysis was applied to study the inter-relationships among the variables. Findings reveal that while empathy of a leader is significantly related to the development of authentic leadership, mindfulness is not. Wider geographical selection and replication of the study in other industry is recommended. The chapter promotes development of OB interventions intended to foster the development of authentic leaders for positive organizational outcomes.

INTRODUCTION

The recent economic crisis in Greece as well as scams such as Vyapam in India calls for leaders who do not deny responsibility, defy their stakeholders or hide information but instead lead with authenticity and integrity. Authentic leadership (AL) that emerges from the earlier theories of social intelligence (Thorndike, 1920) and multiple intelligence (Gardner, 1983; Salovey and Mayer, 1990) has attracted

DOI: 10.4018/978-1-5225-5297-0.ch015

the attention of researchers and practitioners worldwide. Demand for authentic leadership has been on rise due to rising social costs globally and the need for authenticity (Gardner, Avolio, Luthans, May, and Walumbwa, F. 2005, Klenke 2007). Researchers have added that the integration of ideas is paramount to understanding (Tsur, Berkovitz, and Ginzburg, 2016). Empathy and mindfulness have been noted to significantly associate with the development of effective leaders (Wolff, Pescosolido, and Druskat, 2002). While empathy significantly contributes to the leadership success (Cooper and Sawaf, 1997; Yukl, 1998), mindfulness too has been related to leadership (Boyatzis and McKee, 2005). In order to remain competitive, it has become indispensable for business managers to acquire empathy skills so that they can interact effectively with employees from diverse backgrounds and achieve the goals of the organization (Kayworth and Leidner, 2002). There is a need for more effective and 'genuine' leadership skills for the survival of business in current times. Also, mobilising and influencing the followers is a path that treads towards a successful attainment of leadership objectives. One such leadership is authentic leadership. This chapter explores the construct of authentic leadership and seeks to examine how the two constructs of empathy and mindfulness contribute to its development. Authentic leadership, empathy and mindfulness are human constructs and are likely to share relationship among each other. It is therefore important to find how these mentioned variables are interrelated and are likely to contribute towards the development of authentic leadership.

This study aims to test the theoretical relationships among empathy, mindfulness and authentic leadership in millennials aged 18-34 who are eager to take the leap. With more and more millennials joining the work force, managers must ensure that new joinees are regularly challenged and satisfied in the organization. Although many studies and a variety research has been done, there is still room for clarity on what leadership styles are best suited to serve millennials (Lee, C. C., Mullins, K., and Cho, Y. S., 2016).A poll study shows that one in five of millennials plan to quit their day job to start their own business since they are wary and tired of scams (Ellevate, 2015).Millennials already think they have the right skills to become a leader as 55% of them think that relationship building is the most important skill which is closely related to relational transparency of AL(Workplacetrends.com, 2015). They want to learn online and have mentors to develop leadership as a skill. They also stress on the need of companies to create stronger leadership programs (Ellevate, 2015). Young generation, millennials, in particular strongly believe that leaders should be more authentic, approachable, who are able to give proper reasoning and justification behind every decision they make and are open to questions if any, when raised by the followers (Taylor, 2016).

The same motivates the researchers to explore the antecedents that are pivotal in development of the Authentic Leadership in the work force that majorly comprises of millennials.

The authors ask here two research questions: a) how mindfulness relates to authentic leadership, and b) how empathy contributes to the development of authentic leadership. The chapter begins with developing hypothesis and goes on to present method and findings. Finally, the chapter is concluded by discussing the limitations and implications for academicians and practitioners.

LITERATURE REVIEW

Authentic Leadership

Authentic leadership is a relatively fresh concept hence it is still in its developing phase. The scholars are yet to agree on the common definition of authentic leadership. Kernis (2003) defined authenticity as a psychological construct as 'the unobstructed operation of one's true, or core, self in one's daily enterprise' (p.13). Authentic leadership is a complex multidimensional construct wherein followers, groups and the organization are 'true' to themselves without regard to others and the organisation (Avolio and Gardner, 2005; Gardner, Avolio, Luthans, May, and Walumbwa, F. 2005).There are numerous facets to authentic leadership, however key themes that have been identified are:

- A steady level of self-awareness (Avolio and Gardner, 2005; Avolio, Gardner, Walumbwa, Luthans, and May, 2004; Gardner, Avolio, Luthans, May, and Walumbwa, F. 2005; Ilies, Morgeson and Nahrgang, 2005; Walumbwa, Avolio, Gardner, Wernsing and Peterson, 2008; Yammarino, Dionne, Schriesheim, and Dansereau, 2008).
- An ability to know one's true self, awareness of one's own strengths and weaknesses and its acceptance makes a leader better (Avolio and Gardner, 2005; Gardner, Avolio, Luthans, May, and Walumbwa, F. 2005; Walumbwa, Avolio, Gardner, Wernsing and Peterson, 2008).
- Acting truly to oneself and openly with others (Avolio, Gardner, Walumbwa, Luthans, and May, 2004; Avolio and Gardner, 2005; Brown andTrevino, 2006; Walumbwa, Avolio, Gardner, Wernsing and Peterson, 2008).
- Strength and ability to act according to one's own beliefs and values (Avolio, Gardner, Walumbwa, Luthans, and May, 2004; Avolio and Gardner, 2005; Gardner, Avolio, Luthans, May, and Walumbwa, F. 2005; Walumbwa, Avolio, Gardner, Wernsing and Peterson, 2008).

Authentic leadership has emerged as higher-order, multi-dimensional construct comprising self-awareness, balanced processing of information, relational transparency, and internalized moral standards (Gardner, Avolio, Luthans, May and Walumbwa, 2005;Walumbwa, Avolio, Gardner, Wernsing and Peterson, 2008). Self -awareness signifies leader's awareness of his own strengths and weaknesses, and how they compare themselves with the rest of the world. Internalized moral perspective demonstrates intrinsic form of self-regulation. They align their actions with their values and beliefs and do not succumb to external pressures. Balanced processing refers to the leader's unbiased decision making after carefully analysing the situation without conforming to the external influences. The fourth component is relational transparency that depicts as to how a leader presents himself in front of his followers. How genuine he is while presenting his true self to others. All these components of authentic leadership make a workplace healthy and ethical.

AL certainly offers numerous benefits not just to the organisation but also at individual level. Research suggests that people who are true to themselves experience higher self-esteem, have more positive affect and more hope for the future (Harter, 2002). Authenticity has also been positively linked with psychological wellbeing (Kernis and Goldman, 2005a; Sheldon, Rawsthorne and Ilardi, 1997) as well as high self-esteem and life satisfaction (Kernis and Goldman, 2005b).

Mindfulness

Mindfulness can be defined as 'the state of being attentive to and aware of what is taking place in the present' (Brown and Ryan, 2003, p.822). Considerable literature provides evidence of empirically proven benefits of mindfulness. Mindfulness relates itself with lower levels of emotional disturbance, higher level of subjective well-being and eudemonic wellbeing (Brown and Ryan, 2003; Carlson and Brown, 2005), greater understanding and acceptance of emotions, (Baer, Smith and Allen, 2004; Brown and Ryan, 2003), mindfulness regulates behaviour that in turn helps in optimising wellbeing (Brown and Ryan, 2003; Deci and Ryan, 1980; Ryan, 2005) and associates itself with self – congruence (Brown and Ryan, 2003; Thrash and Elliot, 2002). It refers to focussing on the moment, what is occurring at present without thinking of the past or the future. "Mindfulness is the awareness that emerges through paying attention on purpose, in the present moment, and nonjudgmentally to the unfolding of experience moment by moment" (Kabat-Zinn,2003, pp. 145).

Numerous studies highlight that mindfulness enhances relationships and social interactions (Brown, Ryan and Creswell, 2007). Mindfulness training has been generating much interest within the leadership literature as well as in the corporate leadership. Thus, with the number of benefits that mindfulness imparts, it is evident that it has a role to play in development of leadership behaviour. Mindfulness can facilitate the development of authentic leadership in a number of ways including enhancing relationships and compassion, contributing to the leader and follower relationship and more importantly by enhancing self-awareness and self-regulation.

Empathy

Empathy is considered as one of the most coveted virtues of the human beings by the society (Rogers, Dziobek, Hassenstab, Wolf, and Convit, 2006), and is a fundamental part of our social fabric (Baron-Cohen and Wheelwright, 2004). Empathy is the ability to interpret other's feelings and to re-experience them oneself and depicts an important concept central to emotionally intelligent behaviour (Salovey and Mayer, 1990, pp. 194–195).Empathy is also sharing of both positive and negative feelings that promotes bond between individuals (Plutchik, 1987, p. 43). Numerous studies highlight the importance of empathy in strengthening interpersonal relations (Rogers, 1951, pp. 52–54) and in encouraging change and learning (Rogers 1975, p. 3). Empathy can be explained as an individual's tendency to understand the emotions of other people as his own emotions.

Empathy is a multidimensional process and has been measured on two subscales that is Perspective taking and Empathic Concern (Davis, 1983). Perspective taking or role taking, refers to an individual's tendency to understand and adapt another person's point of view and empathetic concern emphasizes on the feelings of sympathy and concern for others. The chapter does not take into account, the other two components i.e. personal distress and fantasy of Interpersonal Reactivity Index scale because number of studies suggests that empathy and personal distress are separate constructs (Eisenberg and Fabes, 1998; Pulos, 2004). The fantasy component was not considered because it is limited to the fictional stories and it is unclear if it measures pure empathy (Baron-Cohen, S. and Wheelwright, S.; in press).

It is pertinent to consider perspective taking of an individual because it does have an effect on an individual's social interaction and hence may have a significant impact on maintaining healthy relationships at the workplace. Effective leaders are able to create resonance with their followers and can guide them to yield more productive and emotional behaviours with empathy (Goleman, Boyatzis and McKee,

2002, p. 50).As against this leaders lacking in empathy often create dissonance (Goleman, Boyatzis, and McKee, 2002, p. 50).To bring in the change, empathy is therefore necessary to establish the interpersonal relationships (Goleman, Boyatzis, and McKee, 2002, p. 50). Developing empathy is important owing to its benefits to the society as it leads to development of leadership potential and reduction in anti-social behaviours (Sadri, 2012; Winning and Boag, 2015).Outstanding leaders vary from leaders that are less effective in terms of higher consideration and are more sensitive to the requirements of their followers (House and Podsakoff, 1994).

HYPOTHESES DEVELOPMENT

Authentic leadership refers to awareness of self, what is going within. An authentic leader observes internally with openness and is non-judgmental and unbiased, he is what he is and therefore, sees himself more clearly. With the surge of emotions and thoughts, authentic leader offers further insight into how to experience life (Kinsler L., 2014). Mindfulness provides the option to experience oneself as an 'ever changing system of concepts, images, sensations and beliefs' (Shapiro, Carlson, Astin, and Freedman, 2006).Mindfulness refers to the awareness of what is going on around one's self and therefore offers a window into the self, which in turn helps a person to enrich self-awareness(Shapiro, Carlson, Astin, and Freedman, 2006). Researchers suggest that mindful leaders do not force upon their ideas on the followers, instead they are more receptive and by promoting positive discourse they are open to the ideas shared (Sethi, 2009). This is similar to balanced processing – an integral component of authentic leadership which suggests that an authentic leader is receptive of opposing views and takes into account all the possible options before considering one for action. Besides, leaders with mindfulness have the ability to connect deeply with their followers. Mindfulness is an activity to remain engaged so that person is more receptive to the information that might not be usually considered by him. Thus mindfulness encourages a more 'empirical stance towards reality' (Brown, Ryan and Creswell, 2007)) which may develop unbiased processing of information, one of the major components of AL. Mindfulness also generates an openness and encourages being receptive to both positive and negative information about the self, thereby leading to greater understanding of one's self. Thus, it is hypothesized that:

H One a: Mindfulness has a positive correlation with authentic Leadership.
H One b: Mindfulness is a predictor of authentic leadership.

Authentic leaders promotes a free expression of one's own feelings, presentation of leader's true interior and self -disclosure (Walumbwa, Avolio, Gardner, Wernsing, and Peterson, 2008). These behaviours generate trust through the leader follower relationship where information is shared and true thoughts, and feelings, are expressed while minimizing expressions of inappropriate feelings (Kernis, 2003). It has been asserted that empathy produces trust which is again crucial in development of authentic leadership (Agote, Aramburu and Lines, 2016; Nadler and Liviatan, 2006). Relational transparency – a vital component of authentic leadership implies as to how open and transparent the sharing of information is between leaders and followers (Avolio and Gardner 2005). Empathy may assist in sharing of perspectives, ideas and suggestions. This may help the leaders in understanding the views of their subordinates and helping them when needed. (Yukl, .2010). The relationship between these attributes of leadership can be believed to be moderately correlated. Research suggests that high levels of empathy in business leaders indicate higher leadership effectiveness (Rahman, 2013). Empathy allows leaders to understand perspectives of the other people and their opinions in a better way which makes the work environment more positive and productive for the employees (Voss, Gruber, and Reppel, 2010).

Empathy can be an interesting predictor of authentic leadership as it enhances leaders potential to listen to their followers, serve them and develop greater understanding of relationships to their fullest potential. This is because empathy enhances a sense of leadership by providing leaders with the awareness to listen, serve their followers, and have greater understanding of interrelationships within the group (Marques, 2010). Empathic concern, a key component of empathy enables leaders to understand what others are thinking by putting oneself in his/her place. Developing empathic concern in the leaders helps them increase interaction among peers and generates greater empathy (Hodges, Kiel, Kramer, Veach and Villanueva, 2010). Similarly, another key component of empathy that is perspective taking can be developed as a skill, which would motivate the employees to understand and deal with negotiation issues in a better way. Leaders can reinforce social bonds by encouraging social interactions and by utilizing self-reflection and self-awareness so that they can see more of themselves in others, thereby stereotyping (Galinsky, Ku and Wang, 2005). Enhancing perspective taking skills enables the leaders to perceive the thoughts and feelings of their followers (Goleman, 1995). In the recent studies, it has been further established that empathy of a leader has a significant relationship with authentic leadership (Mortier, Vlerick and Clays, 2016)

Thus it is hypothesized that:

H Two a: Empathy and its components are positively correlated with authentic leadership.
H Two b: Empathy is a predictor of authentic Leadership.

The proposed framework is shown in Figure 1.

RESEARCH METHODOLOGY

Sampling

The general intent of this exploratory and descriptive study was to find out if empathy and mindfulness lead to the development of authentic leadership. The method used by researchers was simple random sampling and took a sample size of 250 professional with 1- 3 years of experience. The total number of

Figure 1. The proposed theoretical framework

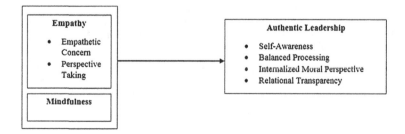

participants filling the paper and pencil questionnaire completely were 200 .The sample was collected from the professionals working in the IT industry in the northern region of India including states of Haryana, Uttar Pradesh and Delhi. The average age was 24.59 years. The sample comprised of 144 male respondents and 56 female respondents. All the respondents were B Tech graduates. The work experience of the sample population has been kept low because, this study aims to gauge the authentic leadership potential of the millennials, the future leaders and whether empathy and mindfulness play a role in the same. Participants were told that participation in this study was voluntary and received no incentive for taking part.

Measures and Psychometric Properties

- **Empathy:** Empathy was assessed by using two subscales of the Interpersonal Reactivity Index model, empathic concern and perspective taking (Davis, 1980, 1983). Specifically, only two components out of four were taken because the rest of the two components are relevant clinically. The component Empathic concern refers to feelings of concern and compassion for others (Davis, 1983) and perspective taking refers to the tendency for employees to create useful ideas for organizations (Grant and Berry, 2011). Both the components comprised of 7 items each with few items with reverse coding. Sample items include: "I often have tender, concerned feelings for people less fortunate than me." "I sometimes try to understand my friends better by imagining how things look from their perspective." Each item had five Likert-type response choices (1-does not describe me at all to 5-describes me very well).

- **Mindfulness:** Mindfulness was measured on 15 items questionnaire i.e. Mindfulness Attention Awareness Scale (Brown, K.W. and Ryan, R.M. (2003). A five-point Likert-style format was used with the response choices as 1 for almost always and 5 for almost never. Sample items include: "I could be experiencing some emotion and not be conscious of it until sometime later." "I tend to walk quickly to get where I'm going without paying attention to what I experience along the way." "I get so focused on the goal I want to achieve that I lose touch with what I'm doing right now to get there."

- **Authentic Leadership:** Authentic leadership is measured on scale developed by Walumbwa et al (2008). This instrument measures authentic leadership as a second-order factor comprised of the four first-order factors namely self-awareness, internalised moral perspective, balanced processing, and relational transparency. ALQ is a valid measure of authentic leadership, which was confirmed by another recent study (Clapp-Smith, Vogelgesang, and Avey, 2009). A five-point Likert-style format was used with the response choices as 1 for strongly agree and 5 for strongly disagree with no right or wrong responses. Sample items include: "I accept the feelings I have about myself (Self Awareness)." "Other people know where I stand on controversial issues (internalized moral perspective)." "I listen very carefully to the ideas of others before making decisions (balanced processing)." "I let others know who I truly am as a person (relational transparency)."

FINDINGS AND ANALYSIS

Descriptive Statistics

The first step involved in the procedure was to test the reliability of each of the measures used. For this Cronbach alpha was calculated for the scale used. Following it was the next step wherein in order to test the hypothesis developed descriptive statistics for authentic leadership and its components, empathy and its components and mindfulness was calculated. Mean and standard deviation of each of the component was calculated. The last step that followed was to calculate the correlation coefficient followed by, stepwise regression analysis was done to study the contribution of each factor to the development of authentic leadership. The findings of the computation have been discussed further.

To test the validity of the instrument, Cronbach's alpha tests were conducted. Cronbach's alpha is calculated to measure the internal consistency and reliability of the instrument. The Cronbach's alpha came to be 0.65, thus the instrument was considered reliable for the study.

Authentic leadership was calculated by taking the means and standard deviations of all the 16 items from the part 4 of the questionnaire (3.63 and .46 respectively).Similarly, means and standard deviation was calculated separately for all the four components of authentic leadership where mean and standard deviation of self-awareness was 3.78 and .59, balanced processing was 3.59 and .59, relational transparency was 3.40 and .75 and internalized moral perspective was 3.69 and .533 respectively.

Next, mean and standard deviation of empathy that consisted of 14 items of part 1 of the questionnaire was calculated. It was calculated to be 3.41 and .49 respectively. Mean and standard deviation of components of empathy i.e. empathetic concern was 3.62 and .59 whereas for perspective taking was 3.21 and .64 respectively.

Thirdly, the mean and standard deviation of mindfulness measured on 15 item scale was calculated as 3.09 and .67 respectively.

Authentic leadership, empathy (and its components) and mindfulness was scored more than average by the respondents as their mean was more than three.

Table 1 shows the descriptive statistics of the variables considered in the study.

Table 1.

Descriptive Statistics	Mean	Std. Deviation
Authentic Leadership	3.6342	.45995
Mindfulness	3.0908	.66581
Empathy	3.4141	.49460
Empathy - Empathetic Concern	3.6215	.59460
Empathy – Perspective taking	3.2128	.64499
AL- Self Awareness	3.7779	.59642
AL- Balanced Processing	3.5897	.59985
AL- Relational Transparency	3.4095	.75335
AL –Internalised Moral Perspective	3.6954	.53381

Correlates and Determinants of Authentic Leadership

The next step after calculating the means and standard deviation of the variables in the studywas to compute the correlation between independent variables and the dependent variables. The dependent variable was authentic leadership that comprised of four components that is self-awareness, balanced processing, relational transparency and internalised moral perspective. The independent variables were empathy and mindfulness. Empathy has two components namely empathetic concern and perspective taking.

Table 2 shows the relationship between the dependent and independent variables along with their components. It was found that empathy has a positive correlation with authentic leadership, r= .371 significant at 0.01 level, *thus accepting our hypothesis Two a*. The components of authentic leadership –balanced processing (r=.314) and relational transparency (r=.383) held significant relationship with empathy at 0.01 level where as self-awareness (r=.175), and internalised moral perspective (r=.171) were significant at 0.05 level. Authentic leaders display higher levels of self-awareness with followers by making the followers believe that leader understands them by making appropriate modifications in his/her behaviour (Avolio and Luthans, 2006).

Here, empathy enhances positive connect between the leader and the follower. Authentic leaders share an open and transparent relationship with followers. This makes them feel emotionally secure with the leaders as they discuss even the sensitive issues with them with transparency. Since, they are aware of the fact that the leaders would provide them with a trusting and a, emotionally secure and a supportive environment comprised of empathy. Empathy relates closely with internalised moral perspective, a key component of authentic leadership (Hannah, 2005). Certain other studies also emphasize that authentic leader's empathy salient in their self-concept by which they can raise their level of internalized moral perspective (Hannah, 2005; Zhu, Avolio et al., 2011). In a recent study too, it has been highlighted that leaders who exhibit empathy are more likely to make ethical relations with their subordinates and act in

Table 2.

	AL	AL- SA	AL- BP	AL – IMP	AL- RT	EMPATHY	EMP-EC	EMP-PT	MIND
AL	1								
AL- SA	.774**	1							
AL- BP	.731**	.432**	1						
AL -IMP	.646**	.438**	.262**	1					
AL- RT	.835**	.536**	.498**	.394**	1				
EMPATHY	.371**	.175*	.314**	.171*	.383**	1			
EMP-EC	.241**	0.136	0.118	0.129	.291**	.771**	1		
EMP-PT	.344**	.149*	.379**	.154*	.298**	.813**	.256**	1	
MIND	-.152*	-0.07	-0.105	-.218**	-0.068	-.179*	-0.078	-.226**	1

*Significant at 0.05 level.

**Significant at 0.01 level.

a responsible manner. This further underlines the relationship between the internalised moral perspective which is an integral component of authentic leadership and empathy. (Dietz and Kleinlogel, 2014).

Empathetic concern – key component of empathy has a significant positive correlation with authentic leadership (r=.241) at 0.01 level. It was interesting to note that relational transparency – major component of authentic leadership is significantly correlated with empathetic concern (.291) at 0.01 level. Component of empathy - perspective taking has individually has a significant positive relationship with authentic leadership (r=.344 at 0.01 level). It is also to be noted that perspective taking also shares positive correlation with all the four components of authentic leadership wherein self-awareness (r=.149) and internalized moral perspective (r=.154) are significant at 0.05 level and balanced processing (r=.379) and relational transparency (r=.298) are significant at 0.01 level. *Thus, the authors accept the hypothesis Two a.* This result also aligns with previous research in the same field. There have been quite a few researches where empathy has been correlated with effective leadership (Atwater and Waldman, 2008; Choi, 2006; Feng, Lazarand Preece, 2004; Goleman, 2000) and the same has been reinforced in this study.

It is however interesting to note that mindfulness is negatively correlated to authentic leadership (r=-.152 significant at 0.05 level) *thus rejecting our hypothesis one a.* One of the components of authentic leadership i.e. internalised moral perspective is significantly negatively correlated to mindfulness (r=-.218) at 0.01 level. The rest of the three components of authentic leadership do not show significant relationship with mindfulness.

Referring to mindfulness having negative correlation with empathy and its components and also with authentic leadership and its components, these findings are contrary to the previous literature which states mindfulness coaching is instrumental in development of authentic leadership. The authors have attributed the significant negative relation of mindfulness both with authentic leadership and empathy to the characteristics of millennials as stated in literature. The authors have cited three such characteristics of millennials that help us explain the negative relationship – 1) millennials stay connected with the laptop, computers and mobile phones, but they use technology to be isolated from the present moment (Layer, R. M,2012).2) Millennials are self-absorbed and impatient (Research centre, 2007). 3) They rely on external locus of control (Astin, 1997) with higher level of individualism, greater emphasis is on autonomy that drifts young professionals from social connectivity thus lowering their levels of mindfulness (Twenge, 2004). Based on these three characteristics, it can be said that millennials may be low on mindfulness but not necessarily on leadership and empathy. In the sample considered for the study, millennials showed low scores on mindfulness but high scores on AL and empathy.

Regression Model

It was expected that authentic leadership will predict the relationships with mindfulness and empathy and advanced hypothesis in this regard. The hypotheses were tested as follows: First, the authors examined the relation between authentic leadership and empathy. Since, the sample size in this study was relatively small to perform SEM analyses (cf. Quintana and Maxwell 1999), hence the researchers used multivariate regression analyses in SPSS to test the predicted direct effects of empathy and mindfulness on authentic leadership.

This section deals with the regression model that contributes to the development of authentic leadership. It examines the strength of the independent variable on the dependent variable. It was assumed that there is a linear relationship between the independent variables and their probability to predict authentic leadership. The regression analysis was carried with the dependent variable as authentic leadership and independent variables as empathy and mindfulness.

The value of multiple r=0.379and R square is .143, thus stating that14% of development of authentic leadership is predicted by empathy. Empathy has Beta value of .367 and correlation coefficient of .371 at 0.01 level, thus significantly contributing to the development of authentic leadership. Based on the finding *the authors accepted the Hypothesis 2 b hypothesis suggesting that empathy is a predictor of authentic leadership.* Based of the above findings *Hypothesis two b was rejected which concluded that mindfulness is not a predictor of authentic leadership.* Empathy enables leaders to create an atmosphere of openness and making them less rigid and open to new ideas thereby making them sensitive to followers' needs and thus leading to effective leadership (Goleman, 2001).Past studies have also suggested that business leaders should increase their empathic concern and perspective taking skills and the same can be developed by active listening and showing true concern for their employees (Rahman, 2013). The empathetic concern and perspective taking can serve as tools to develop empathic skills and authentic leadership, respectively, among business leaders at all levels in the organization. Leaders can be asked to rate their empathy and leadership skills, based on the responses and feedback trainings and mentoring can be provided to them to develop the same in order to be authentic leaders.

Table 3 shows the regression analysis for authentic leadership.

Table 3.

Regression Table for Authentic Leadership

R	R Square	Adjusted R Square	Std. Error of Estimate
.379 a	.144	.139	.43518

Anova

	Sum of Squares	Df	Mean Square	F	Sig.
Regression	5.378	1	5.378	28.397	.000a
Residual	32.005	169	.189		
Total	37.383	170			

Dependent Variable: AL

Coefficients

	Unstandardized Coefficients		Standardized Coefficients	t	Sig.
	B	Std. Error	Beta		
(Constant)	2.443	.228		10.733	.000
Empathy	.351	.066	.379	5.329	.000

Dependent Variable: AL

CONCLUSION

This study supports previous research and provides significant evidence that high levels of empathy skills are play a major role in achieving leadership effectiveness (Gardner and Stough, 2002; Rosete and Ciarrochi, 2005; Shipper, Kincaid, Rotondo and Hoffman, 2003).Authentic leaders displaying empathy can increase the support and positive rating of the leaders which would in turn enhance organizational outcomes gradually (Goldstein, Vezich and Shapiro, 2014).Such display of positive effects by a leader uplifts the moods of the subordinates (Michel, Pichler, and Newness, 2014). Such leaders, by displaying optimistic and empathetic attitude are able to inculcate positive emotions in the followers which in turn motivates them to perform better and contribute to the organization effectively (Damen, van Knippenberg, and van Knippenberg, 2008).The findings in the chapter respond to need of designing and implementation of leadership development intervention strategies intended to foster the development of authentic leaders for positive organizational outcomes. MDPs and workshops for authentic leadership development can be organized across organizations to enhance empathy skills among business leaders that would stimulate leadership effectiveness and organizational performance. The study expands the growing body of knowledge about authentic leadership effectiveness and provides new insight as to how authentic leaders in an organization can improve organizational effectiveness by incorporating empathy to foster productivity. The authors recommend leadership training institutes to include empathy in their training plans when imparting training on leadership and educate the leaders across all levels as to how to develop empathy as a necessary skill to foster productivity in an organization.

There are limitations to this research concerning the sample, the variables, and the methodology. Concerning the sample, this study is limited by the variability of the participants in terms of the organization where they worked and their position in the organization. The sample may therefore be limited to a few positions within each represented organization, and might not be applicable in smaller, private companies and non-business organizations. The methodology might be limited since self-report measures might lead to biasness and participants can exaggerate their level of empathy (Lowenstein, 2005). There are significant opportunities in extending the study based on the existing research of empathy. The study can be extended to other sectors as well and might prove useful. The study would provide valuable insights if higher positions of business leadership like managers, team leaders and supervisors are included in the sample, with more than 5-8 years of experience. Since self - report measures were taken as a base, employee rating should also be included in future research to provide a deeper and more accurate understanding about the impact of empathy on authentic leadership.

REFERENCES

Agote, L., Aramburu, N., & Lines, R. (2016). Authentic leadership perception, trust in the leader, and followers' emotions in organizational change processes. *The Journal of Applied Behavioral Science*, *52*(1), 35–63. doi:10.1177/0021886315617531

Astin, J. A. (1997). Stress reduction through mindfulness meditation: Effects on psychological symptomatology, sense of control, and spiritual experiences. *Psychotherapy and Psychosomatics*, *66*(2), 97–106. doi:10.1159/000289116 PMID:9097338

Atwater, L. E., & Waldman, D. A. (2008). *Leadership, feedback and the open communication gap* (1st ed.). New York: Taylor and Francis Group, LLC.

Avolio, B. J., Gardner, W., Walumbwa, F., Luthans, F., & May, D. R. (2004). Unlocking the mask: A look at the process by which authentic leaders impact follower attitudes and behaviours. *The Leadership Quarterly*, *15*(6), 801–823. doi:10.1016/j.leaqua.2004.09.003

Avolio, B. J., & Gardner, W. L. (2005). Authentic leadership development: Getting to the root of positive forms of leadership. *The Leadership Quarterly*, *16*(3), 315–338. doi:10.1016/j.leaqua.2005.03.001

Avolio, B. J., & Luthans, F. (2006). *High Impact Leader: Moments Matter in Authentic Leadership Development*. McGraw-Hill.

Avolio, B. J., Luthans, F., & Walumbwa, F. o. (2004). *Authentic Leadership: Theory building for veritable sustained performance*. Working Paper. Gallup Leadership Institute, University of Nebraska, Lincoln.

Baer, R. A., Smith, G., & Allen, K. B. (2004). Assessment of mindfulness by self-report: The Kentucky inventory of Mindfulness skills. *Assessment*, *11*(3), 191–206. doi:10.1177/1073191104268029 PMID:15358875

Baron-Cohen, S., & Wheelright, S. (2004). The empathy quotient: An investigation of adults with Asperger syndrome or high-functioning autism and normal sex differences. *Journal of Autism and Developmental Disorders*, *34*(2), 163–175. doi:10.1023/B:JADD.0000022607.19833.00 PMID:15162935

Boyatzis, R. E., & McKee, A. (2005). *Resonant leadership: Renewing yourself and connecting with others through mindfulness, hope, and compassion* (1st ed.). Harvard Business Review Press.

Brown, K. W., & Ryan, M. (2003). The benefits of being present: Mindfulness and its role in psychological well-being. *Journal of Personality and Social Psychology*, *84*(4), 822–848. doi:10.1037/0022-3514.84.4.822 PMID:12703651

Brown, K. W., Ryan, R. M., & Creswell, J. D. (2007). Mindfulness: Theoretical foundations and evidence for its salutary effects. *Psychological Inquiry*, *18*(4), 211–237. doi:10.1080/10478400701598298

Brown, M. E., & Treviño, L. K. (2006). Ethical leadership: A review and future directions. *The Leadership Quarterly*, *17*(6), 595–616. doi:10.1016/j.leaqua.2006.10.004

Carlson, L. E., & Brown, K. W. (2005). Validation of the Mindful attention awareness scale in a cancer population. *Journal of Psychosomatic Research*, *58*(1), 29–33. doi:10.1016/j.jpsychores.2004.04.366 PMID:15771867

Choi, J. (2006). A motivational theory of charismatic leadership: Envisioning, empathy, and empowerment. *Journal of Leadership & Organizational Studies*, *13*(1), 24–43. doi:10.1177/10717919070130010501

Clapp-Smith, R., Vogelgesang, G. R., & Avey, J. B. (2009). Authentic leadership and positive psychological capital the mediating role of trust at the group level of analysis. *Journal of Leadership & Organizational Studies*, *15*(3), 227–240. doi:10.1177/1548051808326596

Cooper, R. K., & Sawaf, A. (1997). *Executive EQ: Emotional intelligence in leadership and organizations*. New York: Grosset/Putman.

Davis, M. H. (1980). A multidimensional approach to individual differences in empathy. *Catalog of Selected Documents in Psychology*, *10*(85). Retrieved from http://www.eckerd.edu/academics/psychology/files/Davis_1980.pdf

Davis, M. H. (1983). Measuring individual differences in empathy: Evidence for a multidimensional approach. *Journal of Personality and Social Psychology*, *44*(1), 113–126. doi:10.1037/0022-3514.44.1.113

Deci, E. L., & Ryan, R. M. (1980). Self-determination theory: When mind mediates behaviour. *Journal of Mind and Behavior*, *1*, 33–43.

Dietz, J., & Kleinlogel, E. P. (2014). Wage cuts and managers' empathy: How a positive emotion can contribute to positive organizational ethics in difficult times. *Journal of Business Ethics*, *119*(4), 461–472. doi:10.1007/s10551-013-1836-6

Dziobek, I., Rogers, K., Fleck, S., Bahnemann, M., Heekeren, H. R., Wolf, O. T., & Convit, A. (2007). Dissociation of cognitive and emotional empathy in adults with Asperger syndrome using the Multifaceted Empathy Test (MET). *Journal of Autism and Developmental Disorders*, *38*(3), 464–473. doi:10.1007/s10803-007-0486-x PMID:17990089

Eisenberg, N., Fabes, R. A., & Spinrad, T. L. (1998). Prosocial development. In Handbook of child psychology. Academic Press.

Ellevate. (2015). *Forbes*. Retrieved 28 September, 2015, from http://www.forbes.com/sites/85broads/2013/11/18/the-millennial-startup-revolution/

Endrissat, N., Muller, W. R., & Kaudela-Baum, S. (2007). En route to an empirically-based understanding of Authentic Leadership. *European Management Journal*, *25*(3), 207–220. doi:10.1016/j.emj.2007.04.004

Feng, J., Lazar, J., & Preece, J. (2004). Empathy and online interpersonal trust: A fragile relationship. *Journal of Behavior and Information Technology*, *23*(2), 97–106. doi:10.1080/01449290310001659240

Galinsky, A. D., Ku, G., & Wang, C. S. (2005). Perspective taking and self-other overlap: Fostering social bonds and facilitating social coordination. *Group Processes & Intergroup Relations*, *8*(2), 109–124. doi:10.1177/1368430205051060

Gardner, H. (1983). *Frames of mind*. New York: Basic Books.

Gardner, L., & Stough, C. (2002). Examining the relationship between leadership and emotional intelligence in senior level managers. *Leadership and Organization Development Journal*, *23*(2), 68–78. doi:10.1108/01437730210419198

Gardner, W., Avolio, B. J., Luthans, F., May, D. R., & Walumbwa, F. (2005). 'Can you see the real me?' A self-based model of authentic leader and follower development. *The Leadership Quarterly*, *16*(3), 343–372. doi:10.1016/j.leaqua.2005.03.003

Gardner, W. L., Avolio, B. J., Luthans, F., May, D. R., & Walumbwa, F. (2005). Can You See the Real Me? A Self-based Model of Authentic Leader and Follower Development. *The Leadership Quarterly*, *16*(3), 343–372. doi:10.1016/j.leaqua.2005.03.003

Goldstein, N. J., Vezich, I. S., & Shapiro, J. R. (2014). Perceived perspective taking: When others walk in our shoes. *Journal of Personality and Social Psychology*, *106*(6), 941–960. doi:10.1037/a0036395 PMID:24841098

Goleman, D. (1995). *Emotional intelligence: Why it can matter more than IQ?* New York: Bantam Books.

Goleman, D. (2000). Leadership that gets results. *Harvard Business Review*, *78*(2), 78–90.

Goleman, D. (2001). An e-based theory of performance. In C. Cherniss & D. Goleman (Eds.), *The emotionally intelligence workplace* (pp. 27–44). San Francisco, CA: Jossey-Bass.

Goleman, D., Boyatzis, R., and McKee, A. (2002). *Primal leadership*. Boston, MA: Harvard Business School Press.

Grant, A. M., & Schwartz, B. (2011). Too much of a good thing the challenge and opportunity of the inverted U. *Perspectives on Psychological Science*, *6*(1), 61–76. doi:10.1177/1745691610393523 PMID:26162116

Hannah, S. T., Lester, P. B., & Vogelgesang, G. R. (2005). Moral leadership: Explicating the moral component of authentic leadership. *Authentic leadership theory and practice: Origins, effects and development, 3*, 43-81.

Harter, S. (2002). Authenticity. In C. R. Snyder & S. J. Lopez (Eds.), *Handbook of positive psychology* (pp. 382–394). New York: Oxford University Press.

Hodges, S. D., Kiel, K. J., Kramer, A. D., Veach, D., & Villanueva, R. (2010). Giving birth to empathy: The effects of similar experience on empathic accuracy, empathic concern, and perceived empathy. *Personality and Social Psychology Bulletin*, *36*(3), 398–409. doi:10.1177/0146167209350326 PMID:19875825

House, R. J., & Podsakoff, P. M. (1994). Leadership effectiveness: Past perspectives and future directions for research. In J. Greenberg (Ed.), Organizational behavior: The state of the science (pp. 45– 82). Hillsdale, NJ: Lawrence Erlbaum Associates.

Ilies, R., Morgeson, F. P., & Nahrgang, J. D. (2005). Authentic Leadership and eudemonic well-being: Understanding leader-follower outcomes. *The Leadership Quarterly*, *16*(3), 373–394. doi:10.1016/j.leaqua.2005.03.002

Kabat-Zinn, J. (1994). *Wherever you go, there you are: mindfulness meditation in everyday life*. Hyperion Books.

Kabat-Zinn, J. (2003). Mindfulness based interventions in context: Past, present, and future. *Clinical Psychology: Science and Practice*, *10*(2), 144–156. doi:10.1093/clipsy.bpg016

Kayworth, T. R., & Leidner, D. E. (2002). Leadership effectiveness in global virtual teams. *Journal of Management Information Systems*, *18*(3), 7–40. doi:10.1080/07421222.2002.11045697

Kernis, M. H. (2003). Toward a conceptualisation of optimal self-esteem. *Psychological Inquiry*, *14*(1), 1–26. doi:10.1207/S15327965PLI1401_01

Kernis, M. H., & Goldman, B. M. (2005a). Authenticity, social motivation, and psychological adjustment. In J. P. Forgas, K. D. Williams, & S. M. Laham (Eds.), *Social motivation: Conscious and unconscious processes* (pp. 210–227). New York: Cambridge University Press.

Kernis, M. H., & Goldman, B. M. (2005b). From thought and experience to behaviour and interpersonal relationships: A multicomponent conceptualization of authenticity. In A. Tesser, J. V. Wood, & D. A. Stapel (Eds.), *On building, defending, and regulating the Self* (pp. 31–52). New York: Psychology Press.

Kinsler, L. (2014, March). International Coaching. *Psychological Review*, *9*(1).

Klenke, K. (2007). Authentic Leadership: A Self, Leader, and Spiritual Identity Perspective. *International Journal of Leadership Studies*, *3*(1), 68–97.

Layer, R. M. (2012). *The Millennial Student: A Strategy for Improved Wellness* (Doctoral dissertation). University of Minnesota.

Lee, C. C., Mullins, K., & Cho, Y. S. (2016). Factors affecting job satisfaction and retention of millennials. Academy of Organizational Culture, Communications and Conflict, 6.

Loewenstein, G. (2005). Hot-cold empathy gaps and medical decision making. *Health Psychology*, *24*(4, Suppl), S49–S56. doi:10.1037/0278-6133.24.4.S49 PMID:16045419

Marques, J. (2010). Spirituality, meaning, interbeing, leadership, and empathy: SMILE. *Interbeing*, *4*(2), 7.

Michel, J., Pichler, S., & Newness, K. (2014). Integrating leader affect, leader work-family spillover, and leadership. *Leadership and Organization Development Journal*, *35*(5), 410–428. doi:10.1108/LODJ-06-12-0074

Mortier, A. V., Vlerick, P., & Clays, E. (2016). Authentic leadership and thriving among nurses: The mediating role of empathy. *Journal of Nursing Management*, *24*(3), 357–365. doi:10.1111/jonm.12329 PMID:26264773

Nadler, A., & Liviatan, I. (2006). Intergroup reconciliation: Effects of adversary's expressions of empathy, responsibility, and recipients' trust. *Personality and Social Psychology Bulletin*, *32*(4), 459–470. doi:10.1177/0146167205276431 PMID:16513799

Plutchik, R. (1987). Evolutionary bases of empathy. In N. Eisenberg & J. Strayer (Eds.), *Empathy and its development* (pp. 38–46). New York Cambridge University Press.

Pulos, S., Elison, J., and Lennon, R. (2004). The hierarchical structure of the Interpersonal Reactivity Index. *Social Behaviour and Personality*, 32355-360.

Quintana, S. M., & Maxwell, S. E. (1999). Implications of recent developments in structural equation modelling for counselling psychology. *The Counseling Psychologist*, *27*(4), 485–527. doi:10.1177/0011000099274002

Rahman, W. A., & Castelli, P. A. (2013). The impact of empathy on leadership effectiveness among business leaders in the United States and Malaysia. *International Journal of Economics Business and Management Studies*, *2*(3), 83–97.

Rogers, C. R. (1951). *Client-Centered therapy*. Boston: Houghton Mifflin.

Rogers, C. R. (1975). Empathic: An unappreciated way of being. *The Counseling Psychologist, 5*(2), 2–10. doi:10.1177/001100007500500202

Rogers, K., Dziobek, I., Hassenstab, J., Wolf, O. T., & Convit, A. (2007). Who cares? Revisiting empathy in Asperger syndrome. *Journal of Autism and Developmental Disorders, 37*(4), 709–715. doi:10.1007/s10803-006-0197-8 PMID:16906462

Rosete, D., & Ciarrochi, J. (2005). Emotional intelligence and its relationship to workplace performance outcomes of leadership effectiveness. *Leadership and Organization Development Journal, 26*(5), 388–399. doi:10.1108/01437730510607871

Ryan, R. M. (2005). The developmental line of autonomy in the etiology, dynamics, and treatment of borderline personality disorders. *Development and Psychopathology, 17*(04), 987–1006. doi:10.1017/S0954579405050467 PMID:16613427

Sadri, G. (2012). Emotional intelligence and leadership development. *Public Personnel Management, 41*(3), 535–548. doi:10.1177/009102601204100308

Salovey, P., & Mayer, J. D. (1990). Emotional intelligence. *Imagination, Cognition and Personality, 9*(3), 185–211. doi:10.2190/DUGG-P24E-52WK-6CDG

Sethi, D. (2009). Mindful leadership. *Leader to Leader, 2009*(51), 7–11. doi:10.1002/ltl.311

Shapiro, S. L., Carlson, L. E., Astin, J. A., & Freedman, B. (2006). Mechanisms of mindfulness. *Journal of Clinical Psychology, 62*(3), 373–386. doi:10.1002/jclp.20237 PMID:16385481

Sheldon, K. M., Ryan, R. M., Rawsthorne, L. J., & Ilardi, B. (1997). Trait self and true self: Cross-role variation in the Big-Five personality traits and its relations with psychological authenticity and subjective well-being. *Journal of Personality and Social Psychology, 73*(6), 1380–1393. doi:10.1037/0022-3514.73.6.1380

Shipper, F., Kincaid, J., Rotondo, D. M., & Hoffman, R. C. IV. (2003). A cross-cultural exploratory study of the linkage between emotional intelligence and managerial effectiveness. *The International Journal of Organizational Analysis, 11*(3), 171–191. doi:10.1108/eb028970

Taylor, S. L. (2016). *Reshaping Millennials As Future Leaders Of The Marine Corps.* Air War College Montgomery United States.

The Pew Research Centre for the People and the Press. (2007). *How young people view their lives, futures and politics: A portrait of "Generation Next."* Author.

Thorndike, E. L. (1920). Intelligence and its use. *Harper's Magazine, 140*, 227–235.

Thrash, T. M., & Elliot, A. J. (2002). Implicit and self-attributed achievement motives: Concordance and predictive validity. *Journal of Personality, 70*(5), 729–755. doi:10.1111/1467-6494.05022 PMID:12322858

Tsur, N., Berkovitz, N., & Ginzburg, K. (2016). Body awareness, emotional clarity, and authentic behavior: The moderating role of mindfulness. *Journal of Happiness Studies, 17*(4), 1451–1472. doi:10.1007/s10902-015-9652-6

Twenge, J. M., Zhang, L., & Im, C. (2004). It's beyond my control: A cross-temporal meta-analysis of increasing externality in locus of control, 1960-2002. *Personality and Social Psychology Review*, *8*(3), 308–319. doi:10.1207/s15327957pspr0803_5 PMID:15454351

Van Kleef, G. A., Homan, A. C., Beersma, B., Van Knippenberg, D., Van Knippenberg, B., & Damen, F. (2009). Searing sentiment or cold calculation? The effects of leader emotional displays on team performance depend on follower epistemic motivation. *Academy of Management Journal*, *52*(3), 562–580. doi:10.5465/AMJ.2009.41331253

Voss, R., Gruber, T., & Reppel, A. (2010). Which classroom service encounters make students happy or unhappy? *International Journal of Education*, *24*(7), 615–636.

Walumbwa, F., Avolio, B. J., Gardner, W., Wernsing, T. S., & Peterson, S. J. (2008). Authentic Leadership: Development and validation of a theory-based measure. *Journal of Management*, *34*(1), 89–126. doi:10.1177/0149206307308913

Winning, A. P., & Boag, S. (2015). Does brief mindfulness training increase empathy? The role of personality. *Personality and Individual Differences*, *86*, 492–498. doi:10.1016/j.paid.2015.07.011

Wolff, S. B., Pescosolido, A. T., & Druskat, V. U. (2002). Emotional intelligence as the basis of leadership emergence in self-managing teams. *The Leadership Quarterly*, *13*(5), 505–522. doi:10.1016/S1048-9843(02)00141-8

Workplacetrendscom. (2015). Retrieved 28 September, 2015, from https://workplacetrends.com/the-millennial-leadership-survey/

Yukl, G. (1998). Leadership in organizations (4th ed.). Prentice Hall.

Zhu, W., Avolio, B. J., Riggio, R. E., & Sosik, J. J. (2011). The effect of authentic transformational leadership on follower and group ethics. *The Leadership Quarterly*, *22*(5), 801–817. doi:10.1016/j.leaqua.2011.07.004

Chapter 16
High Involvement Work Processes:
Implications for Employee Withdrawal Behaviors

Manu Melwin Joy
SCMS School of Technology and Management, India

ABSTRACT

The purpose of this chapter is to examine the effect of high involvement work processes on employee withdrawal behaviors in information technology sector in India. It draws from the structured questionnaire data from 300 software engineers working in Infosys, CTS, and HCL. Data was analyzed to find out details related to the relationship between high involvement work processes and employee withdrawal behaviors. It was found that high involvement work processes have a strong negative impact on withdrawal behaviors. The relationship was found to be stronger in the case of work withdrawal behaviors compared to that of job withdrawal behaviors.

INTRODUCTION

Employee retention has been a crucial issue faced by organizations across the globe. Since the ability to retain the best employees is directly related to performance indicators such as increased sales, enhanced customer satisfaction, satisfied employees etc, organizations are forced to adopt superior retention strategies to maintain their valuable talent. Researchers such as Gberevbie (2008) and Taplin et al. (2003) have found that adoption and implementation of appropriate employee retention strategies will motivate employees to stay with the organization and work for success of the organization. As a result of the knowledge based economy, there is a heightened emphasis on the link of employee retention strategies with firm productivity. This results in human resources becoming important organizational assets and leads to tight linkage of retention strategies with organizational survival. While organizations calculated the overall contribution of employees on manufacturing processes and products in the past, the rise of service industry has shifted focus on individual level contributions and current employers are able to

DOI: 10.4018/978-1-5225-5297-0.ch016

find out the direct effect of each employee to different organizational outcomes. The socio economic trends happening at individual, organizational and industry level has to be reviewed to have a better understanding about the increased need for retention strategies.

From the individual perspective, there are four reasons for retention strategies to be crucial. First, when the "Generation Y" and millennial started moving into the workplace, they bring with them specific values and expectations about work experiences (Twenge & Campbell, 2008). These individuals came with little expectations about job security, pensions or conventional career models. Since their needs are entirely different from the requirements of the baby boomers, organizations have to strive hard to maintain their loyalty by implementing innovative retention strategies appealing to the younger work-force. Secondly, individual expectation of retentions strategies can be considered as an after effect of globalization. In the current global village, individuals could cross borders effortlessly and take advantage of career opportunities, thereby increasing the available job alternatives for skilled professionals. So organizations should convince the employees that their current work environment is better than all other available options and motivate them to stay in their respective jobs. The scarcity of human resource is the third factor leading to the relevance of comprehensive retention strategies. The global dearth of skilled professionals has lead to a wealth of career opportunities for existing employees who possess the right kind of knowledge, skills and attitude. With employee poaching being common place, skilled employees are aware of their leverage and this had resulted in inflated salary and other compensation packages. The emerging interest in the work life balance is the final factor from the individual perspective that underscores the importance of employee retention strategies. Nowadays, employees prefer to stay with organizations that help to maximize their work, family and societal objectives. If firms tend to ignore these trends in work life balances, they may suffer from significant staff losses. Therefore, socio economic trends such as changing work demographics, economic globalization, scarcity of right talent and focus on work life balance has resulted in individuals paying more attention to employee retention strategies.

Two factors from the organizational perspective have led to the increased need for employee retention strategies. First, experts forecast serious shortage of skilled labor in the twenty first century (Judy, 2000) and majority of organizations face dearth of employees with right kind of competencies to excel in the competitive marketplace. Demand for skilled professionals in on a rise because of the frequent technological innovations and the situation is made worse by the mass retirement of baby boomer generations. Today, the wealth of career opportunities available for employees forces the organizations to put in place efficient retention strategies. Second, the cost related to high turnover rates has become too big for organizations to neglect. According to many human resource experts, the replacement cost of skill professions account to as much as 150% of the departing employee's salary, taking into consideration the head hunter's fee, defector's lost contacts, the newcomers depressed productivity and the time co-workers spend guiding him. Simultaneously, high turnover leads to lower employee morale and many workers reportedly experience a sense of personal loss once their colleagues have left the organization. The dissatisfaction heightens with the awareness that the departed colleague has got a better alternative. From the organizational perspective, the socio economic trends such as dearth of skilled labor and spiraling cost of turnover has resulted in the increased relevance of retention practices.

In a nutshell, high turnover rates along with their visible and hidden costs, a change in the labor force demographics, and an environment of aggressive competition for limited and critical human talent creates the need for IT organizations to adopt employee retention issues. Researches of the past decade have argued that high performance work systems act as a panacea to issues related to human capital, especially employee retention. Because of the highly contentious nature of the term employee retention, a more measurable and objective term called employee withdrawal behavior was used to operationalize the concept. In the following section, the theoretical underpinnings of terms High Involvement Work Processes and Employee Withdrawal Behaviors is outlined. Based on the review of literature, a conceptual model linking both variables is proposed. Then, the methodology adopted is outlined and data analysis is depicted. The findings obtained are discussed along with implication for HR practice.

Prior Research on High Involvement Work Processes (HIWP)

Increased interest in different forms of inclusionary practices and processes among managers and researchers resulted from the realization that success partially stems from an emphasis on employee involvement practices and is essential to survival in this age of escalating global and domestic competition. There is a conviction among the important stakeholders that employee involvement has a positive effect on organizational performance and this belief has paved way for many modern managerial practices, such as participative decision making, quality circles and gain sharing. Once introduced, these practices will lead to improved product or service quality, better innovation, bolstered employee motivation, reduced cost but increased speed of production and lesser employee absenteeism and turnover (Lawler, 1996, Leana & Florkowski, 1992).

Likewise, in the past decade, different views and perspectives concerning the definition of involvement, how to construct involvement and how to operationalize involvement in research have evolved (Wagner, 1994, Leana, Locke & Schweiger, 1990). However, no individual approach to constructing involvement has evolved as the definitive approach. The approach to employee involvement applied in the present study is referred to as high involvement work processes (HIWP).

The term high involvement in chosen over the more popular label high performance because of multiple reasons. The first reason is that the HR processes and employee participation is well depicted by the term high involvement (Ledford, 1993; Ramsay, Scholarios, & Harley, 2000; Vandenberg et al., 1999). In addition, this label improves flexibility as it permits for the chances of having employee-centered practices without subsuming organizational outcomes (Wall & Wood, 2005). Even though several research have suggested that well implemented high involvement work systems lead to 'high performance' outcomes, 'high involvement' better depicts the crucial role played by employees in ensuring its correct implementation (Vandenberg et al., 1999; Wall & Wood, 2005).

The second reason is that, contrasting many earlier research studies (Arthur, 1994; Guthrie, 2001; Huselid, 1995), the focal point of the present research is not on 'performance'; it is on the connection between employees' subjective understanding of the various human resources management practices used within their respective firm and individual employee's work attitudes. Vandenberg et al. (1999) argued that HIWP relies on subjective beliefs. Recent researches show that the strength of subjective beliefs about events has more dominant influence over individuals' and organizational effectiveness than does objective assessments of those same events. According to the arguments put forward by Wood (1999) and Wall & Wood (2005), risk in using the term 'high performance management' is that it strengthens specific bundles of management practices before its outcomes are known. On the contrary, high involvement does not subsume outcomes, only processes, rendering it a less restrictive term.

Third, many researchers (Becker & Huselid, 1998) choose the term high performance work systems to widen the focus away from employees' attitudes and commitment (Wood, 1999). Since the present study focuses on employee attitudes, perceptions, and commitment, but not outcomes, it would be inappropriate to use this term. Previous conceptions of high commitment / involvement (Beer, Spector, Lawrence,

Mills & Watson, 1984, Walton, 1985) relate these schemes with a control-oriented human resources management strategy and many scholars argue that that including contingent based pay schemes requires a change of terminology from high commitment / involvement management to high performance. But the current trend agrees that appropriate performance-based-pay schemes such as team and organizational wide incentives can be successfully incorporated in models of high involvement work systems (Lawler et al., 1995, Vandenberg et al., 1999). To put it differently, researcher in the present study is investigating the nature of high involvement work systems from the employees' perspectives rather than that of their managers. It is for this rationale that the term involvement rather than performance is a better descriptor of these systems.

A superficial look at the literature falling under the general rubric of involvement shows that the majority of research has narrowly concentrated on one form of involvement: participative decision making (Wagner, 1994). All these researches have exclusively operationalized participative decision making as the independent variable by identifying characteristic organizational level practices and then connecting relating these practices to effectiveness (Cotton et al., 1988). The role of individual in involvement processes is only indirectly acknowledged by this approach of moving from organizational practices to the outcomes. The common notion is that organizational practices represent individual feelings toward involvement, and the individual's acceptance of those practices as guiding principles.

The reality is that this approach has not been an accurate test which would operationalize involvement through the individual. The characteristics of this type of operationalization is that it acknowledges the need for individual employee to perceive the existence of opportunity for involvement and the employee must support it by actually putting involvement into practice in his or her day-to-day work routine (Lawler, 1996). In a nutshell, a firm may have plenty of written policies regarding involvement, and top management may even assume it is practiced, but these policies and beliefs are worthless until the individual perceives them as something significant to his or her organizational well-being.

The High Involvement Work Processes approach provides a feasible way of bringing the individual into the research picture. Relying heavily on the works of Galbraith (1973) and Lawler (1996), it is evident that HIWP approach does not assign itself to a particular program or practice, such as participative decision making or quality circles alone and its focus lies on four mutually reinforcing attributes. These attributes are (a) the power to perform and take decisions about job in all its aspects; (b) information about processes, quality, customer response, event and business results; (c) rewards linked to business results and development in capability and contribution; and (d) knowledge of the work, the business, and the total work system.

High Involvement Work Processes literature stresses a lot on whether the attributes are the exclusive privilege of only a few individuals in the firm or broadly distributed across all members of the organization (Lawler, 1996). According to Galbraith (1973), the four attributes of involvement such as power, information, reward, and knowledge (PIRK) are found in all organizations but are conventionally restricted to the individuals in the top of management and asserts that the mere existence of the attributes doesn't serve the purpose. For involvement to be high, the four attributes must be evenly distributed at all levels of the organization (Lawler1996) and employees must regard the PIRK attributes as operational characteristics of their jobs.

The main advantage of High Involvement Work Processes approach is that it avoids the pointless dissection that results from discussing over how much decision making one is allowed, over which array of topics and at the result of which type of intervention. Since High Involvement Work Processes completely rely on subjective beliefs, these needless arguments are alleviated. Based on studies done on similar beliefs, it is evident that power of subjective beliefs about incidents exerts a much more dominant influence over individuals' and organizational effectiveness than does objective assessments of those same incidents. Hence, even if a researcher identifies a range of involving practices in place within a firm, those practices will have little impact unless the relevant individuals manifest them in some form and put them to practice in their own ways.

The theoretical positive influence of High Involvement Work Processes on organizations allows them to take advantage of their human capital by both building it and actively connecting it to the firm's performance. Since competitor can imitate similar policies, procedures, and technologies, leverage created by organizations out of various non-human resources may be short lived (Barney, 1991). The benefits gained out of leveraging human capital are supposed to be more important, rare, and hard to imitate, and hence, offer a sustainable advantage (Jackson & Schuler, 1995; Koch & McGrath, 1996).

In highly stable manufacturing industries where the nature of work restricts redesign to provide employees more power and they necessarily have little control over the quantity and quality of their production, High Involvement Work Processes might not be very effective (Lawler, 1996). On the contrary, implementation of High Involvement Work Processes will directly benefit organizations operating in very dynamic environments where employee flexibility and up-to-date knowledge are vital. Firms operating in technology industry or those that rely heavily on knowledge-based work falls under this category

Lawler's influential research on High-Involvement Management summed up the issue of how High Involvement Work Processes maximizes human capital. When people participate in setting goals and getting information about their performance two things happen. First, they set goals that are perceived by them to be achievable. Second, their self-esteem and competence becomes tied to achieving the goals and therefore they are also highly motivated to achieve them (Lawler, 1996).

Vandenberg et al. (1999) refers to the involvement attributes as High Involvement Work Processes. High Involvement Work Processes has to be distinguished from High Performance Work Practices or High Involvement Work Practices (Guthrie, Spell, & Nyamori, 2002) - which are synonymous, in this review, with specific sets of HR practices. Formal and sanctioned work activities that facilitate an organization to achieve its goals – such as training and performance appraisal comes under the purview of practices. The resultant experience of involvement in the work environment is termed as processes.

Definition based on the studies done by Lawler (1992) states that involvement is a management perspective that takes the elements of power, information, rewards, and knowledge to the grass root levels in an organization. The power to act and make decisions about work in all its aspects is defined as power. Information about processes, quality, customer feedback, events and business results is defined as Information. Rewards tied to business results and growth in capability and contribution is defined as rewards. Knowledge of the work, of the business, and of the total work system is defined as knowledge (Lawler, 1992). High Involvement Work Processes expands this general definition by enquiring workers how much of each of these attributes they experience in their jobs (Vandenberg et al., 1999).

Prior Research on Employee Retention and Withdrawal Behaviors (EWB)

Retention is traditionally defined as a voluntary initiative taken by an organization to create an environment which engages employees for the long term. A more elaborate and contemporary definition of the concept of retention is to avoid the loss of skilled and competent employees from leaving productivity and profitability (Chibowa, Sameul & Chipunza, 2010). Many researchers view employee retention as the result of implementation of human resource practices that support employees to remain with the organization since the work environment satisfies their needs. Employee retention, according to Harvard Business Essentials, is the opposite of turnover – turnover being the sum of voluntary and involuntary separation between employee and his employer. Intent to leave work is normally considered as a proxy for real voluntary turnover (Carraher and Buckly, 2008), which is one of the most harmful behaviors from the perspective of organizational effectiveness. Theory of reasoned action states that intention to leave is a psychological precursor to a behavioral act (Ajzen and Fishbein, 1980). Based on this assumption, an employee who nurtures the thought of leaving the job is more likely to do so if the right conditions exist and may reduce their efforts at work. Employees who are not committed to their organizations exhibit withdrawal behaviors, which are defined as a set of actions that employees perform to stay away from work situations – behaviors that may eventually result in leaving the organization (Hulin, 1991). Withdrawal behaviors refer to a bundle of attitudes and behaviors used by employees when they stay at the job but for some reason opt to be less involved (Kaplan et al., 2009).

Researchers have identified employee exit intentions as one of the most proximal predictors of turnover (Griffeth, 2000) and have been generally used as an outcome variable in research studies concentrating on voluntary employee turnover. (Benson, 2006; Finegold, Mohrman & Spreitzer, 2002). On the contrary, employee neglect behaviors such as absence, tardiness and reduced work efforts have not been extensively investigated. Nevertheless, literature review asserts moderate negative correlation between job satisfaction, affective commitment and employee neglect (Johns, 2002; Meyer et.al 2002). Even though these relationships are not as strong as those for intentions and turnover, they need further investigation. There is a general consensus among researcher about the connectedness of withdrawal behaviors and there is evidence that employee withdrawal is progressive, with more minor forms of withdrawal such as neglect behaviors eventually leading to more extreme acts such as turnover (Johns, 2002).

Withdrawal behaviors can be defined as a bundle of attitudes and behaviors adopted by employees when they stay at the job but for some reason decide to be less participative (Kaplan et al., 2009). Many traditional theories including equity theory (Adams, 1965), inducements– contributions theory (March and Simon, 1958), and social exchange theory (Thibault and Kelly, 1959) stressed the role played by withdrawal behavior that forces employees to withhold inputs from an organization. These theories states that withdrawal behaviors are often controllable forms of input reduction. Moreover, withdrawal behaviors allows an employee to reduce the cost of an aversive job by involving in more pleasurable activities while still enjoying the economic benefits offered by the job.

Employee withdrawal intentions consists of various different, yet connected constructs (e.g. thinking of quitting, intention to search and intention to quit), which have been generally studied in relation to withdrawal behavior (e.g. absenteeism, actual turnover). Definition given in the organizational research depicts withdrawal behavior as actions intended to place physical or psychological remoteness between employees and workplace (Rosse and Hulin, 1985). Mobley (1982) and Mobley et al. (1978) suggests the meaning of the label "withdrawal" as a process, which contains diverse, yet related constructs. The turnover model of Mobley et al. (1978) has evaluated various constructs of withdrawal intentions (i.e. thinking of quitting, intention to search and intention to quit) as well as the construct of withdrawal behavior (i.e. actual quit).

Researchers have categorized deviant behavior in the workplace along two dimensions: minor versus serious deviance, and directed at either organizational or personal targets (Fox & Spector, 1999). Behaviours that come under the label of minor organizational deviance which disrupts productivity includes arriving late or leaving early, intentionally working slower, daydreaming instead of working, failing to help a coworker, or withholding work-related information from a co-worker. On contrary, serious organizational deviance is linked to behaviors targeted at property, such as damaging or stealing equipment. While minor interpersonal deviance points towards petty acts against individuals in the workplace, such as gossiping about co-workers or blaming coworkers whereas serious interpersonal deviance denotes acts of aggression or violence directed at individuals in the workplace which includes sexual harassment and verbal or physical abuses.

Considering the classification system discussed above, the category of minor organizational deviance includes many behaviors that overlaps with the concept of psychological withdrawal which implies the little effort that employee puts into work. Many different manifestation of this includes daydreaming, doing personal tasks at work, chatting excessively with co-workers, and letting others do the work (Lehman & Simpson, 1992). Even though some researchers consider psychological withdrawal behaviors as minor deviances when compared to the willful harm of property or persons, work done by Skarlicki and Folger (1997) purports that ignoring mild negative behaviors can have dramatic consequences on organizational functioning. It was observed that psychological withdrawal behaviors have a progressive propensity, whereby one withdrawal behavior affects subsequent withdrawal behaviors (Sagie, et al., 2002). Decreased effort on the job can lead to lateness or leaving early, which can then progress to greater levels of withdrawal such as absenteeism and turnover. Withdrawal behavior phenomenon can be compared to ripple effect where one employee influences behaviors of other employees (Sagie, et al., 2002). For example, late coming of one employee may tempt the others to respond in similar ways resulting in them to become psychologically and behaviorally withdrawn, thereby hampering productivity even further.

In the current study, typology of organizational withdrawal behaviors identified by Hanisch & Hulin (1991) was used. It consists of job and work withdrawal behaviors. When dissatisfied employees exhibit a bundle of behaviors to evade the work situation, they are called job withdrawal behaviors. This kind of behavior is displayed to avoid involvement in dissatisfying work situation. The most common forms of job withdrawal behaviors are turnover intentions, desire to retire or actual resignation. When dissatisfied employees exhibit a bundle of behaviors to evade aspects of their specific work role or reducing the time spent on their specific work tasks while remaining in the organization, they are called work withdrawal behaviors. The most common forms of work withdrawal behaviors are unfavorable job behaviors, lateness, and absenteeism.

Conceptual Model

From the observations made about the constructs, the conceptual model was developed as shown in the Figure 1. The Employee Withdrawal Behavior and High Involvement Work Processes were selected as the dependent and independent variable respectively.

Figure 1. Conceptual model

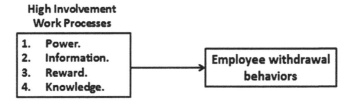

Method

Research Hypothesis

Based on the conceptual framework and inferring from the conceptual focus adopted from this study, the following hypothesis have been proposed for the study.

H1: There is a strong negative relationship between High Involvement Work Processes and employee withdrawal behaviors.

Research Objective

The main objective of the study is to investigate the relationship between High Involvement Work Processes and Employee Withdrawal Behaviors in IT firms in India.

Research Design

The present research has employed both descriptive and explanatory methodologies in the study. The study tries to describe the distribution of employees who have different levels of perception regarding High Involvement Work Processes and Employee Withdrawal Behaviors in their respective firms. The study intends to explain the precedent outcome linkages among the factors of both High Involvement Work Processes and Employee Withdrawal Behaviors and it is thus explanatory in nature.

Data Collection

Since questionnaire survey has been widely recognized as an efficient tool for measuring perception of individuals on a particular subject and survey research is useful to collect data from a large number of respondents in a relatively short period of time, the current study employed questionnaire survey for data collection.

- **Questionnaire on High Involvement Work Processes:** This tool was designed by Riordan and Vandenberg (1999) to assess the perception of employees of the High Involvement Work Processes of selected three organizations along the four dimensions of power, information, reward and knowledge. The final version of the scale consists of a total number of 32 items with 7 items for power, 10 items for information, 7 items for reward and 8 items for Knowledge. Each part of the questionnaire used a 4 – point rating scale with 1 indicating strong disagreement and 4 indicating strong agreement for each dimension of HIWP. The range of the total score possible of the scale was 32 to 128.
- **Questionnaire on Employee Withdrawal Behaviors:** This tool was designed by Hanisch and Hulin (1990) to measure employee withdrawal behaviours. The final version of scale consists of a total number of 18 items with 6 items for job withdrawal behaviours and 12 items for work withdrawal behaviours. The questionnaire used an 8 point scale and the total score possible of the scale was 18 to 144.

Sampling

Multistage random sampling was employed for carrying out the research. The population for the current study was specified through the following progressive sequence. List of IT firms from the selected Techparks was compiled using NASSCOM database to broadly define the population of the study. From this general database, all the large IT firms were filtered using employee strength and years of existence as the criteria. From the pool of large IT firms, Infosys, HCL and CTS were selected based on organization's market share. Small and medium IT firms were avoided because of the unavailability of data regarding High Involvement Work Processes. IT professionals with less than one year of experience were avoided because of their restricted knowledge regarding the various High Involvement Work Processes existing in the organization.

- **Sample Size:** Power analysis used by Krishnan and Singh (2010) was employed to decide the sample size. By forming an explanatory power of .78 and the f2 value of 0.15, it was found that sample size should be 278 but to ensure data sufficiency, researcher has opted for the sample size of 200 samples. The process of Bootstrapping and bolline-shrine plot was used to test the data for outliers so as to enhance the normality of the data. The researcher found out that there were 9 outliers in the study and it was removed using bootstrapping method. The sample adequacy was again ensured by referring to Hoelter index as part of the fit measures of the final structural model of HIWP and HR outcomes. The Hoelter Index at 0.05 significance showed 172 samples as adequate whereas Hoelter Index at 0.01 significance level showed 196 as adequate for the study. Hence the sample of 300 was found to be adequate.
- **Selection of Units of Observation:** 342 responses was collected from 3 firms. Detailed examination of the data based on grossly missing or inappropriate values resulted in deletion of 42 records. Thus, the final data set had 300 usable records that comprise the total sample.

Statistical Analysis

For statistical analyses, regression and Structural Equation Modeling (SEM) was used. The impact of High Involvement Work Processes on Employee Withdrawal Behaviors was analyzed using test like regression. Researcher also tried to test the integrative model for High Involvement Work Processes using Structural Equation Modeling (SEM). Subsequent step was to evaluate the degree of fit of several structural models of use in testing the hypotheses concerning relations among underlying latent variables.

Data Analysis

Descriptive statistics are shown in Tables 1-3.

Table 1. Classification of details based on the gender of IT employees

	Frequency	Percent
Male	172	57
Female	128	43

Table 2. Age group classification of IT employees

	Frequency	Percent
Less than 26	125	40.06
26-30	151	48.39
31-35	35	11.21
36 and above	1	0.32

Table 3. Classification of IT employees based on educational qualification

	Frequency	Percent
Graduate	252	82
Post Graduate	40	16
Doctorate	8	2

Impact of High Performance Work Systems on Employee Withdrawal Behaviors

The hypothesis H1 stated that there is a significant negative relationship between High Involvement Work Processes and Employee Withdrawal Behaviors and it was checked using regression analysis.

Analyses clearly conveyed that perceived High Involvement Work Processes has a strong negative impact on Employee Withdrawal Behaviors at 5% level of significance. Regression analysis further showed that among the four bundles, information and knowledge had the strongest link with employee withdrawal behaviors.

The split – half reliability coefficient for the HIWP dimensions Power, Information, Reward and Knowledge, using the Spearman – Brown formula, was found to be 0.764, 0.803, 0.683 and 0.852. The split half reliability coefficient for the two dimensions of Employee Withdrawal Behaviors using Spearman Brown formula was found to be 0.789 and 0.721.

Table 4. Multiple regression analysis results for high involvement work processes with employee withdrawal behaviors

Variables	Beta Value	Std. Error	Collinearity		Sig	Durbin - Watson	R	R2
			Tolerance	VIF				
Power	-0.102	.211	0.603	1.656	.112	1.773	.453	.203
Information	-0.151	.156	0.502	2.003	.024			
Reward	-0.104	.163	0.542	1.837	.126			
Knowledge	-0.182	.149	0.605	1.663	.003			

Analysis of Structural Model

This section deals with the comprehensive analysis of the structural model which depicts the hypothesized relationships among the variables under study. As represented in table, the hypothesized path between High Involvement Work Processes and Employee Withdrawal Behaviors was found to be meaningful.

FINDINGS AND DISCUSSIONS

It was found that all dimensions of High Involvement Work Processes had strong negative relationship with withdrawal behaviors of individuals. The current analysis clearly conveys that the information and knowledge dimension of High Involvement Work Processes have a stronger impact on withdrawal behaviors compared to two other dimensions of power and reward. The hypothesized relationship between dependant and independent variables is well supported by the analysis. There is ample literature support proving the strong negative relationship between High Involvement Work Processes and Employee Withdrawal Behaviors. According to Koslowsky et al., (1997), High Involvement Work Processes have a significant negative impact on employee lateness. He also argued that tardiness is a behavioral outcome of certain organizational attitudes that is created as a result of the implementation of High Involvement Work Processes. When organization creates an environment of high morality with the help of High Involvement Work Processes, employees may respond by refraining from deviant activities such as withdrawal behaviors (Peterson, 2002). Individuals who perceive the absence of High Involvement Work Processes will have a tendency to engage more in undesirable behaviors such as lateness, absenteeism and turnover (Elovainio et al., 2004). When proper High Involvement Work Processes is in place in the organization, employee's seldom experience the violation of psychological contract which is considered as the root source for all forms of withdrawal behaviors (Purvis & Cropley, 2003). When organizations fail to introduce proper High Involvement Work Processes, personalized attachments are compromised (Bundeson, 2001) and employees try to get back the benefits entitled to them by withdrawing from work (Kickul, 2001). Apart from that, when employees feel uncomfortable due to the lack of High Involvement Work Processes and imposed organizational values, they reciprocate with a lower levels of commitment, which in turn lead to unfavorable work attitudes and behaviors (Bundeson, 2001; Kwantes,2003) depending on the extent of ideological breach.

Table 5. Path significance

Indicators	Values	P-Value	Significance
EWB - HIWP	-.162	.001	**

**Significant at .01 level

Figure 2. Structural paths of the model

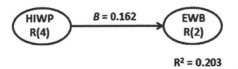

R² = 0.203

CONCLUSION

This study establishes the existence of a significant relationship between High Involvement Work Processes and Employee Withdrawal Behaviors. Therefore, top management should pay extra attention to ensure that comprehensive retention practices are in place to retain talented workforce. This paper moves a step forward by explaining the concept of High Involvement Work Processes in the context of information technology sector. Industry leaders can use the results of this study for bringing down the occurrences of Employee Withdrawal Behaviors. This study reinforces the use of bundle of High Involvement Work Processes to gain maximum benefits compared to the use of individual practices.

Implications to Management Theory and Managerial Practice

This finding may enable researchers in the human resource management to develop more robust understanding of the positive effects of High Involvement Work Processes on Employee Withdrawal Behaviors. Apart from that, this study makes a contribution to the broader Employee Withdrawal Behaviors literature by manifesting the extended relationship path from High Involvement Work Processes to Employee Withdrawal Behaviors, and demonstrating that Employee Withdrawal Behaviors at the organizational level has an effect on employee attitudes and behaviors as well. It also offers practical implications for employers seeking to motivate employees, and provide insights into why employees are engaging in withdrawal behaviors. The High Involvement Work Processes – Employee Withdrawal Behaviors model will enable the management to identify the paths that lead to EWB and chalk out strategies to avoid the same.

LIMITATIONS AND FUTURE RESEARCH

There are many limitations to the study. Only large IT firms operating in Kerala were considered for the study. The medium and small IT firms are excluded because of literature support for the fact that it takes time for an organization to implement, improve and standardize High Involvement Work Processes. The survey instrument and the interviews were limited in several ways such as the individuals' honest answers on the surveys and interview instruments as well as the time allowed during the survey. Apart from large IT companies, future researchers should study perception of High Involvement Work Processes among middle level and small IT firms. To increase the scope of future study, researchers can look for High Involvement Work Processes of IT firms based on classification in terms of product oriented and project or service oriented companies.

REFERENCES

Adams, J. S. (1965). Inequity in social exchange. In L. Berkowitz (Ed.), Advances in Experimental Social Psychology (vol. 2, pp. 267–299). New York, NY: Academic Press.

Ajzen, I., & Fishbein, M. (1980). *Understanding Attitudes and Predicting Social Behavior*. Prentice Hall.

Arthur, J. B. (1994). Effects of human resource systems on manufacturing performance and turnover. *Academy of Management Journal*, *37*(3), 670–687. doi:10.2307/256705

Barney, J. (1991). Firm Resources and Sustained Competitive Advantage. *Journal of Management, 17*(1), 99–120. doi:10.1177/014920639101700108

Becker, B. E., & Huselid, M. A. (1998). High performance work systems and firm performance: A synthesis of research and managerial implications. *Research in Personnel and Human Resources Management, 16*, 53–101.

Beer, M., Spector, B., Lawrence, P., Mills, D., & Walton, R. (1984). *Managing human assets*. New York: Free Press.

Benson, G. S. (2006). Employee development, commitment and intention to turnover: A test of 'employability' policies in action. *Human Resource Management Journal, 16*(2), 173–192. doi:10.1111/j.1748-8583.2006.00011.x

Bundeson, J. S. (2001). How Work Ideologies Shape the Psychological Contract of Professional Employees: Doctors' Response to Perceived Breach. *Journal of Organizational Behavior, 22*(2), 717–741. doi:10.1002/job.112

Carraher, S. M., & Buckley, M. R. (2008). Attitudes towards benefits and behavioral intentions and their relationship to Absenteeism, Performance, and Turnover among nurses. *Academy of Health Care Management Journal, 4*(2), 89–109.

Chiboiwa, M., Samuel, M., & Chipunza, C. (2010). An examination of employee retention strategy in a private organization in Zimbabwe. *African Journal of Business Management, 4*(10), 2103–2109.

Cotton, J. L., Vollrath, D. A., Froggatt, K. L., Lengnick-Hall, M. L., & Jennings, K. R. (1988). Employee Participation: Diverse Forms and Different Outcomes. *Academy of Management Review, 13*(1), 8–22.

Finegold, D., Mohrman, S., & Spreitzer, G. M. (2002). Age effects on the predictors of technical workers' commitment and willingness to turnover. *Journal of Organizational Behavior, 23*(5), 655–674. doi:10.1002/job.159

Fox, S., & Spector, P. E. (1999). A model of work frustration–aggression. *Journal of Organizational Behavior, 20*(6), 915–931. doi:10.1002/(SICI)1099-1379(199911)20:6<915::AID-JOB918>3.0.CO;2-6

Galbraith, J. R. (1973). *Designing complex organizations*. Reading, MA: Addison - Wesley.

Gberevbie, D. E. (2008). *Staff Recruitment, Retention Strategies and Performance of Selected Public and Private Organizations in Nigeria*. College of Business and Social Sciences, Covenant University.

Griffeth, R. W., Hom, P. W., & Gaertner, S. (2000). A Meta-Analysis of Antecedents and Correlates of Employee Turnover: Update, Moderator Tests, and Research Implications for the Next Millennium. *Journal of Management, 26*(3), 463–488. doi:10.1177/014920630002600305

Guthrie, J. P. (2001). High Involvement work practices, turnover and productivity: Evidence from New Zealand. *Academy of Management Journal, 44*(1), 180–190. doi:10.2307/3069345

Guthrie, J. P., Spell, C. S., & Nyamori, R. O. (2002). Correlates and consequences of high involvement work practices: The role of competitive strategy. *International Journal of Human Resource Management, 13*(1), 183–197. doi:10.1080/09585190110085071

Hanisch, K. A., & Hulin, C. (1991). General attitudes and organizational withdrawal: An evaluation of causal model. *Journal of Vocational Behavior*, *39*(1), 110–128. doi:10.1016/0001-8791(91)90006-8

Hulin, C. L. (1991). *Adaptation, Persistence, and Commitment in Organizations*. Palo Alto, CA: Consulting Psychologist Press.

Huselid, M. A. (1995). The impact of human resource management practices on turnover, productivity and corporate financial performance. *Academy of Management Journal*, *38*(3), 635–672. doi:10.2307/256741

Jackson, S. E., & Schuler, R. S. (1995). Understanding Human Resource Management in the Context of Organizations and their Environments. *Annual Review of Psychology*, *46*(1), 237–264. doi:10.1146/annurev.ps.46.020195.001321 PMID:19245335

Johns, G. (1994). How often were you absent? A review of the use of self-reported absence data. *The Journal of Applied Psychology*, *79*(4), 574–591. doi:10.1037/0021-9010.79.4.574

Judy, R. (2000). Labor forecast: Gray skies, worker drought continues. *HRMagazine*, *44*(1), 18–26.

Kaplan, S., Bradley, J. C., Lachman, J. N., & Hayness, D. (2009). On the Role of Positive and Negative Affectivity in Job Performance: A Meta-Analytic Investigation. *The Journal of Applied Psychology*, *94*(1), 162–176. doi:10.1037/a0013115 PMID:19186902

Kickul, J. (2001). Promises Made, Promises Broken: An Exploration of Small Business Attraction and Retention Practices. *Journal of Small Business Management*, *39*(2), 320–335. doi:10.1111/0447-2778.00029

Koch, M. J., & McGrath, R. G. (1996). Improving labor productivity: Human resource management policies do matter. *Strategic Management Journal*, *17*(5), 335–354. doi:10.1002/(SICI)1097-0266(199605)17:5<335::AID-SMJ814>3.0.CO;2-R

Koslowsky, M. (2000). A New Perspective on Employee Lateness. *Applied Psychology*, *49*(3), 390–407. doi:10.1111/1464-0597.00022

Krishnan, S. K., & Singh, M. (2010). Outcomes of intention to quit of Indian IT professionals. *Journal of Human Resource Management, 49*(2), 421-437.

Kwantes, C. T. (2003). Organizational Citizenship and Withdrawal Behaviors in the USA and India: Does Commitment Make a Difference? *International Cultural Management*, *3*(1), 5–26.

Lawler, E. E. (1992). *The ultimate advantage: Creating the high involvement organization*. San Francisco: Jossey-Bass.

Lawler, E. E. (1996). *From the ground up: Six principles for building the new logic corporation*. Jossey – Bass.

Leana, C. R., Ahlbrandt, R. S., & Murrell, A. J. (1992). The effects of employee involvement programs on unionized worker's attitudes, perceptions and preferences in decision making. *Academy of Management Journal*, *35*(4), 861–873. doi:10.2307/256319

Leana, C. R., & Florkowski, G. W. (1992). Employee Involvement Programs: Integrating Psychological Theory and Management Practice. In G. Ferris & K. Rowland (Eds.), *Research in Personnel and Human Resources Management, 10* (pp. 233–270). Greenwich, CT: JAI Press.

Leana, C. R., Locke, E. A., & Schweiger, D. M. (1990). Fact and Fiction in Analyzing Research on Participative Decision Making: A Critique of Cotton, Vollrath, Froggatt, Lengnick-Hall, and Jennings. *Academy of Management Review, 15*(1), 137–146.

Ledford, G. E. Jr, & Mohrman, S. A. (1993). Self-Design for High Involvement: A Large-Scale Organizational Change. *Human Relations, 46*(2), 143–173. doi:10.1177/001872679304600202

Lehman, W. E., & Simpson, D. D. (1992). Employee substance use and on-the-job behaviors. *The Journal of Applied Psychology, 77*(3), 309–321. doi:10.1037/0021-9010.77.3.309 PMID:1601823

Meyer, J. P., Stanley, D. J., Herscovitch, L., & Topolnytsky, L. (2002). Affective, Continuance, and Normative Commitment to the Organization: A Meta-analysis of Antecedents, Correlates, and Consequences. *Journal of Vocational Behavior, 61*(1), 20–52. doi:10.1006/jvbe.2001.1842

Mobley, W., Horner, S., & Hollingsworth, A. (1978). An evaluation of the precursors of hospital employee turnover. *The Journal of Applied Psychology, 63*(4), 408–414. doi:10.1037/0021-9010.63.4.408 PMID:701211

Peterson, D. K. (2002). Deviant workplace behavior and the organization's ethical climate. *Journal of Business and Psychology, 17*(1), 47–61. doi:10.1023/A:1016296116093

Purvis, L. J., & Cropley, M. (2003). The Psychological Contracts of National Health Service Nurses. *Journal of Nursing Management, 11*(2), 107–120. doi:10.1046/j.1365-2834.2003.00357.x PMID:12581399

Ramsay, H., Scholarios, D., & Harley, B. (2000). Employees and High-Performance Work Systems: Testing inside the Black Box. *British Journal of Industrial Relations, 38*(4), 501–531. doi:10.1111/1467-8543.00178

Rosse, J. G., & Hulin, C. L. (1985). Adaptation to work: An analysis of employee health, withdrawal, and change. *Organizational Behavior and Human Decision Processes, 36*(3), 324–347. doi:10.1016/0749-5978(85)90003-2 PMID:10275698

Sagie, A., Birati, A., & Tziner, A. (2002). Assessing the Costs of Behavioral and Psychological Withdrawal: A New Model and an Empirical Illustration. *Applied Psychology, 51*(1), 67–89. doi:10.1111/1464-0597.00079

Skarlicki, D. P., & Folger, R. (1997). Retaliation in the workplace: The roles of distributive, procedural, and interactional justice. *The Journal of Applied Psychology, 82*(3), 434–443. doi:10.1037/0021-9010.82.3.434

Taplin, I. M., Winterton, J., & Winterton, R. (2003). Understanding Labor Turnover in a Labor Intensive Industry: Evidence from British Clothing Industry. *Journal of Management Studies, 40*(2), 4–15.

Thibaut, J. W., & Kelley, H. H. (1959). The Social Psychology of Groups. *Social Research, 27*(2), 252–254.

Twenge, J. M., & Campbell, S. M. (2008). Generational differences in psychological traits and their impact on the workplace. *Journal of Managerial Psychology, 23*(1), 862–877. doi:10.1108/02683940810904367

Vandenberg, R. J., Richardson, H. A., & Eastman, L. J. (1999). The Impact of High Involvement Work Processes on Organizational Effectiveness: A Second-Order Latent Variable Approach. *Group & Organization Management, 24*(3), 300-339.

Wagner, J. A. (1994). On beating dead horses, reconsidering reconsiderations, and ending disputes: Further thoughts about a recent study of research on participation. *Academy of Management Review, 20*, 506–508.

Wall, T. D., & Wood, S. J. (2005). *The romance of HRM and business performance: The case for big science*. Sheffield, UK: University of Sheffield.

Walton, R. E. (1985). From control to commitment in the workplace. *Harvard Business Review, 63*, 77–84.

Wood, S. (1999). Human resource management and performance. *International Journal of Management Reviews, 1*(4), 367–413. doi:10.1111/1468-2370.00020

Chapter 17

Three New Directions for Time Banking Research:
Information Management, Knowledge Management, and the Open Source Model

Lukas Valek
University of Hradec Kralove, Czech Republic

ABSTRACT

This chapter aims to highlight three viable fields of research within the domain of time banking (TB), a time-currency-based complementary economy system that has been implemented in various frameworks now for more than three decades. The areas of information management (IM), knowledge management (KM), and open source software (OSS) are almost totally unexplored within time banking. In information management, attention has mainly been devoted to IM frameworks. One link (among others) between knowledge management and open source software has been found in a core concept of the time bank called co-production. Finally, all three of these fields can be related directly to time banking and should have a place in further research, the results of which could also have applications in the field of complementary economic systems in general.

1. INTRODUCTION

Time Banking has been around for more than thirty years, during which time it has spread from its country of origin, the United States, to other countries around the world (hOurworld.org, 2017b; Timebanks_USA, 2017). In some resources (Miller, 2008), however, the world's first time bank is said to have been founded in Japan in 1973 by Teruko Mizushima, with the idea beginning to spread globally approximately ten years later when E. S. Cahn invented his Time Dollar in the US (Cahn & Rowe, 1992). The TB concept has faced many challenges, and in terms of cultural environment it is often adapted to reflect a particular regional reality (Valek, 2013b), this adaptation including the management of information and knowledge contained within a time bank, but also various information technology solutions. Nowadays many Time Banking movements have emerged around the world, with the number ever-increasing, thus it is quite

DOI: 10.4018/978-1-5225-5297-0.ch017

difficult to determine a precise count (Blanc, 2011). Nevertheless, their focus on social economy gives users a tool to help themselves rather than expect support from authorities. At the present time, more than 30 different web platforms and software (Boyle & Bird, 2014) support TB endeavors as well as efforts to unify time banks into stronger groups or alliances (Valek, 2016).

This goal of this chapter is to show a number of new directions for research in the field of Time Banking. Time Banking is a type of complementary economy, and as TB uses time as a form of currency, it is also considered a complementary currency system. The word "complementary" is important, as we can also find in the literature the term "alternative economy," with the difference being in the fact that an alternative structure is intended as a replacement for current economic systems or for a particular currency, while a complement merely helps in places where a current economy or currency is failing (Lietaer, 2001). Complements are easier to integrate into an economy, and by its influence slowly shifts the economic paradigm. As for complementary economic systems, literature is available, including works on TB, outlining advantages and risks related to various complementary currency systems (Kennedy, 2012). Justifications for existence of complementary economies and their putative place in society are not part of this study, as this is rather extensive topic which has already filled many books.

Thus far, in many places where people have been learning about concepts of Time Banking they are in very hard position to implement it (Valek, 2013a, 2013b, 2015a). Warnings to expect opposition (Cahn, 2004) have been given. It remains important is to build a surrounding environment with people who think the same way, thus a community can be created to further develop the idea and to apply the positive effects of TB. Unfortunately, however, mere enthusiasm is often not enough, since to keep a Time Bank running and sustainable several factors are necessary which are related to the language and other cultural conditions in a respective location, as well as to the number of users and services it offers, how funds are obtained, the readiness of the environment to accept ideas of Time Banking, policies and legal issues, as well as tactical and strategic planning. These points seem to be crucial in all courses of the lifetime of a Time Bank (Valek, 2013b). Aside from this, with the growing professionalization of TB a systemic approach towards managing information and knowledge is necessary. Time Banks are themselves a tool itself to directly target the origin of specific problems, and as tools they should be carefully managed and structured.

Research in field of TB is very scarce. Naughton-Doe has found 80 documents related to Time Banking, out of which only 38 can be considered primary data and 29 qualitative data. Most of topics related to TB implementation, processes, outputs, associations and outcomes. Nevertheless, they often contain limited or unexplained samples, the methodology used was not found to be adequate, or the texts fail to explain the measurements used. In the end, only 11 papers were found usable for scientific research (Naughton-Doe, 2015). In the area of information and Knowledge Management, TB remains unexplored, as none of resources were found to be related to these domains.

Throughout this text, TB is used as abbreviation both for Time Bank and Time Banking, with TBs used in plural for Time Banks except in situations when the use of abbreviated form might hinder understanding. The chapter has the following structure: after this introduction a short background is described which focuses on the non-mainstream economic approaches of which TB is integral part as well as the details of TB. In next section, the three fields of Information Management, Knowledge Management and Information Technology are outlined in the given context. In the discussion, all three are scrutinized in greater depth, from which conclusions are then drawn.

2. BACKGROUND

2.1. Non-Mainstream Economic Approaches in the Digital Age: Complementary Economies

The form of currency generally utilized today alludes to fiat currency. Fiat money is in fact created "out of nothing" and the name itself refers to its enigmatic existence (from Latin *Fiat lux* in the Biblical book of Genesis, meaning "Let there be light," which can be restated as "Let there be money.") (Lietaer, 2001). Critiques of the fiat currency issued by private institutions through the creation of debt have gone as far as to compare it to arsenic, which although it is a deadly poison was used to alleviate short-term symptoms in medicine when no better solution was available (Lietaer et al., 2012). Complementary economic systems are supportive means which provide contextual solutions to problems proceeding from the economy as a whole by the creation of fiat money. An early critique of fiat currency was put forth in the 1930s by Irving Fisher, who proposed the so-called "Chicago Plan," the aim of which was to gradually transfer the responsibility of issuing of fiat currency to governments by forcing commercial banks to back deposits by credits from a government and later lowering the amount of money in circulation by lowering the banks' capital deposits. In the working paper "The Chicago Plan Revisited," authors Jaromir Benes and Michael Kumhof re-evaluate this idea, determining that it could bring many benefits (Benes and Kumhof, 2012), but in the end it would merely signify the transfer of the authority of the "creation" of money to only one intuitional body instead of allowing multiple institutions to control it. Nevertheless, a higher order might be reached by establishing real control over the issuing of fiat money through the prevention of the violent reactions of commercial banks to market events, which is what the Chicago Plan, never instituted, would offer.

Related to the previous statements, the observation can be added that fiat money itself has also now become a commodity (Caroll and Belloti, 2015), although it is difficult to imagine trading in something which does not really exist in material form. Tied to concepts like these, the focus of market economies on economic growth has been long institutionalized, despite the fact that endless unlimited growth has been demonstrated to not be possible (Seyfang and Longhurst, 2012, Holmgren, 2011).

These previous lines might tend toward the utopic or dystopic, but they are put forward here as only a concentrated description of the kind of rhetoric that many of the founders of complementary economic systems use, and from this somewhat moralistic critique the whole scope of what has been referred to as the non-mainstream economy emerges. As noted earlier, history has proven that alternatives to monetary systems in use at a particular time usually do not work, whereas complements to this system actually possess the power and potential to utilize what is "left behind" by the market economy. Several examples have emerged, starting with complementary currencies, through exchange systems, unconditional minimal revenue, Time Banks, gift economies and other structures. Many of these options were first mentioned in the literature decades (or much longer) ago, but the fact that they not only persist but have been shown to thrive in many parts of the world shows their feasibility. All of these have been studied by the Complementary Currency Resource Center (CCRC, 2016).

2.1.1. Most Common Complementary Economies

- **Local Currencies:** These structures represent regionally developed and used currencies of which the main aim is to facilitate exchange within a certain geographically defined region. They have several objectives (Kennedy et al., 2012):

Creating Local Jobs

- Stem the drain of purchasing power from the region.
- To open up new avenues to enable local government to fulfill its designated tasks

Helping to Develop

- Economic stimulation instead of stagnation
- Stabilization or growth of the population
- Increase in regional purchasing power and, by this, improvement in municipal finances
- Positive identification with the region
- Improvements to the infrastructure and increased local autonomy
- A greater sense amongst the population, a sense of participation
- Preservation and development of employment opportunities and incentives for firms to remain in the region

Local currencies stand upon the trust of their users, which is common feature for all complementary currencies. As mentioned above, the main focus is on bringing back activity, prosperity and jobs to a certain region. These could represent either an urban or rural region.

- **LETS (Local Economy Trading System):** LETS represents one of the first working concepts of a trading system, an economy which grows from the needs of community. It resembles a local currency system, as it uses one as a medium, but it sprouts from a need to maintain trading within communities in times of crises (Lietaer, 2001). Standard money might be also used in these transactions, but most exchange is made for the LETS currency (usually a work/service). In this sense, citizens in a particular region can keep trading and working even when official currency is scarce. Scarcity does influence LETS money, as it is generated in the moment when a demand is created, more precisely when a trade is agreed upon. Moreover, currency in a closed system of LETS appears in a strictly reciprocal operation between two parties when at a given time a certain number of units is subtracted on one side and added to on the other side (Martignoni, 2015).
- **Business Exchange:** This regional community currency allows small businesses and individuals to continue to trade and produce even when they would not have enough financial power in the official currency. A business exchange provides credits, in turn allowing trades which would not normally take place. In addition, a safe environment is created which fosters commerce between and among proven business partners. In this sense, it plays a similar supportive role as a TB does in business. One good example is Swiss WIR, the oldest continuous complementary currency system in the Western world, in existence since 1934 (Lietaer, 2001). The WIR exchange includes both businesses and individuals in a system which in 2010 had an annual turnover rate of 1.6

billion WIR francs (1 WIR franc = 1 Swiss franc). Other examples of a business exchange have emerged in the RES in Belgium with its yearly turnover of the equivalent of 35 million Euro, as well as the Business Exchange Scotland, along with others.

- **Electronic Currencies:** In the 21st century, many services which generally remain within the domain of huge corporations, e.g. amongst their subsidiary banking facilities, have come within the grasp ordinary people. They can be "grown" from grassroots instead of installed from top. The emergence of open source systems has by co-production (introduced below) allowed small enterprises or even individuals to develop their own software, including operating systems, a fact which has also had a huge impact in the field of telecommunications. Individuals can even for the first time legally circumvent banks in domains which had previously remained untouchable. As one example for all, in the money transfer sector, the project Transferwise (Transferwise, 2016) allows the complete avoidance of banks and their fees by matching sending and receiving transactions in different countries and currencies, so that the actual payment never leaves the country of origin.

Perhaps the biggest impact in electronic currencies in past few years has been made by the Bitcoin. This public electronic currency founded in 2009 (Bitcoin.cz, 2016) is based on the open source approach. The main critique of the founders of Bitcoin against ordinary money electronic transactions was focused on the necessity within large financial institutions of an intermediary or "middle man" in electronic transactions, with the accompanying cost increases, especially transaction fees, which limit and in fact often completely rule out small casual transactions. Also, the necessity of officially verifying the identities and financial status of the parties involved, and with this the requirements to submit personal information, slow down and complicate transactions. The proposed approach was an electronic payment system based on cryptographic proof instead of "trust" or identity verification, allowing any two willing parties to transact directly with each other without the need for a trusted third party (Nakamoto, 2009). The verification factor and need for the tracking of exchanges is also inherent for TB, as verification requires memory, while paper money leaves no traceable trail. The Time Dollar, or time credit, is counted as an electronic currency, a fact which builds trust, as the present is shaped by the future (Cahn, 2000). Another feature of Bitcoin is that the final resource of money is limited, but the currency can be divided into fractions. By this constraint, it comes much closer to a commodity-based currency. The payment cryptographic engine uses so-called "mining" to create new coins.

However, the Bitcoin system is not without its critics. Firstly, it removes the power over money from banks and places it into uncertain hands of volunteers who run the mining engine on their computers, the combined power of which exceeds the world's 500 fastest supercomputers put together (Economist, 2013), thus the security of transactions may be called into question. At any rate, the success of Bitcoin has paved the way for other similar currencies, which mimic it or have tried to change some features of it, e.g. Litecoin, which offers faster transactions, but keeps the limited coin supply feature. Peercoin, of which there is unlimited supply, but comes with implicit 1% inflation. Anoncoin and Zerocoin both aim for complete anonymity of the transactions. In conclusion, even though Bitcoin has its own disadvantages, it (and its popularity) has proven a point, that this might be the way of imagining and putting into use new kind of money. The decentralization involved move the power over currency from banks to individuals. In the same way as the online music project Napster (eventually determined to be illegal) paved the way for services like iTunes and Spotify (Economist, 2013), the road has paved by Bitcoin for new currency independence.

- **Sharing-Based Economies:** Several systems of exchange deserve mention here. These sharing systems actually save costs of users by virtue of the medium of exchange being shared, thus limiting consumption. Typical examples are car sharing, services like Airbnb and Couchsurfing (through which accommodation is shared), tools sharing (along with other various items) through which people use certain items only occasionally and can borrow them from the community for limited period of time.
- **Gift Economy:** This would seem to be the oldest kind of complementary economy. Gift giving also helps to strengthen social ties, especially in tough times, and it is particularly important in a demanding and unpredictable environment (Lietaer, 2001). In the Czech Republic, one gift economy-based platform has emerged called Hearth.net (Hearth.net), a web platform which creates a community of people who are willing to give. Those who have something to offer (which could be practically anything) give it unconditionally, and those who need ask from the community that it should be given to them.

2.2. Time Banks

This section is based on research on TB conducted by the University of Hradec Kralove, Faculty of Informatics and Management (UHK, FIM), Czech Republic. The long-term project consisted of many methods including questionnaires, semi-structured interviews, study visits, student specific research projects, in-depth analysis and literature reviews. Study visits uncovered particular differences in the understanding of TB concept, with semi-structured interviews with important stakeholders showing management methods of TBs and, finally, a literature review puts everything in scientific context. But as mentioned above, in the fields of Information Management, Knowledge Management and Information Technologies there is little relevant research. Although many initiatives have emerged attempting to develop ideal TB software for their own particular conditions, theoretical research for these groups is also not a priority. In general, the research into TB that does exist is disjointed and often based on anecdotal evidence with lack of appropriate methodology (Naughton-Doe, 2015). As noted earlier, most of the research is related to the performance of existing TBs, e.g. their influence on healthcare, social services, community development, etc. (Boyle & Bird, 2014; Caroll & Belloti, 2015; Granger, 2013; Lasker et al., 2010; Osipov, Volinsky, & Prasikova, 2016; Ozzane, 2010; Ryan-Collins, Stephens, & Coote, 2008; Shih, Bellotti, Han, & Carroll, 2015; Timebanking_UK, 2005).

In addition, TB has no clear, agreed-upon definition. It is usually described by a mere description of the workings of the exchange of the time currency, often called Time Credits (TC), along with how it contributes to community. Sometimes a functioning TB is not even referred to using the words "Time Bank," with one example can be shown in the organization Partners in Care (Partners_in_Care, 2017), where it is described as Time Exchange. While there are various types of TBs, to this date there has been no unified categorization or taxonomy of TBs, although in the past many attempts have been made to classify the category (Ryan-Collins et al., 2008, Naughton-Doe, 2015, Watershed, 2017, Blanc, 2011, Timebanking_UK, 2015, Boyle and Bird, 2014). These attempts have been mostly negatively influenced by a researcher. Still, the very use of a TB remains subjective, i.e. practiced according to the point of view of a particular person or a team. As the most elemental level a division can be made into three usages according to the member base of a TB:

- Person to person TBs, in which only individuals participate in exchanges
- Person to organization TBs, in which individuals exchange with legal bodies
- Organization to organization TBs, in which organizations use their unused resources to exchange with each other

Even though there is no unified definition, a TB can be identified by its key features, defined in literature according to function, core values and main principles. The core principle is called co-production and a TB always employs five core values. If a system uses a time currency, but does not involve co-production (Cahn, 2000), these core values do not reflect what can be called TB, e.g. Ithaca Hours (IthacaHours, 2016), which uses time currency, but works on LETS principles. The core values can be listed as the following (Boyle & Bird, 2014; Cahn, 2000; Granger, 2013; Ozzane, 2010):

1. **We Are all Assets:** TB values people and recognizes that everyone has something special to offer others - knowledge, skills, resources, time. Every human being has the capacity to be a builder and contributor as individual or as a part of an organization. Thus the service offered in a TB could be almost anything, opening up opportunities for exchange – making offers and requests – which are not "marketable," but have value for other members of the TB (both people and organizations).
2. **Redefining Work:** Redefining work means that members are rewarded for any kind of work, whether it would be considered financially profitable or not by market economy standards, as touched upon above. Work in this sense does not necessarily mean a "job."
3. **Reciprocity:** This exchange works in a two-way process. Members can both offer and request at the same time and both the earnings of TC as well as spending TC bring positive feedback.
4. **Social Capital:** The creation of social capital is very important for any community, whether it consists of individuals or a knowledge-based organization (Nonaka, 1991). Social capital, among other functions, solves problems with unemployment, and learning for individuals and facilitates innovation and further development of organizations.
5. **Respect:** Every human being matters. As a mutual understanding of what people and organizations do, this is a key element for the development of positive relationships between entities in a region. A higher level of trust leads to the possibility of further innovation by the facilitating of common projects (Lehaney, 2004)

The core principle of TB so-called co-production (Cahn, 2000). Co-production means that people take responsibility for solving problems in their imminent environment and co-produce results. Thus, rather than waiting for help from outside they take initiative and find ways to resolve problems that needs to be solved. In this sense, TB is a tool which creates and nurtures a community that can co-produce results autonomously. Co-production can also be found in the business world and in the sphere of information technologies, even though it is generally not referred to in this way. This will be introduced below.

3. THE NEW DIRECTIONS

The main topics explored in this chapter are as follows:

- Information Management frameworks
- Knowledge Management in TBs
- Open source software and other tools

3.1. Information Management

Processing information in a IT system is an issue for most organizations, with the creation of a functional and efficient Information Management Framework (IMF) attempting to create an "ideal" situation (Maes, 1999), in order that involved stakeholders have access to information to make optimal decisions (Linderman et al., 2005). An IMF should cover and unify the main topics important for directing information in an organization from point of view of management: strategy, structure and operations. Areas of concern include: business/organizational, information and communication, as well as technology (both systems and infrastructure), and should take into account in its design all of the above (Maes, Rijsenbrij, Truijens, & Goedvolk, 2000). IMF should be considered when developing new software for a TB and also take into account the overall layout of information distribution within a TB. To these ends, a generic Information Management framework will be proposed for a TB environment.

3.2. Knowledge Management

One of main functions of a TB is knowledge and skill sharing, with these knowledge and skills used to perform a service exchanged. Knowledge sharing is one of most important features of a TB (Valek, Kolerova, & Otcenaskova, 2014) and this happens in several ways. At first, TB provides people/members with a safe environment in which to find other people with similar interests who will gather around certain issues (along with other people bound in standard organizations), much like communities of practice in a company (CoP) form informally around problems. A CoP is by one definition a "group of professionals informally bound to one another through exposure to a common class of problems, common pursuit of solutions, and thereby themselves embodying a store of knowledge" (Manville & Foote, 1996). This could be within a firm or any other organization in which a TB is included. Forming CoPs have the same basis as the idea of co-production, the main driving force of TB introduced above. Co-production is based on giving people the tools to be able to solve problems, so those with the appropriate skills, knowledge and interests can naturally join the effort. These individuals will gather around the problem without much facilitation and start solving it themselves; nevertheless, a framework would be handy in these conditions (Valek, 2015b).

CoPs are in essence interest groups who gather informally around a problem to solve it, i.e. in the structured environment of an organization unsolved problems remain, thus people interested in solving those problems with the knowledge to do so gather naturally voluntary around an issue and resolve it. The only difference between interest groups of TB and CoPs is that CoPs form within an existing company, and interest groups (CoPs of a TB) form in an existing and working TB.

Of course, in TB both explicit and tacit knowledge is present. Explicit knowledge easily learned and transferred, for example knowledge contained in books. Tacit knowledge comes only by experiential learning and is gained by an individual over time (Shreiber et al., 2002). To "get out" the knowledge from the individual's mind is very complicated, but a process that must be undertaken so that others can learn from these skills and experience.

Learning from each other's knowledge within a TB is one of the motivations to join one. This raises the competences of all members, a possibility that many are attracted to, including organizations. This learning happens naturally just by the exchange of certain services, but also by other outputs and spin-off events and projects, i.e. by people offering services, including what they like and know how to do, and thus learning becomes a by-product of the exchange of knowledge contained therein. For this reason, educational processes are fundamental part of the framework of a TB. This is in accordance with Nonaka's Spiral of Knowledge (known also as SECI by first letters of its four steps of Socialization, Externalization, Combination and Internalization), whereby explicit knowledge can be extracted out of the tacit, as depicted in Figure 1 (Takeuchi & Nonaka, 2004).

The steps of the spiral are:

- **Socialization:** Seeing how others do it and learning from their knowledge, which happens when people meet and have the opportunity to experience the knowledge of another person, thus be shown how to do things. In TB there are services which are directly aimed at learning, but knowledge is transferred from one person to another also even in those which are not.
- **Externalization:** Now it is possible to formulate and describe the knowledge in a way which is understandable for another person. Part of the knowledge of the other person has been "extracted," after which the learner is now ready to try new tasks and activities him/herself.
- **Combination:** To formulate how the newly gained knowledge could be used. In TB this means developing new competences.
- **Internalization:** Using what has been learned in application. In TB, typically new services can be offered, new interest groups formed, new projects started, etc.

Figure 1. Spiral of Knowledge (or SECI model) by Ikujiro Nonaka
Source (Takeuchi & Nonaka, 2004).

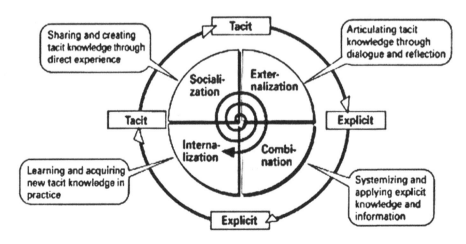

3.3. Information Technologies

As mentioned above, the number of TBs currently in existence is difficult to calculate (Blanc, 2011). To obtain greater support, TBs tend to create networks, such as Timebanks USA in United States of America, Timebanks UK in United Kingdom and the newly-born Timebanking Europe, which has sprouted out of TBUK as a TB support net for other European countries (Valek, 2015), although at the moment it lacks proper financial support. The more extensive software platforms which allow more features are Time and Talents (T&T) from hOurworld (http://hourworld.org/) and Community Weaver from TimeBanks USA (http://timebanks.org/community-weaver-upgrade-to-cw-3-0/). As Timebanks USA states on their website, the network includes more than 200 independent TBs in USA and others in more than 32 other countries, and they have developed the Community Weaver (CW) for the network (http://timebanks.org/about/), which TBs in the TBUSA network are encouraged to use.

On the other hand, T&T is more widely spread, as it includes 507 communities using the software around the world. This includes mostly the USA, UK and a few countries worldwide. Based on discussions with users, several technical issues with CW have emerged, especially with version 2.0. Put simply, the problems were caused by its overcomplicated design, which is based on two platforms: Wordpress and Drupal (www.larks.la/tags/community-weaver). Currently version 3.0 is available and time will prove its relative stability and usefulness. On the other hand, T&T is known for its stability, although the design at first glance might seem overly simple. Due to this stability, simplicity, and easy to use approach, T&T has spread widely in the United Kingdom, replacing the older software Time On Line.

In addition, hOurworld has just launched their mobile application for Android and iOS called hOurmobile, which broadens greatly the accessibility of the service. Another possibility for time bankers is the internet banking software Cyclos, which can be used as a platform for various kinds of Complementary Currencies, including TB. Cyclos is a pay service in its 4.0 version, but can be used free by a social organization if it demonstrates social benefits and non-profit aims. Cyclos 3.0 is offered as open source (although support was ended in 2013), so it can help enthusiasts to create own Complementary Currency trade system (http://www.cyclos.org/products/). To sum it up, most of the solutions described rely on a content management application, as this is easily accessible and not very complicated to manage even for less experienced users (Valek, 2016).

4. DISCUSSION

4.1. Information Management

As noted above, a solid Information Management framework is always necessary so that the involved entities and stakeholders have access to information to make optimal decisions (Linderman et al., 2005). As there is no available theory or research which takes into consideration the TB environment, it is necessary to use an approach from the business world. The structure we have chosen comes from the Generic Framework for Information Management proposed by (Maes, 1999).

Figure 2. Generic framework for information management
Source: (Maes et al., 2000).

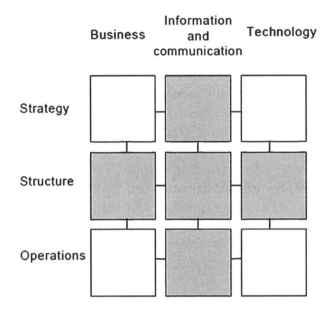

The structure of the proposed Generic Framework for Information Management (GIMF) also seems ideal for TB, as it considers all the important elements, with each cell of the framework being equally important (Maes, 1999). As noted above, the term business might be confusing, so it can be replaced with the word TB for these purposes.

To describe the structure of the GIMF, the columns describe from left to right, business expertise, interpretation of information, and providing technology. The horizontal lines represent from the bottom, the operative, tactical, and strategic levels of these groups (Maes et al., 2000). The adaptation of GIMF to TB environment is shown in Figure 3.

4.1.1. Time Bank Column

Following the bottom up structure, the TB originates from a need of a target group, which turns to its member base, which in turn provides inputs, most importantly their skills, knowledge, assets, resources and time, so the starting cell is one within the Structure line and Time Bank column. In order to root their activity, potential they must adhere to local law and regulations which would lead to the foundation of a base organization (upper cell), the Time Bank. When a TB is in operation, members would start to exchange and they also can form interest groups (lower cell).

4.1.2. Information and Communications Column

The coordinator is the central junction of all information flows, i.e. an information bridge and a cross-roads. Records about all activities and skills, knowledge, assets, resources and time pass through the coordinator so he/she can facilitate function of a TB. The information is used to provide information to the base organization for strategic decision making.

Figure 3. Generic Time Bank Information Management framework (GTBIMF)

	Time Bank	Information and Communication	Technology
Strategy	Law and Regulations – Statutes – Rules Strategic decisions by base organization (organization/community on which a TB is based)	Reporting to base organization	Choosing appropriate IT solution, designing it and/or adapting it to current needs of a TB Both desktop and mobile applications are desirable
Structure	Members Target Groups Inputs including skills, knowledge, assets, resources and time	Coordinator is a center of information flows and connects all elements	Appropriate simple structure which would cover all necessary elements for TB operation
Operations	Exchange activity and feedbacking Forming of interest groups	Proper records of exchanges, time credits, quality and offers and requests, same as, skills, knowledge, assets, resources and time	Main features should be simplicity, ease to use, robustness, accessibility, nearly autopoietic with almost no need for external resources, with running costs very low or free

4.1.3. Technology Column

Taking the bottom up approach, members require a simple, affordable, robust, accessible and easy to use technological solution. The final solution depends on availability, but in general it can be designed from scratch, or an existing solution can be used or adapted if available. The selected solution should not only consist of a desktop version, but also contain a mobile application option. From certain point the system should be ideally autopoietic (Holmgren, 2011), in other words "self-sustainable", using own internal resources to run itself with very little outside inputs.

The table introduced above can be called a Generic Time Bank Information Management framework and it is the first of its kind. It not only explains simplifications in the structure of the Time Credit entity, but also proposes a new way of looking at information flows in a TB.

4.2. Knowledge Management

Probably the strongest relation to Knowledge Management confirmed by our research is knowledge sharing. Introduced above as Communities of Practice (CoP) in (Valek, 2015b), KM is strongly related to the idea of co-production, with the only difference being that in the literature CoPs have in fact already been introduced in the business environment. As KM is mainly about managing how humans can share their knowledge effectively using technical tools where appropriate (Lehaney, 2004), this approach can be applied to any sphere of human activity. In addition, the above-proposed GTBIMF gives a clear framework not only to the information but also to knowledge sharing. Both CoPs and interest groups, which are often naturally created by members in a TB, can exist and operate successfully only when members trust each other, with trust being the cornerstone of a TB. This dependability among members is secured by rules and the coordinator's presence. Knowledge is a bond between the social and professional links among people sharing a common interest in a particular area, which enables them to share experiences and an understanding of potential issues and pitfalls. Membership and choice of community needs to be voluntary, otherwise members may not participate in the knowledge sharing (Lehaney, 2004). If we consider the fact that all TBs are composed of people, whether individuals or groups bound to organizations, this description categorically describes how TB operates in sense of its knowledge sharing potential. The benefits of CoPs are based mostly on the creation of social capital, which allows the further development of an organization. By being part of a CoP, members obtain the benefits of connections and relationships framed within a common context. These ties in fact represent the social capital of the community, which then has the power to enhance the performance of an organization within which a CoP is operating (Lesser & Storck, 2001). In other words, by giving people within an organization the opportunity to participate in a TB we allow creation of CoPs or interest groups in this context, thus enhancing the overall performance of the group.

By exchanging services and knowledge in TBs, experiential learning occurs. Experiential learning relates to the tacit knowledge. Managing this knowledge means surfacing it (making it in some way explicit) (Nonaka, 1991). Experiential knowledge can be converted into fluid knowledge so that others can share it (Lehaney, 2004). The knowledge intensity (Otcenaskova, Bures, & Mikulecka, 2012) of all the participants within a knowledge sharing system such as TB is one of the essential keystones supporting the variability of choice within the system. Put another way, the more the participants of the system know, the more they have to share, thus the more possibilities there are for sharing and, in case of TB, the more opportunities to spend the earned TC they have (Valek, 2015b). This idea of knowledge intensity actually supports the assumption that the more skills, knowledge, assets, resources and time are inputted, the more possibilities TB offers and the more outputs it brings.

Another similarity is that face to face meetings and communications are considered to be most important for developing relationships and learning within CoPs (Lesser & Storck, 2001). Thus it is in TBs, where the personal contact between or among individuals is even more important than the exchange itself (Valek et al., 2014). This does not mean that virtualization is impossible, but, again, it brings both benefits and risks in both situations. Virtualization or non-personal communication raises questions about the legitimacy of exchanges and thus brings another obstacle for participation of members (Hildreth, Kimble, & Wright, 2000), as shown in a previous analysis (Valek, 2015b).

Based on the above, we can say that co-production is a phenomenon which is present both among individuals and in organizations of any kind. We can also say that co-production leads to the creation of CoPs/interest groups and these can give organizations or a TB a much greater potential than solely with pure operation based on original "design" of an organization. To clarify this point, TB is not only a complementary economic system, but it has much other added value in knowledge sharing and co-production. A TB can create a situation which allows the multiplication of the activities of its members, thus strengthening existing positive feedbacks of TB system regarding the outside wider system environment, thus creating completely new solutions and feedbacks, e.g. diverse kinds of knowledge at the various nodes of a TB.

4.3. Information Technologies

As mentioned earlier, contemporary IT solutions are generally limited to adaptations of content management applications, as these adaptations offer the required attributes of low to no cost and are generally accessible even to less skilled developers.

Open source software domains, as they do not require high investments, seem a most promising, if not a proprietary solution in terms of TB software development (Sacks, 2015). And although an original solution needs to be adapted and "forged" into software platforms which would fit to the needs of a particular TB, only a minimal investment of time and money might be required (Anthes, 2016). On the other hand, this adaptation could be also resolved by co-production. Open source attracts various problem-solving communities and thus forms CoPs on the basis of co-production. Regarding co-production in an open source environment, we can say that it has been present in the software development area for long time; it has just not been referred to using this terminology. As open source software has opened completely new ways of innovations and markets, the TB concept, working by the same principles of co-production, opens new opportunities on a societal level by offering so-called diffusion of innovation (Fitzgerald, 2011). This diffusion offers the possibility of innovation to be communicated among members of a social system, such as a TB or an open source community.

Based on open source and with simplicity as one of primary attributes, more extensive potential solutions like ERP systems are already "out of the game." Larger, more complex systems would be a burden to a TB system, as it needs only a simple virtual "marketplace" and two databases. Further, the software would be ideally maintenance free and very robust.

A mobile application extension would also be welcomed. The hOurworld organization has already developed an app for their Time & Talents program called hOurmobile (hOurworld.org, 2017a). Regarding the development of mobile applications, it has been found advisable to implement a cloud solution to a TB software package to handle the synchronicity of data between units within the system (Widodo, Lim, & Atiquzzaman, 2017).

Another possibility is the use of simulation software. If used from the beginning in the implementation stage, it is not complicated to follow all the flows, gather all the data, and use this information for further simulations, or to take a system as it is and try to simulate it in various contexts without preceding data. An idea has already been proposed to try agent-based simulations to determine the viability of the implementation of TB under various conditions and in various geographical areas (Tucnik, Valek, Blecha, & Bures, 2016). Such simulations can be beneficial, not only to determine the feasibility of a TB set up, but also, if feasibility is proven, to convince stakeholders to support the idea. Simulations can be also done ex-post, to determine possible flaws in operation and avoid them in the future.

5. CONCLUSION

This chapter has attempted to demonstrate three new possible directions of TB development: Information Management, Knowledge Management and Information Technologies. In field of Information Management was proposed the Generic Time Bank Information Management framework, which can facilitate the implementation of new TBs, but also review status of an information system within existing structures. This is especially useful from a systemic point of view, based on our contention that a GTBIMF would contain all the essential elements which would have to be considered in building a TB information system. Nevertheless, the approach proposed remains untested, and obviously implementing our framework in real-life situations would be needed to prove its viability and ultimate worth. In Knowledge Management, more commonly known and employed fields emerge, e.g. so-called co-production, which plays an important role, as it essentially relates one of main TB principles to the wider concept of communities of practice (CoPs), a concept already familiar to those involved in Knowledge Management. Co-production phenomena can further be related to open source software development, a movement in which taking initiative is one of main driving forces in the first place. Another interesting notion proceeds from the so-called diffusion of innovation, the worth of which remains to be explored. Diffusion of innovation is a concept by which an existing community holds the tendency not only to solve problems, as in traditional meaning of co-production, but also to co-produce innovations, whether innovations take the form of communal advances in the field of information technologies. In all three of the fields mentioned, further research into the relatively unexplored realm of TB seems quite promising, with a great potential for developing more economical and effective uses of resources within an organization.

REFERENCES

Anthes, G. (2016). Open Source Software No Longer Optional. *Communications of the ACM, 59*(8), 15–17. doi:10.1145/2949684

Boyle, D., & Bird, S. (2014). *Give and Take: How timebanking is transforming healthcare*. Stroud, UK: Timebanking UK.

Cahn, E. S. (2000). No more throw-away people: the co-production imperative. Washington, DC: Academic Press.

Caroll, J. M., & Belloti, V. (2015). *Creating Value Together: The Emerging Design Space of Peer-to-Peer Currency and Exchange*. Paper presented at the Collaborating through Social Media - CSCW 2015, Vancouver, Canada. doi:10.1145/2675133.2675270

Fitzgerald, B. (2011). Adopting Open Source Software: A Practical Guide. Cambridge, MA: The MIT Press. doi:10.7551/mitpress/9780262516358.001.0001

Granger, P. (2013). *Valuing people and pooling resources to alleviate poverty through Time banking*. London: Academic Press.

Hildreth, P., Kimble, C., & Wright, P. (2000). Communities of practice in the distributed international environment. *Journal of Knowledge Management, 4*(1), 27–38.

Holmgren, D. (2011). *Permaculture: Principles & Pathways Beyond Sustainability*. East Meon: Permanent Publications Hyden House Ltd.

hOurworld.org. (2017a). *hOurmobile mobile application on Google Play*. Retrieved from https://play.google.com/store/apps/details?id=edu.psu.ist.mtb_hourworld&hl=en

hOurworld.org. (2017b). *Main Page*. Retrieved from hourworld.org

IthacaHours. (2016). *Main Page*. Retrieved from http://www.ithacahours.com/

Lasker, J., Collom, E., Bealer, T., Niclaus, E., Keefe, J. Y., Kratzer, Z., & Perlow, K. et al. (2010). Time Banking and Health: The Role of a Community Currency Organization in Enhancing Well-Being. *Health Promotion Practice*. doi:10.1177/1524839909353022 PMID:20685912

Lehaney, B. (2004). *Beyond Knowledge Management*. Idea Group Publishing. doi:10.4018/978-1-59140-180-3

Lesser, E. L., & Storck, J. (2001). Communities of practice and organizational performance. *IBM Systems Journal*, *40*(4), 831–841. doi:10.1147/sj.404.0831

Linderman, M., Siegel, B., Ouellet, D., Brichacek, J., Haines, S., Chase, G., & O'May, J. (2005). *A Reference Model for Information Management to Support Coalition Information Sharing Needs*. Academic Press.

Maes, R. (1999). *Reconsidering Information Mangagement Through A Generic Framework*. Academic Press.

Maes, R., Rijsenbrij, D., Truijens, O., & Goedvolk, H. (2000). *Redefining business - IT alingment through a unified frameworks*. Academic Press.

Manville, B., & Foote, N. (1996). Harvest your workers´ knowledge. *Datamation*, 7.

Naughton-Doe, R. (2015). *An evaluation of timebanking in England: What can timebanks contribute to the co-production of preventive social care?* (Dissertation), University of Bristol.

Nonaka, I. (1991). *The Knowledge-Creating Company. Harvard Business Review*.

Osipov, I. V., Volinsky, A. A., & Prasikova, A. Y. (2016). E-Learning Collaborative System for Practicing Foreign Languages with Native Speakers. *International Journal of Advanced Computer Science and Applications*, *7*(3).

Otcenaskova, T., Bures, V., & Mikulecka, J. (2012). *Theoretical Fundaments of Knowledge Intensity Modelling*. Paper presented at the 18th International Business Information Management Association conference, Istanbul, Turkey.

Ozzane, L. K. (2010). Learning to exchange time: Benefits and obstacles to time banking. *International Journal of Community Currency Research*, *14*, A1–A16.

Partners in Care. (2017). Retrieved from http://www.partnersincare.org/

Ryan-Collins, J., Stephens, L., & Coote, A. (2008). *The new wealth of time: How timebanking helps people build better public services*. London: New Economics Foundation.

Sacks, M. (2015). Competition Between Open Source and Proprietary Software: Strategies for Survival. *Journal of Management Information Systems*, *32*(3), 268–295. doi:10.1080/07421222.2015.1099391

Shih, P., Bellotti, V., Han, K., & Carroll, J. (2015). *Unequal Time for Unequal Value: Implications of Differing Motivations for Participation in Timebanking*. Paper presented at the 33rd Annual ACM Conference on Human Factors in Computing Systems, Seoul, South Korea. doi:10.1145/2702123.2702560

Shreiber, G., Akkermans, H., Anjewierden, A., Hoog, R. d., Shadbolt, N., Velde, W. V. d., & Wielinga, B. (2002). Knowledge Engineering and Management. Cambridge, MA: The MIT Press.

Takeuchi, H., & Nonaka, I. (2004). Knowledge creation and dialectics. *Hitotsubashi on Knowledge Management*, 1-27.

Timebanking UK. (2005). *A bridge to tomorrow: Time banking for baby boomers*. Gloucester, UK: TimebanksUK.

Timebanks USA. (2017). *About Timebanks USA*. Retrieved from https://timebanks.org/timebanksusa/

Tucnik, P., Valek, L., Blecha, P., & Bures, V. (2016). Use of Time Banking as a non-monetary component in agent-based computational economics models. *WSEAS Transactions on Business and Economics, 13*.

Valek, L. (2013a). *Time Banks in Czech Republic: Filling an Empty Gap in Time Bank Research*. Norristown, NJ: Int Business Information Management Assoc-Ibima.

Valek, L. (2013b). Time Banks in Russia: Filling an Empty Gap in Time Bank Research. *Tradition and Reform: Social Reconstruction of Europe*, 383-386.

Valek, L. (2015a). *The difference in understanding of time banking in various contexts*. Paper presented at the 6th LUMEN International Conference: Rethinking Social Action. Core Values 2015, Iasi, Romania.

Valek, L. (2015b). *Time Banks and Knowledge Sharing: Link to the Knowledge Management*. Paper presented at the 5th International Conference Lumen 2014, Transdisciplinary and Communicative Action (Lumen-Tca 2014).

Valek, L. (2016). Open Ways for Time Banking Research: Project Management and Beyond. *International Journal of Human Capital and Information Technology Professionals*, 7(1), 35–47. doi:10.4018/IJHCITP.2016010103

Valek, L., Kolerova, K., & Otcenaskova, T. (2014). Time banks and clusters: Similarities of sharing framework. *Global Journal on Technology, 6*, 31-36.

Widodo, R. N. S., Lim, H., & Atiquzzaman, M. (2017). SDM: Smart deduplication for mobile cloud storage. *Future Generation Computer Systems-the International Journal of Escience, 70*, 64–73. doi:10.1016/j.future.2016.06.023

Compilation of References

Abraham, R. (2000). The role of job control as a moderator of emotional dissonance and emotional intelligence - outcome relationships. *The Journal of Psychology, 134*(2), 169–184. doi:10.1080/00223980009600860 PMID:10766109

Abraham, S. (2012). Development of Employee Engagement Programme on the Basis of Employee Satisfaction Survey. *Journal of Economic Development, Management, IT, Finance and Marketing, 4*(1), 27–37.

Adams, J. S. (1965). Inequity in social exchange. In L. Berkowitz (Ed.), Advances in Experimental Social Psychology (vol. 2, pp. 267–299). New York, NY: Academic Press.

Adekola, B. (2012). The impact of organizational commitment on job satisfaction: A study of employees at Nigerian Universities. *International Journal of Human Resource Studies, 2*(2), 1. doi:10.5296/ijhrs.v2i2.1740

Aggarwal, C. C. (2011). *Social Network Data Analytics*. New York: Springer. doi:10.1007/978-1-4419-8462-3

Agote, L., Aramburu, N., & Lines, R. (2016). Authentic leadership perception, trust in the leader, and followers' emotions in organizational change processes. *The Journal of Applied Behavioral Science, 52*(1), 35–63. doi:10.1177/0021886315617531

Agudo, J. E., Rico, M., Sánchez, H., & Valor, M. (2011). Accessing mobile learning records in Moodle through web services. *The IEEE Journal of Latin-American Learning Technologies, 6*(3), 95–102.

Ahmad, N., & Oranye, N. O. (2010). Empowerment, job satisfaction and organizational commitment: A comparative analysis of nurses working in Malaysia and England. *Journal of Nursing Management, 18*(5), 582–591. doi:10.1111/j.1365-2834.2010.01093.x PMID:20636507

Ajzen, I., & Fishbein, M. (1980). *Understanding Attitudes and Predicting Social Behavior*. Prentice Hall.

Akerjordet, K., & Severinsson, E. (2008). Emotionally intelligent nurse leadership: A literature review study. *Journal of Nursing Management, 16*(5), 265–577. doi:10.1111/j.1365-2834.2008.00893.x PMID:18558927

Akerjordet, K., & Severinsson, E. (2009). Emotional intelligence, reaction and thought: A Pilot study. *Nursing & Health Sciences, 11*(3), 213–220. doi:10.1111/j.1442-2018.2009.00435.x PMID:19689628

Akhawe, D., & Felt, A. P. (2013). Alice in wonderland: A large-scale field study of browser security warning effectiveness. *Proceedings of the 22nd USENIX Security Symposium*, 257-272.

Al-Aameri, A. S. (2000). Job satisfaction and organizational commitment for nurses. *Saudi Medical Journal, 21*(6), 531–535. PMID:11500699

Alavi, M., & Leidner, D. E. (2001). Review: Knowledge management and knowledge management systems: Conceptual foundations and research issues. *Management Information Systems Quarterly, 25*(1), 107–136. doi:10.2307/3250961

Aljohani, N. R., & Davis, H. C. (2012). Learning analytics in mobile and ubiquitous learning environments. 11th World Conference on Mobile and Contextual Learning: mLearn 2012.

Al-Khafaji, K. M. K., & Eryilmaz, M. (2017). Auditor technology and privacy control to secure e-learning information on cloud. *Proceedings of International Conference on Progress in Applied Science.*

Allan, A., Noakes-Fry, K., & Mogull, R. (2005). *Management update: How businesses can defend against social engineering attacks.* Gartner Inc.

Allen, B., Ananthakrishnan, R., Chard, K., Foster, I., Madduri, R., Pruyne, J., . . . Tuecke, S. (2017). Globus: a case study in software as a service for scientists. In *Proceedings of the 8ᵗʰ Workshop ScienceCloud'17* (pp. 26-32). Academic Press. doi:10.1145/3086567.3086570

Allen, N. J., & Meyer, J. P. (1990). The measurement and antecedents of affective, continuance, and normative commitment to the organization. *Journal of Occupational Psychology, 63*(1), 1–18. doi:10.1111/j.2044-8325.1990.tb00506.x

Allen, N. J., & Meyer, J. P. (1996). Affective, continuance, and normative commitment to the organization: An examination of construct validity. *Journal of Vocational Behavior, 49*(3), 252–276. doi:10.1006/jvbe.1996.0043 PMID:8980084

Almigo, N., Khan, R. K. A. W., & Hamzah, H. (2014). *Coaches turnover tendency review of job satisfaction and organizational commitment program in the national service.* Academic Press.

Alsinet, T., Barroso, D., Béjar, R., & Planes, J. (2009): A Formal Model of Competence-Based Assessment. *CCIA*, 428-436.

Alvesson, M. (2004). *Knowledge work and knowledge-intensive firms.* Oxford, UK: Oxford University Press.

Alwi, N. H. M., & Fan, I. (2010). E-Learning and Information Security Management. *International Journal of Digital Society, 1*(2), 148–156. doi:10.20533/ijds.2040.2570.2010.0019

Anand, N. (2016). Impact of human resource practices on job satisfaction: Evidence from Indian public sector banks. *International Journal of Engineering Technology Science and Research, 3,* 122–115.

Anderson, E., & Weitz, B. (1989). Determinants of continuity in conventional industrial channel dyad. *Marketing Science, 8*(4), 310–323. doi:10.1287/mksc.8.4.310

Andreassen, C. S., Griffiths, M. D., Hetland, J., & Pallesen, S. (2012). Development of a work addiction scale. *Scandinavian Journal of Psychology, 53*(3), 265–272. doi:10.1111/j.1467-9450.2012.00947.x PMID:22490005

Anguera, M. T. (2008). Metodologías cualitativas: características, procesos y aplicaciones. In *Metodología en la investigación sobre discapacidad. Introducción al uso de las ecuaciones estructurales* (pp. 141–155). Salamanca: Publicaciones del INICO.

Anthes, G. (2016). Open Source Software No Longer Optional. *Communications of the ACM, 59*(8), 15–17. doi:10.1145/2949684

Antunes, F., & Costa, J. P. (2011). *Decision Support Social Network.* Paper presented at the 6th Iberian Conference on Information Systems and Technologies (CISTI), Chaves, Portugal.

Antunes, F., & Costa, J. P. (2012a). *Disentangling Online Social Networking and Decision Support Systems Research Using Social Network Analysis.* Paper presented at the EWG-DSS Liverpool-2012 Workshop on Decision Support Systems & Operations Management Trends and Solutions in Industries, Liverpool, UK.

Antunes, F., & Costa, J. P. (2015). The Impact of Online Social Networks on Decision Support Systems. In L. Mola, F. Pennarola, & S. Za (Eds.), From Information to Smart Society (Vol. 5, pp. 75-85). Springer International Publishing. doi:10.1007/978-3-319-09450-2_7

Antunes, F., & Costa, J. P. (2012b). Integrating decision support and social networks. *Advances in Human-Computer Interaction, 2012*, 1–10. doi:10.1155/2012/574276

Antunes, F., & Costa, J. P. (2014). Reviewing Motivations for Engaging in Decision Support Social Networks. *International Journal of Human Capital and Information Technology Professionals, 5*(1), 1–14. doi:10.4018/ijhcitp.2014010101

Antunes, F., Freire, M., & Costa, J. P. (2016). Semantic web and decision support systems. *Journal of Decision Systems, 25*(1), 79–93. doi:10.1080/12460125.2015.1087293

APWG. (2008-2014). *Phishing attacks trends reports.* Anti-Phishing Working Group.

Aranya, N., Kushnir, P., & Valency, R. (1986). Organisational commitment in a male dominated profession. *Human Relations, 39*(5), 433–448. doi:10.1177/001872678603900504

Arif, S., & Ilyas, M. (2013). Quality of work-life model for teachers of private universities in Pakistan. *Quality Assurance in Education, 21*(3), 282–298. doi:10.1108/QAE-Feb-2012-0006

Arif, T. (2015). The Mathematics of Social Network Analysis: Metrics for Academic Social Networks. *International Journal of Computer Applications Technology and Research, 4*(12), 889–893. doi:10.7753/IJCATR0412.1003

Armstrong, M. (2009). Armstrong's handbook of human resource management practice. London: Kogan Page.

Arnal, J., Rincón, D., & Latorre, A. (1994). *Investigación educativa. Fundamentos y metodología.* Barcelona: Labor.

Arthur, J. B. (1994). Effects of human resource systems on manufacturing performance and turnover. *Academy of Management Journal, 37*(3), 670–687. doi:10.2307/256705

Ashok, A., Hahn, A., & Govindarasu, M. (2014). Cyber-physical security of wide-area monitoring, protection and control in a smart grid environment. *Journal of Advanced Research, 5*(4), 481–489. doi:10.1016/j.jare.2013.12.005 PMID:25685516

Asif, S., & Sargeant, A. (2000). Modelling internal communication in the financial services sector. *European Journal of Marketing, 34*(3/4), 299–317. doi:10.1108/03090560010311867

Astin, J. A. (1997). Stress reduction through mindfulness meditation: Effects on psychological symptomatology, sense of control, and spiritual experiences. *Psychotherapy and Psychosomatics, 66*(2), 97–106. doi:10.1159/000289116 PMID:9097338

Attride-Stirling, J. (2001). Thematic networks: An analytic tool for qualitative research. *Qualitative Research, 1*(3), 385–405. doi:10.1177/146879410100100307

Atwater, L. E., & Waldman, D. A. (2008). *Leadership, feedback and the open communication gap* (1st ed.). New York: Taylor and Francis Group, LLC.

Avolio, B. J., Luthans, F., & Walumbwa, F. o. (2004). *Authentic Leadership: Theory building for veritable sustained performance.* Working Paper. Gallup Leadership Institute, University of Nebraska, Lincoln.

Avolio, B. J., & Gardner, W. L. (2005). Authentic leadership development: Getting to the root of positive forms of leadership. *The Leadership Quarterly, 16*(3), 315–338. doi:10.1016/j.leaqua.2005.03.001

Avolio, B. J., Gardner, W., Walumbwa, F., Luthans, F., & May, D. R. (2004). Unlocking the mask: A look at the process by which authentic leaders impact follower attitudes and behaviours. *The Leadership Quarterly, 15*(6), 801–823. doi:10.1016/j.leaqua.2004.09.003

Avolio, B. J., & Luthans, F. (2006). *High Impact Leader: Moments Matter in Authentic Leadership Development.* McGraw-Hill.

Aydin, Z., & Yildiz, S. (2014). Using wikis to promote collaborative EFL writing. *Language Learning & Technology*, *18*(1), 160–180.

Aydogdu, S., & Asikgil, B. (2011). An empirical study of the relationship among job satisfaction, organizational commitment and turnover intention. *International Review of Management and Marketing, 1*(3), 43.

Azeem, S. M. (2010). Job satisfaction and organizational commitment among employees in the Sultanate of Oman. *Psychology (Irvine, Calif.), 1*(4), 295–300. doi:10.4236/psych.2010.14038

Azeem, S. M., & Akhtar, N. (2014). Job satisfaction and organizational commitment among public sector employees in Saudi Arabia. *International Journal of Business and Social Science, 5*(7).

Azeez, R. O., Jayeoba, F., & Adeoye, A. O. (2016). Job satisfaction, turnover intention and organizational commitment, Bvimsr's. *Journal of Management Research, 8*(2), 102.

Baer, R. A., Smith, G., & Allen, K. B. (2004). Assessment of mindfulness by self-report: The Kentucky inventory of Mindfulness skills. *Assessment, 11*(3), 191–206. doi:10.1177/1073191104268029 PMID:15358875

Balderas, A., Berns, A., Palomo-Duarte, M., Dodero, J. M., & Ruiz-Rube, I. (2017). Retrieving Objective Indicators from Student Logs in Virtual Worlds. *Journal of Information Technology Research, 10*(3), 69–83.

Bandara, I., Ioras, F., & Maher, K. (2014). Cyber security concerns in e-learning education. In *Proceedings of ICERI-2014 Conference* (pp.728-734). Seville, Spain: Academic Press.

Barney, J. (1991). Firm Resources and Sustained Competitive Advantage. *Journal of Management, 17*(1), 99–120. doi:10.1177/014920639101700108

Baron-Cohen, S., & Wheelright, S. (2004). The empathy quotient: An investigation of adults with Asperger syndrome or high-functioning autism and normal sex differences. *Journal of Autism and Developmental Disorders, 34*(2), 163–175. doi:10.1023/B:JADD.0000022607.19833.00 PMID:15162935

Bar-On, R. (1997). *Bar-On Emotional Quotient Inventory (EQ-I): Technical Manual*. Toronto, Canada: Multi-Health Systems.

Barr, H., & Low, H. (2013). *Introducing interprofessional education*. Centre for the Advancement of Interprofessional Education. doi:10.1007/978-94-6209-353-9_16

Batagelj, V., Doreian, P., Ferligoj, A., & Kejzar, A. (2014). Understanding Large Temporal Networks and Spatial Networks: Exploration, Pattern Searching, Visualization and Network Evolution. Chichester, UK: John Wiley & Sons Ltd. doi:10.1002/9781118915370

Baumruk, R., Gorman, B., & Gorman, R. E. (2006). Why managers are crucial to increasing engagement. *Strategic HR Review, 5*(2), 24–27. doi:10.1108/14754390680000863

Becker, B. E., & Huselid, M. A. (1998). High performance work systems and firm performance: A synthesis of research and managerial implications. *Research in Personnel and Human Resources Management, 16*, 53–101.

Beehr, T. A., Jex, S. M., Stacy, B. A., & Murray, M. A. (2001). Work stressors and coworker support as predictors of individual strain and job performance. *Journal of Organizational Behavior, 21*(4), 391–403. doi:10.1002/(SICI)1099-1379(200006)21:4<391::AID-JOB15>3.0.CO;2-9

Beer, M., Spector, B., Lawrence, P., Mills, D., & Walton, R. (1984). *Managing human assets*. New York: Free Press.

Bellotti, F., Kapralos, B., Lee, K., Moreno-Ger, P., & Berta, R. (2013). Assessment in and of serious games: An overview. *Advances in Human-Computer Interaction, 2013*, 1. doi:10.1155/2013/120791

Benevenuto, F., Rodrigues, T., Meeyoung, C., & Almeida, V. (2009, November 4–6,). *Characterizing User Behavior in Online Social Networks.* Paper presented at the Internet Measurement Conference (IMC'09), Chicago, IL. doi:10.1145/1644893.1644900

Benkhoff, B. (1997). Disentangling organisational commitment: the changes of OCQ for research and policy. *Personal Review, 26*(1), 114-20.

Benson, G. S. (2006). Employee development, commitment and intention to turnover: A test of 'employability' policies in action. *Human Resource Management Journal, 16*(2), 173–192. doi:10.1111/j.1748-8583.2006.00011.x

Berki, E. (2001). *Establishing a scientific discipline for capturing the entropy of systems process models: CDM-FILTERS - A computational and dynamic metamodel as a flexible and integrated language for the testing, expression and re-engineering of systems* (PhD Thesis). University of N. London, UK.

Berki, E., & Jäkälä, M. (2009). Cyber-identities and social life in cyberspace. In Hatzipanagos, S. & Warburton, S. (Eds.), Handbook of Research on Social Software and Developing Community Ontologies (pp. 27-39). IGI Global. doi:10.4018/978-1-60566-208-4.ch003

Berki, E., Chaudhary, S., Li, L., & Valtanen, J. (2014). Increasing social awareness through software quality and social computing – Towards effective anti-phishing research strategies. *Proceedings of the 22nd SQM Conference*, 149-164.

Berki, E., Georgiadou, E., & Holcombe, M. (2004). Requirements engineering and process modelling in software quality management – Towards a generic process metamodel. *Software Quality Journal, 12*(3), 265–283. doi:10.1023/B:SQJO.0000034711.87241.f0

Berki, E., Sharma-Kandel, C., Zhao, Y., & Chaudhary, S. (2017). A comparative study of cloud services use by prospective IT professionals in five countries. *Proceedings of the 9th EDULEARN.*

Berki, R. N. (1986). *Security and society: Reflections on Law, order and politics.* London: J. M. Dent & Sons Ltd.

Berlanga, A. J., Sloep, P. B., Brouns, F., Bitter-Rijpkema, M. E., & Koper, R. (2008). Towards a TENCompetence ePortfolio. *International Journal of Emerging Technologies in Learning, 3*, 24–28.

Berns, A., Palomo-Duarte, M., & Dodero, J. M. (2017b). A mobile learning system to allow students developing their own learning resources. In. J. Colpaert, A. Aerts, R. Kern, & M. Kaiser (Eds.), *CALL in context- Proceedings of the 2017 CALL conference* (pp. 83-90). Academic Press.

Berns, A., Palomo-Duarte, M., Dodero, J. M., & Valero-Franco, C. (2013b). Using a 3D online game to assess students' foreign language acquisition and communicative competence. In D. Hernández-Leo, T. Ley, R. Klamma, & A. Harrer (Eds.), Lecture Notes in Computer Science: Vol. 8095. *Scaling up learning for sustained impact: Proceedings of the 8th European Conference, on Technology Enhanced Learning (EC-TEL)* (pp. 19-31). Berlin, Germany: Springer-Verlag. doi:10.1007/978-3-642-40814-4_3

Berns, A., Palomo-Duarte, M., Dodero, J. M., Ruiz-Ladrón, J. M., & Calderón-Márquez, A. (2015). Mobile apps to support and assess foreign language learning. In F. Helm, L. Bradley, M. Guarda, & S. Thouësny (Eds.), *Critical CALL – Proceedings of the 2015 EUROCALL Conference* (pp. 51-56). Academic Press. doi:10.14705/rpnet.2015.000309

Berns, A., Gonzalez-Pardo, A., & Camacho, D. (2013a). Game-like language learning in 3-D virtual environments. *Computers & Education, 60*(1), 210–220. doi:10.1016/j.compedu.2012.07.001

Berns, A., Isla-Montes, J. L., Palomo-Duarte, M., & Dodero, J. M. (2016). Motivation, students' needs and learning outcomes: A hybrid game-based app for enhanced language learning. *SpringerPlus, 5*(1), 1305. doi:10.1186/s40064-016-2971-1 PMID:27547679

Berns, A., & Palomo-Duarte, M. (2015). Supporting Foreign Language Learning through a gamified app. In R. Hernández & P. Rankin (Eds.), *Higher Education and Second Language Learning: Promoting Self-Directed Learning in New Technological and Educational Contexts* (pp. 181–204). Oxford, UK: Peter Lang.

Berns, A., Palomo-Duarte, M., Isla-Montes, J. L., Dodero, J. M., & Delatorre, P. (2017a). Agenda colaborativa para el aprendizaje de idiomas: Del papel al dispositivo móvil. *Revista Iberoamericana de Educación a Distancia RIED, 20*(2), 119–139. doi:10.5944/ried.20.2.17713

Berry, L. M. (1997). *Psychology at work.* San Francisco: McGraw Hill.

Bhuian, S. N., & Mengüç, B. (2002). An Extension And Evoluation Of Job Characteristics, Organizational Commitment And Job Satisfaction In An Expatriate, Quest Worker, Sales Setting. *Journal of Personal Selling & Sales Management, 22*(1), 1–11.

Bigliardi, Dormio, Galati, & Schiuma. (2012). The impact of organizational culture on the job satisfaction of knowledge workers. *VINE, 42*(1), 36 – 51.

Bingöl. (2010). *Dursun.* İstanbul: İnsan Kaynakları Yönetimi, Beta Basım Yayım Dağıtım.

Biswas, S., & Bhatnagar, J. (2013). Mediator Analysis of Employee Engagement: Role of Perceived Organizational Support, P-O Fit, Organizational Commitment and Job Satisfaction. *Vikalpa, 38*(1), 27–40.

Blake, R. (2000). Computer mediated communication: A window on L2 Spanish interlanguage. *Language Learning & Technology, 4*(1), 120–136.

Blanchard, A. L. (2004). The effects of dispersed virtual communities on face-to-face social capital. In Social Capital and Information Technology. MIT Press.

Blanchard, A. L., & Markus, M. L. (2004). The experienced sense of a virtual community: Characteristics and processes. Data Base Advance Information System, 35(1), 65–79.

Blanco, M., & Ginovart, M. (2009). Creating Moodle Quizzes for the Subjects of Mathematics and Statistics Corresponding to the First Years in Engineering Studies. In *Proceedings of the 1st International Conference on Education and New Learning Technologies* (pp. 1984-1883). Barcelona: AITED.

Blau, G. J. (1985). The measurement and prediction of career commitment. *Journal of Occupational Psychology, 58*(4), 277–288. doi:10.1111/j.2044-8325.1985.tb00201.x

Blessing White. (2006). *Employee Engagement Report 2006.* BlessingWhite, Inc. Available: www.blessingwhite.com

Blessing White. (2008). *The Employee Engagement Equation in India.* Presented by BlessingWhite and HR Anexi. Available: www.blessingwhite.com

Bocchino, C. C., Hartman, B. W., & Foley, P. F. (2003). The relationship between person-organization congruence, perceived violations of the psychological contract, and occupational stress symptoms. *Consulting Psychology Journal: Practice and Research, 55*(4), 203–214. doi:10.1037/1061-4087.55.4.203

Bodomo, A. B. (2010). *Computer-Mediated Communication for Linguistics and Literacy: Technology and Natural Language Education.* Hershey, PA: Information Science Reference. doi:10.4018/978-1-60566-868-0

Bolhari, A., Rezaeian, A., Bolhari, J., & Bairamzadeh, S. (2012). Occupational Stress Level among Information Technology Professionals in Iran. *International Journal of Information and Electronics Engineering, 2*(5), 682–685.

Bonneau, J., Herley, C., van Oorschot, P. C., & Stajano, F. (2012). The quest to replace passwords: a framework for comparative evaluation of web authentication schemes. *Proceedings of the IEEE Symposium on Security and Privacy*, 553-567. doi:10.1109/SP.2012.44

Borgatti, S. P. (2009). 2-Mode Concepts in Social Network Analysis. In R. A. Meyers (Ed.), *Encyclopedia of Complexity and System Science* (pp. 8279–8291). Larkspur, CA: Springer. doi:10.1007/978-0-387-30440-3_491

Boshoff, C., & Mels, G. (1995). A Causal Model to Evaluate the Relationships Among Supervision, Role Stress, Organizational Commitment and Internal Service Quality. *European Journal of Marketing*, *29*(2), 23–42. doi:10.1108/03090569510080932

Bouty, I. (2000). Interpersonal and interaction influences on Informal resource exchanges between R&D researchers across organizational boundaries. *Academy of Management Journal*, *43*(1), 50–65. doi:10.2307/1556385

Boyatzis, R. (1982). *The competent manager: a model for effective performance*. New York: John Wiley and Sons.

Boyatzis, R. E., & McKee, A. (2005). *Resonant leadership: Renewing yourself and connecting with others through mindfulness, hope, and compassion* (1st ed.). Harvard Business Review Press.

Boyd, D. M. (2006). The significance of social software. In T. N. Burg & J. Schmidt (Eds.), *BlogTalks Reloaded. Social Software - Research & Cases* (pp. 15–30). Norderstedt, Germany: Books on Demand GmbH.

Boyd, D. M., & Ellison, N. B. (2008). Social network sites: Definition, history, and scholarship. *Journal of Computer-Mediated Communication*, *13*(1), 210–230. doi:10.1111/j.1083-6101.2007.00393.x

Boyle, D., & Bird, S. (2014). *Give and Take: How timebanking is transforming healthcare*. Stroud, UK: Timebanking UK.

Bradley, G. (2007). Job tenure as a moderator of stressor-strain relations: A comparison of experienced and new-start teachers. *Work and Stress*, *21*(1), 48–64. doi:10.1080/02678370701264685

Bravo-Lillo, C., Cranor, L. F., Downs, J., Komanduri, S., Reeder, R. W., Schechter, S., & Sleeper, M. (2013). Your attention please: designing security-decision UIs to make genuine risk harder to ignore. *Proceedings of the Symposium on Usable Privacy and Security*. doi:10.1145/2501604.2501610

Breaugh, J. A., & Mann, R. B. (1984). Recruiting source effects: A test of two alternative explanations. *Journal of Occupational Psychology*, *57*(4), 261–267. doi:10.1111/j.2044-8325.1984.tb00167.x

Briere, J., & Elliott, D. M. (1998). Clinical utility of the Impact of Event Scale: Psychometrics in the general population. *Assessment*, *5*(2), 171–180. doi:10.1177/107319119800500207 PMID:9626392

Briner, R., Harris, C., & Daniels, K. (2004). How do work stress and coping work? Toward a fundamental theoretical reappraisal. *British Journal of Guidance & Counselling*, *32*(2), 223–234. doi:10.1080/03069880410001692256

Brown, K. W., & Ryan, M. (2003). The benefits of being present: Mindfulness and its role in psychological well-being. *Journal of Personality and Social Psychology*, *84*(4), 822–848. doi:10.1037/0022-3514.84.4.822 PMID:12703651

Brown, K. W., Ryan, R. M., & Creswell, J. D. (2007). Mindfulness: Theoretical foundations and evidence for its salutary effects. *Psychological Inquiry*, *18*(4), 211–237. doi:10.1080/10478400701598298

Brown, M. E., & Treviño, L. K. (2006). Ethical leadership: A review and future directions. *The Leadership Quarterly*, *17*(6), 595–616. doi:10.1016/j.leaqua.2006.10.004

Brown, R. I. F. (1993). *Some contributions of the study of gambling to the study of other addictions. In Gambling behavior and problem gambling*. Reno, NV: University of Nevada Press.

Brown, R., & Brooks, I. (2002). Emotion at work: Identifying the emotional climate of night nursing. *Journal of Management in Medicine, 16*(5), 327–344. doi:10.1108/02689230210446517 PMID:12463648

Brown, R., Waring, R., & Donkaewbua, S. (2008). Incidental Vocabulary Acquisition from Reading, Reading-While-Listening, and Listening to Stories. *Reading in a Foreign Language, 20*(2), 136–163.

Bruno, G. (2016). Tasks and assignments in case management models. *Procedia Computer Science, 100*, 156–163. doi:10.1016/j.procs.2016.09.135

Bruno, G. (2017). A dataflow-oriented modeling approach to business processes. *International Journal of Human Capital and Information Technology Professionals, 8*(1), 51–65. doi:10.4018/IJHCITP.2017010104

Buelens, M., & Poelmans, S. A. Y. (2004). Enriching the Spence and Robbins' typology of workaholism: Demographic, motivational, and organizational correlates. *Journal of Organizational Change Management, 17*(5), 440–458. doi:10.1108/09534810410554470

Buendía, L., Colás, P., & Hernández, F. (1997). *Métodos de investigación en psicopedagogía*. Madrid: McGraw-Hill.

Bundeson, J. S. (2001). How Work Ideologies Shape the Psychological Contract of Professional Employees: Doctors' Response to Perceived Breach. *Journal of Organizational Behavior, 22*(2), 717–741. doi:10.1002/job.112

Burd, B., Elahi, A., Russell, I., Barker, L., Pérez, A. F., Siever, B., & Guerra, J. G. et al. (2017). The Internet of Things in CS education: current challenges and future potential. *Proceedings of the 22nd ACM Conference on Innovation and Technology in Computer Science Education*. doi:10.1145/3059009.3081331

Burgos, D., Moreno-Ger, P., Sierra, J. L., & Fernandez-Manjon, B. (2007). Authoring game-based adaptive units of learning with IMS Learning Design and e-Adventure. *International Journal of Learning Technology, 3*(3), 252–268. doi:10.1504/IJLT.2007.015444

Burke, M., Marlow, C., & Lento, T. (2009). *Feed Me: Motivating Newcomer Contribution in Social Network Sites.* Paper presented at the CHI 2009, Boston, MA. doi:10.1145/1518701.1518847

Burkett, S. (2006). Scott Burkett's pothole of the infobahm: The life cycle of online community members [Weblog post]. Retrieved from http://www.scottburkett.com/intek/php/online-communities/2006-01-09/the-lifecycleof- online-community-members.html

Burston, J. (2013). Mobile-assisted language learning: A selected annotated bibliography of implementation studies 1994-2012. *Language Learning & Technology, 17*(3), 157–224.

Busch, T., Fallan, L., & Pettersen, A. (1998). Disciplinary Differences in Job Satisfaction Self- Efficacy, Goal Commitment and Organizational Commitment among Faculty Employees in Norwegian Colleges: An Empirical Assessment of Indicators of Performance. *Quality in Higher Education, 4*(2), 137–157. doi:10.1080/1353832980040204

Butler, . (2005). Community effort in online groups: Who does the work and why. In S. Weisband & L. Atwater (Eds.), *Leadership at a Distance*. Mahwah, NJ: Lawrence Erlbaum Associates Inc.

Bytheway, J. A. (2011). *Vocabulary learning strategies in massively multiplayer online role-playing games* (Master's thesis). University of Wellington.

Caballero-Hernández, J. A., Palomo-Duarte, M., & Dodero, J. M. (2017). Skill assessment in learning experiences based on serious games: A Systematic Mapping Study. *Computers & Education, 113*, 42–60. doi:10.1016/j.compedu.2017.05.008

Cabanillas, C., Resinas, M., Ruiz-Cortés, A., & Awad, A. (2011). Automatic generation of a data-centered view of business processes. In *Lecture Notes in Computer Science, 6741* (pp. 352–366). Heidelberg, Germany: Springer. doi:10.1007/978-3-642-21640-4_27

Cahn, E. S. (2000). No more throw-away people: the co-production imperative. Washington, DC: Academic Press.

Cahyono, D. (2015). Modeling Turnover and Their Antecedents Using the Locus of Control as Moderation: Empirical Study of Public Accountant Firms in Java Indonesia. *International Journal of Finance and Accounting, 4*(1), 40–51.

Calderón-Márquez, A., Palomo-Duarte, M., Berns, A., & Dodero, J. M. (2017). Tendencias y tipos de aprendizaje en MALL: una revisión sistemática de la literatura (2012-2016). *V Congreso Internacional sobre Aprendizaje, Innovación y Competitividad. (CINAIC 2017)*. doi:10.26754/CINAIC.2017.000001_061

Camillo, G. L., Westphall, C. M., Werner, J., & Westphall, C. B. (2017). Preserving privacy with fine-grained authorization in an identity management system. In *Proceedings of the 16th International Conference on Networks* (pp. 75-80), Venice, Italy: Academic Press.

Caplan, R. D., & Jones, K. W. (1975). Effects of Work Load, Role Ambiguity, and Type A Personality on Anxiety, Depression, and Heart Rate. *The Journal of Applied Psychology, 4*(2), 713–719. doi:10.1037/0021-9010.60.6.713 PMID:1194173

Cappelli, P. (2001). A market-driven approach to retaining talent. Harvard Business Review, 27-50.

Cardy, R. L., & Lengnick-Hall, M. L. (2011). Will they stay or will they go? Exploring a customer-oriented approach to employee retention. *Journal of Business and Psychology, 26*(2), 213–217. doi:10.1007/s10869-011-9223-8

Carley, K. M. (1997). Network Text Analysis: The Network Position of Concepts. In C. W. Roberts (Ed.), *Analysis for the Social Sciences: Methods for Drawing Statistical Inferences from Texts and Transcripts* (pp. 79–100). Mahwah, NJ: Laurence Erlbaum Associates, Inc.

Carlson, L. E., & Brown, K. W. (2005). Validation of the Mindful attention awareness scale in a cancer population. *Journal of Psychosomatic Research, 58*(1), 29–33. doi:10.1016/j.jpsychores.2004.04.366 PMID:15771867

Caroll, J. M., & Belloti, V. (2015). *Creating Value Together: The Emerging Design Space of Peer-to-Peer Currency and Exchange*. Paper presented at the Collaborating through Social Media - CSCW 2015, Vancouver, Canada. doi:10.1145/2675133.2675270

Carraher, S. M., & Buckley, M. R. (2008). Attitudes towards benefits and behavioral intentions and their relationship to Absenteeism, Performance, and Turnover among nurses. *Academy of Health Care Management Journal, 4*(2), 89–109.

Casado-Lumbreras, C., Colomo-Palacios, R., Gomez-Berbis, J. M., & Garcia-Crespo, A. (2009). Mentoring programmes: A study of the Spanish software industry. International. *Journal of Learning and Intellectual Capital, 6*(3), 293–302. doi:10.1504/IJLIC.2009.025046

Casado-Lumbreras, C., Colomo-Palacios, R., Soto-Acosta, P., & Misra, S. (2011). Culture dimensions in software development industry: *The effects of mentoring. Scientific Research and Essays, 6*(11), 2403–2412.

CEPIS. (n.d.). *e-Competence Benchmark*. Retrieved July 2017, from https://www.cepisecompetencebenchmark.org/survey/survey/index

Chabungham, P. (2005). *The Soft Art of Being a Tough Leader*. Indian Management Journal.

Chao, P. Y., & Chen, G. D. (2009). Augmenting paper-based learning with mobile phones. *Interacting with Computers, 21*(3), 173–185. doi:10.1016/j.intcom.2009.01.001

Chao, T. (2009). Artifact-based transformation of IBM Global Financing. In *Lecture Notes in Computer Science, 5701* (pp. 261–277). Heidelberg, Germany: Springer.

Chaudhary, S. (2016). *The use of usable security and security education to fight phishing attacks* (PhD Thesis). University of Tampere, Finland.

Chaudhary, S., Zhao, Y., Berki, E., Valtanen, J., Li,L., Helenius, M., & Mystakidis, S. (2015b). A cross-cultural and gender-based perspective for online security: Exploring knowledge, skills and attitudes of higher education students. *IADIS International Journal on WWW/Internet, 13*(1), 57-71.

Chaudhary, S., & Berki, E. (2013). Challenges in designing usable anti-phishing solutions. *Proceedings of the 21st SQM Conference*, 189-200.

Chaudhary, S., Berki, E., Li, L., & Valtanen, J. (2015a). Time Up for phishing with effective anti-phishing research strategies. *International Journal of Human Capital and IT Professionals, 6*(2), 49–64. doi:10.4018/IJHCITP.2015040104

Chaudhary, S., Berki, E., Li, L., Valtanen, J., & Helenius, M. (2017). A socio-cognitive and computational model for decision making and user modelling in social phishing. *Proceedings of the 25th SQM Conference.*

Chaudhary, S., & Rathore, S. (2013). *Developing Emotional Intelligence for Workplace Success. Innovation, Social Networking and Technologies, an Approach.* Bloomsbury Publishing India Pvt. Limited.

Chaudhary, S., Zolotavkin, Y., Berki, E., Helenius, M., Nykänen, P., & Kela, J. (2016). Towards a conceptual framework for privacy protection in the use of interactive 3600 video surveillance. *Proceedings of the IEEE 22nd International Conference on Virtual Systems & Multimedia,.*

Checkland, P., & Scholes, J. (1990). *Soft systems methodology in action.* Wiley & Sons.

Cheetham, G., & Chivers, G. (2005). *Professions, competence, and informal learning.* Cheltenham, UK: Edward Elgar Publishing.

Cheniti-Belcadhi, L., Henze, N., & Braham, R. (2008). Assessment personalization in the Semantic Web. *Journal of Computational Methods in Science and Engineering, 8*(3), 163–182.

Chen, T. Y., Chang, P. L., & Ching, W. Y. (2004). A study of career needs, career development programs, job satisfaction and the turnover intentions of R&D personnel. *Career Development International, 9*(4), 424–437. doi:10.1108/13620430410544364

Chen, Y., & He, W. (2013). Security risks and protection in online learning: A survey. *International Review of Research in Open and Distance Learning, 14*(5), 108–127. doi:10.19173/irrodl.v14i5.1632

Cherrington, D. J. (1980). *The Work Ethic.* New York, NY: American Management Association.

Cheung, F. Y., & Tang, C. S. (2009). The influence of emotional intelligence and affectiv ity on emotional labor strategies at work. *Journal of Individual Differences, 30*(2), 75–86. doi:10.1027/1614-0001.30.2.75

Chiboiwa, M., Samuel, M., & Chipunza, C. (2010). An examination of employee retention strategy in a private organization in Zimbabwe. *African Journal of Business Management, 4*(10), 2103–2109.

Chinnery, G. (2006). Emerging technologies. Going to the mall: Mobile assisted language learning. *Language Learning & Technology, 10*(1), 9–16.

Choi, J. (2006). A motivational theory of charismatic leadership: Envisioning, empathy, and empowerment. *Journal of Leadership & Organizational Studies, 13*(1), 24–43. doi:10.1177/10717919070130010501

Chu. (2010). The benefits of meditation vis-à-vis emotional intelligence, perceived stress and negative mental health. *Stress and Health, 26*(2), 169-180.

Clapp-Smith, R., Vogelgesang, G. R., & Avey, J. B. (2009). Authentic leadership and positive psychological capital the mediating role of trust at the group level of analysis. *Journal of Leadership & Organizational Studies, 15*(3), 227–240. doi:10.1177/1548051808326596

Clugston, M. (2000). The mediating effects of multidimensional commitment on job satisfaction and intent to leave. *Journal of Organizational Behavior, 21*(4), 477–486. doi:10.1002/(SICI)1099-1379(200006)21:4<477::AID-JOB25>3.0.CO;2-7

Coates, T. (2005). An addendum to a definition of Social Software. *PLASTICBAG. ORG, 5*. Retrieved from http://www.plasticbag.org/archives/2005/01/an_addendum_to_a_definition_of_social_software/

Coleman, H., & Unrau, Y. A. (2010). Qualitative Data Analysis. In R. M. Grinnell & Y. A. Unrau (Eds.), *Social Work: Research and Evaluation. Foundations of Evidence-Based Practice* (pp. 447–464). New York: Oxford University Press.

Colombo, B., Antonietti, A., Sala, R., & Caravita, S. C. S. (2013). Blog Content and Structure, Cognitive Style and Metacognition. *International Journal of Technology and Human Interaction, 9*(3), 1–17. doi:10.4018/jthi.2013070101

Colomo Palacios, R., Casado-Lumbreras, C., Soto-Acosta, P., García Peñalvo, F. J., & Caro, E. T. (2013). Competence gaps in software personnel: A multi-organizational study. *Computers in Human Behavior, 29*(2), 456–461. doi:10.1016/j.chb.2012.04.021

Colomo-Palacios, R., Casado-Lumbreras, C., Misra, S., & Soto-Acosta, P. (2014b). Career abandonment intentions among software workers. *Human Factors and Ergonomics in Manufacturing & Service Industries, 24*(6), 641–655. doi:10.1002/hfm.20509

Colomo-Palacios, R., Casado-Lumbreras, C., Soto-Acosta, P., & García-Crespo, Á. (2013). Decisions in software development projects management. *An exploratory study. Behaviour & Information Technology, 32*(11), 1077–1085. doi:10.1080/0144929X.2011.630414

Colomo-Palacios, R., Casado-Lumbreras, C., Soto-Acosta, P., García-Peñalvo, F. J., & Tovar, E. (2014a). Project managers in global software development teams: A study of the effects on productivity and performance. *Software Quality Journal, 22*(1), 3–19. doi:10.1007/s11219-012-9191-x

Colomo-Palacios, R., Casado-Lumbreras, C., Soto-Acosta, P., & Misra, S. (2014). Providing knowledge recommendations: An approach for informal electronic mentoring. *Interactive Learning Environments, 22*(2), 221–240. doi:10.1080/10494820.2012.745430

Connolly, T. M., Stansfield, M., & Hainey, T. (2001). An alternate reality game for language learning: ARGuing for multilingual motivation. *Computers & Education, 57*(1), 1389–1415. doi:10.1016/j.compedu.2011.01.009

Cooper, R. K., & Sawaf, A. (1997). *Executive EQ: Emotional intelligence in leadership and organizations*. New York: Grosset/Putman.

Corbin, J., & Strauss, A. (1990). Grounded Theory Research: Procedures, Canons and Evaluative Criteria. *Qualitative Sociology, 13*(1), 3–21. doi:10.1007/BF00988593

Cornillie, F., Thorne, S. L., & Desmet, P. (2012). ReCALL special issue: Digital games for language learning: challenges and opportunities: Editorial Digital games for language learning: From hype to insight? *ReCALL, 24*(03), 243–256. doi:10.1017/S0958344012000134

Cortiella, C., & Horowitz, S. H. (2014). *The State of learning disabilities: facts, trends and emerging issues*. New York: National Center for Learning Disabilities.

Cothrel, J., & Williams, R. (1999). Online Communities helping them form and grow. *Journal of Knowledge Management*, *3*(1), 54–60. doi:10.1108/13673279910259394

Cotton, J. L., Vollrath, D. A., Froggatt, K. L., Lengnick-Hall, M. L., & Jennings, K. R. (1988). Employee Participation: Diverse Forms and Different Outcomes. *Academy of Management Review*, *13*(1), 8–22.

Cox, T., & Ferguson, E. (1991). Individual Differences, Stress and Coping. In C. L. Cooper & R. Payne (Eds.), *Personality and Stress: Individual Differences in the Stress Process*. Wiley.

Cox, T., & Griffiths, A. (2010). *Work-related stress: a theoretical perspective. In Occupational Health Psychology*. Chichester, UK: Wiley-Blackwell.

Cox, T., Griffiths, A., & Rial-Gonzalez, E. (2000). *Research on Work-Related Stress*. Luxembourg: Office for Official Publications of the European Communities.

Cranny, C. J., Smith, P. C., & Stone, E. F. (1992). *Job satisfaction: How people feel about their jobs and how it affects their performance*. New York, NY: Lexington Book.

Creswell, J. (2005). *Educational Research: Planning, Conducting, and Evaluating Quantitative and Qualitative Research*. Upper Saddle River, NJ: Pearson Education.

Cropanzano, R., Rupp, E. D., & Byrne, S. Z. (2003). The Relationship of Emotional Exhaustion to Work Attitudes, Job Performance, and Organizational Citizenship Behaviors. *The Journal of Applied Psychology*, *88*(4), 160–169. doi:10.1037/0021-9010.88.1.160 PMID:12675403

Dasgupta, H., & Kumar, S. (2009). Role Stress among Doctors Working in a Government Hospital in Shimla (India). *European Journal of Soil Science*, *9*(3), 356–370.

Dasgupta, M., & Gupta, R. K. (2009). Innovation in Organizations: A Review of the Role of Organizational Learning and Knowledge Management. *Global Business Review*, *10*(2), 203–224. doi:10.1177/097215090901000205

Davenport, T. H. (2014). *Big data at work: dispelling the myths, uncovering the opportunities*. Harvard Business School Press. doi:10.15358/9783800648153

Davis, M. H. (1980). A multidimensional approach to individual differences in empathy. *Catalog of Selected Documents in Psychology*, *10*(85). Retrieved from http://www.eckerd.edu/academics/psychology/files/Davis_1980.pdf

Davis, M. H. (1983). Measuring individual differences in empathy: Evidence for a multidimensional approach. *Journal of Personality and Social Psychology*, *44*(1), 113–126. doi:10.1037/0022-3514.44.1.113

Day, A. L., & Carroll, S. A. (2004). Using ability based measure of emotional intelligence to predict individual performance, group performance, and group Citizenship Behaviors. *Personality and Individual Differences*, *36*(6), 1443–1458. doi:10.1016/S0191-8869(03)00240-X

Day, A. L., Therrien, D. L., & Carroll, S. A. (2005). Predicting psychological health: Assessing the incremental validity of emotional intelligence beyond personality, Type A behaviour, and daily hassles. *European Journal of Personality*, *19*(6), 519–536. doi:10.1002/per.552

Day, J. (2007). Strangers on the train the relationship of the IT department with the rest of the business. *Information Technology & People*, *20*(1), 6–31. doi:10.1108/09593840710730536

De Coi, J., Herder, E., Koesling, A., Lofi, C., Olmedilla, D., Papatreou, O., & Siberski, W. (2007). A Model for Competence Gap Analysis. *Proceedings of 3rd International Conference on Web Information Systems and Technologies (WEBIST)*, 304-312.

De Man, H. (2009, January). Case management: A review of modeling approaches. *BPTrends.*

Deci, E. L., & Ryan, R. M. (1980). Self-determination theory: When mind mediates behaviour. *Journal of Mind and Behavior, 1*, 33–43.

Deepa, E., Palaniswamy, R., & Kuppusamy, S. (2014). Effect of Performance Appraisal System in Organizational Commitment, Job Satisfaction and Productivity. *The Journal Contemporary Management Research, 8*(1), 72–82.

Del Blanco, Á., Torrente, J., Moreno-Ger, P., & Fernández-Manjón, B. (2011). Enhancing adaptive learning and assessment in virtual learning environments with educational games. In Q. Jin (Ed.), *Intelligent Learning Systems and Advancements in Computer-Aided Instruction: Emerging Studies* (pp. 144–163). Hershey, PA: Information Science Reference.

Delgado, C. (2014). *Viajando a Ítaca por los mares cuantitativos, manual de ruta para investigar en grado y en postgrado.* Salamanca: Amaru.

Dernovsek, D. (2008). *Creating highly engaged and committed employee starts at the top andends at the bottom line Credit Union Magazine, May 2008.* Credit Union National Association, Inc.

Dhabhar, F. S., Saul, A. N., Daugherty, C., Holmes, T. H., Bouley, D. M., & Oberyszyn, T. M. (2010). Short-term stress enhances cellular immunity and increases early resistance to squamous cell carcinoma. *Brain, Behavior, and Immunity, 24*(1), 127–137. doi:10.1016/j.bbi.2009.09.004 PMID:19765644

Dhamija, R., Tygar, J. D., & Hearst, M. (2006). Why phishing works. *Proceedings of the Conference on Human Factors in Computing Systems*, 581-590.

Di Ciccio, C., Marrella, A., & Russo, A. (2015). Knowledge-intensive processes: Characteristics, requirements and analysis of contemporary approaches. *Journal on Data Semantics, 4*(1), 29–57. doi:10.1007/s13740-014-0038-4

Dierendonck, D. V. (2015). The influence of planning, support and self-concordance on goal progress and job satisfaction-Evidence-based HRM. *A Global Forum for Empirical Scholarship, 3*(3), 206 – 221.

Dietz, J., & Kleinlogel, E. P. (2014). Wage cuts and managers' empathy: How a positive emotion can contribute to positive organizational ethics in difficult times. *Journal of Business Ethics, 119*(4), 461–472. doi:10.1007/s10551-013-1836-6

Dirani, K. M., & Kuchinke, K. P. (2011). Job satisfaction and organizational commitment: Validating the Arabic satisfaction and commitment questionnaire (ASCQ), testing the correlations, and investigating the effects of demographic variables in the Lebanese banking sector. *International Journal of Human Resource Management, 22*(5), 1180–1202. doi:10.1080/09585192.2011.556801

Dolog, P., Thomsen, L. L., Thomsen, B., & Stage, J. (2010). Competence Centered Specialization in Web Engineering Topics in a Software Engineering Masters Degree Programme. *Proceedings of the 1st Educators' Day on Web Engineering Curricula, WECU-2010 in conjunction with International Web Engineering Conference.* http://CEUR-WS.org/Vol-607

Dondlinger, M. J. (2007). Educational video game design: A review of the literature. *Journal of Applied Educational Technology, 4*(1), 21–31.

Dulewicz, V., & Higgs, M. (1998). Emotional intelligence: Can it be measured reliably and validly using competency data? *Competency, 6*(1), 1–15.

Duxbury, L., & Halinski, M. (2014). Dealing with the Grumpy Boomers, Re-engaging the disengaged and retaining talent. *Journal of Organizational Change Management, 27*(4), 660 – 676. <ALIGNMENT.qj></ALIGNMENT>10.1108/JOCM-05-2014-0106

Dziobek, I., Rogers, K., Fleck, S., Bahnemann, M., Heekeren, H. R., Wolf, O. T., & Convit, A. (2007). Dissociation of cognitive and emotional empathy in adults with Asperger syndrome using the Multifaceted Empathy Test (MET). *Journal of Autism and Developmental Disorders*, *38*(3), 464–473. doi:10.1007/s10803-007-0486-x PMID:17990089

e-CF Council Project. (n.d.). Retrieved July 2017, from www.ecfalliance.org

e-Competence Quality. (n.d.). *e-Competence Certificates*. Retrieved July 2017, from http://www.e-competence-quality. com/certification-profiles/

Eggers, D. (2014). *The circle*. Vintage Books.

Eisenberg, N., Fabes, R. A., & Spinrad, T. L. (1998). Prosocial development. In Handbook of child psychology. Academic Press.

eLeaP. (2016). *The Internet of Things' impact on elearning*. Available at: https://www.eleapsoftware.com/the-internet-of-things-impact-on-elearning/

Elizabeth, G., & Zakkariya, K.A. (2015). Job related stress and job satisfaction: a comparative study among bank employees. *Journal of Management Development*, *34*(3), 316 – 329.

Ellevate. (2015). *Forbes*. Retrieved 28 September, 2015, from http://www.forbes.com/sites/85broads/2013/11/18/the-millennial-startup-revolution/

EN 16234-1:2016. (2016). *e-Competence Framework (e-CF) – a Common European Framework for ICT Professionals in All Industry Sectors – Part 1: Framework. European e-Competence Framework. e-CF 3.0 Profiling tool on-line*. Retrieved July 2017, from http://www.ecompetences.eu/e-cf-3-0-and-ict-profiles-on-line-tool

Endrissat, N., Muller, W. R., & Kaudela-Baum, S. (2007). En route to an empirically-based understanding of Authentic Leadership. *European Management Journal*, *25*(3), 207–220. doi:10.1016/j.emj.2007.04.004

Engeström, Y. (1987). *Learning by expanding: an activity-theoretical approach to developmental research*. Helsinki, Finland: Orienta-Konsultit Oy.

Engler, N. (1998). IS managers under stress. *Computing*, *12*, 44–48.

Erickson, T.J. (2005). *Testimony submitted before the US Senate Committee on Health, Education, Labour and Pensions, May 26*. Academic Press.

Eshuis, R., & van Gorp, P. (2012). Synthesizing object life cycles from business process models. In *Lecture Notes in Computer Science, 7532* (pp. 307–320). Heidelberg, Germany: Springer. doi:10.1007/978-3-642-34002-4_24

e-Skills Match Project. (n.d.). Retrieved July 2017, from http://www.eskillsmatch.eu/en/

Eslami, J., & Gharakhani, D. (2012). Organizational commitment and job satisfaction. *ARPN Journal of Science and Technology*, *2*(2), 85–91.

Estes, B., & Wang, J. (2008). Workplace Incivility: Impacts on Individual and Organizational Performance. *Human Resource Development Review*, *7*(2), 218–240. doi:10.1177/1534484308315565

European Commission. (2007). *Proposal For A Recommendation Of The European Parliament And Of The Council On Key Competences For Lifelong Learning*. Council Of The European Union.

European Commission. (n.d.a). *ESCO: European Classification of Skills/Competences, Qualifications and Occupations*. Retrieved July 2017, from https://www.ec.europa.eu/esco/portal/document/en/8e9cf30d-9799-4f95-ae29-e05c725b24c7

European Commission. (n.d.b). *European Qualifications Framework*. Retrieved July 2017, from http://ec.europa.eu/ploteus

Evangelidou, F. (2017). Kavala's 6th Graders towards Mastering Mathematics: A Blended Learning Proposal at Disabled Students' Side. In A. Palalas & P. Pawluk (Eds.), *Blended Learning Theory and Practice Proceedings of the 2nd World Conference on Blended Learning (IABL2017)* (pp. 79-84). Toronto: International Association for Blended Learning and George Brown College.

Expert Group on Future Skills Needs (EGFSN). (2013). *Addressing Future Demand for High-Level ICT Skills (November 2013)*. Forfás / EGFSN.

Farabaugh, R. (2007). "The isle is full of noises": Using Wiki software to establish a discourse community in a Shakespeare classroom. *Language Awareness*, *16*(1), 41–56. doi:10.2167/la428.0

Feng, J., Lazar, J., & Preece, J. (2004). Empathy and online interpersonal trust: A fragile relationship. *Journal of Behavior and Information Technology*, *23*(2), 97–106. doi:10.1080/01449290310001659240

Fernandez, C. P. (2007). Employee engagement. *Journal of Public Health Management and Practice.* Available: http://find.galegroup.com

Fernández-Balandrón, C. (2007). ITIL: Information Technology Infrastructure Library. *BIT Numerical Mathematics*, *160*, 46–49.

Fernández-Sanz, L., & García-García, M.J. (2006). The human factor in software engineering. *Eur. J. Inform. Prof., 7*(1).

Fernández-Sanz, L., Gómez Pérez, J., & Castillo-Martínez, A. (2017). e-Skills Match: A framework for mapping and integrating the main skills, knowledge and competence standards and models for ICT occupations. *Computer Standards & Interfaces*, *51*, 30–42. doi:10.1016/j.csi.2016.11.004

Ferriman, N. (2013). The impact of blended e-learning on undergraduate academic essay writing in English (L2). *Computers & Education*, *60*(1), 243–253. doi:10.1016/j.compedu.2012.07.008

Field, L. K., & Buitendach, J. H. (2011). Happiness, Work Engagement and Organisational Commitment of Support Staff at a Tertiary Education Institution in South Africa. *SA Journal of Industrial Psychology/SA Tydskrif vir Bedryfsielkunde*, *37*(1), 946-955. doi:10.4102/sajip.v37i1.946

Finegold, D., Mohrman, S., & Spreitzer, G. M. (2002). Age effects on the predictors of technical workers' commitment and willingness to turnover. *Journal of Organizational Behavior*, *23*(5), 655–674. doi:10.1002/job.159

Fiorillo, D., & Nappo, N. (2014). Job satisfaction in Italy: Individual characteristics and social relations. *International Journal of Social Economics*, *41*(8), 683–704. doi:10.1108/IJSE-10-2012-0195

Fischer, A. E. (2014). *Improving user protection and security in cyberspace.* Report of Committee on Culture, Science, Education and Media, Council of Europe. Retrieved March 12, 2014, from www.statewatch.org/news/2014/mar/coe-parl-ass-cyberspace-security.pdf

Fitze, M. (2006). Discourse and Participation in ESL face-to-face and written electronic conferences. *Language Learning & Technology*, *10*(1), 67–86.

Fitzgerald, B. (2011). Adopting Open Source Software: A Practical Guide. Cambridge, MA: The MIT Press. doi:10.7551/mitpress/9780262516358.001.0001

Flechais, I., Mascolo, C., & Sasse, M. A. (2007). Integrating security and usability into the requirements and design process. *International Journal of Electronic Security and Digital Forensics*, *1*(1), 12–26. doi:10.1504/IJESDF.2007.013589

Florence, Y. Y. L., & Weiyan, T. (2014). Boosting facility managers' personal and work outcomes through job design. *Facilities*, *32*(13/14), 825–844. doi:10.1108/F-04-2013-0031

Fox, S., & Spector, P. E. (1999). A model of work frustration–aggression. *Journal of Organizational Behavior, 20*(6), 915–931. doi:10.1002/(SICI)1099-1379(199911)20:6<915::AID-JOB918>3.0.CO;2-6

Franco, C. P. (2008). Using Wiki-based Peer-Correction to Develop Writing Skills of Brazilian EFL Learners. *Novitas-ROYAL, 2*(1), 49–59.

Frank, F. D., Finnegan, R. P., & Taylor, C. R. (2004). The race for talent: Retaining and engaging workers in the 21st century. *Human Resource Planning, 27*(3), 12–25.

Freire, M., Antunes, F., & Costa, J. P. (2015a). *Exploring social network analysis techniques on decision support.* Paper presented at the 2nd European Conference on Social Media ECSM 2015, Porto, Portugal.

Freire, M., Antunes, F., & Costa, J. P. (2015b). *Social network analysis to support decision-making.* Paper presented at the Workshop on Assessment Methodologies – energy, mobility and other real world applications (WAM 2015), Coimbra, Portugal.

Freire, M., Antunes, F., & Costa, J. P. (2017). A Semantics Extraction Framework for Decision Support in Context-Specific Social Web Networks. In L. S. Linden I., Colot C (Ed.), Decision Support Systems VII. Data, Information and Knowledge Visualization in Decision Support Systems (pp. 133-147). Springer. doi:10.1007/978-3-319-57487-5_10

Gabor, A. M., Popescu, M. C., & Naaji, A. (2017). Security issues related to e-learning education. *International Journal of Computer Science and Network Security, 17*(1), 60–66.

Gagliardi, F., Hankin, C., Gal-Ezer, J., McGettrick, A., & Meitern, M. (2016). *Advancing cybersecurity research and education in Europe major drivers of growth in the digital landscape.* ACM.

Galbraith, J. R. (1973). *Designing complex organizations.* Reading, MA: Addison - Wesley.

Galinsky, A. D., Ku, G., & Wang, C. S. (2005). Perspective taking and self-other overlap: Fostering social bonds and facilitating social coordination. *Group Processes & Intergroup Relations, 8*(2), 109–124. doi:10.1177/1368430205051060

Gani, S. H. (2012). Job Stress among bank employees: A case study of selected banks. *Internatioanl Journal of Business and Managment Tomorrow, 2*(3), 1–9.

García, M. J., & Fernández-Sanz, L. (2007). Opinión de los profesionales TIC acerca de la formación y las certificaciones personales. *Novatica,* 32-39

García-Crespo, Á., Colomo-Palacios, R., Gómez-Berbís, J. M., & Tovar-Caro, E. (2008). The IT Crowd: Are We Stereotypes? *IT Professional, 10*(6), 24–27. doi:10.1109/MITP.2008.134

García-Peñalvo, F. J. (2008). *Advances in E-Learning: Experiences and Methodologies.* Hershey, PA: Information Science Reference. doi:10.4018/978-1-59904-756-0

García-Peñalvo, F. J., & Colomo-Palacios, R. (2015). Innovative teaching methods in Engineering. *International Journal of Engineering Education, 31*(3), 689–693.

García-Peñalvo, F. J., Colomo-Palacios, R., & Lytras, M. D. (2012). Informal learning in work environments: Training with the Social Web in the workplace. *Behaviour & Information Technology, 31*(8), 753–755. doi:10.1080/0144929X.2012.661548

García-Peñalvo, F. J., Conde, M. A., Alier, M., & Colomo-Palacios, R. (2014). A Case Study for Measuring Informal Learning in PLEs. *International Journal of Emerging Technologies in Learning, 9*(7), 47–55. doi:10.3991/ijet.v9i7.3734

García-Peñalvo, F. J., González-González, J. C., & Murray, M. (2012). MyElvin: A Web-Based Informal Learning Platform for Languages Practice. *International Journal of Knowledge Society Research, 3*(1), 26–39. doi:10.4018/jksr.2012010103

García-Peñalvo, F. J., Johnson, M., Ribeiro Alves, G., & Minovic, M. (2014). Informal learning recognition through a cloud ecosystem. *Future Generation Computer Systems, 32*, 282–294. doi:10.1016/j.future.2013.08.004

Gardner, H. (1983). *Frames of mind.* New York: Basic Books.

Gardner, H. (1983). *Frames of mind: The theory of multiple intelligences.* New York: Basic Books.

Gardner, L., & Stough, C. (2002). Examining the relationship between leadership and emotional intelligence in senior level managers. *Leadership and Organization Development Journal, 23*(2), 68–78. doi:10.1108/01437730210419198

Gardner, W., Avolio, B. J., Luthans, F., May, D. R., & Walumbwa, F. (2005). 'Can you see the real me?' A self-based model of authentic leader and follower development. *The Leadership Quarterly, 16*(3), 343–372. doi:10.1016/j.leaqua.2005.03.003

Garimella, U., & Paruchuri, P. (2015). An Agent for Helping HR with Recruitment. *International Journal of Agent Technologies and Systems, 7*(3), 67–85. doi:10.4018/IJATS.2015070104

Garrison, D. R., & Kanuka, H. (2004). Blended learning: Uncovering its transformative potential in higher education. *The Internet and Higher Education, 7*(2), 95–115. doi:10.1016/j.iheduc.2004.02.001

Garver, M. S., & Mentzer, J. T. (1999). Logistics Research Methods: Employing Structural Equation Modelling to Test for Construct Validity. *Journal of Business Logistics, 20*, 33–57.

Gberevbie, D. E. (2008). *Staff Recruitment, Retention Strategies and Performance of Selected Public and Private Organizations in Nigeria.* College of Business and Social Sciences, Covenant University.

Gefen, D. (2002). Customer loyalty in e-commerce. *Journal of the Association for Information Systems, 3*, 27-51.

Gehrke, N., & Wolf, P. (2010). *Towards Audit 2.0 – A Web 2.0 Community Platform for Auditors.* Paper presented at the 43rd Hawaii International Conference on System Sciences (CD-ROM), Kauai, HI. doi:10.1109/HICSS.2010.407

George, J. M. (2000). Emotions and leadership: The role of emotional intelligence. *Human Relations, 53*(8), 1027–1055. doi:10.1177/0018726700538001

Gikandi, J., Morrow, D., & Davis, N. (2011). Online formative assessment in higher education: A review of the literature. *Computers & Education, 57*(4), 2333–2351. doi:10.1016/j.compedu.2011.06.004

Girão, P. S., Pires, V. F., Dias, O. P., & Martins, J. F. (2010). Development of a mobile learning framework for an analog electronics course. In *Sixth International Conference on Education Engineering (EDUCON) 2010* (pp. 561-567). Madrid: IEEE.

Girard, A., & Fallery, B. (2009). *E-recruitment: new practices, new issues. An exploratory study. In Human Resource Information System* (pp. 39–48). INSTICC Press.

Glaser, B. G., & Strauss, A. L. (1967). *The Discovery of Grounded Theory: Strategies for Qualitative Research.* New York: Aldine. Publishing Company.

Glimmer, V. H. B. (1966). *Industrial psychology.* New York: Mc Graw Hill Book Co. G.

Gohm, C. L., Corser, G. C., & Dalsky, D. J. (2005). Useful, unnecessary, or irrelevant? *Personality and Individual Differences, 39*(1), 1017–1028. doi:10.1016/j.paid.2005.03.018

Goldstein, N. J., Vezich, I. S., & Shapiro, J. R. (2014). Perceived perspective taking: When others walk in our shoes. *Journal of Personality and Social Psychology, 106*(6), 941–960. doi:10.1037/a0036395 PMID:24841098

Goleman, D., Boyatzis, R., and McKee, A. (2002). *Primal leadership.* Boston, MA: Harvard Business School Press.

Goleman, D. (1995). *Emotional intelligence: Why it can matter more than IQ?* New York: Bantam Books.

Goleman, D. (1998). *Working with emotional intelligence.* New York: Bantam.

Goleman, D. (2000). Leadership that gets results. *Harvard Business Review, 78*(2), 78–90.

Goleman, D. (2001). An e-based theory of performance. In C. Cherniss & D. Goleman (Eds.), *The emotionally intelligence workplace* (pp. 27–44). San Francisco, CA: Jossey-Bass.

Gongla, P., & Rizzuto, C. R. (2001). Evolving Communities of Practice: IBM Global Services Experience. *IBM Systems Journal, 40*(4), 842–862. doi:10.1147/sj.404.0842

Gonzalez-Roma, V., Schaufeli, W. B., Bakker, A. B., & Lloret, S. (2006). Burnout and work engagement: Independent factors or opposite poles? *Journal of Vocational Behavior, 68*(1), 165–174. doi:10.1016/j.jvb.2005.01.003

Goodman, C. K. (2011). Work stress can strain marriage. *McClatchy-Tribune Newspapers.* Retrieved from http://articles.chicagotribune.com/2011-06-03/travel/ct-tribu-work-stress-marriage- 20110603_1_strain-marriage-job-stress-couples

Granger, P. (2013). *Valuing people and pooling resources to alleviate poverty through Time banking.* London: Academic Press.

Grant, A. M., & Schwartz, B. (2011). Too much of a good thing the challenge and opportunity of the inverted U. *Perspectives on Psychological Science, 6*(1), 61–76. doi:10.1177/1745691610393523 PMID:26162116

Grant, G. (1979). *On Competence: A Critical Analysis of Competence-based Reforms in Higher Education.* San Francisco: Jossey-Bass.

Grant, J. E., Potenza, M. N., Weinstein, A., & Gorelick, D. A. (2010). Introduction to behavioral addictions. *The American Journal of Drug and Alcohol Abuse, 36*(5), 233–241. doi:10.3109/00952990.2010.491884 PMID:20560821

Greenberg, J. (2005). *Managing behavior in organizations* (4th ed.). Englewood Cliffs, NJ: Prentice-Hall.

Greenhow, C., & Lewin, C. (2016). Social media and education: Reconceptualizing the boundaries of formal and informal learning. *Learning, Media and Technology, 41*(1), 6–30. doi:10.1080/17439884.2015.1064954

Griffeth, R. W., Hom, P. W., & Gaertner, S. (2000). A Meta-Analysis of Antecedents and Correlates of Employee Turnover: Update, Moderator Tests, and Research Implications for the Next Millennium. *Journal of Management, 26*(3), 463–488. doi:10.1177/014920630002600305

Griffiths, M. D. (2005). A components model of addiction within a biopsychological framework. *Journal of Substance Use, 10*(4), 191–197. doi:10.1080/14659890500114359

Griffiths, M. D. (2011). Workaholism: A 21st century addiction. *The Psychologist. Bulletin of the British Psychological Society, 24*, 740–744.

Gross, R., & Acquisti, A. (2005). *Information Revelation and Privacy in Online Social Networks.* Paper presented at the 2005 ACM Workshop on Privacy in the Electronic Society (WPES'05), Alexandria, VA. doi:10.1145/1102199.1102214

Gruneberg, M. M. (1979). *Understanding job satisfaction.* London: The Macmillan Press Ltd. doi:10.1007/978-1-349-03952-4

Grzywacz, J. G., & Marks, N. F. (2000). Reconceptualizing the work family interface: An ecological perspective on the correlates of positive and negative spillover between work and family. *Journal of Occupational Psychology, 5*(1), 111–126. doi:10.1037/1076-8998.5.1.111 PMID:10658890

Guazzini, A., Sarac, A., Donati, C., Nardi, A., Vilone, D., & Meringolo, P. (2017). Participation and privacy perception in virtual environments: The role of sense of community, culture and gender between Italian and Turkish. *Future Internet, 9*(11).

Gulikers, J. T., Bastiaens, T. J., & Kirschner, P. A. (2004). A five-dimensional framework for authentic assessment. *Educational Technology Research and Development, 52*(3), 67–86. doi:10.1007/BF02504676

Guthrie, J. P. (2001). High Involvement work practices, turnover and productivity: Evidence from New Zealand. *Academy of Management Journal, 44*(1), 180–190. doi:10.2307/3069345

Guthrie, J. P., Spell, C. S., & Nyamori, R. O. (2002). Correlates and consequences of high involvement work practices: The role of competitive strategy. *International Journal of Human Resource Management, 13*(1), 183–197. doi:10.1080/09585190110085071

Hacker, A. (2003). Turnover: A silent profit killer. *Information Systems Management, 20*(2), 14–18. doi:10.1201/1078 /43204.20.2.20030301/41465.3

Hadnagy, C. (2011). *Social engineering: The art of human hacking.* Wiley Publishing.

Hair, J., Black, W., Babin, B., & Anderson, R. (2010). Multivariate Data Analysis. Prentice Hall, Inc.

Hakanen, J., & Peeters, M. (2015). How do work engagement, workaholism, and the work-to-family interface affect each other? A 7-year follow-up study. *Journal of Occupational and Environmental Medicine, 57*(6), 601–609. doi:10.1097/ JOM.0000000000000457 PMID:26053362

Halevi, T., Lewis, J., & Memon, N. (2013). A pilot study of cyber security and privacy related behavior and personality traits. *Proceedings of the 22nd International Conference on World Wide Web*, 737-744. doi:10.1145/2487788.2488034

Hallberg, U., & Schaufeli, W. B. (2006). "Same same" but different? Can work engagement be discriminated from job involvement and organizational commitment? *European Psychologist, 11*(2), 119–127. doi:10.1027/1016-9040.11.2.119

Hamari, J., Koivisto, J., & Sarsa, H. (2014). Does gamification work? – a literature review of empirical studies on gamification. In *2014 47th Hawaii International Conference on System Sciences (HICSS)* (pp. 3025-3034). Waikoloa, HI: IEEE.

Hanisch, K. A., & Hulin, C. (1991). General attitudes and organizational withdrawal: An evaluation of causal model. *Journal of Vocational Behavior, 39*(1), 110–128. doi:10.1016/0001-8791(91)90006-8

Hannah, S. T., Lester, P. B., & Vogelgesang, G. R. (2005). Moral leadership: Explicating the moral component of authentic leadership. *Authentic leadership theory and practice: Origins, effects and development, 3*, 43-81.

Hapanchi, A. H., & Aurum, A. (2011). Antecedents to IT personnel's intentions to leave: A systematic literature review. *Journal of Systems and Software, 84*(2), 238–249. doi:10.1016/j.jss.2010.09.022

Haq, G.S.S. (2015). A Study on Job Satisfaction Of It Industry Employees. *Innovative Journal of Business and Management, 4*(1), 1–7.

Härenstam, A., & Group, T. M. R. (2005). Different development trends in working life and increasing occupational stress require new work environment strategies. *Work (Reading, Mass.), 24*(3), 261–277. PMID:15912016

Harley, D. (1998). Re-floating the Titanic: Dealing with social engineering attacks. *Proceedings of the European Expert Group for IT Security.*

Harpaz, I., & Snir, R. (2003). Workaholism: Its definition and nature. *Human Relations, 56*(3), 291–319. doi:10.1177/0018726703056003613

Harrrison, J. K., & Hubbard, R. (1998). Antecedents to organizational commitment among Mexican employees of a US firms in Mexico. *The Journal of Social Psychology*, *138*(5), 609–623. doi:10.1080/00224549809600416

Harter, S. (2002). Authenticity. In C. R. Snyder & S. J. Lopez (Eds.), *Handbook of positive psychology* (pp. 382–394). New York: Oxford University Press.

Hasan, B., Mahmoud, T., Gomez, J. M., Pramode, R., & Kurzhofer, J. (2015). User acceptance identification of restrictions caused by mobile security countermeasures. In *Proceedings of 5ᵗʰ International Conference on Mobile Services, Resources, and Users* (pp.31-37). Brussel, Belgium: Academic Press.

Hauder, M., Pigat, S., & Matthes, F. (2014). Research challenges in adaptive case management: a literature review. In *Proceedings of the 18th IEEE International Enterprise Distributed Object Computing Conference Workshops and Demonstrations* (pp. 98–107). New York: IEEE Press. doi:10.1109/EDOCW.2014.24

Heartfield, R., & Loukas, G. (2016). A taxonomy of attacks and a survey defense mechanisms for semantic social engineering attacks. *ACM Computing Surveys*, *48*(3).

Hemsley, J., & Mason, R. M. (2013). Knowledge and Knowledge Management in the Social Media Age. *Journal of Organizational Computing and Electronic Commerce*, *23*(1-2), 138–167. doi:10.1080/10919392.2013.748614

Herley, C. (2009). So long, and no thanks for the externalities: The rational rejection of security advice by users. *Proceedings of the New Security Paradigms Workshop*, 133-144. doi:10.1145/1719030.1719050

Hernández, R., Fernández, C., & Baptista, P. (2014). *Metodología de la investigación*. McGraw Hill.

Herring, S. (2010). Web Content Analysis: Expanding the Paradigm. In J. Hunsinger, L. Klastrup, & M. Allen (Eds.), *The International Handbook of Internet Research* (pp. 233–249). New York: Springer.

Herring, S. (2013). Discourse in Web 2.0: Familiar, Reconfigured, and Emergent. In D. Tannen & A.-M. Trester (Eds.), *Discourse 2.0: language and new media* (pp. 1–25). Washington, DC: Georgetown University Press.

Herrington, J., & Herrington, A. (1998). Authentic assessment and multimedia: How university students respond to a model of authentic assessment. *Higher Education Research & Development*, *17*(3), 305–322. doi:10.1080/0729436980170304

Higgs, M., & Aitken, P. (2003). An exploration of the relationship between emotional intelligence and leadership potential. *Journal of Managerial Psychology*, *18*(8), 814–823. doi:10.1108/02683940310511890

Hildreth, P., Kimble, C., & Wright, P. (2000). Communities of practice in the distributed international environment. *Journal of Knowledge Management*, *4*(1), 27–38.

Hinkle, L. E. (1973). The Concept of Stress in the Biological and Social Sciences. *Science, Medicine and Man*, *1*(1), 31–48. PMID:4610743

Hippel, E., & Krogh, G. (2003). Open Source Software and the "Private-Collective" Innovation Model: Issues for Organization Science. *Organization Science*, *14*(2), 208–223. doi:10.1287/orsc.14.2.209.14992

Hirschheim, R., & Newman, M. (2010). Houston, we've had a problem...... offshoring, IS employment and the IS discipline: Perception is not reality. *Journal of Information Technology*, *25*(4), 358–372. doi:10.1057/jit.2010.23

Hochschild, A. (1983). *The managed heart: Commercialization of human feeling*. Berkley, CA: University of California Press.

Hodges, S. D., Kiel, K. J., Kramer, A. D., Veach, D., & Villanueva, R. (2010). Giving birth to empathy: The effects of similar experience on empathic accuracy, empathic concern, and perceived empathy. *Personality and Social Psychology Bulletin*, *36*(3), 398–409. doi:10.1177/0146167209350326 PMID:19875825

Hofboll, S. E., Geller, P., & Dunahoo, C. (2003). Women's coping: Communal versus individual orientation. In M. J. Schabracq, J. A. M. Winburst, & C. L. Cooper (Eds.), *The Handbook of Work and Health Psychology*. Wiltshire, UK: John Wiley & Sons.

Holmgren, D. (2011). *Permaculture: Principles & Pathways Beyond Sustainability*. East Meon: Permanent Publications Hyden House Ltd.

Hong, J. (2012). The state of phishing attacks. *Communications of the ACM, 55*(1), 74. doi:10.1145/2063176.2063197

Horwitz, F. M., Heng, C. T., & Quazi, H. A. (2003). Finders, keepers? Attracting, motivating and retaining knowledge workers. *Human Resource Management Journal, 13*(4), 23–44. doi:10.1111/j.1748-8583.2003.tb00103.x

hOurworld.org. (2017a). *hOurmobile mobile application on Google Play*. Retrieved from https://play.google.com/store/apps/details?id=edu.psu.ist.mtb_hourworld&hl=en

hOurworld.org. (2017b). *Main Page*. Retrieved from hourworld.org

House, R. J., & Podsakoff, P. M. (1994). Leadership effectiveness: Past perspectives and future directions for research. In J. Greenberg (Ed.), Organizational behavior: The state of the science (pp. 45– 82). Hillsdale, NJ: Lawrence Erlbaum Associates.

Houseman, S., & Heinrich, C. (2016). The Nature and Role of Temporary Help Work in the U.S. Economy. *Employment Research, 23*(1), 1–4. doi:10.17848/1075-8445.23(1)-1

Ho, V. T., Wong, S. S., & Lee, C. H. (2011). A tale of passion: Linking job passion and cognitive engagement to employee work performance. *Journal of Management Studies, 48*(1), 26–47. doi:10.1111/j.1467-6486.2009.00878.x

HR-XML. (2007). *HR-XML Consortium Competencies*. Retrieved from http://ns.hr-xml.org/2_5/HR-XML-2_5/CPO/Competencies.html

Hu, L., & Bentler, P. M. (1999). Cutoff Criteria for Fit Indexes in Covariance Structure Analysis: Conventional Criteria versus New Alternatives. *Structural Equation Modeling, 6*(1), 1–55. doi:10.1080/10705519909540118

Hulin, C. L. (1991). *Adaptation, Persistence, and Commitment in Organizations*. Palo Alto, CA: Consulting Psychologist Press.

Hull, R. (2008). Artifact-oriented business process models: brief survey of research results and challenges. In *Lecture Notes in Computer Science, 5332* (pp. 1152–1163). Heidelberg, Germany: Springer.

Hull, R. (2011). Introducing the Guard–Stage-Milestone approach for specifying business entity lifecycles. In *Lecture Notes in Computer Science, 6551* (pp. 1–24). Heidelberg, Germany: Springer. doi:10.1007/978-3-642-19589-1_1

Human Resources. (2007). *Research: Employee engagement ROI-rules of engagement*. Available: http://global.factiva.com/ha/default.aspx

Humanante-Ramos, P., García-Peñalvo, F., & Conde-González, M. (2017). Mobile Personal Learning Environments: A systematic literature review. *Revista Iberoamericana de Educación a Distancia, 20*(2), 73–92. doi:10.5944/ried.20.2.17692

Huselid, M. A. (1995). The impact of human resource management practices on turnover, productivity and corporate financial performance. *Academy of Management Journal, 38*(3), 635 672. doi:10.2307/256741

Hüsing, T.,Korte, W. B., & Dashja, E. (2015). *e-Skills in Europe Trends and Forecasts for the European ICT Professional and Digital Leadership Labour Markets (2015-2020)*. Empirica Working Paper, November 2015.

Hwang, G., Tsai, C., & Yang, S. J. H. (2008). Criteria, strategies and research issues of context-aware ubiquitous learning. *Journal of Educational Technology & Society, 11*(2), 81–91.

IEEE Computer Society. (n.d.). Retrieved July 2017, from http://www.computer.org

Ikematsu, K., & Murata, T. (2013). A Fast Method for Detecting Communities from Tripartite Networks. In A. Jatowt, E.-P. Lim, Y. Ding, A. Miura, T. Tezuka, G. Dias, & B. T. Dai et al. (Eds.), *Social Informatics* (pp. 192–205). Springer. doi:10.1007/978-3-319-03260-3_17

Ilahi, M., Cheniti-Belcadhi, L., & Braham, R. (2014b). Scenario Model for Competence-Based Assessment. In *2014 IEEE 14th International Conference on Advanced Learning Technologies* (pp. 344-346). IEEE. doi:10.1109/ICALT.2014.103

Ilahi, M., Cheniti-Belcadhi, L., & Braham, R. (2013). Competence Web–Based Assessment for lifelong learning. *First International Conference On Technological Ecosystems for Enhancing Multiculturality*. doi:10.1145/2536536.2536619

Ilahi, M., Cheniti-Belcadhi, L., & Braham, R. (2014a). Semantic Models for Competence-Based Assessment. *International Journal of Human Capital and Information Technology Professionals, 5*(3), 33–46. doi:10.4018/ijhcitp.2014070103

Ilies, R., Morgeson, F. P., & Nahrgang, J. D. (2005). Authentic Leadership and eudemonic well-being: Understanding leader-follower outcomes. *The Leadership Quarterly, 16*(3), 373–394. doi:10.1016/j.leaqua.2005.03.002

International Labour Organization. (n.d.). *International Standard Classification of Occupations*. Retrieved July 2017, from http://www.ilo.org/public/english/bureau/stat/isco/

Ireland, I. C. T. (Leadership in Information and Communications Technology) & ISA (Irish Software Association). (2011). The need for language skills in the high-tech sector. ICT & ISA.

Iriberri, A., & Leroy, G. (2009). A life cycle perspective on online community Success. *ACM Computing Surveys, 41*(2), 11. doi:10.1145/1459352.1459356

IT Certification Master. (n.d.). *The List of Certifications*. Retrieved July 2017, from http://www.itcertificationmaster.com/list-of-all-it-certifications

IthacaHours. (2016). *Main Page*. Retrieved from http://www.ithacahours.com/

Ivanova, M., & Chatti, M. A. (2011). Competences Mapping for Personal Learning Environment Management. *Proceedings of the PLE Conference 2011*.

Jackson, S. E., & Schuler, R. S. (1995). Understanding Human Resource Management in the Context of Organizations and their Environments. *Annual Review of Psychology, 46*(1), 237–264. doi:10.1146/annurev.ps.46.020195.001321 PMID:19245335

Jagatic, T. N., Johnson, N., Jakobsson, M., Menczer, F. (2007). Social phishing. *Communications of the ACM, 50*(10), 94-100.

Jäkälä, M., & Berki, E. (2013). Communities, communication and online identities. In Digital Identity and Social Media (pp. 1-13). IGI Global.

Jakobsson, M. (2007). The human factor in phishing. *Proceedings of the Privacy and Security of Consumer Information*.

Jakobsson, M., & Myers, S. (2008). Delayed password disclosure. *International Journal of Applied Cryptography, 1*(1), 47–59. doi:10.1504/IJACT.2008.017051

Jansi, A.M., & Anbazhagan, S. (2017). A Study on Personality Traits of Information Technology (IT) Employees and Job Satisfaction. *International Journal of Marketing and Human Resource Management, 8*(2), 1–8.

Jaros, S. J. (1997). An assessment of Meyer and Allen's (1991), three component model of organizational commitment and turnover intentions. *Journal of Vocational Behavior, 51*(3), 319–337. doi:10.1006/jvbe.1995.1553

Jarvenpaa, S.L., & Knoll, K. (1998). Is anybody out there Antecedents of trust in global virtual teams. *Journal of Management Information System, 14*, 29–65.

Jeffrey, L. M., Milne, J., Suddaby, G., & Higgins, A. (2014). Blended learning: How teachers balance the blend of online and classroom components. *Journal of Information Technology Education: Research, 13*, 121–140.

Jiang, K., Lepak, D., Hu, J., & Baer, J. (2012). How does human resource management influence organizational outcomes? A meta-analytic investigation of mediating mechanisms. *Academy of Management Journal, 55*(6), 1264–1294. doi:10.5465/amj.2011.0088

Johns, G. (1996). Theories of Work Motivation. In *Leadership Organizational Behavior*. Harper Collins College Publishers.

Johns, G. (1994). How often were you absent? A review of the use of self-reported absence data. *The Journal of Applied Psychology, 79*(4), 574–591. doi:10.1037/0021-9010.79.4.574

Johnston, M. W., Parasuraman, A., Futrell, C. M., & Black, W. C. (1990). A longitudinal assessment of the impact of selected organisational influences on salespeople's organisational commitment during early employment. *JMR, Journal of Marketing Research, 23*(1), 333–344. doi:10.2307/3172590

Joint Task Force on Computing Curricula Association for Computing Machinery IEEE-Computer Society. (2013). *Computer Science Curricula 2013. e-Competence Quality Self-Assessment Tool*. Retrieved July 2017, from http://www.eskills-quality.eu/results-downloads/self-assessment-tool

Jones, B., Failla, A., & Miller, B. (2007). Tacit Knowledge in Rapidly Evolving Organisational Environments. *International Journal of Technology and Human Interaction, 3*(1), 49–71. doi:10.4018/jthi.2007010104

Joseph, S., Gautam, B., & Bharathi, S. V. (2015). An Empirical Study on the Factors Contributing to Work Family Conflict among Young Employees in the IT Companies. *Indian Journal of Science and Technology, 8*(6), 50–60. doi:10.17485/ijst/2015/v8iS6/62919

Joshi, N. A. (2014). Performance-centric cloud-based e-learning. *The IUP Journal of Information Technology, X*(2), 7–16.

Joung, H.-W., Goh, B. K., Huffman, L., Jingxue, J. Y., & Surles, J. (2015). Investigating relationships between internal marketing practices and employee organizational commitment in the foodservice industry. *International Journal of Contemporary Hospitality Management, 27*(7), 1618–1640. doi:10.1108/IJCHM-05-2014-0269

Judy, R. (2000). Labor forecast: Gray skies, worker drought continues. *HRMagazine, 44*(1), 18–26.

Jung, C., Eitel, A., Feth, D., & Rudolph, M. (2015). Dealing with uncertainty in context-aware mobile applications. In *Proceedings of 5th International Conference on Mobile Services, Resources, and Users* (pp. 1-7). Brussel, Belgium: Academic Press.

Kabat-Zinn, J. (1994). *Wherever you go, there you are: mindfulness meditation in everyday life*. Hyperion Books.

Kabat-Zinn, J. (2003). Mindfulness based interventions in context: Past, present, and future. *Clinical Psychology: Science and Practice, 10*(2), 144–156. doi:10.1093/clipsy.bpg016

Kahn, W. A. (1990). Psychological conditions of personal engagement and disengagement at work. *Academy of Management Journal, 33*(4), 692–724. doi:10.2307/256287

Kainda, R., Flechais, I., & Roscoe, A. W. (2010). Security and Usability: Analysis and Evaluation. *Proceedings of the 5th International Conference on Availability, Reliability and Security*. doi:10.1109/ARES.2010.77

Kaplan, A. M., & Haenlein, M. (2010). Users of the world, unite! The challenges and opportunities of Social Media. *Business Horizons*, *53*(1), 59–68. doi:10.1016/j.bushor.2009.09.003

Kaplan, M., Ogut, E., Kaplan, A., & Aksay, K. (2012). The relationship between job satisfaction and organizational commitment: The case of hospital employees. *World Journal of Management*, *4*(1), 22–29.

Kaplan, S., Bradley, J. C., Lachman, J. N., & Hayness, D. (2009). On the Role of Positive and Negative Affectivity in Job Performance: A Meta-Analytic Investigation. *The Journal of Applied Psychology*, *94*(1), 162–176. doi:10.1037/a0013115 PMID:19186902

Karad, A. (2010). Job Stress in the Information Technology Sector- The cause and effect analysis. *Journal Of Commerce and Management Thought*, *1*(3), 247–271.

Karad, A. (2010). Job Stress in the Information Technology Sector- The cause and effect analysis. *Journal Of Commerce and Management Thought.*, *1*(3), 247–271.

Karad, C. A. (2010). Job Stress in the Information Technology Sector-The cause and effect analysis. *Journal of Commerce and Management Thought*, *1*(3), 247–271.

Karen, L. H., & Julia, L. H. (2002). Workplace Environment in a Professional Services Firm. *Behavioral Research in Accounting*, *14*(1), 105–127. doi:10.2308/bria.2002.14.1.105

Karrasch. (2003). Antecedents and Consequences of Organizational Commitment. *Military Psychology*, *15*(3), 225-36.

Kasim, R., & Abdul, G. C. (2012). Leadership – style, satisfaction and commitment. *Engineering, Construction, and Architectural Management*, *19*(1), 61–85. doi:10.1108/09699981211192571

Kaur, N. (1992). *Team Cohesion, Adjustment and Achievement motivation as related to performance and gender in team sports* (Unpublished Doctoral thesis). Dept of Physical Education, Publish University, Chandigarh, India.

Kayworth, T. R., & Leidner, D. E. (2002). Leadership effectiveness in global virtual teams. *Journal of Management Information Systems*, *18*(3), 7–40. doi:10.1080/07421222.2002.11045697

Kerlinger, F. N. (1973). *Foundations of Behavioral Research*. New York: Rinehart and Winston.

Kernis, M. H. (2003). Toward a conceptualisation of optimal self-esteem. *Psychological Inquiry*, *14*(1), 1–26. doi:10.1207/S15327965PLI1401_01

Kernis, M. H., & Goldman, B. M. (2005a). Authenticity, social motivation, and psychological adjustment. In J. P. Forgas, K. D. Williams, & S. M. Laham (Eds.), *Social motivation: Conscious and unconscious processes* (pp. 210–227). New York: Cambridge University Press.

Kernis, M. H., & Goldman, B. M. (2005b). From thought and experience to behaviour and interpersonal relationships: A multicomponent conceptualization of authenticity. In A. Tesser, J. V. Wood, & D. A. Stapel (Eds.), *On building, defending, and regulating the Self* (pp. 31–52). New York: Psychology Press.

Khan, A. S., & Jan, F. (2015). The Study of Organization Commitment and Job Satisfaction among Hospital Nurses, A Survey of District Hospitals of Dera Ismail Khan. *Global Journal of Management and Business Research*.

Khanna, P., & Sehgal, M. (2016). A study of HRM practices and its effect on employees job satisfaction in private sector banks with special reference to ICICI banks in Ludhiana. *International Journal of Management*, *4*, 36–43.

Khedr, A. E., & Indrees, A. M. (2017). Enhanced e-learning system for e-courses base on cloud computing. *Journal of Computers*, *12*(1), 10–19.

Kickul, J. (2001). Promises Made, Promises Broken: An Exploration of Small Business Attraction and Retention Practices. *Journal of Small Business Management, 39*(2), 320–335. doi:10.1111/0447-2778.00029

Kietzmann, J. H., Hermkens, K., McCarthy, I. P., & Silvestre, B. S. (2011). Social media? Get serious! Understanding the functional building blocks of social media. *Business Horizons, 54*(3), 241–251. doi:10.1016/j.bushor.2011.01.005

Kim, H. (2013). E-learning privacy and security requirements [review]. *Journal of Security Engineering, 10*(5), 591–600. doi:10.14257/jse.2013.10.5.07

Kinast & Partner. (2014). *Social media and data protection.* Retrieved from www.kinast-partner.com/data-protection-law/social-media-and-data-protection/

King, J. E. (2000). White-collar reactions to job insecurity and the role of the psychological contract: Implications for human resource management. *Human Resource Management, 39*(1), 79–92. doi:10.1002/(SICI)1099-050X(200021)39:1<79::AID-HRM7>3.0.CO;2-A

Kinsler, L. (2014, March). International Coaching. *Psychological Review, 9*(1).

Kirlappos, I., & Sasse, M. A. (2012). Security education against phishing: A modest proposal for a major rethink. *IEEE Security and Privacy, 10*(2), 24–32. doi:10.1109/MSP.2011.179

Klein, S. M., & Ritti, R. R. (1984). *Understanding organizational behavior* (2nd ed.). Boston: Kent Publishing Company.

Klenke, K. (2007). Authentic Leadership: A Self, Leader, and Spiritual Identity Perspective. *International Journal of Leadership Studies, 3*(1), 68–97.

Klohnen, E. C. (1996). Conceptual analysis and measurement of the construct of ego-resiliency. *Journal of Personality and Social Psychology, 70*(2), 1067–1079. doi:10.1037/0022-3514.70.5.1067 PMID:8656335

Koch, M. J., & McGrath, R. G. (1996). Improving labor productivity: Human resource management policies do matter. *Strategic Management Journal, 17*(5), 335–354. doi:10.1002/(SICI)1097-0266(199605)17:5<335::AID-SMJ814>3.0.CO;2-R

Kok, S., & Rogers, R. (2016). Rethinking migration in the digital age-transglocalization and the Somali diaspora. *Global Networks*, 1–24.

Kolbitsch, J., & Maurer, H. (2006). The Transformation of the Web: How Emerging Communities Shape the Information We Consume. *Journal of Universal Computer Science, 12*(2), 187–213.

Kol, S., & Schcolnik, M. (2008). Asynchronous Forums in EAP: Assessment Issues. *Language Learning & Technology, 12*(2), 49–70.

Kompaso, S. M., & Sridevi, M. S. (2010). Employee engagement: The key to improving performance. *International Journal of Business and Management, 5*(12), 89. doi:10.5539/ijbm.v5n12p89

Korczynski, M. (2002). *Human resource management in service work.* Hampshire, UK: Palgrave. doi:10.1007/978-1-137-10774-9

Korunka, H. (2006). Evaluating causes and consequences of turnover intention among IT workers: The development of a questionnaire survey. *Behaviour & Information Technology, 25*(5), 381–397. doi:10.1080/01449290500102144

Koslowsky, M. (2000). A New Perspective on Employee Lateness. *Applied Psychology, 49*(3), 390–407. doi:10.1111/1464-0597.00022

Kou, K., Jia, Z., & Wang, Y. (2013). A Comparative Research on Competency and Competence, Competency Model and Competence Model. *Proceedings of the Sixth International Conference on Management Science and Engineering Management. Lecture Notes in Electrical Engineering*, 185, 681-693. doi:10.1007/978-1-4471-4600-1_58

Kovacic, A., Bubas, G., & Zlatovic, M. (2008). *E-tivities with a wiki: Innovative Teaching of English as a Foreign Language*. In *Proceedings of the 14th Congress of the European University Information Systems Organisation* (pp. 1-13). Aarhus, Denmark: Academic Press.

Kozinets, R. (1999). E-tribalized marketing: The strategic implications of virtual communities of consumption. European Management Journal, 17(3), 252-264.

Kożusznik, M. W., Dyląg, A., & Jaworek, M. A. (2014). The Polish adaptation of the short form of the Dutch Work Addiction Scale. In T. Marek, W. Karwowski, M. Frankowicz, J. Kantola, & P. Zgaga (Eds.), *Human Factors of Global Society: A System of Systems Perspective* (pp. 311–318). New York: CRC Press Taylor and Francis Group.

Krashen, S. D. (1985). *The input hypothesis: Issues and implications*. New York: Addison-Wesley Longman Ltd.

Kreitner, R., & Kinicki, A. (1992). *Organizational behavior* (2nd ed.). New York: Irwin.

Krishnan, S. K., & Singh, M. (2010). Outcomes of intention to quit of Indian IT professionals. *Journal of Human Resource Management, 49*(2), 421-437.

Kukulska-Hulme, A. (2016). *Personalization of language learning through mobile technologies: Part of the Cambridge Papers in ELT series*. Cambridge, UK: Cambridge University Press.

Kulshrestha, . (2006). Subjective Well Being in Relation to Emotional Intelligence and Locus of Control among Executives. *Journal of the Indian Academy of Applied Psychology, 32*(2), 93–98.

Kumaraguru, P., Sheng, S., Acquisti, A., Cranor, L. F., & Hong, J. (2007). Teaching Johnny not to fall for phish. *ACM Transactions on Internet Technology, 10*(2).

Kumaran, S., Liu, R., & Wu, F. Y. (2008). On the duality of information-oriented and activity-oriented models of business processes. In *Lecture Notes in Computer Science, 5074* (pp. 32–47). Heidelberg: Springer.

Kumari, G., Joshi, G., & Pandey, K. M. (2014). Job Stress in Software Companies: A Case Study of HCL Bangalore, India. *Global Journal of Computer Science and Technology, 14*(7).

Kumar, M. S., & Siddique, A. M. (2011). A study on occupational stress among IT professionals Chennai. *International Journal of Enterprise Innovation Management Studies, 2*(2), 119–124.

Künzle, V., & Reichert, M. (2011). PHILharmonicFlows: Towards a framework for object-aware process management. *Journal of Software Maintenance and Evolution: Research and Practice, 23*(4), 205–244. doi:10.1002/smr.524

Kuo, C., Parno, B., & Perrig, A. (2007). Browser enhancements for preventing phishing attacks. In M. Jakobsson & S. Myers (Eds.), *Phishing and countermeasures: Understanding the increasing problem of electronic identity theft* (pp. 351–367). John Wiley & Sons, Inc.

Küster, J. M., Ryndina, K., & Gall, H. (2007). Generation of business process models for object life cycle compliance. In *Lecture Notes in Computer Science, 4714* (pp. 165–181). Heidelberg, Germany: Springer. doi:10.1007/978-3-540-75183-0_13

Kwantes, C. T. (2003). Organizational Citizenship and Withdrawal Behaviors in the USA and India: Does Commitment Make a Difference? *International Cultural Management, 3*(1), 5–26.

Landy, F. J., & Conte, J. M. (2004). *Work in 21st century: An introduction to individual and organizational psychology.* New York: McGraw Hill.

Lasker, J., Collom, E., Bealer, T., Niclaus, E., Keefe, J. Y., Kratzer, Z., & Perlow, K. et al. (2010). Time Banking and Health: The Role of a Community Currency Organization in Enhancing Well-Being. *Health Promotion Practice.* doi:10.1177/1524839909353022 PMID:20685912

Lavanya, N. A., Buvana, M., & Shanthi, D. (2017). Detection of security threats and vulnerabilities of e-learning systems in cloud computing. *Advances in Natural and Applied Sciences, 11*(7), 550–559.

Lawler, E. E. (1992). *The ultimate advantage: Creating the high involvement organization.* San Francisco: Jossey-Bass.

Lawler, E. E. (1996). *From the ground up: Six principles for building the new logic corporation.* Jossey – Bass.

Layer, R. M. (2012). *The Millennial Student: A Strategy for Improved Wellness* (Doctoral dissertation). University of Minnesota.

Lazarus. (1993). Coping Theory and Research: Past, Present, and Future. *Psychosomatic Medicine, 55,* 234-247.

Leana, C. R., Ahlbrandt, R. S., & Murrell, A. J. (1992). The effects of employee involvement programs on unionized worker's attitudes, perceptions and preferences in decision making. *Academy of Management Journal, 35*(4), 861–873. doi:10.2307/256319

Leana, C. R., & Florkowski, G. W. (1992). Employee Involvement Programs: Integrating Psychological Theory and Management Practice. In G. Ferris & K. Rowland (Eds.), *Research in Personnel and Human Resources Management, 10* (pp. 233–270). Greenwich, CT: JAI Press.

Leana, C. R., Locke, E. A., & Schweiger, D. M. (1990). Fact and Fiction in Analyzing Research on Participative Decision Making: A Critique of Cotton, Vollrath, Froggatt, Lengnick-Hall, and Jennings. *Academy of Management Review, 15*(1), 137–146.

Ledford, G. E. Jr, & Mohrman, S. A. (1993). Self-Design for High Involvement: A Large-Scale Organizational Change. *Human Relations, 46*(2), 143–173. doi:10.1177/001872679304600202

Lee, C. C., Mullins, K., & Cho, Y. S. (2016). Factors affecting job satisfaction and retention of millennials. Academy of Organizational Culture, Communications and Conflict, 6.

Lee, F.S., Vogel, D., & Limayem, M. (2003). Virtual Community Informatics: A review and research agenda. *The Journal of Information Technology Theory and Application, 5*(1), 47-61.

Lee, K., Carswell, J. J., & Allen, N. J. (2000). A meta-analytic review of occupational commitment: Relations with person and work-related variables. *The Journal of Applied Psychology, 85*(5), 799–811. doi:10.1037/0021-9010.85.5.799 PMID:11055151

Lee, L. (2010). Exploring wiki-mediated collaborative writing: A case-study in an elementary Spanish course. *CALICO Journal, 27*(2), 260–276. doi:10.11139/cj.27.2.260-276

Lehaney, B. (2004). *Beyond Knowledge Management.* Idea Group Publishing. doi:10.4018/978-1-59140-180-3

Lehman, W. E., & Simpson, D. D. (1992). Employee substance use and on-the-job behaviors. *The Journal of Applied Psychology, 77*(3), 309–321. doi:10.1037/0021-9010.77.3.309 PMID:1601823

Leite, N. R. P., Rodrigues, A. C. D. A., & Albuquerque, L. G. D. (2014). Organizational commitment and job satisfaction: What are the potential relationships? *BAR - Brazilian Administration Review, 11*(4), 476–495. doi:10.1590/1807-7692bar2014276

Leskovec, J., Adamic, L. A., & Huberman, B. A. (2007). The Dynamics of Viral Marketing. *ACM Transactions on the Web, 1*(1).

Lesser, E. L., & Storck, J. (2001). Communities of practice and organizational performance. *IBM Systems Journal, 40*(4), 831–841. doi:10.1147/sj.404.0831

Levi, L. (1996). *Managing Physical Stress*. Australia Thomson Delmar Learning.

Li, L. (2013). *A contingency framework to assure the user-centred quality and to support the design of anti-phishing software* (PhD Thesis). University of Tampere, Finland.

Li, L., Berki, E., Helenius, M., & Ovaska, S. (2014). Towards a contingency approach with whitelist- and blacklist-based anti-phishing applications: What do usability tests indicate? *Behaviour & Information Technology, 33*(11), 1136–1147. doi:10.1080/0144929X.2013.875221

Li, L., Berki, E., Helenius, M., & Reijo, S. (2012). New usability metrices for authentication mechanisms. *Proceedings of the SQM and INSPIRE International Conference.*

Li, L., & Helenius, M. (2007). Usability evaluation of anti-phishing toolbars. *Journal of Computer Virology, 3*(2), 163–184. doi:10.1007/s11416-007-0050-4

Li, L., Helenius, M., & Berki, E. (2007). Phishing resistant information systems: security handling with misuse cases design. *Proceedings of the SQM Conference.*

Li, L., Helenius, M., & Berki, E. (2011). How and why phishing and spam messages disturb us? *Proceedings of the IADIS International Conference ICT, Society and Human Beings.*

Li, L., Nummenmaa, T., Berki, E., & Helenius, M. (2015). Phishing Knowledge based User Modelling in Software Design. *Proceedings of the SPLST Conference.*

Lilly, J., & Warnes, M. (2009). Designing mobile games for learning: The mGBL approach. In O. Petrovic & A. Brand (Eds.), Serious Games on the Move (pp. 3-27). Springer-Verlag/Wien.

Linderman, M., Siegel, B., Ouellet, D., Brichacek, J., Haines, S., Chase, G., & O'May, J. (2005). *A Reference Model for Information Management to Support Coalition Information Sharing Needs*. Academic Press.

Linley, P. A., Joseph, S., Harrington, S., & Wood, A. (2006). Positive psychology: Past, present, and(possible) future. *The Journal of Positive Psychology, 1*(1), 3–16. doi:10.1080/17439760500372796

Loewenstein, G. (2005). Hot-cold empathy gaps and medical decision making. *Health Psychology, 24*(4, Suppl), S49–S56. doi:10.1037/0278-6133.24.4.S49 PMID:16045419

Loosemore, M., & Waters, T. (2004). Gender Differences in Occupational Stress among Professionals in the Construction Industry. *Journal of Management Engineering, 20*(3), 126–132. doi:10.1061/(ASCE)0742-597X(2004)20:3(126)

Love, P. E. D., & Irani, Z. (2007). Coping and psychological adjustment among information technology personnel. *Industrial Management & Data Systems, 107*(6), 824–844. doi:10.1108/02635570710758743

Lu, H., Alison, E., While, K., & Barriball, L. (2007). Job satisfaction and its related factors: A questionnaire survey of hospital nurses in Mainland China. *International Journal of Nursing Studies, 44*(4), 574–588. doi:10.1016/j.ijnurstu.2006.07.007 PMID:16962123

Lum, L., Kervin, J., Clark, K., Reid, F., & Sirola, W. (1998). Explaining Nursing Turnover Intention: Job Satisfaction, Pay Satisfaction, or Organizational Commitment? *Journal of Organizational Behavior, 19*(3), 305–320. doi:10.1002/(SICI)1099-1379(199805)19:3<305::AID-JOB843>3.0.CO;2-N

Lumley, E. J., Coetzee, M., Tladinyane, R., & Ferreira, N. (2011). Exploring the job satisfaction and organisational commitment of employees in the information technology environment. *Southern African Business Review*, *15*(1), 100–118.

Lund, A. (2008). Wikis: A Collective Approach to Language Learning. *ReCALL*, *20*(1), 35–54. doi:10.1017/S0958344008000414

Lundgren, B., Jonsson, B., Pangborn, R. M., Sontag, A. M., Barylko-Pikielna, N., Pietrzak, E., & Yoshida, M. et al. (1978). Taste discrimination vs. hedonic response to sucrose. *An interlaboratory study. Chemical Senses*, *3*(3), 249–265. doi:10.1093/chemse/3.3.249

Luthans, F. (1998). *Organizational Behaviour* (8th ed.). Boston: Irwin McGraw-Hill.

Mabry, J. (2015). *Recent progress in biometrics*. Clanrye International.

Macey, W. H., & Schneider, B. (2008). The Meaning of Employee Engagement. *Industrial and Organizational Psychology: Perspectives on Science and Practice*, *1*(01), 3–30. doi:10.1111/j.1754-9434.2007.0002.x

Machlowitz, M. (1980). *Workaholics: Living with them, working with them*. Reading, MA: Addison-Wesley.

Maclaran, P., & Catterall, M. (2002). Researching the social Web: Marketing information from virtual communities. *Marketing Intelligence & Planning*, *20*(6), 319–326. doi:10.1108/02634500210445374

Maes, R. (1999). *Reconsidering Information Mangagement Through A Generic Framework*. Academic Press.

Maes, R., Rijsenbrij, D., Truijens, O., & Goedvolk, H. (2000). *Redefining business - IT alingment through a unified frameworks*. Academic Press.

Magdaleno-Palencia, J.S., García-Valdez, J.M., Castañón-Puga, M., & Gaxiola-Vega, L.A. (2011). On the Modelling of Adaptive Hypermedia Systems Using Agents for Courses with the Competency Approach. *ICSECS,* (3), 624-630.

Ma, H., Gustafson, S., Moitra, A., & Bracewell, D. (2010). Ego-Centric Network Sampling in Viral Marketing Applications. In I.-H. Ting, H.-J. Wu, & T.-H. Ho (Eds.), *Mining and Analyzing Social Networks* (pp. 35–50). Springer. doi:10.1007/978-3-642-13422-7_3

Maher, A. A., Najwa, H. M. A., & Roesnita, I. (2014). Towards an efficient privacy in cloud based e-learning. In *Proceedings of International Conference on Intelligent Systems, Data Mining and Information Technology* (pp.40-45). Bangkok, Thailand: Academic Press.

Mak, B., & Coniam, D. (2008). Using Wikis to enhance and develop writing skills among secondary school students in Hong Kong. System. *An International Journal of Educational Technology and Applied Linguistics*, *36*(3), 437–455.

Malhotra. (1997). Evolution of a virtual community: Understanding design issues through a longitudinal study. *Proceedings of the Eighteenth International Conference on Information Systems*.

Malini, G., Mala, T., & Kannan, A. (2016). Markov model based prediction for effective e-content delivery in the cloud. *Asian Journal of Information Technology*, *15*(17), 3280–3286. Available at http://docsdrive.com/pdfs/medwelljournals/ajit/2016/3280-3286.pdf

Maloney Krichmar, D., & Preece, J. (2005). A multilevel analysis of sociability, usability, and community dynamics in an online health community. ACM Trans. Comput-Hum. Interaction, 12(2), 1-232.

Manca, S., & Ranieri, M. (2016). Facebook and the other. Potentials and obstacles of Social Media for teaching in higher education. *Computers & Education*, *95*(April), 216–230. doi:10.1016/j.compedu.2016.01.012

Mander, J., & McGrath, F. (2017). *Flagship Report Q1 2017 - Time Spent on Social Networks or Services.* Global Web Index Media.

Mannheim, B., Baruch, Y., & Tal, J. (1997). Alternative Models for Antecedents and Outcomes of Work Centrality and Job Satisfaction of High-Tech Personnel. *Human Relations, 50*(12), 1537–1562. doi:10.1177/001872679705001204

Manville, B., & Foote, N. (1996). Harvest your workers´ knowledge. *Datamation, 7.*

Maria, M., Pavlos, S., Eleni, M., Thamme, K., & Constantinidis, T. C. (2010). Greek Registered Nurses' Job Satisfaction in Relation to Work-Related Stress: A Study on Army and Civilian Registered nurses. *Global Journal of Health Science, 2*(1), 44–59. Available at www.ccsenet.org/gjhs

Marin, M., Hull, R., & Vaculín, R. (2013). Data centric BPM and the emerging case management standard: A short survey. *Lecture Notes in Business Information Processing, 132*, 24–30. doi:10.1007/978-3-642-36285-9_4

Marmo, R. (2011). Web Mining and Social Network Analysis. In H. Zhang, R. S. Segall, & M. Cao (Eds.), *Visual Analytics and Interactive Technologies: Data, Text and Web Mining Applications* (pp. 202–211). Hershey, PA: Information Science Reference. doi:10.4018/978-1-60960-102-7.ch012

Marques, J. (2010). Spirituality, meaning, interbeing, leadership, and empathy:SMILE. *Interbeing, 4*(2), 7.

Martin, A., & Roodt, G. (2008). Perceptions of organisational commitment, job satisfaction and turnover intentions in a post-merger South African tertiary institution. *SA Journal of Industrial Psychology, 34*(1), 23–31. doi:10.4102/sajip.v34i1.415

Marty, J. C., & Carron, T. (2011). Observation of collaborative activities in a game-based learning platform. *IEEE Transactions on Learning Technologies, 4*(1), 98–110. doi:10.1109/TLT.2011.1

Maslach, C., Schaufeli, W. B., & Leiter, M. P. (2001). Job burnout. *Annual Review of Psychology, 52*(1), 397–422. doi:10.1146/annurev.psych.52.1.397 PMID:11148311

Mathieu, J. E., & Zajac, D. M. (1990). A review and meta-analysis of the antecedents, correlates, and consequences of organizational commitment. *Psychological Bulletin, 108*(2), 171–194. doi:10.1037/0033-2909.108.2.171

Mayer, J. D., & Salovey, P. (1997). What is emotional intelligence? In P. Salovey & D.J. Sluyter (Eds.), Emotional Development and Emotional Intelligence: Educational Implications (pp. 3-31). New York: Basic Books.

McCanny, J., & Hopper, A. (2016). *Progress and research in cybersecurity: Supporting resilience, trust and digital identities.* The Royal Society.

McDermott, R. (2000). Community Development as a Natural Step: Five Stages of Community Development. *Knowledge Management Review, 3*(5).

McMillan, L. H. W., O'Driscoll, M. P., & Burke, R. J. (2003). Workaholism: A review of theory, research and new directions. In C. L. Cooper & I. T. Robertson (Eds.), *International Review of Industrial and Organizational Psychology* (pp. 167–190). New York: John Wiley.

McMillan, L. H. W., O'Driscoll, M. P., Marsh, N. V., & Brady, E. C. (2001). Understanding workaholism: Data synthesis, theoretical critique, and future design strategies. *International Journal of Stress Management, 8*(2), 69–91. doi:10.1023/A:1009573129142

McPhee, S. D., & Townsend, L. J. (1992). A study of organisational commitment and job satisfaction among Air force occupational therapy officers. *Military Medicine, 153*(3), 117–121. PMID:1603401

McRae, C. M., & Vaughn, R. B. (2007). Phighting the phisher: Using web bugs and honeytokens to investigate the source of phishing attacks. *Proceedings of the 40th Hawaii International Conference on System Sciences*. doi:10.1109/HICSS.2007.435

Melero, J., Hernández-Leo, D., & Manatunga, K. (2015). Group-based mobile learning: Do group size and sharing mobile devices matter? *Computers in Human Behavior*, *44*, 377–385. doi:10.1016/j.chb.2014.11.078

Meyer, A., Pufahl, L., Fahland, D., & Weske, M. (2013). Modeling and enacting complex data dependencies in business processes. In *Lecture Notes in Computer Science, 8094* (pp. 171–186). Heidelberg, Germany: Springer. doi:10.1007/978-3-642-40176-3_14

Meyer, A., & Weske, M. (2014). Activity-oriented and artifact-oriented process model roundtrip. *Lecture Notes in Business Information Processing*, *171*, 167–181. doi:10.1007/978-3-319-06257-0_14

Meyer, J. P., & Allen, N. J. (1991). A three-component conceptualization of organizational commitment. *Human Resource Management Review*, *1*(1), 61–89. doi:10.1016/1053-4822(91)90011-Z

Meyer, J. P., & Allen, N. J. (1997). *Commitment in the workplace: Theory, research, and application*. Newbury Park, CA: Sage.

Meyer, J. P., Allen, N. J., & Smith, C. A. (1993). Commitment to organizations and occupations: Extension and test of a three-component model. *The Journal of Applied Psychology*, *78*(4), 538–551. doi:10.1037/0021-9010.78.4.538

Meyer, J. P., Stanley, D. J., Herscovitch, L., & Topolnytsky, L. (2002). Affective, Continuance, and Normative Commitment to the Organization: A Meta-analysis of Antecedents, Correlates, and Consequences. *Journal of Vocational Behavior*, *61*(1), 20–52. doi:10.1006/jvbe.2001.1842

Michailidis, M., & Georgiou, Y. (2005). Employee occupational stress in banking. *Work (Reading, Mass.)*, *24*(2), 123–137. PMID:15860902

Michailids, M. P., & Elwkai, M. E. A. (2002). Factors contributing to occupational stress experienced by individuals employed in the fast food industry. *Work (Reading, Mass.)*, *21*(2), 125–140. PMID:14501091

Michel, J., Pichler, S., & Newness, K. (2014). Integrating leader affect, leader work-family spillover, and leadership. *Leadership and Organization Development Journal*, *35*(5), 410–428. doi:10.1108/LODJ-06-12-0074

Miles, M. B., & Huberman, A. (1994). *Qualitative Data Analysis: An Expanded Sourcebook*. Newbury Park, CA: SAGE.

Milletary, J. (2013). *Technical trends in phishing attacks*. Retrieved on 16 August 2017 from: https://www.us-cert.gov/sites/default/files/publications/phishing_trends0511.pdf

Minovic, M., Štavljanin, V., & Milovanovic, M. (2012). Educational Games and IT Professionals: Perspectives from the Field. *International Journal of Human Capital and Information Technology Professionals*, *3*(4), 25–38. doi:10.4018/jhcitp.2012100103

Mirkamalia, S. M., & Thanib, F. N. (2011). A Study on the Quality of Work Life (QWL) among faculty members of University of Tehran(UT) and Sharif university of Technology (SUT). *Social and Behavioral Sciences*, *29*, 179–187.

Mislevy, R. J., Steinberg, L. S., & Almond, R. G. (2003). Focus article: On the structure of educational assessments. *Measurement: Interdisciplinary Research and Perspectives*, *1*(1), 3–62. doi:10.1207/S15366359MEA0101_02

Misra, G., & Such, J. M. (2015). Social computing privacy and online relationships. In *AISB Social Aspects of Cognition and Computing Symposium* (pp. 1-6). Academic Press. Available at: http://eprints.lancs.ac.uk/74190/1/SACCS_AISB2015_submission_11.pdf

Mitchell, T. R., Holtom, B. C., & Lee, T. W. (2001). How to keep your best employees: Developing an effective retention policy. *The Academy of Management Executive*, *15*(4), 96–109. doi:10.5465/AME.2001.5897929

Miyazoe, T., & Anderson, T. (2010). Learning outcomes and students' perceptions of online writing: Simultaneous implementation of a forum, blog, and wiki in an EFL blended learning setting. *System: An International Journal of Educational Technology and Applied Linguistics*, *38*(2), 185–199. doi:10.1016/j.system.2010.03.006

Mobley, W., Horner, S., & Hollingsworth, A. (1978). An evaluation of the precursors of hospital employee turnover. *The Journal of Applied Psychology*, *63*(4), 408–414. doi:10.1037/0021-9010.63.4.408 PMID:701211

Mohanty, A., & Lalatendu, K. J. (2016). Work-Life Balance Challenges for Indian Employees: Socio-Cultural Implications and Strategies. *Journal of Human Resource and Sustainability Studies*, *4*(01), 15–21. doi:10.4236/jhrss.2016.41002

Mohsin, A. (2004). Role stress among women in the Indian information technology sector. *Women in Management Review*, *19*(7), 356–363. doi:10.1108/09649420410563412

Mooradian, T., Renzl, B., & Matzler, K. (2006). Who trusts? Personality, trust and knowledge sharing. *Journal of Management Learning*, *37*(4), 523–540. doi:10.1177/1350507606073424

Moreno-Ger, P., Burgos, D., Martínez-Ortiz, I., Sierra, J. L., & Fernández-Manjón, B. (2008). Educational game design for online education. *Computers in Human Behavior*, *24*(6), 2530–2540. doi:10.1016/j.chb.2008.03.012

Morrison, J. (2008). The relationship between emotional intelligence competencies and preferred conflict-handling styles. *Journal of Nursing Management*, *16*(8), 974–983. doi:10.1111/j.1365-2834.2008.00876.x PMID:19094110

Mortier, A. V., Vlerick, P., & Clays, E. (2016). Authentic leadership and thriving among nurses: The mediating role of empathy. *Journal of Nursing Management*, *24*(3), 357–365. doi:10.1111/jonm.12329 PMID:26264773

Moser, C., Groenewegen, P., & Huysman, M. (2013). Extending Social Network Analysis with Discourse Analysis: Combining Relational with Interpretive Data. In T. Özyer, J. Rokne, G. Wagner, & A. Reuser (Eds.), *The Influence of Technology on Social Network Analysis and Mining* (pp. 547–561). New York: Springer. doi:10.1007/978-3-7091-1346-2_24

Mota, J. M., Ruiz-Rube, I., Dodero, J. M., & Figueiredo, M. 2016. Visual environment for designing interactive learning scenarios with augmented reality. In *Proceedings of 12th International Conference on Mobile Learning* (pp. 67–74). Algarve, Portugal: mlearning.

Motahari-Nezhad, H. R., & Swenson, K. D. (2013). Adaptive case management: overview and research challenges. In *Proceedings of the 15th IEEE Conference on Business Informatics* (pp. 264–269). New York: IEEE Press. doi:10.1109/CBI.2013.44

Mowday, R. T., Porter, L. W., & Steers, R. M. (1982). *Employee organizational linkages: The psychology of commitment, absenteeism and turnover*. New York: Academic Press.

Mowday, R. T., Steers, R. M., & Porter, L. W. (1979). The measurement of organizational commitment. *Journal of Vocational Behavior*, *14*(2), 224–247. doi:10.1016/0001-8791(79)90072-1

Mueller, C. W., Boyer, E. M., Price, J. L., & Iverson, R. D. (1994). Employee attachment and non coercive conditions of work. *Work and Occupations*, *21*(2), 179–212. doi:10.1177/0730888494021002002

Müller, D., Reichert, M., & Herbst, J. (2007). Data-driven modeling and coordination of large process structures. In *Lecture Notes in Computer Science, 4803* (pp. 131–149). Heidelberg, Germany: Springer. doi:10.1007/978-3-540-76848-7_10

Mummalaneni, V., & Wilson, D. (1991). *The influence of close personal relationships between a buyer and a seller on the continued stability of the role relationships* (Working Paper 4). Institute for the Study of Business Markets, Pennsylvania State University.

Munson, S. A. (2008). *Motivating and enabling organizational memory with a wrokgroup Wiki.* Paper presented at the WikiSym08 2008 International Symposium on Wikis, Porto, Portugal.

Murata, T. (1989). Petri nets: Properties, analysis and applications. *Proceedings of the IEEE, 77*(4), 541–580. doi:10.1109/5.24143

Murugesan, S. (2010). *Handbook of Research on Web 2.0, 3.0, and X.0- Technologies, Business, and Social Applications.* Hershey, PA: IGI-Global. doi:10.4018/978-1-60566-384-5

Mystakidis, S., Berki, E., & Valtanen, J. (2017). Toward successfully integrating mini learning games into social virtual reality environments: Recommendations for improving open and distance learning. *Proceedings of the 9th EDULEARN.* doi:10.21125/edulearn.2017.1203

NACE. (n.d.). *Eurostat Statistics Explained.* Retrieved July 2017, from http://www.ec.europa.eu/eurostat/statistics-explained/index.php/Main_Page

Nadler, A., & Liviatan, I. (2006). Intergroup reconciliation: Effects of adversary's expressions of empathy, responsibility, and recipients' trust. *Personality and Social Psychology Bulletin, 32*(4), 459–470. doi:10.1177/0146167205276431 PMID:16513799

Najjar, J., Derntl, M., Klobucar, T., Simon, B., Totschnig, M., Grant, S., & Pawlowski, J. (2010). A data model for describing and exchanging Personal Achieved Learning Outcomes (PALO). *International Journal of IT Standards and Standardization Research, 8*(2), 87–104. doi:10.4018/jitsr.2010070107

Nancy, C. M. (1977). *Satisfactions in the White-Collar Job.* Ayer publishing.

Nanjundeswaraswamy, T. S. (2013). Quality of Work life of Employees in Private Technical Institutions. *International Journal of Qualitative Research, 7*(3), 3–14.

Naughton-Doe, R. (2015). *An evaluation of timebanking in England: What can timebanks contribute to the co-production of preventive social care?* (Dissertation), University of Bristol.

Neelamegam, R., & Asrafi, S. (2010). Work Stress Among Employees of Dindigul District Central Cooperative Bank, Tamil Nadu: A Study. The IUP Journal of Management Research, 5(2), 57-69.

Neville, K., & Heavin, C. (2013). Using social media to support the learning needs of future IS security professionals. *Electronic Journal of e-Learning, 11*(1), 29-38.

News.163.com. (2014). *The police raid in Dongguan becomes a spoofing resource.* Retrieved on 12 August 2014 from: http://news.163.com/14/0213/03/9KUCEQKI00014Q4P.html

Nielson, K. B. (2017). Mobile-Assisted Language Learning: Research-Based Best Practices for Maximizing Learner Success. In Blended Learning: Concepts, Methodologies, Tools, and Applications (pp. 818-842). Hershey, PA: IGI Global.

Nigam, A., & Caswell, N. S. (2003). Business artifacts: An approach to operational specification. *IBM Systems Journal, 42*(3), 428–445. doi:10.1147/sj.423.0428

Nikolaou, I., & Tsaousis, I. (2002). Emotional Intelligence in the workplace: Exploring its effects on occupational stress and organizational commitment. *The International Journal of Organizational Analysis, 10*(4), 45–65. doi:10.1108/eb028956

Nikolaou, I., & Tsaousis, I. (2009). Emotional Intelligence in the workplace: Exploring its effects on occupational stress and organizational commitment. *The International Journal of Organizational Analysis, 10*(4), 37–42.

Nitchot, A., Gilbert, L., & Wills, G. B. (2012). *Competence Web-based System for Suggesting Study Materials Links: Approach & Experimental Design.* In EdMedia-World Conference on Educational Media and Technology, Denver, CO.

Nonaka, I. (1991). *The Knowledge-Creating Company. Harvard Business Review.*

Nonnecke, B., & Preece, J. (2001). Why lurkers lurk. *Proceedings of the Seventh Americas Conference on Information Systems.*

Nonnecke, B., & Preece, J. (2000). Lurker demographics: Counting the silent. In *Proceedings of the Sigchil Conference on Human Factors in Computing Systems.* ACM Press. doi:10.1145/332040.332409

Norris, D. R., & Niebuhr, R. E. (1984). Professionalism, organizational commitment and job satisfaction in an accounting organization. *Accounting, Organizations and Society, 9*(1), 49–60. doi:10.1016/0361-3682(84)90029-1

Oates, W. (1971). *Confessions of a workaholic: The facts about work addiction.* New York: World.

Olawumi, O., Väänänen, A., Haataja, U., & Toivanen, P. (2017). Security issues in smart homes and mobile health system: Threat analysis, possible countermeasures and lessons learned. *International Journal on Information Technologies and Security, 9*(1), 31–52.

Oliver, G. R. (2012). *Foundations of the Assumed Business Operations and Strategy Body of Knowledge (BOSBOK): An Outline of Shareable Knowledge.* Sydney: Darlington Press.

Olmo-Gil, M., Berns, A., & Palomo-Duarte, M. (2017). *Exploring the Potential of Commercial Language Apps to Meet Students' Learning Needs when Studying English at High School and University* (Academic dissertation). Retrieved from Universidad de Cádiz institutional repository. (handler 10498/19542)

OMG-BPMN. (2013). *Business Process Model and Notation, V.2.0.2.* Retrieved July 17, 2017, from http://www.omg.org/spec/BPMN/2.0.2/

OMG-CMMN. (2016). *Case Management Model and Notation, V.1.0.* Retrieved July 17, 2017, from http://www.omg.org/spec/CMMN/1.1/

OMG-OCL. (2014). *Object Constraint Language, V.2.4.* Retrieved July 17, 2017, from http://www.omg.org/spec/OCL/2.4/

OMG-UML. (2015). *Unified Modeling Language, V.2.5.* Retrieved July 17, 2017, from http://www.omg.org/spec/UML/2.5/

O'Neill, & Davis, K. (2011 *International Journal of Hospitality Management 30* 2385390 doi:10.1016/j.ijhm.2010.07.007 PMID:23794780

Onyema, E. O. (2014). Assessing the relationship between human resource management and employee job satisfaction: A case study of a food and beverage company. *Journal of Business Administration Research, 3*(1), 71–81. doi:10.5430/jbar.v3n1p71

Orlikowski, W. J., & Iacono, C. S. (2001). Desperately Seeking the "IT" in IT Research - A Call to Theorizing the IT Artifact. *Information Systems Research, 12*(2), 121–134. doi:10.1287/isre.12.2.121.9700

Osipov, I. V., Volinsky, A. A., & Prasikova, A. Y. (2016). E-Learning Collaborative System for Practicing Foreign Languages with Native Speakers. *International Journal of Advanced Computer Science and Applications, 7*(3).

Otcenaskova, T., Bures, V., & Mikulecka, J. (2012). *Theoretical Fundaments of Knowledge Intensity Modelling.* Paper presented at the 18th International Business Information Management Association conference, Istanbul, Turkey.

Ozzane, L. K. (2010). Learning to exchange time: Benefits and obstacles to time banking. *International Journal of Community Currency Research, 14*, A1–A16.

Padgett, D. K. (1998). *Qualitative methods in social work research: Challenges and rewards.* Thousand Oaks, CA: SAGE.

Palomo-Duarte, M., Berns, A., Cejas, A., Dodero, J. M., Caballero, J. A., & Ruiz-Rube, I. (2016). Assessing Foreign Language Learning Through Mobile Game-Based Learning Environments. *International Journal of Human Capital and Information Technology Professionals, 7*(2), 53–67. doi:10.4018/IJHCITP.2016040104

Palomo-Duarte, M., Dodero, J. M., Tocino, J. T., García-Domínguez, A., & Balderas, A. (2012). Competitive evaluation in a video game development course. In *17th ACM Annual Conference on Innovation and Technology in Computer Science Education (ITiCSE '12)*, (pp. 321-326): ACM. doi:10.1145/2325296.2325371

Pandey, S., & Sharma, V. (2014). An Exploratory study on Organisational Crisis in Information Technology industry. *International journal of Research in Computer Application & Management, 4*(9), 22-34.

Pang, B., & Lee, L. (2008). *Opinion Mining and Sentiment Analysis* (Vol. 2). Now Publishers Inc.

Paquette, G., Rogozan, D., & Marino, O. (2012). Competency Comparison Relations for Recommendation in Technology Enhanced Learning Scenarios. *Proceedings of the 2nd Workshop on Recommender Systems for Technology Enhanced Learning (RecSysTEL).*

Pareek, U. (1983). Organizational roles stress. In L. D. Goodstein & J. W. Pfeiffer (Eds.), The 1983 annual (pp. 115-123). San Diego, CA: University Associates.

Pareek, U. (1998).The Pfeiffer Library (2nd ed.). Jossey/Bass.

Pareek, U. (1982). *Organizational role stress scales (manual, scale, answer sheet).* Ahmedabad: Navin Publications.

Pareek, U. (1993). *Making Organizational Roles Effective.* McGraw-Hill.

Pareek, U. (1993). *Making organizational roles effective.* New Delhi: Tata McGraw-Hill Publishing.

Pareek, U. (1993). *Making Organizational Roles Effective.* New Delhi: Tata McGraw-Hill.

Partners in Care. (2017). Retrieved from http://www.partnersincare.org/

Patwardhan, N. C. (2014). Work-Life Balance Initiations for Women Employees in the IT Industry. In P. Verma & H. Shah (Eds.), *Work-life Balance: A Global Perspective.* Delhi: Wisdom Publications.

Pauli, J. J., & Xu, D. (2005). Misuse case-based design and analysis of secure software architecture. *Proceedings of the International Conference on Information Technology: Coding and Computing, 2*, 398-403. doi:10.1109/ITCC.2005.199

Payne, R. (1988). *Individual Differences in the Study of Occupational Stress.* New York: Wiley.

Penna. (2007). *Meaning at Work Research Report.* Available: http:// www. e-penna.com/ newsopinion/research.aspx

Pesic, M., Schonenberg, H., & van der Aalst, W. M. P. (2007). Declare: Full support for loosely-structured processes. In *Proceedings of the 11th IEEE International Conference on Enterprise Distributed Object Computing* (pp. 287-298). New York: IEEE Press. doi:10.1109/EDOC.2007.14

Pestonjee, D. M. (1992). *Stress and Coping. The India experience.* New Delhi: Sage Publication.

Peterson, D. K. (2002). Deviant workplace behavior and the organization's ethical climate. *Journal of Business and Psychology, 17*(1), 47–61. doi:10.1023/A:1016296116093

Peytcheva-Forsyth, R., & Yovkova, B. (2015). How students' experience in e-learning affects their judgements about the quality of an online course. *International Journal of Human Capital and Information Technology Professionals*, 6(1), 14–25. doi:10.4018/ijhcitp.2015010102

Pinto, A. M., Sánchez, M. C., & García, F. J. (2015b). Developing a VLE to Enable the Innovative Learning of English Pronunciation. In *Proceedings of the 3rd International Conference on Technological Ecosystems for Enhancing Multi-culturality* (pp. 83-89). New York: ACM. doi:10.1145/2808580.2808594

Pinto-Llorente, A. M., Sánchez-Gómez, M. C., & García-Peñalvo, F. J. (2014a). Assessing the effectiveness of a technological model to improve written skills in English in higher education. In *Proceedings of the Second International Conference on Technological Ecosystems for Enhancing Multiculturality* (pp. 69-74). New York: ACM.

Pinto-Llorente, A. M., Sánchez-Gómez, M. C., & García-Peñalvo, F. J. (2014c). Students' essential characteristics for learning English in a hypermedia modular model. In *Proceedings of the Second International Conference on Technological Ecosystems for Enhancing Multiculturality* (pp. 107-111). New York: ACM.

Pinto-Llorente, A. M., Sánchez-Gómez, M. C., & García-Peñalvo, F. J. (2015a). To Be or Not to Be Successful? That Does Not Only Depend on Technology, But Also on Human Factors. *Journal of Cases on Information Technology*, 17(1), 51–69. doi:10.4018/JCIT.2015010104

Pinto-Llorente, A. M., Sánchez-Gómez, M. C., & Palacios-Vicario, B. (2014b). Modelo Blended Learning para la enseñanza-aprendizaje del inglés en educación superior. In *Blended Learning en educación superior. Perspectivas de innovación y cambio* (pp. 121–142). Madrid: Editorial Síntesis.

Plutchik, R. (1987). Evolutionary bases of empathy. In N. Eisenberg & J. Strayer (Eds.), *Empathy and its development* (pp. 38–46). New York Cambridge University Press.

Porter, L. W., Steers, R. M., Mowday, R. T., & Boulian, P. V. (1974). Organizational Commitment, Job Satisfaction and Turnover among Psychiatric Technicians. *The Journal of Applied Psychology*, 59(5), 603–609. doi:10.1037/h0037335

Power, D. J., & Phillips-Wren, G. (2012). Impact of Social Media and Web 2.0 on Decision-Making. *Journal of Decision Systems*, 20(3), 249–261. doi:10.3166/jds.20.249-261

Prensky, M. (2005). Computer games and learning: Digital game-based learning. In J. Raessens & J. Goldstein (Eds.), *Handbook of computer game studies* (pp. 97–122). Cambridge, MA: MIT Press.

Provost, F., & Fawcett, T. (2013). *Data Science for Business: What You Need to Know about Data Mining and Data-Analytic Thinking*. O'Reilly Media.

Pulos, S., Elison, J., and Lennon, R. (2004). The hierarchical structure of the Interpersonal Reactivity Index. *Social Behaviour and Personality*, 32355-360.

Purvis, L. J., & Cropley, M. (2003). The Psychological Contracts of National Health Service Nurses. *Journal of Nursing Management*, 11(2), 107–120. doi:10.1046/j.1365-2834.2003.00357.x PMID:12581399

Pyöriä, P., Melin, H., & Blom, R. (2005). *Knowledge workers in the information society*. Tampere: Tampere University Press.

Qi, H., Wang, M., Tong, R., Shen, R., Wang, J., & Gao, Y. (2006). The design and implementation of an interactive mobile learning system. In *The 6th IEEE International Conference on Advanced Learning Technologies 2006* (pp. 947-951). Kerkrade: IEEE.

Quan, J., & Cha, H. (2010). IT certifications, outsourcing and information systems personnel turnover. *Information Technology & People*, 24(4), 330–351. doi:10.1108/09593841011087798

Quintana, S. M., & Maxwell, S. E. (1999). Implications of recent developments in structural equation modelling for counselling psychology. *The Counseling Psychologist*, *27*(4), 485–527. doi:10.1177/0011000099274002

Rafferty, A. M., Maben, J., West, E., & Robinson, D. (2005). *What makes a good employer?* Issue Paper 3 International Council of Nurses Geneva.

Rahman, W. A., & Castelli, P. A. (2013). The impact of empathy on leadership effectiveness among business leaders in the United States and Malaysia. *International Journal of Economics Business and Management Studies*, *2*(3), 83–97.

Ramsay, H., Scholarios, D., & Harley, B. (2000). Employees and High-Performance Work Systems: Testing inside the Black Box. *British Journal of Industrial Relations*, *38*(4), 501–531. doi:10.1111/1467-8543.00178

Ramzan, Z. (2006). *Context-Aware phishing realized*. Retrieved on 15 August 2017 from: https://www.symantec.com/connect/blogs/context-aware-phishing-realized

Rathore, S., & Ahuja, V. (2015). A study of role stress among the IT professionals in India: Examining the impact of demographic factors. *International Journal of Human Capital and IT Professionals*, *6*(2).

Rathore, S., & Ahuja, V. (2015). Examining the impact of Emotional Intelligence on Organizational Role Stress: An empirical study of the Indian IT sector. *International Journal of Human Capital and Information Technology Professionals*, *6*(1), 51–63. doi:10.4018/ijhcitp.2015010105

Rathore, S., Ningthoujam, S., & Medury, Y. (2012). Understanding Emotional Intelligence: Integrating Indo Western Perspectives. *Metamorphosis*. *Journal of Management Research*, *12*(2), 44–54.

Rauhala, E. (2014). *In China, police raid on notorious 'Sin City' greeted with ridicule*. Retrieved on 12 September 2014 from: http://time.com/6064/in-china-police-raid-on-notorious-sin-city-greeted-with-ridicule/

Reddiyoor, N. A., Rajeswari K. S. (2017). Role of Self-Efficacy and Collective Efficacy as Moderators of Occupational Stress Among Software Development Professionals. *International Journal of Human Capital and Information Technology Professionals*, *8*(2), 1-14.

Riahi, G. (2015). E-learning systems based on cloud computing: A review. *Procedia Computer Science*, *62*, 352–359. doi:10.1016/j.procs.2015.08.415

Ridings. (2006). Psychological barriers: Lurker and poster motivations and behaviour in online communities. Commun. AIS, 18, 329–354.

Robinson, B. E. (1999). The work addiction risk test: Development a tentative measure of workaholism. *Perceptual and Motor Skills*, *88*(1), 199–210. doi:10.2466/pms.1999.88.1.199 PMID:10214644

Robinson, B. E. (2000). Workaholism: Bridging the Gap between Workplace, Sociocultural, and Family Research. *Journal of Employment Counseling*, *37*(1), 31–47. doi:10.1002/j.2161-1920.2000.tb01024.x

Robinson, D., Perryman, S., & Hayday, S. (2004). *The Drivers of Employee Engagement Report 408*. Institute for Employment Studies.

Robinson, D., Perryman, S., & Hayday, S. (2004). *The Drivers of Employee Engagement*. Brighton, UK: Institute for Employment Studies.

Robinson, I., Webber, J., & Eifrem, E. (2013). *Graph Databases. Gravenstein Highway North*. Sebastopol, CA: O'Reilly Media, Inc.

Robles, G., González-Barahona, J. M., & Moral, A. (2012). A synchronous on-line competition software to improve and motivate learning. In *Global Engineering Education Conference (EDUCON)*, 2012 (pp. 1-8). Marrakech: IEEE. doi:10.1109/EDUCON.2012.6201118

Rodríguez, A. I., & Riaza, B. G. (2016). Learning Goes Mobile: Devices and APPS for the Practice of Contents at Tertiary Level. In D. Fonseca & E. Redondo (Eds.), *Handbook of Research on Applied E-Learning in Engineering and Architecture Education* (pp. 472–496). Hershey, PA: IGI Global. doi:10.4018/978-1-4666-8803-2.ch021

Rodriguez, D., Patel, R., Bright, A., Gregory, D., & Gowing, M. K. (2002). Developing Competency Models to Promote Integrated Human Resource. *Human Resource Management, 41*(3), 309–324. doi:10.1002/hrm.10043

Roehling, M. V., Cavanaugh, M. A., Moynihan, L. M., & Boswell, W. (2000). The nature of the new employment relationship: A content analysis of the practitioner and academic literatures. *Human Resource Management, 39*(4), 305–320. doi:10.1002/1099-050X(200024)39:4<305::AID-HRM3>3.0.CO;2-V

Rogers, C. R. (1951). *Client-Centered therapy*. Boston: Houghton Mifflin.

Rogers, C. R. (1975). Empathic: An unappreciated way of being. *The Counseling Psychologist, 5*(2), 2–10. doi:10.1177/001100007500500202

Rogers, K., Dziobek, I., Hassenstab, J., Wolf, O. T., & Convit, A. (2007). Who cares? Revisiting empathy in Asperger syndrome. *Journal of Autism and Developmental Disorders, 37*(4), 709–715. doi:10.1007/s10803-006-0197-8 PMID:16906462

Romansky, R., & Noninska, I. (2015a). Globalization and digital privacy. *Electrotechnika & Electronica, 50*(11/12), 36-41. Retrieved from http://ceec.fnts.bg/journal.html

Romansky, R. (2015b). Social computing and digital privacy. *Communication & Cognition, 48*(3-4), 65–82.

Romansky, R. (2017a). *Information servicing in distributed learning environments*. Saarbrüken, Germany: LAP LAMBERT Academic Publishing.

Romansky, R., & Noninska, I. (2016a). Architecture of Combined e-Learning Environment and Investigation of Secure Access and Privacy Protection. *International Journal of Human Capital and Information Technology Professionals, 9*(3), 89–106. doi:10.4018/IJHCITP.2016070107

Romansky, R., & Noninska, I. (2016b). Discrete Formalization and Investigation of Secure Access to Corporative Resources. *International Journal of Engineering Research and Management, 3*(5), 97–101.

Romansky, R., & Noninska, I. (2016c). An Approach for Modelling of Security Procedures for Information Resources Protection. *International Advanced Research Journal in Science. Engineering and Technology, 3*(6), 1–6.

Romansky, R., & Noninska, I. (2017b). Stochastic Investigation of Secure Access to the Resources of a Corporative System. *International Journal of Scientific & Engineering Research, 8*(1), 578–584.

Roschelle, J. (2003). Unlocking the learning value of wireless mobile devices. *Journal of Computer Assisted Learning, 19*(3), 260–272. doi:10.1046/j.0266-4909.2003.00028.x

Rosete, D., & Ciarrochi, J. (2005). Emotional intelligence and its relationship to workplace performance outcomes of leadership effectiveness. *Leadership and Organization Development Journal, 26*(5), 388–399. doi:10.1108/01437730510607871

Rosse, J. G., & Hulin, C. L. (1985). Adaptation to work: An analysis of employee health, withdrawal, and change. *Organizational Behavior and Human Decision Processes, 36*(3), 324–347. doi:10.1016/0749-5978(85)90003-2 PMID:10275698

Rothkrantz, L. (2015). How social media facilitate learning communities and peer groups around MOOCS. *International Journal of Human Capital and Information Technology Professionals, 6*(1), 1–13. doi:10.4018/ijhcitp.2015010101

Rousseau, D. M. (1996). Changing the deal while keeping the people. *The Academy of Management Executive, 10*, 50–58.

Rousseau, D. M. (2001). The idiosyncratic deal: Flexibility versus fairness? *Organizational Dynamics, 29*(4), 260–273. doi:10.1016/S0090-2616(01)00032-8

Rowley, J., & Dawes, J. (2000). Disloyalty: A closer look at non-loyals. *Journal of Consumer Marketing, 17*(6), 538-549.

RSA. (2009). *Phishing, vishing and smishing: Old threats present new risks.* RSA.

Ruggiero, P., & Foote, J. (2011). *Cyber threats to mobile phone.* US-CERT.

Russell, C., & Zinta, S. (2000). The Relationship of Organizational Stress to organizational commitment, and Organizational Citizenship Behaviors. *Journal of Industrial and Organizational Psychology.*

Ryan-Collins, J., Stephens, L., & Coote, A. (2008). *The new wealth of time: How timebanking helps people build better public services.* London: New Economics Foundation.

Ryan, R. M. (2005). The developmental line of autonomy in the etiology, dynamics, and treatment of borderline personality disorders. *Development and Psychopathology, 17*(04), 987–1006. doi:10.1017/S0954579405050467 PMID:16613427

Rydstedt, L. W., Devereux, J., & Furnham, A. F. (2004). Are lay theories of work stress related to distress? A longitudinal study in the British workforce. *Work and Stress, 18*(3), 245–254. doi:10.1080/02628370412331323906

Ryndina, K., Küster, J. M., & Gall, H. (2007). Consistency of business process models and object life cycles. In *Lecture Notes in Computer Science, 4364* (pp. 80–90). Heidelberg, Germany: Springer. doi:10.1007/978-3-540-69489-2_11

Sa'don, N. F., & Iahad, N. A. (2017). Collaborative Mobile Learning: A Systematic Literature Review. In Blended Learning: Concepts, Methodologies, Tools, and Applications (pp. 676-690). Hershey, PA: IGI Global. doi:10.4018/978-1-5225-0783-3.ch033

Sacks, M. (2015). Competition Between Open Source and Proprietary Software: Strategies for Survival. *Journal of Management Information Systems, 32*(3), 268–295. doi:10.1080/07421222.2015.1099391

Sadiq, S., Orlowska, M., Sadiq, W., & Schulz, K. (2005). When workflows will not deliver: the case of contradicting work practice. *Proceedings of the 8th International Conference on Business Information Systems.*

Sadri, G. (2012). Emotional intelligence and leadership development. *Public Personnel Management, 41*(3), 535–548. doi:10.1177/009102601204100308

Sagie, A., Birati, A., & Tziner, A. (2002). Assessing the Costs of Behavioral and Psychological Withdrawal: A New Model and an Empirical Illustration. *Applied Psychology, 51*(1), 67–89. doi:10.1111/1464-0597.00079

Salleh, R., Nair, M. S., & Harun, H. (2012). Job satisfaction, organizational commitment, and turnover intention: A case study on employees of a retail company in Malaysia. *World Academy of Science, Engineering and Technology, 72*(12), 316–323.

Salovey, P., & Mayer, J. D. (1990). Emotional intelligence. *Imagination, Cognition and Personality, 9*(3), 185–211. doi:10.2190/DUGG-P24E-52WK-6CDG

Saltares Márquez, D., & Cejas Sánchez, A. (2014). *Libgdx Cross-platform Game Development Cookbook.* Packt Publishing.

Samani, R., & McFarland, C. (2014). *Hacking the human operating system:Tthe role of social engineering within cybersecurity.* Intel Security McAfee.

Sampson, D., & Fytros, D. (2008). *Competence Models in Technology-enhanced Competence-based Learning. In International Handbook on Information Technologies for Education and Training* (2nd ed.; pp. 155–177). Berlin: Springer. doi:10.1007/978-3-540-74155-8_9

Samuel, O. O., Botha, A., Ford, M., Tolmay, J. P., & Krause, C. (2009). Igloo: Mobile learning system to facilitate and support learners and educators. In A. Gyasi-Agyei, & A. Ogunfunmi (Eds.), *2nd International Conference on Adaptive Science & Technology (ICAST) 2009* (pp. 355-360). Accra: IEEE. doi:10.1109/ICASTECH.2009.5409702

Sánchez-Gómez, M. C. (2015). La dicotomía cualitativo-cuantitativo: posibilidades de integración y diseños mixtos. Campo Abierto. Vol. monográfico, 11-30.

Sánchez-Gómez, M. C., Pinto-Llorente, A. M., & García-Peñalvo, F. J. (2010). Blended learning University students' perception of digital competence. In European Applied Business Research (EABR) and European College Teaching & Learning (ETLC), Dublin, Ireland.

Sánchez, J., & Olivares, R. (2011). Problem solving and collaboration using mobile serious games. *Computers & Education*, *57*(3), 1943–1952. doi:10.1016/j.compedu.2011.04.012

Sánchez, M. C., Pinto, A. M., & García, F. J. (2011). University students' technological competence. A European higher education area (EHEA). Case study. In *CAL 2011 Learning Futures: Education, Technology & Sustainability*. Manchester Metropolitan University.

Sangwan, S. (2005). Virtual Community Success: A Uses and Gratifications Perspective. *Proceedings of the 38th Annual Hawaii International Conference*. doi:10.1109/HICSS.2005.673

Sanz, J. L. C. (2011). Entity-oriented operations modeling for business process management - A multidisciplinary review of the state-of-the-art. In *Proceedings of the 6th IEEE International Symposium on Service Oriented System Engineering* (pp. 152-163). New York: IEEE Press.

Sarwar, S., & Abugre, J. (2013). The Influence of Rewards And Job Satisfaction on Employees In The Service Industry. *The Business & Management Review*, 23-32.

Savignon, S. J., & Roithmeier, W. (2004). Computer-Mediated Communication: Texts and Strategies. *CALICO Journal*, *21*(2), 265–290.

Schaef, A. W., & Fassel, D. (1988). *The Addictive Organization*. Francisco, CA: Harper Row.

Schaufeli, W. B., & Bakker, A. B. (2004). Job demands, job resources, and their relationship with burnout and engagement: A multi-sample study. *Journal of Organizational Behavior*, *25*(3), 293–315. doi:10.1002/job.248

Schaufeli, W. B., Salanova, M., Gonzalez-Roma, V., & Bakker, A. B. (2002a). The measurement of engagement and burnout and: A confirmative analytic approach. *Journal of Happiness Studies*, *3*(1), 71–92. doi:10.1023/A:1015630930326

Schaufeli, W. B., Taris, T. W., & Van, R. W. (2008). Workaholism, burnout and engagement: Three of a kind or three different kinds of employee well-being. *Applied Psychology*, *57*(2), 173–203. doi:10.1111/j.1464-0597.2007.00285.x

Schaufeli, W. S., & Enzmann, D. (1998). *The burnout companion to study and practice: A critical analysis*. London: Taylor & Francis.

Schneider, J., Groza, T., & Passant, A. (2013). A review of argumentation for the Social Semantic Web. *Semantic Web*, *4*(2), 159–218. doi:10.3233/SW-2012-0073

Schneier, B. (2000). *Cryoto-gram*. Retrieved on 24 August 2017 from: https://www.schneier.com/crypto-gram/archives/2000/1015.html

Schonenberg, H., Mans, R., Russell, N., Mulyar, N., & van der Aalst, W. (2008). Process flexibility: A survey of contemporary approaches. *Lecture Notes in Business Information Processing, 10*, 16–30. doi:10.1007/978-3-540-68644-6_2

Schoonover, S. C., Schoonover, H., Nemerov, D., & Ehly, C. (2000). *Competency-Based HR Applications: Results of a Comprehensive Survey.* Andersen/Schoonover/SHRM.

Scott, K. S., Moore, K. S., & Miceli, M. P. (1997). An exploration of the meaning and consequences of workaholism. *Human Relations, 50*(3), 287–314. doi:10.1177/001872679705000304

Seebaluck, A. K., & Seegum, T. D. (2013). Motivation among public primary school teachers in Mauritius. *International Journal of Educational Management, 27*(4), 446–464. doi:10.1108/09513541311316359

Sekaran, U. (2003). *Research methods for business: A skill-building approach* (4th ed.). New York, NY: John Wiley.

Selwyn, N., & Stirling, E. (2016). Social media and education…now the dust has settled. *Learning, Media and Technology, 41*(1), 1–5. doi:10.1080/17439884.2015.1115769

Selye, H. (1997). The general adaptation syndrome and the diseases of adaptation. *The Journal of Clinical Endocrinology, 6*(2), 117–123. doi:10.1210/jcem-6-2-117 PMID:21025115

Sethi, D. (2009). Mindful leadership. *Leader to Leader, 2009*(51), 7–11. doi:10.1002/ltl.311

Sethi, V., King, R. C., & Quick, J. C. (2004). What causes stress in information system professionals? *Communications of the ACM, 47*(3), 99–102. doi:10.1145/971617.971623

Shaffer, H. J., LaPlante, D. A., LaBrie, R. A., Kidman, K. C., Donato, A. N., & Stanton, M. V. (2004). Toward a syndrome model of addiction: Multiple expressions, common etiology. *Harvard Review of Psychiatry, 12*(6), 367–374. doi:10.1080/10673220490905705 PMID:15764471

Shankar, V., Urban, G.L., & Sultan, F. (2002). Online Trust: a stakeholder perspective, concepts, implications and future directions. *Journal of Strategic Information Systems, 11*, 325–344.

Shapiro, S. L., Carlson, L. E., Astin, J. A., & Freedman, B. (2006). Mechanisms of mindfulness. *Journal of Clinical Psychology, 62*(3), 373–386. doi:10.1002/jclp.20237 PMID:16385481

Sharma, E. (2004). Doctors in Jaipur: Working under higher levels of Stress. *Journal of Health Management, 7*, 151-156.

Sharples, M., Taylor, J., & Vavoula, G. (2005). Towards a theory of mobile learning. In H. van der Merwe & T. Brown (Eds.), *Proceedings of 4th World Conference on mLearning (mLearn)* (pp. 1-9). Cape Town: mLearn.

Sheldon, K. M., Ryan, R. M., Rawsthorne, L. J., & Ilardi, B. (1997). Trait self and true self: Cross-role variation in the Big-Five personality traits and its relations with psychological authenticity and subjective well-being. *Journal of Personality and Social Psychology, 73*(6), 1380–1393. doi:10.1037/0022-3514.73.6.1380

Sheng, S., Holbrook, M., Kumaraguru, P., Cranor, L., & Downs, J. (2010). Who Falls for Phish? A demographic analysis of phishing susceptibility and effectiveness of interventions. *Proceedings of the Conference on Human Factors in Computing System.*

Sheng, S., Magnien, B., Kumaraguru, P., Acquisti, A., Cranor, L. F., Hong, J., & Nunge, E. (2007). Anti-phishing Phil: The design and evaluation of a game that teaches people not to fall for phish. *Proceedings of the SOUPS*, 88-99. doi:10.1145/1280680.1280692

Shih, P., Bellotti, V., Han, K., & Carroll, J. (2015). *Unequal Time for Unequal Value: Implications of Differing Motivations for Participation in Timebanking.* Paper presented at the 33rd Annual ACM Conference on Human Factors in Computing Systems, Seoul, South Korea. doi:10.1145/2702123.2702560

Shimazu, A., & Schaufeli, W. B. (2007). Does distraction facilitate problem-focused coping with job stress? A one year longitudinal study. *Journal of Behavioral Medicine, 30*(5), 423–434. doi:10.1007/s10865-007-9109-4 PMID:17522973

Shimazu, A., Schaufeli, W. B., & Taris, T. W. (2010). How does workaholism affect worker health and performance? The mediating role of coping. *International Journal of Behavioral Medicine, 17*(2), 154–160. doi:10.1007/s12529-010-9077-x PMID:20169433

Shipper, F., Kincaid, J., Rotondo, D. M., & Hoffman, R. C. IV. (2003). A cross-cultural exploratory study of the linkage between emotional intelligence and managerial effectiveness. *The International Journal of Organizational Analysis, 11*(3), 171–191. doi:10.1108/eb028970

Shivshankar, S., & Paul, S. (2015). E-Learning Environment – The Security and Privacy Challenges Focusing on the Counter Measures. *Proceedings of the International Conference on Developments of E-Systems Engineering.* doi:10.1109/DeSE.2015.31

Shoukry, L., Göbel, S., & Steinmetz, R. (2014). Learning Analytics and Serious Games: Trends and Considerations. In *Proceedings of the 2014 ACM International Workshop on Serious Games* (pp. 21-26). Orlando, FL: ACM. doi:10.1145/2656719.2656729

Shreiber, G., Akkermans, H., Anjewierden, A., Hoog, R. d., Shadbolt, N., Velde, W. V. d., & Wielinga, B. (2002). Knowledge Engineering and Management. Cambridge, MA: The MIT Press.

Shulman, T. E., & Hemenover, S. H. (2006). Is dispositional emotional Intelligence synonymous with personality? *Self and Identity, 5*(2), 147–171. doi:10.1080/15298860600586206

Shum, S. B., Cannavacciuolo, L., De Liddo, A., Iandoli, L., & Quinto, I. (2011). Using Social Network Analysis to Support Collective Decision-Making Process. *International Journal of Decision Support System Technology, 3*(2), 15–31. doi:10.4018/jdsst.2011040102

Shute, V. J., & Ke, F. (2012). Games, learning, and assessment. In D. Ifenthaler, D., Eseryel & X. Ge (Eds.), Assessment in Game Based Learning (pp. 43-58). New York, NY: Springer. doi:10.1007/978-1-4614-3546-4_4

Shute, V. J., & Ventura, M. (2013). *Stealth assessment: Measuring and supporting learning in video games.* Cambridge, MA: MIT Press.

Sicilia, M. A., Cuadrado, J. J., García, E., Rodríguez, D., & Hilera, J. R. (2005). The evaluation of ontological representation of the SWEBOK as a revision tool. *Proceedings of the 9th Annual International Computer Software and Application Conference (COMPSAC)*, 26-28.

Siemens, G., & Baker, R. (2012). Learning analytics and educational data mining: towards communication and collaboration. In S. Buckingham, D. Gasevic, & R. Ferguson (Eds.), *Proceedings of the 2nd international conference on learning analytics and knowledge* (pp. 252-254). Vancouver: ACM. doi:10.1145/2330601.2330661

Simon, H. A. (1977). *The New Science of Management Decision.* Upper Saddle River, NJ: Prentice Hall.

Simonite, T. (2013). *Google wants to replace your password with a ring.* Retrieved on 16 August 2014 from: http://www.technologyreview.com/news/512051/google-wants-to-replace-all-your-passwords-with-a-ring/

Sindre, G., & Opdahl, A. (2005). Eliciting security requirements with misuse cases. *Requirements Engineering, 10*(1), 34–44. doi:10.1007/s00766-004-0194-4

Singh, A. (2012). Job Satisfaction in Insurance Sector: An Empirical Investigation. *International Journal of Engineering and Management Sciences, 3*(4).

Singh, D. (2007). Emotional Intelligence at Work; A Professional Guide (3rd ed.). Sage Publications.

Singh, S. K., & Singh, S. (2008). Managing Role Stress through Emotional Intelligence: A Study of Indian Medico Professionals. *International Journal of Indian Culture and Business Management, 1*(4), 377–396. doi:10.1504/IJI-CBM.2008.018620

Sinha, V., Abraham, A., Bhaskarna, B., Xavier, K., & Kariat, K. (2014). Role efficacy: Studying the impact on employee engagement, employee motivation and attrition. *International Journal of Human Capital and Information Technology Professionals, 5*(4), 35–54. doi:10.4018/ijhcitp.2014100103

Sinofsky, S. (2011). *Signing in with a picture password*. Retrieved on 16 August 2014 from: http://blogs.msdn.com/b/b8/archive/2011/12/16/signing-in-with-a-picture-password.aspx

Síthigh, D. M. (2011). Legal games: The regulation of content and the challenge of casual gaming. *Journal of Gaming & Virtual Worlds, 3*(1), 3–19. doi:10.1386/jgvw.3.1.3_1

Sitthisak, O., Gilbert, L., & Davis, H.C. (2008). Deriving E-Assessment from a Competency Model. *ICALT*, 327-329 .

Siu, O.-L. (2002). Occupational Stressors and Well-being among Chinese Employees: The Role of Organisational Commitment. *Applied Psychology, 51*(4), 527–544. doi:10.1111/1464-0597.t01-1-00106

Skarlicki, D. P., & Folger, R. (1997). Retaliation in the workplace: The roles of distributive, procedural, and interactional justice. *The Journal of Applied Psychology, 82*(3), 434–443. doi:10.1037/0021-9010.82.3.434

Slaski, M., & Cartwright, S. (2002). Health performance and Emotional Intelligence: An exploratory study of retail managers. *Stress and Health, 18*(2), 63–68. doi:10.1002/smi.926

Smidts, A., Pruyn, A., & Riel, C. (2001). The impact of employee communication and perceived external prestige on organizational identification. *Academy of Management Journal, 49*(5), 1051–1062. doi:10.2307/3069448

Smith, A. (2011). Perceptions of stress at work Human Research. *Human Resource Management Journal, 11*(4), 74–78. doi:10.1111/j.1748-8583.2001.tb00052.x

Solinger, O. N., & Van Oleffen, W. (2008). Beyond the three-component model of organitzacional commitment. *The Journal of Applied Psychology, 93*(1), 70–83. doi:10.1037/0021-9010.93.1.70 PMID:18211136

Sonnentag, S., Brodbeck, F. C., Heinbokel, T., & Stolte, W. (1994). Stressor-burnout Relationship in Software Development Teams. *Journal of Occupational and Organizational Psychology, 67*(4), 25–32. doi:10.1111/j.2044-8325.1994.tb00571.x

Soto-Acosta, P., Martínez-Conesa, I., & Colomo-Palacios, R. (2010). An empirical analysis of the relationship between IT training sources and IT value. *Information Systems Management, 27*(3), 274–283. doi:10.1080/10580530.2010.493847

Spector, P. E. (1997). *Job satisfaction: Application, assessment, cause and consequences*. Thousand Oaks, CA: Sage Publication.

Spence, J. T., & Robbins, A. S. (1992). Workaholism: Definition, measurement, and preliminary results. *Journal of Personality Assessment, 58*(1), 160–178. doi:10.1207/s15327752jpa5801_15 PMID:16370875

Spielberger, C. D., & Reheiser, E. C. (1994). The job stress survey: Measuring gender differences in occupational stress. *Journal of Social Behavior and Personality, 9*, 199–218.

Srikanth, P. B., & Jomon, M. G. (2013). Role ambiguity and role performance Effectiveness: Moderating the Effect of Feedback seeking Behaviour. *Asian Academy of Management Journal, 18*(2), 105–127.

Srivastava, S. (2011). Analyzing the impact of mentoring on job burnout –job satisfaction relationship: An empirical study on Indian managers. *Paradigm, 15*(1/2), 48–57.

Steel, R. P. (2002). Turnover theory at the empirical interface: Problems of fit and function. *Academy of Management Review, 27*, 346–360.

Steer, R. M., Mooday, R. T., & Porter, L. W. (1982). *Employee organisation linkages.* New York: Academic Press.

Steinberg, A., & Ritzmann, R. F. (1990). A Living Systems Approach to Understanding the *Concept of Stress. Behavioral Science, 35*(2), 138–146. doi:10.1002/bs.3830350206 PMID:2327936

Stringer, C., Didham, J., & Theivananthampillai, P. (2011). Motivation, pay satisfaction, and job satisfaction of frontline employees. *Qualitative Research in Accounting & Management, 8*(2), 161–179. doi:10.1108/11766091111137564

Subrahmanyama, K., Reich, S. M., Waechter, N., & Espinoza, G. (2008). Online and offline social networks: Use of social networking sites by emerging adults. *Journal of Applied Developmental Psychology, 29*(6), 420–433. doi:10.1016/j.appdev.2008.07.003

Suki, N. M., Ramayah, T., Ming, M. K. P., & Suki, N. M. (2011). Factors Enhancing Employed Job Seekers Intentions to Use Social Networking Sites as a Job Search Tool. *International Journal of Technology and Human Interaction, 7*(2), 38–54. doi:10.4018/jthi.2011040105

Suma, S., & Lesha, J. (2013). Job satisfaction and organizational commitment: The case of Shkodra municipality. *European Scientific Journal, ESJ, 9*(17).

Sun, P. C., Tsai, R. J., Finger, G., Chen, Y. Y., & Yeh, D. (2008). What drives a successful e-learning? An empirical investigation of the critical factors influencing learner satisfaction. *Computers & Education, 50*(4), 1183–1202. doi:10.1016/j.compedu.2006.11.007

Surowiecki, J. (2005). *The wisdom of crowds.* Anchor Books.

Takeuchi, H., & Nonaka, I. (2004). Knowledge creation and dialectics. *Hitotsubashi on Knowledge Management*, 1-27.

Taplin, I. M., Winterton, J., & Winterton, R. (2003). Understanding Labor Turnover in a Labor Intensive Industry: Evidence from British Clothing Industry. *Journal of Management Studies, 40*(2), 4–15.

Taraghi, B., Ebner, M., Saranti, A., & Schön, M. (2014a). On using Markov chain to evidence the learning structures and difficulty levels of one digit multiplication. In *Proceedings of the 4th International Conference on Learning Analytics and Knowledge* (pp. 68-72). Indianapolis, IN: Academic Press. doi:10.1145/2567574.2567614

Taraghi, B., Saranti, A., Ebner, M., & Schön, M. (2014b). *Markov chain and classification of difficulty levels enhances the learning path in one digit multiplication.* In Lecture Notes in Computer Science: Vol. 8523 (pp. 322–333). Springer. doi:10.1007/978-3-319-07482-5_31

Taras, M. (2002). Using Assessment for Learning and Learning from Assessment. *Assessment & Evaluation in Higher Education, 27*(6), 501–510. doi:10.1080/0260293022000020273

Taris, T. W., Schaufeli, W. B., & Shimazu, A. (2010). The push and pull of work: About the difference between workaholism and work engagement. In A. B. Bakker & M. P. Leiter (Eds.), *Work engagement: A handbook of essential theory and research.* New York: Psychology Press.

Taris, T. W., Schaufeli, W. B., & Verhoeven, L. C. (2005). Internal and external validation of the Dutch Work Addiction Risk Test: Implications for jobs and non-work conflict. *Journal of Applied Psychology: An International Review, 54*, 37–60. doi:10.1111/j.1464-0597.2005.00195.x

Taylor, S. L. (2016). *Reshaping Millennials As Future Leaders Of The Marine Corps*. Air War College Montgomery United States.

Technopedia. (2017). *Definition of cyberattack*. Retrieved on 14 August 2017 from: https://www.techopedia.com/definition/24748/cyberattack

Teigland, R., & Wasko, M. M. (2003). Integrating Knowledge through Information Trading: Examining the Relationship between Boundary Spanning Communication and Individual Performance. *Decision Sciences, 34*(2), 261–286. doi:10.1111/1540-5915.02341

The Pew Research Centre for the People and the Press. (2007). *How young people view their lives, futures and politics: A portrait of "Generation Next."* Author.

Thibaut, J. W., & Kelley, H. H. (1959). The Social Psychology of Groups. *Social Research, 27*(2), 252–254.

Thingujam, N. K. S., & Ram, U. (2000). Emotional Intelligence scale: Indian Norms. *Journal of Education & Psychology, 58*, 40–44.

Thomas, W. H., & Feldman, D. C. (2009). Age, work experience, and the psychological contract. *Journal of Organizational Behavior, 30*(8), 1053–1075. doi:10.1002/job.599

Thorndike, E. L. (1920). Intelligence and its use. *Harper's Magazine, 140*, 227–235.

Thorndike, E. L. (1920). Intelligence and its use. *Harper's Magazine, 140*, 227-235.

Thrash, T. M., & Elliot, A. J. (2002). Implicit and self-attributed achievement motives: Concordance and predictive validity. *Journal of Personality, 70*(5), 729–755. doi:10.1111/1467-6494.05022 PMID:12322858

Timebanking UK. (2005). *A bridge to tomorrow: Time banking for baby boomers*. Gloucester, UK: TimebanksUK.

Timebanks USA. (2017). *About Timebanks USA*. Retrieved from https://timebanks.org/timebanksusa/

Ting, Y. (1997). Determinants of job satisfaction of federal government employees. *Public Personnel Management, 26*(3), 313–335.

Tollinen, A., Jarvinen, J., & Karjaluoto, H. (2012). *Opportunities and Challenges of Social Media Monitoring in the Business to Business Sector*. Paper presented at the The 4th International Business and Social Science Research Conference, Dubai, UAE.

Tomar, J. S. (2017). Employee Engagement Practices in IT Sector Vis-à-Vis Other Sectors in India. *International Journal of Human Capital and Information Technology Professionals, Volume, 8*(3), 7–14.

Tongco, M. D. C. (2007). Purposive Sampling as a Tool for Informant Selection. *A Journal for Plant. People and Applied Research, 5*, 147–158.

Torkelson, E., & Muhonen, T. (2004). The role of gender and job level in coping with occupational stress. *Work and Stress, 18*(3), 267–274. doi:10.1080/02678370412331323915

Torkzadeh, G., & Dhillon, G. (2002). Measuring factors that influence the success of internet commerce. *Information Systems Research, 13*(2), 187–204. doi:10.1287/isre.13.2.187.87

Torrance, H. (1995). *Evaluating authentic assessment: Problems and possibilities in new approaches to assessment*. Open University.

Trevor, C. O. (2001). Interactions among actual ease-of-movement determinants and job satisfaction in the prediction of voluntary turnover. *Academy of Management Journal, 44*(4), 621–638. doi:10.2307/3069407

Trinder, J. (2005). Mobile technologies and systems. In A. Kukulska-Hulme & J. Traxler (Eds.), *Mobile learning. A handbook for educators and trainers* (pp. 7–24). London: Routledge, Taylor & Francis Inc.

Trinidad, A., Carretero, V., & Soriano, R. M. (2006). Teoría fundamentada "Grounded Theory" La construcción de la teoría a través del análisis interpretacional. Madrid: CIS.

Tsai, M. T., & Huang, C. C. (2008). The relationship among ethical climate types, facets of job satisfaction, and the three components of organizational commitment: A study of nurses in Taiwan. *Journal of Business Ethics, 80*(3), 565–581. doi:10.1007/s10551-007-9455-8

Tsur, N., Berkovitz, N., & Ginzburg, K. (2016). Body awareness, emotional clarity, and authentic behavior: The moderating role of mindfulness. *Journal of Happiness Studies, 17*(4), 1451–1472. doi:10.1007/s10902-015-9652-6

Tucnik, P., Valek, L., Blecha, P., & Bures, V. (2016). Use of Time Banking as a non-monetary component in agent-based computational economics models. *WSEAS Transactions on Business and Economics, 13.*

Turner, B. A., & Chelladurai, P. (2005). Organizational and occupational commitment, intention to leave and perceived performance of intercollegiate coaches. *Journal of Sport Management, 19*(2), 193–211. doi:10.1123/jsm.19.2.193

Turnley, W. H., & Feldman, D. C. (1998). Psychological contract violation during corporate restructuring. *Human Resource Management, 37*(1), 71–83. doi:10.1002/(SICI)1099-050X(199821)37:1<71::AID-HRM7>3.0.CO;2-S

Turnley, W. H., & Feldman, D. C. (2000). Re-examining the effects of psychological contract violations: Unmet expectations and job dissatisfaction as mediators. *Journal of Organizational Behavior, 21*(1), 25–42. doi:10.1002/(SICI)1099-1379(200002)21:1<25::AID-JOB2>3.0.CO;2-Z

Turoff, M., Hiltz, S. R., Bieber, M., Fjermstad, J., & Rana, A. (1999). Collaborative Discourse Structures in Computer Mediated Group Communications. *Journal of Computer-Mediated Communication, 4*(4), 1050–1079.

Twenge, J. M., & Campbell, S. M. (2008). Generational differences in psychological traits and their impact on the workplace. *Journal of Managerial Psychology, 23*(1), 862–877. doi:10.1108/02683940810904367

Twenge, J. M., Zhang, L., & Im, C. (2004). It's beyond my control: A cross-temporal meta-analysis of increasing externality in locus of control, 1960-2002. *Personality and Social Psychology Review, 8*(3), 308–319. doi:10.1207/s15327957pspr0803_5 PMID:15454351

Twu, H. (2010). A predictive study of Wiki interaction: Can attitude toward Wiki predict Wiki interaction in High-Context Cultures groups? *Journal of Educational Technology Development and Exchange, 3*(1), 57–68. doi:10.18785/jetde.0301.05

Tziner, E., Fein, E. C., & Oren, L. (2012). Fein, L. Orenn Human motivation and performance outcomes in the context of downsizing. *Is Less Still More, 1*, 103–133. doi:10.1017/CBO9780511791574.008

U.S. Department of Homeland Security. (2013). *What is security and resilience?* Retrieved on 16 August 2014 from: http://www.dhs.gov/what-security-and-resilience

University of Alcalá. (n.d.). *Mapa competencial basado en los marcos europeos e-CF y ESCO.* Retrieved July 2017, from https://www.uah.es/export/sites/uah/es/estudios/.galleries/Archivos-estudios/MU/Unico/AM133_11_1_3_E_MasterDireccionProyectosUAH-mapa-eCF.pdf

Valek, L. (2013a). *Time Banks in Czech Republic: Filling an Empty Gap in Time Bank Research.* Norristown, NJ: Int Business Information Management Assoc-Ibima.

Valek, L. (2013b). Time Banks in Russia: Filling an Empty Gap in Time Bank Research. *Tradition and Reform: Social Reconstruction of Europe*, 383-386.

Valek, L. (2015a). *The difference in understanding of time banking in various contexts.* Paper presented at the 6th LUMEN International Conference: Rethinking Social Action. Core Values 2015, Iasi, Romania.

Valek, L. (2015b). *Time Banks and Knowledge Sharing: Link to the Knowledge Management.* Paper presented at the 5th International Conference Lumen 2014, Transdisciplinary and Communicative Action (Lumen-Tca 2014).

Valek, L., Kolerova, K., & Otcenaskova, T. (2014). Time banks and clusters: Similarities of sharing framework. *Global Journal on Technology, 6,* 31-36.

Valek, L. (2016). Open Ways for Time Banking Research: Project Management and Beyond. *International Journal of Human Capital and Information Technology Professionals, 7*(1), 35–47. doi:10.4018/IJHCITP.2016010103

Valtanen, J. (2016). *What is the Problem? The meaning of problem in problem-based learning context – Towards problem-aware students* (PhD Thesis). University of Tampere, Finland.

Van der Aalst, W. M. P., Weske, M., & Grünbauer, D. (2005). Case handling: A new paradigm for business process support. *Data & Knowledge Engineering, 53*(2), 129–162. doi:10.1016/j.datak.2004.07.003

Van Kleef, G. A., Homan, A. C., Beersma, B., Van Knippenberg, D., Van Knippenberg, B., & Damen, F. (2009). Searing sentiment or cold calculation? The effects of leader emotional displays on team performance depend on follower epistemic motivation. *Academy of Management Journal, 52*(3), 562–580. doi:10.5465/AMJ.2009.41331253

Van Scotter, J. R. (2000). Relationships of task performance and contextual performance with turnover, job satisfaction, and affective commitment. *Human Resource Management Review, 10*(1), 79–95. doi:10.1016/S1053-4822(99)00040-6

Van Zundert, M., Sluijsmans, D., & Van Merriënboer, J. (2010). Effective peer assessment processes: Research findings and future directions. *Learning and Instruction, 20*(4), 270–279. doi:10.1016/j.learninstruc.2009.08.004

Vandenberg, R. J., Richardson, H. A., & Eastman, L. J. (1999). The Impact of High Involvement Work Processes on Organizational Effectiveness: A Second-Order Latent Variable Approach. *Group & Organization Management, 24*(3), 300-339.

Vansteenkiste, M., Neyrinck, B., Niemiec, C. P., Soenens, B., Witte, H., & Broeck, A. (2007). On the relations among work value orientations, psychological need satisfaction and job outcomes: A self-determination theory approach. *Journal of Occupational and Organizational Psychology, 80*(2), 251–277. doi:10.1348/096317906X111024

Vassilev, T. I. (2015). An Approach to Teaching Introductory Programming for IT Professionals Using Games. *International Journal of Human Capital and Information Technology Professionals, 6*(1), 26–38. doi:10.4018/ijhcitp.2015010103

Viberg, O., & Grönlund, Å. (2012). Mobile assisted language learning: A literature review. In *11th World Conference on Mobile and Contextual Learning* (pp. 9-16). Helsinki, Finland: mLearn.

Virtual University of Tunis. (n.d.). Retrieved from http://c2i.uvt.rnu.tn/Sitec2i/index.php?option=com_content&view=article&id=61&Itemid=48

Viti, P. A. F., dos Santos, D. R., Westphall, C. B., Westphall, C. M., & Vieira, K. M. M. (2014). Current issues in cloud computing security and management. In *Proceedings of the 8th International Conference on Emerging Security Information, Systems and Technologies* (pp.36-42). Lisbon, Portugal: Academic Press.

Vogt, K., Hakanen, J. J., Brauchli, R., Gregor, G. J., & Bauer, G. F. (2016). The consequences of job crafting: A three-wave study. *European Journal of Work and Organizational Psychology, 25*(3), 353–362. doi:10.1080/1359432X.2015.1072170

Voss, R., Gruber, T., & Reppel, A. (2010). Which classroom service encounters make students happy or unhappy? *International Journal of Education, 24*(7), 615–636.

Wagner, J. A. (1994). On beating dead horses, reconsidering reconsiderations, and ending disputes: Further thoughts about a recent study of research on participation. *Academy of Management Review, 20,* 506–508.

Wallgren, L. G. (2013). Department of Psychology, University of Gothenburg, Gothenburg, Sweden. *International Journal of Human Capital and Information Technology Professionals, 4*(4), 1–17. doi:10.4018/ijhcitp.2013100101

Wall, T. D., & Wood, S. J. (2005). *The romance of HRM and business performance: The case for big science.* Sheffield, UK: University of Sheffield.

Walton, R. E. (1985). From control to commitment in the workplace. *Harvard Business Review, 63,* 77–84.

Walumbwa, F., Avolio, B. J., Gardner, W., Wernsing, T. S., & Peterson, S. J. (2008). Authentic Leadership: Development and validation of a theory-based measure. *Journal of Management, 34*(1), 89–126. doi:10.1177/0149206307308913

Warren, S. J., & Lin, L. (2013). Ethical considerations for learning game, simulation, and virtual world design and development. In K-12 Education: Concepts, Methodologies, Tools, and Applications (pp. 292-309). Hershey, PA: Information Science Publishing.

Warschauer, M., Said, G. R. E., & Zohry, A. (2002). Language Choice Online: Globalization and Identity in Egypt. *Journal of Computer-Mediated Communication, 7*(4).

Wasko, M. M., & Faraj, S. (2005). Why should I share? Examining social capital and knowledge contribution In electronic networks of practice. *Management Information Systems Quarterly, 29*(1), 35–57.

Wechsler, D. (1958). *The measurement and appraisal of adult intelligence* (4th ed.). Baltimore, MD: The Williams and Wilkins Company. Kerry S. Webb, Texas Woman's University. doi:10.1037/11167-000

Wegner, . (2002). *Cultivating Communities of Practice: A Guide to Managing Knowledge.* Cambridge, MA: Harvard Business School Press.

Wegner, . (2002). *Cultivating Communities of Practice: A Guide to ManagingKnowledge.* Cambridge, MA: Harvard Business School Press.

Wells, J. B., Minor, E., Anger, A., & Amato, N. (2009). Predictors of job stress among staff in juvenile correctional facilities. *Criminal Justice and Behavior, 36*(3), 245–258. doi:10.1177/0093854808329334

Werner, J., Westphal, C. M., & Westphal, C. B. (2017). Cloud identity management: A survey on privacy strategies. *Computer Networks, 122,* 29–42. doi:10.1016/j.comnet.2017.04.030

Whitelock, D., Gilbert, L., & Gale, V. (2013). E-assessment tales: What types of literature are informing day-to-day practice? *International Journal of e-Assessment, 3*(1).

Widodo, R. N. S., Lim, H., & Atiquzzaman, M. (2017). SDM: Smart deduplication for mobile cloud storage. *Future Generation Computer Systems-the International Journal of Escience, 70,* 64–73. doi:10.1016/j.future.2016.06.023

Wiener, Y., & Gechman, A. S. (1977). Commitment: A behavioral approach to job involvement. *Journal of Vocational Behavior, 10*(1), 47–52. doi:10.1016/0001-8791(77)90041-0

Williams, L. J., & Hazer, J. T. (1986). Antecedents and consequences of satisfaction and commitment in turnover models: A re-analysis using latent variable structural equation methods. *The Journal of Applied Psychology, 72*(1), 219–231. doi:10.1037/0021-9010.71.2.219

Wilson, D. T., & Mummalaneni, V. (1990). Bonding and commitment in buyer-seller relationships: a preliminary conceptualisation. In D. Ford (Ed.), *Understanding Business Markets* (pp. 408–420). London: Academic Press, Harcourt Brace Jovanovich.

Wilson, V., & Pirrie, A. (2000). *Multidisciplinary teamworking beyond the barriers? A review of the issues.* Scottish Council of Research in Education SCRE.

Winning, A. P., & Boag, S. (2015). Does brief mindfulness training increase empathy? The role of personality. *Personality and Individual Differences*, *86*, 492–498. doi:10.1016/j.paid.2015.07.011

Wirtz, P. H., Ehlert, U., Kottwitz, M. U., & Semmer, N. K. (2013). Occupational role stress is associated with higher cortisol reactivity to acute stress. *Journal of Occupational Health Psychology*, *18*(2), 121–131. doi:10.1037/a0031802 PMID:23566275

Wolff, S. B., Pescosolido, A. T., & Druskat, V. U. (2002). Emotional intelligence as the basis of leadership emergence in self-managing teams. *The Leadership Quarterly*, *13*(5), 505–522. doi:10.1016/S1048-9843(02)00141-8

Wood, S. (1999). Human resource management and performance. *International Journal of Management Reviews*, *1*(4), 367–413. doi:10.1111/1468-2370.00020

Workplacetrendscom. (2015). Retrieved 28 September, 2015, from https://workplacetrends.com/the-millennial-leadership-survey/

Wu, M., Miller, R. C., & Garfinkel, S. L. (2006). Do security toolbars actually prevent phishing attacks? *Proceedings of the Conference on Human Factors in Computing System*, 601-610. doi:10.1145/1124772.1124863

Yang, C.-T., Yeh, W.-T., & Shih, W.-C. (2017). Implementation and evaluation of an e-learning architecture on cloud environments. *International Journal of Information and Education Technology (IJIET)*, *7*(8), 623–630. doi:10.18178/ijiet.2017.7.8.943

Yee, K. (2004). Aligning security and usability. *IEEE Security and Privacy*, *2*(5), 48–55. doi:10.1109/MSP.2004.64

Yeh, C. H., Lee, G. G., & Pai, J. C. (2011). Influence of CIO'S knowledge-sharing behavior on the quality of the IS/IT strategic planning (ISSP) process in Taiwan. *African Journal of Business Management*, *5*(6), 2465–2.

Yousef, D. A. (1998). Satisfaction with Job Security as a Predictor of Organizational Commitment and Job Performance in a Multicultural Environment. *International Journal of Manpower*, *19*(3), 184–194. doi:10.1108/01437729810216694

Yuan, X., Guo, M., Ren, F., & Peng, F. (2014). Usability analysis of online bank login interface based on eye tracking experiment. *Sensors & Transducers*, *165*(2), 203–212.

Yücel, İ. (2012). Examining the relationships among job satisfaction, organizational commitment, and turnover intention: An empirical study. *International Journal of Business and Management*, *7*(20), 44. doi:10.5539/ijbm.v7n20p44

Yukl, G. (1998). Leadership in organizations (4th ed.). Prentice Hall.

Yu, X., & Xue, Y. (2016). Smart grids: A cyber-physical systems perspective. *Proceedings of the IEEE*, *104*(5), 1058–1070. doi:10.1109/JPROC.2015.2503119

Zehrer, A., Crotts, J. C., & Magnini, V. P. (2011). The perceived usefulness of blog postings: An extension of the expectancy-disconfirmation paradigm. *Tourism Management*, *32*(1), 106–113. doi:10.1016/j.tourman.2010.06.013

Zhu, W., Avolio, B. J., Riggio, R. E., & Sosik, J. J. (2011). The effect of authentic transformational leadership on follower and group ethics. *The Leadership Quarterly*, *22*(5), 801–817. doi:10.1016/j.leaqua.2011.07.004

About the Contributors

Vandana Ahuja has over 18 years of experience across the corporate sector and academia.She is the author of the book on Digital Marketing - published by Oxford University Press.She has worked with the IT Arm of the Jaypee Group and NIIT, India where she was responsible for Business Development and Marketing for Corporate Training Programmes. She has been actively researching the domain of the collaborative web, with focus on its contributions to the fields of Marketing and CRM and has several years of research experience. She has published several manuscripts in International and National Journals. She also serves on the Editorial Board of several International Journals. At Jaypee Business School, she is the Area-Chair, Marketing and teaches Sales and Distribution Management, Social Media and E-Marketing, and Services Marketing. She has organised one National and one International Conference and is now the Conference co-chair for the International Conference on Information Technology and Quantitative Management, 2017 being jointly organised by IAITQM and JBS.

Shubhangini Rathore is a management researcher; with over 9 years of experience in the corporate sector and academia. She is currently working as an adjunct professor at IBS Gurgaon. She holds her Doctorate in the area of Emotional Intelligence, Organizational Stress & Employee Commitment. She has taught and developed HR courses at reputed business schools. After starting her career as a HR professional; she chose to take a step ahead and put her observations to practice, by way of research on various aspects of Human Resource Management. As an active researcher, she has published various research papers in distinguished International Journals. She has also presented her ideas and concepts in various national and international conferences and seminars.

* * *

Shirin Alavi has over 11 years of experience and has earlier worked with the Standard Chartered Bank and has work experience primarily in the domain of CRM operations and International Business and Marketing. She has about eight years of research experience in the domain of Marketing and Customer Relationship Management. She has published several manuscripts in International and National Journals. She also serves on the Editorial Board of International Journals.

Francisco Antunes is an Assistant Professor at the Management and Economics Department. He holds a PhD in Management, by the Beira Interior University. His research interests include electronic commerce, decision support systems and information systems. He is also a Researcher at the Institute of Computer and Systems Engineering of Coimbra, Portugal. He has published in journals such as the European Journal of Operational Research, Advances in Human-Computer Interaction, International Journal of Information Technology & Decision Making, among others. He is also a member of the program committee of conferences such as GDN – Group Decision and Negotiation; CISTI – Iberian Conference on Information Systems and Technologies; KEOD – International Conference on Knowledge Engineering and Ontology Development, as well as a journal referee for several journals.

Eleni Berki is Adjunct Professor of Software Quality and Formal Modelling at the University of Jyväskylä and a Senior Research Fellow at the University of Tampere, Finland. Her teaching and research areas are software/total quality engineering and deep learning/learnability in diverse contexts. She is a member of more than 50 multidisciplinary international committees, and has organised and chaired many international conferences. She studied and mainly worked in the UK, Greece and Finland. Her teaching and research focus on: security testing, confidentiality in e-health and trust/privacy management, social engineering and free/open source software as social innovation. Dr Berki has more than 150 multidisciplinary and international publications with hundreds of references and citations to them worldwide. She supervised 8 PhD researchers, and currently supervises many interdisciplinary PhD theses.

Anke Berns currently holds a position as a Lecturer of German at the University of Cadiz (Spain) receiving her PhD in 2002. Her research interests focus especially on the use of new technologies in the teaching and learning of foreign languages. Anke is particularly interested in design-based research, learner motivation and assessment. She has collaborated on several EU funded projects and has made numerous contributions to peer-reviewed journals and conferences.

Giorgio Bruno is an Associate Professor at Politecnico di Torino, where he teaches courses on software engineering and object-oriented programming. His current interests concern the operational modeling of business processes and collaborative services, and the design of information systems and workflow systems. He has authored two books and over 150 technical papers on the above-mentioned subjects.

Juan Antonio Caballero is a PhD candidate. He works as a web developer in Basebone. His main interest are serious games and learning analytics.

Ana Castillo-Martínez has a BSc (2010), MSc (2012) and PhD (2016) in Computer Science from the University of Alcala, where she is now a researcher in the Computer Science Department, where she has participated in several research projects. Her research interests include mobile devices and energy management. Currently, she has relevant publications on ICT field with publications in high impact international journals. Previously, she was working in Iberia (an IAG company) in the Department of Financial Management.

Alberto Cejas has an MSc in Computer Science from the University of Cadiz. He works as a game developer at Gameloft. His main interests are video game technologies and software development.

Sunil Chaudhary is Lecturer and research coordinator at the Deerwalk Institute of Technology in Kathmandu, Nepal and a former doctoral researcher at the University of Tampere. He obtained his PhD degree on cybersecurity in 2016 from the University of Tampere and completed a BEng in Computer Engineering from Tribhuvan University, Nepal and an MSc in Software Development from the University of Tampere, Finland. His PhD thesis title is: "The use of usable security and security education to fight phishing attacks." (2016). His research interests are: anti-phishing technologies and phishing-resistant systems, software quality criteria, and digital walls and territories. Since 2012 he has been working in industry under the international research project Internet of Things, funded by the Finnish Agency for Research and Innovation TEKES. Sunil investigates privacy, security and usability relating to surveillance, health, and ambient intelligence.

João Paulo Costa is a Full Professor at the Faculty of Economics of the University of Coimbra. He holds a PhD in Economics, by the University of Coimbra. His major field of study is decision support systems. He is also a Researcher at the Institute of Computer and Systems Engineering of Coimbra, Portugal, as well as at the Centre for Business and Economics Research (CeBER). He has published in journals such as the European Journal of Operational Research, Decision Support Systems, Pacific Journal of Optimization, among others. He is also a member of the program committee of conferences such as GDN – Group Decision and Negotiation; CISTI – Iberian Conference on Information Systems and Technologies; as well as referee for journals as the European Journal of Operations Research, the Journal of Group Decision and Negotiation. Current research interests regard multiobjective linear fractional programming, group decision support systems, multicriteria decision aiding and management information systems.

Juan Manuel Dodero has a Computer Science MSc from the Technical University of Madrid and an Engineering PhD from the University Carlos III of Madrid. He is an Associate Professor of the University of Cádiz, Spain. Formerly he was a consultant in ICT companies and a senior lecturer at the University Carlos III of Madrid. His main research field is technology-enhanced learning, with a focus on the application of computing and software technologies for the computer-aided design and assessment of learning processes. He has coordinated and participated a number of national and international R&D projects in relation with these subjects, generating numerous peer-reviewed indexed publications. He has been director of the Open Knowledge and Libre Software Office at his institution.

Luis Fernández-Sanz is an associate professor at Dept. of Computer Science of Universidad de Alcala (UAH). He earned a degree in Computing in 1989 at Universidad Politecnica de Madrid (UPM) and his Ph.D. in Computing with a special award at University of the Basque Country in 1997. With more than 20 years of research and teaching experience (at UPM, Universidad Europea de Madrid and UAH), he is also engaged in the management of the main Spanish Computing Professionals association (ATI: www.ati.es) as vicepresident and he is chairman of ATI Software Quality group. He has been vicepresident of CEPIS (Council of European Professional Informatics Societies: www.cepis.org) from 2011 to 2013 and member of the Board of Directors since 2016. With a large number of contributions in refereed impact international journals, conferences and book chapters, his main research interests include technical fields like software quality and engineering and testing and non technical fields like computing education, especially in multinational settings, IT profession and requirements and skills for IT jobs.

Manuela Freire is a Ph.D student at the Faculty of Economics of the University of Coimbra, in Management - Science Applied to Decision. She received her MSc on Business Management in 2011, by the Faculty of Economics of the University of Algarve. His research interests include social networks, decision making and decision support systems. She also works for a telecommunications company in the area of management and quality control department. In addition, she is also a Researcher at the Institute of Computer and Systems Engineering of Coimbra, Portugal.

Francisco José García-Peñalvo did his undergraduate studies in Computing at the University of Salamanca and University of Valladolid and his Ph.D. at the University of Salamanca. Dr. García-Peñalvo is the head of the research group GRIAL (Research Group Interaction and eLearning). His main research interests focus on eLearning, Computers & Education, Adaptive Systems, Web Engineering, Semantic Web and Software Reuse. He has led and participated in over 50 research and innovation projects. He was Vice Chancellor for Innovation at the University of Salamanca between March 2007 and December 2009. He has published more than 300 articles in international journals and conferences. He has been guest editor of several special issues of international journals (Online Information Review, Computers in Human Behaviour, Interactive Learning Environments...). He is also a member of the program committee of several international conferences and reviewer for several international journals. Now, he is the Editor-in-Chief of the International Journal of Information Technology Research and the Education in the Knowledge Society Journal. Besides he is the coordinator of the multidisciplinary PhD Programme on Education in the Knowledge Society.

Josefa Gómez-Pérez received the BS and MS in Telecommunications Engineering from the University Polytechnic of Cartagena, Spain, in 2005 and 2007, respectively, and the PhD in Informatics Engineering from the University of Alcala, Spain, in 2011. She has participated in several research projects with Spanish and European organizations. Her current research interest is the analysis of ICT skills for users and professionals related to employability and education.

Mounira Ilahi holds doctoral degree in computer science from ENSI, University of Manouba. She has received the Master degree in Intelligent Information Systems from the Higher Institute of Computer Science and Management of Kairouan, Tunisia. Mounira is currently an Assistant professor at the Higher Institute of Specialized Education at the University of Manouba in Tunisia where she is an associate researcher. She is a member of the PRINCE Research laboratory at the University of Sousse in Tunisia. Her research interests include Technology Enhanced Learning, Semantic Web, E-assessment and E-accessibility. She has participated in various doctoral summer schools and conferences in Technology Enhanced Learning.

Manu Joy completed his under graduation in civil engineering from Govt. Engineering College, Thrissur and post graduation in management from Amrita School of Business, Coimbatore. Currently, he has submitted his doctoral thesis in social science at School of management studies, CUSAT. Apart from this, he has acquired post graduation in psychology, psychotherapy, training and development and sociology. At present, he is working as assistant professor at SCMS School of Technology and Management. In addition to his teaching and research expertise, he is a professional management trainer with 10 years of experience and has conducted more than 500 programs across ten states in India. His training clientele includes more than 100 corporate and government organizations with Bharat Matrimony, ICAI and ICWAI to name a few. His writings appear in both scholarly and applied publications.

Linfeng Li is Lecturer and Postdoctoral Researcher at the Department of Computer Sciences of The Beijing Institute of Petrochemical Technology. He obtained a BSc in Computer Science in China and his MSc and PhD from the University of Tampere, Finland. His PhD thesis title is "A contingency framework to assure the user-centred quality and to support the design of anti-phishing software" (2013). Prior to his scholarship for a PhD, Linfeng worked as a software quality engineer in F-Secure. His research focuses on end user behaviour modelling, software quality criteria and metrics, security and usability. He has co-authored many international papers and has many international research partners.

Irina Noninska is Assoc. Professor in Cryptography. She has obtained her PhD degree in Databases and Local Area Networks from Technical University of Sofia. Now she is a lecturer at Computer Systems Department, Technical University of Sofia, delivering courses "Cryptography" and "E-business technologies". Her scientific and research interests are in the area of Information and Network Security, Data Protection, Cryptographic Algorithms and Protocols, Internet of Things, M2M Standards and Applications. She is author and co-author of 87 scientific papers, articles and 8 books.

Manuel Palomo-Duarte has a CS degree from the University of Seville and a PhD from the University of Cadiz. He is currently a lecturer in the University of Cadiz, Spain. His teaching focuses on subjects related to web science and databases using open-source software. His main research interests are collaborative learning technologies and software development, fields in which he has published different contributions in peer-reviewed journals and research conferences.

Shivani Pandey is a HR professional and a researcher. She holds her Doctorate in the area of Human Resource Management. She has worked in the corporate sector as human resources professional and her prime expertise and interest lies in the field of Human Resource Management. She is presently associated with Shipping Industry and simultaneously exploring new prospects for research.

Ana María Pinto-Llorente holds a PhD in Education and Technology, Bachelor in English as a second language (University of Salamanca) and Bachelor in Education (Pontifical University of Salamanca). She is currently working as a professor in the Department of Didactics, Organization and Research Methods at the University of Salamanca. Her areas of work are related to technology, innovation and didactics. She has been the Coordinator of the Postgraduate Programme in Bilingual Education and the Director of the Special Course in Bilingual Education in Infant, Primary and Secondary education. Her research interests focus on Second Language, Blended Learning, E-Learning, and Computers & Education. She has an extensive experience of teaching Technology, Linguistics, Phonetics, English, and Technology in face-to-face and Blended Learning Modality. She has published different articles in national and international journals, and presented several papers in national and international conferences.

Radi Romansky is a full professor in Technical University of Sofia, Bulgaria; Doctor of Science in Informatics and Computer Science, Vice Rector. Hi has over 195 scientific publications and 19published monographies, books and manuals. Participant in 33 scientific research projects in the field of computer systems and technologies, e-learning, etc. Full member of the European Network of Excellence on High Performance and Embedded Architectures and Compilation – HiPEAC. Member of the International Editorial Board of scientific journals (Bulgaria, India, Slovakia, USA, etc.), chairman of the Organizing and Program committee of International Conference on Information Technologies. Scientific areas: Computer systems and architectures, Computer modelling, Information technologies, Personal data protection, etc.

Iván Ruiz-Rube is an associate lecturer at the University of Cadiz, Spain. He has an MSc in Software Engineering and Technology from the University of Seville and a PhD from the University of Cadiz. His fields of research are technology-enhanced learning, software process improvement and data analytics. Previously, he has worked as a software engineer in consulting companies, such as Everis Spain S.L. and Sadiel S.A.

Mª Cruz Sánchez-Gómez, Doctor and Bachelor in Education Sciences at the University of Salamanca, and a Master's degree in Speech Pathology at the Pontifical University of Salamanca. She is a Professor in the Department of Education, Organization and Research Methods at the University of Salamanca with a profile in research and diagnostic methods in education. Her areas of work are related to new technologies (she is a researcher of an excellence research group (GRIAL and IBSAL), groups at risk of social exclusion (coordinator of the researches related to women and disability of INICO, university institute of integration in the community), and educational evaluation (with members of MIDE). In 2008 she received the First National Award of Research of Caja Madrid Social Work and in 2014 the Awards of Innovation and Education Research Perfecta Corselas. She run the Department of Continuing Education at the University of Salamanca from March 2007 until October 2010, and was in charge of all non-formal education at the University of Salamanca: courses, continuing education, summer courses, conferences, seminars and degrees of Salamanca University (specialist, expert, and master). At the moment, Mª Cruz is the head of the Department of Education, Organization and Research Methods at the University of Salamanca.

Santoshi Sengupta, Ph.D. in Management, has been working with Jaypee Institute of Information Technology, Noida, for the past eleven years. After Ph. D, she did her Post-Doctoral research with Universitat Pompeu Fabra, Barcelona and worked in the area of Group Dynamics. She started her career in January 2005 as a faculty in Department of Humanities and Social Sciences in JIIT. She has to her credit several research publications in international and national journals of repute and also as chapters in books. She has presented a number of papers in international conferences both in India and abroad. She teaches Organizational Behavior, Presentation and Communication Skills, English and Group and Co-operative Processes engineering graduates and management post-graduates. She endeavors to augment herself as a committed researcher and a proficient teacher to impart the best to students. She is a highly motivated, inventive and result – oriented academician, who seeks to coalesce academic training in a learning-centric approach.

Swati Sharma, Ph.D in Management, has been working with Jaypee Institute of Information Technology, Noida, for the past eight years. She started her career in Service Industry after her MBA degree and has served various service organizations of repute in the capacity of senior management. With her stint in service industry lasting for 5 years, she has found her interest in academics and has experience of around 12 years of teaching undergraduate and post graduate students. The elective papers taught by her in past few semesters are Service Management and Marketing, Managing and Marketing of Technology and Technology and Culture. She has keen interest in research and has published in international and national journals of repute and also has book chapters to her credit. She has presented a number of papers in international conferences both in India and abroad. Her interest areas include Consumer Behavior, Service Marketing and Cross Cultural Studies.

Aishwarya Singh is a doctoral researcher in human resource management at Jaypee business school, JIIT, Noida. Her research interest includes individual cultural values,leadership studies with special reference to authentic leadership, its effects on creativity. She holds a master's degree in business administration from Banasthali Vidyapith, Rajasthan and a B.A economic honors from the same institution. She has to her credit few research papers in peer reviewed international and national journals and also presented some papers in international conferences in India. Having worked as an assistant professor in OB & HR at management institutions and as HR Head at in her last corporate stint has provided her the much needed work experience to complement her education. With a good teaching and corporate background coupled with a strong set interpersonal and communication skills, she finds herself better equipped as a researcher. She aspires to create an impact in academia with her research and with her determination to walk an extra mile to content her quest for wisdom.

Anita Singh is a Professor in the area of HR at the Institute of Management Studies Ghaziabad and has experience of 23 years in corporate and academia in teaching, research and training. She has earned Ph.D.in the area of Management. She has done Master of Business Administration, Masters in Personnel Management and Industrial Relations and EPHRM from IIM-Calcutta. She has been actively involved in the research, and case study writing, and contributed several manuscripts in International, National journals, and book chapters. She has also presented a number of papers in International Conference in India and abroad. Her recent publication includes 'Rethinking Human Resource: Making of Parental Policy in India', published in International Journal of Intelligent Enterprise, a top journal of Inderscience publishers. Her current research interest includes in the area of human resource management and behavioral science.

Lata Bajpai Singh is an Associate Professor at Institute of Management Studies Ghaziabad. She received her PhD in Human Resource Management from M. J. P. Rohilkhand University, Bareilly U.P. India. Apart from academic interest she took part in research, training and corporate consulting assignments. During her 16 years of academic experience she has contributed many research papers as journal publications, conference proceedings and published case studies. Her current research interests include behavioral issues among the workforce, human resource practices at SME's, HR Practices in Digital era, and employee engagement.

Lukas Valek completed his bachelor´s degree in financial management in 2006 at University of Hradec Kralove, Czech Republic and master´s degree in corporate finance and business in 2009 at Brno University of technology, Czech Republic. Later on, he progressed to non-profit sphere and gained more experience in the area in following years later working as a trainer in non-formal learning approaches. After is appointment in a board of one of major voluntary organizations in Prague he founded his own NGO in the city of Hradec Kalove in 2012. On parallel, he begun a research in the field of complementary economy systems again at University of Hradec Kralove. At this moment he is assistant professor on Institute of Social Work of the University of Hradec Kralove as researcher, lecturer and developing international relations with published over 20 works on international conferences and journals.

Juri Valtanen obtained his PhD degree from the School of Education, the University of Tampere, Finland. The title of his PhD thesis is: "What is the Problem? The Meaning of Problem in Problem-Based Learning Context – Towards Problem-Aware Students" (2016). He completed an MSc degree in Adult Education from the same school; his MSc thesis was about industrial teamwork of team supporters/top managers, team leaders, and team members' experiences. Juri's work interests include problem focused education, question asking, values and quality improvement, valorisation and innovation project management. He has worked as process/product improvement specialist and as a lecturer; also as a trainee in Yle, the Finnish national broadcasting corporation. Other studies and activities include film direction and scriptwriting. His publications are multidisciplinary and have often been internationally cited.

Index

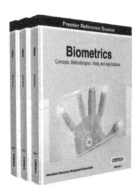

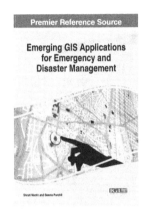 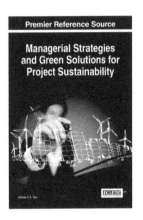  

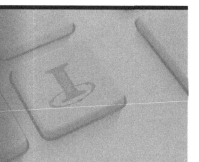

Printed in the United States
By Bookmasters